COPYRIGHT, DESIGNS AND PATENTS ACT 1988 (UK)

Updated as of March 26, 2018

THE LAW LIBRARY

TABLE OF CONTENTS

Introductory Text   4

Part I Copyright   4

Countries to which this Part extends.   119

Application of this Part to countries to which it does not extend   120

Part II Rights in performances   121

Countries to which this Part extends.   164

Part III Design Right   165

Countries to which this Part extends.   188

Part IV Registered Designs   188

Part V Patent Agents and Trade Mark Agents   193

Part VI Patents   200

Part VII Miscellaneous and General   203

Schedules   220

Schedule 1. CERTAIN PERMITTED USES OF ORPHAN WORKS   220

Schedule 2. Regulation of licensing bodies   224

Schedule 3. Copyright: transitional provisions and savings   226

Schedule 4. Rights in performances: permitted acts   238

Schedule 5. LICENSING OF PERFORMERS' ... RIGHTS   258

Schedule 6. Registered designs: minor and consequential amendments of 1949 Act
                                                                                268

Schedule 7. The Registered Designs Act 1949 as amended Arrangement of Sections
                                                                                277

Schedule 8. Patents: miscellaneous amendments   302

Schedule 9. PERMITTED ACTS TO WHICH SECTION 296ZE APPLIES   315

Schedule 10. Provisions for the Benefit of Great Ormond Street Hospital for Children
                                                                                319

Schedule 11. Consequential amendments: general   321

Schedule 12. Repeals   329

Open Government Licence v3.0   330

Introductory Text

Copyright, Designs and Patents Act 1988

1988 CHAPTER 48

An Act to restate the law of copyright, with amendments; to make fresh provision as to the rights of performers and others in performances; to confer a design right in original designs; to amend the Registered Designs Act 1949; to make provision with respect to patent agents and trade mark agents; to confer patents and designs jurisdiction on certain county courts; to amend the law of patents; to make provision with respect to devices designed to circumvent copy-protection of works in electronic form; to make fresh provision penalising the fraudulent reception of transmissions; to make the fraudulent application or use of a trade mark an offence; to make provision for the benefit of the Hospital for Sick Children, Great Ormond Street, London; to enable financial assistance to be given to certain international bodies; and for connected purposes.
[15th November 1988]
Be it enacted by the Queen's most Excellent Majesty, by and with the advice and consent of the Lords Spiritual and Temporal, and Commons, in this present Parliament assembled, and by the authority of the same, as follows:—
Modifications etc. (not altering text)
C1. Act amended by Broadcasting Act 1990 (c. 42, SIF 96), s. 176, Sch. 17 para. 7. (1)

Part I Copyright

Part I Copyright

Modifications etc. (not altering text)
C1. Pt. I (ss. 1-179) modified by S.I. 1989/988, art. 2. (3)
C2. Pt. I (ss. 1-179) extended by S.I. 1989/1293, arts. 2. (3), 3, 4. (4)-(6)
C3. Pt. I (ss. 1-179) applied (with modifications) by S.I. 1993/942, arts. 2. (3), 5, Sch. 4 (with art. 6)
C4. Pt. I (ss. 1-179) applied by S.I. 1993/942, arts. 4, 5, Sch. 4 (with art. 6)
Pt. I (ss. 1-179) applied (with modifications) (22.7.1999) by S.I. 1999/1751, arts. 2. (3), 3, 4. (3)(5), 5, 7, Schs. 2, 4, 5 (as amended (22.4.2003) by S.I. 2003/774, arts. 2-5) (which S.I. and amending S.I. were revoked (1.5.2005) by S.I. 2005/852, art. 8. (b)(d))
C5. Pt. 1 (ss. 1-179) extended in part (with modifications) by The Copyright (Bermuda) Order 2003 (S.I. 2003/1517), art. 2, Sch. (the amendment coming into force in accordance with art. 1 of the amending S.I.)
C6. Pt. 1 (ss. 1-179) modified (31.10.2003) by The Copyright and Related Rights Regulations 2003 (S.I. 2003/2498), reg. 37. (2) (with regs. 31-40)
C7. Pt. 1 (ss. 1-179) extended (with modifications) (1.5.2005) by The Copyright and Performances (Application to Other Countries) Order 2005 (S.I. 2005/852), arts. 2-5, Sch. (with art. 7) (which S.I. was revoked (6.4.2006) by SI 2006/316, art. 1. (3))

C8. Pt. 1 (ss. 1-179) extended in part (with modifications) by The Copyright (Gibraltar) Order 2005 (S.I. 2005/853), art. 2, Sch. (the amendment coming into force in accordance with art. 1 of the amending S.I.)

C9. Pt. 1 (ss. 1-179) extended (with modifications) (6.4.2006) by The Copyright and Performances (Application to Other Countries) Order 2006 (S.I. 2006/316), {arts. 2- 5}, Sch. (with art. 7) (which S.I. was revoked (6.4.2007) by S.I. 2007/273, art. 1. (3))

C10. Pt. 1 (ss. 1-179) extended (with modifications) (6.4.2007) by The Copyright and Performances (Application to Other Countries) Order 2007 (S.I. 2007/273), arts. 2-5, Sch. (with art. 7) (which S.I. was revoked (6.4.2008) by SI 2008/677, art. 1. (3))

C11. Pt. 1 (ss. 1-179) extended (with modifications) (6.4.2008) by The Copyright and Performances (Application to Other Countries) Order 2008 (S.I. 2008/677), arts. 2-5, Sch. (with art. 7)

C12. Pt. 1 extended (with modifications) (6.4.2012) by The Copyright and Performances (Application to Other Countries) Order 2012 (S.I. 2012/799), arts. 1. (1), arts. 2-5, Schs. (with art. 8)

C13. Pt. 1 applied in part (with modifications) (6.4.2013) by The Copyright and Performances (Application to Other Countries) Order 2013 (S.I. 2013/536), arts. 1. (1), 2, 4, 5, Schs. (with art. 8)

C14. Pt. 1 extended in part (Cayman Islands) (with modifications) (coming into force in accordance with art. 1 of the amending Order) by The Copyright (Cayman Islands) Order 2015 (S.I. 2015/795), arts. 1, 2, Sch. (as amended by The Copyright (Cayman Islands) (Amendment) Order 2016 (S.I. 2016/370), arts. 1, 2-40)

C15. Pt. 1 applied (with modifications) (6.4.2017) by The Copyright and Performances (Application to Other Countries) Order 2016 (S.I. 2016/1219), arts. 1. (1), 4 (with art. 13)

C16. Pt. 1 restricted (6.4.2017) by The Copyright and Performances (Application to Other Countries) Order 2016 (S.I. 2016/1219), arts. 1. (1), 6 (with art. 13)

C17. Pt. 1 restricted (6.4.2017) by The Copyright and Performances (Application to Other Countries) Order 2016 (S.I. 2016/1219), arts. 1. (1), 9 (with art. 13)

C18. Pt. 1 applied (with modifications) (6.4.2017) by The Copyright and Performances (Application to Other Countries) Order 2016 (S.I. 2016/1219), arts. 1. (1), 7 (with art. 13)

C19. Pt. 1 restricted (6.4.2017) by The Copyright and Performances (Application to Other Countries) Order 2016 (S.I. 2016/1219), arts. 1. (1), 2 (with art. 13)

C20. Pt. 1 restricted (6.4.2017) by The Copyright and Performances (Application to Other Countries) Order 2016 (S.I. 2016/1219), arts. 1. (1), 3 (with art. 13)

C21. Pt. 1 applied (with modifications) (6.4.2017) by The Copyright and Performances (Application to Other Countries) Order 2016 (S.I. 2016/1219), arts. 1. (1), 5, Sch. Pt. 1 (with art. 13)

C22. Pt. 1 applied (with modifications) (6.4.2017) by The Copyright and Performances (Application to Other Countries) Order 2016 (S.I. 2016/1219), arts. 1. (1), 8 (with art. 13)

C23. Pt. 1: power to extend conferred (27.4.2017) by Digital Economy Act 2017 (c. 30), ss. 118. (1), 119. (7)(8)(a)

Chapter I Subsistence, ownership and duration of copyright

Modifications etc. (not altering text)
C24. Pt. I Ch. 1 (ss. 1-15) applied in part (1.12.1996) by S.I. 1996/2967, reg. 17. (4) (with Pt. III)
1 Copyright and copyright works.
(1) Copyright is a property right which subsists in accordance with this Part in the following descriptions of work—

    (a) original literary, dramatic, musical or artistic works,

    (b) sound recordings, films [F1or broadcasts], and

    (c) the typographical arrangement of published editions.

(2) In this Part "copyright work" means a work of any of those descriptions in which copyright

subsists.

(3) Copyright does not subsist in a work unless the requirements of this Part with respect to qualification for copyright protection are met (see section 153 and the provisions referred to there).

Amendments (Textual)

F1. Words in s. 1. (1)(b) substituted (31.10.2003) by The Copyright and Related Rights Regulations 2003 (S.I. 2003/2498), reg. 5. (2) (with regs. 31-40)

2 Rights subsisting in copyright works.

(1) The owner of the copyright in a work of any description has the exclusive right to do the acts specified in Chapter II as the acts restricted by the copyright in a work of that description.

(2) In relation to certain descriptions of copyright work the following rights conferred by Chapter IV (moral rights) subsist in favour of the author, director or commissioner of the work, whether or not he is the owner of the copyright—

    (a) section 77 (right to be identified as author or director),

    (b) section 80 (right to object to derogatory treatment of work), and

    (c) section 85 (right to privacy of certain photographs and films).

Descriptions of work and related provisions

3 Literary, dramatic and musical works.

(1) In this Part—

"literary work" means any work, other than a dramatic or musical work, which is written, spoken or sung, and accordingly includes—

    (a) a table or compilation [F2other than a database], F3. . .

    (b) a computer program; F4. . .[F5. (c) preparatory design material for a computer program][F6and

    F6. (d)a database]

"dramatic work" includes a work of dance or mime; and

"musical work" means a work consisting of music, exclusive of any words or action intended to be sung, spoken or performed with the music.

(2) Copyright does not subsist in a literary, dramatic or musical work unless and until it is recorded, in writing or otherwise; and references in this Part to the time at which such a work is made are to the time at which it is so recorded.

(3) It is immaterial for the purposes of subsection (2) whether the work is recorded by or with the permission of the author; and where it is not recorded by the author, nothing in that subsection affects the question whether copyright subsists in the record as distinct from the work recorded.

Amendments (Textual)

F2. Words in s. 3. (1)(a) inserted (1.1.1998) by S.I. 1997/3032, reg. 5. (a) (with Pt. IV)

F3. Word in s. 3. (1) omitted (1.1.1993) by virtue of S.I. 1992/3233, reg. 3

F4. Word in s. 3. (1)(b) left out (1.1.1998) by virtue of S.I. 1997/3032, reg. 5. (b) (with Pt. IV)

F5. Word and s. 3. (1)(c) inserted (1.1.1993) by S.I. 1992/3233, reg. 3

F6. S. 3. (1)(d) and word preceding it inserted (1.1.1998) by S.I. 1997/3032, reg. 5. (c) (with Pt. IV)

[F73. A Databases

(1) In this Part "database" means a collection of independent works, data or other materials which—

    (a) are arranged in a systematic or methodical way, and

    (b) are individually accessible by electronic or other means.

(2) For the purposes of this Part a literary work consisting of a database is original if, and only if, by reason of the selection or arrangement of the contents of the database the database constitutes the author's own intellectual creation.]

Amendments (Textual)

F7. S. 3. A inserted (1.1.1998) by S.I. 1997/3032, reg. 6 (with Pt. IV)
4 Artistic works.

(1) In this Part "artistic work" means—

    (a) a graphic work, photograph, sculpture or collage, irrespective of artistic quality,

    (b) a work of architecture being a building or a model for a building, or

    (c) a work of artistic craftsmanship.

(2) In this Part—

"building" includes any fixed structure, and a part of a building or fixed structure;

"graphic work" includes—

    (a) any painting, drawing, diagram, map, chart or plan, and

    (b) any engraving, etching, lithograph, woodcut or similar work;

"photograph" means a recording of light or other radiation on any medium on which an image is produced or from which an image may by any means be produced, and which is not part of a film;

"sculpture" includes a cast or model made for purposes of sculpture.

[F85. A Sound recordings.

(1) In this Part "sound recording" means—

    (a) a recording of sounds, from which the sounds may be reproduced, or

    (b) a recording of the whole or any part of a literary, dramatic or musical work, from which sounds reproducing the work or part may be produced,

regardless of the medium on which the recording is made or the method by which the sounds are reproduced or produced.

(2) Copyright does not subsist in a sound recording which is, or to the extent that it is, a copy taken from a previous sound recording.]

Amendments (Textual)

F8. Ss. 5. A, 5. B substituted for s. 5 (1.1.1996) by S.I. 1995/3297, reg. 9. (1) (with Pt. III)

[F95. B Films.

(1) In this Part "film" means a recording on any medium from which a moving image may by any means be produced.

(2) The sound track accompanying a film shall be treated as part of the film for the purposes of this Part.

(3) Without prejudice to the generality of subsection (2), where that subsection applies—

    (a) references in this Part to showing a film include playing the film sound track to accompany the film,

    [F10. (b)references in this Part to playing a sound recording, or to communicating a sound recording to the public, do not include playing or communicating the film sound track to accompany the film,

    (c) references in this Part to copying a work, so far as they apply to a sound recording, do not include copying the film sound track to accompany the film, and

    (d) references in this Part to the issuing, rental or lending of copies of a work, so far as they apply to a sound recording, do not include the issuing, rental or lending of copies of the sound track to accompany the film.]

(4) Copyright does not subsist in a film which is, or to the extent that it is, a copy taken from a previous film.

(5) Nothing in this section affects any copyright subsisting in a film sound track as a sound recording.]

Amendments (Textual)

F9. Ss. 5. A, 5. B substituted for s. 5 (1.1.1996) by S.I. 1995/3297, reg. 9. (1) (with Pt. III)
F10. S. 5. B(3)(b)-(d) substituted (1.2.2006) for s. 5. B(3)(b) and preceding word by The Performances (Moral Rights, etc.) Regulations 2006 (S.I. 2006/18), reg. 2, Sch. para. 2 (with reg. 8)

5. . . . .

6 Broadcasts.

[F11. (1) In this Part a " broadcast " means an electronic transmission of visual images, sounds or

other information which—
    (a) is transmitted for simultaneous reception by members of the public and is capable of being lawfully received by them, or
    (b) is transmitted at a time determined solely by the person making the transmission for presentation to members of the public,
and which is not excepted by subsection (1. A); and references to broadcasting shall be construed accordingly.
(1. A)Excepted from the definition of "broadcast" is any internet transmission unless it is—
    (a) a transmission taking place simultaneously on the internet and by other means,
    (b) a concurrent transmission of a live event, or
    (c) a transmission of recorded moving images or sounds forming part of a programme service offered by the person responsible for making the transmission, being a service in which programmes are transmitted at scheduled times determined by that person.]
(2) An encrypted transmission shall be regarded as capable of being lawfully received by members of the public only if decoding equipment has been made available to members of the public by or with the authority of the person making the transmission or the person providing the contents of the transmission.
(3) References in this Part to the person making a broadcast, [F12or a transmission which is a broadcast] are—
    (a) to the person transmitting the programme, if he has responsibility to any extent for its contents, and
    (b) to any person providing the programme who makes with the person transmitting it the arrangements necessary for its transmission;
and references in this Part to a programme, in the context of broadcasting, are to any item included in a broadcast.
F13[(4)For the purposes of this Part, the place from which a [F14wireless] broadcast is made is the place where, under the control and responsibility of the person making the broadcast, the programme-carrying signals are introduced into an uninterrupted chain of communication (including, in the case of a satellite transmission, the chain leading to the satellite and down towards the earth).]
F15[(4. A)Subsections (3) and (4) have effect subject to section 6. A (safeguards in case of certain satellite broadcasts).]
(5) References in this Part to the reception of a broadcast include reception of a broadcast relayed by means of a telecommunications system.
[F16. (5. A)The relaying of a broadcast by reception and immediate re-transmission shall be regarded for the purposes of this Part as a separate act of broadcasting from the making of the broadcast which is so re-transmitted.]
(6) Copyright does not subsist in a broadcast which infringes, or to the extent that it infringes, the copyright in another broadcast F17. . . .

Amendments (Textual)
F11. S. 6. (1)(1. A) substituted (31.10.2003) for s. 6. (1) by The Copyright and Related Rights Regulations 2003 (S.I. 2003/2498), reg. 4. (a) (with regs. 31-40)
F12. Words in s. 6. (3) substituted (31.10.2003) by The Copyright and Related Rights Regulations 2003 (S.I. 2003/2498), reg. 4. (b) (with regs. 31-40)
F13. S. 6. (4) substituted (1.12.1996 with effect as mentioned in reg. 28 of the amending S.I.) by S.I. 1996/2967, reg. 5
F14. Word in s. 6. (4) inserted (31.10.2003) by The Copyright and Related Rights Regulations 2003 (S.I. 2003/2498), reg. 4. (c) (with regs. 31-40)
F15. S. 6. (4. A) inserted (1.12.1996 with effect as mentioned in reg. 28 of the amending S.I.) by S.I. 1996/2967, reg. 6. (1)
F16. S. 6. (5. A) inserted (31.10.2003) by The Copyright and Related Rights Regulations 2003 (S.I. 2003/2498), reg. 4. (d) (with regs. 31-40)
F17. Words in s. 6. (6) repealed (31.10.2003) by The Copyright and Related Rights Regulations

2003 (S.I. 2003/2498), reg. 2. (2), Sch. 2 (with regs. 31-40)

[F186. A Safeguards in case of certain satellite broadcasts.

(1) This section applies where the place from which a broadcast by way of satellite transmission is made is located in a country other than an EEA State and the law of that country fails to provide at least the following level of protection—

(a) exclusive rights in relation to [F19wireless] broadcasting equivalent to those conferred by section 20 ([F20infringement by communication to the public]) on the authors of literary, dramatic, musical and artistic works, films and broadcasts;

(b) a right in relation to live [F21wireless] broadcasting equivalent to that conferred on a performer by section 182. (1)(b) (consent required for live broadcast of performance); and

(c) a right for authors of sound recordings and performers to share in a single equitable remuneration in respect of the [F21wireless] broadcasting of sound recordings.

(2) Where the place from which the programme-carrying signals are transmitted to the satellite ("the uplink station") is located in an EEA State—

(a) that place shall be treated as the place from which the broadcast is made, and

(b) the person operating the uplink station shall be treated as the person making the broadcast.

(3) Where the uplink station is not located in an EEA State but a person who is established in an EEA State has commissioned the making of the broadcast—

(a) that person shall be treated as the person making the broadcast, and

(b) the place in which he has his principal establishment in the European Economic Area shall be treated as the place from which the broadcast is made.]

Amendments (Textual)

F18. S. 6. A inserted (1.12.1996 with effect as mentioned in reg. 28 of the amending S.I.) by S.I. 1996/2967, reg. 6. (2)

F19. Words in s. 6. A(1)(a) inserted (31.10.2003) by The Copyright and Related Rights Regulations 2003 (S.I. 2003/2498), reg. 5. (3)(a)(i) (with regs. 31-40)

F20. Words in s. 6. A(1)(a) substituted (31.10.2003) by The Copyright and Related Rights Regulations 2003 (S.I. 2003/2498), reg. 5. (3)(a)(ii) (with regs. 31-40)

F21. Word in s. 6. A(1)(b)(c) inserted (31.10.2003.) by The Copyright and Related Rights Regulations 2003 (S.I. 2003/2498), reg. 5. (3)(b) (with regs. 31-40)

7 Cable programmes.

F22. . . . .

Amendments (Textual)

F22. S. 7 repealed (31.10.2003) by The Copyright and Related Rights Regulations 2003 (S.I. 2003/2498), regs. 2. (2), 5. (1), Sch. 2 (with regs. 31-40)

8 Published editions.

(1) In this Part "published edition", in the context of copyright in the typographical arrangement of a published edition, means a published edition of the whole or any part of one or more literary, dramatic or musical works.

(2) Copyright does not subsist in the typographical arrangement of a published edition if, or to the extent that, it reproduces the typographical arrangement of a previous edition.

Authorship and ownership of copyright

9 Authorship of work.

(1) In this Part "author", in relation to a work, means the person who creates it.

(2) That person shall be taken to be—

F23 [F23. (aa)in the case of a sound recording, the producer;

F23. (ab)in the case of a film, the producer and the principal director;]

(b) in the case of a broadcast, the person making the broadcast (see section 6. (3)) or, in the case of a broadcast which relays another broadcast by reception and immediate re-transmission, the person making that other broadcast;

(c) F24. . . . .

(d) in the case of the typographical arrangement of a published edition, the publisher.

(3) In the case of a literary, dramatic, musical or artistic work which is computer-generated, the author shall be taken to be the person by whom the arrangements necessary for the creation of the work are undertaken.

(4) For the purposes of this Part a work is of "unknown authorship" if the identity of the author is unknown or, in the case of a work of joint authorship, if the identity of none of the authors is known.

(5) For the purposes of this Part the identity of an author shall be regarded as unknown if it is not possible for a person to ascertain his identity by reasonable inquiry; but if his identity is once known it shall not subsequently be regarded as unknown.

Amendments (Textual)

F23. S. 9. (2)(aa)(ab) substituted for s. 9. (2)(a) (1.12.1996 with effect in relation to films made on or after 1.7.1994) by S.I. 1996/2967, regs. 18. (1), 36

F24. S. 9. (2)(c) repealed (31.10.2003) by The Copyright and Related Rights Regulations 2003 (S.I. 2003/2498), regs. 2. (2), 5. (4), Sch. 2 (with regs. 31-40)

10 Works of joint authorship.

(1) In this Part a "work of joint authorship" means a work produced by the collaboration of two or more authors in which the contribution of each author is not distinct from that of the other author or authors.

F25 [(1. A)A film shall be treated as a work of joint authorship unless the producer and the principal director are the same person.]

(2) A broadcast shall be treated as a work of joint authorship in any case where more than one person is to be taken as making the broadcast (see section 6. (3)).

(3) References in this Part to the author of a work shall, except as otherwise provided, be construed in relation to a work of joint authorship as references to all the authors of the work.

Amendments (Textual)

F25. S. 10. (1. A) inserted (1.12.1996 with effet in relation to films made on or after 1.7.1994) by S.I. 1996/2967, regs. 18. (2), 36

[F2610. A Works of co-authorship

(1) In this Part a "work of co-authorship" means a work produced by the collaboration of the author of a musical work and the author of a literary work where the two works are created in order to be used together.

(2) References in this Part to a work or the author of a work shall, except as otherwise provided, be construed in relation to a work of co-authorship as references to each of the separate musical and literary works comprised in the work of co-authorship and to each of the authors of such works.]

Amendments (Textual)

F26. S. 10. A inserted (1.11.2013) by The Copyright and Duration of Rights in Performances Regulations 2013 (S.I. 2013/1782), regs. 1, 4 (with regs. 11-27)

11 First ownership of copyright.

(1) The author of a work is the first owner of any copyright in it, subject to the following provisions.

(2) Where a literary, dramatic, musical or artistic work [F27, or a film,] is made by an employee in the course of his employment, his employer is the first owner of any copyright in the work subject to any agreement to the contrary.

(3) This section does not apply to Crown copyright or Parliamentary copyright (see sections 163 and 165) or to copyright which subsists by virtue of section 168 (copyright of certain international organisations).

Amendments (Textual)

F27. Words in s. 11. (2) inserted (1.12.1996 with effect in relation to films made on or after 1.7.1994) by S.I. 1996/2967, regs. 18. (3), 36

Duration of copyright

[F2812 Duration of copyright in literary, dramatic, musical or artistic works.

(1) The following provisions have effect with respect to the duration of copyright in a literary, dramatic, musical or artistic work.

(2) Copyright expires at the end of the period of 70 years from the end of the calendar year in which the author dies, subject as follows.

(3) If the work is of unknown authorship, copyright expires—

(a) at the end of the period of 70 years from the end of the calendar year in which the work was made, or

(b) if during that period the work is made available to the public, at the end of the period of 70 years from the end of the calendar year in which it is first so made available,

subject as follows.

(4) Subsection (2) applies if the identity of the author becomes known before the end of the period specified in paragraph (a) or (b) of subsection (3).

(5) For the purposes of subsection (3) making available to the public includes—

(a) in the case of a literary, dramatic or musical work—

(i) performance in public, or

[F29. (ii)communication to the public;]

(b) in the case of an artistic work—

(i) exhibition in public,

(ii) a film including the work being shown in public, or

[F30. (iii)communication to the public;]

but in determining generally for the purposes of that subsection whether a work has been made available to the public no account shall be taken of any unauthorised act.

(6) Where the country of origin of the work is not an EEA state and the author of the work is not a national of an EEA state, the duration of copyright is that to which the work is entitled in the country of origin, provided that does not exceed the period which would apply under subsections (2) to (5).

(7) If the work is computer-generated the above provisions do not apply and copyright expires at the end of the period of 50 years from the end of the calendar year in which the work was made.

(8) The provisions of this section are adapted as follows in relation to a work of joint authorship [F31or a work of co-authorship]—

(a) the reference in subsection (2) to the death of the author shall be construed—

(i) if the identity of all the authors is known, as a reference to the death of the last of them to die, and

(ii) if the identity of one or more of the authors is known and the identity of one or more others is not, as a reference to the death of the last whose identity is known;

(b) the reference in subsection (4) to the identity of the author becoming known shall be construed as a reference to the identity of any of the authors becoming known;

(c) the reference in subsection (6) to the author not being a national of an EEA state shall be construed as a reference to none of the authors being a national of an EEA state.

(9) This section does not apply to Crown copyright or Parliamentary copyright (see sections 163 to [F32166. D]) or to copyright which subsists by virtue of section 168 (copyright of certain international organisations).]

Amendments (Textual)

F28. S. 12 substituted (1.1.1996) by S.I. 1995/3297, reg. 5. (1) (with Pt. III)

F29. S. 12. (5)(a)(ii) substituted (31.10.2003) by The Copyright and Related Rights Regulations 2003, (S.I. 2003/2498), reg. 2. (1), {Sch. 1 para. 4. (1)} (with regs. 31-40)

F30. S. 12. (5)(b)(iii) substituted (31.10.2003) by The Copyright and Related Rights Regulations 2003, (S.I. 2003/2498), reg. 2. (1), {Sch. 1 para. 4. (2)} (with regs. 31-40)

F31. Words in s. 12. (8) inserted (1.11.2013) by The Copyright and Duration of Rights in

Performances Regulations 2013 (S.I. 2013/1782), regs. 1, 5 (with regs. 11-27)

F32. Word in s. 12. (9) substituted by Government of Wales Act 2006 (c. 32), s. 160. (1), Sch. 10 para. 23 (with Sch. 11 para. 22), the amending provision coming into force immediately after "the 2007 election" (held on 3.5.2007) subject to s. 161. (4)(5) of the amending Act, which provides for certain provisions to come into force for specified purposes immediately after the end of "the initial period" (which ended with the day of the first appointment of a First Minister on 25.5.2007) - see ss. 46, 161. (1)(4)(5) of the amending Act.

[F3313. A Duration of copyright in sound recordings.

(1) The following provisions have effect with respect to the duration of copyright in a sound recording.

[F34. (2)Subject to subsections (4) and (5) [F35and section 191. HA(4)], copyright expires—

(a) at the end of the period of 50 years from the end of the calendar year in which the recording is made, or

(b) if during that period the recording is published, [F3670] years from the end of the calendar year in which it is first published, or

(c) if during that period the recording is not published but is made available to the public by being played in public or communicated to the public, [F3770] years from the end of the calendar year in which it is first so made available,

but in determining whether a sound recording has been published, played in public or communicated to the public, no account shall be taken of any unauthorised act.]

(3) F38 . . . .

(4) Where the author of a sound recording is not a national of an EEA state, the duration of copyright is that to which the sound recording is entitled in the country of which the author is a national, provided that does not exceed the period which would apply under [F39 subsection (2)] .

(5) If or to the extent that the application of subsection (4) would be at variance with an international obligation to which the United Kingdom became subject prior to 29th October 1993, the duration of copyright shall be as specified in [F39subsection (2)].]

Amendments (Textual)

F33. Ss. 13. A, 13. B substituted for s. 13 (1.1.1996) by S.I. 1995/3297, reg. 6. (1) (with Pt. IV)

F34. S. 13. A(2) substituted (31.10.2003) by The Copyright and Related Rights Regulations 2003 (S.I. 2003/2498), reg. 29. (a) (with regs. 31-40)

F35. Words in s. 13. A(2) inserted (1.11.2013) by The Copyright and Duration of Rights in Performances Regulations 2013 (S.I. 2013/1782), regs. 1, 6. (a) (with regs. 11-27)

F36. Word in s. 13. A(2)(b) substituted (1.11.2013) by The Copyright and Duration of Rights in Performances Regulations 2013 (S.I. 2013/1782), regs. 1, 6. (b) (with regs. 11-27)

F37. Word in s. 13. A(2)(c) substituted (1.11.2013) by The Copyright and Duration of Rights in Performances Regulations 2013 (S.I. 2013/1782), regs. 1, 6. (b) (with regs. 11-27)

F38. S. 13. A(3) repealed (31.10.2003) by The Copyright and Related Rights Regulations 2003 (S.I. 2003/2498), regs. 2. (2), 29. (b), Sch. 2 (with regs. 31-40)

F39. Words in s. 13. A(4)(5) substituted (31.10.2003) by The Copyright and Related Rights Regulations 2003 (S.I.2003/2498), reg. 29. (c) (with regs. 31-40)

[F4013. B Duration of copyright in films.

(1) The following provisions have effect with respect to the duration of copyright in a film.

(2) Copyright expires at the end of the period of 70 years from the end of the calendar year in which the death occurs of the last to die of the following persons—

(a) the principal director,

(b) the author of the screenplay,

(c) the author of the dialogue, or

(d) the composer of music specially created for and used in the film;

subject as follows.

(3) If the identity of one or more of the persons referred to in subsection (2)(a) to (d) is known and the identity of one or more others is not, the reference in that subsection to the death of the last of them to die shall be construed as a reference to the death of the last whose identity is known.

(4) If the identity of the persons referred to in subsection (2)(a) to (d) is unknown, copyright expires at—

(a) the end of the period of 70 years from the end of the calendar year in which the film was made, or

(b) if during that period the film is made available to the public, at the end of the period of 70 years from the end of the calendar year in which it is first so made available.

(5) Subsections (2) and (3) apply if the identity of any of those persons becomes known before the end of the period specified in paragraph (a) or (b) of subsection (4).

(6) For the purposes of subsection (4) making available to the public includes—

(a) showing in public, or

[F41. (b)communicating to the public;]

but in determining generally for the purposes of that subsection whether a film has been made available to the public no account shall be taken of any unauthorised act.

(7) Where the country of origin is not an EEA state and the author of the film is not a national of an EEA state, the duration of copyright is that to which the work is entitled in the country of origin, provided that does not exceed the period which would apply under subsections (2) to (6).

(8) In relation to a film of which there are joint authors, the reference in subsection (7) to the author not being a national of an EEA state shall be construed as a reference to none of the authors being a national of an EEA state.

(9) If in any case there is no person falling within paragraphs (a) to (d) of subsection (2), the above provisions do not apply and copyright expires at the end of the period of 50 years from the end of the calendar year in which the film was made.

(10) For the purposes of this section the identity of any of the persons referred to in subsection (2)(a) to (d) shall be regarded as unknown if it is not possible for a person to ascertain his identity by reasonable inquiry; but if the identity of any such person is once known it shall not subsequently be regarded as unknown.]

Amendments (Textual)

F40. Ss. 13. A, 13. B substituted for s. 13 (1.1.1996) by S.I. 1995/3297, reg. 6. (1) (with Pt. IV)

F41. S. 13. B(6)(b) substituted (31.10.2003) by The Copyright and Related Rights Regulations 2003 (S.I. 2003/2498), reg. 2. (1), Sch. 1 para. 4. (3) (with regs. 31-40)

13. . . . .

[F4314 Duration of copyright in broadcasts F42. . . .

(1) The following provisions have effect with respect to the duration of copyright in a broadcast F44. . . .

(2) Copyright in a broadcast F44. . . expires at the end of the period of 50 years from the end of the calendar year in which the broadcast was made F45. . . , subject as follows.

(3) Where the author of the broadcast F44. . . is not a national of an EEA state, the duration of copyright in the broadcast F44. . . is that to which it is entitled in the country of which the author is a national, provided that does not exceed the period which would apply under subsection (2).

(4) If or to the extent that the application of subsection (3) would be at variance with an international obligation to which the United Kingdom became subject prior to 29th October 1993, the duration of copyright shall be as specified in subsection (2).

(5) Copyright in a repeat broadcast F44. . . expires at the same time as the copyright in the original broadcast F44. . . ; and accordingly no copyright arises in respect of a repeat broadcast F44. . . which is broadcast F46. . . after the expiry of the copyright in the original broadcast F44. . . .

(6) A repeat broadcast F44. . . means one which is a repeat F47. . . of a broadcast previously made F47. . . .]

Amendments (Textual)

F42. Words in s. 14 heading repealed (31.10.2003) by The Copyright and Related Rights Regulations 2003 (S.I. 2003/2498), reg. 2. (2), Sch. 2 (with regs. 31-40)

F43. S. 14 substituted (1.1.1996) by S.I. 1995/3297, reg. 7. (1) (with Pt. IV)

F44. Words in s. 14 repealed (31.10.2003) by The Copyright and Related Rights Regulations 2003 (S.I. 2003/2498), reg. 2. (2), Sch. 2 (with regs. 31-40)

F45. Words in s. 14. (2) repealed (31.10.2003) by The Copyright and Related Rights Regulations 2003 (S.I. 2003/2498), reg. 2. (2), Sch. 2 (with regs. 31-40)

F46. Words in s. 14. (5) repealed (31.10.2003) by The Copyright and Related Rights Regulations 2003 (S.I. 2003/2498), reg. 2. (2), Sch. 2 (with regs. 31-40)

F47. Words in s. 14. (6) repealed (31.10.2003) by The Copyright and Related Rights Regulations 2003 (S.I. 2003/2498), reg. 2. (2), Sch. 2 (with regs. 31-40)

15 Duration of copyright in typographical arrangement of published editions.

Copyright in the typographical arrangement of a published edition expires at the end of the period of 25 years from the end of the calendar year in which the edition was first published.

[F4815. A Meaning of country of origin.

(1) For the purposes of the provisions of this Part relating to the duration of copyright the country of origin of a work shall be determined as follows.

(2) If the work is first published in a Berne Convention country and is not simultaneously published elsewhere, the country of origin is that country.

(3) If the work is first published simultaneously in two or more countries only one of which is a Berne Convention country, the country of origin is that country.

(4) If the work is first published simultaneously in two or more countries of which two or more are Berne Convention countries, then—

(a) if any of those countries is an EEA state, the country of origin is that country; and

(b) if none of those countries is an EEA state, the country of origin is the Berne Convention country which grants the shorter or shortest period of copyright protection.

(5) If the work is unpublished or is first published in a country which is not a Berne Convention country (and is not simultaneously published in a Berne Convention country), the country of origin is—

(a) if the work is a film and the maker of the film has his headquarters in, or is domiciled or resident in a Berne Convention country, that country;

(b) if the work is—

(i) a work of architecture constructed in a Berne Convention country, or

(ii) an artistic work incorporated in a building or other structure situated in a Berne Convention country,

that country;

(c) in any other case, the country of which the author of the work is a national.

(6) In this section—

(a) a "Berne Convention country" means a country which is a party to any Act of the International Convention for the Protection of Literary and Artistic Works signed at Berne on 9th September 1886; and

(b) references to simultaneous publication are to publication within 30 days of first publication.]

Amendments (Textual)

F48. S. 15. A inserted (1.1.1996) by S.I. 1995/3297, reg. 8. (1) (with Pt. IV)

Chapter II Rights of Copyright Owner

Modifications etc. (not altering text)

C25. Pt. I Ch. II (ss. 16-27) applied (with modifications) (1.12.1996) by S.I. 1996/2967, reg. 17. (1) (with Pt. III)

16 The acts restricted by copyright in a work.

(1) The owner of the copyright in a work has, in accordance with the following provisions of this Chapter, the exclusive right to do the following acts in the United Kingdom—

(a) to copy the work (see section 17);

(b) to issue copies of the work to the public (see section 18);

F49[(ba)to rent or lend the work to the public (see section 18. A);]

(c) to perform, show or play the work in public (see section 19);

[F50. (d)to communicate the work to the public (see section 20);]

(e) to make an adaptation of the work or do any of the above in relation to an adaptation (see section 21);

and those acts are referred to in this Part as the "acts restricted by the copyright".

(2) Copyright in a work is infringed by a person who without the licence of the copyright owner does, or authorises another to do, any of the acts restricted by the copyright.

(3) References in this Part to the doing of an act restricted by the copyright in a work are to the doing of it—

(a) in relation to the work as a whole or any substantial part of it, and

(b) either directly or indirectly;

and it is immaterial whether any intervening acts themselves infringe copyright.

(4) This Chapter has effect subject to—

(a) the provisions of Chapter III (acts permitted in relation to copyright works), and

(b) the provisions of Chapter VII (provisions with respect to copyright licensing).

Amendments (Textual)

F49. S. 16. (1)(ba) inserted (1.12.1996) by S.I. 1996/2967, reg. 10. (1) (with Pt. III)

F50. S. 16. (1)(d) substituted (31.10.2003) by The Copyright and Related Rights Regulations 2003 (S.I. 2003/2498), reg. 6. (2) (with regs. 31-40)

17 Infringement of copyright by copying.

(1) The copying of the work is an act restricted by the copyright in every description of copyright work; and references in this Part to copying and copies shall be construed as follows.

(2) Copying in relation to a literary, dramatic, musical or artistic work means reproducing the work in any material form.

This includes storing the work in any medium by electronic means.

(3) In relation to an artistic work copying includes the making of a copy in three dimensions of a two-dimensional work and the making of a copy in two dimensions of a three-dimensional work.

(4) Copying in relation to a film [F51or broadcast] includes making a photograph of the whole or any substantial part of any image forming part of the film [F51or broadcast].

(5) Copying in relation to the typographical arrangement of a published edition means making a facsimile copy of the arrangement.

(6) Copying in relation to any description of work includes the making of copies which are transient or are incidental to some other use of the work.

Amendments (Textual)

F51. Words in s. 17. (4) substituted (31.10.2003) by The Copyright and Related Rights Regulations 2003 (S.I. 2003/2498), regs. 2. (1), 5. (5), Sch. 1 para. 3. (1)(a) (with regs. 31-40)

18 Infringement by issue of copies to the public.

(1) The issue to the public of copies of the work is an act restricted by the copyright in every description of copyright work.

F52[F52. (2)References in this Part to the issue to the public of copies of a work are to—

(a) the act of putting into circulation in the EEA copies not previously put into circulation in the EEA by or with the consent of the copyright owner, or

(b) the act of putting into circulation outside the EEA copies not previously put into circulation in the EEA or elsewhere.

F52. (3)References in this Part to the issue to the public of copies of a work do not include—

(a) any subsequent distribution, sale, hiring or loan of copies previously put into circulation (but see section 18. A: infringement by rental or lending), or

(b) any subsequent importation of such copies into the United Kingdom or another EEA state, except so far as paragraph (a) of subsection (2) applies to putting into circulation in the EEA copies previously put into circulation outside the EEA.]

F53[(4)References in this Part to the issue of copies of a work include the issue of the original.]

Amendments (Textual)

F52. S. 18. (2)(3) substituted (1.12.1996) by S.I. 1996/2967, reg. 9. (2) (with Pt. III)

F53. S. 18. (4) added (1.12.1996) by S.I. 1996/2967, reg. 9. (3) (with Pt. III)

[F54**18. A Infringement by rental or lending of work to the public.**

(1) The rental or lending of copies of the work to the public is an act restricted by the copyright in—

(a) a literary, dramatic or musical work,

(b) an artistic work, other than—

(i) a work of architecture in the form of a building or a model for a building, or

(ii) a work of applied art, or

(c) a film or a sound recording.

(2) In this Part, subject to the following provisions of this section—

(a) "rental" means making a copy of the work available for use, on terms that it will or may be returned, for direct or indirect economic or commercial advantage, and

(b) "lending" means making a copy of the work available for use, on terms that it will or may be returned, otherwise than for direct or indirect economic or commercial advantage, through an establishment which is accessible to the public.

(3) The expressions "rental" and "lending" do not include—

(a) making available for the purpose of public performance, playing or showing in public [F55or communication to the public];

(b) making available for the purpose of exhibition in public; or

(c) making available for on-the-spot reference use.

(4) The expression "lending" does not include making available between establishments which are accessible to the public.

(5) Where lending by an establishment accessible to the public gives rise to a payment the amount of which does not go beyond what is necessary to cover the operating costs of the establishment, there is no direct or indirect economic or commercial advantage for the purposes of this section.

(6) References in this Part to the rental or lending of copies of a work include the rental or lending of the original.]

Amendments (Textual)

F54. S. 18. A inserted (1.12.1996) by S.I. 1996/2967, reg. 10. (2) (with Pt. III)

F55. Words in s. 18. A(3)(a) substituted by The Copyright and Related Rights Regulations 2003 (S.I. 2003/2498), reg. 2. (1), Sch. 1 para. 6. (2)(a) (with regs. 31-40)

19 Infringement by performance, showing or playing of work in public.

(1) The performance of the work in public is an act restricted by the copyright in a literary, dramatic or musical work.

(2) In this Part "performance", in relation to a work—

(a) includes delivery in the case of lectures, addresses, speeches and sermons, and

(b) in general, includes any mode of visual or acoustic presentation, including presentation by means of a sound recording, film [F56or broadcast] of the work.

(3) The playing or showing of the work in public is an act restricted by the copyright in a sound recording, film [F56or broadcast].

(4) Where copyright in a work is infringed by its being performed, played or shown in public by means of apparatus for receiving visual images or sounds conveyed by electronic means, the person by whom the visual images or sounds are sent, and in the case of a performance the performers, shall not be regarded as responsible for the infringement.

Amendments (Textual)

F56. Words in s. 19. (2)(b)(3) substituted (31.10.2003) by The Copyright and Related Rights Regulations 2003 (S.I. 2003/2498), reg. 2. (1), Sch. 1 para. 3. (1)(b)(c) (with regs. 31-40)

[F57**20. Infringement by communication to the public**

(1) The communication to the public of the work is an act restricted by the copyright in—

(a) a literary, dramatic, musical or artistic work,

(b) a sound recording or film, or

(c) a broadcast.

(2) References in this Part to communication to the public are to communication to the public by electronic transmission, and in relation to a work include—

(a) the broadcasting of the work;

(b) the making available to the public of the work by electronic transmission in such a way that members of the public may access it from a place and at a time individually chosen by them.]

Amendments (Textual)

F57. S. 20 substituted (31.10.2003) by The Copyright and Related Rights Regulations 2003 (S.I. 2003/2498), reg. 6. (1) (with regs. 31-40)

21 Infringement by making adaptation or act done in relation to adaptation.

(1) The making of an adaptation of the work is an act restricted by the copyright in a literary, dramatic or musical work.

For this purpose an adaptation is made when it is recorded, in writing or otherwise.

(2) The doing of any of the acts specified in sections 17 to 20, or subsection (1) above, in relation to an adaptation of the work is also an act restricted by the copyright in a literary, dramatic or musical work.

For this purpose it is immaterial whether the adaptation has been recorded, in writing or otherwise, at the time the act is done.

(3) In this Part "adaptation"—

(a) in relation to a literary [F58work, [F59other than a computer program or a database, or in relation to a]] dramatic work, means—

(i) a translation of the work;

(ii) a version of a dramatic work in which it is converted into a non-dramatic work or, as the case may be, of a non-dramatic work in which it is converted into a dramatic work;

(iii) a version of the work in which the story or action is conveyed wholly or mainly by means of pictures in a form suitable for reproduction in a book, or in a newspaper, magazine or similar periodical;

F60[(ab)in relation to a computer program, means an arrangement or altered version of the program or a translation of it;]

F61[(ac)in relation to a database, means an arrangement or altered version of the database or a translation of it;]

(b) in relation to a musical work, means an arrangement or transcription of the work.

(4) In relation to a computer program a "translation" includes a version of the program in which it is converted into or out of a computer language or code or into a different computer language or code F62. . .

(5) No inference shall be drawn from this section as to what does or does not amount to copying a work.

Amendments (Textual)

F58. Words in s. 21. (3)(a) inserted (1.1.1993) by S.I. 1992/3233, reg. 5. (1)

F59. Words in s. 21. (3)(a) substituted (1.1.1998) by S.I. 1997/3032, reg. 7. (a) (with Pt. IV)

F60. S. 21. (3)(ab) inserted (1.1.1993) by S.I. 1992/3233, reg. 5. (2)

F61. S. 21. (3)(ac) inserted (1.1.1998) by S.I. 1997/3032, reg. 7. (b) (with Pt. IV)

F62. Words in s. 21. (4) omitted (1.1.1993) by virtue of S.I. 1992/3233, reg. 5. (3)

Secondary infringement of copyright

22 Secondary infringement: importing infringing copy.

The copyright in a work is infringed by a person who, without the licence of the copyright owner, imports into the United Kingdom, otherwise than for his private and domestic use, an article which is, and which he knows or has reason to believe is, an infringing copy of the work.

23 Secondary infringement: possessing or dealing with infringing copy.

The copyright in a work is infringed by a person who, without the licence of the copyright owner—

(a) possesses in the course of a business,

(b) sells or lets for hire, or offers or exposes for sale or hire,

(c) in the course of a business exhibits in public or distributes, or

(d) distributes otherwise than in the course of a business to such an extent as to affect prejudicially the owner of the copyright,

an article which is, and which he knows or has reason to believe is, an infringing copy of the work.

24 Secondary infringement: providing means for making infringing copies.

(1) Copyright in a work is infringed by a person who, without the licence of the copyright owner—

(a) makes,

(b) imports into the United Kingdom,

(c) possesses in the course of a business, or

(d) sells or lets for hire, or offers or exposes for sale or hire,

an article specifically designed or adapted for making copies of that work, knowing or having reason to believe that it is to be used to make infringing copies.

(2) Copyright in a work is infringed by a person who without the licence of the copyright owner transmits the work by means of a telecommunications system (otherwise than by [F63communication to the public]), knowing or having reason to believe that infringing copies of the work will be made by means of the reception of the transmission in the United Kingdom or elsewhere.

Amendments (Textual)

F63. Words in s. 24. (2) substituted (31.10.2003) by The Copyright and Related Rights Regulations 2003 (S.I. 2003/2498), reg. 2. (1), Sch. 1 para. 5. (a) (with regs. 31-40)

25 Secondary infringement: permitting use of premises for infringing performance.

(1) Where the copyright in a literary, dramatic or musical work is infringed by a performance at a place of public entertainment, any person who gave permission for that place to be used for the performance is also liable for the infringement unless when he gave permission he believed on reasonable grounds that the performance would not infringe copyright.

(2) In this section "place of public entertainment" includes premises which are occupied mainly for other purposes but are from time to time made available for hire for the purposes of public entertainment.

26 Secondary infringement: provision of apparatus for infringing performance, &c.

(1) Where copyright in a work is infringed by a public performance of the work, or by the playing or showing of the work in public, by means of apparatus for—

(a) playing sound recordings,

(b) showing films, or

(c) receiving visual images or sounds conveyed by electronic means,

the following persons are also liable for the infringement.

(2) A person who supplied the apparatus, or any substantial part of it, is liable for the infringement if when he supplied the apparatus or part—

(a) he knew or had reason to believe that the apparatus was likely to be so used as to infringe copyright, or

(b) in the case of apparatus whose normal use involves a public performance, playing or showing, he did not believe on reasonable grounds that it would not be so used as to infringe copyright.

(3) An occupier of premises who gave permission for the apparatus to be brought onto the premises is liable for the infringement if when he gave permission he knew or had reason to believe that the apparatus was likely to be so used as to infringe copyright.

(4) A person who supplied a copy of a sound recording or film used to infringe copyright is liable for the infringement if when he supplied it he knew or had reason to believe that what he supplied, or a copy made directly or indirectly from it, was likely to be so used as to infringe copyright.

Infringing copies

27 Meaning of "infringing copy".

(1) In this Part "infringing copy", in relation to a copyright work, shall be construed in accordance with this section.

(2) An article is an infringing copy if its making constituted an infringement of the copyright in the work in question.

(3) F64. . . An article is also an infringing copy if—

(a) it has been or is proposed to be imported into the United Kingdom, and

(b) its making in the United Kingdom would have constituted an infringement of the copyright in the work in question, or a breach of an exclusive licence agreement relating to that work.

F65. (3. A). . . . .

(4) Where in any proceedings the question arises whether an article is an infringing copy and it is shown—

(a) that the article is a copy of the work, and

(b) that copyright subsists in the work or has subsisted at any time,

it shall be presumed until the contrary is proved that the article was made at a time when copyright subsisted in the work.

(5) Nothing in subsection (3) shall be construed as applying to an article which may lawfully be imported into the United Kingdom by virtue of any enforceable [F66. EU] right within the meaning of section 2. (1) of the M1. European Communities Act 1972.

(6) In this Part "infringing copy" includes a copy falling to be treated as an infringing copy by virtue of any of the following provisions —

- [F67section 29. A(3) (copies for text and data analysis for non-commercial research),]
- [F68section 28. B(7) and (9) (personal copies for private use),]
- [F69section 31. A(5) and (6) (disabled persons: copies of works for personal use),]
- [F70section 31. B(11) (making and supply of accessible copies by authorised bodies),]
- [F67section 35. (5) (recording by educational establishments of broadcasts),]
- [F67section 36. (8) (copying and use of extracts of works by educational establishments),]
- [F67section 42. A(5)(b) (copying by librarians: single copies of published works),]
- [F67section 61. (6)(b) (recordings of folksongs),]
- F71...
- F72...
- F72...
- F72...
- F72...
- section 56. (2) (further copies, adaptations, &c. of work in electronic form retained on transfer of principal copy),
- section 63. (2) (copies made for purpose of advertising artistic work for sale),
- section 68. (4) (copies made for purpose of broadcast F73 . . .),
- [F74section 70. (2) (recording for the purposes of time-shifting),
- section 71. (2) (photographs of broadcasts), or]
- any provision of an order under section 141 (statutory licence for certain reprographic copying by educational establishments).

Amendments (Textual)

F64. Words in s. 27. (3) omitted (1.12.1996) by virtue of S.I. 1996/2967, reg. 9. (4) (with Pt. III)

F65. S. 27. (3. A) omitted (1.12.1996) by virtue of S.I. 1996/2967, reg. 9. (4) (with Pt. III)

F66. Word substituted (22.4.2011) by The Treaty of Lisbon (Changes in Terminology) Order 2011 (S.I. 2011/1043), arts. 3, 6

F67. Words in s. 27. (6) inserted (1.6.2014) by The Copyright and Rights in Performances (Research, Education, Libraries and Archives) Regulations 2014 (S.I. 2014/1372), reg. 1, Sch. para. 2. (b)

F68. Words in s. 27. (6) inserted (1.10.2014) by The Copyright and Rights in Performances (Personal Copies for Private Use) Regulations 2014 (S.I. 2014/2361), regs. 1. (1), 4. (1) (with reg.

5) (but note that the amending S.I. was quashed with prospective effect by the High Court in the case of R (British Academy of Songwriters, Composers and Authors and others) v Secretary of State for Business, Innovation and Skills [2015] EWHC 2041 (Admin), 17 July 2015)
F69. Words in s. 27. (6) substituted (1.6.2014) by The Copyright and Rights in Performances (Disability) Regulations 2014 (S.I. 2014/1384), reg. 1. (1), Sch. para. 1. (a)
F70. Words in s. 27. (6) substituted (1.6.2014) by The Copyright and Rights in Performances (Disability) Regulations 2014 (S.I. 2014/1384), reg. 1. (1), Sch. para. 1. (b)
F71 Words in s. 27. (6) omitted (1.6.2014) by virtue of The Copyright and Rights in Performances (Disability) Regulations 2014 (S.I. 2014/1384) , reg. 1. (1) , Sch. para. 1. (c)
F72. Words in s. 27. (6) omitted (1.6.2014) by virtue of The Copyright and Rights in Performances (Research, Education, Libraries and Archives) Regulations 2014 (S.I. 2014/1372), reg. 1, Sch. para. 2. (a)
F73. Words in s. 27. (6) repealed (31.10.2003) by The Copyright and Related Rights Regulations 2003 (S.I. 2003/2498), reg. 2. (2), Sch. 2 (with regs. 31-40)
F74. S. 27. (6): entries substituted (31.10.2003) for word "or" appearing at end of entry for s. 68. (4) by The Copyright and Related Rights Regulations 2003 (S.I. 2003/2498), reg. 20. (3) (with regs. 31-40)
Marginal Citations
M11972 c. 68.

Chapter III Acts Permitted in relation to Copyright Works

Modifications etc. (not altering text)
C26. Pt. I Ch. III (ss. 28–76) amended by Broadcasting Act 1990 (c. 42, SIF 96), s. 176, Sch. 17 para. 7. (1)
C27. Pt. I Ch. III (ss. 28-76) applied (with modifications) (1.12.1996) by S.I. 1996/2967, reg. 17. (1)-(3) (with Pt. III)
C28. Pt. I Ch. III (ss. 28-76) continued (31.10.2003) by virtue of The Copyright and Related Rights Regulations 2003 (S.I. 2003/2498), reg. 33, (with regs. 31-40)
28 Introductory provisions.
(1) The provisions of this Chapter specify acts which may be done in relation to copyright works notwithstanding the subsistence of copyright; they relate only to the question of infringement of copyright and do not affect any other right or obligation restricting the doing of any of the specified acts.
(2) Where it is provided by this Chapter that an act does not infringe copyright, or may be done without infringing copyright, and no particular description of copyright work is mentioned, the act in question does not infringe the copyright in a work of any description.
(3) No inference shall be drawn from the description of any act which may by virtue of this Chapter be done without infringing copyright as to the scope of the acts restricted by the copyright in any description of work.
(4) The provisions of this Chapter are to be construed independently of each other, so that the fact that an act does not fall within one provision does not mean that it is not covered by another provision.

General

[F7528. AMaking of temporary copies
Copyright in a literary work, other than a computer program or a database, or in a dramatic, musical or artistic work, the typographical arrangement of a published edition, a sound recording or a film, is not infringed by the making of a temporary copy which is transient or incidental, which is an integral and essential part of a technological process and the sole purpose of which is to enable—

(a) a transmission of the work in a network between third parties by an intermediary; or

(b) a lawful use of the work;

and which has no independent economic significance.]

Amendments (Textual)

F75. S. 28. A inserted (31.10.2003) by The Copyright and Related Rights Regulations 2003 (S.I. 2003/2498), reg. 8. (1) (with regs. 31-40)

[F7628. BPersonal copies for private use

(1) The making of a copy of a work, other than a computer program, by an individual does not infringe copyright in the work provided that the copy—

(a) is a copy of—

(i) the individual's own copy of the work, or

(ii) a personal copy of the work made by the individual,

(b) is made for the individual's private use, and

(c) is made for ends which are neither directly nor indirectly commercial.

(2) In this section "the individual's own copy" is a copy which—

(a) has been lawfully acquired by the individual on a permanent basis,

(b) is not an infringing copy, and

(c) has not been made under any provision of this Chapter which permits the making of a copy without infringing copyright.

(3) In this section a "personal copy" means a copy made under this section.

(4) For the purposes of subsection (2)(a), a copy "lawfully acquired on a permanent basis"—

(a) includes a copy which has been purchased, obtained by way of a gift, or acquired by means of a download resulting from a purchase or a gift (other than a download of a kind mentioned in paragraph (b)); and

(b) does not include a copy which has been borrowed, rented, broadcast or streamed, or a copy which has been obtained by means of a download enabling no more than temporary access to the copy.

(5) In subsection (1)(b) "private use" includes private use facilitated by the making of a copy—

(a) as a back up copy,

(b) for the purposes of format-shifting, or

(c) for the purposes of storage, including in an electronic storage area accessed by means of the internet or similar means which is accessible only by the individual (and the person responsible for the storage area).

(6) Copyright in a work is infringed if an individual transfers a personal copy of the work to another person (otherwise than on a private and temporary basis), except where the transfer is authorised by the copyright owner.

(7) If copyright is infringed as set out in subsection (6), a personal copy which has been transferred is for all purposes subsequently treated as an infringing copy.

(8) Copyright in a work is also infringed if an individual, having made a personal copy of the work, transfers the individual's own copy of the work to another person (otherwise than on a private and temporary basis) and, after that transfer and without the licence of the copyright owner, retains any personal copy.

(9) If copyright is infringed as set out in subsection (8), any retained personal copy is for all purposes subsequently treated as an infringing copy.

(10) To the extent that a term of a contract purports to prevent or restrict the making of a copy which, by virtue of this section, would not infringe copyright, that term is unenforceable.]

Amendments (Textual)

F76. S. 28. B inserted (1.10.2014) by The Copyright and Rights in Performances (Personal Copies for Private Use) Regulations 2014 (S.I. 2014/2361), regs. 1. (1), 3. (1) (with reg. 5) (but note that the amending S.I. was quashed with prospective effect by the High Court in the case of R (British Academy of Songwriters, Composers and Authors and others) v Secretary of State for Business, Innovation and Skills [2015] EWHC 2041 (Admin), 17 July 2015)

29 Research and private study.

[F77. (1)Fair dealing with a F78... work for the purposes of research for a non-commercial purpose does not infringe any copyright in the work provided that it is accompanied by a sufficient acknowledgement.]

[F79. (1. B)No acknowledgement is required in connection with fair dealing for the purposes mentioned in subsection (1) where this would be impossible for reasons of practicality or otherwise.

(1. C)Fair dealing with a F80... work for the purposes of private study does not infringe any copyright in the work.]

F81. (2). . . . .

(3) Copying by a person other than the researcher or student himself is not fair dealing if—

[F82. (a)in the case of a librarian, or a person acting on behalf of a librarian, that person does anything which is not permitted under section 42. A (copying by librarians: single copies of published works), or]

(b) in any other case, the person doing the copying knows or has reason to believe that it will result in copies of substantially the same material being provided to more than one person at substantially the same time and for substantially the same purpose.

F83 [(4)It is not fair dealing—

(a) to convert a computer program expressed in a low level language into a version expressed in a higher level language, or

(b) incidentally in the course of so converting the program, to copy it,

(these acts being permitted if done in accordance with section 50. B (decompilation)).]

[F84. (4. A)It is not fair dealing to observe, study or test the functioning of a computer program in order to determine the ideas and principles which underlie any element of the program (these acts being permitted if done in accordance with section 50. BA (observing, studying and testing)).]

[F85. (4. B)To the extent that a term of a contract purports to prevent or restrict the doing of any act which, by virtue of this section, would not infringe copyright, that term is unenforceable.]

(5) F86. . . . .

Amendments (Textual)

F77. S. 29. (1) substituted (31.10.2003) by The Copyright and Related Rights Regulations 2003 (S.I. 2003/2498), reg. 9. (a), (with regs 31-40)

F78. Words in s. 29. (1) omitted (1.6.2014) by virtue of The Copyright and Rights in Performances (Research, Education, Libraries and Archives) Regulations 2014 (S.I. 2014/1372), regs. 1, 3. (1)(a)

F79. S. 29. (1. B)(1. C) substituted (31.10.2003) for s. 29. (1. A) by The Copyright and Related Rights Regulations 2003 (S.I. 2003/2498), reg. 9. (b) (with regs. 31-40)

F80. Words in s. 29. (1. C) omitted (1.6.2014) by virtue of The Copyright and Rights in Performances (Research, Education, Libraries and Archives) Regulations 2014 (S.I. 2014/1372), regs. 1, 3. (1)(b)

F81. S. 29. (2) omitted (1.6.2014) by virtue of The Copyright and Rights in Performances (Research, Education, Libraries and Archives) Regulations 2014 (S.I. 2014/1372), regs. 1, 3. (1)(c)

F82. S. 29. (3)(a) substituted (1.6.2014) by The Copyright and Rights in Performances (Research, Education, Libraries and Archives) Regulations 2014 (S.I. 2014/1372), regs. 1, 3. (1)(d)

F83. S. 29. (4) inserted (1.1.1993) by S.I. 1992/3233, reg. 7

F84. S. 29. (4. A) inserted (31.10.2003) by The Copyright and Related Rights Regulations 2003 (S.I. 2003/2498), reg. 9. (d) (with regs. 31-40)

F85. S. 29. (4. B) inserted (1.6.2014) by The Copyright and Rights in Performances (Research, Education, Libraries and Archives) Regulations 2014 (S.I. 2014/1372), regs. 1, 3. (1)(e)

F86. S. 29. (5) repealed (31.10.2003) by The Copyright and Related Rights Regulations 2003 (S.I. 2003/2498), regs. 2. (2), 9. (e), Sch. 2 (with regs. 31-40)

[F8729. A Copies for text and data analysis for non-commercial research

(1) The making of a copy of a work by a person who has lawful access to the work does not infringe copyright in the work provided that—

(a) the copy is made in order that a person who has lawful access to the work may carry out a computational analysis of anything recorded in the work for the sole purpose of research for a non-commercial purpose, and

(b) the copy is accompanied by a sufficient acknowledgement (unless this would be impossible for reasons of practicality or otherwise).

(2) Where a copy of a work has been made under this section, copyright in the work is infringed if—

(a) the copy is transferred to any other person, except where the transfer is authorised by the copyright owner, or

(b) the copy is used for any purpose other than that mentioned in subsection (1)(a), except where the use is authorised by the copyright owner.

(3) If a copy made under this section is subsequently dealt with—

(a) it is to be treated as an infringing copy for the purposes of that dealing, and

(b) if that dealing infringes copyright, it is to be treated as an infringing copy for all subsequent purposes.

(4) In subsection (3) "dealt with" means sold or let for hire, or offered or exposed for sale or hire.

(5) To the extent that a term of a contract purports to prevent or restrict the making of a copy which, by virtue of this section, would not infringe copyright, that term is unenforceable.]

Amendments (Textual)

F87. S. 29. A inserted (1.6.2014) by The Copyright and Rights in Performances (Research, Education, Libraries and Archives) Regulations 2014 (S.I. 2014/1372), regs. 1, 3. (2)

30 Criticism, review[F88, quotation] and news reporting.

(1) Fair dealing with a work for the purpose of criticism or review, of that or another work or of a performance of a work, does not infringe any copyright in the work provided that it is accompanied by a sufficient acknowledgement [F89 (unless this would be impossible for reasons of practicality or otherwise)] [F90 and provided that the work has been made available to the public].

[F91. (1. ZA)Copyright in a work is not infringed by the use of a quotation from the work (whether for criticism or review or otherwise) provided that—

(a) the work has been made available to the public,

(b) the use of the quotation is fair dealing with the work,

(c) the extent of the quotation is no more than is required by the specific purpose for which it is used, and

(d) the quotation is accompanied by a sufficient acknowledgement (unless this would be impossible for reasons of practicality or otherwise).]

[F92. (1. A)For the purposes of [F93subsections (1) and (1. ZA)] a work has been made available to the public if it has been made available by any means, including—

(a) the issue of copies to the public;

(b) making the work available by means of an electronic retrieval system;

(c) the rental or lending of copies of the work to the public;

(d) the performance, exhibition, playing or showing of the work in public;

(e) the communication to the public of the work,

but in determining generally for the purposes of [F94those subsections] whether a work has been made available to the public no account shall be taken of any unauthorised act.]

(2) Fair dealing with a work (other than a photograph) for the purpose of reporting current events does not infringe any copyright in the work provided that (subject to subsection (3)) it is accompanied by a sufficient acknowledgement.

(3) No acknowledgement is required in connection with the reporting of current events by means of a sound recording, film [F95 or broadcast where this would be impossible for reasons of practicality or otherwise].

[F96. (4)To the extent that a term of a contract purports to prevent or restrict the doing of any act which, by virtue of subsection (1. ZA), would not infringe copyright, that term is unenforceable.]

Amendments (Textual)

F88. Word in s. 30 heading inserted (1.10.2014) by The Copyright and Rights in Performances (Quotation and Parody) Regulations 2014 (S.I. 2014/2356), regs. 1, 3. (2)

F89. Words in s. 30. (1) inserted (1.10.2014) by The Copyright and Rights in Performances (Quotation and Parody) Regulations 2014 (S.I. 2014/2356), regs. 1, 3. (3)

F90. Words in s. 30. (1) inserted (31.10.2003) by The Copyright and Related Rights Regulations 2003 (S.I. 2003/2498), reg. 10. (1)(a) (with regs. 31-40)

F91. S. 30. (1. ZA) inserted (1.10.2014) by The Copyright and Rights in Performances (Quotation and Parody) Regulations 2014 (S.I. 2014/2356), regs. 1, 3. (4)

F92. S. 30. (1. A) inserted (31.10.2003) by The Copyright and Related Rights Regulations 2003 (S.I. 2003/2498), reg. 10. (1)(b) (with regs. 31-40)

F93. Words in s. 30. (1. A) substituted (1.10.2014) by The Copyright and Rights in Performances (Quotation and Parody) Regulations 2014 (S.I. 2014/2356), regs. 1, 3. (5)(a)

F94. Words in s. 30. (1. A) substituted (1.10.2014) by The Copyright and Rights in Performances (Quotation and Parody) Regulations 2014 (S.I. 2014/2356), regs. 1, 3. (5)(b)

F95. Words in s. 30. (3) substituted (31.10.2003) by The Copyright and Related Rights Regulations 2003 (S.I. 2003/2498), reg. 10. (1)(c) (with regs. 31-40)

F96. S. 30. (4) inserted (1.10.2014) by The Copyright and Rights in Performances (Quotation and Parody) Regulations 2014 (S.I. 2014/2356), regs. 1, 3. (6)

[F9730. ACaricature, parody or pastiche

(1) Fair dealing with a work for the purposes of caricature, parody or pastiche does not infringe copyright in the work.

(2) To the extent that a term of a contract purports to prevent or restrict the doing of any act which, by virtue of this section, would not infringe copyright, that term is unenforceable.]

Amendments (Textual)

F97. S. 30. A inserted (1.10.2014) by The Copyright and Rights in Performances (Quotation and Parody) Regulations 2014 (S.I. 2014/2356), regs. 1, 5. (1)

31 Incidental inclusion of copyright material.

(1) Copyright in a work is not infringed by its incidental inclusion in an artistic work, sound recording, film [F98or broadcast].

(2) Nor is the copyright infringed by the issue to the public of copies, or the playing, showing [F99or communication to the public], of anything whose making was, by virtue of subsection (1), not an infringement of the copyright.

(3) A musical work, words spoken or sung with music, or so much of a sound recording [F98or broadcast] as includes a musical work or such words, shall not be regarded as incidentally included in another work if it is deliberately included.

Amendments (Textual)

F98. Words in s. 31. (1)(3) substituted (31.10.2003) by The Copyright and Related Rights Regulations 2003 (S.I. 2003/2498), reg. 2. (1), Sch. 1 para. 3. (1)(d)(e) (with regs. 31-40)

F99. Words in s. 31. (2) substituted (31.10.2003) by The Copyright and Related Rights Regulations 2003 (31.10.2003), reg. 2. (1), {Sch. 1 para. 6. (2)(b)} (with reg. 31-40)

[F100. Disability]

Amendments (Textual)

F100. S. 31. A cross-heading substituted (1.6.2014) by The Copyright and Rights in Performances (Disability) Regulations 2014 (S.I. 2014/1384), regs. 1. (1), 2. (2)

[F10131. A Disabled persons: copies of works for personal use

(1) This section applies if—

(a) a disabled person has lawful possession or lawful use of a copy of the whole or part of a work, and

(b) the person's disability prevents the person from enjoying the work to the same degree as a person who does not have that disability.

(2) The making of an accessible copy of the copy of the work referred to in subsection (1)(a) does not infringe copyright if—

(a) the copy is made by the disabled person or by a person acting on behalf of the disabled person,

(b) the copy is made for the disabled person's personal use, and

(c) the same kind of accessible copies of the work are not commercially available on reasonable terms by or with the authority of the copyright owner.

(3) If a person makes an accessible copy under this section on behalf of a disabled person and charges the disabled person for it, the sum charged must not exceed the cost of making and supplying the copy.

(4) Copyright is infringed by the transfer of an accessible copy of a work made under this section to any person other than—

(a) a person by or for whom an accessible copy of the work may be made under this section, or

(b) a person who intends to transfer the copy to a person falling within paragraph (a), except where the transfer is authorised by the copyright owner.

(5) An accessible copy of a work made under this section is to be treated for all purposes as an infringing copy if it is held by a person at a time when the person does not fall within subsection (4)(a) or (b).

(6) If an accessible copy made under this section is subsequently dealt with—

(a) it is to be treated as an infringing copy for the purposes of that dealing, and

(b) if that dealing infringes copyright, it is to be treated as an infringing copy for all subsequent purposes.

(7) In this section "dealt with" means sold or let for hire or offered or exposed for sale or hire.]
Amendments (Textual)
F101. S. 31. A substituted (1.6.2014) by The Copyright and Rights in Performances (Disability) Regulations 2014 (S.I. 2014/1384), regs. 1. (1), 2. (3)
[F10231. B Making and supply of accessible copies by authorised bodies
(1) If an authorised body has lawful possession of a copy of the whole or part of a published work, the body may, without infringing copyright, make and supply accessible copies of the work for the personal use of disabled persons.
(2) But subsection (1) does not apply if the same kind of accessible copies of the work are commercially available on reasonable terms by or with the authority of the copyright owner.
(3) If an authorised body has lawful access to or lawful possession of the whole or part of a broadcast or a copy of a broadcast, the body may, without infringing copyright—

(a) in the case of a broadcast, make a recording of the broadcast, and make and supply accessible copies of the recording or of any work included in the broadcast, and

(b) in the case of a copy of a broadcast, make and supply accessible copies of that copy or of any work included in the broadcast, for the personal use of disabled persons.

(4) But subsection (3) does not apply if the same kind of accessible copies of the broadcast, or of any work included in it, are commercially available on reasonable terms by or with the authority of the copyright owner.
(5) For the purposes of subsections (1) and (3), supply "for the personal use of disabled persons" includes supply to a person acting on behalf of a disabled person.
(6) An authorised body which is an educational establishment conducted for profit must ensure that any accessible copies which it makes under this section are used only for its educational purposes.
(7) An accessible copy made under this section must be accompanied by—

(a) a statement that it is made under this section, and

(b) a sufficient acknowledgement (unless this would be impossible for reasons of practicality or otherwise).

(8) If an accessible copy is made under this section of a work which is in copy-protected electronic form, the accessible copy must, so far as is reasonably practicable, incorporate the same or equally

effective copy protection (unless the copyright owner agrees otherwise).

(9) An authorised body which has made an accessible copy of a work under this section may supply it to another authorised body which is entitled to make accessible copies of the work under this section for the purposes of enabling that other body to make accessible copies of the work.

(10) If an authorised body supplies an accessible copy it has made under this section to a person or authorised body as permitted by this section and charges the person or body for it, the sum charged must not exceed the cost of making and supplying the copy.

(11) If an accessible copy made under this section is subsequently dealt with—

(a) it is to be treated as an infringing copy for the purposes of that dealing, and

(b) if that dealing infringes copyright, it is to be treated as an infringing copy for all subsequent purposes.

(12) In this section "dealt with" means sold or let for hire or offered or exposed for sale or hire.

Amendments (Textual)

F102. Ss. 31. B, 31. BA, 31. BB substituted (1.6.2014) for s. 31. B by The Copyright and Rights in Performances (Disability) Regulations 2014 (S.I. 2014/1384), regs. 1. (1), 2. (4)

31. BAMaking and supply of intermediate copies by authorised bodies

(1) An authorised body which is entitled to make an accessible copy of a work under section 31. B may, without infringing copyright, make a copy of the work ("an intermediate copy") if this is necessary in order to make the accessible copy.

(2) An authorised body which has made an intermediate copy of a work under this section may supply it to another authorised body which is entitled to make accessible copies of the work under section 31. B for the purposes of enabling that other body to make accessible copies of the work.

(3) Copyright is infringed by the transfer of an intermediate copy made under this section to a person other than another authorised body as permitted by subsection (2), except where the transfer is authorised by the copyright owner.

(4) If an authorised body supplies an intermediate copy to an authorised body under subsection (2) and charges the body for it, the sum charged must not exceed the cost of making and supplying the copy.

Amendments (Textual)

F102. Ss. 31. B, 31. BA, 31. BB substituted (1.6.2014) for s. 31. B by The Copyright and Rights in Performances (Disability) Regulations 2014 (S.I. 2014/1384), regs. 1. (1), 2. (4)

31. BBAccessible and intermediate copies: records and notification

(1) An authorised body must keep a record of—

(a) accessible copies it makes under section 31. B,

(b) intermediate copies it makes under section 31. BA, and

(c) the persons to whom such copies are supplied.

(2) An authorised body must allow the copyright owner or a person acting for the copyright owner, on giving reasonable notice, to inspect at any reasonable time—

(a) records kept under subsection (1), and

(b) records of copies made under sections 31. B and 31. C as those sections were in force before the coming into force of these Regulations.

(3) Within a reasonable time of making an accessible copy under section 31. B, an authorised body must—

(a) notify any body which—

(i) represents particular copyright owners or owners of copyright in the type of work concerned, and

(ii) has given notice to the Secretary of State of the copyright owners, or the classes of copyright owner, represented by it, or

(b) if there is no such body, notify the copyright owner (unless it is not reasonably possible to ascertain the name and address of the copyright owner).]

Amendments (Textual)

F102. Ss. 31. B, 31. BA, 31. BB substituted (1.6.2014) for s. 31. B by The Copyright and Rights in Performances (Disability) Regulations 2014 (S.I. 2014/1384), regs. 1. (1), 2. (4)

F10331. C

. . . .

Amendments (Textual)

F103. Ss. 31. C-31. E repealed (1.6.2014) by The Copyright and Rights in Performances (Disability) Regulations 2014 (S.I. 2014/1384), reg. 1. (1), Sch. para. 8 Table

F10331. D

. . . .

Amendments (Textual)

F103. Ss. 31. C-31. E repealed (1.6.2014) by The Copyright and Rights in Performances (Disability) Regulations 2014 (S.I. 2014/1384), reg. 1. (1), Sch. para. 8 Table

F10331. E

. . . .

Amendments (Textual)

F103. Ss. 31. C-31. E repealed (1.6.2014) by The Copyright and Rights in Performances (Disability) Regulations 2014 (S.I. 2014/1384), reg. 1. (1), Sch. para. 8 Table

[F10431. F Sections 31. A to 31. BB: interpretation and general

(1) This section supplements sections 31. A to 31. BB and includes definitions.

(2) "Disabled person" means a person who has a physical or mental impairment which prevents the person from enjoying a copyright work to the same degree as a person who does not have that impairment, and "disability" is to be construed accordingly.

(3) But a person is not to be regarded as disabled by reason only of an impairment of visual function which can be improved, by the use of corrective lenses, to a level that is normally acceptable for reading without a special level or kind of light.

(4) An "accessible copy" of a copyright work means a version of the work which enables the fuller enjoyment of the work by disabled persons.

(5) An accessible copy—

(a) may include facilities for navigating around the version of the work, but

(b) must not include any changes to the work which are not necessary to overcome the problems suffered by the disabled persons for whom the accessible copy is intended.

(6) "Authorised body" means—

(a) an educational establishment, or

(b) a body that is not conducted for profit.

(7) The "supply" of a copy includes making it available for use, otherwise than for direct or indirect economic or commercial advantage, on terms that it will or may be returned.

(8) To the extent that a term of a contract purports to prevent or restrict the doing of any act which, by virtue of section 31. A, 31. B or 31. BA, would not infringe copyright, that term is unenforceable.]

Amendments (Textual)

F104. S. 31. F substituted (1.6.2014) by The Copyright and Rights in Performances (Disability) Regulations 2014 (S.I. 2014/1384), regs. 1. (1), 2. (5) (with Sch. para. 9)

Education

[F10532. Illustration for instruction

(1) Fair dealing with a work for the sole purpose of illustration for instruction does not infringe copyright in the work provided that the dealing is—

(a) for a non-commercial purpose,

(b) by a person giving or receiving instruction (or preparing for giving or receiving instruction), and

(c) accompanied by a sufficient acknowledgement (unless this would be impossible for reasons of practicality or otherwise).

(2) For the purposes of subsection (1), "giving or receiving instruction" includes setting

examination questions, communicating the questions to pupils and answering the questions.

(3) To the extent that a term of a contract purports to prevent or restrict the doing of any act which, by virtue of this section, would not infringe copyright, that term is unenforceable.]

Amendments (Textual)

F105. S. 32 substituted (1.6.2014) by The Copyright and Rights in Performances (Research, Education, Libraries and Archives) Regulations 2014 (S.I. 2014/1372), regs. 1, 4. (1)

33 Anthologies for educational use.

(1) The inclusion of a short passage from a published literary or dramatic work in a collection which—

(a) is intended for use in educational establishments and is so described in its title, and in any advertisements issued by or on behalf of the publisher, and

(b) consists mainly of material in which no copyright subsists,

does not infringe the copyright in the work if the work itself is not intended for use in such establishments and the inclusion is accompanied by a sufficient acknowledgement.

(2) Subsection (1) does not authorise the inclusion of more than two excerpts from copyright works by the same author in collections published by the same publisher over any period of five years.

(3) In relation to any given passage the reference in subsection (2) to excerpts from works by the same author—

(a) shall be taken to include excerpts from works by him in collaboration with another, and

(b) if the passage in question is from such a work, shall be taken to include excerpts from works by any of the authors, whether alone or in collaboration with another.

(4) References in this section to the use of a work in an educational establishment are to any use for the educational purposes of such an establishment.

34 Performing, playing or showing work in course of activities of educational establishment.

(1) The performance of a literary, dramatic or musical work before an audience consisting of teachers and pupils at an educational establishment and other persons directly connected with the activities of the establishment—

(a) by a teacher or pupil in the course of the activities of the establishment, or

(b) at the establishment by any person for the purposes of instruction,

is not a public performance for the purposes of infringement of copyright.

(2) The playing or showing of a sound recording, film [F106or broadcast] before such an audience at an educational establishment for the purposes of instruction is not a playing or showing of the work in public for the purposes of infringement of copyright.

(3) A person is not for this purpose directly connected with the activities of the educational establishment simply because he is the parent of a pupil at the establishment.

Amendments (Textual)

F106. Words in s. 34. (2) substituted (31.10.2003) by The Copyright and Related Rights Regulations 2003 (S.I. 2003/2498), reg. 2. (1), Sch. 1 para. 3. (1)(f) (with regs. 31-40)

[F10735. Recording by educational establishments of broadcasts

(1) A recording of a broadcast, or a copy of such a recording, may be made by or on behalf of an educational establishment for the educational purposes of that establishment without infringing copyright in the broadcast, or in any work included in it, provided that—

(a) the educational purposes are non-commercial, and

(b) the recording or copy is accompanied by a sufficient acknowledgement (unless this would be impossible for reasons of practicality or otherwise).

(2) Copyright is not infringed where a recording of a broadcast or a copy of such a recording, made under subsection (1), is communicated by or on behalf of the educational establishment to its pupils or staff for the non-commercial educational purposes of that establishment.

(3) Subsection (2) only applies to a communication received outside the premises of the establishment if that communication is made by means of a secure electronic network accessible only by the establishment's pupils and staff.

(4) Acts which would otherwise be permitted by this section are not permitted if, or to the extent

that, licences are available authorising the acts in question and the educational establishment responsible for those acts knew or ought to have been aware of that fact.

(5) If a copy made under this section is subsequently dealt with—

    (a) it is to be treated as an infringing copy for the purposes of that dealing, and

    (b) if that dealing infringes copyright, it is to be treated as an infringing copy for all subsequent purposes.

(6) In this section "dealt with" means—

    (a) sold or let for hire,

    (b) offered or exposed for sale or hire, or

    (c) communicated otherwise than as permitted by subsection (2).]

Amendments (Textual)

F107. S. 35 substituted (1.6.2014) by The Copyright and Rights in Performances (Research, Education, Libraries and Archives) Regulations 2014 (S.I. 2014/1372), regs. 1, 4. (2)

[F10836. Copying and use of extracts of works by educational establishments

(1) The copying of extracts of a relevant work by or on behalf of an educational establishment does not infringe copyright in the work, provided that—

    (a) the copy is made for the purposes of instruction for a non-commercial purpose, and

    (b) the copy is accompanied by a sufficient acknowledgement (unless this would be impossible for reasons of practicality or otherwise).

(2) Copyright is not infringed where a copy of an extract made under subsection (1) is communicated by or on behalf of the educational establishment to its pupils or staff for the purposes of instruction for a non-commercial purpose.

(3) Subsection (2) only applies to a communication received outside the premises of the establishment if that communication is made by means of a secure electronic network accessible only by the establishment's pupils and staff.

(4) In this section "relevant work" means a copyright work other than—

    (a) a broadcast, or

    (b) an artistic work which is not incorporated into another work.

(5) Not more than 5% of a work may be copied under this section by or on behalf of an educational establishment in any period of 12 months, and for these purposes a work which incorporates another work is to be treated as a single work.

(6) Acts which would otherwise be permitted by this section are not permitted if, or to the extent that, licences are available authorising the acts in question and the educational establishment responsible for those acts knew or ought to have been aware of that fact.

(7) The terms of a licence granted to an educational establishment authorising acts permitted by this section are of no effect so far as they purport to restrict the proportion of a work which may be copied (whether on payment or free of charge) to less than that which would be permitted by this section.

(8) If a copy made under this section is subsequently dealt with—

    (a) it is to be treated as an infringing copy for the purposes of that dealing, and

    (b) if that dealing infringes copyright, it is to be treated as an infringing copy for all subsequent purposes.

(9) In this section "dealt with" means—

    (a) sold or let for hire,

    (b) offered or exposed for sale or hire, or

    (c) communicated otherwise than as permitted by subsection (2).]

Amendments (Textual)

F108. S. 36 substituted (1.6.2014) by The Copyright and Rights in Performances (Research, Education, Libraries and Archives) Regulations 2014 (S.I. 2014/1372), regs. 1, 4. (3)

[F10936. A Lending of copies by educational establishments

Copyright in a work is not infringed by the lending of copies of the work by an educational establishment.]

Amendments (Textual)

F109. S. 36. A inserted (1.12.1996) by S.I. 1996/2967, reg. 11. (1) (with Pt. III)

Libraries and archives

F11037. Libraries and archives: introductory.

. . . .

Amendments (Textual)

F110. Ss. 37-40 repealed (1.6.2014) by The Copyright and Rights in Performances (Research, Education, Libraries and Archives) Regulations 2014 (S.I. 2014/1372), reg. 1, Sch. para. 14 Table

F11038. Copying by librarians: articles in periodicals.

. . . .

Amendments (Textual)

F110. Ss. 37-40 repealed (1.6.2014) by The Copyright and Rights in Performances (Research, Education, Libraries and Archives) Regulations 2014 (S.I. 2014/1372), reg. 1, Sch. para. 14 Table

F11039. Copying by librarians: parts of published works.

. . . .

Amendments (Textual)

F110. Ss. 37-40 repealed (1.6.2014) by The Copyright and Rights in Performances (Research, Education, Libraries and Archives) Regulations 2014 (S.I. 2014/1372), reg. 1, Sch. para. 14 Table

F11040. Restriction on production of multiple copies of the same material.

. . . .

Amendments (Textual)

F110. Ss. 37-40 repealed (1.6.2014) by The Copyright and Rights in Performances (Research, Education, Libraries and Archives) Regulations 2014 (S.I. 2014/1372), reg. 1, Sch. para. 14 Table

[F11140. A Lending of copies by libraries or archives.

[F112. (1)Copyright in a work of any description is not infringed by the following acts by a public library in relation to a book within the public lending right scheme—

(a) lending the book;

(b) in relation to an audio-book or e-book, copying or issuing a copy of the book as an act incidental to lending it.

(1. A)In subsection (1)—

(a) " book ", " audio-book " and " e-book " have the meanings given in section 5 of the Public Lending Right Act 1979,

(b) " the public lending right scheme " means the scheme in force under section 1 of that Act,

(c) a book is within the public lending right scheme if it is a book within the meaning of the provisions of the scheme relating to eligibility, whether or not it is in fact eligible, and

(d) " lending " is to be read in accordance with the definition of "lent out" in section 5 of that Act (and section 18. A of this Act does not apply).]

(2) Copyright in a work is not infringed by the lending of copies of the work by a F113 ...library or archive (other than a public library) which is not conducted for profit.]

Amendments (Textual)

F111. S. 40. A inserted (1.12.1996) by S.I. 1996/2967, reg. 11. (2) (with Pt. III)

F112. S. 40. A(1)(1. A) substituted (30.6.2014) for s. 40. A(1) by Digital Economy Act 2010 (c. 24), ss. 43. (7), 47. (3)(d); S.I. 2014/1659, art. 2

F113. Word in s. 40. A(2) omitted (1.6.2014) by virtue of The Copyright and Rights in Performances (Research, Education, Libraries and Archives) Regulations 2014 (S.I. 2014/1372), reg. 1, Sch. para. 3

Modifications etc. (not altering text)

C29. S. 40. A(2) modified (1.12.1996) by S.I. 1996/2967, reg. 35 (with Pt. III)

[F11440. B Libraries and educational establishments etc : making works available through dedicated terminals

(1) Copyright in a work is not infringed by an institution specified in subsection (2)

communicating the work to the public or making it available to the public by means of a dedicated terminal on its premises, if the conditions in subsection (3) are met.

(2) The institutions are—

    (a) a library,

    (b) an archive,

    (c) a museum, and

    (d) an educational establishment.

(3) The conditions are that the work or a copy of the work—

    (a) has been lawfully acquired by the institution,

    (b) is communicated or made available to individual members of the public for the purposes of research or private study, and

    (c) is communicated or made available in compliance with any purchase or licensing terms to which the work is subject.]

Amendments (Textual)

F114. S. 40. B inserted (1.6.2014) by The Copyright and Rights in Performances (Research, Education, Libraries and Archives) Regulations 2014 (S.I. 2014/1372), regs. 1, 5. (1)

[F11541 Copying by librarians: supply of single copies to other libraries

(1) A librarian may, if the conditions in subsection (2) are met, make a single copy of the whole or part of a published work and supply it to another library, without infringing copyright in the work.

(2) The conditions are—

    (a) the copy is supplied in response to a request from a library which is not conducted for profit, and

    (b) at the time of making the copy the librarian does not know, or could not reasonably find out, the name and address of a person entitled to authorise the making of a copy of the work.

(3) The condition in subsection (2)(b) does not apply where the request is for a copy of an article in a periodical.

(4) Where a library makes a charge for supplying a copy under this section, the sum charged must be calculated by reference to the costs attributable to the production of the copy.

(5) To the extent that a term of a contract purports to prevent or restrict the doing of any act which, by virtue of this section, would not infringe copyright, that term is unenforceable.

Amendments (Textual)

F115. Ss. 41-43. A substituted (1.6.2014) for ss. 41-43 by The Copyright and Rights in Performances (Research, Education, Libraries and Archives) Regulations 2014 (S.I. 2014/1372), regs. 1, 5. (2)

42 Copying by librarians etc : replacement copies of works

(1) A librarian, archivist or curator of a library, archive or museum may, without infringing copyright, make a copy of an item in that institution's permanent collection—

    (a) in order to preserve or replace that item in that collection, or

    (b) where an item in the permanent collection of another library, archive or museum has been lost, destroyed or damaged, in order to replace the item in the collection of that other library, archive or museum,

provided that the conditions in subsections (2) and (3) are met.

(2) The first condition is that the item is—

    (a) included in the part of the collection kept wholly or mainly for the purposes of reference on the institution's premises,

    (b) included in a part of the collection not accessible to the public, or

    (c) available on loan only to other libraries, archives or museums.

(3) The second condition is that it is not reasonably practicable to purchase a copy of the item to achieve either of the purposes mentioned in subsection (1).

(4) The reference in subsection (1)(b) to a library, archive or museum is to a library, archive or museum which is not conducted for profit.

(5) Where an institution makes a charge for supplying a copy to another library, archive or museum under subsection (1)(b), the sum charged must be calculated by reference to the costs

attributable to the production of the copy.

(6) In this section "item" means a work or a copy of a work.

(7) To the extent that a term of a contract purports to prevent or restrict the doing of any act which, by virtue of this section, would not infringe copyright, that term is unenforceable.

Amendments (Textual)

F115. Ss. 41-43. A substituted (1.6.2014) for ss. 41-43 by The Copyright and Rights in Performances (Research, Education, Libraries and Archives) Regulations 2014 (S.I. 2014/1372), regs. 1, 5. (2)

42. ACopying by librarians: single copies of published works

(1) A librarian of a library which is not conducted for profit may, if the conditions in subsection (2) are met, make and supply a single copy of—

    (a) one article in any one issue of a periodical, or

    (b) a reasonable proportion of any other published work,

without infringing copyright in the work.

(2) The conditions are—

    (a) the copy is supplied in response to a request from a person who has provided the librarian with a declaration in writing which includes the information set out in subsection (3), and

    (b) the librarian is not aware that the declaration is false in a material particular.

(3) The information which must be included in the declaration is—

    (a) the name of the person who requires the copy and the material which that person requires,

    (b) a statement that the person has not previously been supplied with a copy of that material by any library,

    (c) a statement that the person requires the copy for the purposes of research for a non-commercial purpose or private study, will use it only for those purposes and will not supply the copy to any other person, and

    (d) a statement that to the best of the person's knowledge, no other person with whom the person works or studies has made, or intends to make, at or about the same time as the person's request, a request for substantially the same material for substantially the same purpose.

(4) Where a library makes a charge for supplying a copy under this section, the sum charged must be calculated by reference to the costs attributable to the production of the copy.

(5) Where a person ("P") makes a declaration under this section that is false in a material particular and is supplied with a copy which would have been an infringing copy if made by P—

    (a) P is liable for infringement of copyright as if P had made the copy, and

    (b) the copy supplied to P is to be treated as an infringing copy for all purposes.

(6) To the extent that a term of a contract purports to prevent or restrict the doing of any act which, by virtue of this section, would not infringe copyright, that term is unenforceable.

Amendments (Textual)

F115. Ss. 41-43. A substituted (1.6.2014) for ss. 41-43 by The Copyright and Rights in Performances (Research, Education, Libraries and Archives) Regulations 2014 (S.I. 2014/1372), regs. 1, 5. (2)

43. Copying by librarians or archivists: single copies of unpublished works

(1) A librarian or archivist may make and supply a single copy of the whole or part of a work without infringing copyright in the work, provided that—

    (a) the copy is supplied in response to a request from a person who has provided the librarian or archivist with a declaration in writing which includes the information set out in subsection (2), and

    (b) the librarian or archivist is not aware that the declaration is false in a material particular.

(2) The information which must be included in the declaration is—

    (a) the name of the person who requires the copy and the material which that person requires,

    (b) a statement that the person has not previously been supplied with a copy of that material by any library or archive, and

    (c) a statement that the person requires the copy for the purposes of research for a non-commercial purpose or private study, will use it only for those purposes and will not supply the copy to any other person.

(3) But copyright is infringed if—

(a) the work had been published or communicated to the public before the date it was deposited in the library or archive, or

(b) the copyright owner has prohibited the copying of the work,

and at the time of making the copy the librarian or archivist is, or ought to be, aware of that fact.

(4) Where a library or archive makes a charge for supplying a copy under this section, the sum charged must be calculated by reference to the costs attributable to the production of the copy.

(5) Where a person ("P") makes a declaration under this section that is false in a material particular and is supplied with a copy which would have been an infringing copy if made by P—

(a) P is liable for infringement of copyright as if P had made the copy, and

(b) the copy supplied to P is to be treated as an infringing copy for all purposes.

Amendments (Textual)

F115. Ss. 41-43. A substituted (1.6.2014) for ss. 41-43 by The Copyright and Rights in Performances (Research, Education, Libraries and Archives) Regulations 2014 (S.I. 2014/1372), regs. 1, 5. (2)

43. ASections 40. A to 43: interpretation

(1) The following definitions have effect for the purposes of sections 40. A to 43.

(2) "Library" means—

(a) a library which is publicly accessible, or

(b) a library of an educational establishment.

(3) "Museum" includes a gallery.

(4) "Conducted for profit", in relation to a library, archive or museum, means a body of that kind which is established or conducted for profit or which forms part of, or is administered by, a body established or conducted for profit.

(5) References to a librarian, archivist or curator include a person acting on behalf of a librarian, archivist or curator.]

Amendments (Textual)

F115. Ss. 41-43. A substituted (1.6.2014) for ss. 41-43 by The Copyright and Rights in Performances (Research, Education, Libraries and Archives) Regulations 2014 (S.I. 2014/1372), regs. 1, 5. (2)

44 Copy of work required to be made as condition of export.

If an article of cultural or historical importance or interest cannot lawfully be exported from the United Kingdom unless a copy of it is made and deposited in an appropriate library or archive, it is not an infringement of copyright to make that copy.

[F11644. ALegal deposit libraries

(1) Copyright is not infringed by the copying of a work from the internet by a deposit library or person acting on its behalf if—

(a) the work is of a description prescribed by regulations under section 10. (5) of the 2003 Act,

(b) its publication on the internet, or a person publishing it there, is connected with the United Kingdom in a manner so prescribed, and

(c) the copying is done in accordance with any conditions so prescribed.

(2) Copyright is not infringed by the doing of anything in relation to relevant material permitted to be done under regulations under section 7 of the 2003 Act.

(3) The Secretary of State may by regulations make provision excluding, in relation to prescribed activities done in relation to relevant material, the application of such of the provisions of this Chapter as are prescribed.

(4) Regulations under subsection (3) may in particular make provision prescribing activities—

(a) done for a prescribed purpose,

(b) done by prescribed descriptions of reader,

(c) done in relation to prescribed descriptions of relevant material,

(d) done other than in accordance with prescribed conditions.

(5) Regulations under this section may make different provision for different purposes.

(6) Regulations under this section shall be made by statutory instrument which shall be subject to

annulment in pursuance of a resolution of either House of Parliament.

(7) In this section—

   (a) " the 2003 Act " means the Legal Deposit Libraries Act 2003;

   (b) " deposit library ", " reader " and " relevant material " have the same meaning as in section 7 of the 2003 Act;

   (c) " prescribed " means prescribed by regulations made by the Secretary of State.]

Amendments (Textual)

F116. S. 44. A inserted (1.2.2004) by Legal Deposit Libraries Act 2003 (c. 28), ss. 8. (1), 16. (1) (with s. 16. (4)); S.I. 2004/130, art. 2

[F117. Orphan works

Amendments (Textual)

F117 S. 44. B and cross-heading inserted (29.10.2014) by The Copyright and Rights in Performances (Certain Permitted Uses of Orphan Works) Regulations 2014 (S.I. 2014/2861), regs. 1, 3. (1)

44. BPermitted uses of orphan works

(1) Copyright in an orphan work is not infringed by a relevant body in the circumstances set out in paragraph 1. (1) of Schedule ZA1 (subject to paragraph 6 of that Schedule).

(2) "Orphan work" and "relevant body" have the meanings given by that Schedule.]

Public administration

45 Parliamentary and judicial proceedings.

(1) Copyright is not infringed by anything done for the purposes of parliamentary or judicial proceedings.

(2) Copyright is not infringed by anything done for the purposes of reporting such proceedings; but this shall not be construed as authorising the copying of a work which is itself a published report of the proceedings.

46 Royal Commissions and statutory inquiries.

(1) Copyright is not infringed by anything done for the purposes of the proceedings of a Royal Commission or statutory inquiry.

(2) Copyright is not infringed by anything done for the purpose of reporting any such proceedings held in public; but this shall not be construed as authorising the copying of a work which is itself a published report of the proceedings.

(3) Copyright in a work is not infringed by the issue to the public of copies of the report of a Royal Commission or statutory inquiry containing the work or material from it.

(4) In this section—

"Royal Commission" includes a Commission appointed for Northern Ireland by the Secretary of State in pursuance of the prerogative powers of Her Majesty delegated to him under section 7. (2) of the M2. Northern Ireland Constitution Act 1973; and

"statutory inquiry" means an inquiry held or investigation conducted in pursuance of a duty imposed or power conferred by or under an enactment.

Marginal Citations

M21973 c. 36.

47 Material open to public inspection or on official register.

(1) Where material is open to public inspection pursuant to a statutory requirement, or is on a statutory register, any copyright in the material as a literary work is not infringed by the copying of so much of the material as contains factual information of any description, by or with the authority of the appropriate person, for a purpose which does not involve the issuing of copies to the public.

[F118. (2)Where material is open to public inspection pursuant to a statutory requirement, copyright in the material is not infringed by an act to which subsection (3. A) applies provided that—

(a) the act is done by or with the authority of the appropriate person,

(b) the purpose of the act is—

(i) to enable the material to be inspected at a more convenient time or place, or

(ii) to otherwise facilitate the exercise of any right for the purpose of which the statutory requirement is imposed, and

(c) in the case of the act specified in subsection (3. A)(c), the material is not commercially available to the public by or with the authority of the copyright owner.

(3) Where material which contains information about matters of general scientific, technical, commercial or economic interest is on a statutory register or is open to public inspection pursuant to a statutory requirement, copyright in the material is not infringed by an act to which subsection (3. A) applies provided that—

(a) the act is done by or with the authority of the appropriate person,

(b) the purpose of the act is to disseminate that information, and

(c) in the case of the act specified in subsection (3. A)(c), the material is not commercially available to the public by or with the authority of the copyright owner.

(3. A)This subsection applies to any of the following acts—

(a) copying the material,

(b) issuing copies of the material to the public, and

(c) making the material (or a copy of it) available to the public by electronic transmission in such a way that members of the public may access it from a place and at a time individually chosen by them.]

(4) The Secretary of State may by order provide that subsection (1), (2) or (3) shall, in such cases as may be specified in the order, apply only to copies marked in such manner as may be so specified.

(5) The Secretary of State may by order provide that subsections (1) to (3) apply, to such extent and with such modifications as may be specified in the order—

(a) to material made open to public inspection by—

(i) an international organisation specified in the order, or

(ii) a person so specified who has functions in the United Kingdom under an international agreement to which the United Kingdom is party, or

(b) to a register maintained by an international organisation specified in the order,

as they apply in relation to material open to public inspection pursuant to a statutory requirement or to a statutory register.

(6) In this section—

"appropriate person" means the person required to make the material open to public inspection or, as the case may be, the person maintaining the register;

"statutory register" means a register maintained in pursuance of a statutory requirement; and

"statutory requirement" means a requirement imposed by provision made by or under an enactment.

(7) An order under this section shall be made by statutory instrument which shall be subject to annulment in pursuance of a resolution of either House of Parliament.

Amendments (Textual)

F118. S. 47. (2)-(3. A) substituted for s. 47. (2)(3) (1.6.2014) by The Copyright (Public Administration) Regulations 2014 (S.I. 2014/1385), regs. 1, 2. (1)

Modifications etc. (not altering text)

C30. S. 47. (1) extended with modifications by S.I. 1989/1098, art. 2

C31. S. 47. (6) modified (1.3.2010) by The Scottish Register of Tartans Act 2008 (Consequential Modifications) Order 2010 (S.I. 2010/180), art. 2. (2) (with art. 2. (4))

C32. S. 47. (6) modified (26.2.2015) by The Regulatory Reform (Scotland) Act 2014 (Consequential Modifications) Order 2015 (S.I. 2015/374), arts. 1. (1), 3. (3) (with art. 3. (4))

48 Material communicated to the Crown in the course of public business.

(1) This section applies where a literary, dramatic, musical or artistic work has in the course of public business been communicated to the Crown for any purpose, by or with the licence of the copyright owner and a document or other material thing recording or embodying the work is owned by or in the custody or control of the Crown.

[F119. (2)The Crown may, without infringing copyright in the work, do an act specified in subsection (3) provided that—

(a) the act is done for the purpose for which the work was communicated to the Crown, or any related purpose which could reasonably have been anticipated by the copyright owner, and

(b) the work has not been previously published otherwise than by virtue of this section.]

[F119. (3)The acts referred to in subsection (2) are—

(a) copying the work,

(b) issuing copies of the work to the public, and

(c) making the work (or a copy of it) available to the public by electronic transmission in such a way that members of the public may access it from a place and at a time individually chosen by them.]

(4) In subsection (1) "public business" includes any activity carried on by the Crown.

(5) This section has effect subject to any agreement to the contrary between the Crown and the copyright owner.

[F120. (6) In this section "the Crown" includes a health service body, as defined in section 60. (7) of the National Health Service and Community Care Act 1990, [F121the National Health Service Commissioning Board, a clinical commissioning group established under section 14. D of the National Health Service Act 2006,] F122... , the Care Quality Commission [F123, Health Education England] [F124, the Health Research Authority] and a National Health Service trust established under [F125 section 25 of the National Health Service Act 2006, section 18 of the National Health Service (Wales) Act 2006] or the National Health Service (Scotland) Act 1978 [F126 and an NHS foundation trust] [F127 and also includes a health and social services body, as defined in Article 7. (6) of the Health and Personal Social Services (Northern Ireland) Order 1991, and a Health and Social Services trust established under that Order], and the reference in subsection (1) above to public business shall be construed accordingly.]

Amendments (Textual)

F119. S. 48. (2)(3) substituted (1.6.2014) by The Copyright (Public Administration) Regulations 2014 (S.I. 2014/1385), regs. 1, 2. (2)

F120. S. 48. (6) added by National Health Service and Community Care Act 1990 (c. 19, SIF 113:2), s. 60. (2), Sch. 8 para. 3

F121. Words in s. 48. (6) inserted (1.10.2012) by Health and Social Care Act 2012 (c. 7), s. 306. (4), Sch. 5 para. 44. (a); S.I. 2012/1831, art. 2. (2)

F122. Words in s. 48. (6) omitted (1.4.2013) by virtue of Health and Social Care Act 2012 (c. 7), s. 306. (4), Sch. 5 para. 44. (b); S.I. 2013/160, art. 2. (2) (with arts. 7-9)

F123. Words in s. 48. (6) inserted (1.4.2015) by Care Act 2014 (c. 23), s. 127. (1), Sch. 5 para. 33; S.I. 2014/3186, art. 2. (f)

F124. Words in s. 48. (6) inserted (1.1.2015) by Care Act 2014 (c. 23), s. 127. (1), Sch. 7 para. 25; S.I. 2014/2473, art. 5. (m)

F125. Words in s. 48. (6) substituted (1.3.2007) by National Health Service (Consequential Provisions) Act 2006 (c. 43), ss. 2, 8, Sch. 1 para. 112. (b) (with s. 5, Sch. 3 Pt. 1)

F126. Words in s. 48. (6) inserted (1.4.2004) by Health and Social Care (Community Health and Standards) Act 2003 (c. 43), ss. 34, 199. (1), Sch. 4 para. 72; S.I. 2004/759, art. 2

F127. Words in s. 48. (6) inserted (1.4.1992) by S.I. 1991/194, art. 7. (2), Sch. 2 Pt. I para. 3; S.R. 1991/131, art. 2. (e), Sch. Pt. III

Modifications etc. (not altering text)

C33. S. 48: functions made exercisable by Local Health Boards (E.W.) (1.10.2009) by The Local Health Boards (Directed Functions) (Wales) Regulations 2009 (S.I. 2009/1511), reg. 4, Sch. (subject to reg. 5)

C34. S. 48. (6) modified (temp. from 1.10.2008) by The Health and Social Care Act 2008

(Consequential Amendments and Transitory Provisions) Order 2008 (S.I. 2008/2250), art. 3. (3)
49 Public records.

Material which is comprised in public records within the meaning of the M3. Public Records Act 1958, the M4. Public Records (Scotland) Act 1937 or the M5. Public Records Act (Northern Ireland) 1923 [F128, or in Welsh public records (as defined in the [F129the Government of Wales Act 2006])] which are open to public inspection in pursuance of that Act, may be copied, and a copy may be supplied to any person, by or with the authority of any officer appointed under that Act, without infringement of copyright.

Amendments (Textual)

F128. Words in s. 49 inserted (1.4.1999) by 1998 c. 38, s. 125, Sch. 12 para. 27 (with ss. 139. (2), 143. (2)); S.I. 1999/782, art. 2

F129. Words in s. 49 substituted by Government of Wales Act 2006 (c. 32), s. 160. (1), Sch. 10 para. 24 (with Sch. 11 para. 22), the amending provision coming into force immediately after "the 2007 election" (held on 3.5.2007) subject to s. 161. (4)(5) of the amending Act, which provides for certain provisions to come into force for specified purposes immediately after the end of "the initial period" (which ended with the day of the first appointment of a First Minister on 25.5.2007) - see ss. 46, 161. (1)(4)(5) of the amending Act.

Marginal Citations

M31958 c. 51.

M41937 c. 43.

M51923 c. 20 (N.I.).

50 Acts done under statutory authority.

(1) Where the doing of a particular act is specifically authorised by an Act of Parliament, whenever passed, then, unless the Act provides otherwise, the doing of that act does not infringe copyright.

(2) Subsection (1) applies in relation to an enactment contained in Northern Ireland legislation as it applies in relation to an Act of Parliament.

(3) Nothing in this section shall be construed as excluding any defence of statutory authority otherwise available under or by virtue of any enactment.

Modifications etc. (not altering text)

C35. S. 50 applied by Freedom of Information Act 2000 (c. 36), s. 80. (3) (as added (1.1.2005) by The Freedom of Information (Scotland) Act 2002 (Consequential Modifications) Order 2004 (S.I. 2004/3089), art. 3. (2))

C36. S. 50. (1) modified (1.3.2010) by The Scottish Register of Tartans Act 2008 (Consequential Modifications) Order 2010 (S.I. 2010/180), art. 2. (3) (with art. 2. (4))

C37. S. 50. (1) modified (26.2.2015) by The Regulatory Reform (Scotland) Act 2014 (Consequential Modifications) Order 2015 (S.I. 2015/374), arts. 1. (1), 3. (3) (with art. 3. (4))

[F130. Computer programs: lawful users

Amendments (Textual)

F130. Cross-heading and ss. 50. A-50. C inserted (1.1.1993) by S.I. 1992/3233, reg.8.

F131 50. A Back up copies.

(1) It is not an infringement of copyright for a lawful user of a copy of a computer program to make any back up copy of it which it is necessary for him to have for the purposes of his lawful use.

(2) For the purposes of this section and sections 50. B [F132, 50. BA] and 50. C a person is a lawful user of a computer program if (whether under a licence to do any acts restricted by the copyright in the program or otherwise), he has a right to use the program.

(3) Where an act is permitted under this section, it is irrelevant whether or not there exists any term or condition in an agreement which purports to prohibit or restrict the act (such terms being, by virtue of section 296. A, void).

Amendments (Textual)
F131. Ss. 50. A-50. C inserted (1.1.1993) by S.I. 1992/3233, reg.8.
F132. S. 50. A(2): ", 50. BA" inserted (31.10.2003) by The Copyright and Related Rights Regulations 2003 (S.I. 2003/2498), reg. 15. (2) (with regs. 31-40)

F133 50. B Decompilation.

(1) It is not an infringement of copyright for a lawful user of a copy of a computer program expressed in a low level language—

(a) to convert it into a version expressed in a higher level language, or

(b) incidentally in the course of so converting the program, to copy it,

(that is, to "decompile" it), provided that the conditions in subsection (2) are met.

(2) The conditions are that—

(a) it is necessary to decompile the program to obtain the information necessary to create an independent program which can be operated with the program decompiled or with another program ("the permitted objective"); and

(b) the information so obtained is not used for any purpose other than the permitted objective.

(3) In particular, the conditions in subsection (2) are not met if the lawful user—

(a) has readily available to him the information necessary to achieve the permitted objective;

(b) does not confine the decompiling to such acts as are necessary to achieve the permitted objective;

(c) supplies the information obtained by the decompiling to any person to whom it is not necessary to supply it in order to achieve the permitted objective; or

(d) uses the information to create a program which is substantially similar in its expression to the program decompiled or to do any act restricted by copyright.

(4) Where an act is permitted under this section, it is irrelevant whether or not there exists any term or condition in an agreement which purports to prohibit or restrict the act (such terms being, by virtue of section 296. A, void).

Amendments (Textual)
F133. Ss. 50. A-50. C inserted (1.1.1993) by S.I. 1992/3233, reg.8.

[F13450. BAObserving, studying and testing of computer programs

(1) It is not an infringement of copyright for a lawful user of a copy of a computer program to observe, study or test the functioning of the program in order to determine the ideas and principles which underlie any element of the program if he does so while performing any of the acts of loading, displaying, running, transmitting or storing the program which he is entitled to do.

(2) Where an act is permitted under this section, it is irrelevant whether or not there exists any term or condition in an agreement which purports to prohibit or restrict the act (such terms being, by virtue of section 296. A, void).]

Amendments (Textual)
F134. S. 50. BA inserted (31.10.2003) by The Copyright and Related Rights Regulations 2003 (S.I. 2003/2498), reg. 15. (1) (with regs. 31-40)

F135 50. C Other acts permitted to lawful users.

(1) It is not an infringement of copyright for a lawful user of a copy of a computer program to copy or adapt it, provided that the copying or adapting—

(a) is necessary for his lawful use; and

(b) is not prohibited under any term or condition of an agreement regulating the circumstances in which his use is lawful.

(2) It may, in particular, be necessary for the lawful use of a computer program to copy it or adapt it for the purpose of correcting errors in it.

(3) This section does not apply to any copying or adapting permitted under [F136section 50. A, 50. B or 50. BA].]

Amendments (Textual)
F135. Ss. 50. A-50. C inserted (1.1.1993) by S.I. 1992/3233, reg.8.
F136. Words in s. 50. C(3) substituted (31.10.2003) by The Copyright and Related Rights Regulations 2003 (S.I. 2003/2498), reg. 15. (3) (with regs. 31-40)

[F137. Databases: permitted acts]

Amendments (Textual)
F137. S. 50. D and crossheading inserted (1.1.1998) by S.I. 1997/3032, reg. 9 (with Pt. IV)
50. D[F138 Acts permitted in relation to databases.]

(1) It is not an infringement of copyright in a database for a person who has a right to use the database or any part of the database, (whether under a licence to do any of the acts restricted by the copyright in the database or otherwise) to do, in the exercise of that right, anything which is necessary for the purposes of access to and use of the contents of the database or of that part of the database.

(2) Where an act which would otherwise infringe copyright in a database is permitted under this section, it is irrelevant whether or not there exists any term or condition in any agreement which purports to prohibit or restrict the act (such terms being, by virtue of section 296. B, void).

Amendments (Textual)
F138. S. 50. D inserted (1.1.1998) by S.I. 1997/3032, reg. 9 (with Pt. IV)

Designs

51 Design documents and models.

(1) It is not an infringement of any copyright in a design document or model recording or embodying a design for anything other than an artistic work or a typeface to make an article to the design or to copy an article made to the design.

(2) Nor is it an infringement of the copyright to issue to the public, or include in a film [F139or communicate to the public], anything the making of which was, by virtue of subsection (1), not an infringement of that copyright.

(3) In this section—

"design" means the design of F140...the shape or configuration (whether internal or external) of the whole or part of an article, other than surface decoration; and

"design document" means any record of a design, whether in the form of a drawing, a written description, a photograph, data stored in a computer or otherwise.

Amendments (Textual)
F139. Words in s. 51. (2) substituted (31.10.2003) by The Copyright and Related Rights Regulations 2003 (S.I. 2003/2498), reg. 2. (1), Sch. 1 para. 8. (3) (with regs. 31-40)
F140. Words in s. 51. (3) omitted (1.10.2014) by virtue of Intellectual Property Act 2014 (c. 18), ss. 1. (2), 24. (1); S.I. 2014/2330, art. 3, Sch.
F14152 Effect of exploitation of design derived from artistic work.

. . . .

Amendments (Textual)
F141. S. 52 omitted (28.7.2016) by virtue of Enterprise and Regulatory Reform Act 2013 (c. 24), ss. 74. (2), 103. (3); S.I. 2016/593, arts. 2. (1), 3 (with arts. 4, 5)
53 Things done in reliance on registration of design.

(1) The copyright in an artistic work is not infringed by anything done—

(a) in pursuance of an assignment or licence made or granted by a person registered[F142 —
(i)]under the M6. Registered Designs Act 1949 as the proprietor of a corresponding design, and[F143, or
(ii) under the Community Design Regulation as the right holder of a corresponding registered Community design]

(b) in good faith in reliance on the registration and without notice of any proceedings for the cancellation [F144or invalidation] of the registration or[F145, in a case of registration under the 1949 Act,] for rectifying the relevant entry in the register of designs;

and this is so notwithstanding that the person registered as the proprietor was not the proprietor of the design for the purposes of the 1949 Act[F146 or, in a case of registration under the Community Design Regulation, that the person registered as the right holder was not the right holder of the design for the purposes of the Regulation].

(2) In subsection (1) a "corresponding design", in relation to an artistic work, means a design within the meaning of the 1949 Act which if applied to an article would produce something which would be treated for the purposes of this Part as a copy of the artistic work.

[F147. (3) In subsection (1), a " corresponding registered Community design ", in relation to an artistic work, means a design within the meaning of the Community Design Regulation which if applied to an article would produce something which would be treated for the purposes of this Part as a copy of the artistic work.]

[F148. (4) In this section, " the Community Design Regulation " means Council Regulation (EC) No 6/2002 of 12 December 2001 on Community designs.]

Amendments (Textual)

F142. Word in s. 53. (1)(a) inserted (1.10.2014) by Intellectual Property Act 2014 (c. 18), ss. 5. (2)(a), 24. (1); S.I. 2014/2330, art. 3, Sch.

F143. Words in s. 53. (1)(a) inserted (1.10.2014) by Intellectual Property Act 2014 (c. 18), ss. 5. (2)(b), 24. (1); S.I. 2014/2330, art. 3, Sch.

F144. Words in s. 53. (1)(b) inserted (9.12.2001) by S.I. 2001/3949, reg. 9. (1), Sch. 1 para. 16 (with transitional provisions in regs. 10-14)

F145. Words in s. 53. (1)(b) inserted (1.10.2014) by Intellectual Property Act 2014 (c. 18), ss. 5. (3), 24. (1); S.I. 2014/2330, art. 3, Sch.

F146. Words in s. 53. (1) inserted (1.10.2014) by Intellectual Property Act 2014 (c. 18), ss. 5. (4), 24. (1); S.I. 2014/2330, art. 3, Sch.

F147. S. 53. (3) inserted (1.10.2014) by Intellectual Property Act 2014 (c. 18), ss. 5. (5), 24. (1); S.I. 2014/2330, art. 3, Sch.

F148. S. 53. (4) inserted (1.10.2014) by Intellectual Property Act 2014 (c. 18), ss. 5. (6), 24. (1); S.I. 2014/2330, art. 3, Sch.

Marginal Citations

M61949 c. 88.

Typefaces

54 Use of typeface in ordinary course of printing.

(1) It is not an infringement of copyright in an artistic work consisting of the design of a typeface—

  (a) to use the typeface in the ordinary course of typing, composing text, typesetting or printing,

  (b) to possess an article for the purpose of such use, or

  (c) to do anything in relation to material produced by such use;

and this is so notwithstanding that an article is used which is an infringing copy of the work.

(2) However, the following provisions of this Part apply in relation to persons making, importing or dealing with articles specifically designed or adapted for producing material in a particular typeface, or possessing such articles for the purpose of dealing with them, as if the production of material as mentioned in subsection (1) did infringe copyright in the artistic work consisting of the design of the typeface—

section 24 (secondary infringement: making, importing, possessing or dealing with article for making infringing copy),

sections 99 and 100 (order for delivery up and right of seizure),

section 107. (2) (offence of making or possessing such an article), and

section 108 (order for delivery up in criminal proceedings).

(3) The references in subsection (2) to "dealing with" an article are to selling, letting for hire, or offering or exposing for sale or hire, exhibiting in public, or distributing.

55 Articles for producing material in particular typeface.

(1) This section applies to the copyright in an artistic work consisting of the design of a typeface where articles specifically designed or adapted for producing material in that typeface have been marketed by or with the licence of the copyright owner.

(2) After the period of 25 years from the end of the calendar year in which the first such articles are marketed, the work may be copied by making further such articles, or doing anything for the purpose of making such articles, and anything may be done in relation to articles so made, without infringing copyright in the work.

(3) In subsection (1) "marketed" means sold, let for hire or offered or exposed for sale or hire, in the United Kingdom or elsewhere.

Works in electronic form

56 Transfers of copies of works in electronic form.

(1) This section applies where a copy of a work in electronic form has been purchased on terms which, expressly or impliedly or by virtue of any rule of law, allow the purchaser to copy the work, or to adapt it or make copies of an adaptation, in connection with his use of it.

(2) If there are no express terms—

(a) prohibiting the transfer of the copy by the purchaser, imposing obligations which continue after a transfer, prohibiting the assignment of any licence or terminating any licence on a transfer, or

(b) providing for the terms on which a transferee may do the things which the purchaser was permitted to do,

anything which the purchaser was allowed to do may also be done without infringement of copyright by a transferee; but any copy, adaptation or copy of an adaptation made by the purchaser which is not also transferred shall be treated as an infringing copy for all purposes after the transfer.

(3) The same applies where the original purchased copy is no longer usable and what is transferred is a further copy used in its place.

(4) The above provisions also apply on a subsequent transfer, with the substitution for references in subsection (2) to the purchaser of references to the subsequent transferor.

Miscellaneous: literary, dramatic, musical and artistic works

57 Anonymous or pseudonymous works: acts permitted on assumptions as to expiry of copyright or death of author.

(1) Copyright in a literary, dramatic, musical or artistic work is not infringed by an act done at a time when, or in pursuance of arrangements made at a time when—

(a) it is not possible by reasonable inquiry to ascertain the identity of the author, and

(b) it is reasonable to assume—

(i) that copyright has expired, or

(ii) that the author died [F14970 years] or more before the beginning of the calendar year in which the act is done or the arrangements are made.

(2) Subsection (1)(b)(ii) does not apply in relation to—

(a) a work in which Crown copyright subsists, or

(b) a work in which copyright originally vested in an international organisation by virtue of section 168 and in respect of which an Order under that section specifies a copyright period longer than [F14970 years].

(3) In relation to a work of joint authorship—

(a) the reference in subsection (1) to its being possible to ascertain the identity of the author shall be construed as a reference to its being possible to ascertain the identity of any of the authors, and

(b) the reference in subsection (1)(b)(ii) to the author having died shall be construed as a reference to all the authors having died.

Amendments (Textual)

F149. Words in s. 57. (1)(b)(ii)(2)(b) substituted (with saving) (1.1.1996) by S.I. 1995/3297, regs. 5. (2), 15. (2) (with Pt. III)

58 Use of notes or recordings of spoken words in certain cases.

(1) Where a record of spoken words is made, in writing or otherwise, for the purpose—

(a) of reporting current events, or

(b) of [F150communicating to the public] the whole or part of the work,

it is not an infringement of any copyright in the words as a literary work to use the record or material taken from it (or to copy the record, or any such material, and use the copy) for that purpose, provided the following conditions are met.

(2) The conditions are that—

(a) the record is a direct record of the spoken words and is not taken from a previous record or from a broadcast F151. . . ;

(b) the making of the record was not prohibited by the speaker and, where copyright already subsisted in the work, did not infringe copyright;

(c) the use made of the record or material taken from it is not of a kind prohibited by or on behalf of the speaker or copyright owner before the record was made; and

(d) the use is by or with the authority of a person who is lawfully in possession of the record.

Amendments (Textual)

F150. Words in s. 58. (1) substituted (31.10.2003) by The Copyright and Related Rights Regulations 2003 (S.I. 2003/2498), reg. 2. (1), Sch. 1 para. 12. (a) (with regs. 31-40)

F151. Words in s. 58. (2)(b) repealed (31.10.2003) by The Copyright and Related Rights Regulations 2003 (S.I. 2003/2498), reg. 2. (2), Sch. 2 (with regs. 31-40)

59 Public reading or recitation.

(1) The reading or recitation in public by one person of a reasonable extract from a published literary or dramatic work does not infringe any copyright in the work if it is accompanied by a sufficient acknowledgement.

(2) Copyright in a work is not infringed by the making of a sound recording, or the [F152communication to the public], of a reading or recitation which by virtue of subsection (1) does not infringe copyright in the work, provided that the recording [F153or communication to the public] consists mainly of material in relation to which it is not necessary to rely on that subsection.

Amendments (Textual)

F152. Words in s. 59. (2) substituted (31.10.2003) by The Copyright and Related Rights Regulations 2003 (S.I. 2003/2498), reg. 2. (1), Sch. 1 para. 5. (b) (with regs. 31-40)

F153. Words in s. 59. (2) substituted (31.10.2003) by The Copyright and Related Rights Regulations 2003 (S.I. 2003/2498), reg. 2. (1), Sch. 1 para. 9. (1)(a) (with regs. 31-40)

60 Abstracts of scientific or technical articles.

(1) Where an article on a scientific or technical subject is published in a periodical accompanied by an abstract indicating the contents of the article, it is not an infringement of copyright in the abstract, or in the article, to copy the abstract or issue copies of it to the public.

(2) This section does not apply if or to the extent that there is a licensing scheme certified for the purposes of this section under section 143 providing for the grant of licences.

61 Recordings of folksongs.

(1) A sound recording of a performance of a song may be made for the purpose of including it in an archive maintained by a [F154body not established or conducted for profit] without infringing any copyright in the words as a literary work or in the accompanying musical work, provided the conditions in subsection (2) below are met.

(2) The conditions are that—

(a) the words are unpublished and of unknown authorship at the time the recording is made,

(b) the making of the recording does not infringe any other copyright, and

(c) its making is not prohibited by any performer.

[F155. (3)A single copy of a sound recording made in reliance on subsection (1) and included in an archive referred to in that subsection may be made and supplied by the archivist without infringing copyright in the recording or the works included in it, provided that—

(a) the copy is supplied in response to a request from a person who has provided the archivist with a declaration in writing which includes the information set out in subsection (4), and

(b) the archivist is not aware that the declaration is false in a material particular.

(4) The information which must be included in the declaration is—

(a) the name of the person who requires the copy and the sound recording which is the subject of the request,

(b) a statement that the person has not previously been supplied with a copy of that sound recording by any archivist, and

(c) a statement that the person requires the copy for the purposes of research for a non-commercial purpose or private study, will use it only for those purposes and will not supply the copy to any other person.

(5) Where an archive makes a charge for supplying a copy under this section, the sum charged must be calculated by reference to the costs attributable to the production of the copy.

(6) Where a person ("P") makes a declaration under this section that is false in a material particular and is supplied with a copy which would have been an infringing copy if made by P—

(a) P is liable for infringement of copyright as if P had made the copy, and

(b) the copy supplied to P is to be treated as an infringing copy for all purposes.

(7) In this section references to an archivist include a person acting on behalf of an archivist.]

Amendments (Textual)

F154. Words in s. 61. (1) substituted (1.6.2014) by The Copyright and Rights in Performances (Research, Education, Libraries and Archives) Regulations 2014 (S.I. 2014/1372), regs. 1, 7. (1)

F155. S. 61. (3)-(7) substituted (1.6.2014) for s. 61. (3)-(6) by The Copyright and Rights in Performances (Research, Education, Libraries and Archives) Regulations 2014 (S.I. 2014/1372), regs. 1, 7. (2)

62 Representation of certain artistic works on public display.

(1) This section applies to—

(a) buildings, and

(b) sculptures, models for buildings and works of artistic craftsmanship, if permanently situated in a public place or in premises open to the public.

(2) The copyright in such a work is not infringed by—

(a) making a graphic work representing it,

(b) making a photograph or film of it, or

(c) [F156making a broadcast of] a visual image of it.

(3) Nor is the copyright infringed by the issue to the public of copies, or the [F157communication to the public], of anything whose making was, by virtue of this section, not an infringement of the copyright.

Amendments (Textual)

F156. Words in s. 62. (2)(c) substituted (31.10.2003) by The Copyright and Related Rights Regulations 2003 (S.I. 2003/2498), reg. 2. (1), Sch. 1 para. 14 (with regs. 31-40)

F157. Words in s. 62. (3)(c) substituted (31.10.2003) by The Copyright and Related Rights Regulations 2003 (S.I. 2003/2498), reg. 2. (1), Sch. 1 para. 5. (c) (with regs. 31-40)

63 Advertisement of sale of artistic work.

(1) It is not an infringement of copyright in an artistic work to copy it, or to issue copies to the public, for the purpose of advertising the sale of the work.

(2) Where a copy which would otherwise be an infringing copy is made in accordance with this section but is subsequently dealt with for any other purpose, it shall be treated as an infringing copy for the purposes of that dealing, and if that dealing infringes copyright for all subsequent purposes.

For this purpose "dealt with" means sold or let for hire, offered or exposed for sale or hire, exhibited in public [F158, distributed or communicated to the public].

Amendments (Textual)
F158. Words in s. 63. (2) substituted (31.10.2003) by The Copyright and Related Rights
Regulations 2003 (S.I. 2003/2498), reg. 17 (with regs. 31-40)
64 Making of subsequent works by same artist.

Where the author of an artistic work is not the copyright owner, he does not infringe the copyright
by copying the work in making another artistic work, provided he does not repeat or imitate the
main design of the earlier work.

65 Reconstruction of buildings.

Anything done for the purposes of reconstructing a building does not infringe any copyright—

(a) in the building, or

(b) in any drawings or plans in accordance with which the building was, by or with the licence
of the copyright owner, constructed.

F159 [Miscellaneous: lending of works and playing of sound recordings]

Amendments (Textual)
F159. S. 66 and crossheading substituted (1.12.1996) by S.I. 1996/2967, reg. 11. (3) (with Pt. III)
66[F160 Lending to public of copies of certain works.]

(1) The Secretary of State may by order provide that in such cases as may be specified in the order
the lending to the public of copies of literary, dramatic, musical or artistic works, sound recordings
or films shall be treated as licensed by the copyright owner subject only to the payment of such
reasonable royalty or other payment as may be agreed or determined in default of agreement by
the Copyright Tribunal.

(2) No such order shall apply if, or to the extent that, there is a licensing scheme certified for the
purposes of this section under section 143 providing for the grant of licences.

(3) An order may make different provision for different cases and may specify cases by reference
to any factor relating to the work, the copies lent, the lender or the circumstances of the lending.

(4) An order shall be made by statutory instrument; and no order shall be made unless a draft of it
has been laid before and approved by a resolution of each House of Parliament.

(5) Nothing in this section affects any liability under section 23 (secondary infringement:
possessing or dealing with infringing copy) in respect of the lending of infringing copies.

Amendments (Textual)
F160. S. 66 substituted (1.12.1996) by S.I. 1996/2967, reg. 11. (3) (with Pt. III)

[F161. MISCellaneous: films and sound recordings]

Amendments (Textual)
F161. S. 66. A and crossheading inserted (1.1.1996) by S.I. 1995/3297, reg. 6. (2) (with Pt. III)
66. A[F162 Films: acts permitted on assumptions as to expiry of copyright, &c.]

(1) Copyright in a film is not infringed by an act done at a time when, or in pursuance of
arrangements made at a time when—

(a) it is not possible by reasonable inquiry to ascertain the identity of any of the persons referred
to in section 13. B(2)(a) to (d) (persons by reference to whose life the copyright period is
ascertained), and

(b) it is reasonable to assume—

(i) that copyright has expired, or

(ii) that the last to die of those persons died 70 years or more before the beginning of the calendar
year in which the act is done or the arrangements are made.

(2) Subsection (1)(b)(ii) does not apply in relation to—

(a) a film in which Crown copyright subsists, or

(b) a film in which copyright originally vested in an international organisation by virtue of section 168 and in respect of which an Order under that section specifies a copyright period longer than 70 years.

Amendments (Textual)

F162. S. 66. A inserted (1.1.1996) by S.I. 1995/3297, reg. 6. (2) (with Pt. III)

67 Playing of sound recordings for purposes of club, society, &c.

F163. . . . .

Amendments (Textual)

F163. S. 67 omitted (1.1.2011) by virtue of The Copyright, Designs and Patents Act 1988 (Amendment) Regulations 2010 (S.I. 2010/2694), art. 3. (1)

Miscellaneous: broadcasts F164. . .

Amendments (Textual)

F164. Words in heading before s. 68 repealed (31.10.2003) by The Copyright and Related Rights Regulations 2003 (S.I. 2003/2498), reg. 2. (2), Sch. 2 (with regs. 32, 33)

68 Incidental recording for purposes of broadcast F165. . . .

(1) This section applies where by virtue of a licence or assignment of copyright a person is authorised to broadcast F166. . . —

(a) a literary, dramatic or musical work, or an adaptation of such a work,

(b) an artistic work, or

(c) a sound recording or film.

(2) He shall by virtue of this section be treated as licensed by the owner of the copyright in the work to do or authorise any of the following for the purposes of the broadcast F166. . . —

(a) in the case of a literary, dramatic or musical work, or an adaptation of such a work, to make a sound recording or film of the work or adaptation;

(b) in the case of an artistic work, to take a photograph or make a film of the work;

(c) in the case of a sound recording or film, to make a copy of it.

(3) That licence is subject to the condition that the recording, film, photograph or copy in question—

(a) shall not be used for any other purpose, and

(b) shall be destroyed within 28 days of being first used for broadcasting the work F166. . . .

(4) A recording, film, photograph or copy made in accordance with this section shall be treated as an infringing copy—

(a) for the purposes of any use in breach of the condition mentioned in subsection (3)(a), and

(b) for all purposes after that condition or the condition mentioned in subsection (3)(b) is broken.

Amendments (Textual)

F165. Words in s. 68 heading repealed (31.10.2003) by The Copyright and Related Rights Regulations 2003 (S.I. 2003/2498), reg. 2. (2), Sch. 2 (with regs. 31-40)

F166. Words in s. 68. (1)(2)(3)(b) repealed (31.10.2003) by The Copyright and Related Rights Regulations 2003 (S.I. 2003/2498), reg. 2. (2), Sch. 2 (with regs. 31-40)

69 Recording for purposes of supervision and control of broadcasts and [F167other services].

(1) Copyright is not infringed by the making or use by the British Broadcasting Corporation, for the purpose of maintaining supervision and control over programmes broadcast by them [F168or included in any on-demand programme service provided by them], of recordings of those programmes.

 F169 [F170. (2)Copyright is not infringed by anything done in pursuance of—

 [F171. (a)section 167. (1) of the Broadcasting Act 1990, section 115. (4) or (6) or 117 of the Broadcasting Act 1996 or paragraph 20 of Schedule 12 to the Communications Act 2003;]

 (b) a condition which, [F172 by virtue of section 334. (1) of the Communications Act 2003] , is included in a licence granted under Part I or III of that Act or Part I or II of the Broadcasting Act

1996; F173 . . .

(c) a direction given under section 109. (2) of the Broadcasting Act 1990 (power of [F174. OFCOM] to require production of recordings etc).

[F175. (d)section 334. (3) [F176, 368. O(1) or (3)] of the Communications Act 2003.]

[F170. (3) Copyright is not infringed by the use by OFCOM in connection with the performance of any of their functions under the Broadcasting Act 1990, the Broadcasting Act 1996 or the Communications Act 2003 of—

(a) any recording, script or transcript which is provided to them under or by virtue of any provision of those Acts; or

(b) any existing material which is transferred to them by a scheme made under section 30 of the Communications Act 2003.]]

(4) In subsection (3), "existing material" means—

(a) any recording, script or transcript which was provided to the Independent Television Commission or the Radio Authority under or by virtue of any provision of the Broadcasting Act 1990 or the Broadcasting Act 1996; and

(b) any recording or transcript which was provided to the Broadcasting Standards Commission under section 115. (4) or (6) or 116. (5) of the Broadcasting Act 1996.

[F177. (5)Copyright is not infringed by the use by an appropriate regulatory authority designated under section 368. B of the Communications Act 2003, in connection with the performance of any of their functions under that Act, of any recording, script or transcript which is provided to them under or by virtue of any provision of that Act.

(6) In this section " on-demand programme service " has the same meaning as in the Communications Act 2003 (see section 368. A of that Act).]

Amendments (Textual)

F167. Words in s. 69 heading substituted (31.10.2003) by The Copyright and Related Rights Regulations 2003 (S.I. 2003/2498), reg. 2. (1), Sch. 1 para. 2. (1) (with regs. 31-40)

F168. Words in s. 69. (1) inserted (19.12.2009) by The Audiovisual Media Services Regulations 2009 (S.I. 2009/2979), reg. 12. (2)(a)

F169. S. 69. (2)(3) substituted (1.10.1996 for specified purposes and otherwise 1.4.1997) by 1996 c. 55, s. 148. (1), Sch. 10 Pt. III para. 31 (with s. 43. (6)); S.I. 1996/2120, art. 4, Sch. 1; S.I. 1997/1005, art. 4

F170. S. 69. (3)(4) substituted (29.12.2003) for s. 69. (3) by Communications Act 2003 (c. 21), ss. 406, 411, Sch. 17 para. 91. (3) (with Sch. 18); S.I. 2003/3142, art. 3, Sch. 1 (with art. 11)

F171. S. 69. (2)(a) substituted (29.12.2003) by Communications Act 2003 (c. 21), ss. 406, 411, Sch. 17 para. 91. (2)(a) (with Sch. 18); S.I. 2003/3142, art. 3, Sch. 1 (with art. 11)

F172. Words in s. 69. (2)(b) substituted (29.12.2003) by Communications Act 2003 (c. 21), ss. 406, 411, Sch. 17 para. 91. (2)(b) (with Sch. 18); S.I. 2003/3142, art. 3, Sch. 1 (with art. 11)

F173. Word in s. 69. (2)(b) repealed (29.12.2003) by Communications Act 2003 (c. 21), ss. 406, 411, Sch. 19. (1) (with Sch. 18, Sch. 19. (1) Note 1); S.I. 2003/3142, art. 3, Sch. 1 (with art. 11)

F174. Words in s. 69. (2)(c) substituted (29.12.2003) by Communications Act 2003 (c. 21), ss. 406, 411, Sch. 17 para. 91. (2)(c) (with Sch. 18); S.I. 2003/3142, art. 3, Sch. 1 (with art. 11)

F175. S. 69. (2)(d) inserted (29.12.2003) by Communications Act 2003 (c. 21), ss. 406, 411, Sch. 17 para. 91. (2)(d) (with Sch. 18); S.I. 2003/3142, art. 3, Sch. 1 (with art. 11)

F176. Words in s. 69. (2)(d) inserted (19.12.2009) by The Audiovisual Media Services Regulations 2009 (S.I. 2009/2979), reg. 12. (2)(b)

F177. S. 69. (5)(6) inserted (19.12.2009) by The Audiovisual Media Services Regulations 2009 (S.I. 2009/2979), reg. 12. (2)(c)

Modifications etc. (not altering text)

C38. S. 69 modified (20.7.2004) The Contracting Out (Functions relating to Broadcast Advertising) and Specification of Relevant Functions Order 2004 (S.I. 2004/1975), art. 9. (1)(2) (with reg. 5)

70 Recording for purposes of time-shifting.

[F178. (1)]The making [F179 in domestic premises] for private and domestic use of a recording of a broadcast F180. . . solely for the purpose of enabling it to be viewed or listened to at a more convenient time does not infringe any copyright in the broadcast F180. . . or in any work included in it.

[F181. (2)Where a copy which would otherwise be an infringing copy is made in accordance with this section but is subsequently dealt with—

(a) it shall be treated as an infringing copy for the purposes of that dealing; and

(b) if that dealing infringes copyright, it shall be treated as an infringing copy for all subsequent purposes.

(3) In subsection (2), " dealt with " means sold or let for hire, offered or exposed for sale or hire or communicated to the public.]

Amendments (Textual)

F178. S. 70 renumbered (31.10.2003) as s. 70. (1) by The Copyright and Related Rights Regulations 2003 (S.I. 2003/2498), reg. 19. (1) (with regs. 31-40)

F179. Words in s. 70. (1) inserted (31.10.2003) by The Copyright and Related Rights Regulations 2003 (S.I. 2003/2498), reg. 19. (2) (with regs. 31-40)

F180. Words in s. 70. (1) repealed (31.10.2003) by The Copyright and Related Rights Regulations 2003 (S.I. 2003/2498), reg. 2. (2), Sch. 2 (with regs. 31-40)

F181. S. 70. (2)(3) inserted (31.10.2003) by The Copyright and Related Rights Regulations 2003 (S.I. 2003/2498), reg. 19. (2) (with regs. 31-40)

[F18271. Photographs of broadcasts

(1) The making in domestic premises for private and domestic use of a photograph of the whole or any part of an image forming part of a broadcast, or a copy of such a photograph, does not infringe any copyright in the broadcast or in any film included in it.

(2) Where a copy which would otherwise be an infringing copy is made in accordance with this section but is subsequently dealt with—

(a) it shall be treated as an infringing copy for the purposes of that dealing; and

(b) if that dealing infringes copyright, it shall be treated as an infringing copy for all subsequent purposes.

(3) In subsection (2), " dealt with " means sold or let for hire, offered or exposed for sale or hire or communicated to the public.]

Amendments (Textual)

F182. S. 71 substituted (31.10.2003) by The Copyright and Related Rights Regulations 2003 (S.I. 2003/2498), reg. 20. (1) (with regs. 31-40)

72 Free public showing or playing of broadcast F183. . . .

(1) The showing or playing in public of a broadcast F184. . . to an audience who have not paid for admission to the place where the broadcast F184. . . is to be seen or heard does not infringe any copyright in—

[F185. (a)the broadcast; [F186or]

(b) any sound recording (except so far as it is an excepted sound recording) included in it F187...

F188. (c). . . . .]

[F189. (1. A)For the purposes of this Part an "excepted sound recording" is a sound recording—

(a) whose author is not the author of the broadcast in which it is included; and

(b) which is a recording of music with or without words spoken or sung.

(1. B)Where by virtue of subsection (1) the copyright in a broadcast shown or played in public is not infringed, copyright in any [F190film or] excepted sound recording included in it is not infringed if the playing or showing of that broadcast in public—

(a) F191 . . . .

(b) is necessary for the purposes of—

(i) repairing equipment for the reception of broadcasts;

(ii) demonstrating that a repair to such equipment has been carried out; or

(iii) demonstrating such equipment which is being sold or let for hire or offered or exposed for sale or hire.]

47

(2) The audience shall be treated as having paid for admission to a place—

(a) if they have paid for admission to a place of which that place forms part; or

(b) if goods or services are supplied at that place (or a place of which it forms part)—

(i) at prices which are substantially attributable to the facilities afforded for seeing or hearing the broadcast F192. . . , or

(ii) at prices exceeding those usually charged there and which are partly attributable to those facilities.

(3) The following shall not be regarded as having paid for admission to a place—

(a) persons admitted as residents or inmates of the place;

(b) persons admitted as members of a club or society where the payment is only for membership of the club or society and the provision of facilities for seeing or hearing broadcasts F193. . . is only incidental to the main purposes of the club or society.

(4) Where the making of the broadcast F194. . . was an infringement of the copyright in a sound recording or film, the fact that it was heard or seen in public by the reception of the broadcast F194. . . shall be taken into account in assessing the damages for that infringement.

Amendments (Textual)

F183. Words in s. 72 heading repealed (31.10.2003) by The Copyright and Related Rights Regulations 2003 (S.I. 2003/2498), reg. 2. (2), Sch. 2 (with regs. 31-40)

F184. Words in S. 72. (1) repealed (31.10.2003) by The Copyright and Related Rights Regulations 2003 (S.I. 2003/2498), reg. 2. (2), Sch. 2 (with regs. 31-40)

F185. S. 72. (1)(a)-(c) substituted (31.10.2003) for s. 72. (1)(a)(b) by The Copyright and Related Rights Regulations 2003 (S.I. 2003/2498), reg. 21. (1)(a) (with regs. 31-40)

F186. Word in s. 72. (1)(a) inserted (15.6.2016) by The Copyright (Free Public Showing or Playing) (Amendment) Regulations 2016 (S.I. 2016/565), regs. 1, 3. (a)

F187. Word in s. 72. (1)(b) omitted (15.6.2016) by virtue of The Copyright (Free Public Showing or Playing) (Amendment) Regulations 2016 (S.I. 2016/565), regs. 1, 3. (b)

F188. S. 72. (1)(c) omitted (15.6.2016) by virtue of The Copyright (Free Public Showing or Playing) (Amendment) Regulations 2016 (S.I. 2016/565), regs. 1, 3. (c)

F189. S. 72. (1. A)(1. B) inserted (31.10.2003) by The Copyright and Related Rights Regulations 2003 (S.I. 2003/2498), reg. 21. (1)(b) (with regs. 31-40)

F190. Words in s. 72. (1. B) inserted (15.6.2016) by The Copyright (Free Public Showing or Playing) (Amendment) Regulations 2016 (S.I. 2016/565), regs. 1, 3. (d)

F191. S. 72. (1. B)(a) omitted (1.1.2011) by virtue of The Copyright, Designs and Patents Act 1988 (Amendment) Regulations 2010 (S.I. 2010/2694), art. 4. (1)

F192. Words in S. 72. (2)(b)(i) repealed (31.10.2003) by The Copyright and Related Rights Regulations 2003 (S.I. 2003/2498), reg. 2. (2), Sch. 2 (with regs. 31-40)

F193. Words in S. 72. (3)(b) repealed (31.10.2003) by The Copyright and Related Rights Regulations 2003 (S.I. 2003/2498), reg. 2. (2), Sch. 2 (with regs. 31-40)

F194. Words in S. 72. (4) repealed (31.10.2003) by The Copyright and Related Rights Regulations 2003 (S.I. 2003/2498), reg. 2. (2), Sch. 2 (with regs. 31-40)

F19573 Reception and re-transmission of wireless broadcast by cable.

. . . .

Amendments (Textual)

F195. S. 73 repealed (31.7.2017) by Digital Economy Act 2017 (c. 30), ss. 34. (1)(a), 118. (6); S.I. 2017/765, reg. 2. (n)

F19673. A Royalty or other sum payable in pursuance of section 73. (4).

. . . .

Amendments (Textual)

F196. S. 73. A repealed (31.7.2017) by Digital Economy Act 2017 (c. 30), ss. 34. (1)(a), 118. (6); S.I. 2017/765, reg. 2. (n)

F19774

. . . .

Amendments (Textual)

F197. S. 74 repealed (1.6.2014) by The Copyright and Rights in Performances (Disability) Regulations 2014 (S.I. 2014/1384), reg. 1. (1), Sch. para. 8 Table

[F19875. Recording of broadcast for archival purposes

(1) A recording of a broadcast or a copy of such a recording may be made for the purpose of being placed in an archive maintained by a body which is not established or conducted for profit without infringing any copyright in the broadcast or in any work included in it.

(2) To the extent that a term of a contract purports to prevent or restrict the doing of any act which, by virtue of this section, would not infringe copyright, that term is unenforceable.]

Amendments (Textual)

F198. S. 75 substituted (1.6.2014) by The Copyright and Rights in Performances (Research, Education, Libraries and Archives) Regulations 2014 (S.I. 2014/1372), regs. 1, 8. (1)

Adaptations

76 Adaptations.

An act which by virtue of this Chapter may be done without infringing copyright in a literary, dramatic or musical work does not, where that work is an adaptation, infringe any copyright in the work from which the adaptation was made.

[F199. CHAPTER 3. ACERTAIN PERMITTED USES OF ORPHAN WORKS

Amendments (Textual)

F199. Pt. 1 Ch. 3. A inserted (29.10.2014) by The Copyright and Rights in Performances (Certain Permitted Uses of Orphan Works) Regulations 2014 (S.I. 2014/2861), regs. 1, 3. (2)

76. ACertain permitted uses of orphan works

Schedule ZA1 makes provision about the use by relevant bodies of orphan works.]

Chapter IV Moral Rights

77 Right to be identified as author or director.

(1) The author of a copyright literary, dramatic, musical or artistic work, and the director of a copyright film, has the right to be identified as the author or director of the work in the circumstances mentioned in this section; but the right is not infringed unless it has been asserted in accordance with section 78.

(2) The author of a literary work (other than words intended to be sung or spoken with music) or a dramatic work has the right to be identified whenever—

    (a) the work is published commercially, performed in public [F200or communicated to the public]; or

    (b) copies of a film or sound recording including the work are issued to the public;

and that right includes the right to be identified whenever any of those events occur in relation to an adaptation of the work as the author of the work from which the adaptation was made.

(3) The author of a musical work, or a literary work consisting of words intended to be sung or spoken with music, has the right to be identified whenever—

    (a) the work is published commercially;

    (b) copies of a sound recording of the work are issued to the public; or

    (c) a film of which the sound-track includes the work is shown in public or copies of such a film are issued to the public;

and that right includes the right to be identified whenever any of those events occur in relation to an adaptation of the work as the author of the work from which the adaptation was made.

(4) The author of an artistic work has the right to be identified whenever—

(a) the work is published commercially or exhibited in public, or a visual image of it is [F201communicated to the public];

(b) a film including a visual image of the work is shown in public or copies of such a film are issued to the public; or

(c) in the case of a work of architecture in the form of a building or a model for a building, a sculpture or a work of artistic craftsmanship, copies of a graphic work representing it, or of a photograph of it, are issued to the public.

(5) The author of a work of architecture in the form of a building also has the right to be identified on the building as constructed or, where more than one building is constructed to the design, on the first to be constructed.

(6) The director of a film has the right to be identified whenever the film is shown in public [F200or communicated to the public] or copies of the film are issued to the public.

(7) The right of the author or director under this section is—

(a) in the case of commercial publication or the issue to the public of copies of a film or sound recording, to be identified in or on each copy or, if that is not appropriate, in some other manner likely to bring his identity to the notice of a person acquiring a copy,

(b) in the case of identification on a building, to be identified by appropriate means visible to persons entering or approaching the building, and

(c) in any other case, to be identified in a manner likely to bring his identity to the attention of a person seeing or hearing the performance, exhibition, showing [F202or communication to the public] in question;

and the identification must in each case be clear and reasonably prominent.

(8) If the author or director in asserting his right to be identified specifies a pseudonym, initials or some other particular form of identification, that form shall be used; otherwise any reasonable form of identification may be used.

(9) This section has effect subject to section 79 (exceptions to right).

Amendments (Textual)

F200. Words in s. 77. (2)(a)(6) substituted (31.10.2003) by The Copyright and Related Rights Regulations 2003 (S.I. 2003/2498), reg. 2. (1), Sch. 1 para. 8. (1)(a)(b) (with regs. 31-40)

F201. Words in s. 77. (4)(a) substituted (31.10.2003) by The Copyright and Related Rights Regulations 2003 (S.I. 2003/2498), reg. 2. (1), Sch. 1 para. 8. (2)(a) (with regs. 31-40)

F202. Words in s. 77. (7)(c) substituted (31.10.2003) by The Copyright and Related Rights Regulations 2003 (S.I. 2003/2498), reg. 2. (1), Sch. 1 para. 9. (1)(b) (with regs. 31-40)

78 Requirement that right be asserted.

(1) A person does not infringe the right conferred by section 77 (right to be identified as author or director) by doing any of the acts mentioned in that section unless the right has been asserted in accordance with the following provisions so as to bind him in relation to that act.

(2) The right may be asserted generally, or in relation to any specified act or description of acts—

(a) on an assignment of copyright in the work, by including in the instrument effecting the assignment a statement that the author or director asserts in relation to that work his right to be identified, or

(b) by instrument in writing signed by the author or director.

(3) The right may also be asserted in relation to the public exhibition of an artistic work—

(a) by securing that when the author or other first owner of copyright parts with possession of the original, or of a copy made by him or under his direction or control, the author is identified on the original or copy, or on a frame, mount or other thing to which it is attached, or

(b) by including in a licence by which the author or other first owner of copyright authorises the making of copies of the work a statement signed by or on behalf of the person granting the licence that the author asserts his right to be identified in the event of the public exhibition of a copy made in pursuance of the licence.

(4) The persons bound by an assertion of the right under subsection (2) or (3) are—

(a) in the case of an assertion under subsection (2)(a), the assignee and anyone claiming through him, whether or not he has notice of the assertion;

(b) in the case of an assertion under subsection (2)(b), anyone to whose notice the assertion is brought;

(c) in the case of an assertion under subsection (3)(a), anyone into whose hands that original or copy comes, whether or not the identification is still present or visible;

(d) in the case of an assertion under subsection (3)(b), the licensee and anyone into whose hands a copy made in pursuance of the licence comes, whether or not he has notice of the assertion.

(5) In an action for infringement of the right the court shall, in considering remedies, take into account any delay in asserting the right.

79 Exceptions to right.

(1) The right conferred by section 77 (right to be identified as author or director) is subject to the following exceptions.

(2) The right does not apply in relation to the following descriptions of work—

(a) a computer program;

(b) the design of a typeface;

(c) any computer-generated work.

(3) The right does not apply to anything done by or with the authority of the copyright owner where copyright in the work originally [F203 vested in the author's or director's employer by virtue of section 11. (2) (works produced in the course of employment).]

(4) The right is not infringed by an act which by virtue of any of the following provisions would not infringe copyright in the work—

(a) section 30 (fair dealing for certain purposes), so far as it relates to the reporting of current events by means of a sound recording, film [F204or broadcast];

(b) section 31 (incidental inclusion of work in an artistic work, sound recording, film [F204or broadcast]);

F205. (c). . . . .

(d) section 45 (parliamentary and judicial proceedings);

(e) section 46. (1) or (2) (Royal Commissions and statutory inquiries);

(f) section 51 (use of design documents and models);

F206. (g). . . . .

(h) [F207section 57 or 66. A (acts permitted on assumptions as to expiry of copyright, &c.)];

[F208. (4. A)The right is also not infringed by any act done for the purposes of an examination which by virtue of any provision of Chapter 3 of Part 1 would not infringe copyright.]

(5) The right does not apply in relation to any work made for the purpose of reporting current events.

(6) The right does not apply in relation to the publication in—

(a) a newspaper, magazine or similar periodical, or

(b) an encyclopaedia, dictionary, yearbook or other collective work of reference,

of a literary, dramatic, musical or artistic work made for the purposes of such publication or made available with the consent of the author for the purposes of such publication.

(7) The right does not apply in relation to—

(a) a work in which Crown copyright or Parliamentary copyright subsists, or

(b) a work in which copyright originally vested in an international organisation by virtue of section 168,

unless the author or director has previously been identified as such in or on published copies of the work.

Amendments (Textual)

F203. Words in s. 79. (3) substituted (31.10.2003) by The Copyright and Related Rights Regulations 2003 (S.I. 2003/2498), reg. 2. (1), Sch. 1 para. 18. (1) (with regs. 31-40)

F204. Words in s. 79. (4)(a)(b) substituted (31.10.2003) by The Copyright and Related Rights Regulations 2003 (S.I. 2003/2498), reg. 2. (1), Sch. 1 para. 3. (1)(g)(h) (with regs. 31-40)

F205. S. 79. (4)(c) omitted (1.6.2014) by virtue of The Copyright and Rights in Performances

(Research, Education, Libraries and Archives) Regulations 2014 (S.I. 2014/1372), reg. 1, Sch. para. 4. (a)

F206. S. 79. (4)(g) omitted (28.7.2016) by virtue of Enterprise and Regulatory Reform Act 2013 (c. 24), ss. 74. (3)(a), 103. (3); S.I. 2016/593, arts. 2. (1), 3 (with arts. 4, 5)

F207. Words in s. 79. (4) substituted (1.1.1996) by S.I. 1995/3297, reg. 5. (3) (with Pt. III)

F208. S. 79. (4. A) inserted (1.6.2014) by The Copyright and Rights in Performances (Research, Education, Libraries and Archives) Regulations 2014 (S.I. 2014/1372), reg. 1, Sch. para. 4. (b)

Right to object to derogatory treatment of work

80 Right to object to derogatory treatment of work.

(1) The author of a copyright literary, dramatic, musical or artistic work, and the director of a copyright film, has the right in the circumstances mentioned in this section not to have his work subjected to derogatory treatment.

(2) For the purposes of this section—

(a) "treatment" of a work means any addition to, deletion from or alteration to or adaptation of the work, other than—

(i) a translation of a literary or dramatic work, or

(ii) an arrangement or transcription of a musical work involving no more than a change of key or register; and

(b) the treatment of a work is derogatory if it amounts to distortion or mutilation of the work or is otherwise prejudicial to the honour or reputation of the author or director;

and in the following provisions of this section references to a derogatory treatment of a work shall be construed accordingly.

(3) In the case of a literary, dramatic or musical work the right is infringed by a person who—

(a) publishes commercially, performs in public [F209or communicates to the public] a derogatory treatment of the work; or

(b) issues to the public copies of a film or sound recording of, or including, a derogatory treatment of the work.

(4) In the case of an artistic work the right is infringed by a person who—

(a) publishes commercially or exhibits in public a derogatory treatment of the work, [F210or communicates to the public] a visual image of a derogatory treatment of the work,

(b) shows in public a film including a visual image of a derogatory treatment of the work or issues to the public copies of such a film, or

(c) in the case of—

(i) a work of architecture in the form of a model for a building,

(ii) a sculpture, or

(iii) a work of artistic craftsmanship,

issues to the public copies of a graphic work representing, or of a photograph of, a derogatory treatment of the work.

(5) Subsection (4) does not apply to a work of architecture in the form of a building; but where the author of such a work is identified on the building and it is the subject of derogatory treatment he has the right to require the identification to be removed.

(6) In the case of a film, the right is infringed by a person who—

(a) shows in public [F209or communicates to the public] a derogatory treatment of the film; or

(b) issues to the public copies of a derogatory treatment of the film,

F211. . .

(7) The right conferred by this section extends to the treatment of parts of a work resulting from a previous treatment by a person other than the author or director, if those parts are attributed to, or are likely to be regarded as the work of, the author or director.

(8) This section has effect subject to sections 81 and 82 (exceptions to and qualifications of right).

Amendments (Textual)

F209. Words in s. 80. (3)(a)(6)(a) substituted (31.10.2003) by The Copyright and Related Rights Regulations 2003 (S.I. 2003/2498), reg. 2. (1), Sch. 1 para. 10. (1) (with regs. 31-40)

F210. Words in s. 80. (4)(a) substituted (31.10.2003) by The Copyright and Related Rights Regulations 2003 (S.I. 2003/2498), reg. 2. (1), Sch. 1 para. 13. (2) (with regs. 31-40)

F211. Words in s. 80. (6) omitted (1.1.1996) by virtue of S.I. 1995/3297, reg. 9. (2) (with Pt. III)

81 Exceptions to right.

(1) The right conferred by section 80 (right to object to derogatory treatment of work) is subject to the following exceptions.

(2) The right does not apply to a computer program or to any computer-generated work.

(3) The right does not apply in relation to any work made for the purpose of reporting current events.

(4) The right does not apply in relation to the publication in—

    (a) a newspaper, magazine or similar periodical, or

    (b) an encyclopaedia, dictionary, yearbook or other collective work of reference,

of a literary, dramatic, musical or artistic work made for the purposes of such publication or made available with the consent of the author for the purposes of such publication.

Nor does the right apply in relation to any subsequent exploitation elsewhere of such a work without any modification of the published version.

(5) The right is not infringed by an act which by virtue of [F212section 57 or 66. A (acts permitted on assumptions as to expiry of copyright, &c.)] would not infringe copyright.

(6) The right is not infringed by anything done for the purpose of—

    (a) avoiding the commission of an offence,

    (b) complying with a duty imposed by or under an enactment, or

    (c) in the case of the British Broadcasting Corporation, avoiding the inclusion in a programme broadcast by them of anything which offends against good taste or decency or which is likely to encourage or incite to crime or to lead to disorder or to be offensive to public feeling,

provided, where the author or director is identified at the time of the relevant act or has previously been identified in or on published copies of the work, that there is a sufficient disclaimer.

Amendments (Textual)

F212. Words in s. 81. (5) substituted (1.1.1996) by S.I. 1995/3297, reg. 5. (3) (with Pt. III)

82 Qualification of right in certain cases.

(1) This section applies to—

    (a) works in which copyright originally vested in the author's [F213 or director's] employer by virtue of section 11. (2) (works produced in course of employment) F214. . .

    (b) works in which Crown copyright or Parliamentary copyright subsists, and

    (c) works in which copyright originally vested in an international organisation by virtue of section 168.

(2) The right conferred by section 80 (right to object to derogatory treatment of work) does not apply to anything done in relation to such a work by or with the authority of the copyright owner unless the author or director—

    (a) is identified at the time of the relevant act, or

    (b) has previously been identified in or on published copies of the work;

and where in such a case the right does apply, it is not infringed if there is a sufficient disclaimer.

Amendments (Textual)

F213. Words in s. 82. (1)(a) inserted (31.10.2003) by The Copyright and Related Rights Regulations 2003 (S.I. 2003/2498), reg. 2. (1), Sch. 1 para. 18. (2) (with regs. 31-40)

F214. Words in s. 82. (1)(a) repealed (31.10.2003) by The Copyright and Related Rights Regulations 2003 (S.I. 2003/2498), reg. 2, Sch. 1 para. 18. (2), Sch. 2 (with regs. 31-40)

83 Infringement of right by possessing or dealing with infringing article.

(1) The right conferred by section 80 (right to object to derogatory treatment of work) is also infringed by a person who—

    (a) possesses in the course of a business, or

    (b) sells or lets for hire, or offers or exposes for sale or hire, or

(c) in the course of a business exhibits in public or distributes, or

(d) distributes otherwise than in the course of a business so as to affect prejudicially the honour or reputation of the author or director,

an article which is, and which he knows or has reason to believe is, an infringing article.

(2) An "infringing article" means a work or a copy of a work which—

(a) has been subjected to derogatory treatment within the meaning of section 80, and

(b) has been or is likely to be the subject of any of the acts mentioned in that section in circumstances infringing that right.

False attribution of work

84 False attribution of work.

(1) A person has the right in the circumstances mentioned in this section—

(a) not to have a literary, dramatic, musical or artistic work falsely attributed to him as author, and

(b) not to have a film falsely attributed to him as director;

and in this section an "attribution", in relation to such a work, means a statement (express or implied) as to who is the author or director.

(2) The right is infringed by a person who—

(a) issues to the public copies of a work of any of those descriptions in or on which there is a false attribution, or

(b) exhibits in public an artistic work, or a copy of an artistic work, in or on which there is a false attribution.

(3) The right is also infringed by a person who—

(a) in the case of a literary, dramatic or musical work, performs the work in public [F215or communicates it to the public] as being the work of a person, or

(b) in the case of a film, shows it in public [F215or communicates it to the public] as being directed by a person,

knowing or having reason to believe that the attribution is false.

(4) The right is also infringed by the issue to the public or public display of material containing a false attribution in connection with any of the acts mentioned in subsection (2) or (3).

(5) The right is also infringed by a person who in the course of a business—

(a) possesses or deals with a copy of a work of any of the descriptions mentioned in subsection (1) in or on which there is a false attribution, or

(b) in the case of an artistic work, possesses or deals with the work itself when there is a false attribution in or on it,

knowing or having reason to believe that there is such an attribution and that it is false.

(6) In the case of an artistic work the right is also infringed by a person who in the course of a business—

(a) deals with a work which has been altered after the author parted with possession of it as being the unaltered work of the author, or

(b) deals with a copy of such a work as being a copy of the unaltered work of the author,

knowing or having reason to believe that that is not the case.

(7) References in this section to dealing are to selling or letting for hire, offering or exposing for sale or hire, exhibiting in public, or distributing.

(8) This section applies where, contrary to the fact—

(a) a literary, dramatic or musical work is falsely represented as being an adaptation of the work of a person, or

(b) a copy of an artistic work is falsely represented as being a copy made by the author of the artistic work,

as it applies where the work is falsely attributed to a person as author.

Amendments (Textual)

F215. Words in s. 84. (3)(a)(b) substituted (31.10.2003) by The Copyright and Related Rights Regulations 2003 (S.I. 2003/2498), reg. 2. (1), Sch. 1 para. 10. (2) (with regs. 31-40)

Right to privacy of certain photographs and films

85 Right to privacy of certain photographs and films.

(1) A person who for private and domestic purposes commissions the taking of a photograph or the making of a film has, where copyright subsists in the resulting work, the right not to have—

   (a) copies of the work issued to the public,

   (b) the work exhibited or shown in public, or

   (c) the work [F216communicated to the public];

and, except as mentioned in subsection (2), a person who does or authorises the doing of any of those acts infringes that right.

(2) The right is not infringed by an act which by virtue of any of the following provisions would not infringe copyright in the work—

   (a) section 31 (incidental inclusion of work in an artistic work, film [F217or broadcast]);

   (b) section 45 (parliamentary and judicial proceedings);

   (c) section 46 (Royal Commissions and statutory inquiries);

   (d) section 50 (acts done under statutory authority);

   (e) [F218section 57 or 66. A (acts permitted on assumptions as to expiry of copyright, &c.)].

Amendments (Textual)

F216. Words in s. 85. (1)(c) substituted (31.10.2003) by The Copyright and Related Rights Regulations 2003 (S.I. 2003/2498), reg. 2. (1), Sch. 1 para. 8. (2)(b) (with regs. 31-40)

F217. Words in s. 85. (2)(a) substituted (31.10.2003) by The Copyright and Related Rights Regulations 2003 (S.I. 2003/2498), reg. 2. (1), Sch. 1 para. 3. (1)(i) (with regs. 31-40)

F218. Words in s. 85. (2) substituted (1.1.1996) by S.I. 1995/3297, reg. 6. (3) (with Pt. III)

Supplementary

86 Duration of rights.

(1) The rights conferred by section 77 (right to be identified as author or director), section 80 (right to object to derogatory treatment of work) and section 85 (right to privacy of certain photographs and films) continue to subsist so long as copyright subsists in the work.

(2) The right conferred by section 84 (false attribution) continues to subsist until 20 years after a person's death.

87 Consent and waiver of rights.

(1) It is not an infringement of any of the rights conferred by this Chapter to do any act to which the person entitled to the right has consented.

(2) Any of those rights may be waived by instrument in writing signed by the person giving up the right.

(3) A waiver—

   (a) may relate to a specific work, to works of a specified description or to works generally, and may relate to existing or future works, and

   (b) may be conditional or unconditional and may be expressed to be subject to revocation;

and if made in favour of the owner or prospective owner of the copyright in the work or works to which it relates, it shall be presumed to extend to his licensees and successors in title unless a contrary intention is expressed.

(4) Nothing in this Chapter shall be construed as excluding the operation of the general law of contract or estoppel in relation to an informal waiver or other transaction in relation to any of the rights mentioned in subsection (1).

88 Application of provisions to joint works.

(1) The right conferred by section 77 (right to be identified as author or director) is, in the case of

a work of joint authorship, a right of each joint author to be identified as a joint author and must be asserted in accordance with section 78 by each joint author in relation to himself.

(2) The right conferred by section 80 (right to object to derogatory treatment of work) is, in the case of a work of joint authorship, a right of each joint author and his right is satisfied if he consents to the treatment in question.

(3) A waiver under section 87 of those rights by one joint author does not affect the rights of the other joint authors.

(4) The right conferred by section 84 (false attribution) is infringed, in the circumstances mentioned in that section—

    (a) by any false statement as to the authorship of a work of joint authorship, and

    (b) by the false attribution of joint authorship in relation to a work of sole authorship;

and such a false attribution infringes the right of every person to whom authorship of any description is, whether rightly or wrongly, attributed.

(5) The above provisions also apply (with any necessary adaptations) in relation to a film which was, or is alleged to have been, jointly directed, as they apply to a work which is, or is alleged to be, a work of joint authorship.

A film is "jointly directed" if it is made by the collaboration of two or more directors and the contribution of each director is not distinct from that of the other director or directors.

(6) The right conferred by section 85 (right to privacy of certain photographs and films) is, in the case of a work made in pursuance of a joint commission, a right of each person who commissioned the making of the work, so that—

    (a) the right of each is satisfied if he consents to the act in question, and

    (b) a waiver under section 87 by one of them does not affect the rights of the others.

89 Application of provisions to parts of works.

(1) The rights conferred by section 77 (right to be identified as author or director) and section 85 (right to privacy of certain photographs and films) apply in relation to the whole or any substantial part of a work.

(2) The rights conferred by section 80 (right to object to derogatory treatment of work) and section 84 (false attribution) apply in relation to the whole or any part of a work.

Chapter V Dealings with Rights in Copyright Works

Modifications etc. (not altering text)

C39. Pt. I Ch. V (ss. 90-95) applied (with modifications) (1.12.1996) by S.I. 1996/2967, reg. 17. (1)-(3) (with Pt. III)

90 Assignment and licences.

(1) Copyright is transmissible by assignment, by testamentary disposition or by operation of law, as personal or moveable property.

(2) An assignment or other transmission of copyright may be partial, that is, limited so as to apply—

    (a) to one or more, but not all, of the things the copyright owner has the exclusive right to do;

    (b) to part, but not the whole, of the period for which the copyright is to subsist.

(3) An assignment of copyright is not effective unless it is in writing signed by or on behalf of the assignor.

(4) A licence granted by a copyright owner is binding on every successor in title to his interest in the copyright, except a purchaser in good faith for valuable consideration and without notice (actual or constructive) of the licence or a person deriving title from such a purchaser; and references in this Part to doing anything with, or without, the licence of the copyright owner shall be construed accordingly.

Modifications etc. (not altering text)

C40. Ss. 90-93, 96-98, 101, 102 applied (1.1.1998) by S.I. 1997/3032, reg. 23 (with Pt. IV)

91 Prospective ownership of copyright.

(1) Where by an agreement made in relation to future copyright, and signed by or on behalf of the prospective owner of the copyright, the prospective owner purports to assign the future copyright (wholly or partially) to another person, then if, on the copyright coming into existence, the assignee or another person claiming under him would be entitled as against all other persons to require the copyright to be vested in him, the copyright shall vest in the assignee or his successor in title by virtue of this subsection.

(2) In this Part—

"future copyright" means copyright which will or may come into existence in respect of a future work or class of works or on the occurrence of a future event; and

"prospective owner" shall be construed accordingly, and includes a person who is prospectively entitled to copyright by virtue of such an agreement as is mentioned in subsection (1).

(3) A licence granted by a prospective owner of copyright is binding on every successor in title to his interest (or prospective interest) in the right, except a purchaser in good faith for valuable consideration and without notice (actual or constructive) of the licence or a person deriving title from such a purchaser; and references in this Part to doing anything with, or without, the licence of the copyright owner shall be construed accordingly.

Modifications etc. (not altering text)

C41. Ss. 90-93, 96-98, 101, 102 applied (1.1.1998) by S.I. 1997/3032, reg. 23 (with Pt. IV)

92 Exclusive licences.

(1) In this Part an "exclusive licence" means a licence in writing signed by or on behalf of the copyright owner authorising the licensee to the exclusion of all other persons, including the person granting the licence, to exercise a right which would otherwise be exercisable exclusively by the copyright owner.

(2) The licensee under an exclusive licence has the same rights against a successor in title who is bound by the licence as he has against the person granting the licence.

Modifications etc. (not altering text)

C42. Ss. 90-93, 96-98, 101, 102 applied (1.1.1998) by S.I. 1997/3032, reg. 23 (with Pt. IV)

93 Copyright to pass under will with unpublished work.

Where under a bequest (whether specific or general) a person is entitled, beneficially or otherwise, to—

    (a) an original document or other material thing recording or embodying a literary, dramatic, musical or artistic work which was not published before the death of the testator, or

    (b) an original material thing containing a sound recording or film which was not published before the death of the testator,

the bequest shall, unless a contrary intention is indicated in the testator's will or a codicil to it, be construed as including the copyright in the work in so far as the testator was the owner of the copyright immediately before his death.

Modifications etc. (not altering text)

C43. Ss. 90-93, 96-98, 101, 102 applied (1.1.1998) by S.I. 1997/3032, reg. 23 (with Pt. IV)

[F21993. A Presumption of transfer of rental right in case of film production agreement.

(1) Where an agreement concerning film production is concluded between an author and a film producer, the author shall be presumed, unless the agreement provides to the contrary, to have transferred to the film producer any rental right in relation to the film arising by virtue of the inclusion of a copy of the author's work in the film.

(2) In this section "author" means an author, or prospective author, of a literary, dramatic, musical or artistic work.

(3) Subsection (1) does not apply to any rental right in relation to the film arising by virtue of the inclusion in the film of the screenplay, the dialogue or music specifically created for and used in the film.

(4) Where this section applies, the absence of signature by or on behalf of the author does not exclude the operation of section 91. (1) (effect of purported assignment of future copyright).

(5) The reference in subsection (1) to an agreement concluded between an author and a film producer includes any agreement having effect between those persons, whether made by them

directly or through intermediaries.

(6) Section 93. B (right to equitable remuneration on transfer of rental right) applies where there is a presumed transfer by virtue of this section as in the case of an actual transfer.]

Amendments (Textual)

F219. S. 93. A inserted (1.12.1996) by S.I. 1996/2967, reg. 12 (with Pt. III)

Modifications etc. (not altering text)

C44. S. 93. A applied (with modifications) (1.12.1996) by S.I. 1996/2967, reg. 32. (1) (with Pt. III)

F220[Right to equitable remuneration where rental right transferred

Amendments (Textual)

F220. S. 93. B and crossheading inserted (1.12.1996) by S.I. 1996/2967, reg. 14. (1) (with Pt. III)

F22193. B Right to equitable remuneration where rental right transferred.

(1) Where an author to whom this section applies has transferred his rental right concerning a sound recording or a film to the producer of the sound recording or film, he retains the right to equitable remuneration for the rental.

The authors to whom this section applies are—

    (a) the author of a literary, dramatic, musical or artistic work, and

    (b) the principal director of a film.

(2) The right to equitable remuneration under this section may not be assigned by the author except to a collecting society for the purpose of enabling it to enforce the right on his behalf.

The right is, however, transmissible by testamentary disposition or by operation of law as personal or moveable property; and it may be assigned or further transmitted by any person into whose hands it passes.

(3) Equitable remuneration under this section is payable by the person for the time being entitled to the rental right, that is, the person to whom the right was transferred or any successor in title of his.

(4) The amount payable by way of equitable remuneration is as agreed by or on behalf of the persons by and to whom it is payable, subject to section 93. C (reference of amount to Copyright Tribunal).

(5) An agreement is of no effect in so far as it purports to exclude or restrict the right to equitable remuneration under this section.

(6) References in this section to the transfer of rental right by one person to another include any arrangement having that effect, whether made by them directly or through intermediaries.

(7) In this section a "collecting society" means a society or other organisation which has as its main object, or one of its main objects, the exercise of the right to equitable remuneration under this section on behalf of more than one author.

Amendments (Textual)

F221. S. 93. B inserted (1.12.1996) by S.I. 1996/2967, reg. 14. (1) (with Pt. III)

Modifications etc. (not altering text)

C45. S. 93. B applied (with modifications) (1.12.1996) by S.I. 1996/2967, reg. 32. (2) (with Pt. III)

C46. S. 93. B restricted (1.12.1996) by S.I. 1996/2967, reg. 33 (with Pt. III)

F22293. C Equitable remuneration: reference of amount to Copyright Tribunal.

(1) In default of agreement as to the amount payable by way of equitable remuneration under section 93. B, the person by or to whom it is payable may apply to the Copyright Tribunal to determine the amount payable.

(2) A person to or by whom equitable remuneration is payable under that section may also apply to the Copyright Tribunal—

    (a) to vary any agreement as to the amount payable, or

    (b) to vary any previous determination of the Tribunal as to that matter; but except with the special leave of the Tribunal no such application may be made within twelve months from the date of a previous determination.

An order made on an application under this subsection has effect from the date on which it is made or such later date as may be specified by the Tribunal.

(3) On an application under this section the Tribunal shall consider the matter and make such order as to the method of calculating and paying equitable remuneration as it may determine to be reasonable in the circumstances, taking into account the importance of the contribution of the author to the film or sound recording.

(4) Remuneration shall not be considered inequitable merely because it was paid by way of a single payment or at the time of the transfer of the rental right.

(5) An agreement is of no effect in so far as it purports to prevent a person questioning the amount of equitable remuneration or to restrict the powers of the Copyright Tribunal under this section.]

Amendments (Textual)

F222. S. 93. C inserted (1.12.1996) by S.I. 1996/2967, reg. 14. (1) (with Pt. III)

Moral rights

94 Moral rights not assignable.

The rights conferred by Chapter IV (moral rights) are not assignable.

95 Transmission of moral rights on death.

(1) On the death of a person entitled to the right conferred by section 77 (right to identification of author or director), section 80 (right to object to derogatory treatment of work) or section 85 (right to privacy of certain photographs and films)—

   (a) the right passes to such person as he may by testamentary disposition specifically direct,

   (b) if there is no such direction but the copyright in the work in question forms part of his estate, the right passes to the person to whom the copyright passes, and

   (c) if or to the extent that the right does not pass under paragraph (a) or (b) it is exercisable by his personal representatives.

(2) Where copyright forming part of a person's estate passes in part to one person and in part to another, as for example where a bequest is limited so as to apply—

   (a) to one or more, but not all, of the things the copyright owner has the exclusive right to do or authorise, or

   (b) to part, but not the whole, of the period for which the copyright is to subsist,

any right which passes with the copyright by virtue of subsection (1) is correspondingly divided.

(3) Where by virtue of subsection (1)(a) or (b) a right becomes exercisable by more than one person—

   (a) it may, in the case of the right conferred by section 77 (right to identification of author or director), be asserted by any of them;

   (b) it is, in the case of the right conferred by section 80 (right to object to derogatory treatment of work) or section 85 (right to privacy of certain photographs and films), a right exercisable by each of them and is satisfied in relation to any of them if he consents to the treatment or act in question; and

   (c) any waiver of the right in accordance with section 87 by one of them does not affect the rights of the others.

(4) A consent or waiver previously given or made binds any person to whom a right passes by virtue of subsection (1).

(5) Any infringement after a person's death of the right conferred by section 84 (false attribution) is actionable by his personal representatives.

(6) Any damages recovered by personal representatives by virtue of this section in respect of an infringement after a person's death shall devolve as part of his estate as if the right of action had subsisted and been vested in him immediately before his death.

Chapter VI Remedies for Infringement

Modifications etc. (not altering text)

C47. Pt. I Ch. VI (ss. 96-115) applied (with modifications) (1.12.1996) by S.I. 1996/2967, reg. 17 (with Pt. III)

96 Infringement actionable by copyright owner.

(1) An infringement of copyright is actionable by the copyright owner.

(2) In an action for infringement of copyright all such relief by way of damages, injunctions, accounts or otherwise is available to the plaintiff as is available in respect of the infringement of any other property right.

(3) This section has effect subject to the following provisions of this Chapter.

Modifications etc. (not altering text)

C48. Ss. 90-93, 96-98, 101, 102 applied (1.1.1998) by S.I. 1997/3032, reg. 23 (with Pt. IV)

97 Provisions as to damages in infringement action.

(1) Where in an action for infringement of copyright it is shown that at the time of the infringement the defendant did not know, and had no reason to believe, that copyright subsisted in the work to which the action relates, the plaintiff is not entitled to damages against him, but without prejudice to any other remedy.

(2) The court may in an action for infringement of copyright having regard to all the circumstances, and in particular to—

   (a) the flagrancy of the infringement, and

   (b) any benefit accruing to the defendant by reason of the infringement,

award such additional damages as the justice of the case may require.

Modifications etc. (not altering text)

C49. Ss. 90-93, 96-98, 101, 102 applied (1.1.1998) by S.I. 1997/3032, reg. 23 (with Pt. IV)

[F22397. AInjunctions against service providers

(1) The High Court (in Scotland, the Court of Session) shall have power to grant an injunction against a service provider, where that service provider has actual knowledge of another person using their service to infringe copyright.

(2) In determining whether a service provider has actual knowledge for the purpose of this section, a court shall take into account all matters which appear to it in the particular circumstances to be relevant and, amongst other things, shall have regard to—

   (a) whether a service provider has received a notice through a means of contact made available in accordance with regulation 6. (1)(c) of the Electronic Commerce (EC Directive) Regulations 2002 (SI 2002/2013); and

   (b) the extent to which any notice includes—

(i) the full name and address of the sender of the notice;

(ii) details of the infringement in question.

(3) In this section " service provider " has the meaning given to it by regulation 2 of the Electronic Commerce (EC Directive) Regulations 2002.]

Amendments (Textual)

F223. S. 97. A inserted (31.10.2003) by The Copyright and Related Rights Regulations 2003 (S.I. 2003/2498), reg. 27. (1) (with regs. 31-40)

98 Undertaking to take licence of right in infringement proceedings.

(1) If in proceedings for infringement of copyright in respect of which a licence is available as of right under section 144 (powers exercisable in consequence of report of [F224. Competition and Markets Authority]) the defendant undertakes to take a licence on such terms as may be agreed or, in default of agreement, settled by the Copyright Tribunal under that section—

   (a) no injunction shall be granted against him,

   (b) no order for delivery up shall be made under section 99, and

   (c) the amount recoverable against him by way of damages or on an account of profits shall not exceed double the amount which would have been payable by him as licensee if such a licence on those terms had been granted before the earliest infringement.

(2) An undertaking may be given at any time before final order in the proceedings, without any admission of liability.

(3) Nothing in this section affects the remedies available in respect of an infringement committed before licences of right were available.

Amendments (Textual)

F224. Words in s. 98. (1) substituted (1.4.2014) by The Enterprise and Regulatory Reform Act 2013 (Competition) (Consequential, Transitional and Saving Provisions) Order 2014 (S.I. 2014/892), art. 1. (1), Sch. 1 para. 56 (with art. 3)

Modifications etc. (not altering text)

C50. Ss. 90-93, 96-98, 101, 102 applied (1.1.1998) by S.I. 1997/3032, reg. 23 (with Pt. IV)

99 Order for delivery up.

(1) Where a person—

(a) has an infringing copy of a work in his possession, custody or control in the course of a business, or

(b) has in his possession, custody or control an article specifically designed or adapted for making copies of a particular copyright work, knowing or having reason to believe that it has been or is to be used to make infringing copies,

the owner of the copyright in the work may apply to the court for an order that the infringing copy or article be delivered up to him or to such other person as the court may direct.

(2) An application shall not be made after the end of the period specified in section 113 (period after which remedy of delivery up not available); and no order shall be made unless the court also makes, or it appears to the court that there are grounds for making, an order under section 114 (order as to disposal of infringing copy or other article).

(3) A person to whom an infringing copy or other article is delivered up in pursuance of an order under this section shall, if an order under section 114 is not made, retain it pending the making of an order, or the decision not to make an order, under that section.

(4) Nothing in this section affects any other power of the court.

Modifications etc. (not altering text)

C51. S. 99 extended by S.I. 1991/724, art. 2. (1)(n)

100 Right to seize infringing copies and other articles.

(1) An infringing copy of a work which is found exposed or otherwise immediately available for sale or hire, and in respect of which the copyright owner would be entitled to apply for an order under section 99, may be seized and detained by him or a person authorised by him.

The right to seize and detain is exercisable subject to the following conditions and is subject to any decision of the court under section 114.

(2) Before anything is seized under this section notice of the time and place of the proposed seizure must be given to a local police station.

(3) A person may for the purpose of exercising the right conferred by this section enter premises to which the public have access but may not seize anything in the possession, custody or control of a person at a permanent or regular place of business of his, and may not use any force.

(4) At the time when anything is seized under this section there shall be left at the place where it was seized a notice in the prescribed form containing the prescribed particulars as to the person by whom or on whose authority the seizure is made and the grounds on which it is made.

(5) In this section—

"premises" includes land, buildings, moveable structures, vehicles, vessels, aircraft and hovercraft; and "prescribed" means prescribed by order of the Secretary of State.

(6) An order of the Secretary of State under this section shall be made by statutory instrument which shall be subject to annulment in pursuance of a resolution of either House of Parliament.

Rights and remedies of exclusive licensee

101 Rights and remedies of exclusive licensee.

(1) An exclusive licensee has, except against the copyright owner, the same rights and remedies in respect of matters occurring after the grant of the licence as if the licence had been an assignment.

(2) His rights and remedies are concurrent with those of the copyright owner; and references in the relevant provisions of this Part to the copyright owner shall be construed accordingly.

(3) In an action brought by an exclusive licensee by virtue of this section a defendant may avail himself of any defence which would have been available to him if the action had been brought by the copyright owner.

Modifications etc. (not altering text)

C52. Ss. 90-93, 96-98, 101, 102 applied (1.1.1998) by S.I. 1997/3032, reg. 23 (with Pt. IV)

[F225101. ACertain infringements actionable by a non-exclusive licensee

(1) A non-exclusive licensee may bring an action for infringement of copyright if—

   (a) the infringing act was directly connected to a prior licensed act of the licensee; and

   (b) the licence—

(i) is in writing and is signed by or on behalf of the copyright owner; and

(ii) expressly grants the non-exclusive licensee a right of action under this section.

(2) In an action brought under this section, the non-exclusive licensee shall have the same rights and remedies available to him as the copyright owner would have had if he had brought the action.

(3) The rights granted under this section are concurrent with those of the copyright owner and references in the relevant provisions of this Part to the copyright owner shall be construed accordingly.

(4) In an action brought by a non-exclusive licensee by virtue of this section a defendant may avail himself of any defence which would have been available to him if the action had been brought by the copyright owner.

(5) Subsections (1) to (4) of section 102 shall apply to a non-exclusive licensee who has a right of action by virtue of this section as it applies to an exclusive licensee.

(6) In this section a " non-exclusive licensee " means the holder of a licence authorising the licensee to exercise a right which remains exercisable by the copyright owner.]

Amendments (Textual)

F225. S. 101. A inserted (31.10.2003) by The Copyright and Related Rights Regulations 2003 (S.I. 2003/2498), reg. 28 (with regs. 31-40)

102 Exercise of concurrent rights.

(1) Where an action for infringement of copyright brought by the copyright owner or an exclusive licensee relates (wholly or partly) to an infringement in respect of which they have concurrent rights of action, the copyright owner or, as the case may be, the exclusive licensee may not, without the leave of the court, proceed with the action unless the other is either joined as a plaintiff or added as a defendant.

(2) A copyright owner or exclusive licensee who is added as a defendant in pursuance of subsection (1) is not liable for any costs in the action unless he takes part in the proceedings.

(3) The above provisions do not affect the granting of interlocutory relief on an application by a copyright owner or exclusive licensee alone.

(4) Where an action for infringement of copyright is brought which relates (wholly or partly) to an infringement in respect of which the copyright owner and an exclusive licensee have or had concurrent rights of action—

   (a) the court shall in assessing damages take into account—

(i) the terms of the licence, and

(ii) any pecuniary remedy already awarded or available to either of them in respect of the infringement;

   (b) no account of profits shall be directed if an award of damages has been made, or an account of profits has been directed, in favour of the other of them in respect of the infringement; and

   (c) the court shall if an account of profits is directed apportion the profits between them as the court considers just, subject to any agreement between them;

and these provisions apply whether or not the copyright owner and the exclusive licensee are both parties to the action.

(5) The copyright owner shall notify any exclusive licensee having concurrent rights before applying for an order under section 99 (order for delivery up) or exercising the right conferred by section 100 (right of seizure); and the court may on the application of the licensee make such order under section 99 or, as the case may be, prohibiting or permitting the exercise by the copyright owner of the right conferred by section 100, as it thinks fit having regard to the terms of the licence.

Modifications etc. (not altering text)

C53. Ss. 90-93, 96-98, 101, 102 applied (1.1.1998) by S.I. 1997/3032, reg. 23 (with Pt. IV)

C54. S. 102. (5) extended by S.I.1991/724, art. 2. (1)(n)

Remedies for infringement of moral rights

103 Remedies for infringement of moral rights.

(1) An infringement of a right conferred by Chapter IV (moral rights) is actionable as a breach of statutory duty owed to the person entitled to the right.

(2) In proceedings for infringement of the right conferred by section 80 (right to object to derogatory treatment of work) the court may, if it thinks it is an adequate remedy in the circumstances, grant an injunction on terms prohibiting the doing of any act unless a disclaimer is made, in such terms and in such manner as may be approved by the court, dissociating the author or director from the treatment of the work.

Presumptions

104 Presumptions relevant to literary, dramatic, musical and artistic works.

(1) The following presumptions apply in proceedings brought by virtue of this Chapter with respect to a literary, dramatic, musical or artistic work.

(2) Where a name purporting to be that of the author appeared on copies of the work as published or on the work when it was made, the person whose name appeared shall be presumed, until the contrary is proved—

(a) to be the author of the work;

(b) to have made it in circumstances not falling within section 11. (2), 163, 165 or 168 (works produced in course of employment, Crown copyright, Parliamentary copyright or copyright of certain international organisations).

(3) In the case of a work alleged to be a work of joint authorship, subsection (2) applies in relation to each person alleged to be one of the authors.

(4) Where no name purporting to be that of the author appeared as mentioned in subsection (2) but—

(a) the work qualifies for copyright protection by virtue of section 155 (qualification by reference to country of first publication), and

(b) a name purporting to be that of the publisher appeared on copies of the work as first published,

the person whose name appeared shall be presumed, until the contrary is proved, to have been the owner of the copyright at the time of publication.

(5) If the author of the work is dead or the identity of the author cannot be ascertained by reasonable inquiry, it shall be presumed, in the absence of evidence to the contrary—

(a) that the work is an original work, and

(b) that the plaintiff's allegations as to what was the first publication of the work and as to the country of first publication are correct.

105 Presumptions relevant to sound recordings and films.

(1) In proceedings brought by virtue of this Chapter with respect to a sound recording, where copies of the recording as issued to the public bear a label or other mark stating—

(a) that a named person was the owner of copyright in the recording at the date of issue of the copies, or

(b) that the recording was first published in a specified year or in a specified country,

the label or mark shall be admissible as evidence of the facts stated and shall be presumed to be correct until the contrary is proved.

(2) In proceedings brought by virtue of this Chapter with respect to a film, where copies of the film as issued to the public bear a statement—

(a) that a named person was the [F226director or producer] of the film,

F227[(aa)that a named person was the principal director, the author of the screenplay, the author of the dialogue or the composer of music specifically created for and used in the film,]

(b) that a named person was the owner of copyright in the film at the date of issue of the copies, or

(c) that the film was first published in a specified year or in a specified country,

the statement shall be admissible as evidence of the facts stated and shall be presumed to be correct until the contrary is proved.

(3) In proceedings brought by virtue of this Chapter with respect to a computer program, where copies of the program are issued to the public in electronic form bearing a statement—

(a) that a named person was the owner of copyright in the program at the date of issue of the copies, or

(b) that the program was first published in a specified country or that copies of it were first issued to the public in electronic form in a specified year,

the statement shall be admissible as evidence of the facts stated and shall be presumed to be correct until the contrary is proved.

(4) The above presumptions apply equally in proceedings relating to an infringement alleged to have occurred before the date on which the copies were issued to the public.

(5) In proceedings brought by virtue of this Chapter with respect to a film, where the film as shown in public [F228or communicated to the public] bears a statement—

(a) that a named person was the [F226director or producer] of the film, or

F229[(aa)that a named person was the principal director of the film, the author of the screenplay, the author of the dialogue or the composer of music specifically created for and used in the film, or,]

(b) that a named person was the owner of copyright in the film immediately after it was made,

the statement shall be admissible as evidence of the facts stated and shall be presumed to be correct until the contrary is proved.

This presumption applies equally in proceedings relating to an infringement alleged to have occurred before the date on which the film was shown in public, broadcast or included in a cable programme service.

F230[(6)For the purposes of this section, a statement that a person was the director of a film shall be taken, unless a contrary indication appears, as meaning that he was the principal director of the film.]

Amendments (Textual)

F226. Words in s. 105. (2)(a)(5)(a) substituted (1.12.1996 with effect in relation to films made on or after 1.7.1994) by S.I. 1996/2967, regs. 18. (4)(a), 36 (with Pt. III)

F227. S. 105. (2)(aa) inserted (1.1.1996) by S.I. 1995/3297, Pt. II reg. 5. (4) (with Pt. III)

F228. Words in s. 105. (5) substituted (31.10.2003) by The Copyright and Related Rights Regulations 2003 (S.I. 2003/2498), reg. 2. (1), Sch. 1 para. 8. (1)(c) (with regs. 31-40)

F229. S. 105. (5)(aa) inserted (1.12.1996 with effect in relation to films made on or after 1.7.1994) by S.I. 1996/2967, reg. 18. (4)(b) (with Pt. III)

F230. S. 105. (6) added (1.12.1996 with effect in relation to films made on or after 1.7.1994) by S.I. 1996/2967, reg. 18. (4)(c) (with Pt. III)

106 Presumptions relevant to works subject to Crown copyright.

In proceedings brought by virtue of this Chapter with respect to a literary, dramatic or musical work in which Crown copyright subsists, where there appears on printed copies of the work a statement of the year in which the work was first published commercially, that statement shall be admissible as evidence of the fact stated and shall be presumed to be correct in the absence of evidence to the contrary.

Offences

107 Criminal liability for making or dealing with infringing articles, &c.

(1) A person commits an offence who, without the licence of the copyright owner—

(a) makes for sale or hire, or

(b) imports into the United Kingdom otherwise than for his private and domestic use, or

(c) possesses in the course of a business with a view to committing any act infringing the copyright, or

(d) in the course of a business —

(i) sells or lets for hire, or

(ii) offers or exposes for sale or hire, or

(iii) exhibits in public, or

(iv) distributes, or

(e) distributes otherwise than in the course of a business to such an extent as to affect prejudicially the owner of the copyright,

an article which is, and which he knows or has reason to believe is, an infringing copy of a copyright work.

(2) A person commits an offence who—

(a) makes an article specifically designed or adapted for making copies of a particular copyright work, or

(b) has such an article in his possession,

knowing or having reason to believe that it is to be used to make infringing copies for sale or hire or for use in the course of a business.

[F231. (2. A)A person ("P") who infringes copyright in a work by communicating the work to the public commits an offence if P—

(a) knows or has reason to believe that P is infringing copyright in the work, and

(b) either—

(i) intends to make a gain for P or another person, or

(ii) knows or has reason to believe that communicating the work to the public will cause loss to the owner of the copyright, or will expose the owner of the copyright to a risk of loss.

(2. B)For the purposes of subsection (2. A)—

(a) "gain" and "loss"—

(i) extend only to gain or loss in money, and

(ii) include any such gain or loss whether temporary or permanent, and

(b) "loss" includes a loss by not getting what one might get.]

(3) Where copyright is infringed (otherwise than by reception of a [F232communication to the public])—

(a) by the public performance of a literary, dramatic or musical work, or

(b) by the playing or showing in public of a sound recording or film,

any person who caused the work to be so performed, played or shown is guilty of an offence if he knew or had reason to believe that copyright would be infringed.

(4) A person guilty of an offence under subsection (1)(a), (b), (d)(iv) or (e) is liable—

(a) on summary conviction to imprisonment for a term not exceeding six months or [F233a fine], or both;

(b) on conviction on indictment to a fine or imprisonment for a term not exceeding [F234ten] years, or both.

[F235. (4. A)A person guilty of an offence under subsection (2. A) is liable—

(a) on summary conviction to imprisonment for a term not exceeding three months or [F236a fine], or both;

(b) on conviction on indictment to a fine or imprisonment for a term not exceeding [F237ten] years, or both.]

(5) A person guilty of any other offence under this section is liable on summary conviction to imprisonment for a term not exceeding [F238three] months or a fine not exceeding level 5 on the standard scale, or both.

(6) Sections 104 to 106 (presumptions as to various matters connected with copyright) do not apply to proceedings for an offence under this section; but without prejudice to their application in proceedings for an order under section 108 below.

Amendments (Textual)

F231. S. 107. (2. A)(2. B) substituted for s. 107. (2. A) (1.10.2017) by Digital Economy Act 2017 (c. 30), ss. 32. (2), 118. (6) (with s. 32. (6)); S.I. 2017/765, reg. 3. (a)

F232. Words in s. 107. (3) substituted (31.10.2003) by The Copyright and Related Rights Regulations 2003 (S.I. 2003/2498), reg. 2. (1), Sch. 1 para. 9. (2) (with regs. 31-40)

F233. Words in s. 107. (4)(a) substituted (12.3.2015) by The Legal Aid, Sentencing and Punishment of Offenders Act 2012 (Fines on Summary Conviction) Regulations 2015 (S.I. 2015/664), reg. 1. (1), Sch. 4 para. 17. (2)(a) (with reg. 5. (1))

F234. Word in s. 107. (4)(b) substituted (20.11.2002) by 2002 c. 25, s. 1. (2)(5); S.I. 2002/2749, art. 2

F235. S. 107. (4. A) inserted (31.10.2003) by The Copyright and Related Rights Regulations 2003 (S.I. 2003/2498), reg. 26. (1)(b) (with regs. 31-40)

F236. Words in s. 107. (4. A)(a) substituted (12.3.2015) by The Legal Aid, Sentencing and Punishment of Offenders Act 2012 (Fines on Summary Conviction) Regulations 2015 (S.I. 2015/664), reg. 1. (1), Sch. 4 para. 17. (2)(b) (with reg. 5. (1))

F237. Word in s. 107. (4. A)(b) substituted (1.10.2017) by Digital Economy Act 2017 (c. 30), ss. 32. (3), 118. (6) (with s. 32. (6)); S.I. 2017/765, reg. 3. (a)

F238. Word in s. 107. (5) substituted (1.1.2011) by The Copyright, Designs and Patents Act 1988 (Amendment) Regulations 2010 (S.I. 2010/2694), art. 5

[F239107. A Enforcement by local weights and measures authority.

(1) It is the duty of every local weights and measures authority to enforce within their area the provisions of section 107.

F240. (2). . . . .

(3) Subsection (1) above does not apply in relation to the enforcement of section 107 in Northern Ireland, but it is the duty of the Department of Economic Development to enforce that section in Northern Ireland.

F241...

[F242. (3. A)For the investigatory powers available to a local weights and measures authority or the Department of Enterprise, Trade and Investment in Northern Ireland for the purposes of the duties in this section, see Schedule 5 to the Consumer Rights Act 2015.]

(4) Any enactment which authorises the disclosure of information for the purpose of facilitating the enforcement of the Trade Descriptions Act 1968 shall apply as if section 107 were contained in that Act and as if the functions of any person in relation to the enforcement of that section were functions under that Act.

(5) Nothing in this section shall be construed as authorising a local weights and measures authority to bring proceedings in Scotland for an offence.]

Amendments (Textual)

F239. S. 107. A inserted (6.4.2007) by 1994 c. 33, ss. 165. (2), 172. (2); S.I. 2007/621, art. 2

F240. S. 107. A(2) omitted (1.10.2015) by virtue of Consumer Rights Act 2015 (c. 15), s. 100. (5), Sch. 6 para. 49. (2); S.I. 2015/1630, art. 3. (i) (with art. 8)

F241. Words in s. 107. A(3) omitted (1.10.2015) by virtue of Consumer Rights Act 2015 (c. 15), s. 100. (5), Sch. 6 para. 49. (3); S.I. 2015/1630, art. 3. (i) (with art. 8)

F242. S. 107. A(3. A) inserted (1.10.2015) by Consumer Rights Act 2015 (c. 15), s. 100. (5), Sch. 6 para. 49. (4); S.I. 2015/1630, art. 3. (i)

108 Order for delivery up in criminal proceedings.

(1) The court before which proceedings are brought against a person for an offence under section 107 may, if satisfied that at the time of his arrest or charge—

(a) he had in his possession, custody or control in the course of a business an infringing copy of a copyright work, or

(b) he had in his possession, custody or control an article specifically designed or adapted for making copies of a particular copyright work, knowing or having reason to believe that it had been or was to be used to make infringing copies,

order that the infringing copy or article be delivered up to the copyright owner or to such other person as the court may direct.

(2) For this purpose a person shall be treated as charged with an offence—

(a) in England, Wales and Northern Ireland, when he is orally charged or is served with a summons or indictment;

(b) in Scotland, when he is cautioned, charged or served with a complaint or indictment.

(3) An order may be made by the court of its own motion or on the application of the prosecutor (or, in Scotland, the Lord Advocate or procurator-fiscal), and may be made whether or not the person is convicted of the offence, but shall not be made—

(a) after the end of the period specified in section 113 (period after which remedy of delivery up not available), or

(b) if it appears to the court unlikely that any order will be made under section 114 (order as to disposal of infringing copy or other article).

(4) An appeal lies from an order made under this section by a magistrates' court—

(a) in England and Wales, to the Crown Court, and

(b) in Northern Ireland, to the county court;

and in Scotland, where an order has been made under this section, the person from whose possession, custody or control the infringing copy or article has been removed may, without prejudice to any other form of appeal under any rule of law, appeal against that order in the same manner as against sentence.

(5) A person to whom an infringing copy or other article is delivered up in pursuance of an order under this section shall retain it pending the making of an order, or the decision not to make an order, undersection 114.

(6) Nothing in this section affects the powers of the court under [F243section 143 of the Powers of Criminal Courts (Sentencing)Act 2000], [F244. Part II of the Proceeds of Crime (Scotland) Act 1995] or [F245. Article 11 of the Criminal Justice (Northern Ireland) Order 1994] (general provisions as to forfeiture in criminal proceedings).

Amendments (Textual)

F243. Words in s. 108. (6) substituted (25.8.2000) by 2000 c. 6, ss. 165. (3), 168. (1), Sch. 9 para. 115

F244. Words in s. 108. (6) substituted (1.4.1996) by virtue of 1995 c. 40, ss. 5, 7. (2), Sch. 4 para. 70. (2)

F245. Words in s. 108. (6) substituted (9.1.1995) by S.I. 1994/2795 (N.I. 15), art. 26. (1), Sch. 2 para. 13; S.R. 1994/446, art. 2

109 Search warrants.

(1) Where a justice of the peace (in Scotland, a sheriff or justice of the peace) is satisfied by information on oath given by a constable (in Scotland, by evidence on oath) that there are reasonable grounds for believing—

(a) that an offence under [F246section 107. (1), (2) or (2. A)] has been or is about to be committed in any premises, and

(b) that evidence that such an offence has been or is about to be committed is in those premises,

he may issue a warrant authorising a constable to enter and search the premises, using such reasonable force as is necessary.

(2) The power conferred by subsection (1) does not, in England and Wales, extend to authorising a search for material of the kinds mentioned in section 9. (2) of the M7. Police and Criminal

Evidence Act 1984 (certain classes of personal or confidential material).

(3) A warrant under this section—

(a) may authorise persons to accompany any constable executing the warrant, and

(b) remains in force for [F247three months] from the date of its issue.

(4) In executing a warrant issued under this section a constable may seize an article if he reasonably believes that it is evidence that any offence under [F248section 107. (1), (2) or (2. A)] has been or is about to be committed.

(5) In this section "premises" includes land, buildings [F249fixed or], moveable structures, vehicles, vessels, aircraft and hovercraft.

Amendments (Textual)

F246. Words in s. 109. (1)(a) substituted (31.10.2003) by The Copyright and Related Rights Regulations 2003 (S.I. 2003/2498), reg. 26. (2)(i) (with regs. 31-40)

F247. Words in s. 109. (3)(b) substituted (1.1.2006) by Serious Organised Crime and Police Act 2005 (c. 15), ss. 174. (1), 178, Sch. 16 para. 6. (2); S.I. 2005/3495, art. 2. (1)(s) (subject to art. 2. (2))

F248. Words in s. 109. (4) substituted (31.10.2003) by The Copyright and Related Rights Regulations 2003 (S.I. 2003/2498), reg. 26. (2)(ii) (with regs. 31-40)

F249. Words in s. 109. (5) inserted (20.11.2002) by 2002 c. 25, s. 2. (2)(c); S.I. 2002/2749, art. 2

Modifications etc. (not altering text)

C55. S. 109. (4): power of seizure extended (1.4.2003) by 2001 c. 16, ss. 50, 52-54, 68, 138. (2) Sch. 1 Pt. 1 para. 48; S.I. 2003/708, art. 2

S. 109. (4) modified (E.W.N.I.) (1.4.2003) by 2001 c. 16, ss. 55, 68, 138. (2), Sch. 1 Pt. 3 para. 106 (with s. 57. (3)); S.I. 2003/708, art. 2

Marginal Citations

M71984 c. 60.

110 Offence by body corporate: liability of officers.

(1) Where an offence under section 107 committed by a body corporate is proved to have been committed with the consent or connivance of a director, manager, secretary or other similar officer of the body, or a person purporting to act in any such capacity, he as well as the body corporate is guilty of the offence and liable to be proceeded against and punished accordingly.

(2) In relation to a body corporate whose affairs are managed by its members "director" means a member of the body corporate.

Provision for preventing importation of infringing copies

111 Infringing copies may be treated as prohibited goods.

(1) The owner of the copyright in a published literary, dramatic or musical work may give notice in writing to the Commissioners of Customs and Excise—

(a) that he is the owner of the copyright in the work, and

(b) that he requests the Commissioners, for a period specified in the notice, to treat as prohibited goods printed copies of the work which are infringing copies.

(2) The period specified in a notice under subsection (1) shall not exceed five years and shall not extend beyond the period for which copyright is to subsist.

(3) The owner of the copyright in a sound recording or film may give notice in writing to the Commissioners of Customs and Excise—

(a) that he is the owner of the copyright in the work,

(b) that infringing copies of the work are expected to arrive in the United Kingdom at a time and a place specified in the notice, and

(c) that he requests the Commissioners to treat the copies as prohibited goods.

F250[F251. (3. A)The Commissioners may treat as prohibited goods only infringing copies of works which arrive in the United Kingdom—

(a) from outside the European Economic Area, or

(b) from within that Area but not having been entered for free circulation.

[F251. (3. B)This section does not apply to goods placed in, or expected to be placed in, one of the situations referred to in Article 1. (1), in respect of which an application may be made under Article 5. (1), of Council Regulation (EC) No 1383/2003 concerning customs action against goods suspected of infringing certain intellectual property rights and the measures to be taken against goods found to have infringed such rights.]]

(4) When a notice is in force under this section the importation of goods to which the notice relates, otherwise than by a person for his private and domestic use, [F252subject to subsections (3. A) and (3. B), is prohibited]; but a person is not by reason of the prohibition liable to any penalty other than forfeiture of the goods.

Amendments (Textual)

F250. S. 111. (3. A)(3. B) inserted (1.7.1995) by S.I. 1995/1445, reg. 2. (2)

F251. S. 111. (3. B) substituted (1.7.2004) by The Goods Infringing Intellectual Property Rights (Customs) Regulations 2004 (S.I. 2004/1473), reg. 12 (with reg. 2. (2)(3))

F252. Words in s. 111. (4) substituted (1.7.1995) by S.I. 1995/1445, reg. 2. (3)

112 Power of Commissioners of Customs and Excise to make regulations.

(1) The Commissioners of Customs and Excise may make regulations prescribing the form in which notice is to be given under section 111 and requiring a person giving notice—

(a) to furnish the Commissioners with such evidence as may be specified in the regulations, either on giving notice or when the goods are imported, or at both those times, and

(b) to comply with such other conditions as may be specified in the regulations.

(2) The regulations may, in particular, require a person giving such a notice—

(a) to pay such fees in respect of the notice as may be specified by the regulations;

(b) to give such security as may be so specified in respect of any liability or expense which the Commissioners may incur in consequence of the notice by reason of the detention of any article or anything done to an article detained;

(c) to indemnify the Commissioners against any such liability or expense, whether security has been given or not.

(3) The regulations may make different provision as respects different classes of case to which they apply and may include such incidental and supplementary provisions as the Commissioners consider expedient.

(4) Regulations under this section shall be made by statutory instrument which shall be subject to annulment in pursuance of a resolution of either House of Parliament.

(5) F253. . . . .

Amendments (Textual)

F253. S. 112. (5) repealed (18.4.2005) by Commissioners for Revenue and Customs Act 2005 (c. 11), ss. 50. (6), 52. (2), 53. (1), Sch. 4 para. 38, Sch. 5; S.I. 2005/1126, art. 2. (2)(h)(i)

Supplementary

113 Period after which remedy of delivery up not available.

(1) An application for an order under section 99 (order for delivery up in civil proceedings) may not be made after the end of the period of six years from the date on which the infringing copy or article in question was made, subject to the following provisions.

(2) If during the whole or any part of that period the copyright owner—

(a) is under a disability, or

(b) is prevented by fraud or concealment from discovering the facts entitling him to apply for an order,

an application may be made at any time before the end of the period of six years from the date on which he ceased to be under a disability or, as the case may be, could with reasonable diligence have discovered those facts.

(3) In subsection (2) "disability"—

(a) in England and Wales, has the same meaning as in the M8. Limitation Act 1980;

(b) in Scotland, means legal disability within the meaning of the M9. Prescription and Limitation (Scotland) Act 1973;

(c) in Northern Ireland, has the same meaning as in the M10. Statute of Limitations (Northern Ireland) 1958.

(4) An order under section 108 (order for delivery up in criminal proceedings) shall not, in any case, be made after the end of the period of six years from the date on which the infringing copy or article in question was made.

Marginal Citations

M81980 c. 58.

M91973 c. 52.

M101958 c. 10 (N.I.).

114 Order as to disposal of infringing copy or other article.

(1) An application may be made to the court for an order that an infringing copy or other article delivered up in pursuance of an order under section 99 or 108, or seized and detained in pursuance of the right conferred by section 100, shall be—

(a) forfeited to the copyright owner, or

(b) destroyed or otherwise dealt with as the court may think fit,

or for a decision that no such order should be made.

(2) In considering what order (if any) should be made, the court shall consider whether other remedies available in an action for infringement of copyright would be adequate to compensate the copyright owner and to protect his interests.

(3) Provision shall be made by rules of court as to the service of notice on persons having an interest in the copy or other articles, and any such person is entitled—

(a) to appear in proceedings for an order under this section, whether or not he was served with notice, and

(b) to appeal against any order made, whether or not he appeared;

and an order shall not take effect until the end of the period within which notice of an appeal may be given or, if before the end of that period notice of appeal is duly given, until the final determination or abandonment of the proceedings on the appeal.

(4) Where there is more than one person interested in a copy or other article, the court shall make such order as it thinks just and may (in particular) direct that the article be sold, or otherwise dealt with, and the proceeds divided.

(5) If the court decides that no order should be made under this section, the person in whose possession, custody or control the copy or other article was before being delivered up or seized is entitled to its return.

(6) References in this section to a person having an interest in a copy or other article include any person in whose favour an order could be made in respect of it

[F254. (a)under this section or under section 204 or 231 of this Act;

(b) under section 24. D of the Registered Designs Act 1949;

(c) under section 19 of Trade Marks Act 1994 (including that section as applied by regulation 4 of the Community Trade Mark Regulations 2006 (SI 2006/1027)); or

(d) under regulation 1. C of the Community Design Regulations 2005 (SI 2005/2339).]

Amendments (Textual)

F254. Words in s. 114. (6) substituted (29.4.2006) by The Intellectual Property (Enforcement, etc.) Regulations 2006 (S.I. 2006/1028), reg. 2. (1), Sch. 2 para. 7

Modifications etc. (not altering text)

C56. S. 114 extended by S.I. 1991/724, art. 2. (1)(n)

[F255114. A Forfeiture of infringing copies, etc.: England and Wales or Northern Ireland

(1) In England and Wales or Northern Ireland where there have come into the possession of any person in connection with the investigation or prosecution of a relevant offence—

(a) infringing copies of a copyright work, or

(b) articles specifically designed or adapted for making copies of a particular copyright work, that person may apply under this section for an order for the forfeiture of the infringing copies or articles.

(2) For the purposes of this section "relevant offence" means—

(a) an offence under [F256section 107. (1), (2) or (2. A)] (criminal liability for making or dealing with infringing articles, etc.),

(b) an offence under the Trade Descriptions Act 1968 (c. 29),

[F257. (ba)an offence under the Business Protection from Misleading Marketing Regulations 2008,

(bb) an offence under the Consumer Protection from Unfair Trading Regulations 2008, or]

(c) an offence involving dishonesty or deception.

(3) An application under this section may be made—

(a) where proceedings have been brought in any court for a relevant offence relating to some or all of the infringing copies or articles, to that court, or

(b) where no application for the forfeiture of the infringing copies or articles has been made under paragraph (a), by way of complaint to a magistrates' court.

(4) On an application under this section, the court shall make an order for the forfeiture of any infringing copies or articles only if it is satisfied that a relevant offence has been committed in relation to the infringing copies or articles.

(5) A court may infer for the purposes of this section that such an offence has been committed in relation to any infringing copies or articles if it is satisfied that such an offence has been committed in relation to infringing copies or articles which are representative of the infringing copies or articles in question (whether by reason of being of the same design or part of the same consignment or batch or otherwise).

(6) Any person aggrieved by an order made under this section by a magistrates' court, or by a decision of such a court not to make such an order, may appeal against that order or decision—

(a) in England and Wales, to the Crown Court, or

(b) in Northern Ireland, to the county court.

(7) An order under this section may contain such provision as appears to the court to be appropriate for delaying the coming into force of the order pending the making and determination of any appeal (including any application under section 111 of the Magistrates' Courts Act 1980 (c. 43) or Article 146 of the Magistrates' Courts (Northern Ireland) Order 1981 (S.I. 1981/1675 (N.I. 26)) (statement of case)).

(8) Subject to subsection (9), where any infringing copies or articles are forfeited under this section they shall be destroyed in accordance with such directions as the court may give.

(9) On making an order under this section the court may direct that the infringing copies or articles to which the order relates shall (instead of being destroyed) be forfeited to the owner of the copyright in question or dealt with in such other way as the court considers appropriate.]

Amendments (Textual)

F255. Ss. 114. A, 114. B inserted (20.11.2002) by 2002 c. 25, s. 3; S.I. 2002/2749, art. 2

F256. Words in s. 114. A(2)(a) substituted (31.10.2003) by The Copyright and Related Rights Regulations 2003 (S.I. 2003/2498), reg. 26. (2)(iii) (with regs. 31-40)

F257. S. 114. A(2)(ba)(bb) and word substituted (26.5.2008) for word by The Consumer Protection from Unfair Trading Regulations 2008 (S.I. 2008/1277), reg. 1, Sch. 2 para. 40 (with reg. 28. (2)(3))

F258114. B Forfeiture of infringing copies, etc.: Scotland

(1) In Scotland the court may make an order under this section for the forfeiture of any—

(a) infringing copies of a copyright work, or

(b) articles specifically designed or adapted for making copies of a particular copyright work.

(2) An order under this section may be made—

(a) on an application by the procurator-fiscal made in the manner specified in section 134 of the Criminal Procedure (Scotland) Act 1995 (c. 46), or

(b) where a person is convicted of a relevant offence, in addition to any other penalty which the court may impose.

(3) On an application under subsection (2)(a), the court shall make an order for the forfeiture of any infringing copies or articles only if it is satisfied that a relevant offence has been committed in relation to the infringing copies or articles.

(4) The court may infer for the purposes of this section that such an offence has been committed in relation to any infringing copies or articles if it is satisfied that such an offence has been committed in relation to infringing copies or articles which are representative of the infringing copies or articles in question (whether by reason of being of the same design or part of the same consignment or batch or otherwise).

(5) The procurator-fiscal making the application under subsection (2)(a) shall serve on any person appearing to him to be the owner of, or otherwise to have an interest in, the infringing copies or articles to which the application relates a copy of the application, together with a notice giving him the opportunity to appear at the hearing of the application to show cause why the infringing copies or articles should not be forfeited.

(6) Service under subsection (5) shall be carried out, and such service may be proved, in the manner specified for citation of an accused in summary proceedings under the Criminal Procedure (Scotland) Act 1995.

(7) Any person upon whom notice is served under subsection (5) and any other person claiming to be the owner of, or otherwise to have an interest in, infringing copies or articles to which an application under this section relates shall be entitled to appear at the hearing of the application to show cause why the infringing copies or articles should not be forfeited.

(8) The court shall not make an order following an application under subsection (2)(a)—

(a) if any person on whom notice is served under subsection (5) does not appear, unless service of the notice on that person is proved, or

(b) if no notice under subsection (5) has been served, unless the court is satisfied that in the circumstances it was reasonable not to serve such notice.

(9) Where an order for the forfeiture of any infringing copies or articles is made following an application under subsection (2)(a), any person who appeared, or was entitled to appear, to show cause why infringing copies or articles should not be forfeited may, within 21 days of the making of the order, appeal to the High Court by Bill of Suspension.

(10) Section 182. (5)(a) to (e) of the Criminal Procedure (Scotland) Act 1995 (c. 46) shall apply to an appeal under subsection (9) as it applies to a stated case under Part 2 of that Act.

(11) An order following an application under subsection (2)(a) shall not take effect—

(a) until the end of the period of 21 days beginning with the day after the day on which the order is made, or

(b) if an appeal is made under subsection (9) above within that period, until the appeal is determined or abandoned.

(12) An order under subsection (2)(b) shall not take effect—

(a) until the end of the period within which an appeal against the order could be brought under the Criminal Procedure (Scotland) Act 1995, or

(b) if an appeal is made within that period, until the appeal is determined or abandoned.

(13) Subject to subsection (14), infringing copies or articles forfeited under this section shall be destroyed in accordance with such directions as the court may give.

(14) On making an order under this section the court may direct that the infringing copies or articles to which the order relates shall (instead of being destroyed) be forfeited to the owner of the copyright in question or dealt with in such other way as the court considers appropriate.

(15) For the purposes of this section—

[F259"relevant offence" means—

- an offence under section 107. (1), (2) or (2. A) (criminal liability for making or dealing with infringing articles, etc),

- an offence under the Trade Descriptions Act 1968,

- an offence under the Business Protection from Misleading Marketing Regulations 2008,

- an offence under the Consumer Protection from Unfair Trading Regulations 2008, or

- any offence involving dishonesty or deception;]

"the court" means—
    - in relation to an order made on an application under subsection (2)(a), the sheriff, and
    - in relation to an order made under subsection (2)(b), the court which imposed the penalty.
Amendments (Textual)
F258. Ss. 114. A, 114. B inserted (20.11.2002) by 2002 c. 25, s. 3; S.I. 2002/2749, art. 2
F259. Words in s. 114. B(15) substituted (26.5.2008) by The Consumer Protection from Unfair Trading Regulations 2008 (S.I. 2008/1277), reg. 1, Sch. 2 para. 41 (with reg. 28. (2)(3))
115 Jurisdiction of county court and sheriff court.
(1) In England [F260and Wales the county court and in] Northern Ireland a county court may entertain proceedings under—
section 99 (order for delivery up of infringing copy or other article),
section 102. (5) (order as to exercise of rights by copyright owner where exclusive licensee has concurrent rights), or
section 114 (order as to disposal of infringing copy or other article),
[F261save that, in Northern Ireland, a county court may entertain such proceedings only] where the value of the infringing copies and other articles in question does not exceed the county court limit for actions in tort.
(2) In Scotland proceedings for an order under any of those provisions may be brought in the sheriff court.
(3) Nothing in this section shall be construed as affecting the jurisdiction of the High Court or, in Scotland, the Court of Session.
Amendments (Textual)
F260. Words in s. 115. (1) substituted (22.4.2014) by Crime and Courts Act 2013 (c. 22), s. 61. (3), Sch. 9 para. 72; S.I. 2014/954, art. 2. (c) (with art. 3) (with transitional provisions and savings in S.I. 2014/956, arts. 3-11)
F261. Words in s. 115. (1) inserted by S.I. 1991/724, art. 2. (8), Schedule Pt. I

Chapter VII Copyright Licensing

Modifications etc. (not altering text)
C57. Pt. I Ch. VII (ss. 116-144) applied (with modifications) (1.12.1996) by S.I. 1996/2967, reg. 17. (1)-(3) (with Pt. III)
116 Licensing schemes and licensing bodies.
(1) In this Part a "licensing scheme" means a scheme setting out—
    (a) the classes of case in which the operator of the scheme, or the person on whose behalf he acts, is willing to grant copyright licences, and
    (b) the terms on which licences would be granted in those classes of case;
and for this purpose a "scheme" includes anything in the nature of a scheme, whether described as a scheme or as a tariff or by any other name.
(2) In this Chapter a "licensing body" means
    [F262. (a)a society or other organisation which has as its main object, or one of its main objects, the negotiation or granting, either as owner or prospective owner of copyright or as agent for him, of copyright licences, and whose objects include the granting of licences covering works of more than one author] [F263, or,
    (b) any other organisation which is a collective management organisation as defined by regulation 2 of the Collective Management of Copyright (EU Directive) Regulations 2016].
(3) In this section "copyright licences" means licences to do, or authorise the doing of, any of the acts restricted by copyright.
(4) References in this Chapter to licences or licensing schemes covering works of more than one author do not include licences or schemes covering only—
    (a) a single collective work or collective works of which the authors are the same, or
    (b) works made by, or by employees of or commissioned by, a single individual, firm, company

or group of companies.

For this purpose a group of companies means a holding company and its subsidiaries, within the meaning of [F264section 1159 of the Companies Act 2006].

[F265. (5)Schedule A1 confers powers to provide for the regulation of licensing bodies.]

Amendments (Textual)

F262. Words in s. 116. (2) renumbered as s. 116. (2)(a) (10.4.2016) by The Collective Management of Copyright (EU Directive) Regulations 2016 (S.I. 2016/221), regs. 1, 44. (a)

F263. S. 116. (2)(b) and word inserted (10.4.2016) by The Collective Management of Copyright (EU Directive) Regulations 2016 (S.I. 2016/221), regs. 1, 44. (b)

F264. Words in s. 116. (4) substituted (1.10.2009) by The Companies Act 2006 (Consequential Amendments, Transitional Provisions and Savings) Order 2009 (S.I. 2009/1941), art. 2. (1), Sch. 1 para. 98. (a) (with art. 10)

F265. S. 116. (5) inserted (25.4.2013) by Enterprise and Regulatory Reform Act 2013 (c. 24), ss. 77. (2), 103. (1)

[F266. Orphan works licensing and extended collective licensing

Amendments (Textual)

F266. Ss. 116. A-116. D and cross-heading inserted (25.4.2013) by Enterprise and Regulatory Reform Act 2013 (c. 24), ss. 77. (3), 103. (1)

116. APower to provide for licensing of orphan works

(1) The Secretary of State may by regulations provide for the grant of licences in respect of works that qualify as orphan works under the regulations.

(2) The regulations may—

(a) specify a person or a description of persons authorised to grant licences, or

(b) provide for a person designated in the regulations to specify a person or a description of persons authorised to grant licences

(3) The regulations must provide that, for a work to qualify as an orphan work, it is a requirement that the owner of copyright in it has not been found after a diligent search made in accordance with the regulations.

(4) The regulations may provide for the granting of licences to do, or authorise the doing of, any act restricted by copyright that would otherwise require the consent of the missing owner.

(5) The regulations must provide for any licence—

(a) to have effect as if granted by the missing owner;

(b) not to give exclusive rights;

(c) not to be granted to a person authorised to grant licences.

(6) The regulations may apply to a work although it is not known whether copyright subsists in it, and references to a missing owner and a right or interest of a missing owner are to be read as including references to a supposed owner and a supposed right or interest.

116. BExtended collective licensing

(1) The Secretary of State may by regulations provide for a licensing body that applies to the Secretary of State under the regulations to be authorised to grant copyright licences in respect of works in which copyright is not owned by the body or a person on whose behalf the body acts.

(2) An authorisation must specify—

(a) the types of work to which it applies, and

(b) the acts restricted by copyright that the licensing body is authorised to license.

(3) The regulations must provide for the copyright owner to have a right to limit or exclude the grant of licences by virtue of the regulations.

(4) The regulations must provide for any licence not to give exclusive rights.

(5) In this section " copyright licences " has the same meaning as in section 116.

(6) Nothing in this section applies in relation to Crown copyright or Parliamentary copyright.

116. CGeneral provision about licensing under sections 116. A and 116. B

(1) This section and section 116. D apply to regulations under sections 116. A and 116. B.

(2) The regulations may provide for a body to be or remain authorised to grant licences only if specified requirements are met, and for a question whether they are met to be determined by a person, and in a manner, specified in the regulations.

(3) The regulations may specify other matters to be taken into account in any decision to be made under the regulations as to whether to authorise a person to grant licences.

(4) The regulations must provide for the treatment of any royalties or other sums paid in respect of a licence, including—

(a) the deduction of administrative costs;

(b) the period for which sums must be held;

(c) the treatment of sums after that period (as bona vacantia or otherwise).

(5) The regulations must provide for circumstances in which an authorisation to grant licences may be withdrawn, and for determining the rights and obligations of any person if an authorisation is withdrawn.

(6) The regulations may include other provision for the purposes of authorisation and licensing, including in particular provision—

(a) for determining the rights and obligations of any person if a work ceases to qualify as an orphan work (or ceases to qualify by reference to any copyright owner), or if a rights owner exercises the right referred to in section 116. B(3), while a licence is in force;

(b) about maintenance of registers and access to them;

(c) permitting the use of a work for incidental purposes including an application or search;

(d) for a right conferred by section 77 to be treated as having been asserted in accordance with section 78;

(e) for the payment of fees to cover administrative expenses.

116. DRegulations under sections 116. A and 116. B

(1) The power to make regulations includes power—

(a) to make incidental, supplementary or consequential provision, including provision extending or restricting the jurisdiction of the Copyright Tribunal or conferring powers on it;

(b) to make transitional, transitory or saving provision;

(c) to make different provision for different purposes.

(2) Regulations under any provision may amend this Part, or any other enactment or subordinate legislation passed or made before that provision comes into force, for the purpose of making consequential provision or extending or restricting the jurisdiction of the Copyright Tribunal or conferring powers on it.

(3) Regulations may make provision by reference to guidance issued from time to time by any person.

(4) The power to make regulations is exercisable by statutory instrument.

(5) A statutory instrument containing regulations may not be made unless a draft of the instrument has been laid before and approved by a resolution of each House of Parliament.]

References and applications with respect to licensing schemes

[F267117 Licensing schemes to which following sections apply.

Sections 118 to 123 (references and applications with respect to licensing schemes) apply to licensing schemes which are operated by licensing bodies and cover works of more than one author, so far as they relate to licences for—

(a) copying the work,

(b) rental or lending of copies of the work to the public,

(c) performing, showing or playing the work in public, or

[F268. (d)communicating the work to the public;]

and references in those sections to a licensing scheme shall be construed accordingly.]

Amendments (Textual)

F267. S. 117 substituted (1.12.1996) by S.I. 1996/2967, reg. 15. (2) (with Pt. III)

F268. S. 117. (d) substituted (31.10.2003) by The Copyright and Related Rights Regulations 2003 (S.I. 2003/2498), reg. 2. (1), Sch. 1 para. 4. (4) (with regs. 31-40)

118 Reference of proposed licensing scheme to tribunal.

(1) The terms of a licensing scheme proposed to be operated by a licensing body may be referred to the Copyright Tribunal by an organisation claiming to be representative of persons claiming that they require licences in cases of a description to which the scheme would apply, either generally or in relation to any description of case.

(2) The Tribunal shall first decide whether to entertain the reference, and may decline to do so on the ground that the reference is premature.

(3) If the Tribunal decides to entertain the reference it shall considerthe matter referred and make such order, either confirming or varying the proposed scheme, either generally or so far as it relates to cases of the description to which the reference relates, as the Tribunal may determine to be reasonable in the circumstances.

(4) The order may be made so as to be in force indefinitely or for such period as the Tribunal may determine.

119 Reference of licensing scheme to tribunal.

(1) If while a licensing scheme is in operation a dispute arises between the operator of the scheme and—

   (a) a person claiming that he requires a licence in a case of a description to which the scheme applies, or

   (b) an organisation claiming to be representative of such persons,

that person or organisation may refer the scheme to the Copyright Tribunal in so far as it relates to cases of that description.

(2) A scheme which has been referred to the Tribunal under this section shall remain in operation until proceedings on the reference are concluded.

(3) The Tribunal shall consider the matter in dispute and make such order, either confirming or varying the scheme so far as it relates to cases of the description to which the reference relates, as the Tribunal may determine to be reasonable in the circumstances.

(4) The order may be made so as to be in force indefinitely or for such period as the Tribunal may determine.

120 Further reference of scheme to tribunal.

(1) Where the Copyright Tribunal has on a previous reference of a licensing scheme under [F269section 118, 119 or 128. A], or under this section, made an order with respect to the scheme, then, while the order remains in force—

   (a) the operator of the scheme,

   (b) a person claiming that he requires a licence in a case of the description to which the order applies, or

   (c) an organisation claiming to be representative of such persons,

may refer the scheme again to the Tribunal so far as it relates to cases of that description.

(2) A licensing scheme shall not, except with the special leave of the Tribunal, be referred again to the Tribunal in respect of the same description of cases—

   (a) within twelve months from the date of the order on the previous reference, or

   (b) if the order was made so as to be in force for 15 months or less, until the last three months before the expiry of the order.

(3) A scheme which has been referred to the Tribunal under this section shall remain in operation until proceedings on the reference are concluded.

(4) The Tribunal shall consider the matter in dispute and make such order, either confirming, varying or further varying the scheme so far as it relates to cases of the description to which the reference relates, as the Tribunal may determine to be reasonable in the circumstances.

(5) The order may be made so as to be in force indefinitely or for such period as the Tribunal may determine.

Amendments (Textual)

F269. Words in s. 120. (1) substituted (31.10.2003) by The Copyright and Related Rights Regulations 2003 (S.I. 2003/2498), reg. 21. (4) (with regs. 31-40)

121 Application for grant of licence in connection with licensing scheme.

(1) A person who claims, in a case covered by a licensing scheme, that the operator of the scheme has refused to grant him or procure the grant to him of a licence in accordance with the scheme, or has failed to do so within a reasonable time after being asked, may apply to the Copyright Tribunal.

(2) A person who claims, in a case excluded from a licensing scheme, that the operator of the scheme either—

(a) has refused to grant him a licence or procure the grant to him of a licence, or has failed to do so within a reasonable time of being asked, and that in the circumstances it is unreasonable that a licence should not be granted, or

(b) proposes terms for a licence which are unreasonable,

may apply to the Copyright Tribunal.

(3) A case shall be regarded as excluded from a licensing scheme for the purposes of subsection (2) if—

(a) the scheme provides for the grant of licences subject to terms excepting matters from the licence and the case falls within such an exception, or

(b) the case is so similar to those in which licences are granted under the scheme that it is unreasonable that it should not be dealt with in the same way.

(4) If the Tribunal is satisfied that the claim is well-founded, it shall make an order declaring that, in respect of the matters specified in the order, the applicant is entitled to a licence on such terms as the Tribunal may determine to be applicable in accordance with the scheme or, as the case may be, to be reasonable in the circumstances.

(5) The order may be made so as to be in force indefinitely or for such period as the Tribunal may determine.

122 Application for review of order as to entitlement to licence.

(1) Where the Copyright Tribunal has made an order under section 121 that a person is entitled to a licence under a licensing scheme, the operator of the scheme or the original applicant may apply to the Tribunal to review its order.

(2) An application shall not be made, except with the special leave of the Tribunal—

(a) within twelve months from the date of the order, or of the decision on a previous application under this section, or

(b) if the order was made so as to be in force for 15 months or less, or as a result of the decision on a previous application under this section is due to expire within 15 months of that decision, until the last three months before the expiry date.

(3) The Tribunal shall on an application for review confirm or vary its order as the Tribunal may determine to be reasonable having regard to the terms applicable in accordance with the licensing scheme or, as the case may be, the circumstances of the case.

123 Effect of order of tribunal as to licensing scheme.

(1) A licensing scheme which has been confirmed or varied by the Copyright Tribunal—

(a) under section 118 (reference of terms of proposed scheme), or

(b) under section 119 or 120 (reference of existing scheme to Tribunal),

shall be in force or, as the case may be, remain in operation, so far as it relates to the description of case in respect of which the order was made, so long as the order remains in force.

(2) While the order is in force a person who in a case of a class to which the order applies—

(a) pays to the operator of the scheme any charges payable under the scheme in respect of a licence covering the case in question or, if the amount cannot be ascertained, gives an undertaking to the operator to pay them when ascertained, and

(b) complies with the other terms applicable to such a licence under the scheme,

shall be in the same position as regards infringement of copyright as if he had at all material times been the holder of a licence granted by the owner of the copyright in question in accordance with the scheme.

(3) The Tribunal may direct that the order, so far as it varies the amount of charges payable, has effect from a date before that on which it is made, but not earlier than the date on which the reference was made or, if later, on which the scheme came into operation.

If such a direction is made—

(a) any necessary repayments, or further payments, shall be made in respect of charges already paid, and

(b) the reference in subsection (2)(a) to the charges payable under the scheme shall be construed as a reference to the charges so payable by virtue of the order.

No such direction may be made where subsection (4) below applies.

(4) An order of the Tribunal under section 119 or 120 made with respect to a scheme which is certified for any purpose under section 143 has effect, so far as it varies the scheme by reducing the charges payable for licences, from the date on which the reference was made to the Tribunal.

(5) Where the Tribunal has made an order under section 121 (order as to entitlement to licence under licensing scheme) and the order remains in force, the person in whose favour the order is made shall if he—

(a) pays to the operator of the scheme any charges payable in accordance with the order or, if the amount cannot be ascertained, gives an undertaking to pay the charges when ascertained, and

(b) complies with the other terms specified in the order,

be in the same position as regards infringement of copyright as if he had at all material times been the holder of a licence granted by the owner of the copyright in question on the terms specified in the order.

References and applications with respect to licensing by licensing bodies

[F270124 Licences to which following sections apply.

Sections 125 to 128 (references and applications with respect to licensing by licensing bodies) apply to licences which are granted by a licensing body otherwise than in pursuance of a licensing scheme and cover works of more than one author, so far as they authorise—

(a) copying the work,

(b) rental or lending of copies of the work to the public,

(c) performing, showing or playing the work in public, or

[F271. (d)communicating the work to the public;]

and references in those sections to a licence shall be construed accordingly.]

Amendments (Textual)

F270. S. 124 substituted (1.12.1996) by S.I. 1996/2967, reg. 15. (3) (with Pt. III)

F271. S. 124. (d) substituted (31.10.2003) by The Copyright and Related Rights Regulations 2003 (S.I. 2003/2498), reg. 2. (1), Sch. 1 para. 4. (4) (with regs. 31-40)

125 Reference to tribunal of proposed licence.

(1) The terms on which a licensing body proposes to grant a licence may be referred to the Copyright Tribunal by the prospective licensee.

(2) The Tribunal shall first decide whether to entertain the reference, and may decline to do so on the ground that the reference is premature.

(3) If the Tribunal decides to entertain the reference it shall consider the terms of the proposed licence and make such order, either confirming or varying the terms, as it may determine to be reasonable in the circumstances.

(4) The order may be made so as to be in force indefinitely or for such period as the Tribunal may determine.

126 Reference to tribunal of expiring licence.

(1) A licensee under a licence which is due to expire, by effluxion of time or as a result of notice given by the licensing body, may apply to the Copyright Tribunal on the ground that it is unreasonable in the circumstances that the licence should cease to be in force.

(2) Such an application may not be made until the last three months before the licence is due to expire.

(3) A licence in respect of which a reference has been made to the Tribunal shall remain in operation until proceedings on the reference are concluded.

(4) If the Tribunal finds the application well-founded, it shall make an order declaring that the licensee shall continue to be entitled to the benefit of the licence on such terms as the Tribunal may determine to be reasonable in the circumstances.

(5) An order of the Tribunal under this section may be made so as to be in force indefinitely or for such period as the Tribunal may determine.

127 Application for review of order as to licence.

(1) Where the Copyright Tribunal has made an order under [F272section 125, 126 or 128. B (where that order did not relate to a licensing scheme)], the licensing body or the person entitled to the benefit of the order may apply to the Tribunal to review its order.

(2) An application shall not be made, except with the special leave of the Tribunal—

   (a) within twelve months from the date of the order or of the decision on a previous application under this section, or

   (b) if the order was made so as to be in force for 15 months or less, or as a result of the decision on a previous application under this section is due to expire within 15 months of that decision, until the last three months before the expiry date.

(3) The Tribunal shall on an application for review confirm or vary its order as the Tribunal may determine to be reasonable in the circumstances.

Amendments (Textual)

F272. Words in s. 127. (1) substituted (31.10.2003) by The Copyright and Related Rights Regulations 2003 (S.I. 2003/2498), reg. 21. (5) (with regs. 31-40)

128 Effect of order of tribunal as to licence.

(1) Where the Copyright Tribunal has made an order under section 125 or 126 and the order remains in force, the person entitled to the benefit of the order shall if he—

   (a) pays to the licensing body any charges payable in accordance with the order or, if the amount cannot be ascertained, gives an undertaking to pay the charges when ascertained, and

   (b) complies with the other terms specified in the order,

be in the same position as regards infringement of copyright as if he had at all material times been the holder of a licence granted by the owner of the copyright in question on the terms specified in the order.

(2) The benefit of the order may be assigned—

   (a) in the case of an order under section 125, if assignment is not prohibited under the terms of the Tribunal's order; and

   (b) in the case of an order under section 126, if assignment was not prohibited under the terms of the original licence.

(3) The Tribunal may direct that an order under section 125 or 126, or an order under section 127 varying such an order, so far as it varies the amount of charges payable, has effect from a date before that on which it is made, but not earlier than the date on which the reference or application was made or, if later, on which the licence was granted or, as the case may be, was due to expire. If such a direction is made—

   (a) any necessary repayments, or further payments, shall be made in respect of charges already paid, and

   (b) the reference in subsection (1)(a) to the charges payable in accordance with the order shall be construed, where the order is varied by a later order, as a reference to the charges so payable by virtue of the later order.

[F273128. ANotification of licence or licensing scheme for excepted sound recordings

F274 . . . .

Amendments (Textual)

F273. Ss. 128. A, 128. B inserted (31.10.2003) by The Copyright and Related Rights Regulations 2003 (S.I. 2003/2498), reg. 21. (3) (with regs. 31-40)

F274. S. 128. A omitted (1.1.2011) by virtue of The Copyright, Designs and Patents Act 1988 (Amendment) Regulations 2010 (S.I. 2010/2694), art. 6

128. BReferences to the Tribunal by the Secretary of State under section 128. A

F275 . . . .]

Amendments (Textual)

F273. Ss. 128. A, 128. B inserted (31.10.2003) by The Copyright and Related Rights Regulations 2003 (S.I. 2003/2498), reg. 21. (3) (with regs. 31-40)

F275. S. 128. B omitted (1.1.2011) by virtue of The Copyright, Designs and Patents Act 1988 (Amendment) Regulations 2010 (S.I. 2010/2694), art. 6

Factors to be taken into account in certain classes of case

129 General considerations: unreasonable discrimination.

In determining what is reasonable on a reference or application under this Chapter relating to a licensing scheme or licence, the Copyright Tribunal shall have regard to—

    (a) the availability of other schemes, or the granting of other licences, to other persons in similar circumstances, and

    (b) the terms of those schemes or licences,

and shall exercise its powers so as to secure that there is no unreasonable discrimination between licensees, or prospective licensees, under the scheme or licence to which the reference or application relates and licensees under other schemes operated by, or other licences granted by, the same person.

130 Licences for reprographic copying.

Where a reference or application is made to the Copyright Tribunal under this Chapter relating to the licensing of reprographic copying of published literary, dramatic, musical or artistic works, or the typographical arrangement of published editions, the Tribunal shall have regard to—

    (a) the extent to which published editions of the works in question are otherwise available,

    (b) the proportion of the work to be copied, and

    (c) the nature of the use to which the copies are likely to be put.

131 Licences for educational establishments in respect of works included in broadcasts F276. . . .

(1) This section applies to references or applications under this Chapter relating to licences for the recording by or on behalf of educational establishments of broadcasts F277. . . which include copyright works, or the making of copies of such recordings, for educational purposes.

(2) The Copyright Tribunal shall, in considering what charges (if any) should be paid for a licence, have regard to the extent to which the owners of copyright in the works included in the broadcast F277. . . have already received, or are entitled to receive, payment in respect of their inclusion.

Amendments (Textual)

F276. Words in s. 131 heading repealed (31.10.2003) by The Copyright and Related Rights Regulations 2003 (S.I. 2003/2498), reg. 2. (2), Sch. 2 (with regs. 31-40)

F277. Words in s. 131. (1)(2) repealed (31.10.2003) by The Copyright and Related Rights Regulations 2003 (S.I. 2003/2498), reg. 2. (2), Sch. 2 (with regs. 31-40)

132 Licences to reflect conditions imposed by promoters of events.

(1) This section applies to references or applications under this Chapter in respect of licences relating to sound recordings, films [F278or broadcasts] which include, or are to include, any entertainment or other event.

(2) The Copyright Tribunal shall have regard to any conditions imposed by the promoters of the entertainment or other event; and, in particular, the Tribunal shall not hold a refusal or failure to grant a licence to be unreasonable if it could not have been granted consistently with those conditions.

(3) Nothing in this section shall require the Tribunal to have regard to any such conditions in so far as they—

    (a) purport to regulate the charges to be imposed in respect of the grant of licences, or

(b) relate to payments to be made to the promoters of any event in consideration of the grant of facilities for making the recording, film [F279or broadcast].

Amendments (Textual)

F278. Words in s. 132. (1) substituted (31.10.2003) by The Copyright and Related Rights Regulations 2003 (S.I. 2003/2498), reg. 2. (1), Sch. 3 para. 3. (2)(a) (with regs. 31-40)

F279. Words in s. 132. (3)(b) substituted (31.10.2003) by The Copyright and Related Rights Regulations 2003 (S.I. 2003/2498), reg. 2. (1), Sch. 1 para. 3. (1)(j) (with regs. 31-40)

133 Licences to reflect payments in respect of underlying rights.

F280 [(1)In considering what charges should be paid for a licence—

(a) on a reference or application under this Chapter relating to licences for the rental or lending of copies of a work, or

(b) on an application under section 142 (royalty or other sum payable for lending of certain works), the Copyright Tribunal shall take into account any reasonable payments which the owner of the copyright in the work is liable to make in consequence of the granting of the licence, or of the acts authorised by the licence, to owners of copyright in works included in that work.]

(2) On any reference or application under this Chapter relating to licensing in respect of the copyright in sound recordings, films [F281or broadcasts], the Copyright Tribunal shall take into account, in considering what charges should be paid for a licence, any reasonable payments which the copyright owner is liable to make in consequence of the granting of the licence, or of the acts authorised by the licence, in respect of any performance included in the recording, film [F282or broadcast].

Amendments (Textual)

F280. S. 133. (1) substituted (1.12.1996) by S.I. 1996/2967, reg. 13. (1) (with Pt. III)

F281. Words in s. 133. (2) substituted (31.10.2003) by The Copyright and Related Rights Regulations 2003 (S.I. 2003/2498), reg. 2. (1), Sch. 3 para. 3. (2)(b) (with regs. 31-40)

F282. Words in s. 133. (2) substituted (31.10.2003) by The Copyright and Related Rights Regulations 2003 (S.I. 2003/2498), reg. 2. (1), Sch. 3 para. 3. (1)(k) (with regs. 31-40)

134 Licences in respect of works included in re-transmissions.

(1) F283... this section applies to references or applications under this Chapter relating to licences to include in a broadcast F284... —

(a) literary, dramatic, musical or artistic works, or,

(b) sound recordings or films,

where one broadcast F284... ("the first transmission") is, by reception and immediate re-transmission, to be further broadcast F284... ("the further transmission").

(2) So far as the further transmission is to the same area as the first transmission, the Copyright Tribunal shall, in considering what charges (if any) should be paid for licences for either transmission, have regard to the extent to which the copyright owner has already received, or is entitled to receive, payment for the other transmission which adequately remunerates him in respect of transmissions to that area.

(3) So far as the further transmission is to an area outside that to which the first transmission was made, the Tribunal shall F284... leave the further transmission out of account in considering what charges (if any) should be paid for licences for the first transmission.

F285. (3. A). . . . .

F286. (4). . . . .

Amendments (Textual)

F283. Words in s. 134. (1) repealed (31.7.2017) by Digital Economy Act 2017 (c. 30), ss. 34. (2)(a)(i), 118. (6); S.I. 2017/765, reg. 2. (n)

F284. Words in s. 134. (1)(3) repealed (31.10.2003) by The Copyright and Related Rights Regulations 2003 (S.I. 2003/2498), reg. 2. (2), Sch. 2 (with regs. 31-40)

F285. S. 134. (3. A) repealed (31.7.2017) by Digital Economy Act 2017 (c. 30), ss. 34. (2)(a)(i), 118. (6); S.I. 2017/765, reg. 2. (n)

F286. S. 134. (4) repealed by Broadcasting Act 1990 (c. 42, SIF 96), s. 203. (3), Sch. 21

135 Mention of specific matters not to exclude other relevant considerations.

The mention in sections 129 to 134 of specific matters to which the Copyright Tribunal is to have regard in certain classes of case does not affect the Tribunal's general obligation in any case to have regard to all relevant considerations.

[F287 Use as of right of sound recordings in broadcasts F288 . . .

Amendments (Textual)

F287. Ss. 135. A–135. G inserted by Broadcasting Act 1990 (c. 42, SIF 96), s. 175. (1)

F288. Words in heading preceding s. 135. A repealed (31.10.2003) by The Copyright and Related Rights Regulations 2003 (S.I. 2003/2498), reg. 2. (2), Sch. 2 (with regs. 31-40)

135. A Circumstances in which right available.

(1) Section 135. C applies to the inclusion in a broadcast F289 . . . of any sound recordings if—

(a) a licence to include those recordings in the broadcast F289 . . . could be granted by a licensing body or such a body could procure the grant of a licence to do so,

(b) the condition in subsection (2) or (3) applies, and

(c) the person including those recordings in the broadcast F289 . . . has complied with section 135. B.

(2) Where the person including the recordings in the broadcast F289 . . . does not hold a licence to do so, the condition is that the licensing body refuses to grant, or procure the grant of, such a licence, being a licence—

(a) whose terms as to payment for including the recordings in the broadcast F289 . . . would be acceptable to him or comply with an order of the Copyright Tribunal under section 135. D relating to such a licence or any scheme under which it would be granted, and

(b) allowing unlimited needletime or such needletime as he has demanded.

(3) Where he holds a licence to include the recordings in the broadcast F289 . . . , the condition is that the terms of the licence limit needletime and the licensing body refuses to substitute or procure the substitution of terms allowing unlimited needletime or such needletime as he has demanded, or refuses to do so on terms that fall within subsection (2)(a).

(4) The references in subsection (2) to refusing to grant, or procure the grant of, a licence, and in subsection (3) to refusing to substitute or procure the substitution of terms, include failing to do so within a reasonable time of being asked.

(5) In the group of sections from this section to section 135. G—

[F290 " broadcast " does not include any broadcast which is a transmission of the kind specified in section 6. (1. A)(b) or (c);]

" needletime " means the time in any period (whether determined as a number of hours in the period or a proportion of the period, or otherwise) in which any recordings may be included in a broadcast F289 . . . ;

" sound recording " does not include a film sound track when accompanying a film.

(6) In sections 135. B to 135. G, " terms of payment " means terms as to payment for including sound recordings in a broadcast F289 . . . .]

Amendments (Textual)

F289. Words in s. 135. A repealed (31.10.2003) by The Copyright and Related Rights Regulations 2003 (S.I. 2003/2498), reg. 2. (2), Sch. 2 (with regs. 31-40)

F290. S. 135. A(5): definition of "broadcast" inserted (31.10.2003) by The Copyright and Related Rights Regulations 2003 (S.I. 2003/2498), reg. 2. (1), Sch. 1 para. 15. (1) (with regs. 31-40)

[F291135. B Notice of intention to exercise right.

(1) A person intending to avail himself of the right conferred by section 135. C must—

(a) give notice to the licensing body of his intention to exercise the right, asking the body to propose terms of payment, and

(b) after receiving the proposal or the expiry of a reasonable period, give reasonable notice to the licensing body of the date on which he proposes to begin exercising that right, and the terms of payment in accordance with which he intends to do so.

(2) Where he has a licence to include the recordings in a broadcast F292 . . . , the date specified in a notice under subsection (1)(b) must not be sooner than the date of expiry of that licence except in a case falling within section 135. A(3).

(3) Before the person intending to avail himself of the right begins to exercise it, he must—

(a) give reasonable notice to the Copyright Tribunal of his intention to exercise the right, and of the date on which he proposes to begin to do so, and

(b) apply to the Tribunal under section 135. D to settle the terms of payment.]

Amendments (Textual)

F291. Ss. 135. A–135. G inserted by Broadcasting Act 1990 (c. 42, SIF 96), s. 175. (1)

F292. Words in s. 135. B(2) repealed (31.10.2003) by The Copyright and Related Rights Regulations 2003 (S.I. 2003/2498), reg. 2. (2), Sch. 2 (with regs. 31-40)

[F293135. C Conditions for exercise of right.

(1) A person who, on or after the date specified in a notice under section 135. B(1)(b), includes in a broadcast F294 . . . any sound recordings in circumstances in which this section applies, and who—

(a) complies with any reasonable condition, notice of which has been given to him by the licensing body, as to inclusion in the broadcast F294 . . . of those recordings,

(b) provides that body with such information about their inclusion in the broadcast F294 . . . as it may reasonably require, and

(c) makes the payments to the licensing body that are required by this section, shall be in the same position as regards infringement of copyright as if he had at all material times been the holder of a licence granted by the owner of the copyright in question.

(2) Payments are to be made at not less than quarterly intervals in arrears.

(3) The amount of any payment is that determined in accordance with any order of the Copyright Tribunal under section 135. D or, if no such order has been made—

(a) in accordance with any proposal for terms of payment made by the licensing body pursuant to a request under section 135. B, or

(b) where no proposal has been so made or the amount determined in accordance with the proposal so made is unreasonably high, in accordance with the terms of payment notified to the licensing body under section 135. B(1)(b).

(4) Where this section applies to the inclusion in a broadcast F294 . . . of any sound recordings, it does so in place of any licence.]

Amendments (Textual)

F293. Ss. 135. A–135. G inserted by Broadcasting Act 1990 (c. 42, SIF 96), s. 175. (1)

F294. Words in s. 135. C(1)(4) repealed (31.10.2003) by The Copyright and Related Rights Regulations 2003 (S.I. 2003/2498), reg. 2. (2), Sch. 2 (with regs. 31-40)

[F295135. D Applications to settle payments.

(1) On an application to settle the terms of payment, the Copyright Tribunal shall consider the matter and make such order as it may determine to be reasonable in the circumstances.

(2) An order under subsection (1) has effect from the date the applicant begins to exercise the right conferred by section 135. C and any necessary repayments, or further payments, shall be made in respect of amounts that have fallen due.]

Amendments (Textual)

F295. Ss. 135. A–135. G inserted by Broadcasting Act 1990 (c. 42, SIF 96), s. 175. (1)

[F296135. E References etc. about conditions, information and other terms.

(1) A person exercising the right conferred by section 135. C, or who has given notice to the Copyright Tribunal of his intention to do so, may refer to the Tribunal—

(a) any question whether any condition as to the inclusion in a broadcast F297 . . . of sound recordings, notice of which has been given to him by the licensing body in question, is a reasonable condition, or

(b) any question whether any information is information which the licensing body can reasonably require him to provide.

(2) On a reference under this section, the Tribunal shall consider the matter and make such order

as it may determine to be reasonable in the circumstances.]

Amendments (Textual)

F296. Ss. 135. A–135. G inserted by Broadcasting Act 1990 (c. 42, SIF 96), s. 175. (1)

F297. Words in s. 135. E(1)(a) repealed (31.10.2003) by The Copyright and Related Rights Regulations 2003 (S.I. 2003/2498), reg. 2. (2), Sch. 2 (with regs. 31-40)

[F298135. F Application for review of order.

(1) A person exercising the right conferred by section 135. C or the licensing body may apply to the Copyright Tribunal to review any order under section 135. D or 135. E.

(2) An application shall not be made, except with the special leave of the Tribunal—

(a) within twelve months from the date of the order, or of the decision on a previous application under this section, or

(b) if the order was made so as to be in force for fifteen months or less, or as a result of a decision on a previous application is due to expire within fifteen months of that decision, until the last three months before the expiry date.

(3) On the application the Tribunal shall consider the matter and make such order confirming or varying the original order as it may determine to be reasonable in the circumstances.

(4) An order under this section has effect from the date on which it is made or such later date as may be specified by the Tribunal.]

Amendments (Textual)

F298. Ss. 135. A–135. G inserted by Broadcasting Act 1990 (c. 42, SIF 96), s. 175. (1)

[F299135. G Factors to be taken into account.

(1) In determining what is reasonable on an application or reference under section 135. D or 135. E, or on reviewing any order under section 135. F, the Copyright Tribunal shall—

(a) have regard to the terms of any orders which it has made in the case of persons in similar circumstances exercising the right conferred by section 135. C, and

(b) exercise its powers so as to secure that there is no unreasonable discrimination between persons exercising that right against the same licensing body.

(2) In settling the terms of payment under section 135. D, the Tribunal shall not be guided by any order it has made under any enactment other than that section.

(3) Section 134 (factors to be taken into account: retransmissions) applies on an application or reference under sections 135. D to 135. F as it applies on an application or reference relating to a licence.]

Amendments (Textual)

F299. Ss. 135. A–135. G inserted by Broadcasting Act 1990 (c. 42, SIF 96), s. 175. (1)

[F300135. H Power to amend sections 135. A to 135. G.

(1) The Secretary of State may by order, subject to such transitional provision as appears to him to be appropriate, amend sections 135. A to 135. G so as—

(a) to include in any reference to sound recordings any works of a description specified in the order; or

(b) to exclude from any reference to a broadcast F301 . . . any broadcast F301 . . . of a description so specified.

(2) An order shall be made by statutory instrument; and no order shall be made unless a draft of it has been laid before and approved by resolution of each House of Parliament.]

Amendments (Textual)

F300. S. 135. H inserted (1.11.1996) by 1996 c. 55, s. 139. (1) (with s. 43. (6)); S.I. 1996/2120, art. 5, Sch. 2

F301. Words in s. 135. H(1)(b) repealed (31.10.2003) by The Copyright and Related Rights Regulations 2003 (S.I. 2003/2498), reg. 2. (2), Sch. 2 (with regs. 31-40)

Implied indemnity in schemes or licences for reprographic copying

136 Implied indemnity in certain schemes and licences for reprographic copying.

(1) This section applies to—

(a) schemes for licensing reprographic copying of published literary, dramatic, musical or artistic works, or the typographical arrangement of published editions, and

(b) licences granted by licensing bodies for such copying,

where the scheme or licence does not specify the works to which it applies with such particularity as to enable licensees to determine whether a work falls within the scheme or licence by inspection of the scheme or licence and the work.

(2) There is implied—

(a) in every scheme to which this section applies an undertaking by the operator of the scheme to indemnify a person granted a licence under the scheme, and

(b) in every licence to which this section applies an undertaking by the licensing body to indemnify the licensee,

against any liability incurred by him by reason of his having infringed copyright by making or authorising the making of reprographic copies of a work in circumstances within the apparent scope of his licence.

(3) The circumstances of a case are within the apparent scope of a licence if—

(a) it is not apparent from inspection of the licence and the work that it does not fall within the description of works to which the licence applies; and

(b) the licence does not expressly provide that it does not extend to copyright of the description infringed.

(4) In this section "liability" includes liability to pay costs; and this section applies in relation to costs reasonably incurred by a licensee in connection with actual or contemplated proceedings against him for infringement of copyright as it applies to sums which he is liable to pay in respect of such infringement.

(5) A scheme or licence to which this section applies may contain reasonable provision—

(a) with respect to the manner in which, and time within which, claims under the undertaking implied by this section are to be made;

(b) enabling the operator of the scheme or, as the case may be, the licensing body to take over the conduct of any proceedings affecting the amount of his liability to indemnify.

Reprographic copying by educational establishments

137 Power to extend coverage of scheme or licence.

(1) This section applies to—

(a) a licensing scheme to which sections 118 to 123 apply (see section 117) and which is operated by a licensing body, or

(b) a licence to which sections 125 to 128 apply (see section 124),

so far as it provides for the grant of licences, or is a licence, authorising the making by or on behalf of educational establishments for the purposes of instruction of reprographic copies of published literary, dramatic, musical or artistic works, or of the typographical arrangement of published editions.

(2) If it appears to the Secretary of State with respect to a scheme or licence to which this section applies that—

(a) works of a description similar to those covered by the scheme or licence are unreasonably excluded from it, and

(b) making them subject to the scheme or licence would not conflict with the normal exploitation of the works or unreasonably prejudice the legitimate interests of the copyright owners,

he may by order provide that the scheme or licence shall extend to those works.

(3) Where he proposes to make such an order, the Secretary of State shall give notice of the proposal to—

(a) the copyright owners,

(b) the licensing body in question, and

(c) such persons or organisations representative of educational establishments, and such other persons or organisations, as the Secretary of State thinks fit.

(4) The notice shall inform those persons of their right to make written or oral representations to the Secretary of State about the proposal within six months from the date of the notice; and if any of them wishes to make oral representations, the Secretary of State shall appoint a person to hear the representations and report to him.

(5) In considering whether to make an order the Secretary of State shall take into account any representations made to him in accordance with subsection (4), and such other matters as appear to him to be relevant.

Modifications etc. (not altering text)

C58. Ss. 137–141 extended by S.I. 1989/1067, art. 2

138 Variation or discharge of order extending scheme or licence.

(1) The owner of the copyright in a work in respect of which an order is in force under section 137 may apply to the Secretary of State for the variation or discharge of the order, stating his reasons for making the application.

(2) The Secretary of State shall not entertain an application made within two years of the making of the original order, or of the making of an order on a previous application under this section, unless it appears to him that the circumstances are exceptional.

(3) On considering the reasons for the application the Secretary of State may confirm the order forthwith; if he does not do so, he shall give notice of the application to—

(a) the licensing body in question, and

(b) such persons or organisations representative of educational establishments, and such other persons or organisations, as he thinks fit.

(4) The notice shall inform those persons of their right to make written or oral representations to the Secretary of State about the application within the period of two months from the date of the notice; and if any of them wishes to make oral representations, the Secretary of State shall appoint a person to hear the representations and report to him.

(5) In considering the application the Secretary of State shall take into account the reasons for the application, any representations made to him in accordance with subsection (4), and such other matters as appear to him to be relevant.

(6) The Secretary of State may make such order as he thinks fit confirming or discharging the order (or, as the case may be, the order as previously varied), or varying (or further varying) it so as to exclude works from it.

Modifications etc. (not altering text)

C59. Ss. 137–141 extended by S.I. 1989/1067, art. 2

139 Appeals against orders.

(1) The owner of the copyright in a work which is the subject of an order under section 137 (order extending coverage of scheme or licence) may appeal to the Copyright Tribunal which may confirm or discharge the order, or vary it so as to exclude works from it, as it thinks fit having regard to the considerations mentioned in subsection (2) of that section.

(2) Where the Secretary of State has made an order under section 138 (order confirming, varying or discharging order extending coverage of scheme or licence)—

(a) the person who applied for the order, or

(b) any person or organisation representative of educational establishments who was given notice of the application for the order and made representations in accordance with subsection (4) of that section,

may appeal to the Tribunal which may confirm or discharge the order or make any other order which the Secretary of State might have made.

(3) An appeal under this section shall be brought within six weeks of the making of the order or such further period as the Tribunal may allow.

(4) An order under section 137 or 138 shall not come into effect until the end of the period of six

weeks from the making of the order or, if an appeal is brought before the end of that period, until the appeal proceedings are disposed of or withdrawn.

(5) If an appeal is brought after the end of that period, any decision of the Tribunal on the appeal does not affect the validity of anything done in reliance on the order appealed against before that decision takes effect.

Modifications etc. (not altering text)

C60. Ss. 137–141 extended by S.I. 1989/1067, art. 2

140 Inquiry whether new scheme or general licence required.

(1) The Secretary of State may appoint a person to inquire into the question whether new provision is required (whether by way of a licensing scheme or general licence) to authorise the making by or on behalf of educational establishments for the purposes of instruction of reprographic copies of—

  (a) published literary, dramatic, musical or artistic works, or

  (b) the typographical arrangement of published editions,

of a description which appears to the Secretary of State not to be covered by an existing licensing scheme or general licence and not to fall within the power conferred by section 137 (power to extend existing schemes and licences to similar works).

(2) The procedure to be followed in relation to an inquiry shall be such as may be prescribed by regulations made by the Secretary of State.

(3) The regulations shall, in particular, provide for notice to be given to—

  (a) persons or organisations appearing to the Secretary of State to represent the owners of copyright in works of that description, and

  (b) persons or organisations appearing to the Secretary of State to represent educational establishments,

and for the making of written or oral representations by such persons; but without prejudice to the giving of notice to, and the making of representations by, other persons and organisations.

(4) The person appointed to hold the inquiry shall not recommend the making of new provision unless he is satisfied—

  (a) that it would be of advantage to educational establishments to be authorised to make reprographic copies of the works in question, and

  (b) that making those works subject to a licensing scheme or general licence would not conflict with the normal exploitation of the works or unreasonably prejudice the legitimate interests of the copyright owners.

(5) If he does recommend the making of new provision he shall specify any terms, other than terms as to charges payable, on which authorisation under the new provision should be available.

(6) Regulations under this section shall be made by statutory instrument which shall be subject to annulment in pursuance of a resolution of either House of Parliament.

(7) In this section (and section 141) a "general licence" means a licence granted by a licensing body which covers all works of the description to which it applies.

Modifications etc. (not altering text)

C61. Ss. 137–141 extended by S.I. 1989/1067, art. 2

141 Statutory licence where recommendation not implemented.

(1) The Secretary of State may, within one year of the making of a recommendation under section 140 by order provide that if, or to the extent that, provision has not been made in accordance with the recommendation, the making by or on behalf of an educational establishment, for the purposes of instruction, of reprographic copies of the works to which the recommendation relates shall be treated as licensed by the owners of the copyright in the works.

(2) For that purpose provision shall be regarded as having been made in accordance with the recommendation if—

  (a) a certified licensing scheme has been established under which a licence is available to the establishment in question, or

  (b) a general licence has been—

(i) granted to or for the benefit of that establishment, or

(ii) referred by or on behalf of that establishment to the Copyright Tribunal under section 125 (reference of terms of proposed licence), or

(iii) offered to or for the benefit of that establishment and refused without such a reference,

and the terms of the scheme or licence accord with the recommendation.

(3) The order shall also provide that any existing licence authorising the making of such copies (not being a licence granted under a certified licensing scheme or a general licence) shall cease to have effect to the extent that it is more restricted or more onerous than the licence provided for by the order.

(4) The order shall provide for the licence to be free of royalty but, as respects other matters, subject to any terms specified in the recommendation and to such other terms as the Secretary of State may think fit.

(5) The order may provide that where a copy which would otherwise be an infringing copy is made in accordance with the licence provided by the order but is subsequently dealt with, it shall be treated as an infringing copy for the purposes of that dealing, and if that dealing infringes copyright for all subsequent purposes.

In this subsection "dealt with" means sold or let for hire, offered or exposed for sale or hire, or exhibited in public.

(6) The order shall not come into force until at least six months after it is made.

(7) An order may be varied from time to time, but not so as to include works other than those to which the recommendation relates or remove any terms specified in the recommendation, and may be revoked.

(8) An order under this section shall be made by statutory instrument which shall be subject to annulment in pursuance of a resolution of either House of Parliament.

(9) In this section a "certified licensing scheme" means a licensing scheme certified for the purposes of this section under section 143.

Modifications etc. (not altering text)

C62. Ss. 137–141 extended by S.I. 1989/1067, art. 2

F302 [Royalty or other sum payable for lending of certain works]

Amendments (Textual)

F302. S. 142 and crossheading substituted (1.12.1996) by S.I. 1996/2967, reg. 13. (2) (with Pt. III)

142[F303 Royalty or other sum payable for lending of certain works.]

(1) An application to settle the royalty or other sum payable in pursuance of section 66 (lending of copies of certain copyright works) may be made to the Copyright Tribunal by the copyright owner or the person claiming to be treated as licensed by him.

(2) The Tribunal shall consider the matter and make such order as it may determine to be reasonable in the circumstances.

(3) Either party may subsequently apply to the Tribunal to vary the order, and the Tribunal shall consider the matter and make such order confirming or varying the original order as it may determine to be reasonable in the circumstances.

(4) An application under subsection (3) shall not, except with the special leave of the Tribunal, be made within twelve months from the date of the original order or of the order on a previous application under that subsection.

(5) An order under subsection (3) has effect from the date on which it is made or such later date as may be specified by the Tribunal.

Amendments (Textual)

F303. S. 142 substituted (1.12.1996) by S.I. 1996/2967, reg. 13. (2) (with Pt. III)

Certification of licensing schemes

143 Certification of licensing schemes.

(1) A person operating or proposing to operate a licensing scheme may apply to the Secretary of State to certify the scheme for the purposes of—

F304. (a). . . . .

(b) section 60 (abstracts of scientific or technical articles),

[F305. (c)section 66 (lending to public of copies of certain works),]

F306. (d). . . . .

(e) section 141 (reprographic copying of published works by educational establishments).

(2) The Secretary of State shall by order made by statutory instrument certify the scheme if he is satisfied that it—

(a) enables the works to which it relates to be identified with sufficient certainty by persons likely to require licences, and

(b) sets out clearly the charges (if any) payable and the other terms on which licences will be granted.

(3) The scheme shall be scheduled to the order and the certification shall come into operation for the purposes of section F307... 60, 66. F308... or 141, as the case may be—

(a) on such date, not less than eight weeks after the order is made, as may be specified in the order, or

(b) if the scheme is the subject of a reference under section 118 (reference of proposed scheme), any later date on which the order of the Copyright Tribunal under that section comes into force or the reference is withdrawn.

(4) A variation of the scheme is not effective unless a corresponding amendment of the order is made; and the Secretary of State shall make such an amendment in the case of a variation ordered by the Copyright Tribunal on a reference under section 118, 119 or 120, and may do so in any other case if he thinks fit.

(5) The order shall be revoked if the scheme ceases to be operated and may be revoked if it appears to the Secretary of State that it is no longer being operated according to its terms.

Amendments (Textual)

F304. S. 143. (1)(a) omitted (1.6.2014) by virtue of The Copyright and Rights in Performances (Research, Education, Libraries and Archives) Regulations 2014 (S.I. 2014/1372), reg. 1, Sch. para. 5. (a)

F305. S. 143. (1)(c) substituted (1.12.1996) by S.I. 1996/2967, reg. 11. (4) (with Pt. III)

F306. S. 143. (1)(d) omitted (1.6.2014) by virtue of The Copyright and Rights in Performances (Disability) Regulations 2014 (S.I. 2014/1384), reg. 1. (1), Sch. para. 2. (a)

F307. Word in s. 143. (3) omitted (1.6.2014) by virtue of The Copyright and Rights in Performances (Research, Education, Libraries and Archives) Regulations 2014 (S.I. 2014/1372), reg. 1, Sch. para. 5. (b)

F308. Word in s. 143. (3) omitted (1.6.2014) by virtue of The Copyright and Rights in Performances (Disability) Regulations 2014 (S.I. 2014/1384), reg. 1. (1), Sch. para. 2. (b)

Powers exercisable in consequence of competition report

144 Powers exercisable in consequence of report of [F309. Competition and Markets Authority].

[F310. (1)Subsection (1. A) applies where whatever needs to be remedied, mitigated or prevented by the Secretary of State [F311or (as the case may be) the Competition and Markets Authority] under section 12. (5) of the Competition Act 1980 or section 41. (2), 55. (2), 66. (6), 75. (2), 83. (2), 138. (2), 147. (2)[F312, 147. A(2)] or 160. (2) of, or paragraph 5. (2) or 10. (2) of Schedule 7 to, the Enterprise Act 2002 (powers to take remedial action following references to the [F313. Competition and Markets Authority] in connection with public bodies and certain other persons, mergers or market investigations) consists of or includes—

(a) conditions in licences granted by the owner of copyright in a work restricting the use of the work by the licensee or the right of the copyright owner to grant other licences; or

(b) a refusal of a copyright owner to grant licences on reasonable terms.

(1. A)The powers conferred by Schedule 8 to the Enterprise Act 2002 include power to cancel or modify those conditions and, instead or in addition, to provide that licences in respect of the copyright shall be available as of right.

(2)The references to anything permitted by Schedule 8 to the Enterprise Act 2002 in section 12. (5. A) of the Competition Act 1980 and in sections 75. (4)(a), 83. (4)(a), 84. (2)(a), 89. (1), 160. (4)(a), 161. (3)(a) and 164. (1) of, and paragraphs 5, 10 and 11 of Schedule 7 to, the Act of 2002 shall be construed accordingly.]

(2) The references in sections 56. (2) and 73. (2) of that Act, and [F314section] 12. (5) of the M11. Competition Act 1980, to the powers specified in that Part of that Schedule shall be construed accordingly.

(3) [F315. The Secretary of State [F316or (as the case may be) the Competition and Markets Authority]] shall only exercise the powers available by virtue of this section if he [F317or it] is satisfied that to do so does not contravene any Convention relating to copyright to which the United Kingdom is a party.

(4) The terms of a licence available by virtue of this section shall, in default of agreement, be settled by the Copyright Tribunal on an application by the person requiring the licence; and terms so settled shall authorise the licensee to do everything in respect of which a licence is so available.

(5) Where the terms of a licence are settled by the Tribunal, the licence has effect from the date on which the application to the Tribunal was made.

Amendments (Textual)

F309. Words in s. 144 heading substituted (1.4.2014) by The Enterprise and Regulatory Reform Act 2013 (Competition) (Consequential, Transitional and Saving Provisions) Order 2014 (S.I. 2014/892), art. 1. (1), Sch. 1 para. 57. (4) (with art. 3)

F310. S. 144. (1)(1. A)(2) substituted (20.6.2003 for certain purposes and 29.12.2004 otherwise) for s. 144. (1)(2) by 2002 c. 40, ss. 278. (1), 279, Sch. 25 para. 18. (2); S.I. 2003/1397, arts. 2, 3. (1), Sch. (with arts. 4-12); S.I. 2004/3233, art. 2, Sch. (with arts. 3-5)

F311. Words in s. 144. (1) substituted (1.4.2014) by The Enterprise and Regulatory Reform Act 2013 (Competition) (Consequential, Transitional and Saving Provisions) Order 2014 (S.I. 2014/892), art. 1. (1), Sch. 1 para. 57. (2)(a) (with art. 3)

F312. Word in s. 144. (1) inserted (1.4.2014) by The Enterprise and Regulatory Reform Act 2013 (Competition) (Consequential, Transitional and Saving Provisions) Order 2014 (S.I. 2014/892), art. 1. (1), Sch. 1 para. 57. (2)(b) (with art. 3)

F313. Words in s. 144. (1) substituted (1.4.2014) by The Enterprise and Regulatory Reform Act 2013 (Competition) (Consequential, Transitional and Saving Provisions) Order 2014 (S.I. 2014/892), art. 1. (1), Sch. 1 para. 57. (2)(c) (with art. 3)

F314. Words in s. 144. (2) substituted (1.3.2000) by S.I. 2000/311, art. 22. (2)

F315. Words in s. 144. (3) substituted (20.6.2003 for certain purposes and 29.12.2004 otherwise) by 2002 c. 40, ss. 278. (1), 279, Sch. 25 para. 18. (3)(a); S.I. 2003/1397, arts. 2, 3. (1), Sch. (with arts. 4-12); S.I. 2004/3233, art. 2, Sch. (with arts. 3-5)

F316. Words in s. 144. (3) substituted (1.4.2014) by The Enterprise and Regulatory Reform Act 2013 (Competition) (Consequential, Transitional and Saving Provisions) Order 2014 (S.I. 2014/892), art. 1. (1), Sch. 1 para. 57. (3) (with art. 3)

F317. Words in s. 144. (3) inserted (20.6.2003 for certain purposes and 29.12.2004 otherwise) by 2002 c. 40, ss. 278. (1), 279, Sch. 25 para. 18. (3)(b); S.I. 2003/1397, arts. 2, 3. (1), Sch. (with arts. 4-12); S.I. 2004/3233, art. 2, Sch. (with arts. 3-5)

Modifications etc. (not altering text)

C63. S. 144. (1) amended (20.6.2003) by The Enterprise Act 2002 (Protection of Legitimate Interests) Order 2003 (S.I. 2003/1592), art. 16, Sch. 4 para. 7. (1)(a) (as amended (1.4.2014) by S.I. 2014/891, arts. 1, 19. (3) (with arts. 20-23))

C64. S. 144. (2) amended (20.6.2003) by The Enterprise Act 2002 (Protection of Legitimate Interests) Order 2003 (S.I. 2003/1592), art. 16, Sch. 4 para. 7. (1)(b)

[F318. Compulsory collective administration of certain rights]

Amendments (Textual)
F318. S. 144. A and crossheading inserted (1.12.1996) by S.I. 1996/2967, reg. 7 (with Pt. III)
[F319144. A Collective exercise of certain rights in relation to cable re-transmission.
(1) This section applies to the right of the owner of copyright in a literary, dramatic, musical or artistic work, sound recording or film to grant or refuse authorisation for cable re-transmission of a [F320wireless] broadcast from another EEA F321. . . state in which the work is included. That right is referred to below as "cable re-transmission right".
(2) Cable re-transmission right may be exercised against a cable operator only through a licensing body.
(3) Where a copyright owner has not transferred management of his cable re-transmission right to a licensing body, the licensing body which manages rights of the same category shall be deemed to be mandated to manage his right. Where more than one licensing body manages rights of that category, he may choose which of them is deemed to be mandated to manage his right.
(4) A copyright owner to whom subsection (3) applies has the same rights and obligations resulting from any relevant agreement between the cable operator and the licensing body as have copyright owners who have transferred management of their cable re-transmission right to that licensing body.
(5) Any rights to which a copyright owner may be entitled by virtue of subsection (4) must be claimed within the period of three years beginning with the date of the cable re-transmission concerned.
(6) This section does not affect any rights exercisable by the maker of the broadcast, whether in relation to the broadcast or a work included in it.
[F322. (7)In this section—
" cable operator " means a person responsible for cable re-transmission of a wireless broadcast; and
" cable re-transmission " means the reception and immediate re-transmission by cable, including the transmission of microwave energy between terrestrial fixed points, of a wireless broadcast.]]
Amendments (Textual)
F319. S. 144. A inserted (1.12.1996) by S.I. 1996/2967, reg. 7 (with Pt. III)
F320. Word in s. 144. A(1) inserted (31.10.2003) by The Copyright and Related Rights Regulations 2003 (S.I. 2003/2498), reg. 5. (6) (with regs. 31-40)
F321. Word in s. 144. A(1) repealed (29.4.2006) by The Intellectual Property (Enforcement, etc.) Regulations 2006 (S.I. 2006/1028), reg. 2. (4), Sch. 4
F322. S. 144. A(7) substituted (31.10.2003) by The Copyright and Related Rights Regulations 2003 (S.I. 2003/2498), reg. 2. (1), Sch. 1 para. 15. (2) (with regs. 31-40)

Chapter VIII The Copyright Tribunal

Modifications etc. (not altering text)
C65. Pt. I Ch. VIII (ss. 145-152) applied (1.12.1996) by S.I. 1996/2967, reg. 17. (4) (with Pt. III)
Pt. I Ch. VIII (ss. 145-152) applied (1.1.1998) by S.I. 1997/3032, reg. 25. (2) (with Pt. IV)
145 The Copyright Tribunal.
(1) The Tribunal established under section 23 of the M12. Copyright Act 1956 is renamed the Copyright Tribunal.
(2) The Tribunal shall consist of a chairman and two deputy chairmen appointed by the Lord Chancellor, after consultation with the Lord Advocate, and not less than two or more than eight ordinary members appointed by the Secretary of State.

(3) A person is not eligible for appointment as chairman or deputy chairman [F323unless—

[F324. (a)he satisfies the judicial-appointment eligibility condition on a 5-year basis;]

(b) he is an advocate or solicitor in Scotland of at least [F3255] years' standing;

(c) he is a member of the Bar of Northern Ireland or [F326solicitor of the Court of Judicature of Northern Ireland] of at least [F3255] years' standing; or

(d) he has held judicial office.]

Amendments (Textual)

F323. Words substituted by Courts and Legal Services Act 1990 (c. 41, SIF 37), s. 71. (2), Sch. 10 para. 73

F324. S. 145. (3)(a) substituted (21.7.2008) by Tribunals, Courts and Enforcement Act 2007 (c. 15), ss. 50. (6), 148, Sch. 10 para. 20. (2); S.I. 2008/1653, art. 2. (b)(d) (with arts. 3, 4)

F325. Words in s. 145. (3)(b)(c) substituted (21.7.2008) by Tribunals, Courts and Enforcement Act 2007 (c.15), ss. 50. (6), 148, Sch. 10 para. 20. (3); S.I. 2008/1653, art. 2. (b)(d) (with arts. 3, 4)

F326. S. 145. (3)(c): words wherever they occur in any enactment substituted (1.10.2009) by virtue of Constitutional Reform Act 2005 (c. 4), ss. 59, 148, Sch. 11 para. 5; S.I. 2009/1604, art. 2

Modifications etc. (not altering text)

C66. S. 145: functions of the Lord Advocate transferred to the Secretary of State, and all property, rights and liabilities to which the Lord Advocate is entitled or subject in connection with any such function transferred to the Secretary of State for Scotland (19.5.1999) by S.I. 1999/678, arts. 2, 3, Sch. (with art. 7)

S. 145 modified (30.6.1999) by S.I. 1999/1748, art. 3, Sch. 1 para. 10

C67. S. 145. (2): transfer of certain functions (1.7.1999) by S.I. 1999/1750, arts. 1, 2, Sch. 1. (with art. 7); S.I. 1998/3178, art. 3

Marginal Citations

M121956 c. 74.

146 Membership of the Tribunal.

(1) The members of the Copyright Tribunal shall hold and vacate office in accordance with their terms of appointment, subject to the following provisions.

(2) A member of the Tribunal may resign his office by notice in writing to the Secretary of State or, in the case of the chairman or a deputy chairman, to the Lord Chancellor.

(3) The Secretary of State or, in the case of the chairman or a deputy chairman, the Lord Chancellor may by notice in writing to the member concerned remove him from office if—

(a) he has become bankrupt or made an arrangement with his creditors or, in Scotland, his estate has been sequestrated or he has executed a trust deed for his creditors or entered into a composition contract, or

(b) he is incapacitated by physical or mental illness,

or if he is in the opinion of the Secretary of State or, as the case may be, the Lord Chancellor otherwise unable or unfit to perform his duties as member.

[F327. (3. A)A person who is the chairman or a deputy chairman of the Tribunal shall vacate his office on the day on which he attains the age of 70 years; but this subsection is subject to section 26. (4) to (6) of the Judicial Pensions and Retirement Act 1993 (power to authorise continuance in office up to the age of 75 years).]

(4) If a member of the Tribunal is by reason of illness, absence or other reasonable cause for the time being unable to perform the duties of his office, either generally or in relation to particular proceedings, a person may be appointed to discharge his duties for a period not exceeding six months at one time or, as the case may be, in relation to those proceedings.

(5) The appointment shall be made—

(a) in the case of the chairman or deputy chairman, by the Lord Chancellor, who shall appoint a person who would be eligible for appointment to that office, and

(b) in the case of an ordinary member, by the Secretary of State;

and a person so appointed shall have during the period of his appointment, or in relation to the proceedings in question, the same powers as the person in whose place he is appointed.

(6) The Lord Chancellor shall consult the Lord Advocate before exercising his powers under this section.

[F328. (7)The Lord Chancellor may exercise his powers to remove a person under subsection (3) or to appoint a person under subsection (4) only with the concurrence of the appropriate senior judge.

(8) The appropriate senior judge is the Lord Chief Justice of England and Wales, unless—

(a) the person to be removed exercises functions [F329, or the person to be appointed is to exercise functions,] wholly or mainly in Scotland, in which case it is the Lord President of the Court of Session, or

(b) the person to be removed exercises functions [F329, or the person to be appointed is to exercise functions,] wholly or mainly in Northern Ireland, in which case it is the Lord Chief Justice of Northern Ireland.

(9) The Lord Chief Justice of England and Wales may nominate a judicial office holder (as defined in section 109. (4) of the Constitutional Reform Act 2005) to exercise his functions under subsection (7) in relation to the appointment of a person under subsection (4).

(10) The Lord President of the Court of Session may nominate a judge of the Court of Session who is a member of the First or Second Division of the Inner House of that Court to exercise his functions under subsection (7) in relation to the appointment of a person under subsection (4).

(11) The Lord Chief Justice of Northern Ireland may nominate any of the following to exercise his functions under subsection (7) in relation to the appointment of a person under subsection (4)—

(a) the holder of one of the offices listed in Schedule 1 to the Justice (Northern Ireland) Act 2002;

(b) a Lord Justice of Appeal (as defined in section 88 of that Act).]

Amendments (Textual)

F327. S. 146. (3. A) inserted (31.3.1995) by 1993 c. 8, s. 26, Sch. 6 para.49; S.I. 1995/631, art. 2

F328. S. 146. (7)-(11) inserted (3.4.2006) by Constitutional Reform Act 2005 (c. 4), ss. 15. (1), 148, Sch. 4 para. 199. (2); S.I. 2006/1014, art. 2. (a), Sch. 1 paras. 10, 11. (r)

F329. Words in s. 146. (8) inserted (3.4.2006) by The Lord Chancellor (Transfer of Functions and Supplementary Provisions) (No.2) Order 2006 (S.I. 2006/1016), art. 4, Sch. 3

147 Financial provisions.

(1) There shall be paid to the members of the Copyright Tribunal such remuneration (whether by way of salaries or fees), and such allowances, as the Secretary of State with the approval of the Treasury may determine.

(2) The Secretary of State may appoint such staff for the Tribunal as, with the approval of the Treasury as to numbers and remuneration, he may determine.

(3) The remuneration and allowances of members of the Tribunal, the remuneration of any staff and such other expenses of the Tribunal as the Secretary of State with the approval of the Treasury may determine shall be paid out of money provided by Parliament.

148 Constitution for purposes of proceedings.

(1) For the purposes of any proceedings the Copyright Tribunal shall consist of—

(a) a chairman, who shall be either the chairman or a deputy chairman of the Tribunal, and

(b) two or more ordinary members.

(2) If the members of the Tribunal dealing with any matter are not unanimous, the decision shall be taken by majority vote; and if, in such a case, the votes are equal the chairman shall have a further, casting vote.

(3) Where part of any proceedings before the Tribunal has been heard and one or more members of the Tribunal are unable to continue, the Tribunal shall remain duly constituted for the purpose of those proceedings so long as the number of members is not reduced to less than three.

(4) If the chairman is unable to continue, the chairman of the Tribunal shall—

(a) appoint one of the remaining members to act as chairman, and

(b) appoint a suitably qualified person to attend the proceedings and advise the members on any questions of law arising.

(5) A person is "suitably qualified" for the purposes of subsection (4)(b) if he is, or is eligible for

appointment as, a deputy chairman of the Tribunal.

Jurisdiction and procedure

149 Jurisdiction of the Tribunal.

[F330. The Copyright Tribunal has jurisdiction under this Part] to hear and determine proceedings under—

F331. (za). . . . .

F332 [(zb)section 93. C (application to determine amount of equitable remuneration under section 93. B);]

(a) section 118, 119, or 120 (reference of licensing scheme);

(b) section 121 or 122 (application with respect to entitlement to licence under licensing scheme);

(c) section 125, 126 or 127 (reference or application with respect to licensing by licensing body);

[F333. (ca)section 128. B (reference by the Secretary of State under section 128. A);]

[F334. (cc) section 135. D or 135. E (application or reference with respect to use as of right of sound recordings in broadcasts F335 . . .);]

(d) section 139 (appeal against order as to coverage of licensing scheme or licence);

(e) section 142 (application to settle royalty or other sum payable for [F336lending of certain works];

(f) section 144. (4) (application to settle terms of copyright licence available as of right);

[F337. (fa)paragraph 7 of Schedule ZA1 (application to determine compensation for use of orphan works).]

F338. (g). . . . .

F338. (h). . . . .

Amendments (Textual)

F330. Words in s. 149 substituted (1.12.1996) by S.I. 1996/2967, reg. 24. (2)(a) (with Pt. III)

F331. S. 149. (za) repealed (31.7.2017) by Digital Economy Act 2017 (c. 30), ss. 34. (2)(a)(ii), 118. (6); S.I. 2017/765, reg. 2. (n)

F332. S. 149. (zb) inserted (1.12.1996) by S.I. 1996/2967, reg. 14. (2) (with Pt. III)

F333. S. 149. (ca) inserted (31.10.2003) by The Copyright and Related Rights Regulations 2003 (S.I. 2003/2498), reg. 21. (6) (with regs. 31-40)

F334. S. 149. (cc) inserted by Broadcasting Act 1990 (c. 42, SIF 96), s. 175. (2)

F335. Words in s. 149. (cc) repealed (31.10.2003) by The Copyright and Related Rights Regulations 2003 (S.I. 2003/2498), reg. 2. (2), Sch. 2 (with regs. 31-40)

F336. Words in s. 149. (e) substituted (1.12.1996) by S.I. 1996/2967, reg. 13. (3) (with Pt. III)

F337. S. 149. (fa) inserted (29.10.2014) by The Copyright and Rights in Performances (Certain Permitted Uses of Orphan Works) Regulations 2014 (S.I. 2014/2861), regs. 1, 3. (3)

F338. S. 149. (g)(h) omitted (1.12.1996) by virtue of S.I. 1996/2967, reg. 24. (2)(b) (with Pt. III)

Modifications etc. (not altering text)

C68. S. 149 amended by Broadcasting Act 1990 (c. 42, SIF 96), s. 176, Sch. 17 para. 7. (1)

150 General power to make rules.

(1) The Lord Chancellor may, after consultation with the Lord Advocate, make rules for regulating proceedings before the Copyright Tribunal and, subject to the approval of the Treasury, as to the fees chargeable in respect of such proceedings.

F339[(2)The rules may apply in relation to the Tribunal, as respects proceedings in England and Wales or Northern Ireland, any of the provisions of Part I of the Arbitration Act 1996.]

(3) Provision shall be made by the rules—

(a) prohibiting the Tribunal from entertaining a reference under section 118, 119 or 120 by a representative organisation unless the Tribunal is satisfied that the organisation is reasonably representative of the class of persons which it claims to represent;

(b) specifying the parties to any proceedings and enabling the Tribunal to make a party to the proceedings any person or organisation satisfying the Tribunal that they have a substantial interest in the matter; and

(c) requiring the Tribunal to give the parties to proceedings an opportunity to state their case, in writing or orally as the rules may provide.

(4) The rules may make provision for regulating or prescribing any matters incidental to or consequential upon any appeal from the Tribunal under section 152 (appeal to the court on point of law).

(5) Rules under this section shall be made by statutory instrument which shall be subject to annulment in pursuance of a resolution of either House of Parliament.

Amendments (Textual)

F339. S. 150. (2) substituted (31.1.1997) by 1996 c. 23, s. 107. (1), Sch. 3 para. 50 (with s. 81. (2)); S.I. 1996/3146, art. 3 (with Sch. 2)

Modifications etc. (not altering text)

C69. S. 150: functions of the Lord Advocate transferred to the Secretary of State, and all property, rights and liabilities to which the Lord Advocate is entitled or subject in connection with any such function transferred to the Secretary of State for Scotland (19.5.1999) by S.I. 1999/678, arts. 2, 3, Sch. (with art. 7)

S. 150 modified (30.6.1999) by S.I. 1999/1748, art. 3, Sch. 1 para. 10

C70. S. 150. (1): transfer of certain functions (1.7.1999) by S.I. 1999/1750, arts. 1, 2, Sch. 1 (with art. 7); S.I. 1998/3178, art. 3

151 Costs, proof of orders, &c.

(1) The Copyright Tribunal may order that the costs of a party to proceedings before it shall be paid by such other party as the Tribunal may direct; and the Tribunal may tax or settle the amount of the costs, or direct in what manner they are to be taxed.

(2) A document purporting to be a copy of an order of the Tribunal and to be certified by the chairman to be a true copy shall, in any proceedings, be sufficient evidence of the order unless the contrary is proved.

(3) As respect proceedings in Scotland, the Tribunal has the like powers for securing the attendance of witnesses and the production of documents, and with regard to the examination of witnesses on oath, as an arbiter under a submission.

[F340151. A Award of interest.

(1) Any of the following, namely—

(a) a direction under section 123. (3) so far as relating to a licence for [F341communicating a work to the public];

(b) a direction under section 128. (3) so far as so relating;

(c) an order under section 135. D(1); and

(d) an order under section 135. F confirming or varying an order under section 135. D(1),

may award simple interest at such rate and for such period, beginning not earlier than the relevant date and ending not later than the date of the order, as the Copyright Tribunal thinks reasonable in the circumstances.

(2) In this section " the relevant date " means—

(a) in relation to a direction under section 123. (3), the date on which the reference was made;

(b) in relation to a direction under section 128. (3), the date on which the reference or application was made;

(c) in relation to an order section 135. D(1), the date on which the first payment under section 135. C(2) became due; and

(d) in relation to an order under section 135. F, the date on which the application was made.]

Amendments (Textual)

F340. S. 151. A inserted (1.11.1996 with effect as mentioned in s. 139. (3)) by 1996 c. 55, s. 139. (2) (with s. 43. (6)); S.I. 1996/2120, art. 5, Sch. 2

F341. Words in s. 151. A(1)(a) substituted (31.10.2003) by The Copyright and Related Rights Regulations 2003 (S.I.2003/2498), reg. 2. (1), Sch. 1 para. 7 (with regs. 31-40)

Appeals

152 Appeal to the court on point of law.

(1) An appeal lies on any point of law arising from a decision of the Copyright Tribunal to the High Court or, in the case of proceedings of the Tribunal in Scotland, to the Court of Session.

(2) Provision shall be made by rules under section 150 limiting the time within which an appeal may be brought.

(3) Provision may be made by rules under that section—

(a) for suspending, or authorising or requiring the Tribunal to suspend, the operation of orders of the Tribunal in cases where its decision is appealed against;

(b) for modifying in relation to an order of the Tribunal whose operation is suspended the operation of any provision of this Act as to the effect of the order;

(c) for the publication of notices or the taking of other steps for securing that persons affected by the suspension of an order of the Tribunal will be informed of its suspension.

Chapter IX Qualification for and Extent of Copyright Protection

153 Qualification for copyright protection.

(1) Copyright does not subsist in a work unless the qualification requirements of this Chapter are satisfied as regards—

(a) the author (see section 154), or

(b) the country in which the work was first published (see section 155), or

(c) in the case of a broadcast F342. . . , the country from which the broadcast was made F342. . . (see section 156).

(2) Subsection (1) does not apply in relation to Crown copyright or Parliamentary copyright (see sections 163 to [F343166. D]) or to copyright subsisting by virtue of section 168 (copyright of certain international organisations).

(3) If the qualification requirements of this Chapter, or section 163, 165 or 168, are once satisfied in respect of a work, copyright does not cease to subsist by reason of any subsequent event.

Amendments (Textual)

F342. Words in s. 153. (1)(c) repealed (31.10.2003) by The Copyright and Related Rights Regulations 2003 (S.I. 2003/2498), reg. 2. (2), Sch. 2 (with regs. 31-40)

F343. Word in s. 153. (2) substituted by Government of Wales Act 2006 (c. 32), s. 160. (1), Sch. 10 para. 25 (with Sch. 11 para. 22), the amending provision coming into force immediately after "the 2007 election" (held on 3.5.2007) subject to s. 161. (4)(5) of the amending Act, which provides for certain provisions to come into force for specified purposes immediately after the end of "the initial period" (which ended with the day of the first appointment of a First Minister on 25.5.2007) - see ss. 46, 161. (1)(4)(5) of the amending Act.

Modifications etc. (not altering text)

C71. Ss. 153, 154 extended by S.I. 1989/988, art. 2. (1)

C72. S. 153 extended (1.7.1992) by S.I. 1992/1313, art. 2

C73. Ss. 153, 154 applied (with modifications) (4.5.1993) by S.I. 1993/942, arts. 2, 3, 4, 5, Sch. 4 (with art. 6)

Ss. 153-155 applied (with modifications) (22.7.1999) by S.I. 1999/1751, arts. 2. (1)(2), 5, Sch. 1, Sch. 5 (as amended 22.4.2003 by S.I. 2003/774, arts. 2-5)

Ss. 153, 154, 155 applied (with modifications) (22.7.1999) by S.I. 1999/1751, arts. 2. (1)(2), 3, 5, Sch. 1, Sch. 2, Sch. 5 (as amended 22.4.2003 by S.I. 2003/774, arts. 2-5)

Ss. 153, 154, 156 applied (with modifications) (22.7.1999) by S.I. 1999/1751, arts. 4. (1)(2)(5), 5 (as amended 22.4.2003 by S.I. 2003/774, arts. 2-5)

154 Qualification by reference to author.

(1) A work qualifies for copyright protection if the author was at the material time a qualifying

person, that is—

(a) a British citizen, [F344a national of another EEA state,] a British Dependent Territories citizen, a British National (Overseas), a British Overseas citizen, a British subject or a British protected person within the meaning of the M13. British Nationality Act 1981, or

[F345. (b)an individual domiciled or resident in the United Kingdom or another EEA state or in the Channel Islands, the Isle of Man or Gibraltar or in a country to which the relevant provisions of this Part extend,] or

[F346. (c)a body incorporated under the law of a part of the United Kingdom or another EEA state or of the Channel Islands, the Isle of Man or Gibraltar or of a country to which the relevant provisions of this Part extend.]

(2) Where, or so far as, provision is made by Order under section 159 (application of this Part to countries to which it does not extend), a work also qualifies for copyright protection if at the material time the author was a citizen or subject of, an individual domiciled or resident in, or a body incorporated under the law of, a country to which the Order relates.

(3) A work of joint authorship qualifies for copyright protection if at the material time any of the authors satisfies the requirements of subsection (1) or (2); but where a work qualifies for copyright protection only under this section, only those authors who satisfy those requirements shall be taken into account for the purposes of—

section 11. (1) and (2) (first ownership of copyright; entitlement of author or author's employer), [F347section 12 (duration of copyright), and section 9. (4) (meaning of "unknown authorship") so far as it applies for the purposes of section 12, and]

- section 57 (anonymous or pseudonymous works: acts permitted on assumptions as to expiry of copyright or death of author).

(4) The material time in relation to a literary, dramatic, musical or artistic work is—

(a) in the case of an unpublished work, when the work was made or, if the making of the work extended over a period, a substantial part of that period;

(b) in the case of a published work, when the work was first published or, if the author had died before that time, immediately before his death.

(5) The material time in relation to other descriptions of work is as follows—

(a) in the case of a sound recording or film, when it was made;

(b) in the case of a broadcast, when the broadcast was made;

(c) F348. . . . .

(d) in the case of the typographical arrangement of a published edition, when the edition was first published.

Amendments (Textual)

F344. Words in s. 154. (1)(a) inserted (1.12.2016 for specified purposes, 6.4.2017 in so far as not already in force) by Intellectual Property Act 2014 (c. 18), ss. 22. (1)(a), 24. (1); S.I. 2016/1139, arts. 2, 3 (with art. 4)

F345. S. 154. (1)(b) substituted (1.12.2016 for specified purposes, 6.4.2017 in so far as not already in force) by Intellectual Property Act 2014 (c. 18), ss. 22. (1)(b), 24. (1); S.I. 2016/1139, arts. 2, 3 (with art. 4)

F346. S. 154. (1)(c) substituted (1.12.2016 for specified purposes, 6.4.2017 in so far as not already in force) by Intellectual Property Act 2014 (c. 18), ss. 22. (1)(c), 24. (1); S.I. 2016/1139, arts. 2, 3 (with art. 4)

F347. Paragraph in s. 154. (3) substituted (1.1.1996) by S.I. 1995/3297, reg. 5. (3) (with Pt. III)

F348. S. 154. (5)(c) repealed (31.10.2003) by The Copyright and Related Rights Regulations 2003 (S.I. 2003/2498), reg. 2. (2), Sch. 2 (with regs. 31-40)

Modifications etc. (not altering text)

C15. Pt. 1 applied (with modifications) (6.4.2017) by The Copyright and Performances (Application to Other Countries) Order 2016 (S.I. 2016/1219), arts. 1. (1), 4 (with art. 13)

C16. Pt. 1 restricted (6.4.2017) by The Copyright and Performances (Application to Other Countries) Order 2016 (S.I. 2016/1219), arts. 1. (1), 6 (with art. 13)

C17. Pt. 1 restricted (6.4.2017) by The Copyright and Performances (Application to Other

Countries) Order 2016 (S.I. 2016/1219), arts. 1. (1), 9 (with art. 13)

C18. Pt. 1 applied (with modifications) (6.4.2017) by The Copyright and Performances (Application to Other Countries) Order 2016 (S.I. 2016/1219), arts. 1. (1), 7 (with art. 13)

C19. Pt. 1 restricted (6.4.2017) by The Copyright and Performances (Application to Other Countries) Order 2016 (S.I. 2016/1219), arts. 1. (1), 2 (with art. 13)

C20. Pt. 1 restricted (6.4.2017) by The Copyright and Performances (Application to Other Countries) Order 2016 (S.I. 2016/1219), arts. 1. (1), 3 (with art. 13)

C21. Pt. 1 applied (with modifications) (6.4.2017) by The Copyright and Performances (Application to Other Countries) Order 2016 (S.I. 2016/1219), arts. 1. (1), 5, Sch. Pt. 1 (with art. 13)

C22. Pt. 1 applied (with modifications) (6.4.2017) by The Copyright and Performances (Application to Other Countries) Order 2016 (S.I. 2016/1219), arts. 1. (1), 8 (with art. 13)

C74. Ss. 153, 154 extended by S.I. 1989/988, art. 2. (1)

C75. S. 154 extended (1.7.1992) by S.I. 1992/1313, art. 2

C76. Ss. 153, 154 applied (with modifications) (4.5.1993) by S.I. 1993/942, arts. 2, 3, 4, 5, Sch. 4 (with art. 6)

Ss. 153-155 applied (with modifications) (22.7.1999) by S.I. 1999/1751, arts. 2. (1)(2), 5, Sch. 1, Sch. 5 (as amended 22.4.2003 by S.I. 2003/774, arts. 2-5)

Ss. 153, 154, 155 applied (with modifications) (22.7.1999) by S.I. 1999/1751, arts. 2. (1)(2), 3, 5, Sch. 1, Sch. 2, Sch. 5 (as amended 22.4.2003 by S.I. 2003/774, arts. 2-5)

Ss. 153, 154, 156 applied (with modifications) (22.7.1999) by S.I. 1999/1751, arts. 4. (1)(2)(5), 5, Sch. 5 (as amended 22.4.2003 by S.I. 2003/774, arts. 2-5)

Marginal Citations

M131981 c. 61.

155 Qualification by reference to country of first publication.

(1) A literary, dramatic, musical or artistic work, a sound recording or film, or the typographical arrangement of a published edition, qualifies for copyright protection if it is first published—

(a) in the United Kingdom[F349, another EEA state, the Channel Islands, the Isle of Man or Gibraltar], or

(b) in [F350a country] to which the relevant provisions of this Part extend.

(2) Where, or so far as, provision is made by Order under section 159 (application of this Part to countries to which it does not extend), such a work also qualifies for copyright protection if it is first published in a country to which the Order relates.

(3) For the purposes of this section, publication in one country shall not be regarded as other than the first publication by reason of simultaneous publication elsewhere; and for this purpose publication elsewhere within the previous 30 days shall be treated as simultaneous.

Amendments (Textual)

F349. Words in s. 155. (1)(a) inserted (1.12.2016 for specified purposes, 6.4.2017 in so far as not already in force) by Intellectual Property Act 2014 (c. 18), ss. 22. (2)(a), 24. (1); S.I. 2016/1139, arts. 2, 3 (with art. 4)

F350. Words in s. 155. (1)(b) substituted (1.12.2016 for specified purposes, 6.4.2017 in so far as not already in force) by Intellectual Property Act 2014 (c. 18), ss. 22. (2)(b), 24. (1); S.I. 2016/1139, arts. 2, 3 (with art. 4)

Modifications etc. (not altering text)

C15. Pt. 1 applied (with modifications) (6.4.2017) by The Copyright and Performances (Application to Other Countries) Order 2016 (S.I. 2016/1219), arts. 1. (1), 4 (with art. 13)

C16. Pt. 1 restricted (6.4.2017) by The Copyright and Performances (Application to Other Countries) Order 2016 (S.I. 2016/1219), arts. 1. (1), 6 (with art. 13)

C17. Pt. 1 restricted (6.4.2017) by The Copyright and Performances (Application to Other Countries) Order 2016 (S.I. 2016/1219), arts. 1. (1), 9 (with art. 13)

C18. Pt. 1 applied (with modifications) (6.4.2017) by The Copyright and Performances (Application to Other Countries) Order 2016 (S.I. 2016/1219), arts. 1. (1), 7 (with art. 13)

C19. Pt. 1 restricted (6.4.2017) by The Copyright and Performances (Application to Other

Countries) Order 2016 (S.I. 2016/1219), arts. 1. (1), 2 (with art. 13)

C20. Pt. 1 restricted (6.4.2017) by The Copyright and Performances (Application to Other Countries) Order 2016 (S.I. 2016/1219), arts. 1. (1), 3 (with art. 13)

C21. Pt. 1 applied (with modifications) (6.4.2017) by The Copyright and Performances (Application to Other Countries) Order 2016 (S.I. 2016/1219), arts. 1. (1), 5, Sch. Pt. 1 (with art. 13)

C22. Pt. 1 applied (with modifications) (6.4.2017) by The Copyright and Performances (Application to Other Countries) Order 2016 (S.I. 2016/1219), arts. 1. (1), 8 (with art. 13)

C77. S. 155 extended with modifications by S.I. 1989/1293, arts. 2. (1), 3, 5, 6, Schs. 1, 2, 3, 4

C78. S. 155 extended (1.7.1992) by S.I. 1992/1313, art.2

C79. S. 155 applied (with modifications) (4.5.1993) by S.I. 1993/942, arts.2, 3, 5, Sch. 4 (with art. 6)

Ss. 153-155 applied (with modifications) (22.7.1999) by S.I. 1999/1751, arts. 2. (1)(2), 5, Sch. 1, Sch. 5 (as amended 22.4.2003 by S.I. 2003/774, arts. 2-5)

Ss. 153, 154, 155 applied (with modifications) (22.7.1999) by S.I. 1999/1751, arts. 2. (1)(2), 3, 5, Sch. 1, Sch. 2, Sch. 5 (as amended 22.4.2003 by S.I. 2003/774, arts. 2-5)

156 Qualification by reference to place of transmission.

(1) F351. A broadcast qualifies for copyright protection if it is made from . . . a place in—

(a) the United Kingdom[F352, another EEA state, the Channel Islands, the Isle of Man or Gibraltar], or

(b) [F353a country] to which the relevant provisions of this Part extend.

(2) Where, or so far as, provision is made by Order under section 159 (application of this Part to countries to which it does not extend), a broadcast F351. . . also qualifies for copyright protection if it is made from F351. . . a place in a country to which the Order relates.

Amendments (Textual)

F351. Words in s. 156. (1)(2) repealed (31.10.2003) by The Copyright and Related Rights Regulations 2003 (S.I. 2003/2498), reg. 2. (2), Sch. 2 (with regs. 31-40)

F352. Words in s. 156. (1)(a) inserted (1.12.2016 for specified purposes, 6.4.2017 in so far as not already in force) by Intellectual Property Act 2014 (c. 18), ss. 22. (3)(a), 24. (1); S.I. 2016/1139, arts. 2, 3 (with art. 4)

F353. Words in s. 156. (1)(b) substituted (1.12.2016 for specified purposes, 6.4.2017 in so far as not already in force) by Intellectual Property Act 2014 (c. 18), ss. 22. (3)(b), 24. (1); S.I. 2016/1139, arts. 2, 3 (with art. 4)

Modifications etc. (not altering text)

C15. Pt. 1 applied (with modifications) (6.4.2017) by The Copyright and Performances (Application to Other Countries) Order 2016 (S.I. 2016/1219), arts. 1. (1), 4 (with art. 13)

C16. Pt. 1 restricted (6.4.2017) by The Copyright and Performances (Application to Other Countries) Order 2016 (S.I. 2016/1219), arts. 1. (1), 6 (with art. 13)

C17. Pt. 1 restricted (6.4.2017) by The Copyright and Performances (Application to Other Countries) Order 2016 (S.I. 2016/1219), arts. 1. (1), 9 (with art. 13)

C18. Pt. 1 applied (with modifications) (6.4.2017) by The Copyright and Performances (Application to Other Countries) Order 2016 (S.I. 2016/1219), arts. 1. (1), 7 (with art. 13)

C19. Pt. 1 restricted (6.4.2017) by The Copyright and Performances (Application to Other Countries) Order 2016 (S.I. 2016/1219), arts. 1. (1), 2 (with art. 13)

C20. Pt. 1 restricted (6.4.2017) by The Copyright and Performances (Application to Other Countries) Order 2016 (S.I. 2016/1219), arts. 1. (1), 3 (with art. 13)

C21. Pt. 1 applied (with modifications) (6.4.2017) by The Copyright and Performances (Application to Other Countries) Order 2016 (S.I. 2016/1219), arts. 1. (1), 5, Sch. Pt. 1 (with art. 13)

C22. Pt. 1 applied (with modifications) (6.4.2017) by The Copyright and Performances (Application to Other Countries) Order 2016 (S.I. 2016/1219), arts. 1. (1), 8 (with art. 13)

C80. S. 156 extended (1.7.1992) by S.I. 1992/1313, art.2

C81. S. 156 applied (with modifications) (4.5.1993) by S.I. 1993/942, art.4, 5, Sch. 4 (with art. 6)

Ss. 153, 154, 156 applied (with modifications) (22.7.1999) by S.I. 1999/1751, arts. 4. (1)(2)(5), 5 (as amended 22.4.2003 by S.I. 2003/774, arts. 2-5)

Extent and application of this Part

157 Countries to which this Part extends.

(1) This Part extends to England and Wales, Scotland and Northern Ireland.

(2) Her Majesty may by Order in Council direct that this Part shall extend, subject to such exceptions and modifications as may be specified in the Order, to—

(a) any of the Channel Islands,

(b) the Isle of Man, or

(c) any colony.

(3) That power includes power to extend, subject to such exceptions and modifications as may be specified in the Order, any Order in Council made under the following provisions of this Chapter.

(4) The legislature of a country to which this Part has been extended may modify or add to the provisions of this Part, in their operation as part of the law of that country, as the legislature may consider necessary to adapt the provisions to the circumstances of that country—

(a) as regards procedure and remedies, or

(b) as regards works qualifying for copyright protection by virtue of a connection with that country.

(5) Nothing in this section shall be construed as restricting the extent of paragraph 36 of Schedule 1 (transitional provisions: dependent territories where the M14. Copyright Act 1956 or the M15. Copyright Act 1911 remains in force) in relation to the law of a dependent territory to which this Part does not extend.

Modifications etc. (not altering text)

C15. Pt. 1 applied (with modifications) (6.4.2017) by The Copyright and Performances (Application to Other Countries) Order 2016 (S.I. 2016/1219), arts. 1. (1), 4 (with art. 13)

C16. Pt. 1 restricted (6.4.2017) by The Copyright and Performances (Application to Other Countries) Order 2016 (S.I. 2016/1219), arts. 1. (1), 6 (with art. 13)

C17. Pt. 1 restricted (6.4.2017) by The Copyright and Performances (Application to Other Countries) Order 2016 (S.I. 2016/1219), arts. 1. (1), 9 (with art. 13)

C18. Pt. 1 applied (with modifications) (6.4.2017) by The Copyright and Performances (Application to Other Countries) Order 2016 (S.I. 2016/1219), arts. 1. (1), 7 (with art. 13)

C19. Pt. 1 restricted (6.4.2017) by The Copyright and Performances (Application to Other Countries) Order 2016 (S.I. 2016/1219), arts. 1. (1), 2 (with art. 13)

C20. Pt. 1 restricted (6.4.2017) by The Copyright and Performances (Application to Other Countries) Order 2016 (S.I. 2016/1219), arts. 1. (1), 3 (with art. 13)

C21. Pt. 1 applied (with modifications) (6.4.2017) by The Copyright and Performances (Application to Other Countries) Order 2016 (S.I. 2016/1219), arts. 1. (1), 5, Sch. Pt. 1 (with art. 13)

C22. Pt. 1 applied (with modifications) (6.4.2017) by The Copyright and Performances (Application to Other Countries) Order 2016 (S.I. 2016/1219), arts. 1. (1), 8 (with art. 13)

C23. Pt. 1: power to extend conferred (27.4.2017) by Digital Economy Act 2017 (c. 30), ss. 118. (1), 119. (7)(8)(a)

C82. S. 157. (2)(c) extended (8.4.2010) by Digital Economy Act 2010 (c. 24), ss. 46. (4), 47. (2)(c)

C83. S. 157. (2)(c): power to extend conferred (27.4.2017) by Digital Economy Act 2017 (c. 30), ss. 118. (1), 119. (9)

Marginal Citations

M141956 c. 74.

M151911 c. 46.

158 Countries ceasing to be colonies.

(1) The following provisions apply where a country to which this Part has been extended ceases to be a colony of the United Kingdom.

(2) As from the date on which it ceases to be a colony it shall cease to be regarded as a country to which this Part extends for the purposes of—

(a) section 160. (2)(a) (denial of copyright protection to citizens of countries not giving adequate protection to British works), and

(b) sections 163 and 165 (Crown and Parliamentary copyright).

(3) But it shall continue to be treated as a country to which this Part extends for the purposes of sections 154 to 156 (qualification for copyright protection) until—

(a) an Order in Council is made in respect of that country under section 159 (application of this Part to countries to which it does not extend), or

(b) an Order in Council is made declaring that it shall cease to be so treated by reason of the fact that the provisions of this Part as part of the law of that country have been repealed or amended.

(4) A statutory instrument containing an Order in Council under subsection (3)(b) shall be subject to annulment in pursuance of a resolution of either House of Parliament.

Modifications etc. (not altering text)

C15. Pt. 1 applied (with modifications) (6.4.2017) by The Copyright and Performances (Application to Other Countries) Order 2016 (S.I. 2016/1219), arts. 1. (1), 4 (with art. 13)

C16. Pt. 1 restricted (6.4.2017) by The Copyright and Performances (Application to Other Countries) Order 2016 (S.I. 2016/1219), arts. 1. (1), 6 (with art. 13)

C17. Pt. 1 restricted (6.4.2017) by The Copyright and Performances (Application to Other Countries) Order 2016 (S.I. 2016/1219), arts. 1. (1), 9 (with art. 13)

C18. Pt. 1 applied (with modifications) (6.4.2017) by The Copyright and Performances (Application to Other Countries) Order 2016 (S.I. 2016/1219), arts. 1. (1), 7 (with art. 13)

C19. Pt. 1 restricted (6.4.2017) by The Copyright and Performances (Application to Other Countries) Order 2016 (S.I. 2016/1219), arts. 1. (1), 2 (with art. 13)

C20. Pt. 1 restricted (6.4.2017) by The Copyright and Performances (Application to Other Countries) Order 2016 (S.I. 2016/1219), arts. 1. (1), 3 (with art. 13)

C21. Pt. 1 applied (with modifications) (6.4.2017) by The Copyright and Performances (Application to Other Countries) Order 2016 (S.I. 2016/1219), arts. 1. (1), 5, Sch. Pt. 1 (with art. 13)

C22. Pt. 1 applied (with modifications) (6.4.2017) by The Copyright and Performances (Application to Other Countries) Order 2016 (S.I. 2016/1219), arts. 1. (1), 8 (with art. 13)

C23. Pt. 1: power to extend conferred (27.4.2017) by Digital Economy Act 2017 (c. 30), ss. 118. (1), 119. (7)(8)(a)

[F354159. Application of this Part to countries to which it does not extend

(1) Where a country is a party to the Berne Convention or a member of the World Trade Organisation, this Part, so far as it relates to literary, dramatic, musical and artistic works, films and typographical arrangements of published editions—

(a) applies in relation to a citizen or subject of that country or a person domiciled or resident there as it applies in relation to a person who is a British citizen or is domiciled or resident in the United Kingdom,

(b) applies in relation to a body incorporated under the law of that country as it applies in relation to a body incorporated under the law of a part of the United Kingdom, and

(c) applies in relation to a work first published in that country as it applies in relation to a work first published in the United Kingdom.

(2) Where a country is a party to the Rome Convention, this Part, so far as it relates to sound recordings and broadcasts—

(a) applies in relation to that country as mentioned in paragraphs (a), (b) and (c) of subsection (1), and

(b) applies in relation to a broadcast made from that country as it applies to a broadcast made from the United Kingdom.

(3) Where a country is a party to the WPPT, this Part, so far as relating to sound recordings,

applies in relation to that country as mentioned in paragraphs (a), (b) and (c) of subsection (1).

(4) Her Majesty may by Order in Council—

(a) make provision for the application of this Part to a country by subsection (1), (2) or (3) to be subject to specified restrictions;

(b) make provision for applying this Part, or any of its provisions, to a specified country;

(c) make provision for applying this Part, or any of its provisions, to any country of a specified description;

(d) make provision for the application of legislation to a country under paragraph (b) or (c) to be subject to specified restrictions.

(5) Provision made under subsection (4) may apply generally or in relation to such classes of works, or other classes of case, as are specified.

(6) Her Majesty may not make an Order in Council containing provision under subsection (4)(b) or (c) unless satisfied that provision has been or will be made under the law of the country or countries in question, in respect of the classes to which the provision under subsection (4)(b) or (c) relates, giving adequate protection to the owners of copyright under this Part.

(7) Application under subsection (4)(b) or (c) is in addition to application by subsections (1) to (3).

(8) Provision made under subsection (4)(c) may cover countries that become (or again become) of the specified description after the provision comes into force.

(9) In this section—

"the Berne Convention" means any Act of the International Convention for the Protection of Literary and Artistic Works signed at Berne on 9 September 1886;

"the Rome Convention" means the International Convention for the Protection of Performers, Producers of Phonograms and Broadcasting Organisations done at Rome on 26 October 1961;

"the WPPT" means the World Intellectual Property Organisation Performances and Phonograms Treaty adopted in Geneva on 20 December 1996.

(10) A statutory instrument containing an Order in Council under this section is subject to annulment in pursuance of a resolution of either House of Parliament.]

Amendments (Textual)

F354. S. 159 substituted (1.12.2016 for specified purposes, 6.4.2017 in so far as not already in force) by Intellectual Property Act 2014 (c. 18), ss. 22. (4), 24. (1); S.I. 2016/1139, arts. 2, 3 (with art. 4)

Modifications etc. (not altering text)

C15. Pt. 1 applied (with modifications) (6.4.2017) by The Copyright and Performances (Application to Other Countries) Order 2016 (S.I. 2016/1219), arts. 1. (1), 4 (with art. 13)

C16. Pt. 1 restricted (6.4.2017) by The Copyright and Performances (Application to Other Countries) Order 2016 (S.I. 2016/1219), arts. 1. (1), 6 (with art. 13)

C17. Pt. 1 restricted (6.4.2017) by The Copyright and Performances (Application to Other Countries) Order 2016 (S.I. 2016/1219), arts. 1. (1), 9 (with art. 13)

C18. Pt. 1 applied (with modifications) (6.4.2017) by The Copyright and Performances (Application to Other Countries) Order 2016 (S.I. 2016/1219), arts. 1. (1), 7 (with art. 13)

C19. Pt. 1 restricted (6.4.2017) by The Copyright and Performances (Application to Other Countries) Order 2016 (S.I. 2016/1219), arts. 1. (1), 2 (with art. 13)

C20. Pt. 1 restricted (6.4.2017) by The Copyright and Performances (Application to Other Countries) Order 2016 (S.I. 2016/1219), arts. 1. (1), 3 (with art. 13)

C21. Pt. 1 applied (with modifications) (6.4.2017) by The Copyright and Performances (Application to Other Countries) Order 2016 (S.I. 2016/1219), arts. 1. (1), 5, Sch. Pt. 1 (with art. 13)

C22. Pt. 1 applied (with modifications) (6.4.2017) by The Copyright and Performances (Application to Other Countries) Order 2016 (S.I. 2016/1219), arts. 1. (1), 8 (with art. 13)

C23. Pt. 1: power to extend conferred (27.4.2017) by Digital Economy Act 2017 (c. 30), ss. 118. (1), 119. (7)(8)(a)

160 Denial of copyright protection to citizens of countries not giving adequate protection to British works.

(1) If it appears to Her Majesty that the law of a country fails to give adequate protection to British works to which this section applies, or to one or more classes of such works, Her Majesty may make provision by Order in Council in accordance with this section restricting the rights conferred by this Part in relation to works of authors connected with that country.

(2) An Order in Council under this section shall designate the country concerned and provide that, for the purposes specified in the Order, works first published after a date specified in the Order shall not be treated as qualifying for copyright protection by virtue of such publication if at that time the authors are—

(a) citizens or subjects of that country (not domiciled or resident in the United Kingdom or another country to which the relevant provisions of this Part extend), or

(b) bodies incorporated under the law of that country;

and the Order may make such provision for all the purposes of this Part or for such purposes as are specified in the Order, and either generally or in relation to such class of cases as are specified in the Order, having regard to the nature and extent of that failure referred to in subsection (1).

(3) This section applies to literary, dramatic, musical and artistic works, sound recordings and films; and "British works" means works of which the author was a qualifying person at the material time within the meaning of section 154.

(4) A statutory instrument containing an Order in Council under this section shall be subject to annulment in pursuance of a resolution of either House of Parliament.

Modifications etc. (not altering text)

C15. Pt. 1 applied (with modifications) (6.4.2017) by The Copyright and Performances (Application to Other Countries) Order 2016 (S.I. 2016/1219), arts. 1. (1), 4 (with art. 13)

C16. Pt. 1 restricted (6.4.2017) by The Copyright and Performances (Application to Other Countries) Order 2016 (S.I. 2016/1219), arts. 1. (1), 6 (with art. 13)

C17. Pt. 1 restricted (6.4.2017) by The Copyright and Performances (Application to Other Countries) Order 2016 (S.I. 2016/1219), arts. 1. (1), 9 (with art. 13)

C18. Pt. 1 applied (with modifications) (6.4.2017) by The Copyright and Performances (Application to Other Countries) Order 2016 (S.I. 2016/1219), arts. 1. (1), 7 (with art. 13)

C19. Pt. 1 restricted (6.4.2017) by The Copyright and Performances (Application to Other Countries) Order 2016 (S.I. 2016/1219), arts. 1. (1), 2 (with art. 13)

C20. Pt. 1 restricted (6.4.2017) by The Copyright and Performances (Application to Other Countries) Order 2016 (S.I. 2016/1219), arts. 1. (1), 3 (with art. 13)

C21. Pt. 1 applied (with modifications) (6.4.2017) by The Copyright and Performances (Application to Other Countries) Order 2016 (S.I. 2016/1219), arts. 1. (1), 5, Sch. Pt. 1 (with art. 13)

C22. Pt. 1 applied (with modifications) (6.4.2017) by The Copyright and Performances (Application to Other Countries) Order 2016 (S.I. 2016/1219), arts. 1. (1), 8 (with art. 13)

C23. Pt. 1: power to extend conferred (27.4.2017) by Digital Economy Act 2017 (c. 30), ss. 118. (1), 119. (7)(8)(a)

Supplementary

161 Territorial waters and the continental shelf.

(1) For the purposes of this Part the territorial waters of the United Kingdom shall be treated as part of the United Kingdom.

(2) This Part applies to things done in the United Kingdom sector of the continental shelf on a structure or vessel which is present there for purposes directly connected with the exploration of the sea bed or subsoil or the exploitation of their natural resources as it applies to things done in the United Kingdom.

(3) The United Kingdom sector of the continental shelf means the areas designated by order under section 1. (7) of the M16. Continental Shelf Act 1964.

Modifications etc. (not altering text)

C84. Ss. 161, 162, 171. (1)(3), 172-179 applied (1.12.1996) by S.I. 1996/2967, reg. 17. (4) (with Pt. III)

Marginal Citations

M161964 c. 29.

162 British ships, aircraft and hovercraft.

(1) This Part applies to things done on a British ship, aircraft or hovercraft as it applies to things done in the United Kingdom.

(2) In this section—

"British ship" means a ship which is a British ship for the purposes of the [F355. Merchant Shipping Act 1995] otherwise than by virtue of registration in a country outside the United Kingdom; and

"British aircraft" and "British hovercraft" mean an aircraft or hovercraft registered in the United Kingdom.

Amendments (Textual)

F355. Words in s. 162. (2) substituted (1.1.1996) by 1995 c. 21, ss. 314. (2), 316. (2), Sch. 13 para. 84. (a) (with s. 312. (1))

Modifications etc. (not altering text)

C85. Ss. 161, 162, 171. (1)(3), 172-179 applied (1.12.1996) by S.I. 1996/2967, reg. 17. (4) (with Pt. III)

Chapter X Miscellaneous and General

163 Crown copyright.

(1) Where a work is made by Her Majesty or by an officer or servant of the Crown in the course of his duties—

(a) the work qualifies for copyright protection notwithstanding section 153. (1) (ordinary requirement as to qualification for copyright protection), and

(b) Her Majesty is the first owner of any copyright in the work.

(1. A)F356. . . . .

(2) Copyright in such a work is referred to in this Part as "Crown copyright", notwithstanding that it may be, or have been, assigned to another person.

(3) Crown copyright in a literary, dramatic, musical or artistic work continues to subsist—

(a) until the end of the period of 125 years from the end of the calendar year in which the work was made, or

(b) if the work is published commercially before the end of the period of 75 years from the end of the calendar year in which it was made, until the end of the period of 50 years from the end of the calendar year in which it was first so published.

(4) In the case of a work of joint authorship where one or more but not all of the authors are persons falling within subsection (1), this section applies only in relation to those authors and the copyright subsisting by virtue of their contribution to the work.

(5) Except as mentioned above, and subject to any express exclusion elsewhere in this Part, the provisions of this Part apply in relation to Crown copyright as to other copyright.

(6) This section does not apply to a work if, or to the extent that, Parliamentary copyright subsists in the work (see sections 165 [F357to [F358166. D]]).

Amendments (Textual)

F356. S. 163. (1. A) repealed by Government of Wales Act 2006 (c. 32), ss. 160. (1), 163, Sch. 10 para. 26. (2), Sch. 12 (with Sch. 11 para. 22), the amending provision coming into force immediately after "the 2007 election" (held on 3.5.2007) subject to s. 161. (4)(5) of the amending Act, which provides for certain provisions to come into force for specified purposes immediately after the end of "the initial period" (which ended with the day of the first appointment of a First Minister on 25.5.2007) - see ss. 46, 161. (1)(4)(5) of the amending Act.

F357. Words in s. 163. (6) substituted (6.5.1999) by 1998 c. 46, s. 125. (1), Sch. 8 para. 25. (4);

S.I. 1998/3178, art. 2. (2), Sch. 3

F358. Word in s. 163. (6) substituted by Government of Wales Act 2006 (c. 32), s. 160. (1), Sch. 10 para. 26. (3) (with Sch. 11 para. 22), the amending provision coming into force immediately after "the 2007 election" (held on 3.5.2007) subject to s. 161. (4)(5) of the amending Act, which provides for certain provisions to come into force for specified purposes immediately after the end of "the initial period" (which ended with the day of the first appointment of a First Minister on 25.5.2007) - see ss. 46, 161. (1)(4)(5) of the amending Act.

164 Copyright in Acts and Measures.

(1) Her Majesty is entitled to copyright in every Act of Parliament [F359. Act of the Scottish Parliament][F360, [F361. Measure of the National Assembly for Wales, Act of the National Assembly for Wales,] Act of the Northern Ireland Assembly] or Measure of the General Synod of the Church of England.

(2) The copyright subsists

[F362. (a)in the case of an Act or a Measure of the General Synod of the Church of England, until the end of the period of 50 years from the end of the calendar year in which Royal Assent was given, and

(b) in the case of a Measure of the National Assembly for Wales, until the end of the period of 50 years from the end of the calendar year in which the Measure was approved by Her Majesty in Council.]

(3) References in this Part to Crown copyright (except in section 163) include copyright under this section; and, except as mentioned above, the provisions of this Part apply in relation to copyright under this section as to other Crown copyright.

(4) No other copyright, or right in the nature of copyright, subsists in an Act or Measure.

Amendments (Textual)

F359. Words in s. 164. (1) inserted (6.5.1999) by 1998 c. 46, s. 125. (1), Sch. 8 para. 25. (5); S.I. 1998/3178, art. 2. (2), Sch. 3

F360. Words in s. 164. (1) inserted (2.12.1999) by 1998 c. 47, s. 99, Sch. 13 para. 8. (5) (with s. 95); S.I. 1999/3209, art. 2, Sch.

F361. Words in s. 164. (1) inserted by Government of Wales Act 2006 (c. 32), s. 160. (1), Sch. 10 para. 27. (2) (with Sch. 11 para. 22), the amending provision coming into force immediately after "the 2007 election" (held on 3.5.2007) subject to s. 161. (4)(5) of the amending Act, which provides for certain provisions to come into force for specified purposes immediately after the end of "the initial period" (which ended with the day of the first appointment of a First Minister on 25.5.2007) - see ss. 46, 161. (1)(4)(5) of the amending Act.

F362. S. 164. (2)(a)(b) substituted for words in s. 164. (2) by Government of Wales Act 2006 (c. 32), s. 160. (1), Sch. 10 para. 27. (3) (with Sch. 11 para. 22), the amending provision coming into force immediately after "the 2007 election" (held on 3.5.2007) subject to s. 161. (4)(5) of the amending Act, which provides for certain provisions to come into force for specified purposes immediately after the end of "the initial period" (which ended with the day of the first appointment of a First Minister on 25.5.2007) - see ss. 46, 161. (1)(4)(5) of the amending Act.

165 Parliamentary copyright.

(1) Where a work is made by or under the direction or control of the House of Commons or the House of Lords—

(a) the work qualifies for copyright protection notwithstanding section 153. (1) (ordinary requirement as to qualification for copyright protection), and

(b) the House by whom, or under whose direction or control, the work is made is the first owner of any copyright in the work, and if the work is made by or under the direction or control of both Houses, the two Houses are joint first owners of copyright.

(2) Copyright in such a work is referred to in this Part as "Parliamentary copyright", notwithstanding that it may be, or have been, assigned to another person.

(3) Parliamentary copyright in a literary, dramatic, musical or artistic work continues to subsist until the end of the period of 50 years from the end of the calendar year in which the work was made.

(4) For the purposes of this section, works made by or under the direction or control of the House of Commons or the House of Lords include—

(a) any work made by an officer or employee of that House in the course of his duties, and

(b) any sound recording, film [F363or live broadcast] of the proceedings of that House;

but a work shall not be regarded as made by or under the direction or control of either House by reason only of its being commissioned by or on behalf of that House.

(5) In the case of a work of joint authorship where one or more but not all of the authors are acting on behalf of, or under the direction or control of, the House of Commons or the House of Lords, this section applies only in relation to those authors and the copyright subsisting by virtue of their contribution to the work.

(6) Except as mentioned above, and subject to any express exclusion elsewhere in this Part, the provisions of this Part apply in relation to Parliamentary copyright as to other copyright.

(7) The provisions of this section also apply, subject to any exceptions or modifications specified by Order in Council, to works made by or under the direction or control of any other legislative body of a country to which this Part extends; and references in this Part to "Parliamentary copyright" shall be construed accordingly.

(8) A statutory instrument containing an Order in Council under subsection (7) shall be subject to annulment in pursuance of a resolution of either House of Parliament.

Amendments (Textual)

F363. Words in s. 165. (4)(b) substituted (31.10.2003) by The Copyright and Related Rights Regulations 2003 (S.I. 2003/2498), reg. 2. (1), Sch. 1 para. 11. (b) (with regs. 31-40)

Modifications etc. (not altering text)

C86. S. 165 modified (6.5.1999) by S.I. 1999/676, art. 2

S. 165 modified (2.12.1999) by S.I. 1999/3146, arts. 1. (1), 2; S.I. 1999/3208, art. 2

C87. S. 165 modified (3.5.2007 in accordance with art. 1. (2) of the amending S.I.) by The Parliamentary Copyright (National Assembly for Wales) Order 2007 (S.I. 2007/1116), art. 2

166 Copyright in Parliamentary Bills.

(1) Copyright in every Bill introduced into Parliament belongs, in accordance with the following provisions, to one or both of the Houses of Parliament.

(2) Copyright in a public Bill belongs in the first instance to the House into which the Bill is introduced, and after the Bill has been carried to the second House to both Houses jointly, and subsists from the time when the text of the Bill is handed in to the House in which it is introduced.

(3) Copyright in a private Bill belongs to both Houses jointly and subsists from the time when a copy of the Bill is first deposited in either House.

(4) Copyright in a personal Bill belongs in the first instance to the House of Lords, and after the Bill has been carried to the House of Commons to both Houses jointly, and subsists from the time when it is given a First Reading in the House of Lords.

(5) Copyright under this section ceases—

(a) on Royal Assent, or

(b) if the Bill does not receive Royal Assent, on the withdrawal or rejection of the Bill or the end of the Session:

Provided that, copyright in a Bill continues to subsist notwithstanding its rejection in any Session by the House of Lords if, by virtue of the Parliament Acts 1911 and 1949, it remains possible for it to be presented for Royal Assent in that Session.

(6) References in this Part to Parliamentary copyright (except in section 165) include copyright under this section; and, except as mentioned above, the provisions of this Part apply in relation to copyright under this section as to other Parliamentary copyright.

(7) No other copyright, or right in the nature of copyright, subsists in a Bill after copyright has once subsisted under this section; but without prejudice to the subsequent operation of this section in relation to a Bill which, not having passed in one Session, is reintroduced in a subsequent Session.

[F364166. A Copyright in Bills of the Scottish Parliament.

(1) Copyright in every Bill introduced into the Scottish Parliament belongs to the Scottish

Parliamentary Corporate Body.

(2) Copyright under this section subsists from the time when the text of the Bill is handed in to the Parliament for introduction—

(a) until the Bill receives Royal Assent, or

(b) if the Bill does not receive Royal Assent, until it is withdrawn or rejected or no further parliamentary proceedings may be taken in respect of it.

(3) References in this Part to Parliamentary copyright (except in section 165) include copyright under this section; and, except as mentioned above, the provisions of this Part apply in relation to copyright under this section as to other Parliamentary copyright.

(4) No other copyright, or right in the nature of copyright, subsists in a Bill after copyright has once subsisted under this section; but without prejudice to the subsequent operation of this section in relation to a Bill which, not having received Royal Assent, is later reintroduced into the Parliament.]

Amendments (Textual)

F364. S. 166. A inserted (6.5.1999) by 1998 c. 46, s. 125. (1), Sch. 8 para. 25. (6); S.I. 1998/3178, art. 2. (2), Sch. 3

[F365166. B Copyright in Bills of the Northern Ireland Assembly.

(1) Copyright in every Bill introduced into the Northern Ireland Assembly belongs to the Northern Ireland Assembly Commission.

(2) Copyright under this section subsists from the time when the text of the Bill is handed in to the Assembly for introduction—

(a) until the Bill receives Royal Assent, or

(b) if the Bill does not receive Royal Assent, until it is withdrawn or rejected or no further proceedings of the Assembly may be taken in respect of it.

(3) References in this Part to Parliamentary copyright (except in section 165) include copyright under this section; and, except as mentioned above, the provisions of this Part apply in relation to copyright under this section as to other Parliamentary copyright.

(4) No other copyright, or right in the nature of copyright, subsists in a Bill after copyright has once subsisted under this section; but without prejudice to the subsequent operation of this section in relation to a Bill which, not having received Royal Assent, is later reintroduced into the Assembly.]

Amendments (Textual)

F365. S. 166. B inserted (2.12.1999) by 1998 c. 47, s. 99, Sch. 13 para. 8. (6) (with s. 95); S.I. 1999/3209, art. 2, Sch.

[F366166. CCopyright in proposed Measures of the National Assembly for Wales

(1) Copyright in every proposed Assembly Measure introduced into the National Assembly for Wales belongs to the National Assembly for Wales Commission.

(2) Copyright under this section subsists from the time when the text of the proposed Assembly Measure is handed in to the Assembly for introduction—

(a) until the proposed Assembly Measure is approved by Her Majesty in Council, or

(b) if the proposed Assembly Measure is not approved by Her Majesty in Council, until it is withdrawn or rejected or no further proceedings of the Assembly may be taken in respect of it.

(3) References in this Part to Parliamentary copyright (except in section 165) include copyright under this section; and, except as mentioned above, the provisions of this Part apply in relation to copyright under this section as to other Parliamentary copyright.

(4) No other copyright, or right in the nature of copyright, subsists in a proposed Assembly Measure after copyright has once subsisted under this section; but without prejudice to the subsequent operation of this section in relation to a proposed Assembly Measure which, not having been approved by Her Majesty in Council, is later reintroduced into the Assembly.

Amendments (Textual)

F366. Ss. 166. C, 166. D inserted by Government of Wales Act 2006 (c. 32), s. 160. (1), Sch. 10 para. 28 (with Sch. 11 para. 22), the amending provision coming into force immediately after "the 2007 election" (held on 3.5.2007) subject to s. 161. (4)(5) of the amending Act, which provides for certain provisions to come into force for specified purposes immediately after the end of "the initial period" (which ended with the day of the first appointment of a First Minister on 25.5.2007) - see ss. 46, 161. (1)(4)(5) of the amending Act.

166. DCopyright in Bills of the National Assembly for Wales

(1) Copyright in every Bill introduced into the National Assembly for Wales belongs to the National Assembly for Wales Commission.

(2) Copyright under this section subsists from the time when the text of the Bill is handed in to the Assembly for introduction—

(a) until the Bill receives Royal Assent, or

(b) if the Bill does not receive Royal Assent, until it is withdrawn or rejected or no further proceedings of the Assembly may be taken in respect of it.

(3) References in this Part to Parliamentary copyright (except in section 165) include copyright under this section; and, except as mentioned above, the provisions of this Part apply in relation to copyright under this section as to other Parliamentary copyright.

(4) No other copyright, or right in the nature of copyright, subsists in a Bill after copyright has once subsisted under this section; but without prejudice to the subsequent operation of this section in relation to a Bill which, not having received Royal Assent, is later reintroduced into the Assembly.]

Amendments (Textual)

F366. Ss. 166. C, 166. D inserted by Government of Wales Act 2006 (c. 32), s. 160. (1), Sch. 10 para. 28 (with Sch. 11 para. 22), the amending provision coming into force immediately after "the 2007 election" (held on 3.5.2007) subject to s. 161. (4)(5) of the amending Act, which provides for certain provisions to come into force for specified purposes immediately after the end of "the initial period" (which ended with the day of the first appointment of a First Minister on 25.5.2007) - see ss. 46, 161. (1)(4)(5) of the amending Act.

167 Houses of Parliament: supplementary provisions with respect to copyright.

(1) For the purposes of holding, dealing with and enforcing copyright, and in connection with all legal proceedings relating to copyright, each House of Parliament shall be treated as having the legal capacities of a body corporate, which shall not be affected by a prorogation or dissolution.

(2) The functions of the House of Commons as owner of copyright shall be exercised by the Speaker on behalf of the House; and if so authorised by the Speaker, or in case of a vacancy in the office of Speaker, those functions may be discharged by the Chairman of Ways and Means or a Deputy Chairman.

(3) For this purpose a person who on the dissolution of Parliament was Speaker of the House of Commons, Chairman of Ways and Means or a Deputy Chairman may continue to act until the corresponding appointment is made in the next Session of Parliament.

(4) The functions of the House of Lords as owner of copyright shall be exercised by the Clerk of the Parliaments on behalf of the House; and if so authorised by him, or in case of a vacancy in the office of Clerk of the Parliaments, those functions may be discharged by the Clerk Assistant or the Reading Clerk.

(5) Legal proceedings relating to copyright—

(a) shall be brought by or against the House of Commons in the name of "The Speaker of the House of Commons"; and

(b) shall be brought by or against the House of Lords in the name of "The Clerk of the Parliaments".

Other miscellaneous provisions

168 Copyright vesting in certain international organisations.

(1) Where an original literary, dramatic, musical or artistic work—

(a) is made by an officer or employee of, or is published by, an international organisation to which this section applies, and

(b) does not qualify for copyright protection under section 154 (qualification by reference to author) or section 155 (qualification by reference to country of first publication),
copyright nevertheless subsists in the work by virtue of this section and the organisation is first owner of that copyright.

(2) The international organisations to which this section applies are those as to which Her Majesty has by Order in Council declared that it is expedient that this section should apply.

(3) Copyright of which an international organisation is first owner by virtue of this section continues to subsist until the end of the period of 50 years from the end of the calendar year in which the work was made or such longer period as may be specified by Her Majesty by Order in Council for the purpose of complying with the international obligations of the United Kingdom.

(4) An international organisation to which this section applies shall be deemed to have, and to have had at all material times, the legal capacities of a body corporate for the purpose of holding, dealing with and enforcing copyright and in connection with all legal proceedings relating to copyright.

(5) A statutory instrument containing an Order in Council under this section shall be subject to annulment in pursuance of a resolution of either House of Parliament.

169 Folklore, &c.: anonymous unpublished works.

(1) Where in the case of an unpublished literary, dramatic, musical or artistic work of unknown authorship there is evidence that the author (or, in the case of a joint work, any of the authors) was a qualifying individual by connection with a country outside the United Kingdom, it shall be presumed until the contrary is proved that he was such a qualifying individual and that copyright accordingly subsists in the work, subject to the provisions of this Part.

(2) If under the law of that country a body is appointed to protect and enforce copyright in such works, Her Majesty may by Order in Council designate that body for the purposes of this section.

(3) A body so designated shall be recognised in the United Kingdom as having authority to do in place of the copyright owner anything, other than assign copyright, which it is empowered to do under the law of that country; and it may, in particular, bring proceedings in its own name.

(4) A statutory instrument containing an Order in Council under this section shall be subject to annulment in pursuance of a resolution of either House of Parliament.

(5) In subsection (1) a "qualifying individual" means an individual who at the material time (within the meaning of section 154) was a person whose works qualified under that section for copyright protection.

(6) This section does not apply if there has been an assignment of copyright in the work by the author of which notice has been given to the designated body; and nothing in this section affects the validity of an assignment of copyright made, or licence granted, by the author or a person lawfully claiming under him.

Transitional provisions and savings

170 Transitional provisions and savings.

[F367. (1)]Schedule 1 contains transitional provisions and savings relating to works made, and acts or events occurring, before the commencement of this Part, and otherwise with respect to the operation of the provisions of this Part.

[F368. (2)The Secretary of State may by regulations amend Schedule 1 to reduce the duration of copyright in existing works which are unpublished, other than photographs or films.

(3) The regulations may provide for the copyright to expire—

   (a) with the end of the term of protection of copyright laid down by Directive 2006/116/ EC or at any later time;

   (b) subject to that, on the commencement of the regulations or at any later time.

(4) " Existing works " has the same meaning as in Schedule 1.

(5) Regulations under subsection (2) may—

   (a) make different provision for different purposes;

(b) make supplementary or transitional provision;

(c) make consequential provision, including provision amending any enactment or subordinate legislation passed or made before that subsection comes into force.

(6) The power to make regulations under subsection (2) is exercisable by statutory instrument.

(7) A statutory instrument containing regulations under subsection (2) may not be made unless a draft of the instrument has been laid before and approved by resolution of each House of Parliament.]

Amendments (Textual)

F367. S. 170 renumbered as s. 170. (1) (25.4.2013) by Enterprise and Regulatory Reform Act 2013 (c. 24), ss. 76. (2), 103. (1)

F368. S. 170. (2)-(7) inserted (25.4.2013) by Enterprise and Regulatory Reform Act 2013 (c. 24), ss. 76. (3), 103. (1)

171 Rights and privileges under other enactments or the common law.

(1) Nothing in this Part affects—

(a) any right or privilege of any person under any enactment (except where the enactment is expressly repealed, amended or modified by this Act);

(b) any right or privilege of the Crown subsisting otherwise than under an enactment;

(c) any right or privilege of either House of Parliament;

(d) the right of the Crown or any person deriving title from the Crown to sell, use or otherwise deal with articles forfeited under the laws relating to customs and excise;

(e) the operation of any rule of equity relating to breaches of trust or confidence.

(2) Subject to those savings, no copyright or right in the nature of copyright shall subsist otherwise than by virtue of this Part or some other enactment in that behalf.

(3) Nothing in this Part affects any rule of law preventing or restricting the enforcement of copyright, on grounds of public interest or otherwise.

(4) Nothing in this Part affects any right of action or other remedy, whether civil or criminal, available otherwise than under this Part in respect of acts infringing any of the rights conferred by Chapter IV (moral rights).

(5) The savings in subsection (1) have effect subject to section 164. (4) and section 166. (7) (copyright in Acts, Measures and Bills: exclusion of other rights in the nature of copyright).

Modifications etc. (not altering text)

C88. Ss. 161, 162, 171. (1)(3), 172-179 applied (1.12.1996) by S.I. 1996/2967, reg. 17. (4) (with Pt. III)

Interpretation

172 General provisions as to construction.

(1) This Part restates and amends the law of copyright, that is, the provisions of the M17. Copyright Act 1956, as amended.

(2) A provision of this Part which corresponds to a provision of the previous law shall not be construed as departing from the previous law merely because of a change of expression.

(3) Decisions under the previous law may be referred to for the purpose of establishing whether a provision of this Part departs from the previous law, or otherwise for establishing the true construction of this Part.

Modifications etc. (not altering text)

C89. Ss. 161, 162, 171. (1)(3), 172-179 applied (1.12.1996) by S.I. 1996/2967, reg. 17. (4) (with Pt. III)

Marginal Citations

M171956 c. 74.

[F369[F370172. A Meaning of EEA and related expressions.

[F371. (1)In this Part—

" the EEA " means the European Economic Area; and

" EEA state " means a member State, Iceland, Liechtenstein or Norway.]]

(2) References in this Part to a person being [F372a national of an EEA State] shall be construed in relation to a body corporate as references to its being incoporated under the law of an EEA state.

(3) F373. . . . .]

Amendments (Textual)

F369. S. 172. A inserted (1.1.1996) by S.I. 1995/3297, reg. 11. (1) (with Pt. III)

F370. S. 172. A(1) and sidenote substituted (1.12.1996) by S.I. 1996/2967, reg. 9. (5) (with Pt. III)

F371. S. 172. A(1) substituted (29.4.2006) by The Intellectual Property (Enforcement, etc.) Regulations 2006 (S.I. 2006/1028), reg. 2. (2), Sch. 2 para. 8. (2)

F372. Words in s. 172. A(2) substituted (29.4.2006) by The Intellectual Property (Enforcement, etc.) Regulations 2006 (S.I. 2006/1028), reg. 2. (2), Sch. 2 para. 8. (3)

F373. S. 172. A(3) repealed (29.4.2006) by The Intellectual Property (Enforcement, etc.) Regulations 2006 (S.I. 2006/1028), reg. 2. (4), Sch. 4

Modifications etc. (not altering text)

C90. Ss. 161, 162, 171. (1)(3), 172-179 applied (1.12.1996) by S.I. 1996/2967, reg. 17. (4) (with Pt. III)

173 Construction of references to copyright owner.

(1) Where different persons are (whether in consequence of a partial assignment or otherwise) entitled to different aspects of copyright in a work, the copyright owner for any purpose of this Part is the person who is entitled to the aspect of copyright relevant for that purpose.

(2) Where copyright (or any aspect of copyright) is owned by more than one person jointly, references in this Part to the copyright owner are to all the owners, so that, in particular, any requirement of the licence of the copyright owner requires the licence of all of them.

Modifications etc. (not altering text)

C91. Ss. 161, 162, 171. (1)(3), 172-179 applied (1.12.1996) by S.I. 1996/2967, reg. 17. (4) (with Pt. III)

174 Meaning of "educational establishment" and related expressions.

(1) The expression "educational establishment" in a provision of this Part means—

(a) any school, and

(b) any other description of educational establishment specified for the purposes of this Part, or that provision, by order of the Secretary of State.

(2) The Secretary of State may by order provide that the provisions of this Part relating to educational establishments shall apply, with such modifications and adaptations as may be specified in the order, in relation to teachers who are employed by a [F374local authority (as defined in section 579. (1) of the Education Act 1996) or (in Northern Ireland) a local education authority,] to give instruction elsewhere to pupils who are unable to attend an educational establishment.

(3) In subsection (1)(a) "school"—

(a) in relation to England and Wales, has the same meaning as in [F375the Education Act 1996];

(b) in relation to Scotland, has the same meaning as in the M18. Education (Scotland) Act 1962, except that it includes an approved school within the meaning of the M19. Social Work (Scotland) Act 1968; and

(c) in relation to Northern Ireland, has the same meaning as in the M20. Education and Libraries (Northern Ireland) Order 1986.

(4) An order under subsection (1)(b) may specify a description of educational establishment by reference to the instruments from time to time in force under any enactment specified in the order.

(5) In relation to an educational establishment the expressions "teacher" and "pupil" in this Part include, respectively, any person who gives and any person who receives instruction.

(6) References in this Part to anything being done "on behalf of" an educational establishment are to its being done for the purposes of that establishment by any person.

(7) An order under this section shall be made by statutory instrument which shall be subject to

annulment in pursuance of a resolution of either House of Parliament.

Amendments (Textual)

F374. Words in s. 174. (2) substituted (5.5.2010) by The Local Education Authorities and Children's Services Authorities (Integration of Functions) Order 2010 (S.I. 2010/1158), arts. 1, 5. (1), Sch. 2 para. 36

F375. Words in s. 174. (3) substituted (1.11.1996) by 1996 c. 56, ss. 582. (1), 583. (2), Sch. 37 Pt. I para. 83 (with Sch. 39)

Modifications etc. (not altering text)

C92. Ss. 161, 162, 171. (1)(3), 172-179 applied (1.12.1996) by S.I. 1996/2967, reg. 17. (4) (with Pt. III)

Marginal Citations

M181962 c. 47.

M191968 c. 49.

M20. S.I. 1986/594 (N.I.3).

175 Meaning of publication and commercial publication.

(1) In this Part "publication", in relation to a work—

    (a) means the issue of copies to the public, and

    (b) includes, in the case of a literary, dramatic, musical or artistic work, making it available to the public by means of an electronic retrieval system;

and related expressions shall be construed accordingly.

(2) In this Part "commercial publication", in relation to a literary, dramatic, musical or artistic work means—

    (a) issuing copies of the work to the public at a time when copies made in advance of the receipt of orders are generally available to the public, or

    (b) making the work available to the public by means of an electronic retrieval system;

and related expressions shall be construed accordingly.

(3) In the case of a work of architecture in the form of a building, or an artistic work incorporated in a building, construction of the building shall be treated as equivalent to publication of the work.

(4) The following do not constitute publication for the purposes of this Part and references to commercial publication shall be construed accordingly—

    (a) in the case of a literary, dramatic or musical work—

(i) the performance of the work, or

(ii) the [F376communication to the public of the work] (otherwise than for the purposes of an electronic retrieval system);

    (b) in the case of an artistic work—

(i) the exhibition of the work,

(ii) the issue to the public of copies of a graphic work representing, or of photographs of, a work of architecture in the form of a building or a model for a building, a sculpture or a work of artistic craftsmanship,

(iii) the issue to the public of copies of a film including the work, or

(iv) the [F376communication to the public of the work] (otherwise than for the purposes of an electronic retrieval system);

    (c) in the case of a sound recording or film—

(i) the work being played or shown in public, or

(ii) the [F376communication to the public of the work].

(5) References in this Part to publication or commercial publication do not include publication which is merely colourable and not intended to satisfy the reasonable requirements of the public.

(6) No account shall be taken for the purposes of this section of any unauthorised act.

Amendments (Textual)

F376. Words in s. 175. (4)(a)(ii)(b)(iv)(c)(ii) substituted (31.10.2003) by The Copyright and Related Rights Regulations 2003 (S.I. 2003/2498), reg. 2. (1), Sch. 1 para. 6. (1) (with regs. 31-40)

Modifications etc. (not altering text)

C93. Ss. 161, 162, 171. (1)(3), 172-179 applied (1.12.1996) by S.I. 1996/2967, reg. 17. (4) (with

176 Requirement of signature: application in relation to body corporate.

(1) The requirement in the following provisions that an instrument be signed by or on behalf of a person is also satisfied in the case of a body corporate by the affixing of its seal—

section 78. (3)(b) (assertion by licensor of right to identification of author in case of public exhibition of copy made in pursuance of the licence),

section 90. (3) (assignment of copyright),

section 91. (1) (assignment of future copyright),

section 92. (1) (grant of exclusive licence).

(2) The requirement in the following provisions that an instrument be signed by a person is satisfied in the case of a body corporate by signature on behalf of the body or by the affixing of its seal—

section 78. (2)(b) (assertion by instrument in writing of right to have author identified),

section 87. (2) (waiver of moral rights).

Modifications etc. (not altering text)

C94. Ss. 161, 162, 171. (1)(3), 172-179 applied (1.12.1996) by S.I. 1996/2967, reg. 17. (4) (with Pt. III)

177 Adaptation of expressions for Scotland.

In the application of this Part to Scotland—

"account of profits" means accounting and payment of profits;

"accounts" means count, reckoning and payment;

"assignment" means assignation;

"costs" means expenses;

"defendant" means defender;

"delivery up" means delivery;

"estoppel" means personal bar;

"injunction" means interdict;

"interlocutory relief" means interim remedy; and

"plaintiff" means pursuer.

Modifications etc. (not altering text)

C95. Ss. 161, 162, 171. (1)(3), 172-179 applied (1.12.1996) by S.I. 1996/2967, reg. 17. (4) (with Pt. III)

178 Minor definitions.

In this Part—

"article", in the context of an article in a periodical, includes an item of any description;

"business"includes a trade or profession;

"collective work" means—

- a work of joint authorship, or

- a work in which there are distinct contributions by different authors or in which works or parts of works of different authors are incorporated;

"computer-generated", in relation to a work, means that the work is generated by computer in circumstances such that there is no human author of the work;

"country" includes any territory;

"the Crown" includes the Crown in right of [F377the Scottish Administration [F378, of the Welsh Assembly Government] or of] Her Majesty's Government in Northern Ireland or in any country outside the United Kingdom to which this Part extends;

"electronic" means actuated by electric, magnetic, electro-mechanical energy, and "in electronic form" means in a form usable only by electronic means;

"employed", "employee", "employer", and "employment" refer to employment under a contract of service or of apprenticeship;

"facsimile copy" includes a copy which is reduced or enlarged in scale;

"international organisation" means an organisation the members of which include one or more states;

"judicial proceedings"includes proceedings before any court, tribunal or person having authority to decide any matter affecting a person's legal rights or liabilities;

"parliamentary proceedings" includes proceedings of the Northern Ireland Assembly [F379of the Scottish Parliament][F380, of the New Northern Ireland Assembly] or of the European Parliament [F381and Assembly proceedings within the meaning of section 1. (5) of the Government of Wales Act 2006];

[F382 " private study " does not include any study which is directly or indirectly for a commercial purpose;]

[F383"producer", in relation to a sound recording or a film, means the person by whom the arrangements necessary for the making of the sound recording or film are undertaken;]

[F384"public library" means a library administered by or on behalf of—

- in England and Wales, a library authority within the meaning of the Public Libraries and Museums Act 1964;

- in Scotland, a statutory library authority within the meaning of the Public Libraries (Scotland) Act 1955;

- in Northern Ireland, an Education and Library Board within the meaning of the Education and Libraries (Northern Ireland) Order 1986;]

F385. . . . .

[F386"rental right" means the right of a copyright owner to authorise or prohibit the rental of copies of the work (see section 18. A);]

"reprographic copy" and "reprographic copying" refer to copying by means of a reprographic process;

"reprographic process" means a process—

- for making facsimile copies, or

- involving the use of an appliance for making multiple copies,

and includes, in relation to a work held in electronic form, any copying by electronic means, but does not include the making of a film or sound recording;

"sufficient acknowledgement" means an acknowledgement identifying the work in question by its title or other description, and identifying the author unless—

- in the case of a published work, it is published anonymously;

- in the case of an unpublished work, it is not possible for a person to ascertain the identity of the author by reasonable inquiry;

"sufficient disclaimer", in relation to an act capable of infringing the right conferred by section 80 (right to object to derogatory treatment of work), means a clear and reasonably prominent indication—

- given at the time of the act, and

- if the author or director is then identified, appearing along with the identification,

that the work has been subjected to treatment to which the author or director has not consented,

"telecommunications system" means a system for conveying visual images, sounds or other information by electronic means;

"typeface" includes an ornamental motif used in printing;

"unauthorised", as regards anything done in relation to a work, means done otherwise than—

- by or with the licence of the copyright owner, or

- if copyright does not subsist in the work, by or with the licence of the author or, in a case where section 11. (2) would have applied, the author's employer or, in either case, persons lawfully claiming under him, or

- in pursuance of section 48 (copying, &c of certain material by the Crown);

[F387 " wireless broadcast " means a broadcast by means of wireless telegraphy;]

"wireless telegraphy" means the sending of electro-magnetic energy over paths not provided by a material substance constructed or arranged for that purpose [F388, but does not include the transmission of microwave energy between terrestrial fixed points];

"writing" includes any form of notation or code, whether by hand or otherwise and regardless of the method by which, or medium in or on which, it is recorded, and "written" shall be construed accordingly

Amendments (Textual)

F377. Words in s. 178 inserted (6.5.1999) by 1998 c. 46, s. 125. (1), Sch. 8 para. 25. (7)(a); S.I. 1998/3178, art. 2. (2), Sch. 3

F378. S. 178: words in definition of "the Crown" inserted by Government of Wales Act 2006 (c. 32), s. 160. (1), Sch. 10 para. 29. (2) (with Sch. 11 para. 22), the amending provision coming into force immediately after "the 2007 election" (held on 3.5.2007) subject to s. 161. (4)(5) of the amending Act, which provides for certain provisions to come into force for specified purposes immediately after the end of "the initial period" (which ended with the day of the first appointment of a First Minister on 25.5.2007) - see ss. 46, 161. (1)(4)(5) of the amending Act.

F379. Words in s. 178 inserted (6.5.1999) by 1998 c. 46, s. 125. (1), Sch. 8 para. 25. (7)(b); S.I. 1998/3178, art. 2. (2), Sch. 3

F380. Words in s. 178 cease to have effect (2.12.1999) by virtue of 1998 c. 47, s. 99, Sch. 13 para. 8. (7) (with s. 95); S.I. 1999/3209, art. 2, Sch.

F381. S. 178: words in definition of "parliamentary proceedings" inserted by Government of Wales Act 2006 (c. 32), s. 160. (1), Sch. 10 para. 29. (3) (with Sch. 11 para. 22), the amending provision coming into force immediately after "the 2007 election" (held on 3.5.2007) subject to s. 161. (4)(5) of the amending Act, which provides for certain provisions to come into force for specified purposes immediately after the end of "the initial period" (which ended with the day of the first appointment of a First Minister on 25.5.2007) - see ss. 46, 161. (1)(4)(5) of the amending Act.

F382. S. 178: definition of "private study" inserted (31.10.2003) by The Copyright and Related Rights Regulations 2003 (S.I. 2003/2498), reg. 2. (1), Sch. 1 para. 15. (3) (with regs. 31-40)

F383. Definition in s. 178 inserted (1.12.1996 with effect in relation to films made on or after 31.7.1994) by S.I. 1996/2967, regs. 18. (5), 36 (with Pt. III)

F384. Definition in s. 178 inserted (1.12.1996) by S.I. 1996/2967, reg. 11. (5) (with Pt. III)

F385. Definition in s. 178 omitted (1.12.1996) by virtue of S.I. 1996/2967, reg. 10. (3) (with Pt. III)

F386. Definition in s. 178 inserted (1.12.1996) by S.I. 1996/2967, reg. 10. (3) (with Pt. III)

F387. S. 178: definition of "wireless broadcast" inserted (31.10.2003) by The Copyright and Related Rights Regulations 2003 (S.I. 2003/2498), reg. 2. (1), Sch. 1 para. 15. (3) (with regs. 31-40)

F388. Words in s. 178 inserted (1.12.1996) by S.I. 1996/2967, reg. 8 (with Pt. III)

Modifications etc. (not altering text)

C96. Ss. 161, 162, 171. (1)(3), 172-179 applied (1.12.1996) by S.I. 1996/2967, reg. 17. (4) (with Pt. III)

179 Index of defined expressions.

The following Table shows provisions defining or otherwise explaining expressions used in this Part (other than provisions defining or explaining an expression used only in the same section)—

[F389accessible copy (in sections 31A to 31F) | section 31F(4)] |

account of profits and accounts (in Scotland) | section 177 |

acts restricted by copyright | section 16(1) |

adaptation | section 21(3) |

F390. . . | F390. . . |

[F391archivist (in sections 40A to 43) | section 43A(5)] |

article (in a periodical) | section 178 |

artistic work | section 4(1) |

assignment (in Scotland) | section 177 |

author | sections 9 and 10(3) |

[F392authorised body (in sections 31B to 31BB) | section 31F(6)] |

broadcast (and related expressions) | section 6 |

building | section 4(2) |

business | section 178 |

F393. . . | F394. . . . . |

collective work | section 178 |

commencement (in Schedule 1) | paragraph 1(2) of that Schedule |

commercial publication | section 175 |

[F395communication to the public | section 20] |

computer-generated | section 178 |

[F396conducted for profit (in sections 40A to 43) | section 43A(4)] |

copy and copying | section 17 |

copyright (generally) | section 1 |

copyright (in Schedule 1) | paragraph 2(2) of that Schedule |

copyright owner | sections 101(2) and 173 |

Copyright Tribunal | section 145 |

copyright work | section 1(2) |

costs (in Scotland) | section 177 |

country | section 178 |

[F397country of origin] | [F397section 15A.] |

the Crown | section 178 |

Crown copyright | sections 163(2) and 164(3) |

[F396curator (in sections 40A to 43) | section 43A(5)] |

[F398database] | [F398section 3A(1)] |

defendant (in Scotland) | section 177 |

delivery up (in Scotland) | section 177 |

[F392disabled person (in sections 31A to 31F) | section 31F(2) and (3)] |

dramatic work | section 3(1) |

educational establishment | sections 174(1) to (4) |

electronic and electronic form | section 178 |

employed, employee, employer and employment | section 178 |

[F399excepted sound recording | section 72(1A)] |

exclusive licence | section 92(1) |

[F400 the EEA , EEA state and national of an EEA state] | [F401section 172A] |

existing works (in Schedule 1) | paragraph 1(3) of that Schedule |

facsimile copy | section 178 |

film | [F402section 5B] |

future copyright | section 91(2) |

general licence (in sections 140 and 141) | section 140(7) |

graphic work | section 4(2) |

infringing copy | section 27 |

injunction (in Scotland) | section 177 |

interlocutory relief (in Scotland) | section 177 |

international organisation | section 178 |

issue of copies to the public | [F403section 18] |

joint authorship (work of) | sections 10(1) and (2) |

judicial proceedings | section 178 |

[F404lawful user (in sections 50A to 50C)] | [F404section 50A(2).] |

[F405lending] | [F405section 18A(2) to (6)] |

[F406librarian (in sections 40A to 43 | section 43A(5)] |

[F396library (in sections 40A to 43) | section 43A(2)] |

licence (in sections 125 to 128) | section 124 |

licence of copyright owner | sections 90(4), 91(3) and 173 |

licensing body (in Chapter VII) | section 116(2) |

licensing scheme (generally) | section 116(1) |

licensing scheme (in sections 118 to 121) | section 117 |

literary work | section 3(1) |

made (in relation to a literary, dramatic or musical work) | section 3(2) |

[F396museum (in sections 40A to 43) | section 43A(3)] |

musical work | section 3(1) |

[F407needletime] | [F407section 135A] |

the new copyright provisions (in Schedule 1) | paragraph 1(1) of that Schedule |

the 1911 Act (in Schedule 1) | paragraph 1(1) of that Schedule |

the 1956 Act (in Schedule 1) | paragraph 1(1) of that Schedule |

on behalf of (in relation to an educational establishment) | section 174(5) |

[F398original (in relation to a database)] | [F398section 3A(2)] |

Parliamentary copyright | sections 165(2) and (7) [F408166(6) [F409166A(3) [F410166B(3) 166C(3) and 166D(3)]]]] |

parliamentary proceedings | section 178 |

performance | section 19(2) |

photograph | section 4(2) |

plaintiff (in Scotland) | section 177 |

F411... | F411... |

F411... | F411... |

[F412private study | section 178] |

[F413producer (in relation to a sound recording or film] | [F413section 178.] |

programme (in the context of broadcasting) | section 6(3) |

prospective owner (of copyright) | section 91(2) |

[F414public library] | [F414section 178.] |

publication and related expressions | section 175 |

published edition (in the context of copyright in the typographical arrangement) | section 8 |

pupil | section 174(5) |

rental | [F415section 18A(2) to (6)] |

[F405rental right] | [F405section 178.] |

reprographic copies and reprographic copying | section 178 |

reprographic process | section 178 |

sculpture | section 4(2) |

signed | section 176 |

sound recording | [F416sections 5A and 135A] |

sufficient acknowledgement | section 178 |

sufficient disclaimer | section 178 |

[F392supply (in sections 31B to 31BB) | section 31F(7)] |

teacher | section 174(5) |

telecommunications system | section 178 |

[F407terms of payment] | [F407section 135A] |

typeface | section 178 |

unauthorised (as regards things done in relation to a work) | section 178 |

unknown (in relation to the author of a work) | section 9(5) |

unknown authorship (work of) | section 9(4) |

F390... | F390... |

[F417wireless broadcast | section 178] |

wireless telegraphy | section 178 |

work (in Schedule 1) | paragraph 2(1) of that Schedule |

work of more than one author (in Chapter VII) | section 116(4) |

writing and written | section 178 |

Amendments (Textual)

F389. Words in s. 179 substituted (1.6.2014) by The Copyright and Rights in Performances (Disability) Regulations 2014 (S.I. 2014/1384), reg. 1. (1), Sch. para. 3. (a)

F390. Words in s. 179 omitted (1.6.2014) by virtue of The Copyright and Rights in Performances (Disability) Regulations 2014 (S.I. 2014/1384), reg. 1. (1), Sch. para. 3. (c)

F391. Words in s. 179 substituted (1.6.2014) by The Copyright and Rights in Performances (Research, Education, Libraries and Archives) Regulations 2014 (S.I. 2014/1372), reg. 1, Sch. para. 6. (a)

F392. Words in s. 179 inserted (1.6.2014) by The Copyright and Rights in Performances (Disability) Regulations 2014 (S.I. 2014/1384), reg. 1. (1), Sch. para. 3. (b)

F393. S. 179: entry for "cable programme, cable programme service (and related expressions)" repealed (31.10.2003) by The Copyright and Related Rights Regulations 2003 (S.I. 2003/2498), reg. 2. (2), Sch. 2 (with regs. 31-40)

F394. Words in s. 179 repealed (31.10.2003) by The Copyright and Related Rights Regulations 2003 (S.I. 2003/2498), reg. 2. (2), Sch. 2 (with regs. 32, 33)

F395. Words in s. 179 inserted (31.10.2003) by The Copyright and Related Rights Regulations 2003 (S.I. 2003/2498), reg. 2. (1), Sch. 1 para. 15. (4) (with regs. 31-40)

F396. Words in s. 179 inserted (1.6.2014) by The Copyright and Rights in Performances (Research, Education, Libraries and Archives) Regulations 2014 (S.I. 2014/1372), reg. 1, Sch. para. 6. (c)

F397. Words in s. 179 inserted (1.1.1996) by S.I. 1995/3297, reg. 8. (2) (with Pt. III)

F398. Words in s. 179 inserted (1.1.1998) by S.I. 1997/3032, reg. 11 (with Pt. IV)

F399. Words in s. 179 inserted (31.10.2003) by The Copyright and Related Rights Regulations 2003 (S.I. 2003/2498), reg. 21. (7) (with regs. 31-40)

F400. Words in s. 179 substituted (29.4.2006) by The Intellectual Property (Enforcement, etc.) Regulations 2006 (S.I. 2006/1028), reg. 2. (2), Sch. 2 para. 9

F401. Words in s. 179 inserted (1.1.1996) by S.I. 1995/3297, reg. 11. (2) (with Pt. III)

F402. Words in s. 179 substituted (1.1.1996) by S.I. 1995/3297, reg. 9. (5)(a) (with Pt. III)

F403. Words in s. 179 inserted (1.12.1996) by S.I. 1996/2967, reg. 9. (6)(b) (with Pt. III)

F404. Words in s. 179 inserted (1.1.1993) by S.I. 1992/3233, reg. 9

F405. Words in s. 179 inserted (1.12.1996) by S.I. 1996/2967, reg. 10. (4) (with Pt. III)

F406. Words in s. 179 substituted (1.6.2014) by The Copyright and Rights in Performances (Research, Education, Libraries and Archives) Regulations 2014 (S.I. 2014/1372), reg. 1, Sch. para. 6. (b)

F407. Words inserted by Broadcasting Act 1990 (c.42, SIF 96), s. 175. (3)

F408. Words in s. 179 substituted (6.5.1999) by 1998 c. 46, s. 125. (1), Sch. 8 para. 25. (8); S.I. 1998/3178, art. 2. (2), Sch. 3

F409. Words in s. 179 substituted (2.12.1999) by 1998 c. 47, s. 99, Sch. 13 para. 8. (8) (with s. 95); S.I. 1999/3209, art. 2, Sch.

F410. Words in s. 179 substituted by Government of Wales Act 2006 (c. 32), s. 160. (1), Sch. 10 para. 30 (with Sch. 11 para. 22), the amending provision coming into force immediately after "the 2007 election" (held on 3.5.2007) subject to s. 161. (4)(5) of the amending Act, which provides for certain provisions to come into force for specified purposes immediately after the end of "the initial period" (which ended with the day of the first appointment of a First Minister on 25.5.2007) - see ss. 46, 161. (1)(4)(5) of the amending Act.

F411. Words in s. 179 omitted (1.6.2014) by virtue of The Copyright and Rights in Performances (Research, Education, Libraries and Archives) Regulations 2014 (S.I. 2014/1372), reg. 1, Sch. para. 6. (d)

F412. Words in s. 179 inserted (31.10.2003) by The Copyright and Related Rights Regulations 2003 (S.I. 2003/2498), reg. 2. (1), Sch. 1 para. 15. (4) (with regs. 31-40)

F413. Words in s. 179 inserted (1.12.1996 with effect in relation to films made on or after 1.7.1994) by S.I. 1996/2967, regs. 18. (6), 36 (with Pt. III)

F414. Words in s. 179 inserted (1.12.1996) by S.I. 1996/2967, reg. 11. (6) (with Pt. III)

F415. Words in s. 179 substituted (1.12.1996) by S.I. 1996/2967, reg. 10. (4) (with Pt. III)

F416. Words in s. 179 substituted (1.1.1996) by S.I. 1995/3297, reg. 9. (5)(b) (with Pt. III)

F417. Words in s. 179 inserted (31.10.2003) by The Copyright and Related Rights Regulations 2003 (S.I. 2003/2498), reg. 2. (1), Sch. 1 para. 15. (4) (with regs. 31-40)

Modifications etc. (not altering text)

C97. Ss. 161, 162, 171. (1)(3), 172-179 applied (1.12.1996) by S.I. 1996/2967, reg. 17. (4) (with Pt. III)

Countries to which this Part extends.

157 Countries to which this Part extends.

(1) This Part extends to England and Wales, Scotland and Northern Ireland.

(2) Her Majesty may by Order in Council direct that this Part shall extend, subject to such exceptions and modifications as may be specified in the Order, to—

  (a) any of the Channel Islands,

  (b) the Isle of Man, or

  (c) any colony.

(3) That power includes power to extend, subject to such exceptions and modifications as may be specified in the Order, any Order in Council made under the following provisions of this Chapter.

(4) The legislature of a country to which this Part has been extended may modify or add to the provisions of this Part, in their operation as part of the law of that country, as the legislature may consider necessary to adapt the provisions to the circumstances of that country—

  (a) as regards procedure and remedies, or

  (b) as regards works qualifying for copyright protection by virtue of a connection with that country.

(5) Nothing in this section shall be construed as restricting the extent of paragraph 36 of Schedule 1 (transitional provisions: dependent territories where the M1. Copyright Act 1956 or the M2. Copyright Act 1911 remains in force) in relation to the law of a dependent territory to which this Part does not extend.

Modifications etc. (not altering text)

C1. Pt. 1 applied (with modifications) (6.4.2017) by The Copyright and Performances (Application to Other Countries) Order 2016 (S.I. 2016/1219), arts. 1. (1), 4 (with art. 13)

C2. Pt. 1 restricted (6.4.2017) by The Copyright and Performances (Application to Other Countries) Order 2016 (S.I. 2016/1219), arts. 1. (1), 6 (with art. 13)

C3. Pt. 1 restricted (6.4.2017) by The Copyright and Performances (Application to Other Countries) Order 2016 (S.I. 2016/1219), arts. 1. (1), 9 (with art. 13)

C4. Pt. 1 applied (with modifications) (6.4.2017) by The Copyright and Performances (Application to Other Countries) Order 2016 (S.I. 2016/1219), arts. 1. (1), 7 (with art. 13)

C5. Pt. 1 restricted (6.4.2017) by The Copyright and Performances (Application to Other Countries) Order 2016 (S.I. 2016/1219), arts. 1. (1), 2 (with art. 13)

C6. Pt. 1 restricted (6.4.2017) by The Copyright and Performances (Application to Other Countries) Order 2016 (S.I. 2016/1219), arts. 1. (1), 3 (with art. 13)

C7. Pt. 1 applied (with modifications) (6.4.2017) by The Copyright and Performances (Application to Other Countries) Order 2016 (S.I. 2016/1219), arts. 1. (1), 5, Sch. Pt. 1 (with art. 13)

C8. Pt. 1 applied (with modifications) (6.4.2017) by The Copyright and Performances (Application to Other Countries) Order 2016 (S.I. 2016/1219), arts. 1. (1), 8 (with art. 13)

C9. Pt. 1: power to extend conferred (27.4.2017) by Digital Economy Act 2017 (c. 30), ss. 118. (1), 119. (7)(8)(a)

C10. S. 157. (2)(c) extended (8.4.2010) by Digital Economy Act 2010 (c. 24), ss. 46. (4), 47. (2)(c)

C11. S. 157. (2)(c): power to extend conferred (27.4.2017) by Digital Economy Act 2017 (c. 30), ss. 118. (1), 119. (9)

Marginal Citations

M11956 c. 74.

M21911 c. 46.

Application of this Part to countries to which it does not extend

[F1159. Application of this Part to countries to which it does not extend

(1) Where a country is a party to the Berne Convention or a member of the World Trade Organisation, this Part, so far as it relates to literary, dramatic, musical and artistic works, films and typographical arrangements of published editions—

(a) applies in relation to a citizen or subject of that country or a person domiciled or resident there as it applies in relation to a person who is a British citizen or is domiciled or resident in the United Kingdom,

(b) applies in relation to a body incorporated under the law of that country as it applies in relation to a body incorporated under the law of a part of the United Kingdom, and

(c) applies in relation to a work first published in that country as it applies in relation to a work first published in the United Kingdom.

(2) Where a country is a party to the Rome Convention, this Part, so far as it relates to sound recordings and broadcasts—

(a) applies in relation to that country as mentioned in paragraphs (a), (b) and (c) of subsection (1), and

(b) applies in relation to a broadcast made from that country as it applies to a broadcast made from the United Kingdom.

(3) Where a country is a party to the WPPT, this Part, so far as relating to sound recordings, applies in relation to that country as mentioned in paragraphs (a), (b) and (c) of subsection (1).

(4) Her Majesty may by Order in Council—

(a) make provision for the application of this Part to a country by subsection (1), (2) or (3) to be subject to specified restrictions;

(b) make provision for applying this Part, or any of its provisions, to a specified country;

(c) make provision for applying this Part, or any of its provisions, to any country of a specified description;

(d) make provision for the application of legislation to a country under paragraph (b) or (c) to be subject to specified restrictions.

(5) Provision made under subsection (4) may apply generally or in relation to such classes of works, or other classes of case, as are specified.

(6) Her Majesty may not make an Order in Council containing provision under subsection (4)(b) or (c) unless satisfied that provision has been or will be made under the law of the country or countries in question, in respect of the classes to which the provision under subsection (4)(b) or (c) relates, giving adequate protection to the owners of copyright under this Part.

(7) Application under subsection (4)(b) or (c) is in addition to application by subsections (1) to (3).

(8) Provision made under subsection (4)(c) may cover countries that become (or again become) of the specified description after the provision comes into force.

(9) In this section—

"the Berne Convention" means any Act of the International Convention for the Protection of Literary and Artistic Works signed at Berne on 9 September 1886;

"the Rome Convention" means the International Convention for the Protection of Performers, Producers of Phonograms and Broadcasting Organisations done at Rome on 26 October 1961;

"the WPPT" means the World Intellectual Property Organisation Performances and Phonograms Treaty adopted in Geneva on 20 December 1996.

(10) A statutory instrument containing an Order in Council under this section is subject to annulment in pursuance of a resolution of either House of Parliament.]

Amendments (Textual)

F1. S. 159 substituted (1.12.2016 for specified purposes, 6.4.2017 in so far as not already in force) by Intellectual Property Act 2014 (c. 18), ss. 22. (4), 24. (1); S.I. 2016/1139, arts. 2, 3 (with art. 4)

Modifications etc. (not altering text)

C1. Pt. 1 applied (with modifications) (6.4.2017) by The Copyright and Performances (Application to Other Countries) Order 2016 (S.I. 2016/1219), arts. 1. (1), 4 (with art. 13)

C2. Pt. 1 restricted (6.4.2017) by The Copyright and Performances (Application to Other Countries) Order 2016 (S.I. 2016/1219), arts. 1. (1), 6 (with art. 13)

C3. Pt. 1 restricted (6.4.2017) by The Copyright and Performances (Application to Other Countries) Order 2016 (S.I. 2016/1219), arts. 1. (1), 9 (with art. 13)

C4. Pt. 1 applied (with modifications) (6.4.2017) by The Copyright and Performances (Application to Other Countries) Order 2016 (S.I. 2016/1219), arts. 1. (1), 7 (with art. 13)

C5. Pt. 1 restricted (6.4.2017) by The Copyright and Performances (Application to Other Countries) Order 2016 (S.I. 2016/1219), arts. 1. (1), 2 (with art. 13)

C6. Pt. 1 restricted (6.4.2017) by The Copyright and Performances (Application to Other Countries) Order 2016 (S.I. 2016/1219), arts. 1. (1), 3 (with art. 13)

C7. Pt. 1 applied (with modifications) (6.4.2017) by The Copyright and Performances (Application to Other Countries) Order 2016 (S.I. 2016/1219), arts. 1. (1), 5, Sch. Pt. 1 (with art. 13)

C8. Pt. 1 applied (with modifications) (6.4.2017) by The Copyright and Performances (Application to Other Countries) Order 2016 (S.I. 2016/1219), arts. 1. (1), 8 (with art. 13)

C9. Pt. 1: power to extend conferred (27.4.2017) by Digital Economy Act 2017 (c. 30), ss. 118. (1), 119. (7)(8)(a)

Part II Rights in performances

Part II Rights in performances

Modifications etc. (not altering text)

C1. Pt. 2 (ss. 180-212) restricted (22.4.2003) by The Performances (Reciprocal Protection) (Convention Countries and Isle of Man) Order 2003 (S.I. 2003/773), art. 3 (which S.I. was revoked (1.5.2005) by S.I. 2005/852, art. 8. (c))

C2. Pt. 2 (ss. 180-212) extended (with modifications) (1.5.2005) by The Copyright and Performances (Application to Other Countries) Order 2005 (S.I. 2005/852), art. 6, Sch. (with art. 7) (which S.I. was revoked (6.4.2006) by S.I. 2006/316, art. 1. (3))

C3. Pt. 2 (ss. 180-212) extended (with modifications) (6.4.2006) by The Copyright and Performances (Application to Other Countries) Order 2006 (S.I. 2006/316), art. 6, Sch. (with art. 7) (which S.I. was revoked (6.4.2007) by S.I. 2007/273, art. 1. (3))

C4. Pt. 2 (ss. 180-212) extended (with modifications) (6.4.2007) by The Copyright and Performances (Application to Other Countries) Order 2007 (S.I. 2007/273), art. 6, Sch. (with art. 7) (which S.I. was revoked (6.4.2008) by S.I. 2008/677, art. 1. (3))

C5. Pt. 2 (ss. 180-212) extended (with modifications) (6.4.2008) by The Copyright and Performances (Application to Other Countries) Order 2008 (S.I. 2008/677), art. 6, Sch. (with art. 7)

C6. Pt. 2 extended (with modifications) (6.4.2012) by The Copyright and Performances (Application to Other Countries) Order 2012 (S.I. 2012/799), arts. 1. (1), 6, 7, Schs. (with art. 8)

C7. Pt. 2 applied in part (with modifications) (6.4.2013) by The Copyright and Performances (Application to Other Countries) Order 2013 (S.I. 2013/536), arts. 1. (1), 6, 7, Schs. (with art. 8)

C8. Pt. 2 applied (with modifications) (6.4.2017) by The Copyright and Performances (Application to Other Countries) Order 2016 (S.I. 2016/1219), arts. 1. (1), 12, Sch. Pt. 2 (with art. 13)

C9. Pt. 2 applied (with modifications) (6.4.2017) by The Copyright and Performances (Application to Other Countries) Order 2016 (S.I. 2016/1219), arts. 1. (1), 11, Sch. Pt. 2 (with art.

13)
C10. Pt. 2 applied (with modifications) (6.4.2017) by The Copyright and Performances (Application to Other Countries) Order 2016 (S.I. 2016/1219), arts. 1. (1), 10 (with art. 13)

[F1. Chapter 1. INTRODUCTORY

Amendments (Textual)
F1. Cross-headings before ss. 180, 181 omitted (1.2.2006) and ss. 180, 181 become Pt. 2 Ch. 1 by virtue of The Performances (Moral Rights, etc.) Regulations 2006 (S.I. 2006/18), reg. 4. (1)-(3) (with reg. 8)

X1180 Rights conferred on performers and persons having recording rights.

(1) [F2. Chapter 2 of this Part (economic rights)] confers rights—

(a) on a performer, by requiring his consent to the exploitation of his performances (see sections 181 to 184), and

(b) on a person having recording rights in relation to a performance, in relation to recordings made without his consent or that of the performer (see sections 185 to 188),

and creates offences in relation to dealing with or using illicit recordings and certain other related acts (see sections 198 and 201).

[F3. (1. A)Rights are also conferred on a performer by the following provisions of Chapter 3 of this Part (moral rights)—

(a) section 205. C (right to be identified);

(b) section 205. F (right to object to derogatory treatment of performance).]

(2) In this Part — "performance" means —

(a) a dramatic performance (which includes dance and mime),

(b) a musical performance,

(c) a reading or recitation of a literary work, or

(d) a performance of a variety act or any similar presentation,

which is, or so far as it is, a live performance given by one or more individuals; and "recording", in relation to a performance, means a film or sound recording—

(a) made directly from the live performance,

(b) made from a broadcast of F4. . . the performance, or

(c) made, directly or indirectly, from another recording of the performance.

(3) The rights conferred by this Part apply in relation to performances taking place before the commencement of this Part; but no act done before commencement, or in pursuance of arrangements made before commencement, shall be regarded as infringing those rights.

(4) The rights conferred by this Part are independent of—

(a) any copyright in, or moral rights relating to, any work performed or any film or sound recording of, or broadcast F5. . . the performance, and

(b) any other right or obligation arising otherwise than under this Part.

Editorial Information
X1. The insertion of the new headings "Chapter 1 Introductory", "Chapter 2 Economic Rights", "Chapter 3 Moral Rights" and "Chapter 4 Qualification for Protection, Extent and Interpretation" in Pt. II on 1.2.2006 gives rise to a change in the structure of this legislation on SLD which breaks the continuity of historical versions of the existing provisions which are now brought under those new headings.

Amendments (Textual)
F2. Words in s. 180. (1) substituted (1.2.2006) by The Performances (Moral Rights, etc.) Regulations 2006 (S.I. 2006/18), reg. 5. (1) (with reg. 8)

F3. S. 180. (1. A) inserted 1.2.2006) by The Performances (Moral Rights, etc.) Regulations 2006 (S.I. 2006/18), reg. 5. (2) (with reg. 8)
F4. Words in s. 180. (1)(4)(a) repealed (31.10.2003) by The Copyright and Related Rights Regulations 2003 (S.I. 2003/2498), reg. 2. (2), Sch. 2 (with regs. 31-40)
F5. Words in s. 180. (1)(4)(a) repealed (31.10.2003) by The Copyright and Related Rights Regulations 2003 (S.I. 2003/2498), reg. 2. (2), Sch. 2 (with regs. 32, 33)

X2181 Qualifying performances.

A performance is a qualifying performance for the purposes of the provisions of this Part relating to performers' right if it is given by a qualifying individual (as defined in section 206) or takes place in a qualifying country (as so defined).]

Editorial Information

X2. The insertion of the new headings "Chapter 1 Introductory", "Chapter 2 Economic Rights", "Chapter 3 Moral Rights" and "Chapter 4 Qualification for Protection, Extent and Interpretation" in Pt. II on 1.2.2006 gives rise to a change in the structure of this legislation on SLD which breaks the continuity of historical versions of the existing provisions which are now brought under those new headings.

[F6. Chapter 2. ECONOMIC RIGHTS

Amendments (Textual)

F6. Ss. 182-205. B become Pt. 2 Ch. 2 (1.2.2006) by virtue of The Performances (Moral Rights, etc.) Regulations 2006 (S.I. 2006/18), reg. 4. (4) (with reg. 8)

Editorial Information

X3. The insertion of the new headings "Chapter 1 Introductory", "Chapter 2 Economic Rights", "Chapter 3 Moral Rights" and "Chapter 4 Qualification for Protection, Extent and Interpretation" in Pt. II on 1.2.2006 gives rise to a change in the structure of this legislation on SLD which breaks the continuity of historical versions of the existing provisions which are now brought under those new headings.

Amendments (Textual)

F7. Pt. 2 Ch. 2: cross-heading inserted (1.2.2006) at beginning of Chapter by The Performances (Moral Rights, etc.) Regulations 2006 (S.I. 2006/18), reg. 4. (5) (with reg. 8)

X4[F8182 Consent required for recording, &c. of live performance.

(1) A performer's rights are infringed by a person who, without his consent—

   (a) makes a recording of the whole or any substantial part of a qualifying performance directly from the live performance,

   (b) broadcasts live, F9. . . the whole or any substantial part of a qualifying performance,

   (c) makes a recording of the whole or any substantial part of a qualifying performance directly from a broadcast of, F10. . . the live performance.

(2) F11. . . . .

(3) In an action for infringement of a performer's rights brought by virtue of this section damages shall not be awarded against a defendant who shows that at the time of the infringement he believed on reasonable grounds that consent had been given.]

Editorial Information

X4. The insertion of the new headings "Chapter 1 Introductory", "Chapter 2 Economic Rights", "Chapter 3 Moral Rights" and "Chapter 4 Qualification for Protection, Extent and Interpretation" in Pt. II on 1.2.2006 gives rise to a change in the structure of this legislation on SLD which breaks the continuity of historical versions of the existing provisions which are now brought under those new headings.

Amendments (Textual)

F8. S. 182 substituted (1.12.1996) by S.I. 1996/2967, reg. 20. (1) (with Pt. III)

F9. Words in s. 182. (1)(b) repealed (31.10.2003) by The Copyright and Related Rights Regulations 2003 (S.I. 2003/2498), reg. 2. (2), Sch. 2 (with regs. 31-40)

F10. Words in s. 182. (1)(c) repealed (31.10.2003) by The Copyright and Related Rights Regulations 2003 (S.I. 2003/2498), reg. 2. (2), Sch. 2 (with regs. 31-40)

F11. S. 182. (2) repealed (31.10.2003) by The Copyright and Related Rights Regulations 2003 (S.I. 2003/2498), reg. 2. (2), Sch. 2 (with regs. 31-40)

X5[F12182. A Consent required for copying of recording.

(1) A performer's rights are infringed by a person who, without his consent, makes F13. . . . a copy of a recording of the whole or any substantial part of a qualifying performance.

[F14. (1. A)In subsection (1), making a copy of a recording includes making a copy which is transient or is incidental to some other use of the original recording.]

(2) It is immaterial whether the copy is made directly or indirectly.

(3) The right of a performer under this section to authorise or prohibit the making of such copies is referred to in [F15this Chapter] as "reproduction right".]

Editorial Information

X5. The insertion of the new headings "Chapter 1 Introductory", "Chapter 2 Economic Rights", "Chapter 3 Moral Rights" and "Chapter 4 Qualification for Protection, Extent and Interpretation" in Pt. II on 1.2.2006 gives rise to a change in the structure of this legislation on SLD which breaks the continuity of historical versions of the existing provisions which are now brought under those new headings.

Amendments (Textual)

F12. S. 182. A inserted (1.12.1996) by S.I. 1996/2967, reg. 20. (2) (with Pt. III)

F13. Words in s. 182. A(1) repealed (31.10.2003) by The Copyright and Related Rights Regulations 2003 (S.I.2003/2498), reg. 2. (2), Sch. 2 (with regs. 31-40)

F14. S. 182. A(1. A) inserted (31.10.2003) by The Copyright and Related Rights Regulations 2003 (S.I. 2003/2498), reg. 8. (3) (with regs. 31-40)

F15. Words in S. 182. A(3) substituted (1.2.2006) by The Performances (Moral Rights, etc.) Regulations 2006 (S.I. 2006/18), reg. 2, Sch. para. 8 (with reg. 8)

X6[F16182. B Consent required for issue of copies to public.

(1) A performer's rights are infringed by a person who, without his consent, issues to the public copies of a recording of the whole or any substantial part of a qualifying performance.

(2) References in this Part to the issue to the public of copies of a recording are to—

(a) the act of putting into circulation in the EEA copies not previously put into circulation in the EEA by or with the consent of the performer, or

(b) the act of putting into circulation outside the EEA copies not previously put into circulation in the EEA or elsewhere.

(3) References in this Part to the issue to the public of copies of a recording do not include—

(a) any subsequent distribution, sale, hiring or loan of copies previously put into circulation (but see section 182. C: consent required for rental or lending), or

(b) any subsequent importation of such copies into the United Kingdom or another EEA state, except so far as paragraph (a) of subsection (2) applies to putting into circulation in the EEA copies previously put into circulation outside the EEA.

(4) References in this Part to the issue of copies of a recording of a performance include the issue of the original recording of the live performance.

(5) The right of a performer under this section to authorise or prohibit the issue of copies to the public is referred to in [F17this Chapter] as "distribution right".]

Editorial Information

X6. The insertion of the new headings "Chapter 1 Introductory", "Chapter 2 Economic Rights", "Chapter 3 Moral Rights" and "Chapter 4 Qualification for Protection, Extent and Interpretation" in Pt. II on 1.2.2006 gives rise to a change in the structure of this legislation on SLD which breaks the continuity of historical versions of the existing provisions which are now brought under those new headings.

Amendments (Textual)

F16. S. 182. B inserted (1.12.1996) by S.I. 1996/2967, reg. 20. (2) (with Pt. III)

F17. Words in s. 182. B(5) substituted (1.2.2006) by The Performances (Moral Rights, etc.) Regulations 2006 (S.I. 2006/18), reg. 2, Sch. para. 8 (with reg. 8)

X7[F18182. C Consent required for rental or lending of copies to public.

(1) A performer's rights are infringed by a person who, without his consent, rents or lends to the public copies of a recording of the whole or any substantial part of a qualifying performance.

(2) In [F19this Chapter], subject to the following provisions of this section—

(a) "rental" means making a copy of a recording available for use, on terms that it will or may be returned, for direct or indirect economic or commercial advantage, and

(b) "lending" means making a copy of a recording available for use, on terms that it will or may be returned, otherwise than for direct or indirect economic or commercial advantage, through an establishment which is accessible to the public.

(3) The expressions "rental" and "lending" do not include—

(a) making available for the purpose of public performance, playing or showing in public [F20or communication to the public];

(b) making available for the purpose of exhibition in public; or

(c) making available for on-the-spot reference use.

(4) The expression "lending" does not include making available between establishments which are accessible to the public.

(5) Where lending by an establishment accessible to the public gives rise to a payment the amount of which does not go beyond what is necessary to cover the operating costs of the establishment, there is no direct or indirect economic or commercial advantage for the purposes of this section.

(6) References in [F19this Chapter] to the rental or lending of copies of a recording of a performance include the rental or lending of the original recording of the live performance.

(7) In [F19this Chapter]—

"rental right" means the right of a performer under this section to authorise or prohibit the rental of copies to the public, and

"lending right" means the right of a performer under this section to authorise or prohibit the lending of copies to the public.]

Editorial Information

X7. The insertion of the new headings "Chapter 1 Introductory", "Chapter 2 Economic Rights", "Chapter 3 Moral Rights" and "Chapter 4 Qualification for Protection, Extent and Interpretation" in Pt. II on 1.2.2006 gives rise to a change in the structure of this legislation on SLD which breaks the continuity of historical versions of the existing provisions which are now brought under those new headings.

Amendments (Textual)

F18. S. 182. C inserted (1.12.1996) by S.I. 1996/2967, reg. 20. (2) (with Pt. III)

F19. Words in s. 182. C(2)(6)(7) substituted (1.2.2006) by The Performances (Moral Rights, etc.) Regulations 2006 (S.I. 2006/18), reg. 2, Sch. para. 8 (with reg. 8)

F20. Words in s. 182. C(3)(a) substituted (31.10.2003) by The Copyright and Related Rights Regulations 2003 (S.I. 2003/2498), reg.2. (1), Sch. 1 para. 6. (2)(c) (with regs. 31-40)

X8[F21182. CAConsent required for making available to the public

(1) A performer's rights are infringed by a person who, without his consent, makes available to the public a recording of the whole or any substantial part of a qualifying performance by electronic transmission in such a way that members of the public may access the recording from a place and at a time individually chosen by them.

(2) The right of a performer under this section to authorise or prohibit the making available to the public of a recording is referred to in [F22this Chapter] as "making available right.]

Editorial Information

X8. The insertion of the new headings "Chapter 1 Introductory", "Chapter 2 Economic Rights", "Chapter 3 Moral Rights" and "Chapter 4 Qualification for Protection, Extent and Interpretation" in Pt. II on 1.2.2006 gives rise to a change in the structure of this legislation on SLD which breaks the continuity of historical versions of the existing provisions which are now brought under those new headings.

Amendments (Textual)

F21. S. 182. CA inserted (31.10.2003) by The Copyright and Related Rights Regulations 2003 (S.I. 2003/2498), reg. 7. (1) (with regs. 31-40)

F22. Words in s. 182. CA(2) substituted (1.2.2006) by The Performances (Moral Rights, etc.) Regulations 2006 (S.I. 2006/18), reg. 2, Sch. para. 8 (with reg. 8)

X9 [F23 182. D Right to equitable remuneration for exploitation of sound recording.

(1) Where a commercially published sound recording of the whole or any substantial part of a qualifying performance—

(a) is played in public, or

[F24. (b)is communicated to the public otherwise than by its being made available to the public in the way mentioned in section 182. CA(1),]

the performer is entitled to equitable remuneration from the owner of the copyright in the sound recording [F25or, where copyright in the sound recording has expired pursuant to section 191. HA(4), from a person who plays the sound recording in public or communicates the sound recording to the public].

[F26. (1. A)In subsection (1), the reference to publication of a sound recording includes making it available to the public by electronic transmission in such a way that members of the public may access it from a place and at a time individually chosen by them.]

(2) The right to equitable remuneration under this section may not be assigned by the performer except to a collecting society for the purpose of enabling it to enforce the right on his behalf. The right is, however, transmissible by testamentary disposition or by operation of law as personal or moveable property; and it may be assigned or further transmitted by any person into whose hands it passes.

(3) The amount payable by way of equitable remuneration is as agreed by or on behalf of the persons by and to whom it is payable, subject to the following provisions.

(4) In default of agreement as to the amount payable by way of equitable remuneration, the person by or to whom it is payable may apply to the Copyright Tribunal to determine the amount payable.

(5) A person to or by whom equitable remuneration is payable may also apply to the Copyright Tribunal—

(a) to vary any agreement as to the amount payable, or

(b) to vary any previous determination of the Tribunal as to that matter;

but except with the special leave of the Tribunal no such application may be made within twelve months from the date of a previous determination.

An order made on an application under this subsection has effect from the date on which it is made or such later date as may be specified by the Tribunal.

(6) On an application under this section the Tribunal shall consider the matter and make such order as to the method of calculating and paying equitable remuneration as it may determine to be reasonable in the circumstances, taking into account the importance of the contribution of the performer to the sound recording.

(7) An agreement is of no effect in so far as it purports—

(a) to exclude or restrict the right to equitable remuneration under this section, or

(b) to prevent a person questioning the amount of equitable remuneration or to restrict the powers of the Copyright Tribunal under this section.

[F27. (8) In this section " collecting society " means a society or other organisation which has as its main object, or one of its main objects, the exercise of the right to equitable remuneration on behalf of more than one performer.]]

Editorial Information

X9. The insertion of the new headings "Chapter 1 Introductory", "Chapter 2 Economic Rights", "Chapter 3 Moral Rights" and "Chapter 4 Qualification for Protection, Extent and Interpretation" in Pt. II on 1.2.2006 gives rise to a change in the structure of this legislation on SLD which breaks the continuity of historical versions of the existing provisions which are now brought under those new headings.

Amendments (Textual)

F23. S. 182. D inserted (1.12.1996) by S.I. 1996/2967, reg. 20. (2) (with Pt. III)

F24. S. 182. D(1)(b) substituted (31.10.2003) by The Copyright and Related Rights Regulations 2003 (S.I. 2003/2498), reg. 7. (2) (with regs. 31-40)

F25. Words in s. 182. D(1) inserted (1.11.2013) by The Copyright and Duration of Rights in Performances Regulations 2013 (S.I. 2013/1782), regs. 1, 7 (with regs. 11-27)

F26. S. 182. D(1. A) inserted (1.2.2006) by The Performances (Moral Rights, etc.) Regulations 2006 (S.I. 2006/18), reg. 2, Sch. para. 3. (2) (with reg. 8)

F27. S. 182. D(8) inserted (1.2.2006) by The Performances (Moral Rights, etc.) Regulations 2006 (S.I. 2006/18), reg. 2, Sch. para. 3. (3) (with reg. 8)

Modifications etc. (not altering text)

C11. S. 182. D modified (31.10.2003) by The Copyright and Related Rights Regulations 2003 (S.I. 2003/2498), reg. 34 (with regs. 31-40)

X10183 Infringement of performer's rights by use of recording made without consent.

A performer's rights are infringed by a person who, without his consent—

(a) shows or plays in public the whole or any substantial part of a qualifying performance, or

(b) [F28communicates to the public] the whole or any substantial part of a qualifying performance,

by means of a recording which was, and which that person knows or has reason to believe was, made without the performer's consent.

Editorial Information

X10. The insertion of the new headings "Chapter 1 Introductory", "Chapter 2 Economic Rights", "Chapter 3 Moral Rights" and "Chapter 4 Qualification for Protection, Extent and Interpretation" in Pt. II on 1.2.2006 gives rise to a change in the structure of this legislation on SLD which breaks the continuity of historical versions of the existing provisions which are now brought under those new headings.

Amendments (Textual)

F28. Words in s. 183. (b) substituted (31.10.2003) by The Copyright and Related Rights Regulations 2003 (S.I. 2003/2498), reg. 2. (1), Sch. 1 para. 13. (1)(a) (with regs. 31-40)

X11184 Infringement of performer's rights by importing, possessing or dealing with illicit recording.

(1) A performer's rights are infringed by a person who, without his consent—

(a) imports into the United Kingdom otherwise than for his private and domestic use, or

(b) in the course of a business possesses, sells or lets for hire, offers or exposes for sale or hire, or distributes,

a recording of a qualifying performance which is, and which that person knows or has reason to believe is, an illicit recording.

(2) Where in an action for infringement of a performer's rights brought by virtue of this section a defendant shows that the illicit recording was innocently acquired by him or a predecessor in title of his, the only remedy available against him in respect of the infringement is damages not exceeding a reasonable payment in respect of the act complained of.

(3) In subsection (2) "innocently acquired" means that the person acquiring the recording did not know and had no reason to believe that it was an illicit recording.

Editorial Information

X11. The insertion of the new headings "Chapter 1 Introductory", "Chapter 2 Economic Rights", "Chapter 3 Moral Rights" and "Chapter 4 Qualification for Protection, Extent and Interpretation" in Pt. II on 1.2.2006 gives rise to a change in the structure of this legislation on SLD which breaks the continuity of historical versions of the existing provisions which are now brought under those new headings.

X12 Rights of person having recording rights

X12. The insertion of the new headings "Chapter 1 Introductory", "Chapter 2 Economic Rights", "Chapter 3 Moral Rights" and "Chapter 4 Qualification for Protection, Extent and Interpretation" in Pt. II on 1.2.2006 gives rise to a change in the structure of this legislation on SLD which breaks the continuity of historical versions of the existing provisions which are now brought under those new headings.

X13 185 Exclusive recording contracts and persons having recording rights.

(1) In [F29this Chapter] an "exclusive recording contract" means a contract between a performer and another person under which that person is entitled to the exclusion of all other persons (including the performer) to make recordings of one or more of his performances with a view to their commercial exploitation.

(2) References in [F29this Chapter] to a "person having recording rights", in relation to a performance, are (subject to subsection (3)) to a person—

(a) who is party to and has the benefit of an exclusive recording contract to which the performance is subject, or

(b) to whom the benefit of such a contract has been assigned,

and who is a qualifying person.

(3) If a performance is subject to an exclusive recording contract but the person mentioned in subsection (2) is not a qualifying person, references in [F29this Chapter] to a "person having recording rights" in relation to the performance are to any person—

(a) who is licensed by such a person to make recordings of the performance with a view to their commercial exploitation, or

(b) to whom the benefit of such a licence has been assigned,

and who is a qualifying person.

(4) In this section "with a view to commercial exploitation" means with a view to the recordings being sold or let for hire, or shown or played in public.

Editorial Information

X13. The insertion of the new headings "Chapter 1 Introductory", "Chapter 2 Economic Rights", "Chapter 3 Moral Rights" and "Chapter 4 Qualification for Protection, Extent and Interpretation" in Pt. II on 1.2.2006 gives rise to a change in the structure of this legislation on SLD which breaks the continuity of historical versions of the existing provisions which are now brought under those new headings.

Amendments (Textual)

F29. Words in s. 185. (1)-(3) substituted (1.2.2006) by The Performances (Moral Rights, etc.) Regulations 2006 (S.I. 2006/18), reg. 2, Sch. para. 8 (with reg. 8)

X14 186 Consent required for recording of performance subject to exclusive contract.

(1) A person infringes the rights of a person having recording rights in relation to a performance who, without his consent or that of the performer, makes a recording of the whole or any substantial part of the performance F30. . . .

(2) In an action for infringement of those rights brought by virtue of this section damages shall not be awarded against a defendant who shows that at the time of the infringement he believed on reasonable grounds that consent had been given.

Editorial Information

X14. The insertion of the new headings "Chapter 1 Introductory", "Chapter 2 Economic Rights", "Chapter 3 Moral Rights" and "Chapter 4 Qualification for Protection, Extent and Interpretation" in Pt. II on 1.2.2006 gives rise to a change in the structure of this legislation on SLD which breaks the continuity of historical versions of the existing provisions which are now brought under those new headings.

Amendments (Textual)

F30. Words in s. 186. (1) repealed (31.10.2003) by The Copyright and Related Rights Regulations 2003 (S.I. 2003/2498), reg. 2. (2), Sch. 2 (with regs. 31-40)

X15 187 Infringement of recording rights by use of recording made without consent.

(1) A person infringes the rights of a person having recording rights in relation to a performance

who, without his consent or, in the case of a qualifying performance, that of the performer—

(a) shows or plays in public the whole or any substantial part of the performance, or

(b) [F31communicates to the public] the whole or any substantial part of the performance,

by means of a recording which was, and which that person knows or has reason to believe was, made without the appropriate consent.

(2) The reference in subsection (1) to "the appropriate consent" is to the consent of—

(a) the performer, or

(b) the person who at the time the consent was given had recording rights in relation to the performance (or, if there was more than one such person, of all of them).

Editorial Information

X15. The insertion of the new headings "Chapter 1 Introductory", "Chapter 2 Economic Rights", "Chapter 3 Moral Rights" and "Chapter 4 Qualification for Protection, Extent and Interpretation" in Pt. II on 1.2.2006 gives rise to a change in the structure of this legislation on SLD which breaks the continuity of historical versions of the existing provisions which are now brought under those new headings.

Amendments (Textual)

F31. Words in s. 187. (1)(b) substituted (31.10.2003) by The Copyright and Related Rights Regulations 2003 (S.I. 2003/2498), reg. 2. (1), Sch. 1 para. 13. (1)(b) (with regs. 31-40)

X16188 Infringement of recording rights by importing, possessing or dealing with illicit recording.

(1) A person infringes the rights of a person having recording rights in relation to a performance who, without his consent or, in the case of a qualifying performance, that of the performer—

(a) imports into the United Kingdom otherwise than for his private and domestic use, or

(b) in the course of a business possesses, sells or lets for hire, offers or exposes for sale or hire, or distributes,

a recording of the performance which is, and which that person knows or has reason to believe is, an illicit recording.

(2) Where in an action for infringement of those rights brought by virtue of this section a defendant shows that the illicit recording was innocently acquired by him or a predecessor in title of his, the only remedy available against him in respect of the infringement is damages not exceeding a reasonable payment in respect of the act complained of.

(3) In subsection (2) "innocently acquired" means that the person acquiring the recording did not know and had no reason to believe that it was an illicit recording.

Editorial Information

X16. The insertion of the new headings "Chapter 1 Introductory", "Chapter 2 Economic Rights", "Chapter 3 Moral Rights" and "Chapter 4 Qualification for Protection, Extent and Interpretation" in Pt. II on 1.2.2006 gives rise to a change in the structure of this legislation on SLD which breaks the continuity of historical versions of the existing provisions which are now brought under those new headings.

X17 Exceptions to rights conferred

Editorial Information

X17. The insertion of the new headings "Chapter 1 Introductory", "Chapter 2 Economic Rights", "Chapter 3 Moral Rights" and "Chapter 4 Qualification for Protection, Extent and Interpretation" in Pt. II on 1.2.2006 gives rise to a change in the structure of this legislation on SLD which breaks the continuity of historical versions of the existing provisions which are now brought under those new headings.

X18189 Acts permitted notwithstanding rights conferred by [F32this Chapter].

The provisions of Schedule 2 specify acts which may be done notwithstanding the rights conferred by [F33this Chapter], being acts which correspond broadly to certain of those specified in Chapter III of Part I (acts permitted notwithstanding copyright).

Editorial Information
X18. The insertion of the new headings "Chapter 1 Introductory", "Chapter 2 Economic Rights", "Chapter 3 Moral Rights" and "Chapter 4 Qualification for Protection, Extent and Interpretation" in Pt. II on 1.2.2006 gives rise to a change in the structure of this legislation on SLD which breaks the continuity of historical versions of the existing provisions which are now brought under those new headings.

Amendments (Textual)

F32. Words in heading to s. 189 substituted (1.2.2006) by The Performances (Moral Rights, etc.) Regulations 2006 (S.I. 2006/18), reg. 2, Sch. para. 8 (with reg. 8)

F33. Words in s. 189 substituted (1.2.2006) by The Performances (Moral Rights, etc.) Regulations 2006 (S.I. 2006/18), reg. 2, Sch. para. 8 (with reg. 8)

X19190 Power of tribunal to give consent on behalf of performer in certain cases.

[F34. (1)The Copyright Tribunal may, on the application of a person wishing to make a copy of a recording of a performance, give consent in a case where the identity or whereabouts of the person entitled to the reproduction right cannot be ascertained by reasonable inquiry.]

(2) Consent given by the Tribunal has effect as consent of [F35the person entitled to the reproduction right] for the purposes of—

(a) the provisions of [F36this Chapter] relating to performers' rights, and

(b) section 198. (3)(a) (criminal liability: sufficient consent in relation to qualifying performances),

and may be given subject to any conditions specified in the Tribunal's order.

(3) The Tribunal shall not give consent under subsection (1)(a) except after the service or publication of such notices as may be required by rules made under section 150 (general procedural rules) or as the Tribunal may in any particular case direct.

F37. (4). . . . .

(5) In any case the Tribunal shall take into account the following factors—

(a) whether the original recording was made with the performer's consent and is lawfully in the possession or control of the person proposing to make the further recording;

(b) whether the making of the further recording is consistent with the obligations of the parties to the arrangements under which, or is otherwise consistent with the purposes for which, the original recording was made.

(6) Where the Tribunal gives consent under this section it shall, in default of agreement between the applicant and [F38the person entitled to the reproduction right], make such order as it thinks fit as to the payment to be made to [F39that person] in consideration of consent being given.

Editorial Information
X19. The insertion of the new headings "Chapter 1 Introductory", "Chapter 2 Economic Rights", "Chapter 3 Moral Rights" and "Chapter 4 Qualification for Protection, Extent and Interpretation" in Pt. II on 1.2.2006 gives rise to a change in the structure of this legislation on SLD which breaks the continuity of historical versions of the existing provisions which are now brought under those new headings.

Amendments (Textual)

F34. S. 190. (1) substituted (1.12.1996) by S.I. 1996/2967, reg. 23. (2) (with Pt. III)

F35. Words in s. 190. (2) substituted (1.12.1996) by S.I. 1996/2967, reg. 23. (3) (with Pt. III)

F36. Words in s. 190. (2)(a) substituted (1.2.2006) by The Performances (Moral Rights, etc.) Regulations 2006 (S.I. 2006/18), reg. 2, Sch. para. 8 (with reg. 8)

F37. S. 190. (4) omitted (1.12.1996) by virtue of S.I. 1996/2967, reg. 23. (4) (with Pt. III)

F38. Words in s. 190. (6) substituted (1.12.1996) by S.I. 1996/2967, reg. 23. (5)(a) (with Pt. III)

F39. Words in s. 190. (6) substituted (1.12.1996) by S.I. 1996/2967, reg. 23. (5)(b) (with Pt. III)

X20. F40[Duration of rights]

Editorial Information

X20. The insertion of the new headings "Chapter 1 Introductory", "Chapter 2 Economic Rights", "Chapter 3 Moral Rights" and "Chapter 4 Qualification for Protection, Extent and Interpretation" in Pt. II on 1.2.2006 gives rise to a change in the structure of this legislation on SLD which breaks the continuity of historical versions of the existing provisions which are now brought under those new headings.

Amendments (Textual)

F40. Crossheading substituted (1.12.1996) by S.I. 1996/2967, reg. 21. (5)(a) (with Pt. III)

X21 [F41 191 Duration of rights.]

(1) The following provisions have effect with respect to the duration of the rights conferred by [F42this Chapter].

(2) The rights conferred by [F42this Chapter] in relation to a performance expire—

(a) at the end of the period of 50 years from the end of the calendar year in which the performance takes place, or

(b) if during that period a recording of the performance[F43, other than a sound recording,] is released, 50 years from the end of the calendar year in which it is released, [F44or

(c) if during that period a sound recording of the performance is released, 70 years from the end of the calendar year in which it is released,]

subject as follows.

(3) For the purposes of subsection (2) a recording is "released" when it is first published, played or shown in public [F45 or communicated to the public]; but in determining whether a recording has been released no account shall be taken of any unauthorised act.

(4) Where a performer is not a national of an EEA state, the duration of the rights conferred by [F42 this Chapter] in relation to his performance is that to which the performance is entitled in the country of which he is a national, provided that does not exceed the period which would apply under subsections (2) and (3).

(5) If or to the extent that the application of subsection (4) would be at variance with an international obligation to which the United Kingdom became subject prior to 29th October 1993, the duration of the rights conferred by [F42this Chapter] shall be as specified in subsections (2) and (3).]

Editorial Information

X21. The insertion of the new headings "Chapter 1 Introductory", "Chapter 2 Economic Rights", "Chapter 3 Moral Rights" and "Chapter 4 Qualification for Protection, Extent and Interpretation" in Pt. II on 1.2.2006 gives rise to a change in the structure of this legislation on SLD which breaks the continuity of historical versions of the existing provisions which are now brought under those new headings.

Amendments (Textual)

F41. S. 191 substituted (1.1.1996) by S.I. 1995/3297, reg. 10 (with Pt. III)

F42. Words in s. 191. (1)(2)(4)(5) substituted (1.2.2006) by The Performances (Moral Rights, etc.) Regulations 2006 (S.I. 2006/18), reg. 2, Sch. para. 8 (with reg. 8)

F43. Words in s. 191. (2)(b) inserted (1.11.2013) by The Copyright and Duration of Rights in Performances Regulations 2013 (S.I. 2013/1782), regs. 1, 8. (a) (with regs. 11-27)

F44. S. 191. (2)(c) and word inserted (1.11.2013) by The Copyright and Duration of Rights in Performances Regulations 2013 (S.I. 2013/1782), regs. 1, 8. (b) (with regs. 11-27)

F45. Words in s. 191. (3) substituted (31.10.2003) by The Copyright and Related Rights Regulations 2003 (S.I. 2003/2498), reg. 2. (1), Sch. 1 para. 8. (2)(d) (with regs. 31-40)

X22[F46. Performers' property rights]

Editorial Information

X22. The insertion of the new headings "Chapter 1 Introductory", "Chapter 2 Economic Rights", "Chapter 3 Moral Rights" and "Chapter 4 Qualification for Protection, Extent and Interpretation" in Pt. II on 1.2.2006 gives rise to a change in the structure of this legislation on SLD which breaks

the continuity of historical versions of the existing provisions which are now brought under those new headings.

Amendments (Textual)

F46. Crossheading inserted (1.12.1996) by S.I. 1996/2967, reg. 21. (1) (with Pt. III)

X23[F47191. A Performers' property rights.

(1) The following rights conferred by [F48this Chapter] on a performer—
- reproduction right (section 182. A),
- distribution right (section 182. B),
- rental right and lending right (section 182. C),
- [F49making available right (section 182. CA),]

are property rights ("F50. . . performer's property rights").

(2) References in [F48this Chapter] to the consent of the performer shall be construed in relation to a performer's property rights as references to the consent of the rights owner.

(3) Where different persons are (whether in consequence of a partial assignment or otherwise) entitled to different aspects of a performer's property rights in relation to a performance, the rights owner for any purpose of [F48this Chapter] is the person who is entitled to the aspect of those rights relevant for that purpose.

(4) Where a performer's property rights (or any aspect of them) is owned by more than one person jointly, references in [F48this Chapter] to the rights owner are to all the owners, so that, in particular, any requirement of the licence of the rights owner requires the licence of all of them.]

Editorial Information

X23. The insertion of the new headings "Chapter 1 Introductory", "Chapter 2 Economic Rights", "Chapter 3 Moral Rights" and "Chapter 4 Qualification for Protection, Extent and Interpretation" in Pt. II on 1.2.2006 gives rise to a change in the structure of this legislation on SLD which breaks the continuity of historical versions of the existing provisions which are now brought under those new headings.

Amendments (Textual)

F47. Ss. 191. A-191. M inserted (1.12.1996) by S.I. 1996/2967, reg. 21. (1) (with Pt. III)

F48. Words in s. 191. A(1)-(4) substituted (1.2.2006) by The Performances (Moral Rights, etc.) Regulations 2006 (S.I. 2006/18), reg. 2, Sch. para. 8 (with reg. 8)

F49. Words in s. 191. A(1) inserted (31.10.2003) by The Copyright and Related Rights Regulations 2003 (S.I. 2003/2498), reg. 7. (3) (with regs. 31-40)

F50. Word in s. 191. A(1) omitted by virtue of The Performances (Moral Rights, etc.) Regulations 2006 (S.I. 2006/18), reg. 2, Sch. para. 4 (with reg. 8)

X24[F51191. B Assignment and licences.

(1) A performer's property rights are transmissible by assignment, by testamentary disposition or by operation of law, as personal or moveable property.

(2) An assignment or other transmission of a performer's property rights may be partial, that is, limited so as to apply—
  (a) to one or more, but not all, of the things requiring the consent of the rights owner;
  (b) to part, but not the whole, of the period for which the rights are to subsist.

(3) An assignment of a performer's property rights is not effective unless it is in writing signed by or on behalf of the assignor.

(4) A licence granted by the owner of a performer's property rights is binding on every successor in title to his interest in the rights, except a purchaser in good faith for valuable consideration and without notice (actual or constructive) of the licence or a person deriving title from such a purchaser; and references in [F52this Chapter] to doing anything with, or without, the licence of the rights owner shall be construed accordingly.]

Editorial Information

X24. The insertion of the new headings "Chapter 1 Introductory", "Chapter 2 Economic Rights", "Chapter 3 Moral Rights" and "Chapter 4 Qualification for Protection, Extent and Interpretation" in Pt. II on 1.2.2006 gives rise to a change in the structure of this legislation on SLD which breaks the continuity of historical versions of the existing provisions which are now brought under those new headings.

Amendments (Textual)

F51. Ss. 191. A-191. M inserted (1.12.1996) by S.I. 1996/2967, reg. 21. (1) (with Pt. III)

F52. Words in s. 191. B(4) substituted (1.2.2006) by The Performances (Moral Rights, etc.) Regulations 2006 (S.I. 2006/18), reg. 2, Sch. para. 8 (with reg. 8)

X25[F53191. C Prospective ownership of a performer's property rights.

(1) This section applies where by an agreement made in relation to a future recording of a performance, and signed by or on behalf of the performer, the performer purports to assign his performer's property rights (wholly or partially) to another person.

(2) If on the rights coming into existence the assignee or another person claiming under him would be entitled as against all other persons to require the rights to be vested in him, they shall vest in the assignee or his successor in title by virtue of this subsection.

(3) A licence granted by a prospective owner of a performer's property rights is binding on every successor in title to his interest (or prospective interest) in the rights, except a purchaser in good faith for valuable consideration and without notice (actual or constructive) of the licence or a person deriving title from such a purchaser.

References in [F54this Chapter] to doing anything with, or without, the licence of the rights owner shall be construed accordingly.

(4) In subsection (3) "prospective owner" in relation to a performer's property rights means a person who is prospectively entitled to those rights by virtue of such an agreement as is mentioned in subsection (1).]

Editorial Information

X25. The insertion of the new headings "Chapter 1 Introductory", "Chapter 2 Economic Rights", "Chapter 3 Moral Rights" and "Chapter 4 Qualification for Protection, Extent and Interpretation" in Pt. II on 1.2.2006 gives rise to a change in the structure of this legislation on SLD which breaks the continuity of historical versions of the existing provisions which are now brought under those new headings.

Amendments (Textual)

F53. Ss. 191. A-191. M inserted (1.12.1996) by S.I. 1996/2967, reg. 21. (1) (with Pt. III)

F54. Words in s. 191. C(3) substituted (1.2.2006) by The Performances (Moral Rights, etc.) Regulations 2006 (S.I. 2006/18), reg. 2, Sch. para. 8 (with reg. 8)

X26[F55191. D Exclusive licences.

(1) In [F56this Chapter] an "exclusive licence" means a licence in writing signed by or on behalf of the owner of a performer's property rights authorising the licensee to the exclusion of all other persons, including the person granting the licence, to do anything requiring the consent of the rights owner.

(2) The licensee under an exclusive licence has the same rights against a successor in title who is bound by the licence as he has against the person granting the licence.]

Editorial Information

X26. The insertion of the new headings "Chapter 1 Introductory", "Chapter 2 Economic Rights", "Chapter 3 Moral Rights" and "Chapter 4 Qualification for Protection, Extent and Interpretation" in Pt. II on 1.2.2006 gives rise to a change in the structure of this legislation on SLD which breaks the continuity of historical versions of the existing provisions which are now brought under those new headings.

Amendments (Textual)

F55. Ss. 191. A-191. M inserted (1.12.1996) by S.I. 1996/2967, reg. 21. (1) (with Pt. III)

F56. Words in s. 191. D(1) substituted (1.2.2006) by The Performances (Moral Rights, etc.) Regulations 2006 (S.I. 2006/18), reg. 2, Sch. para. 8 (with reg. 8)

X27[F57191. E Performer's property right to pass under will with unpublished original recording. Where under a bequest (whether general or specific) a person is entitled beneficially or otherwise to any material thing containing an original recording of a performance which was not published before the death of the testator, the bequest shall, unless a contrary intention is indicated in the testator's will or a codicil to it, be construed as including any performer's rights in relation to the recording to which the testator was entitled immediately before his death.]

Editorial Information

X27. The insertion of the new headings "Chapter 1 Introductory", "Chapter 2 Economic Rights", "Chapter 3 Moral Rights" and "Chapter 4 Qualification for Protection, Extent and Interpretation" in Pt. II on 1.2.2006 gives rise to a change in the structure of this legislation on SLD which breaks the continuity of historical versions of the existing provisions which are now brought under those new headings.

Amendments (Textual)

F57. Ss. 191. A-191. M inserted (1.12.1996) by S.I. 1996/2967, reg. 21. (1) (with Pt. III)

X28[F58191. F Presumption of transfer of rental right in case of film production agreement.

(1) Where an agreement concerning film production is concluded between a performer and a film producer, the performer shall be presumed, unless the agreement provides to the contrary, to have transferred to the film producer any rental right in relation to the film arising from the inclusion of a recording of his performance in the film.

(2) Where this section applies, the absence of signature by or on behalf of the performer does not exclude the operation of section 191. C (effect of purported assignment of future rights).

(3) The reference in subsection (1) to an agreement concluded between a performer and a film producer includes any agreement having effect between those persons, whether made by them directly or through intermediaries.

(4) Section 191. G (right to equitable remuneration on transfer of rental right) applies where there is a presumed transfer by virtue of this section as in the case of an actual transfer.]

Editorial Information

X28. The insertion of the new headings "Chapter 1 Introductory", "Chapter 2 Economic Rights", "Chapter 3 Moral Rights" and "Chapter 4 Qualification for Protection, Extent and Interpretation" in Pt. II on 1.2.2006 gives rise to a change in the structure of this legislation on SLD which breaks the continuity of historical versions of the existing provisions which are now brought under those new headings.

Amendments (Textual)

F58. Ss. 191. A-191. M inserted (1.12.1996) by S.I. 1996/2967, reg. 21. (1) (with Pt. III)

Modifications etc. (not altering text)

C12. S. 191. F applied (1.12.1996) by S.I. 1996/2967, reg. 32. (1) (with Pt. III)

X29[F59191. G Right to equitable remuneration where rental right transferred.

(1) Where a performer has transferred his rental right concerning a sound recording or a film to the producer of the sound recording or film, he retains the right to equitable remuneration for the rental.

The reference above to the transfer of rental right by one person to another includes any arrangement having that effect, whether made by them directly or through intermediaries.

(2) The right to equitable remuneration under this section may not be assigned by the performer except to a collecting society for the purpose of enabling it to enforce the right on his behalf.

The right is, however, transmissible by testamentary disposition or by operation of law as personal or moveable property; and it may be assigned or further transmitted by any person into whose hands it passes.

(3) Equitable remuneration under this section is payable by the person for the time being entitled to the rental right, that is, the person to whom the right was transferred or any successor in title of his.

(4) The amount payable by way of equitable remuneration is as agreed by or on behalf of the persons by and to whom it is payable, subject to section 191. H (reference of amount to Copyright Tribunal).

(5) An agreement is of no effect in so far as it purports to exclude or restrict the right to equitable remuneration under this section.

(6) In this section a "collecting society" means a society or other organisation which has as its main object, or one of its main objects, the exercise of the right to equitable remuneration on behalf of more than one performer.]

X29. The insertion of the new headings "Chapter 1 Introductory", "Chapter 2 Economic Rights", "Chapter 3 Moral Rights" and "Chapter 4 Qualification for Protection, Extent and Interpretation" in Pt. II on 1.2.2006 gives rise to a change in the structure of this legislation on SLD which breaks the continuity of historical versions of the existing provisions which are now brought under those new headings.

Amendments (Textual)

F59. Ss. 191. A-191. M inserted (1.12.1996) by S.I. 1996/2967, reg. 21. (1) (with Pt. III)

Modifications etc. (not altering text)

C13. S. 191. G applied (with modifications) (1.12.1996) by S.I. 1996/2967, reg. 32. (2) (with Pt. III)

C14. S. 191. G restricted (1.12.1996) by S.I. 1996/2967, reg. 33 (with Pt. III)

X30[F60191. H Equitable remuneration: reference of amount to Copyright Tribunal.

(1) In default of agreement as to the amount payable by way of equitable remuneration under section 191. G, the person by or to whom it is payable may apply to the Copyright Tribunal to determine the amount payable.

(2) A person to or by whom equitable remuneration is payable may also apply to the Copyright Tribunal—

    (a) to vary any agreement as to the amount payable, or

    (b) to vary any previous determination of the Tribunal as to that matter;

but except with the special leave of the Tribunal no such application may be made within twelve months from the date of a previous determination.

An order made on an application under this subsection has effect from the date on which it is made or such later date as may be specified by the Tribunal.

(3) On an application under this section the Tribunal shall consider the matter and make such order as to the method of calculating and paying equitable remuneration as it may determine to be reasonable in the circumstances, taking into account the importance of the contribution of the performer to the film or sound recording.

(4) Remuneration shall not be considered inequitable merely because it was paid by way of a single payment or at the time of the transfer of the rental right.

(5) An agreement is of no effect in so far as it purports to prevent a person questioning the amount of equitable remuneration or to restrict the powers of the Copyright Tribunal under this section.]

Editorial Information

X30. The insertion of the new headings "Chapter 1 Introductory", "Chapter 2 Economic Rights", "Chapter 3 Moral Rights" and "Chapter 4 Qualification for Protection, Extent and Interpretation" in Pt. II on 1.2.2006 gives rise to a change in the structure of this legislation on SLD which breaks the continuity of historical versions of the existing provisions which are now brought under those new headings.

Amendments (Textual)

F60. Ss. 191. A-191. M inserted (1.12.1996) by S.I. 1996/2967, reg. 21. (1) (with Pt. III)

[F61191. HAAssignment of performer's property rights in a sound recording

(1) This section applies where a performer has [F62by an agreement] assigned the following rights concerning a sound recording to the producer of the sound recording—

    (a) reproduction, distribution and making available rights, or

    (b) performer's property rights.

(2) If, at the end of the 50-year period, the producer has failed to meet one or both of the following conditions, the performer may give a notice in writing to the producer of the performer's intention to terminate the agreement—

    (a) condition 1 is to issue to the public copies of the sound recording in sufficient quantities;

    (b) condition 2 is to make the sound recording available to the public by electronic transmission in such a way that a member of the public may access the recording from a place and at a time chosen by him or her.

(3) If, at any time after the end of the 50-year period, the producer, having met one or both of the

conditions referred to in subsection (2), fails to do so, the performer may give a notice in writing to the producer of the performer's intention to terminate the agreement.

(4) If at the end of the period of 12 months beginning with the date of the notice, the producer has not met the conditions referred to in subsection (2), the agreement terminates and the copyright in the sound recording expires with immediate effect.

(5) An agreement is of no effect in so far as it purports to exclude or restrict the right to give a notice under subsection (2) or (3).

(6) A reference in this section to the assignment of rights includes any arrangement having that effect, whether made directly between the parties or through intermediaries.

(7) In this section—

"50-year period" means

- where the sound recording is published during the initial period, the period of 50 years from the end of the calendar year in which the sound recording is first published, or

- where during the initial period the sound recording is not published but is made available to the public by being played in public or communicated to the public, the period of 50 years from the end of the calendar year in which it was first made available to the public,

but in determining whether a sound recording has been published, played in public or communicated to the public, no account shall be taken of any unauthorised act,

"initial period" means the period beginning on the date the recording is made and ending 50 years from the end of the calendar year in which the sound recording is made,

"producer" means the person for the time being entitled to the copyright in the sound recording,

"sufficient quantities" means such quantity as to satisfy the reasonable requirements of the public for copies of the sound recording,

"unauthorised act" has the same meaning as in section 178.

Amendments (Textual)

F61. Ss. 191. HA-191. HB inserted (1.11.2013) by The Copyright and Duration of Rights in Performances Regulations 2013 (S.I. 2013/1782), regs. 1, 9 (with regs. 11-27)

F62. Words in s. 191. HA(1) inserted (6.4.2014) by The Copyright and Duration of Rights in Performances (Amendment) Regulations 2014 (S.I. 2014/434), regs. 1, 2

191. HBPayment in consideration of assignment

(1) A performer who, under an agreement relating to the assignment of rights referred to in section 191. HA(1) (an "assignment agreement"), is entitled to a non-recurring payment in consideration of the assignment, is entitled to an annual payment for each relevant period from—

(a) the producer, or

(b) where the producer has granted an exclusive licence of the copyright in the sound recording, the licensee under the exclusive licence (the "exclusive licensee").

(2) In this section, "relevant period" means—

(a) the period of 12 months beginning at the end of the 50-year period, and

(b) each subsequent period of 12 months beginning with the end of the previous period, until the date on which copyright in the sound recording expires.

(3) The producer or, where relevant, the exclusive licensee gives effect to the entitlement under subsection (1) by remitting to a collecting society for distribution to the performer in accordance with its rules an amount for each relevant period equal to 20% of the gross revenue received during that period in respect of—

(a) the reproduction and issue to the public of copies of the sound recording, and

(b) the making available to the public of the sound recording by electronic transmission in such a way that members of the public may access it from a place and at a time individually chosen by them.

(4) The amount required to be remitted under subsection (3) is payable within 6 months of the end of each relevant period and is recoverable by the collecting society as a debt.

(5) Subsection (6) applies where—

(a) the performer makes a written request to the producer or, where relevant, the exclusive licensee for information in that person's possession or under that person's control to enable the performer—

(i) to ascertain the amount of the annual payment to which the performer is entitled under subsection (1), or

(ii) to secure its distribution by the collecting society, and

   (b) the producer or, where relevant, the exclusive licensee does not supply the information within the period of 90 days beginning with the date of the request.

(6) The performer may apply to the county court, or in Scotland to the sheriff, for an order requiring the producer or, where relevant, the exclusive licensee to supply the information.

(7) An agreement is of no effect in so far as it purports to exclude or restrict the entitlement under subsection (1).

(8) In the event of any dispute as to the amount required to be remitted under subsection (3), the performer may apply to the Copyright Tribunal to determine the amount payable.

(9) Where a performer is entitled under an assignment agreement to recurring payments in consideration of the assignment, the payments must, from the end of the 50-year period, be made in full, regardless of any provision in the agreement which entitles the producer to withhold or deduct sums from the amounts payable.

(10) In this section—

"producer" and "50-year period" each has the same meaning as in section 191. HA,

"exclusive licence" has the same meaning as in section 92, and

"collecting society" has the same meaning as in section 191. G.]

Amendments (Textual)

F61. Ss. 191. HA-191. HB inserted (1.11.2013) by The Copyright and Duration of Rights in Performances Regulations 2013 (S.I. 2013/1782), regs. 1, 9 (with regs. 11-27)

X31[F63191. I Infringement actionable by rights owner.

(1) An infringement of a performer's property rights is actionable by the rights owner.

(2) In an action for infringement of a performer's property rights all such relief by way of damages, injunctions, accounts or otherwise is available to the plaintiff as is available in respect of the infringement of any other property right.

(3) This section has effect subject to the following provisions of [F64this Chapter].]

Editorial Information

X31. The insertion of the new headings "Chapter 1 Introductory", "Chapter 2 Economic Rights", "Chapter 3 Moral Rights" and "Chapter 4 Qualification for Protection, Extent and Interpretation" in Pt. II on 1.2.2006 gives rise to a change in the structure of this legislation on SLD which breaks the continuity of historical versions of the existing provisions which are now brought under those new headings.

Amendments (Textual)

F63. Ss. 191. A-191. M inserted (1.12.1996) by S.I. 1996/2967, reg. 21. (1) (with Pt. III)

F64. Words in s. 191. I(3) substituted (1.2.2006) by The Performances (Moral Rights, etc.) Regulations 2006 (S.I. 2006/18), reg. 2, Sch. para. 8 (with reg. 8)

X32[F65191. J Provisions as to damages in infringement action.

(1) Where in an action for infringement of a performer's property rights it is shown that at the time of the infringement the defendant did not know, and had no reason to believe, that the rights subsisted in the recording to which the action relates, the plaintiff is not entitled to damages against him, but without prejudice to any other remedy.

(2) The court may in an action for infringement of a performer's property rights having regard to all the circumstances, and in particular to—

   (a) the flagrancy of the infringement, and

   (b) any benefit accruing to the defendant by reason of the infringement,

award such additional damages as the justice of the case may require.]

Editorial Information

X32. The insertion of the new headings "Chapter 1 Introductory", "Chapter 2 Economic Rights", "Chapter 3 Moral Rights" and "Chapter 4 Qualification for Protection, Extent and Interpretation" in Pt. II on 1.2.2006 gives rise to a change in the structure of this legislation on SLD which breaks

the continuity of historical versions of the existing provisions which are now brought under those new headings.

Amendments (Textual)

F65. Ss. 191. A-191. M inserted (1.12.1996) by S.I. 1996/2967, reg. 21. (1) (with Pt. III)

X33[F66191. JAInjunctions against service providers

(1) The High Court (in Scotland, the Court of Session) shall have power to grant an injunction against a service provider, where that service provider has actual knowledge of another person using their service to infringe a performer's property right.

(2) In determining whether a service provider has actual knowledge for the purpose of this section, a court shall take into account all matters which appear to it in the particular circumstances to be relevant and, amongst other things, shall have regard to—

(a) whether a service provider has received a notice through a means of contact made available in accordance with regulation 6. (1)(c) of the Electronic Commerce (EC Directive) Regulations 2002 (SI 2002/2013); and

(b) the extent to which any notice includes—

(i) the full name and address of the sender of the notice;

(ii) details of the infringement in question.

(3) In this section " service provider " has the meaning given to it by regulation 2 of the Electronic Commerce (EC Directive) Regulations 2002.

(4) Section 177 applies in respect of this section as it applies in respect of Part 1.]

Editorial Information

X33. The insertion of the new headings "Chapter 1 Introductory", "Chapter 2 Economic Rights", "Chapter 3 Moral Rights" and "Chapter 4 Qualification for Protection, Extent and Interpretation" in Pt. II on 1.2.2006 gives rise to a change in the structure of this legislation on SLD which breaks the continuity of historical versions of the existing provisions which are now brought under those new headings.

Amendments (Textual)

F66. S. 191. JA inserted (31.10.2003) by The Copyright and Related Rights Regulations 2003 (S.I. 2003/2498), reg. 27. (2) (with regs. 32, 33)

X34[F67191. K Undertaking to take licence of right in infringement proceedings.

(1) If in proceedings for infringement of a performer's property rights in respect of which a licence is available as of right under paragraph 17 of Schedule 2. A (powers exercisable in consequence of competition report) the defendant undertakes to take a licence on such terms as may be agreed or, in default of agreement, settled by the Copyright Tribunal under that paragraph—

(a) no injunction shall be granted against him,

(b) no order for delivery up shall be made under section 195, and

(c) the amount recoverable against him by way of damages or on an account of profits shall not exceed double the amount which would have been payable by him as licensee if such a licence on those terms had been granted before the earliest infringement.

(2) An undertaking may be given at any time before final order in the proceedings, without any admission of liability.

(3) Nothing in this section affects the remedies available in respect of an infringement committed before licences of right were available.]

Editorial Information

X34. The insertion of the new headings "Chapter 1 Introductory", "Chapter 2 Economic Rights", "Chapter 3 Moral Rights" and "Chapter 4 Qualification for Protection, Extent and Interpretation" in Pt. II on 1.2.2006 gives rise to a change in the structure of this legislation on SLD which breaks the continuity of historical versions of the existing provisions which are now brought under those new headings.

Amendments (Textual)

F67. Ss. 191. A-191. M inserted (1.12.1996) by S.I. 1996/2967, reg. 21. (1) (with Pt. III)

X35[F68191. L Rights and remedies for exclusive licensee.

(1) An exclusive licensee has, except against the owner of a performer's property rights, the same rights and remedies in respect of matters occurring after the grant of the licence as if the licence had been an assignment.

(2) His rights and remedies are concurrent with those of the rights owner; and references in the relevant provisions of [F69this Chapter] to the rights owner shall be construed accordingly.

(3) In an action brought by an exclusive licensee by virtue of this section a defendant may avail himself of any defence which would have been available to him if the action had been brought by the rights owner.]

Editorial Information

X35. The insertion of the new headings "Chapter 1 Introductory", "Chapter 2 Economic Rights", "Chapter 3 Moral Rights" and "Chapter 4 Qualification for Protection, Extent and Interpretation" in Pt. II on 1.2.2006 gives rise to a change in the structure of this legislation on SLD which breaks the continuity of historical versions of the existing provisions which are now brought under those new headings.

Amendments (Textual)

F68. Ss. 191. A-191. M inserted (1.12.1996) by S.I. 1996/2967, reg. 21. (1) (with Pt. III)

F69. Words in s. 191. L(2) substituted (1.2.2006) by The Performances (Moral Rights, etc.) Regulations 2006 (S.I. 2006/18), reg. 2, Sch. para. 8 (with reg. 8)

X36[F70191. M Exercise of concurrent rights.

(1) Where an action for infringement of a performer's property rights brought by the rights owner or an exclusive licensee relates (wholly or partly) to an infringement in respect of which they have concurrent rights of action, the rights owner or, as the case may be, the exclusive licensee may not, without the leave of the court, proceed with the action unless the other is either joined as plaintiff or added as a defendant.

(2) A rights owner or exclusive licensee who is added as a defendant in pursuance of subsection (1) is not liable for any costs in the action unless he takes part in the proceedings.

(3) The above provisions do not affect the granting of interlocutory relief on an application by the rights owner or exclusive licensee alone.

(4) Where an action for infringement of a performer's property rights is brought which relates (wholly or partly) to an infringement in respect of which the rights owner and an exclusive licensee have or had concurrent rights of action—

(a) the court shall in assessing damages take into account—

(i) the terms of the licence, and

(ii) any pecuniary remedy already awarded or available to either of them in respect of the infringement;

(b) no account of profits shall be directed if an award of damages has been made, or an account of profits has been directed, in favour of the other of them in respect of the infringement; and

(c) the court shall if an account of profits is directed apportion the profits between them as the court considers just, subject to any agreement between them; and these provisions apply whether or not the rights owner and the exclusive licensee are both parties to the action.

(5) The owner of a performer's property rights shall notify any exclusive licensee having concurrent rights before applying for an order under section 195 (order for delivery up) or exercising the right conferred by section 196 (right of seizure); and the court may on the application of the licensee make such order under section 195 or, as the case may be, prohibiting or permitting the exercise by the rights owner of the right conferred by section 196, as it thinks fit having regard to the terms of the licence.]

Editorial Information

X36. The insertion of the new headings "Chapter 1 Introductory", "Chapter 2 Economic Rights", "Chapter 3 Moral Rights" and "Chapter 4 Qualification for Protection, Extent and Interpretation" in Pt. II on 1.2.2006 gives rise to a change in the structure of this legislation on SLD which breaks the continuity of historical versions of the existing provisions which are now brought under those new headings.

Amendments (Textual)

X37[F71. Non-property rights]

Editorial Information

X37. The insertion of the new headings "Chapter 1 Introductory", "Chapter 2 Economic Rights", "Chapter 3 Moral Rights" and "Chapter 4 Qualification for Protection, Extent and Interpretation" in Pt. II on 1.2.2006 gives rise to a change in the structure of this legislation on SLD which breaks the continuity of historical versions of the existing provisions which are now brought under those new headings.

Amendments (Textual)

F71. Ss. 192. A, 192. B and crossheading substituted for s. 192 (1.12.1996) by S.I. 1996/2967, reg. 21. (2) (with Pt. III)

 X38 [F72 192. A Performers' non-property rights.

(1) the rights conferred on a performer by -

section 182 (consent required for recording, &c. of live performance),

 section 183 (infringement of performer's rights by use of recording made without consent), F73 ...

section 184 (infringement of performer's rights importing, possessing or dealing with illicit recording),

[F74section 191. HA (assignment of performer's property rights in a sound recording), and section 191. HB (payment in consideration of assignment),]

are not assignable or transmissible, except to the following extent.

 They are referred to in [F75 this Chapter] as " F76 . . . performer's non-property rights".

(2) On the death of a person entitled to any such right—

(a) the right passes to such person as he may by testamentary disposition specifically direct, and

(b) if or to the extent that there is no such direction, the right is exercisable by his personal representatives.

(3) References in [F75this Chapter] to the performer, in the context of the person having any such right, shall be construed as references to the person for the time being entitled to exercise those rights.

(4) Where by virtue of subsection (2)(a) a right becomes exercisable by more than one person, it is exercisable by each of them independently of the other or others.

(5) Any damages recovered by personal representatives by virtue of this section in respect of an infringement after a person's death shall devolve as part of his estate as if the right of action had subsisted and been vested in him immediately before his death.]

Editorial Information

X38. The insertion of the new headings "Chapter 1 Introductory", "Chapter 2 Economic Rights", "Chapter 3 Moral Rights" and "Chapter 4 Qualification for Protection, Extent and Interpretation" in Pt. II on 1.2.2006 gives rise to a change in the structure of this legislation on SLD which breaks the continuity of historical versions of the existing provisions which are now brought under those new headings.

Amendments (Textual)

F72. Ss. 192. A, 192. B and crossheading substituted for s. 192 (1.12.1996) by S.I. 1996/2967, reg. 21. (2) (with Pt. III)

F73. Word in s. 192. A(1) deleted (1.11.2013) by The Copyright and Duration of Rights in Performances Regulations 2013 (S.I. 2013/1782), regs. 1, 10 (with regs. 11-27)

F74. Words in s. 192. A(1) inserted (1.11.2013) by The Copyright and Duration of Rights in Performances Regulations 2013 (S.I. 2013/1782), regs. 1, 10 (with regs. 11-27)

F75. Words in s. 192. A(1)(3) substituted (1.2.2006) by The Performances (Moral Rights, etc.) Regulations 2006 (S.I. 2006/18), reg. 2, Sch. para. 8 (with reg. 8)

F76. Word in s. 192. A(1) omitted by virtue of The Performances (Moral Rights, etc.) Regulations 2006 (S.I. 2006/18), reg. 2, Sch. para. 5 (with reg. 8)

X39[F77192. B Transmissibility of rights of person having recording rights.

(1) The rights conferred by [F78this Chapter] on a person having recording rights are not assignable or transmissible.

(2) This does not affect section 185. (2)(b) or (3)(b), so far as those provisions confer rights under [F78this Chapter] on a person to whom the benefit of a contract or licence is assigned.]

Editorial Information

X39. The insertion of the new headings "Chapter 1 Introductory", "Chapter 2 Economic Rights", "Chapter 3 Moral Rights" and "Chapter 4 Qualification for Protection, Extent and Interpretation" in Pt. II on 1.2.2006 gives rise to a change in the structure of this legislation on SLD which breaks the continuity of historical versions of the existing provisions which are now brought under those new headings.

Amendments (Textual)

F77. Ss. 192. A, 192. B and crossheading substituted for s. 192 (1.12.1996) by S.I. 1996/2967, reg. 21. (2) (with Pt. III)

F78. Words in s. 192. B(1)(2) substituted (1.2.2006) by The Performances (Moral Rights, etc.) Regulations 2006 (S.I. 2006/18), reg. 2, Sch. para. 8 (with reg. 8)

X40193 Consent.

(1) Consent for the purposes of [F79this Chapter][F80by a person having a performer's non-property rights, or by a person having recording rights,] may be given in relation to a specific performance, a specified description of performances or performances generally, and may relate to past or future performances.

(2) A person having recording rights in a performance is bound by any consent given by a person through whom he derives his rights under the exclusive recording contract or licence in question, in the same way as if the consent had been given by him.

(3) Where [F81a performer's non-property right] passes to another person, any consent binding on the person previously entitled binds the person to whom the right passes in the same way as if the consent had been given by him.

Editorial Information

X40. The insertion of the new headings "Chapter 1 Introductory", "Chapter 2 Economic Rights", "Chapter 3 Moral Rights" and "Chapter 4 Qualification for Protection, Extent and Interpretation" in Pt. II on 1.2.2006 gives rise to a change in the structure of this legislation on SLD which breaks the continuity of historical versions of the existing provisions which are now brought under those new headings.

Amendments (Textual)

F79. Words in s. 193. (1) substituted (1.2.2006) by The Performances (Moral Rights, etc.) Regulations 2006 (S.I. 2006/18), reg. 2, Sch. para. 8 (with reg. 8)

F80. Words in s. 193. (1) inserted (1.12.1996) by S.I. 1996/2967, reg. 21. (3)(a) (with Pt. III)

F81. Words in s. 193. (3) substituted (1.12.1996) by S.I. 1996/2967, reg. 21. (3)(b) (with Pt. III)

X41. F82. . .

Editorial Information

X41. The insertion of the new headings "Chapter 1 Introductory", "Chapter 2 Economic Rights", "Chapter 3 Moral Rights" and "Chapter 4 Qualification for Protection, Extent and Interpretation" in Pt. II on 1.2.2006 gives rise to a change in the structure of this legislation on SLD which breaks the continuity of historical versions of the existing provisions which are now brought under those new headings.

Amendments (Textual)

F82. Crossheading before s. 194 omitted (1.12.1996) by virtue of S.I. 1996/2967, reg. 21. (5)(b) (with Pt. III)

X42194 Infringement actionable as breach of statutory duty.

An infringement of [F83—

(a) a performer's non-property rights, or

(b) any right conferred by [F84this Chapter] on a person having recording rights,]

is actionable by the person entitled to the right as a breach of statutory duty.

Editorial Information

X42. The insertion of the new headings "Chapter 1 Introductory", "Chapter 2 Economic Rights", "Chapter 3 Moral Rights" and "Chapter 4 Qualification for Protection, Extent and Interpretation" in Pt. II on 1.2.2006 gives rise to a change in the structure of this legislation on SLD which breaks the continuity of historical versions of the existing provisions which are now brought under those new headings.

Amendments (Textual)

F83. Words in s. 194 substituted (1.12.1996) by S.I. 1996/2967, reg. 21. (4) (with Pt. III)

F84. Words in s. 194. (b) substituted (1.2.2006) by The Performances (Moral Rights, etc.) Regulations 2006 (S.I. 2006/18), reg. 2, Sch. para. 8 (with reg. 8)

X43[F85. Delivery up or seizure of illicit recordings]

Editorial Information

X43. The insertion of the new headings "Chapter 1 Introductory", "Chapter 2 Economic Rights", "Chapter 3 Moral Rights" and "Chapter 4 Qualification for Protection, Extent and Interpretation" in Pt. II on 1.2.2006 gives rise to a change in the structure of this legislation on SLD which breaks the continuity of historical versions of the existing provisions which are now brought under those new headings.

Amendments (Textual)

F85. Heading before s. 195 inserted (1.12.1996) by S.I. 1996/2967, reg. 21. (5)(c) (with Pt. III)

X44195 Order for delivery up.

(1) Where a person has in his possession, custody or control in the course of a business an illicit recording of a performance, a person having performer's rights or recording rights in relation to the performance under [F86this Chapter] may apply to the court for an order that the recording be delivered up to him or to such other person as the court may direct.

(2) An application shall not be made after the end of the period specified in section 203; and no order shall be made unless the court also makes, or it appears to the court that there are grounds for making, an order under section 204 (order as to disposal of illicit recording).

(3) A person to whom a recording is delivered up in pursuance of an order under this section shall, if an order under section 204 is not made, retain it pending the making of an order, or the decision not to make an order, under that section.

(4) Nothing in this section affects any other power of the court.

Editorial Information

X44. The insertion of the new headings "Chapter 1 Introductory", "Chapter 2 Economic Rights", "Chapter 3 Moral Rights" and "Chapter 4 Qualification for Protection, Extent and Interpretation" in Pt. II on 1.2.2006 gives rise to a change in the structure of this legislation on SLD which breaks the continuity of historical versions of the existing provisions which are now brought under those new headings.

Amendments (Textual)

F86. Words in s. 195. (1) substituted (1.2.2006) by The Performances (Moral Rights, etc.) Regulations 2006 (S.I. 2006/18), reg. 2, Sch. para. 8 (with reg. 8)

Modifications etc. (not altering text)

C15. S. 195 extended by S.I. 1991/724, art. 2. (1)(n)

X45196 Right to seize illicit recordings.

(1) An illicit recording of a performance which is found exposed or otherwise immediately available for sale or hire, and in respect of which a person would be entitled to apply for an order under section 195, may be seized and detained by him or a person authorised by him.

The right to seize and detain is exercisable subject to the following conditions and is subject to any decision of the court under section 204 (order as to disposal of illicit recording).

(2) Before anything is seized under this section notice of the time and place of the proposed seizure must be given to a local police station.

(3) A person may for the purpose of exercising the right conferred by this section enter premises to which the public have access but may not seize anything in the possession, custody or control of a person at a permanent or regular place of business of his and may not use any force.

(4) At the time when anything is seized under this section there shall be left at the place where it was seized a notice in the prescribed form containing the prescribed particulars as to the person by whom or on whose authority the seizure is made and the grounds on which it is made.

(5) In this section—

"premises" includes land, buildings, fixed or moveable structures, vehicles, vessels, aircraft and hovercraft; and

"prescribed" means prescribed by order of the Secretary of State.

(6) An order of the Secretary of State under this section shall be made by statutory instrument which shall be subject to annulment in pursuance of a resolution of either House of Parliament.

Editorial Information

X45. The insertion of the new headings "Chapter 1 Introductory", "Chapter 2 Economic Rights", "Chapter 3 Moral Rights" and "Chapter 4 Qualification for Protection, Extent and Interpretation" in Pt. II on 1.2.2006 gives rise to a change in the structure of this legislation on SLD which breaks the continuity of historical versions of the existing provisions which are now brought under those new headings.

X46197 Meaning of "illicit recording".

(1) In [F87this Chapter]"illicit recording", in relation to a performance, shall be construed in accordance with this section.

(2) For the purposes of a performer's rights, a recording of the whole or any substantial part of a performance of his is an illicit recording if it is made, otherwise than for private purposes, without his consent.

(3) For the purposes of the rights of a person having recording rights, a recording of the whole or any substantial part of a performance subject to the exclusive recording contract is an illicit recording if it is made, otherwise than for private purposes, without his consent or that of the performer.

(4) For the purposes of sections 198 and 199 (offences and orders for delivery up in criminal proceedings), a recording is an illicit recording if it is an illicit recording for the purposes mentioned in subsection (2) or subsection (3).

(5) In [F87this Chapter]"illicit recording" includes a recording falling to be treated as an illicit recording by virtue of any of the following provisions of Schedule 2—

- [F88paragraph 1. D(3) (copies for text and data analysis for non-commercial research),]
- [F89paragraph 3. A(5) or (6) or 3. B(10) (accessible copies of recordings made for disabled persons)]
- [F90paragraph 1. B(5) and (7) (personal copies of recordings for private use),]
- F91...
- [F92paragraph 6. (5) (recording by educational establishments of broadcasts),]
- [F88paragraph 6. F(5)(b) (copying by librarians: single copies of published recordings),]
- [F88paragraph 6. G(5)(b) (copying by librarians or archivists: single copies of unpublished recordings),]
- [F88paragraph 6. ZA(7) (copying and use of extracts of recordings by educational establishments),]
- paragraph 12. (2) (recordings of performance in electronic form retained on transfer of principal recording), F93. . .
- [F88paragraph 14. (6)(b) (recordings of folksongs),]
- paragraph 16. (3) (recordings made for purposes of broadcast F94. . .),
- [F95paragraph 17. A(2) (recording for the purposes of time-shifting), or
- paragraph 17. B(2) (photographs of broadcasts),]

but otherwise does not include a recording made in accordance with any of the provisions of that Schedule.

(6) It is immaterial for the purposes of this section where the recording was made.

Editorial Information

X46. The insertion of the new headings "Chapter 1 Introductory", "Chapter 2 Economic Rights", "Chapter 3 Moral Rights" and "Chapter 4 Qualification for Protection, Extent and Interpretation" in Pt. II on 1.2.2006 gives rise to a change in the structure of this legislation on SLD which breaks the continuity of historical versions of the existing provisions which are now brought under those new headings.

Amendments (Textual)

F87. Words in s. 197. (1)(5) substituted (1.2.2006) by The Performances (Moral Rights, etc.) Regulations 2006 (S.I. 2006/18), reg. 2, Sch. para. 8 (with reg. 8)

F88. Words in s. 197. (5) inserted (1.6.2014) by The Copyright and Rights in Performances (Research, Education, Libraries and Archives) Regulations 2014 (S.I. 2014/1372), reg. 1, Sch. para. 7. (a)

F89. Words in s. 197. (5) inserted (1.6.2014) by The Copyright and Rights in Performances (Disability) Regulations 2014 (S.I. 2014/1384), reg. 1. (1), Sch. para. 4

F90. Words in s. 197. (5) inserted (1.10.2014) by The Copyright and Rights in Performances (Personal Copies for Private Use) Regulations 2014 (S.I. 2014/2361), regs. 1. (1), 4. (2) (with reg. 5) (but note that the amending S.I. was quashed with prospective effect by the High Court in the case of R (British Academy of Songwriters, Composers and Authors and others) v Secretary of State for Business, Innovation and Skills [2015] EWHC 2041 (Admin), 17 July 2015)

F91. Words in s. 197. (5) omitted (1.6.2014) by virtue of The Copyright and Rights in Performances (Research, Education, Libraries and Archives) Regulations 2014 (S.I. 2014/1372), reg. 1, Sch. para. 7. (b)

F92. Words in s. 197. (5) substituted (1.6.2014) by The Copyright and Rights in Performances (Research, Education, Libraries and Archives) Regulations 2014 (S.I. 2014/1372), reg. 1, Sch. para. 7. (c)

F93. Words in s. 197. (5) repealed (31.10.2003) by The Copyright and Related Rights Regulations 2003 (S.I. 2003/2498), reg. 2. (2), Sch. 2 (with regs. 31-40)

F94. Words in s. 197. (5) repealed (31.10.2003) by The Copyright and Related Rights Regulations 2003 (S.I. 2003/2498), reg. 2. (2), Sch. 2 (with regs. 31-40)

F95. Words in s. 197. (5) inserted (31.10.2003) by The Copyright and Related Rights Regulations 2003 (S.I. 2003/2498), reg. 20. (4) (with regs. 31-40)

[F96197. APresumptions relevant to recordings of performances

(1) In proceedings brought by virtue of this Part with respect to the rights in a performance, where copies of a recording of the performance as issued to the public bear a statement that a named person was the performer, the statement shall be admissible as evidence of the fact stated and shall be presumed to be correct until the contrary is proved.

(2) Subsection (1) does not apply to proceedings for an offence under section 198 (criminal liability for making etc. illicit recordings); but without prejudice to its application in proceedings for an order under section 199 (order for delivery up in criminal proceedings).]

Amendments (Textual)

F96. S. 197. A inserted (29.4.2006) by The Intellectual Property (Enforcement, etc.) Regulations 2006 (S.I. 2006/1028), reg. 2. (2), Sch. 2 para. 10

X47 Offences

Editorial Information

X47. The insertion of the new headings "Chapter 1 Introductory", "Chapter 2 Economic Rights", "Chapter 3 Moral Rights" and "Chapter 4 Qualification for Protection, Extent and Interpretation" in Pt. II on 1.2.2006 gives rise to a change in the structure of this legislation on SLD which breaks

the continuity of historical versions of the existing provisions which are now brought under those new headings.

X48198 Criminal liability for making, dealing with or using illicit recordings.

(1) A person commits an offence who without sufficient consent—

(a) makes for sale or hire, or

(b) imports into the United Kingdom otherwise than for his private and domestic use, or

(c) possesses in the course of a business with a view to committing any act infringing the rights conferred by [F97this Chapter], or

(d) in the course of a business—

(i) sells or lets for hire, or

(ii) offers or exposes for sale or hire, or

(iii) distributes,

a recording which is, and which he knows or has reason to believe is, an illicit recording.

[F98. (1. A)A person ("P") who infringes a performer's making available right in a recording commits an offence if P—

(a) knows or has reason to believe that P is infringing the right, and

(b) either—

(i) intends to make a gain for P or another person, or

(ii) knows or has reason to believe that infringing the right will cause loss to the owner of the right, or expose the owner of the right to a risk of loss.

(1. B)For the purposes of subsection (1. A)—

(a) "gain" and "loss"—

(i) extend only to gain or loss in money, and

(ii) include any such gain or loss whether temporary or permanent, and

(b) "loss" includes a loss by not getting what one might get.]

(2) A person commits an offence who causes a recording of a performance made without sufficient consent to be—

(a) shown or played in public, or

[F99. (b)communicated to the public,]

thereby infringing any of the rights conferred by [F97this Chapter], if he knows or has reason to believe that those rights are thereby infringed.

(3) In subsections (1) and (2) "sufficient consent" means—

(a) in the case of a qualifying performance, the consent of the performer, and

(b) in the case of a non-qualifying performance subject to an exclusive recording contract—

(i) for the purposes of subsection (1)(a) (making of recording), the consent of the performer or the person having recording rights, and

(ii) for the purposes of subsection (1)(b), (c) and (d) and subsection (2) (dealing with or using recording), the consent of the person having recording rights.

The references in this subsection to the person having recording rights are to the person having those rights at the time the consent is given or, if there is more than one such person, to all of them.

(4) No offence is committed under subsection (1) or (2) by the commission of an act which by virtue of any provision of Schedule 2 may be done without infringing the rights conferred by [F97this Chapter].

(5) A person guilty of an offence under subsection (1)(a), (b) or (d)(iii) is liable—

(a) on summary conviction to imprisonment for a term not exceeding six months or [F100a fine], or both;

(b) on conviction on indictment to a fine or imprisonment for a term not exceeding [F101ten] years, or both.

[F102. (5. A)A person guilty of an offence under subsection (1. A) is liable—

(a) on summary conviction to imprisonment for a term not exceeding three months or [F103a fine], or both;

(b) on conviction on indictment to a fine or imprisonment for a term not exceeding [F104 ten] years, or both.]

(6) A person guilty of any other offence under this section is liable on summary conviction to a fine not exceeding level 5 on the standard scale or imprisonment for a term not exceeding six months, or both.

Editorial Information

X48. The insertion of the new headings "Chapter 1 Introductory", "Chapter 2 Economic Rights", "Chapter 3 Moral Rights" and "Chapter 4 Qualification for Protection, Extent and Interpretation" in Pt. II on 1.2.2006 gives rise to a change in the structure of this legislation on SLD which breaks the continuity of historical versions of the existing provisions which are now brought under those new headings.

Amendments (Textual)

F97. Words in s. 198. (1)(c)(2)(4) substituted (1.2.2006) by The Performances (Moral Rights, etc.) Regulations 2006 (S.I. 2006/18), reg. 2, Sch. para. 8 (with reg. 8)

F98. S. 198. (1. A)(1. B) substituted for s. 198. (1. A) (1.10.2017) by Digital Economy Act 2017 (c. 30), ss. 32. (4), 118. (6) (with s. 32. (6)); S.I. 2017/765, reg. 3. (a)

F99. S. 198. (2)(b) substituted (31.10.2003) by The Copyright and Related Rights Regulations 2003 (S.I. 2003/2498), reg. 2. (1), Sch. 1 para. 4. (5) (with regs. 31-40)

F100. Words in s. 198. (5)(a) substituted (12.3.2015) by The Legal Aid, Sentencing and Punishment of Offenders Act 2012 (Fines on Summary Conviction) Regulations 2015 (S.I. 2015/664), reg. 1. (1), Sch. 4 para. 17. (3)(a) (with reg. 5. (1))

F101. S. 198. (5)(b) substituted (20.11.2002) by 2002 c. 25, s. 1. (3)(5); S.I. 2002/2749, art. 2

F102. S. 198. (5. A) inserted (31.10.2003) by The Copyright and Related Rights Regulations 2003 (S.I. 2003/2498), reg. 26. (3)(b) (with regs. 31-40)

F103. Words in s. 198. (5. A)(a) substituted (12.3.2015) by The Legal Aid, Sentencing and Punishment of Offenders Act 2012 (Fines on Summary Conviction) Regulations 2015 (S.I. 2015/664), reg. 1. (1), Sch. 4 para. 17. (3)(b) (with reg. 5. (1))

F104. Word in s. 198. (5. A)(b) substituted (1.10.2017) by Digital Economy Act 2017 (c. 30), ss. 32. (5), 118. (6) (with s. 32. (6)); S.I. 2017/765, reg. 3. (a)

X49[F105198. A Enforcement by local weights and measures authority.

(1) It is the duty of every local weights and measures authority to enforce within their area the provisions of section 198.

F106. (2). . . . .

(3) Subsection (1) above does not apply in relation to the enforcement of section 198 in Northern Ireland, but it is the duty of the Department of Economic Development to enforce that section in Northern Ireland.

F107...

[F108. (3. A)For the investigatory powers available to a local weights and measures authority or the Department of Enterprise, Trade and Investment in Northern Ireland for the purposes of the duties in this section, see Schedule 5 to the Consumer Rights Act 2015.]

(4) Any enactment which authorises the disclosure of information for the purpose of facilitating the enforcement of the Trade Descriptions Act 1968 shall apply as if section 198 were contained in that Act and as if the functions of any person in relation to the enforcement of that section were functions under that Act.

(5) Nothing in this section shall be construed as authorising a local weights and measures authority to bring proceedings in Scotland for an offence.]

Editorial Information

X49. The insertion of the new headings "Chapter 1 Introductory", "Chapter 2 Economic Rights", "Chapter 3 Moral Rights" and "Chapter 4 Qualification for Protection, Extent and Interpretation" in Pt. II on 1.2.2006 gives rise to a change in the structure of this legislation on SLD which breaks the continuity of historical versions of the existing provisions which are now brought under those new headings.

Amendments (Textual)

F105. S. 198. A inserted (6.4.2007) by 1994 c. 33, ss. 165. (3), 172. (2); S.I. 2007/621, art. 2

F106. S. 198. A(2) omitted (1.10.2015) by virtue of Consumer Rights Act 2015 (c. 15), s. 100. (5), Sch. 6 para. 50. (2); S.I. 2015/1630, art. 3. (i) (with art. 8)

F107. Words in s. 198. A(3) omitted (1.10.2015) by virtue of Consumer Rights Act 2015 (c. 15), s. 100. (5), Sch. 6 para. 50. (3); S.I. 2015/1630, art. 3. (i) (with art. 8)

F108. S. 198. A(3. A) inserted (1.10.2015) by Consumer Rights Act 2015 (c. 15), s. 100. (5), Sch. 6 para. 50. (4); S.I. 2015/1630, art. 3. (i)

X50199 Order for delivery up in criminal proceedings.

(1) The court before which proceedings are brought against a person for an offence under section 198 may, if satisfied that at the time of his arrest or charge he had in his possession, custody or control in the course of a business an illicit recording of a performance, order that it be delivered up to a person having performers' rights or recording rights in relation to the performance or to such other person as the court may direct.

(2) For this purpose a person shall be treated as charged with an offence—

(a) in England, Wales and Northern Ireland, when he is orally charged or is served with a summons or indictment;

(b) in Scotland, when he is cautioned, charged or served with a complaint or indictment.

(3) An order may be made by the court of its own motion or on the application of the prosecutor (or, in Scotland, the Lord Advocate or procurator-fiscal), and may be made whether or not the person is convicted of the offence, but shall not be made—

(a) after the end of the period specified in section 203 (period after which remedy of delivery up not available), or

(b) if it appears to the court unlikely that any order will be made under section 204 (order as to disposal of illicit recording).

(4) An appeal lies from an order made under this section by a magistrates' court—

(a) in England and Wales, to the Crown Court, and

(b) in Northern Ireland, to the county court;

and in Scotland, where an order has been made under this section, the person from whose possession, custody or control the illicit recording has been been removed may, without predudice to any other form of appeal under any rule of law, appeal against that order in the same manner as against sentence.

(5) A person to whom an illicit recording is delivered up in pursuance of an order under this section shall retain it pending the making of an order, or the decision not to make an order, under section 204.

(6) Nothing in in this section affects the powers of the court under [F109section 143 of the Powers of Criminal Courts (Sentencing) Act 2000], [F110. Part II of the Proceeds of Crime (Scotland) Act 1995] or [F111. Article 11 of the Criminal Justice (Northern Ireland) Order 1994] (general provisions as to forfeiture in criminal proceedings).

Editorial Information

X50. The insertion of the new headings "Chapter 1 Introductory", "Chapter 2 Economic Rights", "Chapter 3 Moral Rights" and "Chapter 4 Qualification for Protection, Extent and Interpretation" in Pt. II on 1.2.2006 gives rise to a change in the structure of this legislation on SLD which breaks the continuity of historical versions of the existing provisions which are now brought under those new headings.

Amendments (Textual)

F109. Words in s. 199. (6) substituted (25.8.2000) by 2000 c. 6 ss. 165, 168, Sch. 9 para. 116

F110. Words in s. 199. (6) substituted (1.4.1996) by 1995 c. 20, ss. 5, 7. (2), Sch. 4 para. 70. (3)

F111. Words in s. 199. (6) substituted (9.1.1995) by S.I. 1994/2795 (N.I. 15), art. 26. (1), Sch. 2 para. 14; S.R. 1994/446, art. 2

X51200 Search warrants.

(1) Where a justice of the peace (in Scotland, a sheriff or justice of the peace) is satisfied by information on oath given by a constable (in Scotland, by evidence on oath) that there are reasonable grounds for believing—

(a) that an offence under [F112section 198. (1) or (1. A)](offences of making, importing [F113, possessing, selling etc.] or distributing illicit recordings) has been or is about to be committed in any premises, and

(b) that evidence that such an offence has been or is about to be committed is in those premises, he may issue a warrant authorising a constable to enter and search the premises, using such reasonable force as is necessary.

(2) The power conferred by subsection (1) does not, in England and Wales, extend to authorising a search for material of the kinds mentioned in section 9. (2) of the M1. Police and Criminal Evidence Act 1984 (certain classes of personal or confidential material).

(3) A warrant under subsection (1)—

(a) may authorise persons to accompany any constable executing the warrant, and

(b) remains in force for [F114three months] from the date of its issue.

[F115. (3. A)In executing a warrant issued under subsection (1) a constable may seize an article if he reasonably believes that it is evidence that any offence under [F116section 198. (1) or (1. A)] has been or is about to be committed.]

(4) In this section "premises" includes land, buildings, fixed or moveable structures, vehicles, vessels, aircraft and hovercraft.

Editorial Information

X51. The insertion of the new headings "Chapter 1 Introductory", "Chapter 2 Economic Rights", "Chapter 3 Moral Rights" and "Chapter 4 Qualification for Protection, Extent and Interpretation" in Pt. II on 1.2.2006 gives rise to a change in the structure of this legislation on SLD which breaks the continuity of historical versions of the existing provisions which are now brought under those new headings.

Amendments (Textual)

F112. Words in s. 200. (1)(a) substituted (31.10.2003) by The Copyright and Related Rights Regulations 2003 (S.I. 2003/2498), reg. 26. (4)(a) (with regs. 31-40)

F113. Words in s. 200. (1)(a) inserted (20.11.2002) by 2002 c. 25, s. 2. (3)(a)(ii); S.I. 2002/2749, art. 2

F114. Words in s. 200. (3)(b) substituted (1.1.2006) by Serious Organised Crime and Police Act 2005 (c. 15), ss. 174. (1), 178, Sch. 16 para. 6. (3); S.I. 2005/3495, art. 2. (1)(s) (subject to art. 2. (2))

F115. S. 200. (3. A) inserted (20.11.2002) by 2002 c. 25, s. 2. (3)(b); S.I. 2002/2749, art. 2

F116. Words in s. 200. (3. A) substituted (31.10.2003) by The Copyright and Related Rights Regulations 2003 (S.I. 2003/2498), reg. 26. (4)(b) (with reg. 31-40)

Marginal Citations

M11984 c. 60.

X52201 False representation of authority to give consent.

(1) It is an offence for a person to represent falsely that he is authorised by any person to give consent for the purposes of [F117this Chapter] in relation to a performance, unless he believes on reasonable grounds that he is so authorised.

(2) A person guilty of an offence under this section is liable on summary conviction to imprisonment for a term not exceeding six months or a fine not exceeding level 5 on the standard scale or both.

Editorial Information

X52. The insertion of the new headings "Chapter 1 Introductory", "Chapter 2 Economic Rights", "Chapter 3 Moral Rights" and "Chapter 4 Qualification for Protection, Extent and Interpretation" in Pt. II on 1.2.2006 gives rise to a change in the structure of this legislation on SLD which breaks the continuity of historical versions of the existing provisions which are now brought under those new headings.

Amendments (Textual)

F117. Words in s. 201. (1) substituted (1.2.2006) by The Performances (Moral Rights, etc.) Regulations 2006 (S.I. 2006/18), reg. 2, Sch. para. 8 (with reg. 8)

X53202 Offence by body corporate: liability of officers.

(1) Where an offence under [F118this Chapter] committed by a body corporate is proved to have

been committed with the consent or connivance of a director, manager, secretary or other similar officer of the body, or a person purporting to act in any such capacity, he as well as the body corporate is guilty of the offence and liable to be proceeded against and punished accordingly.

(2) In relation to a body corporate whose affairs are managed by its members "director" means a member of the body corporate.

Editorial Information

X53. The insertion of the new headings "Chapter 1 Introductory", "Chapter 2 Economic Rights", "Chapter 3 Moral Rights" and "Chapter 4 Qualification for Protection, Extent and Interpretation" in Pt. II on 1.2.2006 gives rise to a change in the structure of this legislation on SLD which breaks the continuity of historical versions of the existing provisions which are now brought under those new headings.

Amendments (Textual)

F118. Words in s. 202. (1) substituted (1.2.2006) by The Performances (Moral Rights, etc.) Regulations 2006 (S.I. 2006/18), reg. 2, Sch. para. 8 (with reg. 8)

X54 Supplementary provisions with respect to delivery up and seizure

Editorial Information

X54. The insertion of the new headings "Chapter 1 Introductory", "Chapter 2 Economic Rights", "Chapter 3 Moral Rights" and "Chapter 4 Qualification for Protection, Extent and Interpretation" in Pt. II on 1.2.2006 gives rise to a change in the structure of this legislation on SLD which breaks the continuity of historical versions of the existing provisions which are now brought under those new headings.

X55203 Period after which remedy of delivery up not available.

(1) An application for an order under section 195 (order for delivery up in civil proceedings) may not be made after the end of the period of six years from the date on which the illicit recording in question was made, subject to the following provisions.

(2) If during the whole or any part of that period a person entitled to apply for an order—

(a) is under a disability, or

(b) is prevented by fraud or concealment from discovering the facts entitling him to apply,

an application may be made by him at any time before the end of the period of six years from the date on which he ceased to be under a disability or, as the case may be, could with reasonable diligence have discovered those facts.

(3) In subsection (2) "disability"—

(a) in England and Wales, has the same meaning as in the M2. Limitation Act 1980;

(b) in Scotland, means legal disability within the meaning of the M3. Prescription and Limitations (Scotland) Act 1973;

(c) in Northern Ireland, has the same meaning as in the M4. Statute of Limitation (Northern Ireland) 1958.

(4) An order under section 199 (order for delivery up in criminal proceedings) shall not, in any case, be made after the end of the period of six years from the date on which the illicit recording in question was made.

Editorial Information

X55. The insertion of the new headings "Chapter 1 Introductory", "Chapter 2 Economic Rights", "Chapter 3 Moral Rights" and "Chapter 4 Qualification for Protection, Extent and Interpretation" in Pt. II on 1.2.2006 gives rise to a change in the structure of this legislation on SLD which breaks the continuity of historical versions of the existing provisions which are now brought under those new headings.

Marginal Citations

M21980 c. 58.

M31973 c. 52.

M41958 c. 10 (N.I.).

X56204 Order as to disposal of illicit recording.

(1) An application may be made to the court for an order that an illicit recording of a performance delivered up in pursuance of an order under section 195 or 199, or seized and detained in pursuance of the right conferred by section 196, shall be—

 (a) forfeited to such person having performer's rights or recording rights in relation to the performance as the court may direct, or

 (b) destroyed or otherwise dealt with as the court may think fit,

or for a decision that no such order should be made.

(2) In considering what order (if any) should be made, the court shall consider whether other remedies available in an action for infringement of the rights conferred by [F119this Chapter] would be adequate to compensate the person or persons entitled to the rights and to protect their interests.

(3) Provision shall be made by rules of court as to the service of notice on persons having an interest in the recording, and any such person is entitled—

 (a) to appear in proceedings for an order under this section, whether or not he was served with notice, and

 (b) to appeal against any order made, whether or not he appeared;

and an order shall not take effect until the end of the period within which notice of an appeal may be given or, if before the end of that period notice of appeal is duly given, until the final determination or abandonment of the proceedings on the appeal.

(4) Where there is more than one person interested in a recording, the court shall make such order as it thinks just and may (in particular) direct that the recording be sold, or otherwise dealt with, and the proceeds divided.

(5) If the court decides that no order should be made under this section, the person in whose possession, custody or control the recording was before being delivered up or seized is entitled to its return.

(6) References in this section to a person having an interest in a recording include any person in whose favour an order could be made in respect of the recording

 [F120. (a)under this section or under section 114 or 231 of this Act;

 (b) under section 24. D of the Registered Designs Act 1949;

 (c) under section 19 of Trade Marks Act 1994 (including that section as applied by regulation 4 of the Community Trade Mark Regulations 2006 (SI 2006/1027)); or

 (d) under regulation 1. C of the Community Design Regulations 2005 (SI 2005/2339).]

Editorial Information

X56. The insertion of the new headings "Chapter 1 Introductory", "Chapter 2 Economic Rights", "Chapter 3 Moral Rights" and "Chapter 4 Qualification for Protection, Extent and Interpretation" in Pt. II on 1.2.2006 gives rise to a change in the structure of this legislation on SLD which breaks the continuity of historical versions of the existing provisions which are now brought under those new headings.

Amendments (Textual)

F119. Words in s. 204. (2) substituted (1.2.2006) by The Performances (Moral Rights, etc.) Regulations 2006 (S.I. 2006/18), reg. 2, Sch. para. 8 (with reg. 8)

F120. Words in s. 204. (6) substituted (29.4.2006) by The Intellectual Property (Enforcement, etc.) Regulations 2006 (S.I. 2006/1028), reg. 2. (2), Sch. 2 para. 11

Modifications etc. (not altering text)

C16. S. 204 extended by S.I. 1991/724, art. 2. (1)(n)

X57[F121204. A Forfeiture of illicit recordings: England and Wales or Northern Ireland

(1) In England and Wales or Northern Ireland where illicit recordings of a performance have come into the possession of any person in connection with the investigation or prosecution of a relevant offence, that person may apply under this section for an order for the forfeiture of the illicit recordings.

(2) For the purposes of this section "relevant offence" means—

(a) an offence under [F122section 198. (1) or (1. A)](criminal liability for making or dealing with illicit recordings),

(b) an offence under the Trade Descriptions Act 1968 (c. 29),

[F123. (ba)an offence under the Business Protection from Misleading Marketing Regulations 2008,

(bb) an offence under the Consumer Protection from Unfair Trading Regulations 2008, or]

(c) an offence involving dishonesty or deception.

(3) An application under this section may be made—

(a) where proceedings have been brought in any court for a relevant offence relating to some or all of the illicit recordings, to that court, or

(b) where no application for the forfeiture of the illicit recordings has been made under paragraph (a), by way of complaint to a magistrates' court.

(4) On an application under this section, the court shall make an order for the forfeiture of any illicit recordings only if it is satisfied that a relevant offence has been committed in relation to the illicit recordings.

(5) A court may infer for the purposes of this section that such an offence has been committed in relation to any illicit recordings if it is satisfied that such an offence has been committed in relation to illicit recordings which are representative of the illicit recordings in question (whether by reason of being part of the same consignment or batch or otherwise).

(6) Any person aggrieved by an order made under this section by a magistrates' court, or by a decision of such a court not to make such an order, may appeal against that order or decision—

(a) in England and Wales, to the Crown Court, or

(b) in Northern Ireland, to the county court.

(7) An order under this section may contain such provision as appears to the court to be appropriate for delaying the coming into force of the order pending the making and determination of any appeal (including any application under section 111 of the Magistrates' Courts Act 1980 (c. 43) or Article 146 of the Magistrates' Courts (Northern Ireland) Order 1981 (S.I. 1987/1675 (N.I. 26)) (statement of case)).

(8) Subject to subsection (9), where any illicit recordings are forfeited under this section they shall be destroyed in accordance with such directions as the court may give.

(9) On making an order under this section the court may direct that the illicit recordings to which the order relates shall (instead of being destroyed) be forfeited to the person having the performers' rights or recording rights in question or dealt with in such other way as the court considers appropriate.]

Editorial Information

X57. The insertion of the new headings "Chapter 1 Introductory", "Chapter 2 Economic Rights", "Chapter 3 Moral Rights" and "Chapter 4 Qualification for Protection, Extent and Interpretation" in Pt. II on 1.2.2006 gives rise to a change in the structure of this legislation on SLD which breaks the continuity of historical versions of the existing provisions which are now brought under those new headings.

Amendments (Textual)

F121. S. 204. A inserted (20.11.2002) by 2002 c. 25, s. 4; S.I. 2002/2749, art. 2

F122. Words in s. 204. A(2)(a) substituted (31.10.2003) by The Copyright and Related Rights Regulations 2003 (S.I. 2003/2498), reg. 26. (4)(c) (with regs. 31-40)

F123. S. 204. A(2)(ba)(bb) and word substituted (26.5.2008) for word by The Consumer Protection from Unfair Trading Regulations 2008 (S.I. 2008/1277), reg. 1, Sch. 2 para. 42 (with reg. 28. (2)(3))

X58. F124204. B Forfeiture: Scotland

(1) In Scotland the court may make an order under this section for the forfeiture of any illicit recordings.

(2) An order under this section may be made—

(a) on an application by the procurator-fiscal made in the manner specified in section 134 of the Criminal Procedure (Scotland) Act 1995 (c. 46), or

(b) where a person is convicted of a relevant offence, in addition to any other penalty which the court may impose.

(3) On an application under subsection (2)(a), the court shall make an order for the forfeiture of any illicit recordings only if it is satisfied that a relevant offence has been committed in relation to the illicit recordings.

(4) The court may infer for the purposes of this section that such an offence has been committed in relation to any illicit recordings if it is satisfied that such an offence has been committed in relation to illicit recordings which are representative of the illicit recordings in question (whether by reason of being part of the same consignment or batch or otherwise).

(5) The procurator-fiscal making the application under subsection (2)(a) shall serve on any person appearing to him to be the owner of, or otherwise to have an interest in, the illicit recordings to which the application relates a copy of the application, together with a notice giving him the opportunity to appear at the hearing of the application to show cause why the illicit recordings should not be forfeited.

(6) Service under subsection (5) shall be carried out, and such service may be proved, in the manner specified for citation of an accused in summary proceedings under the Criminal Procedure (Scotland) Act 1995.

(7) Any person upon whom notice is served under subsection (5) and any other person claiming to be the owner of, or otherwise to have an interest in, illicit recordings to which an application under this section relates shall be entitled to appear at the hearing of the application to show cause why the illicit recordings should not be forfeited.

(8) The court shall not make an order following an application under subsection (2)(a)—

(a) if any person on whom notice is served under subsection (5) does not appear, unless service of the notice on that person is proved, or

(b) if no notice under subsection (5) has been served, unless the court is satisfied that in the circumstances it was reasonable not to serve such notice.

(9) Where an order for the forfeiture of any illicit recordings is made following an application under subsection (2)(a), any person who appeared, or was entitled to appear, to show cause why the illicit recordings should not be forfeited may, within 21 days of the making of the order, appeal to the High Court by Bill of Suspension.

(10) Section 182. (5)(a) to (e) of the Criminal Procedure (Scotland) Act 1995 shall apply to an appeal under subsection (9) as it applies to a stated case under Part 2 of that Act.

(11) An order following an application under subsection (2)(a) shall not take effect—

(a) until the end of the period of 21 days beginning with the day after the day on which the order is made, or

(b) if an appeal is made under subsection (9) above within that period, until the appeal is determined or abandoned.

(12) An order under subsection (2)(b) shall not take effect—

(a) until the end of the period within which an appeal against the order could be brought under the Criminal Procedure (Scotland) Act 1995 (c. 46), or

(b) if an appeal is made within that period, until the appeal is determined or abandoned.

(13) Subject to subsection (14), illicit recordings forfeited under this section shall be destroyed in accordance with such directions as the court may give.

(14) On making an order under this section the court may direct that the illicit recordings to which the order relates shall (instead of being destroyed) be forfeited to the person having the performers' rights or recording rights in question or dealt with in such other way as the court considers appropriate.

(15) For the purposes of this section—

[F125"relevant offence" means—

- an offence under section 198. (1) or (1. A) (criminal liability for making or dealing with illicit recordings),

- an offence under the Trade Descriptions Act 1968,

- an offence under the Business Protection from Misleading Marketing Regulations 2008,

- an offence under the Consumer Protection from Unfair Trading Regulations 2008, or

- any offence involving dishonesty or deception;]

"the court" means—

- in relation to an order made on an application under subsection (2)(a), the sheriff, and

- in relation to an order made under subsection (2)(b), the court which imposed the penalty.

Editorial Information

X58. The insertion of the new headings "Chapter 1 Introductory", "Chapter 2 Economic Rights", "Chapter 3 Moral Rights" and "Chapter 4 Qualification for Protection, Extent and Interpretation" in Pt. II on 1.2.2006 gives rise to a change in the structure of this legislation on SLD which breaks the continuity of historical versions of the existing provisions which are now brought under those new headings.

Amendments (Textual)

F124. S. 204. B inserted (20.11.2002) by 2002 c. 25, s. 4; S.I. 2002/2749, art. 2

F125. Words in s. 204. (15) substituted (26.5.2008) by The Consumer Protection from Unfair Trading Regulations 2008 (S.I. 2008/1277), reg. 1, Sch. 2 para. 43 (with reg. 28. (2)(3))

X59205 Jurisdiction of county court and sheriff court.

(1) In England [F126and Wales the county court and in] Northern Ireland a county court may entertain proceedings under—

section 195 (order for delivery up of illicit recording), or

section 204 (order as to disposal of illicit recording),

[F127save that, in Northern Ireland, a county court may entertain such proceedings only]where the value of the illicit recordings in question does not exceed the county court limit for actions in tort.

(2) In Scotland proceedings for an order under either of those provisions may be brought in the sheriff court.

(3) Nothing in this section shall be construed as affecting the jurisdiction of the High Court or, in Scotland, the Court of Session.

Editorial Information

X59. The insertion of the new headings "Chapter 1 Introductory", "Chapter 2 Economic Rights", "Chapter 3 Moral Rights" and "Chapter 4 Qualification for Protection, Extent and Interpretation" in Pt. II on 1.2.2006 gives rise to a change in the structure of this legislation on SLD which breaks the continuity of historical versions of the existing provisions which are now brought under those new headings.

Amendments (Textual)

F126. Words in s. 205. (1) substituted (22.4.2014) by Crime and Courts Act 2013 (c. 22), s. 61. (3), Sch. 9 para. 72; S.I. 2014/954, art. 2. (c) (with art. 3) (with transitional provisions and savings in S.I. 2014/956, arts. 3-11)

F127. Words in s. 205. (1) inserted by S.I. 1991/724, art. 2. (8), Schedule Part I

X60. F128[Licensing of performers' F129... rights]

Editorial Information

X60. The insertion of the new headings "Chapter 1 Introductory", "Chapter 2 Economic Rights", "Chapter 3 Moral Rights" and "Chapter 4 Qualification for Protection, Extent and Interpretation" in Pt. II on 1.2.2006 gives rise to a change in the structure of this legislation on SLD which breaks the continuity of historical versions of the existing provisions which are now brought under those new headings.

Amendments (Textual)

F128. S. 205. A and crossheading inserted (1.12.1996) by S.I. 1996/2967, reg. 22. (1) (with Pt. III)

F129. Word in s. 205. A cross-heading omitted (25.4.2013) by virtue of Enterprise and Regulatory Reform Act 2013 (c. 24), s. 103. (1), Sch. 22 para. 6

 X61 [F131 205. A Licensing of performers' F130... rights.

 The provisions of Schedule 2. A have effect with respect to the licensing of performers' F130 ...

rights.]

Editorial Information

X61. The insertion of the new headings "Chapter 1 Introductory", "Chapter 2 Economic Rights", "Chapter 3 Moral Rights" and "Chapter 4 Qualification for Protection, Extent and Interpretation" in Pt. II on 1.2.2006 gives rise to a change in the structure of this legislation on SLD which breaks the continuity of historical versions of the existing provisions which are now brought under those new headings.

Amendments (Textual)

F130. Word in s. 205. A omitted (25.4.2013) by virtue of Enterprise and Regulatory Reform Act 2013 (c. 24), s. 103. (1), Sch. 22 para. 6

F131. S. 205. A inserted (1.12.1996) by S.I. 1996/2967, reg. 22. (1) (with Pt. III)

X62. F132[Jurisdiction of Copyright Tribunal]

Editorial Information

X62. The insertion of the new headings "Chapter 1 Introductory", "Chapter 2 Economic Rights", "Chapter 3 Moral Rights" and "Chapter 4 Qualification for Protection, Extent and Interpretation" in Pt. II on 1.2.2006 gives rise to a change in the structure of this legislation on SLD which breaks the continuity of historical versions of the existing provisions which are now brought under those new headings.

Amendments (Textual)

F132. S. 205. B and crossheading inserted (1.12.1996) by S.I. 1996/2967, reg. 24 (with Pt. III)

X63[F133205. B Jurisdiction of Copyright Tribunal.

(1) The Copyright Tribunal has jurisdiction under [F134this Chapter] to hear and determine proceedings under—

(a) section 182. D (amount of equitable remuneration for exploitation of commercial sound recording);

(b) section 190 (application to give consent on behalf of owner of reproduction right);

(c) section 191. H (amount of equitable remuneration on transfer of rental right);

F135. (cc). . . . .

(d) paragraph 3, 4 or 5 of Schedule 2. A (reference of licensing scheme);

(e) paragraph 6 or 7 of that Schedule (application with respect to licence under licensing scheme);

(f) paragraph 10, 11 or 12 of that Schedule (reference or application with respect to licensing by licensing body);

(g) paragraph 15 of that Schedule (application to settle royalty for certain lending);

(h) paragraph 17 of that Schedule (application to settle terms of licence available as of right).

(2) The provisions of Chapter VIII of Part I (general provisions relating to the Copyright Tribunal) apply in relation to the Tribunal when exercising any jurisdiction under [F134this Chapter].

(3) Provision shall be made by rules under section 150 prohibiting the Tribunal from entertaining a reference under paragraph 3, 4 or 5 of Schedule 2. A (reference of licensing scheme) by a representative organisation unless the Tribunal is satisfied that the organisation is reasonably representative of the class of persons which it claims to represent.]

Editorial Information

X63. The insertion of the new headings "Chapter 1 Introductory", "Chapter 2 Economic Rights", "Chapter 3 Moral Rights" and "Chapter 4 Qualification for Protection, Extent and Interpretation" in Pt. II on 1.2.2006 gives rise to a change in the structure of this legislation on SLD which breaks the continuity of historical versions of the existing provisions which are now brought under those new headings.

Amendments (Textual)

F133. S. 205. B inserted (1.12.1996) by S.I. 1996/2967, reg. 24 (with Pt. III)

F134. Words in s. 205. B(1)(2) substituted (1.2.2006) by The Performances (Moral Rights, etc.)

Regulations 2006 (S.I. 2006/18), reg. 2, Sch. para. 8 (with reg. 8)

F135. S. 205. B(1)(cc) repealed (31.7.2017) by Digital Economy Act 2017 (c. 30), ss. 34. (2)(a)(iii), 118. (6); S.I. 2017/765, reg. 2. (n)

[F136. Chapter 3. MORAL RIGHTS

Amendments (Textual)

F136. Ss. 205. C-205. N and cross-headings inserted (1.2 2006) by The Performances (Moral Rights, etc.) Regulations 2006 (S.I. 2006/18), art. 6 (with reg. 8) (which inserted provisions accordingly become Pt. 2 Ch. 3 (1.2.2006) by virtue of S.I. 2006/18, art. 4. (6) (with reg. 8))

205. CRight to be identified as performer

(1) Whenever a person—

(a) produces or puts on a qualifying performance that is given in public,

(b) broadcasts live a qualifying performance,

(c) communicates to the public a sound recording of a qualifying performance, or

(d) issues to the public copies of such a recording,

the performer has the right to be identified as such.

(2) The right of the performer under this section is—

(a) in the case of a performance that is given in public, to be identified in any programme accompanying the performance or in some other manner likely to bring his identity to the notice of a person seeing or hearing the performance,

(b) in the case of a performance that is broadcast, to be identified in a manner likely to bring his identity to the notice of a person seeing or hearing the broadcast,

(c) in the case of a sound recording that is communicated to the public, to be identified in a manner likely to bring his identity to the notice of a person hearing the communication,

(d) in the case of a sound recording that is issued to the public, to be identified in or on each copy or, if that is not appropriate, in some other manner likely to bring his identity to the notice of a person acquiring a copy,

or (in any of the above cases) to be identified in such other manner as may be agreed between the performer and the person mentioned in subsection (1).

(3) The right conferred by this section in relation to a performance given by a group (or so much of a performance as is given by a group) is not infringed—

(a) in a case falling within paragraph (a), (b) or (c) of subsection (2), or

(b) in a case falling within paragraph (d) of that subsection in which it is not reasonably practicable for each member of the group to be identified,

if the group itself is identified as specified in subsection (2).

(4) In this section "group" means two or more performers who have a particular name by which they may be identified collectively.

(5) If the assertion under section 205. D specifies a pseudonym, initials or some other particular form of identification, that form shall be used; otherwise any reasonable form of identification may be used.

(6) This section has effect subject to section 205. E (exceptions to right).

205. DRequirement that right be asserted

(1) A person does not infringe the right conferred by section 205. C (right to be identified as performer) by doing any of the acts mentioned in that section unless the right has been asserted in accordance with the following provisions so as to bind him in relation to that act.

(2) The right may be asserted generally, or in relation to any specified act or description of acts—

(a) by instrument in writing signed by or on behalf of the performer, or

(b) on an assignment of a performer's property rights, by including in the instrument effecting the assignment a statement that the performer asserts in relation to the performance his right to be identified.

(3) The persons bound by an assertion of the right under subsection (2) are—

(a) in the case of an assertion under subsection (2)(a), anyone to whose notice the assertion is brought;

(b) in the case of an assertion under subsection (2)(b), the assignee and anyone claiming through him, whether or not he has notice of the assertion.

(4) In an action for infringement of the right the court shall, in considering remedies, take into account any delay in asserting the right.

205. EExceptions to right

(1) The right conferred by section 205. C (right to be identified as performer) is subject to the following exceptions.

(2) The right does not apply where it is not reasonably practicable to identify the performer (or, where identification of a group is permitted by virtue of section 205. C(3), the group).

(3) The right does not apply in relation to any performance given for the purposes of reporting current events.

(4) The right does not apply in relation to any performance given for the purposes of advertising any goods or services.

(5) The right is not infringed by an act which by virtue of any of the following provisions of Schedule 2 would not infringe any of the rights conferred by Chapter 2—

(a) paragraph 2. (1. A) (news reporting);

(b) paragraph 3 (incidental inclusion of a performance or recording);

(c) paragraph 4. (2) (things done for the purposes of examination);

(d) paragraph 8 (parliamentary and judicial proceedings);

(e) paragraph 9 (Royal Commissions and statutory inquiries).

Right to object to derogatory treatment

205. FRight to object to derogatory treatment of performance

(1) The performer of a qualifying performance has a right which is infringed if—

(a) the performance is broadcast live, or

(b) by means of a sound recording the performance is played in public or communicated to the public,

with any distortion, mutilation or other modification that is prejudicial to the reputation of the performer.

(2) This section has effect subject to section 205. G (exceptions to right).

205. GExceptions to right

(1) The right conferred by section 205. F (right to object to derogatory treatment of performance) is subject to the following exceptions.

(2) The right does not apply in relation to any performance given for the purposes of reporting current events.

(3) The right is not infringed by modifications made to a performance which are consistent with normal editorial or production practice.

(4) Subject to subsection (5), the right is not infringed by anything done for the purpose of—

(a) avoiding the commission of an offence,

(b) complying with a duty imposed by or under an enactment, or

(c) in the case of the British Broadcasting Corporation, avoiding the inclusion in a programme broadcast by them of anything which offends against good taste or decency or which is likely to encourage or incite crime or lead to disorder or to be offensive to public feeling.

(5) Where—

(a) the performer is identified in a manner likely to bring his identity to the notice of a person seeing or hearing the performance as modified by the act in question; or

(b) he has previously been identified in or on copies of a sound recording issued to the public,

subsection (4) applies only if there is sufficient disclaimer.

(6) In subsection (5) "sufficient disclaimer", in relation to an act capable of infringing the right,

means a clear and reasonably prominent indication—

(a) given in a manner likely to bring it to the notice of a person seeing or hearing the performance as modified by the act in question, and

(b) if the performer is identified at the time of the act, appearing along with the identification, that the modifications were made without the performer's consent.

205. HInfringement of right by possessing or dealing with infringing article

(1) The right conferred by section 205. F (right to object to derogatory treatment of performance) is also infringed by a person who—

(a) possesses in the course of business, or

(b) sells or lets for hire, or offers or exposes for sale or hire, or

(c) distributes,

an article which is, and which he knows or has reason to believe is, an infringing article.

(2) An "infringing article" means a sound recording of a qualifying performance with any distortion, mutilation or other modification that is prejudicial to the reputation of the performer.

Supplementary

205. IDuration of rights

(1) A performer's rights under this Chapter in relation to a performance subsist so long as that performer's rights under Chapter 2 subsist in relation to the performance.

(2) In subsection (1) "performer's rights" includes rights of a performer that are vested in a successor of his.

205. JConsent and waiver of rights

(1) It is not an infringement of the rights conferred by this Chapter to do any act to which consent has been given by or on behalf of the person entitled to the right.

(2) Any of those rights may be waived by instrument in writing signed by or on behalf of the person giving up the right.

(3) A waiver—

(a) may relate to a specific performance, to performances of a specified description or to performances generally, and may relate to existing or future performances, and

(b) may be conditional or unconditional and may be expressed to be subject to revocation,

and if made in favour of the owner or prospective owner of a performer's property rights in the performance or performances to which it relates, it shall be presumed to extend to his licensees and successors in title unless a contrary intention is expressed.

(4) Nothing in this Chapter shall be construed as excluding the operation of the general law of contract or estoppel in relation to an informal waiver or other transaction in relation to either of the rights conferred by this Chapter.

205. KApplication of provisions to parts of performances

(1) The right conferred by section 205. C (right to be identified as performer) applies in relation to the whole or any substantial part of a performance.

(2) The right conferred by section 205. F (right to object to derogatory treatment of performance) applies in relation to the whole or any part of a performance.

205. LMoral rights not assignable

The rights conferred by this Chapter are not assignable.

205. MTransmission of moral rights on death

(1) On the death of a person entitled to a right conferred by this Chapter—

(a) the right passes to such person as he may by testamentary disposition specifically direct,

(b) if there is no such direction but the performer's property rights in respect of the performance in question form part of his estate, the right passes to the person to whom the property rights pass,

(c) if or to the extent that the right does not pass under paragraph (a) or (b) it is exercisable by his personal representatives.

(2) Where a performer's property rights pass in part to one person and in part to another, as for

example where a bequest is limited so as to apply—

(a) to one or more, but not all, of the things to which the owner has the right to consent, or

(b) to part, but not the whole, of the period for which the rights subsist,

any right which by virtue of subsection (1) passes with the performer's property rights is correspondingly divided.

(3) Where by virtue of subsection (1)(a) or (1)(b) a right becomes exercisable by more than one person—

(a) it is, in the case of the right conferred by section 205. F (right to object to derogatory treatment of performance), a right exercisable by each of them and is satisfied in relation to any of them if he consents to the treatment or act in question, and

(b) any waiver of the right in accordance with section 205. J by one of them does not affect the rights of the others.

(4) A consent or waiver previously given or made binds any person to whom a right passes by virtue of subsection (1).

(5) Any damages recovered by personal representatives by virtue of this section in respect of an infringement after a person's death shall devolve as part of his estate as if the right of action had subsisted and been vested in him immediately before his death.

205. NRemedies for infringement of moral rights

(1) An infringement of a right conferred by this Chapter is actionable as a breach of statutory duty owed to the person entitled to the right.

(2) Where—

(a) there is an infringement of a right conferred by this Chapter,

(b) a person falsely claiming to act on behalf of a performer consented to the relevant conduct or purported to waive the right, and

(c) there would have been no infringement if he had been so acting,

that person shall be liable, jointly and severally with any person liable in respect of the infringement by virtue of subsection (1), as if he himself had infringed the right.

(3) Where proceedings for infringement of the right conferred on a performer by this Chapter, it shall be a defence to prove—

(a) that a person claiming to act on behalf of the performer consented to the defendant's conduct or purported to waive the right, and

(b) that the defendant reasonably believed that the person was acting on behalf of the performer.

(4) In proceedings for infringement of the right conferred by section 205. F the court may, if it thinks it an adequate remedy in the circumstances, grant an injunction on terms prohibiting the doing of any act unless a disclaimer is made, in such terms and in such manner as may be approved by the court, dissociating the performer from the broadcast or sound recording of the performance.]

[F137. Chapter 4. QUALIFICATION FOR PROTECTION, EXTENT AND INTERPRETATION

Amendments (Textual)

F137. Ss. 206-212 become Pt. 2 Ch. 4 (1.2.2006) by virtue of The Performances (Moral Rights, etc.) Regulations 2006 (S.I. 2006/18), reg. 4. (7) (with reg. 8)

Editorial Information

X64. The insertion of the new headings "Chapter 1 Introductory", "Chapter 2 Economic Rights", "Chapter 3 Moral Rights" and "Chapter 4 Qualification for Protection, Extent and Interpretation" in Pt. II on 1.2.2006 gives rise to a change in the structure of this legislation on SLD which breaks the continuity of historical versions of the existing provisions which are now brought under those new headings.

X65206 Qualifying countries, individuals and persons.

(1) In this Part—

"qualifying country" means—

(a) the United Kingdom,

[F138. (b) another EEA state,]

[F139. (ba)the Channel Islands, the Isle of Man or Gibraltar,] or

[F140. (bb)a country which is a party to the Rome Convention,] or

(c) to the extent that an Order under section 208 so provides, a country designated under that section as enjoying reciprocal protection;

"qualifying individual" means a citizen or subject of, or an individual resident in, a qualifying country; and

"qualifying person" means a qualifying individual or a body corporate or other body having legal personality which—

(a) is formed under the law of a part of the United Kingdom or another qualifying country, and

(b) has in any qualifying country a place of business at which substantial business activity is carried on.

(2) The reference in the definition of "qualifying individual" to a person's being a citizen or subject of a qualifying country shall be construed—

(a) in relation to the United Kingdom, as a reference to his being a British citizen, and

(b) in relation to a colony of the United Kingdom, as a reference to his being a British Dependent Territories' citizen by connection with that colony.

(3) In determining for the purpose of the definition of "qualifying person" whether substantial business activity is carried on at a place of business in any country, no account shall be taken of dealings in goods which are at all material times outside that country.

[F141. (4)Her Majesty may by Order in Council—

(a) make provision for the application of this Part to a country by virtue of paragraph (bb) or (c) of the definition of "qualifying country" in subsection (1) to be subject to specified restrictions;

(b) amend the definition of "qualifying country" in subsection (1) so as to add a country which is not a party to the Rome Convention;

(c) make provision for the application of this Part to a country added under paragraph (b) to be subject to specified restrictions.

(5) A statutory instrument containing an Order in Council under this section is subject to annulment in pursuance of a resolution of either House of Parliament.]

[F142. (6)In this section, "the Rome Convention" means the International Convention for the Protection of Performers, Producers of Phonograms and Broadcasting Organisations done at Rome on 26 October 1961.]

Editorial Information

X65. The insertion of the new headings "Chapter 1 Introductory", "Chapter 2 Economic Rights", "Chapter 3 Moral Rights" and "Chapter 4 Qualification for Protection, Extent and Interpretation" in Pt. II on 1.2.2006 gives rise to a change in the structure of this legislation on SLD which breaks the continuity of historical versions of the existing provisions which are now brought under those new headings.

Amendments (Textual)

F138. Words in s. 206. (1) substituted (1.12.2016 for specified purposes, 6.4.2017 in so far as not already in force) by Intellectual Property Act 2014 (c. 18), ss. 22. (5)(a), 24. (1); S.I. 2016/1139, arts. 2, 3 (with art. 4)

F139. Words in s. 206. (1) inserted (1.12.2016 for specified purposes, 6.4.2017 in so far as not already in force) by Intellectual Property Act 2014 (c. 18), ss. 22. (5)(b), 24. (1); S.I. 2016/1139, arts. 2, 3 (with art. 4)

F140. Words in s. 206. (1) inserted (1.12.2016 for specified purposes, 6.4.2017 in so far as not already in force) by Intellectual Property Act 2014 (c. 18), ss. 22. (5)(c), 24. (1); S.I. 2016/1139, arts. 2, 3 (with art. 4)

F141. S. 206. (4)(5) inserted (1.12.2016 for specified purposes, 6.4.2017 in so far as not already in force) by Intellectual Property Act 2014 (c. 18), ss. 22. (6), 24. (1); S.I. 2016/1139, arts. 2, 3 (with art. 4)

F142. S. 206. (6) inserted (1.12.2016 for specified purposes, 6.4.2017 in so far as not already in force) by Intellectual Property Act 2014 (c. 18), ss. 22. (7), 24. (1); S.I. 2016/1139, arts. 2, 3 (with art. 4)

X66207 Countries to which this Part extends.

This Part extends to England and Wales, Scotland and Northern Ireland.

Editorial Information

X66. The insertion of the new headings "Chapter 1 Introductory", "Chapter 2 Economic Rights", "Chapter 3 Moral Rights" and "Chapter 4 Qualification for Protection, Extent and Interpretation" in Pt. II on 1.2.2006 gives rise to a change in the structure of this legislation on SLD which breaks the continuity of historical versions of the existing provisions which are now brought under those new headings.

X67208 Countries enjoying reciprocal protection.

(1) Her Majesty may by Order in Council designate as enjoying reciprocal protection under this Part—

(a) a Convention country, or

(b) a country as to which Her Majesty is satisfied that provision has been or will be made under its law giving adequate protection for British performances.

(2) A "Convention country" means a country which is a party to a Convention relating to performers' rights to which the United Kingdom is also a party.

(3) A "British performance" means a performance—

(a) given by an individual who is a British citizen or resident in the United Kingdom, or

(b) taking place in the United Kingdom.

(4) If the law of that country provides adequate protection only for certain descriptions of performance, an Order under subsection (1)(b) designating that country shall contain provision limiting to a corresponding extent the protection afforded by this Part in relation to performances connected with that country.

(5) The power conferred by subsection (1)(b) is exercisable in relation to F143... any colony of the United Kingdom, as in relation to a foreign country.

(6) A statutory instrument containing an Order in Council under this section shall be subject to annulment in pursuance of a resolution of either House of Parliament.

Editorial Information

X67. The insertion of the new headings "Chapter 1 Introductory", "Chapter 2 Economic Rights", "Chapter 3 Moral Rights" and "Chapter 4 Qualification for Protection, Extent and Interpretation" in Pt. II on 1.2.2006 gives rise to a change in the structure of this legislation on SLD which breaks the continuity of historical versions of the existing provisions which are now brought under those new headings.

Amendments (Textual)

F143. Words in s. 208. (5) omitted (1.12.2016 for specified purposes, 6.4.2017 in so far as not already in force) by virtue of Intellectual Property Act 2014 (c. 18), ss. 22. (8), 24. (1); S.I. 2016/1139, arts. 2, 3 (with art. 4)

X68209 Territorial waters and the continental shelf.

(1) For the purposes of this Part the territorial waters of the United Kingdom shall be treated as part of the United Kingdom.

(2) This Part applies to things done in the United Kingdom sector of the continental shelf on a structure or vessel which is present there for purposes directly connected with the exploration of the sea bed or subsoil or the exploitation of their natural resources as it applies to things done in the United Kingdom.

(3) The United Kingdom sector of the continental shelf means the areas designated by order under section 1. (7) of the M5. Continental Shelf Act 1964.

Editorial Information

X68. The insertion of the new headings "Chapter 1 Introductory", "Chapter 2 Economic Rights", "Chapter 3 Moral Rights" and "Chapter 4 Qualification for Protection, Extent and Interpretation" in Pt. II on 1.2.2006 gives rise to a change in the structure of this legislation on SLD which breaks

the continuity of historical versions of the existing provisions which are now brought under those new headings.

Marginal Citations

M51964 c. 29.

X69210 British ships, aircraft and hovercraft.

(1) This Part applies to things done on a British ship, aircraft or hovercraft as it applies to things done in the United Kingdom.

(2) In this section—

"British ship" means a ship which is a British ship for the purposes of the [F144. Merchant Shipping Act 1995] otherwise than by virtue of registration in a country outside the United Kingdom; and

"British aircraft" and "British hovercraft" mean an aircraft or hovercraft registered in the United Kingdom.

Editorial Information

X69. The insertion of the new headings "Chapter 1 Introductory", "Chapter 2 Economic Rights", "Chapter 3 Moral Rights" and "Chapter 4 Qualification for Protection, Extent and Interpretation" in Pt. II on 1.2.2006 gives rise to a change in the structure of this legislation on SLD which breaks the continuity of historical versions of the existing provisions which are now brought under those new headings.

Amendments (Textual)

F144. Words in s. 210. (2) substituted (1.1.1996) by 1995 c. 21, ss. 314. (2), 316. (2), Sch. 13 para. 84. (b) (with s. 312. (1))

[F145210. A

Requirement of signature: application in relation to body corporate

(1) The requirement in the following provisions that an instrument be signed by or on behalf of a person is also satisfied in the case of a body corporate by the affixing of its seal—

section 191. B(3) (assignment of performer's property rights);

section 191. C(1) (assignment of future performer's property rights);

section 191. D(1) (grant of exclusive licence).

(2) The requirement in the following provisions that an instrument be signed by a person is also satisfied in the case of a body corporate by signature on behalf of the body or by the affixing of its seal—

section 205. D(2)(a) (assertion of performer's moral rights);

section 205. J(2) (waiver of performer's moral rights).]

Amendments (Textual)

F145. S. 210. A inserted (1.2.2006) by The Performances (Moral Rights, etc.) Regulations 2006 (S.I. 2006/18), reg. 7 (with reg. 8)

X70 Interpretation

Editorial Information

X70. The insertion of the new headings "Chapter 1 Introductory", "Chapter 2 Economic Rights", "Chapter 3 Moral Rights" and "Chapter 4 Qualification for Protection, Extent and Interpretation" in Pt. II on 1.2.2006 gives rise to a change in the structure of this legislation on SLD which breaks the continuity of historical versions of the existing provisions which are now brought under those new headings.

X71211 Expressions having same meaning as in copyright provisions.

(1) The following expressions have the same meaning in this Part as in Part I (copyright)—

[F146assignment (in Scotland),]

broadcast,

business,

F147. . . . .

F148. . . . .

[F149communication to the public,]

country,

defendant (in Scotland),

delivery up (in Scotland),

[F150the EEA,]

[F150. EEA state,]

film,

[F151injunction (in Scotland)]

literary work,

published, F152. . .

[F153signed,]

[F154sound recording, and]

[F155wireless broadcast.]

(2) [F156 The provisions of—

   (a) section 5. B(2) and (3) (supplementary provisions relating to films), and

   (b) section 6. (3) to (5. A) and section 19. (4) (supplementary provisions relating to broadcasting),

apply] for the purposes of this Part, and in relation to an infringement of the rights conferred by this Part, as they apply for the purposes of Part I and in relation to an infringement of copyright.

Editorial Information

X71. The insertion of the new headings "Chapter 1 Introductory", "Chapter 2 Economic Rights", "Chapter 3 Moral Rights" and "Chapter 4 Qualification for Protection, Extent and Interpretation" in Pt. II on 1.2.2006 gives rise to a change in the structure of this legislation on SLD which breaks the continuity of historical versions of the existing provisions which are now brought under those new headings.

Amendments (Textual)

F146. S. 211. (1): entry inserted (1.2.2006) by The Performances (Moral Rights, etc.) Regulations 2006 (S.I. 2006/18), reg. 2, Sch. para. 6. (2) (with reg. 8)

F147. S. 211. (1): entry repealed (31.10.2003) by The Copyright and Related Rights Regulations 2003 (S.I. 2003/2498), reg. 2. (2), Sch. 2 (with regs. 31-40)

F148. S. 211. (1): entry repealed (31.10.2003) by The Copyright and Related Rights Regulations 2003 (S.I. 2003/2498), reg. 2. (2), Sch. 2 (with regs. 31-40)

F149. S. 211. (1): entry inserted (31.10.2003) by The Copyright and Related Rights Regulations 2003 (S.I. 2003/2498), reg. 2. (1), Sch. 1 para. 15. (5)(a)(i) (with regs. 31-40)

F150. S. 211. (1): entries relating to "the EEA," and "EEA state," substituted (29.4.2006) for entry relating to "EEA national," by The Intellectual Property (Enforcement, etc.) Regulations 2006 (S.I. 2006/1028), reg. 2. (2), Sch. 2 para. 12

F151. S. 211. (1): entry inserted (31.10.2003) by The Copyright and Related Rights Regulations 2003 (S.I. 2003/2498), reg. 2. (1), Sch. 1 para. 15. (5)(a)(i) (with regs. 31-40)

F152. Word in s. 211. (1) repealed (31.10.2003) by The Copyright and Related Rights Regulations 2003 (S.I. 2003/2498), reg. 2. (2), Sch. 2 (with regs. 31-40)

F153. S. 211. (1): entry inserted (1.2.2006) by The Performances (Moral Rights, etc.) Regulations 2006 (S.I. 2006/18), reg. 2, Sch. para. 6. (2) (with reg. 8)

F154. S. 211. (1): entry substituted (31.10.2003) by The Copyright and Related Rights Regulations 2003 (S.I. 2003/2498), reg. 2. (1), {Sch. 1para. 15. (5)(a)(ii)} (with regs. 31-40)

F155. S. 211. (1): entry inserted (31.10.2003) by The Copyright and Related Rights Regulations 2003 (S.I. 2003/2498), reg. 2. (1), Sch. 1 para. 15. (5)(a)(i) (with regs. 31-40)

F156. Words in s. 211. (2) substituted (1.2.2006) by The Performances (Moral Rights, etc.) Regulations 2006 (S.I. 2006/18), reg. 2, Sch. para. 6. (3) (with reg. 8)

X72212 Index of defined expressions.

The following Table shows provisions defining or otherwise explaining expressions used in this Part (other than provisions defining or explaining an expression used only in the same section)—

[F157accessible copy (in paragraphs 3A to 3E of Schedule 2) | paragraph 3E(4) of Schedule 2] |

[F158assignment (in Scotland) | section 211(1) (and section 177);] |

broadcast (and related expressions) | section 211 (and section 6) |

business | section 211(1) (and section 178) |

F159. . . . . | |

[F160communication to the public | section 211(1) (and section 20)] |

[F161consent of performer (in relation to performer's property rights)] | [F162section 191A(2)] |

country | section 211(1) (and section 178) |

defendant (in Scotland) | section 211(1) (and section 177) |

delivery up (in Scotland) | section 211(1) (and section 177) |

[F157disabled person (in paragraphs 3A to 3E of Schedule 2) | paragraph 3E(2) and (3) of Schedule 2] |

[F163distribution right] | [F164section 182B(5)] |

[F165the EEA and EEA state] | [F166section 211(1) (and section 172A)] |

exclusive recording contract | section 185(1) |

film | section 211(1) (and [F167section 5B]) |

[F168group | section 205C(4);] |

illicit recording | section 197 |

[F169injunction (in Scotland) | section 211(1) (and section 177)] |

[F170issue to the public | section 182B;] |

literary work | section 211(1) (and section 3(1)) |

[F171lending right] | [F172section 182C(7)] |

[F173making available right | section 182CA] |

performance | section 180(2) |

[F174performer's non-property rights] | [F175section 192A(1)] |

[F176performer's property rights] | [F177section 191A(1)] |

published | section 211(1) (and section 175) |

qualifying country | section 206(1) |

qualifying individual | section 206(1) and (2) |

qualifying performance | section 181 |

qualifying person | section 206(1) and (3) |

recording (of a performance) | section 180(2) |

recording rights (person having) | section 185(2) and (3) |

[F178rental right]] | [F179section 182C(7)] |

[F180reproduction right] | [F181section 182A(3)] |

[F182rights owner (in relation to performer's property rights)] | [F183 section 191A(3) and (4).] |

[F184signed | section 211(1) (and section 176);] |

sound recording | section 211(1) (and [F185section 5A]). |

[F186wireless broadcast | section 211(1) (and section 178).]] |

Editorial Information

X72. The insertion of the new headings "Chapter 1 Introductory", "Chapter 2 Economic Rights", "Chapter 3 Moral Rights" and "Chapter 4 Qualification for Protection, Extent and Interpretation" in Pt. II on 1.2.2006 gives rise to a change in the structure of this legislation on SLD which breaks the continuity of historical versions of the existing provisions which are now brought under those new headings.

Amendments (Textual)

F157. Words in s. 212 inserted (1.6.2014) by The Copyright and Rights in Performances (Disability) Regulations 2014 (S.I. 2014/1384), reg. 1. (1), Sch. para. 5

F158. S. 212: entry inserted (1.2.2006) by The Performances (Moral Rights, etc.) Regulations 2006 (S.I. 2006/18), reg. 2, Sch. para. 7 (with reg. 8)

F159. S. 212: entry repealed (31.10.2003) by The Copyright and Related Rights Regulations 2003 (S.I. 2003/2498), reg. 2. (2), Sch. 2 (with regs. 31-40)

F160. S. 212: entry inserted (31.10.2003) by The Copyright and Related Rights Regulations 2003

(S.I. 2003/2498), reg. 2. (1), Sch. 1 para. 15. (6) (with regs. 31-40)

F161. Words in s. 212 inserted (1.12.1996) by S.I. 1996/2967, reg. 21. (6) (with Pt. III)

F162. Words in s. 212 inserted (1.12.1996) by S.I. 1996/2967, reg. 21. (6) (with Pt. III)

F163. Words in s. 212 inserted (1.12.1996) by S.I. 1996/2967, reg. 20. (4) (with Pt. III)

F164. Words in s. 212 inserted (1.12.1996) by S.I. 1996/2967, reg. 20. (4) (with Pt. III)

F165. S. 212: words in entry substituted (29.4.2006) by The Intellectual Property (Enforcement, etc.) Regulations 2006 (S.I. 2006/1028), reg. 2. (2), Sch. 2 para. 13

F166. Words in s. 212 inserted (1.1.1996) by S.I. 1995/3297, reg. 11. (4) (with Pt. III)

F167. Words in s. 212 substituted (1.1.1996) by S.I. 1995/3297, reg. 9. (6)(a) (with Pt. III)

F168. S. 212: entry inserted (1.2.2006) by The Performances (Moral Rights, etc.) Regulations 2006 (S.I. 2006/18), reg. 2, Sch. para. 7 (with reg. 8)

F169. S. 212: entry inserted (31.10.2003) by The Copyright and Related Rights Regulations 2003 (S.I. 2003/2498), reg. 2. (1), Sch. 1 para. 15. (6) (with regs. 31-40)

F170. S. 212: entry inserted (1.2.2006) by The Performances (Moral Rights, etc.) Regulations 2006 (S.I. 2006/18), reg. 2, Sch. para. 7 (with reg. 8)

F171. Words in s. 212 inserted (1.12.1996) by S.I. 1996/2967, reg. 20. (4) (with Pt. III)

F172. Words in s. 212 inserted (1.12.1996) by S.I. 1996/2967, reg. 20. (4) (with Pt. III)

F173. S. 212: entry inserted (31.10.2003) by The Copyright and Related Rights Regulations 2003 (S.I. 2003/2498), reg. 2. (1), Sch. 1 para. 15. (6) (with regs. 31-40)

F174. Words in s. 212 inserted (1.12.1996) by S.I. 1996/2967, reg. 21. (6) (with Pt. III)

F175. Words in s. 212 inserted (1.12.1996) by S.I. 1996/2967, reg. 21. (6) (with Pt. III)

F176. Words in s. 212 inserted (1.12.1996) by S.I. 1996/2967, reg. 21. (6) (with Pt. III)

F177. Words in s. 212 inserted (1.12.1996) by S.I. 1996/2967, reg. 21. (6) (with Pt. III)

F178. Words in s. 212 inserted (1.12.1996) by S.I. 1996/2967, reg. 20. (4) (with Pt. III)

F179. Words in s. 212 inserted (1.12.1996) by S.I. 1996/2967, reg. 20. (4) (with Pt. III)

F180. Words in s. 212 inserted (1.12.1996) by S.I. 1996/2967, reg. 20. (4) (with Pt. III)

F181. Words in s. 212 inserted (1.12.1996) by S.I. 1996/2967, reg. 20. (4) (with Pt. III)

F182. Words in s. 212 inserted (1.12.1996) by S.I. 1996/2967, reg. 21. (6) (with Pt. III)

F183. Words in s. 212 inserted (1.12.1996) by S.I. 1996/2967, reg. 21. (6) (with Pt. III)

F184. S. 212: entry inserted (1.2.2006) by The Performances (Moral Rights, etc.) Regulations 2006 (S.I. 2006/18), reg. 2, Sch. para. 7 (with reg. 8)

F185. Words in s. 212 substituted (1.1.1996) by S.I. 1995/3297, reg. 9. (6)(b) (with Pt. III)

F186. S. 212: entry inserted (1.2.2006) by The Performances (Moral Rights, etc.) Regulations 2006 (S.I. 2006/18), reg. 2, Sch. para. 7 (with reg. 8)

[F187. Supplementary

Amendments (Textual)

F187. S. 212. A and cross-heading inserted (1.12.2016 for specified purposes, 6.4.2017 in so far as not already in force) by Intellectual Property Act 2014 (c. 18), ss. 22. (9), 24. (1); S.I. 2016/1139, arts. 2, 3 (with art. 4)

212. APower to amend in consequence of changes to international law

(1) The Secretary of State may by order amend this Part in consequence of changes to international law in the area of performance rights.

(2) An order under this section must be made by statutory instrument; and no order may be made unless a draft of it has been laid before and approved by a resolution of each House of Parliament.]

Countries to which this Part extends.

X1[F1207 Countries to which this Part extends.

This Part extends to England and Wales, Scotland and Northern Ireland.]

Editorial Information

X1. The insertion of the new headings "Chapter 1 Introductory", "Chapter 2 Economic Rights", "Chapter 3 Moral Rights" and "Chapter 4 Qualification for Protection, Extent and Interpretation" in Pt. II on 1.2.2006 gives rise to a change in the structure of this legislation on SLD which breaks the continuity of historical versions of the existing provisions which are now brought under those new headings.

Amendments (Textual)

F1. Ss. 206-212 become Pt. 2 Ch. 4 (1.2.2006) by virtue of The Performances (Moral Rights, etc.) Regulations 2006 (S.I. 2006/18), reg. 4. (7) (with reg. 8)

Modifications etc. (not altering text)

C1. Pt. 2 applied (with modifications) (6.4.2017) by The Copyright and Performances (Application to Other Countries) Order 2016 (S.I. 2016/1219), arts. 1. (1), 12, Sch. Pt. 2 (with art. 13)

C2. Pt. 2 applied (with modifications) (6.4.2017) by The Copyright and Performances (Application to Other Countries) Order 2016 (S.I. 2016/1219), arts. 1. (1), 11, Sch. Pt. 2 (with art. 13)

C3. Pt. 2 applied (with modifications) (6.4.2017) by The Copyright and Performances (Application to Other Countries) Order 2016 (S.I. 2016/1219), arts. 1. (1), 10 (with art. 13)

Part III Design Right

Part III Design Right

Modifications etc. (not altering text)
C1. Pt. III (ss. 213–264) modified by S.I. 1989/1100, art. 3

Chapter I Design right in original designs

213 Design right.

(1) Design right is a property right which subsists in accordance with this Part in an original design.

(2) In this Part "design" means the design of F1... the shape or configuration (whether internal or external) of the whole or part of an article.

(3) Design right does not subsist in—

(a) a method or principle of construction,

(b) features of shape or configuration of an article which—

(i) enable the article to be connected to, or placed in, around or against, another article so that either article may perform its function, or

(ii) are dependent upon the appearance of another article of which the article is intended by the designer to form an integral part, or

(c) surface decoration.

(4) A design is not "original" for the purposes of this Part if it is commonplace [F2in a qualifying country] in the design field in question at the time of its creation[F3; and "qualifying country" has the meaning given in section 217. (3)].

(5) Design right subsists in a design only if the design qualifies for design right protection by reference to—

(a) the designer or the person by whom [F4the designer was employed] (see sections 218 and 219), or

(b) the person by whom and country in which articles made to the design were first marketed (see section 220), or in accordance with any Order under section 221 (power to make further provision with respect to qualification).

 F5 [(5. A) Design right does not subsist in a design which consists of or contains a controlled representation within the meaning of the Olympic Symbol etc. (Protection) Act 1995.]

(6) Design right does not subsist unless and until the design has been recorded in a design document or an article has been made to the design.

(7) Design right does not subsist in a design which was so recorded, or to which an article was made, before the commencement of this Part.

Amendments (Textual)

F1. Words in s. 213. (2) omitted (1.10.2014) by virtue of Intellectual Property Act 2014 (c. 18), ss. 1. (1), 24. (1); S.I. 2014/2330, art. 3, Sch.

F2. Words in s. 213. (4) inserted (1.10.2014) by Intellectual Property Act 2014 (c. 18), ss. 1. (3)(a), 24. (1) (with s. 1. (4)); S.I. 2014/2330, art. 3, Sch.

F3. Words in s. 213. (4) inserted (1.10.2014) by Intellectual Property Act 2014 (c. 18), ss. 1. (3)(b), 24. (1) (with s. 1. (4)); S.I. 2014/2330, art. 3, Sch.

F4. Words in s. 213. (5)(a) substituted (1.10.2014) by Intellectual Property Act 2014 (c. 18), ss. 2. (2)(a), 24. (1) (with s. 2. (3)); S.I. 2014/2330, art. 3, Sch.

F5. S. 213. (5. A) inserted (20.9.1995 with effect as mentioned in s. 14. (2)(3) of the amending Act) by 1995 c. 32, s. 14. (1); S.I. 1995/2472, art. 2

214 The designer.

(1) In this Part the "designer", in relation to a design, means the person who creates it.

(2) In the case of a computer-generated design the person by whom the arrangements necessary for the creation of the design are undertaken shall be taken to be the designer.

215 Ownership of design right.

(1) The designer is the first owner of any design right in a design which is not created F6... in the course of employment.

F7. (2). . . . .

(3) Where F8... a design is created by an employee in the course of his employment, his employer is the first owner of any design right in the design.

(4) If a design qualifies for design right protection by virtue of section 220 (qualification by reference to first marketing of articles made to the design), the above rules do not apply and the person by whom the articles in question are marketed is the first owner of the design right.

Amendments (Textual)

F6. Words in s. 215. (1) omitted (1.10.2014) by virtue of Intellectual Property Act 2014 (c. 18), ss. 2. (1)(a), 24. (1) (with s. 2. (3)); S.I. 2014/2330, art. 3, Sch.

F7. S. 215. (2) omitted (1.10.2014) by virtue of Intellectual Property Act 2014 (c. 18), ss. 2. (1)(b), 24. (1) (with s. 2. (3)); S.I. 2014/2330, art. 3, Sch.

F8. Words in s. 215. (3) omitted (1.10.2014) by virtue of Intellectual Property Act 2014 (c. 18), ss. 2. (1)(c), 24. (1) (with s. 2. (3)); S.I. 2014/2330, art. 3, Sch.

216 Duration of design right.

(1) Design right expires—

    (a) fifteen years from the end of the calendar year in which the design was first recorded in a design document or an article was first made to the design, whichever first occurred, or

    (b) if articles made to the design are made available for sale or hire within five years from the end of that calendar year, ten years from the end of the calendar year in which that first occurred.

(2) The reference in subsection (1) to articles being made available for sale or hire is to their being made so available anywhere in the world by or with the licence of the design right owner.

Qualification for design right protection

217 Qualifying individuals and qualifying persons.

(1) In this Part—

F9...

[F10 " qualifying person " means—

    (a) an individual habitually resident in a qualifying country, or

    (b) a body corporate or other body having legal personality which—

(i) is formed under the law of a part of the United Kingdom or another qualifying country, and

(ii) has in any qualifying country a place of business at which substantial business activity is carried on.]

(2) References in this Part to a qualifying person include the Crown and the government of any other qualifying country.

(3) In this section "qualifying country" means—

    (a) the United Kingdom,

    (b) a country to which this Part extends by virtue of an Order under section 255,

    (c) another member State of the [F11. European Union], or

    (d) to the extent that an Order under section 256 so provides, a country designated under that section as enjoying reciprocal protection.

F12. (4). . . . .

(5) In determining for the purpose of the definition of "qualifying person" whether substantial business activity is carried on at a place of business in any country, no account shall be taken of dealings in goods which are at all material times outside that country.

Amendments (Textual)

F9. Words in s. 217. (1) omitted (1.10.2014) by virtue of Intellectual Property Act 2014 (c. 18), ss. 3. (1)(a), 24. (1) (with s. 3. (6)); S.I. 2014/2330, art. 3, Sch.

F10. Words in s. 217. (1) substituted (1.10.2014) by Intellectual Property Act 2014 (c. 18), ss. 3. (1)(b), 24. (1) (with s. 3. (6)); S.I. 2014/2330, art. 3, Sch.

F11. Words substituted (22.4.2011) by The Treaty of Lisbon (Changes in Terminology) Order 2011 (S.I. 2011/1043), arts. 3, 4

F12. S. 217. (4) omitted (1.10.2014) by virtue of Intellectual Property Act 2014 (c. 18), ss. 3. (2), 24. (1) (with s. 3. (6)); S.I. 2014/2330, art. 3, Sch.

218 Qualification by reference to designer.

(1) This section applies to a design which is not created F13...in the course of employment.

(2) A design to which this section applies qualifies for design right protection if the designer is F14... a qualifying person.

(3) A joint design to which this section applies qualifies for design right protection if any of the designers is F15... a qualifying person.

(4) Where a joint design qualifies for design right protection under this section, only those designers who are F16... qualifying persons are entitled to design right under section 215. (1) (first ownership of design right: entitlement of designer).

Amendments (Textual)

F13. Words in s. 218. (1) omitted (1.10.2014) by virtue of Intellectual Property Act 2014 (c. 18), ss. 2. (2)(b), 24. (1) (with s. 2. (3)); S.I. 2014/2330, art. 3, Sch.

F14. Words in s. 218. (2) omitted (1.10.2014) by virtue of Intellectual Property Act 2014 (c. 18), ss. 3. (3)(a), 24. (1) (with s. 3. (6)); S.I. 2014/2330, art. 3, Sch.

F15. Words in s. 218. (3) omitted (1.10.2014) by virtue of Intellectual Property Act 2014 (c. 18), ss. 3. (3)(b), 24. (1) (with s. 3. (6)); S.I. 2014/2330, art. 3, Sch.

F16. Words in s. 218. (4) omitted (1.10.2014) by virtue of Intellectual Property Act 2014 (c. 18), ss. 3. (3)(c), 24. (1) (with s. 3. (6)); S.I. 2014/2330, art. 3, Sch.

219 [F17. Qualification by reference to employer].

(1) A design qualifies for design right protection if it is created [F18in the course of employment with] a qualifying person.

(2) In the case of F19... joint employment a design qualifies for design right protection if any of the F19... employers is a qualifying person.

(3) Where a design which is F20... created in the course of joint employment qualifies for design right protection under this section, only those F20... employers who are qualifying persons are

entitled to design right under section [F21215. (3)] (first ownership of design right: entitlement of F20... employer).

Amendments (Textual)

F17. S. 219 heading substituted (1.10.2014) by Intellectual Property Act 2014 (c. 18), ss. 2. (2)(c), 24. (1) (with s. 2. (3)); S.I. 2014/2330, art. 3, Sch.

F18. Words in s. 219. (1) substituted (1.10.2014) by Intellectual Property Act 2014 (c. 18), ss. 2. (2)(c), 24. (1) (with s. 2. (3)); S.I. 2014/2330, art. 3, Sch.

F19. Words in s. 219. (2) omitted (1.10.2014) by virtue of Intellectual Property Act 2014 (c. 18), ss. 2. (2)(d), 24. (1) (with s. 2. (3)); S.I. 2014/2330, art. 3, Sch.

F20. Words in s. 219. (3) omitted (1.10.2014) by virtue of Intellectual Property Act 2014 (c. 18), ss. 2. (2)(e), 24. (1) (with s. 2. (3)); S.I. 2014/2330, art. 3, Sch.

F21. Word in s. 219. (3) substituted (1.10.2014) by Intellectual Property Act 2014 (c. 18), ss. 2. (2)(f), 24. (1) (with s. 2. (3)); S.I. 2014/2330, art. 3, Sch.

220 Qualification by reference to first marketing.

(1) A design which does not qualify for design right protection under section 218 or 219 (qualification by reference to designerF22... or employer) qualifies for design right protection if the first marketing of articles made to the design—

(a) is by a qualifying person F23..., and

(b) takes place in the United Kingdom, another country to which this Part extends by virtue of an Order under section 255, or another member State of the [F24. European Union].

(2) If the first marketing of articles made to the design is done jointly by two or more persons, the design qualifies for design right protection if any of those persons meets the [F25 requirement] specified in subsection (1)(a).

(3) In such a case only the persons who meet [F26that requirement] are entitled to design right under section 215. (4) (first ownership of design right: entitlement of first marketer of articles made to the design).

F27. (4). . . . .

Amendments (Textual)

F22. Word in s. 220. (1) omitted (1.10.2014) by virtue of Intellectual Property Act 2014 (c. 18), ss. 2. (2)(g), 24. (1) (with s. 2. (3)); S.I. 2014/2330, art. 3, Sch.

F23. Words in s. 220. (1)(a) omitted (1.10.2014) by virtue of Intellectual Property Act 2014 (c. 18), ss. 3. (4)(a), 24. (1) (with s. 3. (6)); S.I. 2014/2330, art. 3, Sch.

F24. Words substituted (22.4.2011) by The Treaty of Lisbon (Changes in Terminology) Order 2011 (S.I. 2011/1043), arts. 3, 4

F25. Word in s. 220. (2) substituted (1.10.2014) by Intellectual Property Act 2014 (c. 18), ss. 3. (4)(b), 24. (1) (with s. 3. (6)); S.I. 2014/2330, art. 3, Sch.

F26. Words in s. 220. (3) substituted (1.10.2014) by Intellectual Property Act 2014 (c. 18), ss. 3. (4)(c), 24. (1) (with s. 3. (6)); S.I. 2014/2330, art. 3, Sch.

F27. S. 220. (4) omitted (1.10.2014) by virtue of Intellectual Property Act 2014 (c. 18), ss. 3. (4)(d), 24. (1) (with s. 3. (6)); S.I. 2014/2330, art. 3, Sch.

221 Power to make further provision as to qualification.

(1) Her Majesty may, with a view to fulfilling an international obligation of the United Kingdom, by Order in Council provide that a design qualifies for design right protection if such requirements as are specified in the Order are met.

(2) An Order may make different provision for different descriptions of design or article; and may make such consequential modifications of the operation of sections 215 (ownership of design right) and sections 218 to 220 (other means of qualification) as appear to Her Majesty to be appropriate.

(3) A statutory instrument containing an Order in Council under this section shall be subject to annulment in pursuance of a resolution of either House of Parliament.

Dealings with design right

222 Assignment and licences.

(1) Design right is transmissible by assignment, by testamentary disposition or by operation of law, as personal or moveable property.

(2) An assignment or other transmission of design right may be partial, that is, limited so as to apply—

    (a) to one or more, but not all, of the things the design right owner has the exclusive right to do;

    (b) to part, but not the whole, of the period for which the right is to subsist.

(3) An assignment of design right is not effective unless it is in writing signed by or on behalf of the assignor.

(4) A licence granted by the owner of design right is binding on every successor in title to his interest in the right, except a purchaser in good faith for valuable consideration and without notice (actual or constructive) of the licence or a person deriving title from such a purchaser; and references in this Part to doing anything with, or without, the licence of the design right owner shall be construed accordingly.

223 Prospective ownership of design right.

(1) Where by an agreement made in relation to future design right, and signed by or on behalf of the prospective owner of the design right, the prospective owner purports to assign the future design right (wholly or partially) to another person, then if, on the right coming into existence, the assignee or another person claiming under him would be entitled as against all other persons to require the right to be vested in him, the right shall vest in him by virtue of this section.

(2) In this section—

"future design right" means design right which will or may come into existence in respect of a future design or class of designs or on the occurrence of a future event; and

"prospective owner" shall be construed accordingly, and includes a person who is prospectively entitled to design right by virtue of such an agreement as is mentioned in subsection (1).

(3) A licence granted by a prospective owner of design right is binding on every successor in title to his interest (or prospective interest) in the right, except a purchaser in good faith for valuable consideration and without notice (actual or constructive) of the licence or a person deriving title from such a purchaser; and references in this Part to doing anything with, or without, the licence of the design right owner shall be construed accordingly.

224 Assignment of right in registered design presumed to carry with it design right.

Where a design consisting of a design in which design right subsists is registered under the M1. Registered Designs Act 1949 and the proprietor of the registered design is also the design right owner, an assignment of the right in the registered design shall be taken to be also an assignment of the design right, unless a contrary intention appears.

Marginal Citations

M11949 c. 88.

225 Exclusive licences.

(1) In this Part an "exclusive licence" means a licence in writing signed by or on behalf of the design right owner authorising the licensee to the exclusion of all other persons, including the person granting the licence, to exercise a right which would otherwise be exercisable exclusively by the design right owner.

(2) The licensee under an exclusive licence has the same rights against any successor in title who is bound by the licence as he has against the person granting the licence.

Chapter II Rights of Design Right Owner and Remedies

226 Primary infringement of design right.

(1) The owner of design right in a design has the exclusive right to reproduce the design for commercial purposes—

    (a) by making articles to that design, or

(b) by making a design document recording the design for the purpose of enabling such articles to be made.

(2) Reproduction of a design by making articles to the design means copying the design so as to produce articles exactly or substantially to that design, and references in this Part to making articles to a design shall be construed accordingly.

(3) Design right is infringed by a person who without the licence of the design right owner does, or authorises another to do, anything which by virtue of this section is the exclusive right of the design right owner.

(4) For the purposes of this section reproduction may be direct or indirect, and it is immaterial whether any intervening acts themselves infringe the design right.

(5) This section has effect subject to the provisions of Chapter III (exceptions to rights of design right owner).

227 Secondary infringement: importing or dealing with infringing article.

(1) Design right is infringed by a person who, without the licence of the design right owner—

    (a) imports into the United Kingdom for commercial purposes, or

    (b) has in his possession for commercial purposes, or

    (c) sells, lets for hire, or offers or exposes for sale or hire, in the course of a business,

an article which is, and which he knows or has reason to believe is, an infringing article.

(2) This section has effect subject to the provisions of Chapter III (exceptions to rights of design right owner).

228 Meaning of "infringing article".

(1) In this Part "infringing article", in relation to a design, shall be construed in accordance with this section.

(2) An article is an infringing article if its making to that design was an infringement of design right in the design.

(3) An article is also an infringing article if—

    (a) it has been or is proposed to be imported into the United Kingdom, and

    (b) its making to that design in the United Kingdom would have been an infringement of design right in the design or a breach of an exclusive licence agreement relating to the design.

(4) Where it is shown that an article is made to a design in which design right subsists or has subsisted at any time, it shall be presumed until the contrary is proved that the article was made at a time when design right subsisted.

(5) Nothing in subsection (3) shall be construed as applying to an article which may lawfully be imported into the United Kingdom by virtue of any enforceable [F28. EU] right within the meaning of section 2. (1) of the M2. European Communities Act 1972.

(6) The expression "infringing article" does not include a design document, notwithstanding that its making was or would have been an infringement of design right.

Amendments (Textual)

F28. Word substituted (22.4.2011) by The Treaty of Lisbon (Changes in Terminology) Order 2011 (S.I. 2011/1043), arts. 3, 6

Marginal Citations

M21972 c. 68.

Remedies for infringement

229 Rights and remedies of design right owner.

(1) An infringement of design right is actionable by the design right owner.

(2) In an action for infringement of design right all such relief by way of damages, injunctions, accounts or otherwise is available to the plaintiff as is available in respect of the infringement of any other property right.

(3) The court may in an action for infringement of design right, having regard to all the circumstances and in particular to—

(a) the flagrancy of the infringement, and

(b) any benefit accruing to the defendant by reason of the infringement,

award such additional damages as the justice of the case may require.

(4) This section has effect subject to section 233 (innocent infringement).

230 Order for delivery up.

(1) Where a person—

(a) has in his possession, custody or control for commercial purposes an infringing article, or

(b) has in his possession, custody or control anything specifically designed or adapted for making articles to a particular design, knowing or having reason to believe that it has been or is to be used to make an infringing article,

the owner of the design right in the design in question may apply to the court for an order that the infringing article or other thing be delivered up to him or to such other person as the court may direct.

(2) An application shall not be made after the end of the period specified in the following provisions of this section; and no order shall be made unless the court also makes, or it appears to the court that there are grounds for making, an order under section 231 (order as to disposal of infringing article, &c.).

(3) An application for an order under this section may not be made after the end of the period of six years from the date on which the article or thing in question was made, subject to subsection (4).

(4) If during the whole or any part of that period the design right owner—

(a) is under a disability, or

(b) is prevented by fraud or concealment from discovering the facts entitling him to apply for an order,

an application may be made at any time before the end of the period of six years from the date on which he ceased to be under a disability or, as the case may be, could with reasonable diligence have discovered those facts.

(5) In subsection (4) "disability"—

(a) in England and Wales, has the same meaning as in the M3. Limitation Act 1980;

(b) in Scotland, means legal disability within the meaning of the M4. Prescription and Limitation (Scotland) Act 1973;

(c) in Northern Ireland, has the same meaning as in the M5. Statute of Limitations (Northern Ireland) 1958.

(6) A person to whom an infringing article or other thing is delivered up in pursuance of an order under this section shall, if an order under section 231 is not made, retain it pending the making of an order, or the decision not to make an order, under that section.

(7) Nothing in this section affects any other power of the court.

Modifications etc. (not altering text)

C2. S. 230 extended by S.I.1991/724, art. 2. (1)(n)

Marginal Citations

M31980 c. 58.

M41973 c. 52.

M51958 c. 10 (N.I.).

231 Order as to disposal of infringing articles, &c.

(1) An application may be made to the court for an order that an infringing article or other thing delivered up in pursuance of an order under section 230 shall be—

(a) forfeited to the design right owner, or

(b) destroyed or otherwise dealt with as the court may think fit,

or for a decision that no such order should be made.

(2) In considering what order (if any) should be made, the court shall consider whether other remedies available in an action for infringement of design right would be adequate to compensate the design right owner and to protect his interests.

(3) Provision shall be made by rules of court as to the service of notice on persons having an

interest in the article or other thing, and any such person is entitled—

(a) to appear in proceedings for an order under this section, whether or not he was served with notice, and

(b) to appeal against any order made, whether or not he appeared;

and an order shall not take effect until the end of the period within which notice of an appeal may be given or, if before the end of that period notice of appeal is duly given, until the final determination or abandonment of the proceedings on the appeal.

(4) Where there is more than one person interested in an article or other thing, the court shall make such order as it thinks just and may (in particular) direct that the thing be sold, or otherwise dealt with, and the proceeds divided.

(5) If the court decides that no order should be made under this section, the person in whose possession, custody or control the article or other thing was before being delivered up F29. . . is entitled to its return.

(6) References in this section to a person having an interest in an article or other thing include any person in whose favour an order could be made in respect of it

[F30. (a)under this section or under section 114 or 204 of this Act;

(b) under section 24. D of the Registered Designs Act 1949;

(c) under section 19 of Trade Marks Act 1994 (including that section as applied by regulation 4 of the Community Trade Mark Regulations 2006 (SI 2006/1027)); or

(d) under regulation 1. C of the Community Design Regulations 2005 (SI 2005/2339).]

Amendments (Textual)

F29. Words in s. 231. (5) repealed (29.4.2006) by The Intellectual Property (Enforcement, etc.) Regulations 2006 (S.I. 2006/1028), reg. 2. (4), Sch. 4

F30. Words in s. 231. (6) substituted (29.4.2006) by The Intellectual Property (Enforcement, etc.) Regulations 2006 (S.I. 2006/1028), reg. 2. (2), Sch. 2 para. 14

Modifications etc. (not altering text)

C3. S. 231 extended by S.I. 1991/724, art. 2. (1)(n)

232 Jurisdiction of county court and sheriff court.

(1) In England [F31and Wales the county court and in] Northern Ireland a county court may entertain proceedings under—

section 230 (order for delivery up of infringing article, &c.),

section 231 (order as to disposal of infringing article, &c.), or

section 235. (5) (application by exclusive licensee having concurrent rights),

[F32save that, in Northern Ireland, a county court may entertain such proceedings only] where the value of the infringing articles and other things in question does not exceed the county court limit for actions in tort.

(2) In Scotland proceedings for an order under any of those provisions may be brought in the sheriff court.

(3) Nothing in this section shall be construed as affecting the jurisdiction of the High Court or, in Scotland, the Court of Session.

Amendments (Textual)

F31. Words in s. 232. (1) substituted (22.4.2014) by Crime and Courts Act 2013 (c. 22), s. 61. (3), Sch. 9 para. 72; S.I. 2014/954, art. 2. (c) (with art. 3) (with transitional provisions and savings in S.I. 2014/956, arts. 3-11)

F32. Words in s. 232. (1) inserted by S.I. 1991/724, art. 2. (8), Schedule Part I

233 Innocent infringement.

(1) Where in an action for infringement of design right brought by virtue of section 226 (primary infringement) it is shown that at the time of the infringement the defendant did not know, and had no reason to believe, that design right subsisted in the design to which the action relates, the plaintiff is not entitled to damages against him, but without prejudice to any other remedy.

(2) Where in an action for infringement of design right brought by virtue of section 227 (secondary infringement) a defendant shows that the infringing article was innocently acquired by him or a predecessor in title of his, the only remedy available against him in respect of the

infringement is damages not exceeding a reasonable royalty in respect of the act complained of.

(3) In subsection (2) "innocently acquired" means that the person acquiring the article did not know and had no reason to believe that it was an infringing article.

234 Rights and remedies of exclusive licensee.

(1) An exclusive licensee has, except against the design right owner, the same rights and remedies in respect of matters occurring after the grant of the licence as if the licence had been an assignment.

(2) His rights and remedies are concurrent with those of the design right owner; and references in the relevant provisions of this Part to the design right owner shall be construed accordingly.

(3) In an action brought by an exclusive licensee by virtue of this section a defendant may avail himself of any defence which would have been available to him if the action had been brought by the design right owner.

235 Exercise of concurrent rights.

(1) Where an action for infringement of design right brought by the design right owner or an exclusive licensee relates (wholly or partly) to an infringement in respect of which they have concurrent rights of action, the design right owner or, as the case may be, the exclusive licensee may not, without the leave of the court, proceed with the action unless the other is either joined as a plaintiff or added as a defendant.

(2) A design right owner or exclusive licensee who is added as a defendant in pursuance of subsection (1) is not liable for any costs in the action unless he takes part in the proceedings.

(3) The above provisions do not affect the granting of interlocutory relief on the application of the design right owner or an exclusive licensee.

(4) Where an action for infringement of design right is brought which relates (wholly or partly) to an infringement in respect of which the design right owner and an exclusive licensee have concurrent rights of action—

(a) the court shall, in assessing damages, take into account—

(i) the terms of the licence, and

(ii) any pecuniary remedy already awarded or available to either of them in respect of the infringement;

(b) no account of profits shall be directed if an award of damages has been made, or an account of profits has been directed, in favour of the other of them in respect of the infringement; and

(c) the court shall if an account of profits is directed apportion the profits between them as the court considers just, subject to any agreement between them;

and these provisions apply whether or not the design right owner and the exclusive licensee are both parties to the action.

(5) The design right owner shall notify any exclusive licensee having concurrent rights before applying for an order under section 230 (order for delivery up of infringing article, &c.); and the court may on the application of the licensee make such order under that section as it thinks fit having regard to the terms of the licence.

Modifications etc. (not altering text)

C4. S. 235. (5) extended by S.I. 1991/724, art. 2. (1)(n)

Chapter III Exceptions to Rights of Design Right Owners

236 Infringement of copyright.

Where copyright subsists in a work which consists of or includes a design in which design right subsists, it is not an infringement of design right in the design to do anything which is an infringement of the copyright in that work.

Availability of licences of right

237 Licences available in last five years of design right.

(1) Any person is entitled as of right to a licence to do in the last five years of the design right term anything which would otherwise infringe the design right.

(2) The terms of the licence shall, in default of agreement, be settled by the comptroller.

(3) The Secretary of State may if it appears to him necessary in order to—

(a) comply with an international obligation of the United Kingdom, or

(b) secure or maintain reciprocal protection for British designs in other countries,

by order exclude from the operation of subsection (1) designs of a description specified in the order or designs applied to articles of a description so specified.

(4) An order shall be made by statutory instrument; and no order shall be made unless a draft of it has been laid before and approved by a resolution of each House of Parliament.

238 Powers exercisable for protection of the public interest.

[F33. (1) Subsection (1. A) applies where whatever needs to be remedied, mitigated or prevented by the Secretary of State [F34 or (as the case may be) the Competition and Markets Authority] under section 12. (5) of the Competition Act 1980 or section 41. (2), 55. (2), 66. (6), 75. (2), 83. (2), 138. (2), 147. (2) [F35 , 147. A(2)] or 160. (2) of, or paragraph 5. (2) or 10. (2) of Schedule 7 to, the Enterprise Act 2002 (powers to take remedial action following references to the [F36 Competition and Markets Authority] in connection with public bodies and certain other persons, mergers or market investigations etc.) consists of or includes—

(a) conditions in licences granted by a design right owner restricting the use of the design by the licensee or the right of the design right owner to grant other licences, or

(b) a refusal of a design right owner to grant licences on reasonable terms.

(1. A)The powers conferred by Schedule 8 to the Enterprise Act 2002 include power to cancel or modify those conditions and, instead or in addition, to provide that licences in respect of the design right shall be available as of right.

(2)The references to anything permitted by Schedule 8 to the Enterprise Act 2002 in section 12. (5. A) of the Competition Act 1980 and in sections 75. (4)(a), 83. (4)(a), 84. (2)(a), 89. (1), 160. (4)(a), 161. (3)(a) and 164. (1) of, and paragraphs 5, 10 and 11 of Schedule 7 to, the Act of 2002 shall be construed accordingly.]

(3) The terms of a licence available by virtue of this section shall, in default of agreement, be settled by the comptroller.

Amendments (Textual)

F33. S. 238. (1)(1. A)(2) substituted (20.6.2003 for certain purposes and 29.12.2004 otherwise) for s. 238. (1)(2) by 2002 c. 40, ss. 278. (1), 279, Sch. 25 para. 18. (4); S.I. 2003/1397, arts. 2, 3. (1), Sch. (with arts. 4-12); S.I. 2004/3233, art. 2, Sch. (with arts. 3-5)

F34. Words in s. 238. (1) substituted (1.4.2014) by The Enterprise and Regulatory Reform Act 2013 (Competition) (Consequential, Transitional and Saving Provisions) Order 2014 (S.I. 2014/892), art. 1. (1), Sch. 1 para. 58. (a) (with art. 3)

F35. Word in s. 238. (1) inserted (1.4.2014) by The Enterprise and Regulatory Reform Act 2013 (Competition) (Consequential, Transitional and Saving Provisions) Order 2014 (S.I. 2014/892), art. 1. (1), Sch. 1 para. 58. (b) (with art. 3)

F36. Words in s. 238. (1) substituted (1.4.2014) by The Enterprise and Regulatory Reform Act 2013 (Competition) (Consequential, Transitional and Saving Provisions) Order 2014 (S.I. 2014/892), art. 1. (1), Sch. 1 para. 58. (c) (with art. 3)

Modifications etc. (not altering text)

C5. S. 238. (1) amended (20.6.2003) by The Enterprise Act 2002 (Protection of Legitimate Interests) Order 2003 (S.I. 2003/1592), Sch. 4 para. 7. (2)(a)

C6. S. 238. (2) amended (20.6.2003) by The Enterprise Act 2002 (Protection of Legitimate Interests) Order 2003 (S.I. 2003/1592), Sch. 4 para. 7. (2)(a)

239 Undertaking to take licence of right in infringement proceedings.

(1) If in proceedings for infringement of design right in a design in respect of which a licence is available as of right under section 237 or 238 the defendant undertakes to take a licence on such terms as may be agreed or, in default of agreement, settled by the comptroller under that section—

(a) no injunction shall be granted against him,

(b) no order for delivery up shall be made under section 230, and

(c) the amount recoverable against him by way of damages or on an account of profits shall not exceed double the amount which would have been payable by him as licensee if such a licence on those terms had been granted before the earliest infringement.

(2) An undertaking may be given at any time before final order in the proceedings, without any admission of liability.

(3) Nothing in this section affects the remedies available in respect of an infringement committed before licences of right were available.

Crown use of designs

240 Crown use of designs.

(1) A government department, or a person authorised in writing by a government department, may without the licence of the design right owner—

(a) do anything for the purpose of supplying articles for the services of the Crown, or

(b) dispose of articles no longer required for the services of the Crown;

and nothing done by virtue of this section infringes the design right.

(2) References in this Part to "the services of the Crown" are to—

(a) the defence of the realm,

(b) foreign defence purposes, and

(c) health service purposes.

(3) The reference to the supply of articles for "foreign defence purposes" is to their supply—

(a) for the defence of a country outside the realm in pursuance of an agreement or arrangement to which the government of that country and Her Majesty's Government in the United Kingdom are parties; or

(b) for use by armed forces operating in pursuance of a resolution of the United Nations or one of its organs.

(4) The reference to the supply of articles for "health service purposes" are to their supply for the purpose of providing—

[F37. (za)primary medical services or primary dental services under [F38the National Health Service Act 2006 or the National Health Service (Wales) Act 2006,][F39or primary medical services under Part 1 of the National Health Service (Scotland) Act 1978]]

F40[(a)pharmaceutical services, general medical services or general dental services under— [F41. (i)Chapter 1 of Part 7 of the National Health Service Act 2006, or Chapter 1 of Part 7 of the National Health Service (Wales) Act 2006 (in the case of pharmaceutical services),]

(ii) Part II of the National Health Service (Scotland) Act 1978 [F42. (in the case of pharmaceutical services or general dental services)], or

(iii) the corresponding provisions of the law in force in Northern Ireland; or

(b) personal medical services or personal dental services in accordance with arrangements made under—

(i) F43. . . . .

(ii) section 17. C of the 1978 Act [F44. (in the case of personal dental services)], or

(iii) the corresponding provisions of the law in force in Northern Ireland][F45or

(c) local pharmaceutical services provided under[F46 the National Health Service Act 2006 or the National Health Service (Wales) Act 2006].]

(5) In this Part—

"Crown use", in relation to a design, means the doing of anything by virtue of this section which would otherwise be an infringement of design right in the design; and

"the government department concerned", in relation to such use, means the government department by whom or on whose authority the act was done.

(6) The authority of a government department in respect of Crown use of a design may be given to a person either before or after the use and whether or not he is authorised, directly or indirectly, by

the design right owner to do anything in relation to the design.

(7) A person acquiring anything sold in the exercise of powers conferred by this section, and any person claiming under him, may deal with it in the same manner as if the design right were held on behalf of the Crown.

Amendments (Textual)

F37. S. 240. (4)(za) inserted (1.4.2004) by Health and Social Care (Community Health and Standards) Act 2003 (c. 43), ss. 184, 199. (1), Sch. 11 para. 52. (a); S.I. 2004/288, art. 5 (with art. 8) (as amended by S.I. 2004/866, art. 2) and by S.I. 2004/480, art. 4 (with art. 7) (as amended by S.I. 2004/1019, art. 2)

F38. Words in s. 240. (4)(za) substituted (1.3.2007) by National Health Service (Consequential Provisions) Act 2006 (c. 43), ss. 2, 8, Sch. 1 para. 113. (a) (with s. 5, Sch. 3 Pt. 1)

F39. Words in s. 240. (4)(za) inserted (1.4.2004) by The Primary Medical Services (Scotland) Act 2004 (Consequential Modifications) Order 2004 (S.I. 2004/957), art. 2, Sch. para. 5. (a)

F40. S. 240. (4)(a)(b) substituted (1.4.1998) by 1997 c. 46, s. 41. (10), Sch. 2 Pt. I para. 63; S.I. 1998/631, art. 2. (1)(b), Sch. 2 (subject to arts. 3-5)

F41. S. 240. (4)(a)(i) substituted (1.3.2007) by National Health Service (Consequential Provisions) Act 2006 (c. 43), ss. 2, 8, Sch. 1 para. 113. (b) (with s. 5, Sch. 3 Pt. 1)

F42. Words in s. 240. (4)(a)(ii) inserted (1.4.2004) by The Primary Medical Services (Scotland) Act 2004 (Consequential Modifications) Order 2004 (S.I. 2004/957), art. 2, Sch. para. 5. (b)

F43. S. 240. (4)(b)(i) repealed (1.4.2004) by Health and Social Care (Community Health and Standards) Act 2003 (c. 43), ss. 184, 196, 199. (1), Sch. 11 para. 52. (c), Sch. 14 Pt. 4; S.I. 2004/288, art. 5 (with art. 8) (as amended by S.I. 2004/866, art. 2) and by S.I. 2004/480, art. 4 (with art. 7) (as amended by S.I. 2004/1019, art. 2)

F44. Words in s. 240. (4)(b)(ii) inserted (1.4.2004) by The Primary Medical Services (Scotland) Act 2004 (Consequential Modifications) Order 2004 (S.I. 2004/957), art. 2, Sch. para. 5. (c)

F45. S. 240. (4)(c) and the word "or" immediately preceding it inserted (1.7.2002 for W. and 1.1.2003 for E.) by 2001 c. 15, ss. 67. (1), 70. (2), Sch. 5 Pt. 1 para. 7 (with ss. 64. (9), 65. (4)); S.I. 2002/1475, art. 2. (1), Sch. Pt. I; S.I. 2003/53, art. 2

F46. Words in s. 240. (4)(c) substituted (1.3.2007) for s. 240. (4)(c)(i)(ii) by National Health Service (Consequential Provisions) Act 2006 (c. 43), ss. 2, 8, Sch. 1 para. 113. (c) (with s. 5, Sch. 3 Pt. 1)

241 Settlement of terms for Crown use.

(1) Where Crown use is made of a design, the government department concerned shall—

(a) notify the design right owner as soon as practicable, and

(b) give him such information as to the extent of the use as he may from time to time require, unless it appears to the department that it would be contrary to the public interest to do so or the identity of the design right owner cannot be ascertained on reasonable inquiry.

(2) Crown use of a design shall be on such terms as, either before or after the use, are agreed between the government department concerned and the design right owner with the approval of the Treasury or, in default of agreement, are determined by the court.

In the application of this subsection to Northern Ireland the reference to the Treasury shall, where the government department referred to in that subsection is a Northern Ireland department, be construed as a reference to the Department of Finance and Personnel.

[F47. In the application of this subsection to Scotland, where the government department referred to in that subsection is any part of the Scottish Administration, the words "with the approval of the Treasury" are omitted.]

(3) Where the identity of the design right owner cannot be ascertained on reasonable inquiry, the government department concerned may apply to the court who may order that no royalty or other sum shall be payable in respect of Crown use of the design until the owner agrees terms with the department or refers the matter to the court for determination.

Amendments (Textual)

F47. Paragraph in s. 241. (2) inserted (1.7.1999) by S.I. 1999/1820, arts. 1. (2), 4, Sch. 2 Pt. I para. 93. (2); S.I. 1998/3178, art. 3

242 Rights of third parties in case of Crown use.

(1) The provisions of any licence, assignment or agreement made between the design right owner (or anyone deriving title from him or from whom he derives title) and any person other than a government department are of no effect in relation to Crown use of a design, or any act incidental to Crown use, so far as they—

(a) restrict or regulate anything done in relation to the design, or the use of any model, document or other information relating to it, or

(b) provide for the making of payments in respect of, or calculated by reference to such use; and the copying or issuing to the public of copies of any such model or document in connection with the thing done, or any such use, shall be deemed not to be an infringement of any copyright in the model or document.

(2) Subsection (1) shall not be construed as authorising the disclosure of any such model, document or information in contravention of the licence, assignment or agreement.

(3) Where an exclusive licence is in force in respect of the design—

(a) if the licence was granted for royalties—

(i) any agreement between the design right owner and a government department under section 241 (settlement of terms for Crown use) requires the consent of the licensee, and

(ii) the licensee is entitled to recover from the design right owner such part of the payment for Crown use as may be agreed between them or, in default of agreement, determined by the court;

(b) if the licence was granted otherwise than for royalties—

(i) section 241 applies in relation to anything done which but for section 240 (Crown use) and subsection (1) above would be an infringement of the rights of the licensee with the substitution for references to the design right owner of references to the licensee, and

(ii) section 241 does not apply in relation to anything done by the licensee by virtue of an authority given under section 240.

(4) Where the design right has been assigned to the design right owner in consideration of royalties—

(a) section 241 applies in relation to Crown use of the design as if the references to the design right owner included the assignor, and any payment for Crown use shall be divided between them in such proportion as may be agreed or, in default of agreement, determined by the court; and

(b) section 241 applies in relation to any act incidental to Crown use as it applies in relation to Crown use of the design.

(5) Where any model, document or other information relating to a design is used in connection with Crown use of the design, or any act incidental to Crown use, section 241 applies to the use of the model, document or other information with the substitution for the references to the design right owner of references to the person entitled to the benefit of any provision of an agreement rendered inoperative by subsection (1) above.

(6) In this section—

"act incidental to Crown use" means anything done for the services of the Crown to the order of a government department by the design right owner in respect of a design;

"payment for Crown use" means such amount as is payable by the government department concerned by virtue of section 241; and

"royalties" includes any benefit determined by reference to the use of the design.

243 Crown use: compensation for loss of profit.

(1) Where Crown use is made of a design, the government department concerned shall pay—

(a) to the design right owner, or

(b) if there is an exclusive licence in force in respect of the design, to the exclusive licensee, compensation for any loss resulting from his not being awarded a contract to supply the articles made to the design.

(2) Compensation is payable only to the extent that such a contract could have been fulfilled from his existing manufacturing capacity; but is payable notwithstanding the existence of circumstances rendering him ineligible for the award of such a contract.

(3) In determining the loss, regard shall be had to the profit which would have been made on such

a contract and to the extent to which any manufacturing capacity was under-used.

(4) No compensation is payable in respect of any failure to secure contracts for the supply of articles made to the design otherwise than for the services of the Crown.

(5) The amount payable shall, if not agreed between the design right owner or licensee and the government department concerned with the approval of the Treasury, be determined by the court on a reference under section 252; and it is in addition to any amount payable under section 241 or 242.

(6) In the application of this section to Northern Ireland, the reference in subsection (5) to the Treasury shall, where the government department concerned is a Northern Ireland department, be construed as a reference to the Department of Finance and Personnel.

[F48. (7)In the application of this section to Scotland, where the government department referred to in subsection (5) is any part of the Scottish Administration, the words "with the approval of the Treasury" in that subsection are omitted.]

Amendments (Textual)

F48. S. 243. (7) inserted (1.7.1999) by S.I. 1999/1820, arts. 1. (2), 4, Sch. 2 Pt. I para. 93. (3); S.I. 1998/3178, art. 3

244 Special provision for Crown use during emergency.

(1) During a period of emergency the powers exercisable in relation to a design by virtue of section 240 (Crown use) include power to do any act which would otherwise be an infringement of design right for any purpose which appears to the government department concerned necessary or expedient—

(a) for the efficient prosecution of any war in which Her Majesty may be engaged;

(b) for the maintenance of supplies and services essential to the life of the community;

(c) for securing a sufficiency of supplies and services essential to the well-being of the community;

(d) for promoting the productivity of industry, commerce and agriculture;

(e) for fostering and directing exports and reducing imports, or imports of any classes, from all or any countries and for redressing the balance of trade;

(f) generally for ensuring that the whole resources of the community are available for use, and are used, in a manner best calculated to serve the interests of the community; or

(g) for assisting the relief of suffering and the restoration and distribution of essential supplies and services in any country outside the United Kingdom which is in grave distress as the result of war.

(2) References in this Part to the services of the Crown include, as respects a period of emergency, those purposes; and references to "Crown use" include any act which would apart from this section be an infringement of design right.

(3) In this section "period of emergency" means a period beginning with such date as may be declared by Order in Council to be the beginning, and ending with such date as may be so declared to be the end, of a period of emergency for the purposes of this section.

(4) No Order in Council under this section shall be submitted to Her Majesty unless a draft of it has been laid before and approved by a resolution of each House of Parliament.

[F49. Miscellaneous

Amendments (Textual)

F49. Ss. 244. A, 244. B and cross-heading inserted (1.10.2014) by Intellectual Property Act 2014 (c. 18), ss. 4, 24. (1); S.I. 2014/2330, art. 3, Sch.

244. AException for private acts, experiments and teaching

Design right is not infringed by—

(a) an act which is done privately and for purposes which are not commercial;

(b) an act which is done for experimental purposes; or

(c) an act of reproduction for teaching purposes or for the purpose of making citations provided that—

(i) the act of reproduction is compatible with fair trade practice and does not unduly prejudice the normal exploitation of the design, and

(ii) mention is made of the source.

244. BException for overseas ships and aircraft

Design right is not infringed by—

(a) the use of equipment on ships or aircraft which are registered in another country but which are temporarily in the United Kingdom;

(b) the importation into the United Kingdom of spare parts or accessories for the purpose of repairing such ships or aircraft; or

(c) the carrying out of repairs on such ships or aircraft.]

General

245 Power to provide for further exceptions.

(1) The Secretary of State may if it appears to him necessary in order to—

(a) comply with an international obligation of the United Kingdom, or

(b) secure or maintain reciprocal protection for British designs in other countries,

by order provide that acts of a description specified in the order do not infringe design right.

(2) An order may make different provision for different descriptions of design or article.

(3) An order shall be made by statutory instrument and no order shall be made unless a draft of it has been laid before and approved by a resolution of each House of Parliament.

Chapter IV Jurisdiction of the Comptroller and the Court

246 Jurisdiction to decide matters relating to design right.

(1) A party to a dispute as to any of the following matters may refer the dispute to the comptroller for his decision—

(a) the subsistence of design right,

(b) the term of design right, or

(c) the identity of the person in whom design right first vested;

and the comptroller's decision on the reference is binding on the parties to the dispute.

(2) No other court or tribunal shall decide any such matter except—

(a) on a reference or appeal from the comptroller,

(b) in infringement or other proceedings in which the issue arises incidentally, or

(c) in proceedings brought with the agreement of the parties or the leave of the comptroller.

(3) The comptroller has jurisdiction to decide any incidental question of fact or law arising in the course of a reference under this section.

247 Application to settle terms of licence of right.

(1) A person requiring a licence which is available as of right by virtue of—

(a) section 237 (licences available in last five years of design right), or

(b) an order under section 238 (licences made available in the public interest),

may apply to the comptroller to settle the terms of the licence.

(2) No application for the settlement of the terms of a licence available by virtue of section 237 may be made earlier than one year before the earliest date on which the licence may take effect under that section.

(3) The terms of a licence settled by the comptroller shall authorise the licensee to do—

(a) in the case of licence available by virtue of section 237, everything which would be an infringement of the design right in the absence of a licence;

(b) in the case of a licence available by virtue of section 238, everything in respect of which a licence is so available.

(4) In settling the terms of a licence the comptroller shall have regard to such factors as may be

prescribed by the Secretary of State by order made by statutory instrument.

(5) No such order shall be made unless a draft of it has been laid before and approved by a resolution of each House of Parliament.

(6) Where the terms of a licence are settled by the comptroller, the licence has effect—

    (a) in the case of an application in respect of a licence available by virtue of section 237 made before the earliest date on which the licence may take effect under that section, from that date;

    (b) in any other case, from the date on which the application to the comptroller was made.

248 Settlement of terms where design right owner unknown.

(1) This section applies where a person making an application under section 247 (settlement of terms of licence of right) is unable on reasonable inquiry to discover the identity of the design right owner.

(2) The comptroller may in settling the terms of the licence order that the licence shall be free of any obligation as to royalties or other payments.

(3) If such an order is made the design right owner may apply to the comptroller to vary the terms of the licence with effect from the date on which his application is made.

(4) If the terms of a licence are settled by the comptroller and it is subsequently established that a licence was not available as of right, the licensee shall not be liable in damages for, or for an account of profits in respect of, anything done before he was aware of any claim by the design right owner that a licence was not available.

249 Appeals as to terms of licence of right.

(1) An appeal lies from any decision of the comptroller under section 247 or 248 (settlement of terms of licence of right) to [F50a person appointed under section 27. A of the Registered Designs Act 1949].

F51. (2). . . . .

Amendments (Textual)

F50. Words in s. 249. (1) substituted (6.4.2015) by Intellectual Property Act 2014 (c. 18), ss. 10. (7)(a), 24. (1); S.I. 2015/165, art. 3

F51. S. 249. (2) omitted (6.4.2015) by virtue of Intellectual Property Act 2014 (c. 18), ss. 10. (7)(b), 24. (1); S.I. 2015/165, art. 3

[F52249. AOpinions service

The descriptions of designs which may be specified in regulations under subsection (1)(b) of section 28. A of the Registered Designs Act 1949 (requests to the comptroller for opinions on designs) include, in particular—

    (a) designs in which design right subsists in accordance with this Part, and

    (b) designs in relation to which there is a question whether design right so subsists.]

Amendments (Textual)

F52. S. 249. A inserted (1.10.2014) by Intellectual Property Act 2014 (c. 18), ss. 11. (2), 24. (1); S.I. 2014/2330, art. 3, Sch.

250 Rules.

(1) The Secretary of State may make rules for regulating the procedure to be followed in connection with any proceeding before the comptroller under this Part.

(2) Rules may, in particular, make provision—

    (a) prescribing forms;

    (b) requiring fees to be paid;

    (c) authorising the rectification of irregularities of procedure;

    (d) regulating the mode of giving evidence and empowering the comptroller to compel the attendance of witnesses and the discovery of and production of documents;

    (e) providing for the appointment of advisers to assist the comptroller in proceedings before him;

    (f) prescribing time limits for doing anything required to be done (and providing for the alteration of any such limit); and

    (g) empowering the comptroller to award costs and to direct how, to what party and from what parties, costs are to be paid.

(3) Rules prescribing fees require the consent of the Treasury.

(4) The remuneration of an adviser appointed to assist the comptroller shall be determined by the Secretary of State with the consent of the Treasury and shall be defrayed out of money provided by Parliament.

(5) Rules shall be made by statutory instrument which shall be subject to annulment in pursuance of a resolution of either House of Parliament.

Jurisdiction of the court

251 References and appeals on design right matters.

(1) In any proceedings before him under section 246 (reference of matter relating to design right), the comptroller may at any time order the whole proceedings or any question or issue (whether of fact or law) to be referred, on such terms as he may direct, to the High Court or, in Scotland, the Court of Session.

(2) The comptroller shall make such an order if the parties to the proceedings agree that he should do so.

(3) On a reference under this section the court may exercise any power available to the comptroller by virtue of this Part as respects the matter referred to it and, following its determination, may refer any matter back to the comptroller.

(4) An appeal lies from any decision of the comptroller in proceedings before him under section 246 (decisions on matters relating to design right) to [F53—

    (a)]the High Court or, in Scotland, the Court of Session [F54, or

    (b) a person appointed under section 27. A of the Registered Designs Act 1949].

Amendments (Textual)

F53. Words in s. 251. (4) renumbered as s. 251. (4)(a) (6.4.2015) by Intellectual Property Act 2014 (c. 18), ss. 10. (8)(a), 24. (1); S.I. 2015/165, art. 3

F54. S. 251. (4)(b) and word preceding it inserted (6.4.2015) by Intellectual Property Act 2014 (c. 18), ss. 10. (8)(b), 24. (1); S.I. 2015/165, art. 3

252 Reference of disputes relating to Crown use.

(1) A dispute as to any matter which falls to be determined by the court in default of agreement under—

    (a) section 241 (settlement of terms for Crown use),

    (b) section 242 (rights of third parties in case of Crown use), or

    (c) section 243 (Crown use: compensation for loss of profit),

may be referred to the court by any party to the dispute.

(2) In determining a dispute between a government department and any person as to the terms for Crown use of a design the court shall have regard to—

    (a) any sums which that person or a person from whom he derives title has received or is entitled to receive, directly or indirectly, from any government department in respect of the design; and

    (b) whether that person or a person from whom he derives title has in the court's opinion without reasonable cause failed to comply with a request of the department for the use of the design on reasonable terms.

(3) One of two or more joint owners of design right may, without the concurrence of the others, refer a dispute to the court under this section, but shall not do so unless the others are made parties; and none of those others is liable for any costs unless he takes part in the proceedings.

(4) Where the consent of an exclusive licensee is required by section 242. (3)(a)(i) to the settlement by agreement of the terms for Crown use of a design, a determination by the court of the amount of any payment to be made for such use is of no effect unless the licensee has been notified of the reference and given an opportunity to be heard.

(5) On the reference of a dispute as to the amount recoverable as mentioned in section 242. (3)(a)(ii) (right of exclusive licensee to recover part of amount payable to design right owner) the

court shall determine what is just having regard to any expenditure incurred by the licensee—

(a) in developing the design, or

(b) in making payments to the design right owner in consideration of the licence (other than royalties or other payments determined by reference to the use of the design).

(6) In this section "the court" means—

(a) in England and Wales, the High [F55. Court,]

(b) in Scotland, the Court of Session, and

(c) in Northern Ireland, the High Court.

Amendments (Textual)

F55. Word in s. 252. (6)(a) substituted (1.10.2013) by Crime and Courts Act 2013 (c. 22), s. 61. (3), Sch. 9 para. 30. (2); S.I. 2013/1725, art. 3. (c)

Chapter V Miscellaneous and General

Amendments (Textual)

F56. S. 253 253 and crossheading substituted for (1.10.2017) by Intellectual Property (Unjustified Threats) Act 2017 (c. 14), ss. 5. (2), 8 (with art. 7. (4)); S.I. 2017/771, reg. 2. (1)(b) (with reg. 3)

253. Threats of infringement proceedings

(1) A communication contains a "threat of infringement proceedings" if a reasonable person in the position of a recipient would understand from the communication that—

(a) design right subsists in a design, and

(b) a person intends to bring proceedings (whether in a court in the United Kingdom or elsewhere) against another person for infringement of the design right by—

(i) an act done in the United Kingdom, or

(ii) an act which, if done, would be done in the United Kingdom.

(2) References in this section and in section 253. C to a "recipient" include, in the case of a communication directed to the public or a section of the public, references to a person to whom the communication is directed.

253. AActionable threats

(1) Subject to subsections (2) to (5), a threat of infringement proceedings made by any person is actionable by any person aggrieved by the threat.

(2) A threat of infringement proceedings is not actionable if the infringement is alleged to consist of—

(a) making an article for disposal, or

(b) importing an article for disposal.

(3) A threat of infringement proceedings is not actionable if the infringement is alleged to consist of an act which, if done, would constitute an infringement of a kind mentioned in subsection (2)(a) or (b).

(4) A threat of infringement proceedings is not actionable if the threat—

(a) is made to a person who has done, or intends to do, an act mentioned in subsection (2)(a) or (b) in relation to an article, and

(b) is a threat of proceedings for an infringement alleged to consist of doing anything else in relation to that article.

(5) A threat of infringement proceedings which is not an express threat is not actionable if it is contained in a permitted communication.

(6) In sections 253. C and 253. D an "actionable threat" means a threat of infringement proceedings that is actionable in accordance with this section.

253. BPermitted communications

(1) For the purposes of section 253. A(5), a communication containing a threat of infringement proceedings is a "permitted communication" if—

(a) the communication, so far as it contains information that relates to the threat, is made for a permitted purpose;

(b) all of the information that relates to the threat is information that—

(i) is necessary for that purpose (see subsection (5)(a) to (c) for some examples of necessary information), and

(ii) the person making the communication reasonably believes is true.

(2) Each of the following is a "permitted purpose"—

(a) giving notice that design right subsists in a design;

(b) discovering whether, or by whom, design right in a design has been infringed by an act mentioned in section 253. A(2)(a) or (b);

(c) giving notice that a person has a right in or under the design right in a design, where another person's awareness of the right is relevant to any proceedings that may be brought in respect of the design right in the design.

(3) The court may, having regard to the nature of the purposes listed in subsection (2)(a) to (c), treat any other purpose as a "permitted purpose" if it considers that it is in the interests of justice to do so.

(4) But the following may not be treated as a "permitted purpose"—

(a) requesting a person to cease doing, for commercial purposes, anything in relation to an article made to a design,

(b) requesting a person to deliver up or destroy an article made to a design, or

(c) requesting a person to give an undertaking relating to an article made to a design.

(5) If any of the following information is included in a communication made for a permitted purpose, it is information that is "necessary for that purpose" (see subsection (1)(b)(i))—

(a) a statement that design right subsists in a design;

(b) details of the design, or of a right in or under the design right in the design, which—

(i) are accurate in all material respects, and

(ii) are not misleading in any material respect; and

(c) information enabling the identification of articles that are alleged to be infringing articles in relation to the design.

253. CRemedies and defences

(1) Proceedings in respect of an actionable threat may be brought against the person who made the threat for—

(a) a declaration that the threat is unjustified;

(b) an injunction against the continuance of the threat;

(c) damages in respect of any loss sustained by the aggrieved person by reason of the threat.

(2) It is a defence for the person who made the threat to show that the act in respect of which proceedings were threatened constitutes (or if done would constitute) an infringement of design right.

(3) It is a defence for the person who made the threat to show—

(a) that, despite having taken reasonable steps, the person has not identified anyone who has done an act mentioned in section 253. A(2)(a) or (b) in relation to the article which is the subject of the threat, and

(b) that the person notified the recipient, before or at the time of making the threat, of the steps taken.

253. DProfessional advisers

(1) Proceedings in respect of an actionable threat may not be brought against a professional adviser (or any person vicariously liable for the actions of that professional adviser) if the conditions in subsection (3) are met.

(2) In this section "professional adviser" means a person who, in relation to the making of the communication containing the threat—

(a) is acting in a professional capacity in providing legal services or the services of a trade mark attorney or a patent attorney, and

(b) is regulated in the provision of legal services, or the services of a trade mark attorney or a patent attorney, by one or more regulatory bodies (whether through membership of a regulatory body, the issue of a licence to practise or any other means).

(3) The conditions are that—

(a) in making the communication the professional adviser is acting on the instructions of another person, and

(b) when the communication is made the professional adviser identifies the person on whose instructions the adviser is acting.

(4) This section does not affect any liability of the person on whose instructions the professional adviser is acting.

(5) It is for a person asserting that subsection (1) applies to prove (if required) that at the material time—

(a) the person concerned was acting as a professional adviser, and

(b) the conditions in subsection (3) were met.

253. ESupplementary: proceedings for delivery up etc.

In section 253. (1)(b) the reference to proceedings for infringement of design right includes a reference to—

(a) proceedings for an order under section 230 (order for delivery up), and

(b) proceedings for an order under section 231 (order as to disposal of infringing articles).]

[F57. Licensee under licence of right not to claim connection with design right owner]

Amendments (Textual)

F57. S. 254 cross-heading inserted (1.10.2017) by Intellectual Property (Unjustified Threats) Act 2017 (c. 14), ss. 5. (3), 8; S.I. 2017/771, reg. 2. (1)(b) (with reg. 3)

254 Licensee under licence of right not to claim connection with design right owner.

(1) A person who has a licence in respect of a design by virtue of section 237 or 238 (licences of right) shall not, without the consent of the design right owner—

(a) apply to goods which he is marketing, or proposes to market, in reliance on that licence a trade description indicating that he is the licensee of the design right owner, or

(b) use any such trade description in an advertisement in relation to such goods.

(2) A contravention of subsection (1) is actionable by the design right owner.

(3) In this section "trade description", the reference to applying a trade description to goods and "advertisement" have the same meaning as in the M6. Trade Descriptions Act 1968.

Marginal Citations

M61968 c. 29.

Extent of operation of this Part

255 Countries to which this Part extends.

(1) This Part extends to England and Wales, Scotland and Northern Ireland.

(2) Her Majesty may by Order in Council direct that this Part shall extend, subject to such exceptions and modifications as may be specified in the Order, to—

(a) any of the Channel Islands,

(b) the Isle of Man, or

(c) any colony.

(3) That power includes power to extend, subject to such exceptions and modifications as may be specified in the Order, any Order in Council made under section 221 (further provision as to qualification for design right protection) or section 256 (countries enjoying reciprocal protection).

(4) The legislature of a country to which this Part has been extended may modify or add to the provisions of this Part, in their operation as part of the law of that country, as the legislature may consider necessary to adapt the provisions to the circumstances of that country; but not so as to deny design right protection in a case where it would otherwise exist.

(5) Where a country to which this Part extends ceases to be a colony of the United Kingdom, it shall continue to be treated as such a country for the purposes of this Part until—

(a) an Order in Council is made under section 256 designating it as a country enjoying reciprocal protection, or

(b) an Order in Council is made declaring that it shall cease to be so treated by reason of the fact that the provisions of this Part as part of the law of that country have been amended or repealed.

(6) A statutory instrument containing an Order in Council under subsection (5)(b) shall be subject to annulment in pursuance of a resolution of either House of Parliament.

256 Countries enjoying reciprocal protection.

(1) Her Majesty may, if it appears to Her that the law of a country provides adequate protection for British designs, by Order in Council designate that country as one enjoying reciprocal protection under this Part.

(2) If the law of a country provides adequate protection only for certain classes of British design, or only for designs applied to certain classes of article, any Order designating that country shall contain provision limiting, to a corresponding extent, the protection afforded by this Part in relation to designs connected with that country.

(3) An Order under this section shall be subject to annulment in pursuance of a resolution of either House of Parliament.

257 Territorial waters and the continental shelf.

(1) For the purposes of this Part the territorial waters of the United Kingdom shall be treated as part of the United Kingdom.

(2) This Part applies to things done in the United Kingdom sector of the continental shelf on a structure or vessel which is present there for purposes directly connected with the exploration of the sea bed or subsoil or the exploitation of their natural resources as it applies to things done in the United Kingdom.

(3) The United Kingdom sector of the continental shelf means the areas designated by order under section 1. (7) of the M7. Continental Shelf Act 1964.

Marginal Citations

M71964 c. 29.

Interpretation

258 Construction of references to design right owner.

(1) Where different persons are (whether in consequence of a partial assignment or otherwise) entitled to different aspects of design right in a work, the design right owner for any purpose of this Part is the person who is entitled to the right in the respect relevant for that purpose.

(2) Where design right (or any aspect of design right) is owned by more than one person jointly, references in this Part to the design right owner are to all the owners, so that, in particular, any requirement of the licence of the design right owner requires the licence of all of them.

259 Joint designs.

(1) In this Part a "joint design" means a design produced by the collaboration of two or more designers in which the contribution of each is not distinct from that of the other or others.

(2) References in this Part to the designer of a design shall, except as otherwise provided, be construed in relation to a joint design as references to all the designers of the design.

260 Application of provisions to articles in kit form.

(1) The provisions of this Part apply in relation to a kit, that is, a complete or substantially complete set of components intended to be assembled into an article, as they apply in relation to the assembled article.

(2) Subsection (1) does not affect the question whether design right subsists in any aspect of the design of the components of a kit as opposed to the design of the assembled article.

261 Requirement of signature: application in relation to body corporate.

The requirement in the following provisions that an instrument be signed by or on behalf of a person is also satisfied in the case of a body corporate by the affixing of its seal—

section 222. (3) (assignment of design right),

section 223. (1) (assignment of future design right),

section 225. (1) (grant of exclusive licence).

262 Adaptation of expressions in relation to Scotland.

In the application of this Part to Scotland—

"account of profits" means accounting and payment of profits;

"accounts" means count, reckoning and payment;

"assignment" means assignation;

"costs" means expenses;

[F58"declaration" means "declarator";]

"defendant" means defender;

"delivery up" means delivery;

"injunction" means interdict;

"interlocutory relief" means interim remedy; and

"plaintiff" means pursuer.

Amendments (Textual)

F58. Words in s. 262 inserted (1.10.2017) by Intellectual Property (Unjustified Threats) Act 2017 (c. 14), ss. 5. (4), 8; S.I. 2017/771, reg. 2. (1)(b) (with reg. 3)

263 Minor definitions.

(1) In this Part—

"British design" means a design which qualifies for design right protection by reason of a connection with the United Kingdom of the designer or the person by whom F59... the designer is employed;

"business" includes a trade or profession;

F60...

"the comptroller" means the Comptroller-General of Patents, Designs and Trade Marks;

"computer-generated", in relation to a design, means that the design is generated by computer in circumstances such that there is no human designer,

"country" includes any territory;

"the Crown" includes the Crown in right of Her Majesty's Government in Northern Ireland [F61and the Crown in right of the Scottish Administration][F62and the Crown in right of the Welsh Assembly Government];

"design document" means any record of a design, whether in the form of a drawing, a written description, a photograph, data stored in a computer or otherwise;

"employee", "employment" and "employer" refer to employment under a contract of service or of apprenticeship;

"government department" includes a Northern Ireland department [F63and any part of the Scottish Administration][F64and any part of the Welsh Assembly Government].

(2) References in this Part to "marketing", in relation to an article, are to its being sold or let for hire, or offered or exposed for sale or hire, in the course of a business, and related expressions shall be construed accordingly; but no account shall be taken for the purposes of this Part of marketing which is merely colourable and not intended to satisfy the reasonable requirements of the public.

(3) References in this Part to an act being done in relation to an article for "commercial purposes" are to its being done with a view to the article in question being sold or hired in the course of a business.

Amendments (Textual)

F59. Words in s. 263. (1) omitted (1.10.2014) by virtue of Intellectual Property Act 2014 (c. 18), ss. 2. (2)(i), 24. (1) (with s. 2. (3)); S.I. 2014/2330, art. 3, Sch.

F60. Words in s. 263. (1) omitted (1.10.2014) by virtue of Intellectual Property Act 2014 (c. 18), ss. 2. (2)(j), 24. (1) (with s. 2. (3)); S.I. 2014/2330, art. 3, Sch.

F61. Words in definition of "the Crown" in s. 263. (1) inserted (1.7.1999) by S.I. 1999/1820, arts.

1. (2), 4, Sch. 2 Pt. I para. 93. (4)(a); S.I. 1998/3178, art. 3

F62. S. 263. (1): words in definition of "the Crown" inserted by Government of Wales Act 2006 (c. 32), s. 160. (1), Sch. 10 para. 31. (2) (with Sch. 11 para. 22), the amending provision coming into force immediately after "the 2007 election" (held on 3.5.2007) subject to s. 161. (4)(5) of the amending Act, which provides for certain provisions to come into force for specified purposes immediately after the end of "the initial period" (which ended with the day of the first appointment of a First Minister on 25.5.2007) - see ss. 46, 161. (1)(4)(5) of the amending Act.

F63. Words in definition of "government department" in s. 263. (1) inserted (1.7.1999) by S.I. 1999/1820, arts. 1. (2), 4, Sch. 2 Pt. I para. 93. (4)(b); S.I. 1998/3178, art. 3

F64. S. 263. (1): words in definition of "government department" inserted by Government of Wales Act 2006 (c. 32), s. 160. (1), Sch. 10 para. 31. (3) (with Sch. 11 para. 22), the amending provision coming into force immediately after "the 2007 election" (held on 3.5.2007) subject to s. 161. (4)(5) of the amending Act, which provides for certain provisions to come into force for specified purposes immediately after the end of "the initial period" (which ended with the day of the first appointment of a First Minister on 25.5.2007) - see ss. 46, 161. (1)(4)(5) of the amending Act.

264 Index of defined expressions.

The following Table shows provisions defining or otherwise explaining expressions used in this Part (other than provisions defining or explaining an expression used only in the same section)—

account of profits and accounts (in Scotland) | section 262 |
assignment (in Scotland) | section 262 |
British designs | section 263(1) |
business | section 263(1) |
commercial purposes | section 263(3) |
F65. . . | F65. . . |
the comptroller | section 263(1) |
computer-generated | section 263(1) |
costs (in Scotland) | section 262 |
country | section 263(1) |
the Crown | section 263(1) |
Crown use | sections 240(5) and 244(2) |
defendant (in Scotland) | section 262 |
delivery up (in Scotland) | section 262 |
design | section 213(2) |
design document | section 263(1) |
designer | sections 214 and 259(2) |
design right | section 213(1) |
design right owner | sections 234(2) and 258 |
employee, employment and employer | section 263(1) |
exclusive licence | section 225(1) |
government department | section 263(1) |
government department concerned (in relation to Crown use) | section 240(5) |
infringing article | section 228 |
injunction (in Scotland) | section 262 |
interlocutory relief (in Scotland) | section 262 |
joint design | section 259(1) |
licence (of the design right owner) | sections 222(4), 223(3) and 258 |
making articles to a design | section 226(2) |
marketing (and related expressions) | section 263(2) |
original | section 213(4) |
plaintiff (in Scotland) | section 262 |
F66. . . | F66. . . |
qualifying person | sections 217(1) and (2) |

signed | section 261 |

Amendments (Textual)

F65. Words in s. 264 omitted (1.10.2014) by virtue of Intellectual Property Act 2014 (c. 18), ss. 2. (2)(k), 24. (1) (with s. 2. (3)); S.I. 2014/2330, art. 3, Sch.

F66. Words in s. 264 omitted (1.10.2014) by virtue of Intellectual Property Act 2014 (c. 18), ss. 3. (5), 24. (1) (with s. 3. (6)); S.I. 2014/2330, art. 3, Sch.

Countries to which this Part extends.

255 Countries to which this Part extends.

(1) This Part extends to England and Wales, Scotland and Northern Ireland.

(2) Her Majesty may by Order in Council direct that this Part shall extend, subject to such exceptions and modifications as may be specified in the Order, to—

    (a) any of the Channel Islands,

    (b) the Isle of Man, or

    (c) any colony.

(3) That power includes power to extend, subject to such exceptions and modifications as may be specified in the Order, any Order in Council made under section 221 (further provision as to qualification for design right protection) or section 256 (countries enjoying reciprocal protection).

(4) The legislature of a country to which this Part has been extended may modify or add to the provisions of this Part, in their operation as part of the law of that country, as the legislature may consider necessary to adapt the provisions to the circumstances of that country; but not so as to deny design right protection in a case where it would otherwise exist.

(5) Where a country to which this Part extends ceases to be a colony of the United Kingdom, it shall continue to be treated as such a country for the purposes of this Part until—

    (a) an Order in Council is made under section 256 designating it as a country enjoying reciprocal protection, or

    (b) an Order in Council is made declaring that it shall cease to be so treated by reason of the fact that the provisions of this Part as part of the law of that country have been amended or repealed.

(6) A statutory instrument containing an Order in Council under subsection (5)(b) shall be subject to annulment in pursuance of a resolution of either House of Parliament.

Part IV Registered Designs

Part IV Registered Designs

Modifications etc. (not altering text)

C1. Pt. IV (ss. 265-273) extended (with modifications) (Isle of Man) (9.12.2001) by S.I. 2001/3678, art. 3, Sch. 3

C2. Pt. 4 extended (Isle of Man) (with modifications) (11.11.2013) by The Registered Designs (Isle of Man) Order 2013 (S.I. 2013/2533), arts. 1, 3. (2), Sch. 2

F1265. . . . .

Amendments (Textual)

F1. S. 265 repealed (9.12.2001) by S.I. 2001/3949, reg. 9. (2), Sch. 2 (with transitional provisions in regs. 10-14)

266 Provisions with respect to certain designs registered in

pursuance of application made before commencement.

(1) Where a design is registered under the Registered Designs Act 1949 in pursuance of an application made after 12th January 1988 and before the commencement of this part which could not have been registered under section 1 of that Act as substituted by section 265 above—

   (a) the right in the registered design expires ten years after the commencement of this part, if it does not expire earlier in accordance with the 1949 Act, and

   (b) any person is, after the commencement of this Part, entitled as of right to a licence to do anything which would otherwise infringe the right in the registered design.

(2) The terms of a licence available by virtue of this section shall, in default of agreement, be settled by the registrar on an application by the person requiring the licence; and the terms so settled shall authorise the licensee to do everything which would be an infringement of the right in the registered design in the absence of a licence.

(3) In settling the terms of a licence the registrar shall have regard to such factors as may be prescribed by the Secretary of State by order made by statutory instrument.
No such order shall be made unless a draft of it has been laid before and approved by a resolution of each House of Parliament.

(4) Where the terms of a licence are settled by the registrar, the licence has effect from the date on which the application to the registrar was made.

(5) Section 11. B of the 1949 Act (undertaking to take licence of right in infringement proceedings), as inserted by section 270 below, applies where a licence is available as of right under this section, as it applies where a licence is available as of right under section 11. A of that Act.

(6) Where a licence is available as of right under this section, a person to whom a licence was granted before the commencement of this part may apply to the registrar for an order adjusting the terms of that licence.

(7) an appeal lies from any decision of the registrar under this section.

(8) This section shall be construed as one with the Registered Designs Act 1949.

267 Authorship and first ownership of designs.

(1) Section 2 of the Registered Designs Act 1949 (proprietorship of designs) is amended as follows.

(2) For subsection (1) substitute—

"(1)The author of a design shall be treated for the purposes of this Act as the original proprietor of the design, subject to the following provisions.

(1. A)Where a design is created in pursuance of a commission for money or money's worth, the person commissioning the design shall be treated as the original proprietor of the design.

(1. B)Where, in a case not falling within subsection (1. A), a design is created by an employee in the course of his employment, his employer shall be treated as the original proprietor of the design.".

(3) After subsection (2) insert—

"(3)In this Act the "author" of a design means the person who creates it.

(4) In the case of a design generated by computer in circumstances such that there is no human author, the person by whom the arrangements necessary for the creation of thee design are made shall be taken to be the author.".

(4) The amendments made by this section do not apply in relation to an application for registration made before the commencement of this Part.

F2268. . . . .

Amendments (Textual)
F2. S. 268 repealed (9.12.2001) by S.I. 2001/3949, reg. 9. (2), Sch. 2 (with transitional provisions in regs. 10-14)

269 Duration of right in registered design.

(1) For section 8 of the M1. Registered Designs Act 1949 (period of right) substitute—

"8 Duration of right in registered design.

(1) The right in a registered design subsists in the first instance for a period of five years from the date of the registration of the design.

(2) The period for which the right subsists may be extended for a second, third, fourth and fifth period of five years, by applying to the registrar for an extension and paying the prescribed renewal fee.

(3) If the first, second, third or fourth period expires without such application and payment being made, the right shall cease to have effect; and the registrar shall, in accordance with rules made by the Secretary of State, notify the proprietor of that fact.

(4) If during the period of six months immediately following the end of that period an application for extension is made and the prescribed renewal fee and any prescribed additional fee is paid, the right shall be treated as if it had never expired, with the result that—

(a) anything done under or in relation to the right during that further period shall be treated as valid,

(b) an act which would have constituted an infringement of the right if it had not expired shall be treated as an infringement, and

(c) an act which would have constituted use of the design for the services of the Crown if the right had not expired shall be treated as such use.

(5) Where it is shown that a registered design—

(a) was at the time it was registered a corresponding design in relation to an artistic work in which copyright subsists, and

(b) by reason of a previous use of that work would not have been registrable but for section 6. (4) of this Act (registration despite certain prior applications of design),

the right in the registered design expires when the copyright in that work expires, if that is earlier than the time at which it would otherwise expire, and it may not thereafter be renewed.

(6) The above provisions have effect subject to the proviso to section 4. (1) (registration of same design in respect of other articles, &c.).

8. A Restoration of lapsed right in design.

(1) Where the right in a registered design has expired by reason of a failure to extend, in accordance with section 8. (2) or (4), the period for which the right subsists, an application for the restoration of the right in the design may be made to the registrar within the prescribed period.

(2) The application may be made by the person who was the registered proprietor of the design or by any other person who would have been entitled to the right in the design if it had not expired; and where the design was held by two or more persons jointly, the application may, with the leave of the registrar, be made by one or more of them without joining the others.

(3) Notice of the application shall be published by the registrar in the prescribed manner.

(4) If the registrar is satisfied that the proprietor took reasonable care to see that the period for which the right subsisted was extended in accordance with section 8. (2) or (4), he shall, on payment of any unpaid renewal fee and any prescribed additional fee, order the restoration of the right in the design.

(5) The order may be made subject to such conditions as the registrar thinks fit, and if the proprietor of the design does not comply with any condition the registrar may revoke the order and give such consequential directions as he thinks fit.

(6) Rules altering the period prescribed for the purposes of subsection (1) may contain such transitional provisions and savings as appear to the Secretary of State to be necessary or expedient.

8. B Effect of order for restoration of right.

(1)

The effect of an order under section 8. A for the restoration of the right in a registered design is as follows.

(2) Anything done under or in relation to the right during the period between expiry and restoration shall be treated as valid.

(3) Anything done during that period which would have constituted an infringement if the right had not expired shall be treated as an infringement—

    (a) if done at a time when it was possible for an application for extension to be made under section 8. (4); or

    (b) if it was a continuation or repetition of an earlier infringing act.

(4) If, after it was no longer possible for such an application for extension to be made and before publication of notice of the application for restoration, a person—

    (a) began in good faith to do an act which would have constituted an infringement of the right in the design if it had not expired, or

    (b) made in good faith effective and serious preparations to do such an act,

he has the right to continue to do the act or, as the case may be, to do the act, notwithstanding the restoration of the right in the design; but this does not extend to granting a licence to another person to do the act.

(5) If the act was done, or the preparations were made, in the course of a business, the person entitled to the right conferred by subsection (4) may—

    (a) authorise the doing of that act by any partners of his for the time being in that business, and

    (b) assign that right, or transmit it on death (or in the case of a body corporate on its dissolution), to any person who acquires that part of the business in the course of which the act was done or the preparations were made.

(6) Where an article is disposed of to another in exercise of the rights conferred by subsection (4) or subsection (5), that other and any person claiming through him may deal with the article in the same way as if it had been disposed of by the registered proprietor of the design.

(7) The above provisions apply in relation to the use of a registered design for the services of the Crown as they apply in relation to infringement of the right in the design.".

(2) The above amendment does not apply in relation to the right in a design registered in pursuance of an application made before the commencement of this Part.

Marginal Citations

M1 1949 c. 88.

270 Powers exercisable for protection of the public interest.

In the M2. Registered Designs Act 1949 after section 11 insert—

"11. A Powers exercisable for protection of the public interest.

(1) Where a report of the Monopolies and Mergers Commission has been laid before Parliament containing conclusions to the effect—

    (a) on a monopoly reference, that a monopoly situation exists and facts found by the Commission operate or may be expected to operate against the public interest,

    (b) on a merger reference, that a merger situation qualifying for investigation has been created and the creation of the situation, or particular elements in or consequences of it specified in the report, operate or may be expected to operate against the public interest,

    (c) on a competition reference, that a person was engaged in an anti-competitive practice which operated or may be expected to operate against the public interest, or

    (d) on a reference under section 11 of the Competition Act 1980 (reference of public bodies and certain other persons), that a person is pursuing a course of conduct which operates against the public interest,

the appropriate Minister or Ministers may apply to the registrar to take action under this section.

(2) Before making an application the appropriate Minister or Ministers shall publish, in such a manner as he or they think appropriate, a notice describing the nature of the proposed application and shall consider any representations which may be made within 30 days of such publication by persons whose interests appear to him or them to be affected.

(3) If on an application under this section it appears to the registrar that the matters specified in the Commission's report as being those which in the Commission's opinion operate or operated or may be expected to operate against the public interest include—

(a) conditions in licences granted in respect of a registered design by its proprietor restricting the use of the design by the licensee or the right of the proprietor to grant other licences, or

(b) a refusal by the proprietor of a registered design to grant licences on reasonable terms, he may by order cancel or modify any such condition or may, instead or in addition, make an entry in the register to the effect that licences in respect of the design are to be available as of right.

(4) The terms of a licence available by virtue of this section shall, in default of agreement, be settled by the registrar on an application by the person requiring the licence; and terms so settled shall authorise the licensee to do everything which would be an infringement of the right in the registered design in the absence of a licence.

(5) Where the terms of a licence are settled by the registrar the licence has effect from the date on which the application to him was made.

(6) An appeal lies from any order of the registrar under this section.

(7) In this section "the appropriate Minister or Ministers" means the Minister or Ministers to whom the report of the Monopolies and Mergers Commission was made.

11. B Undertaking to take licence of right in infringement proceedings.

(1) If in proceedings for infringement of the right in a registered design in respect of which a licence is available as of right under section 11. A of this Act the defendant undertakes to take a licence on such terms as may be agreed or, in default of agreement, settled by the registrar under that section—

(a) no injunction shall be granted against him, and

(b) the amount recoverable against him by way of damages or on an account of profits shall not exceed double the amount which would have been payable by him as licensee if such a licence on those terms had been granted before the earliest infringement.

(2) An undertaking may be given at any time before final order in the proceedings, without any admission of liability.

(3) Nothing in this section affects the remedies available in respect of an infringement committed before licences of right were available.".

Marginal Citations

M21949 c. 88.

271 Crown use: compensation for loss of profit.

(1) In Schedule 1 to the M3. Registered Designs Act 1949 (Crown use), after paragraph 2 insert—

2. A(1)Where Crown use is made of a registered design, the government department concerned shall pay—

(a) to the registered proprietor, or

(b) if there is an exclusive licence in force in respect of the design, to the exclusive licensee, compensation for any loss resulting from his not being awarded a contract to supply the articles to which the design is applied.

(2) Compensation is payable only to the extent that such a contract could have been fulfilled from his existing manufacturing capacity; but is payable notwithstanding the existence of circumstances rendering him ineligible for the award of such a contract.

(3) In determining the loss, regard shall be had to the profit which would have been made on such a contract and to the extent to which any manufacturing capacity was underused.

(4) No compensation is payable in respect of any failure to secure contracts for the supply of

articles to which the design is applied otherwise than for the services of the Crown.

(5) The amount payable under this paragraph shall, if not agreed between the registered proprietor or licensee and the government department concerned with the approval of the Treasury, be determined by the court on a reference under paragraph 3; and it is in addition to any amount payable under paragraph 1 or 2 of this Schedule.

(6) In this paragraph—

"Crown use", in relation to a design, means the doing of anything by virtue of paragraph 1 which would otherwise be an infringement of the right in the design; and

"the government department concerned", in relation to such use, means the government department by whom or on whose authority the act was done.".

(2) In paragraph 3 of that Schedule (reference of disputes as to Crown use), for sub-paragraph (1) substitute—

"(1)Any dispute as to—

(a) the exercise by a Government department, or a person authorised by a Government department, of the powers conferred by paragraph 1 of this Schedule,

(b) terms for the use of a design for the services of the Crown under that paragraph,

(c) the right of any person to receive any part of a payment made under paragraph 1. (3), or

(d) the right of any person to receive a payment under paragraph 2. A,

may be referred to the court by either party to the dispute.".

(3) The above amendments apply in relation to any Crown use of a registered design after the commencement of this section, even if the terms for such use were settled before commencement.

Marginal Citations

M31949 c. 88.

272 Minor and consequential amendments.

The M4. Registered Designs Act 1949 is further amended in accordance with Schedule 3 which contains minor amendments and amendments consequential upon the provisions of this Act.

Marginal Citations

M41949 c. 88.

Supplementary

273 Text of Registered Designs Act 1949 as amended.

Schedule 4 contains the text of the Registered Designs Act 1949 as amended.

Part V Patent Agents and Trade Mark Agents

Part V Patent Agents and Trade Mark Agents

274 Persons permitted to carry on business of a patent agent.

(1) Any individual, partnership or body corporate may, subject to the following provisions of this Part [F1and to the Legal Services Act 2007] , carry on the business of acting as agent for others for the purpose of—

(a) applying for or obtaining patents, in the United Kingdom or elsewhere, or

(b) conducting proceedings before the comptroller relating to applications for, or otherwise in connection with, patents.

(2) This does not affect any restriction under the European Patent Convention as to who may act on behalf of another for any purpose relating to European patents.

Amendments (Textual)

F1. Words in s. 274. (1) inserted (1.1.2010) by Legal Services Act 2007 (c. 29), ss. 185. (2), 211 (with ss. 29, 192, 193); S.I. 2009/3250, art. 2. (f)(i) (with art. 9)

[F2275. The register of patent attorneys

(1) There is to continue to be a register of persons who act as agent for others for the purpose of applying for or obtaining patents.

(2) In this Part a registered patent attorney means an individual whose name is entered on the register kept under this section.

(3) The register is to be kept by the Chartered Institute of Patent Attorneys.

(4) The Secretary of State may, by order, amend subsection (3) so as to require the register to be kept by the person specified in the order.

(5) Before making an order under subsection (4), the Secretary of State must consult the Legal Services Board.

(6) An order under this section must be made by statutory instrument.

(7) An order under this section may not be made unless a draft of it has been laid before, and approved by a resolution of, each House of Parliament.]

Amendments (Textual)

F2. Ss. 275, 275. A substituted (1.1.2010) for s. 275 by Legal Services Act 2007 (c. 29), {ss. 185. (3)}, 211 (with ss. 29, 192, 193); S.I. 2009/3250, art. 2. (f)(i) (with art. 9)

[F3275. ARegulation of patent attorneys

(1) The person who keeps the register under section 275 may make regulations which regulate—
    (a) the keeping of the register and the registration of persons;
    (b) the carrying on of patent attorney work by registered persons.

(2) Those regulations may, amongst other things, make—
    (a) provision as to the educational and training qualifications, and other requirements, which must be satisfied before an individual may be registered or for an individual to remain registered;
    (b) provision as to the requirements which must be met by a body (corporate or unincorporate) before it may be registered, or for it to remain registered, including provision as to the management and control of the body;
    (c) provision as to the educational, training and other requirements to be met by regulated persons;
    (d) provision regulating the practice, conduct and discipline of registered persons or regulated persons;
    (e) provision authorising in such cases as may be specified in the regulations the erasure from the register of the name of any person registered in it, or the suspension of a person's registration;
    (f) provision requiring the payment of such fees as may be specified in or determined in accordance with the regulations;
    (g) provision about the provision to be made by registered persons in respect of complaints made against them;
    (h) provision about the keeping by registered persons or regulated persons of records and accounts;
    (i) provision for reviews of or appeals against decisions made under the regulations;
    (j) provision as to the indemnification of registered persons or regulated persons against losses arising from claims in respect of civil liability incurred by them.

(3) Regulations under this section may make different provision for different purposes.

(4) Regulations under this section which are not regulatory arrangements within the meaning of the Legal Services Act 2007 are to be treated as such arrangements for the purposes of that Act.

(5) Before the appointed day, regulations under this section may be made only with the approval of the Secretary of State.

(6) The powers conferred to make regulations under this section are not to be taken to prejudice—

(a) any other power which the person who keeps the register may have to make rules or regulations (however they may be described and whether they are made under an enactment or otherwise);

(b) any rules or regulations made by that person under any such power.

(7) In this section—

"appointed day" means the day appointed for the coming into force of paragraph 1 of Schedule 4 to the Legal Services Act 2007;

"manager", in relation to a body, has the same meaning as in the Legal Services Act 2007 (see section 207);

"patent attorney work" means work done in the course of carrying on the business of acting as agent for others for the purpose of—

- applying for or obtaining patents, in the United Kingdom or elsewhere, or

- conducting proceedings before the comptroller relating to applications for, or otherwise in connection with, patents;

"registered person" means—

- a registered patent attorney, or

- a body (corporate or unincorporate) registered in the register kept under section 275;

"regulated person" means a person who is not a registered person but is a manager or employee of a body which is a registered person.]

Amendments (Textual)

F3. Ss. 275, 275. A substituted (1.1.2010) for s. 275 by Legal Services Act 2007 (c. 29), {ss. 185. (3)}, 211 (with ss. 29, 192, 193); S.I. 2009/3250, art. 2. (f)(i) (with art. 9)

276 Persons entitled to describe themselves as patent agents.

(1) An individual who is not a [F4registered patent attorney] shall not—

(a) carry on a business (otherwise than in partnership) under any name or other description which contains the words "patent agent" or "patent attorney"; or

(b) in the course of a business otherwise describe himself, or permit himself to be described, as a "patent agent" or "patent attorney".

(2) A partnership [F5or other unincorporated body] shall not—

(a) carry on a business under any name or other description which contains the words "patent agent" or "patent attorney"; or

(b) in the course of a business otherwise describe itself, or permit itself to be described as, a firm of "patent agents" or "patent attorneys",

unless [F6the partnership or other body is registered in the register kept under section 275].

(3) A body corporate shall not—

(a) carry on a business (otherwise than in partnership) under any name or other description which contains the words "patent agent" or "patent attorney"; or

(b) in the course of a business otherwise describe itself, or permit itself to be described as, a "patent agent" or "patent attorney",

unless [F7the body corporate is registered in the register kept under section 275.]

(4) Subsection (3) does not apply to a company which began to carry on business as a patent agent before 17th November 1917 if the name of a director or the manager of the company who is a registered patent [F8attorney] is mentioned as being so registered in all professional advertisements, circulars or letters issued by or with the company's consent on which its name

appears.

(5) Where this section would be contravened by the use of the words "patent agent" or "patent attorney" in reference to an individual, partnership or body corporate, it is equally contravened by the use of other expressions in reference to that person, or his business or place of business, which are likely to be understood as indicating that he is entitled to be described as a "patent agent" or "patent attorney".

(6) A person who contravenes this section commits an offence and is liable on summary conviction to a fine not exceeding level 5 on the standard scale; and proceedings for such an offence may be begun at any time within a year from the date of the offence.

(7) This section has effect subject to—

    (a) section 277 (persons entitled to describe themselves as European patent attorneys, &c.), and

    (b) section 278. (1) (use of term "patent attorney" in reference to solicitors).

Amendments (Textual)

F4. Words in s. 276. (1) substituted (1.1.2010) by Legal Services Act 2007 (c. 29), ss. 208. (1), 211, {Sch. 21 para. 76. (a)} (with ss. 29, 192, 193); S.I. 2009/3250, art. 2. (h) (with art. 9)

F5. Words in s. 276. (2) substituted (1.1.2010) by Legal Services Act 2007 (c. 29), ss. 185. (4)(a)(i), 211 (with ss. 29, 192, 193); S.I. 2009/3250, art. 2. (f)(i) (with art. 9)

F6. Words in s. 276. (2) substituted (1.1.2010) by Legal Services Act 2007 (c. 29), ss. 185. (4)(a)(ii), 211 (with ss. 29, 192, 193); S.I. 2009/3250, art. 2. (f)(i) (with art. 9)

F7. Words in s. 276. (3) substituted (1.1.2010) by Legal Services Act 2007 (c. 29), ss. 185. (4)(b), 211 (with ss. 29, 192, 193); S.I. 2009/3250, art. 2. (f)(i) (with art. 9)

F8. Words in s. 276. (4) substituted (1.1.2010) by Legal Services Act 2007 (c. 29), ss. 208. (1), 211, {Sch. 21 para. 76. (b)} (with ss. 29, 192, 193); S.I. 2009/3250, art. 2. (h) (with art. 9)

Modifications etc. (not altering text)

C1. S. 276. (7)(b) amended (E.W.) (1.1.1992) by S.I. 1991/2684 arts. 2, 4, Sch.1

C2. S. 276. (7)(b) applied (with modifications) (23.12.2011) by The Legal Services Act 2007 (Designation as a Licensing Authority) (No. 2) Order 2011 (S.I. 2011/2866), arts. 1. (2), 8. (1)(2), Sch. 2

277 Persons entitled to describe themselves as European patent attorneys, &c.

(1) The term "European patent attorney" or "European patent agent" may be used in the following cases without any contravention of section 276.

(2) An individual who is on the European list may—

    (a) carry on business under a name or other description which contains the words "European patent attorney" or "European patent agent", or

    (b) otherwise describe himself, or permit himself to be described, as a "European patent attorney" or "European patent agent".

(3) A partnership of which not less than the prescribed number or proportion of partners is on the European list may—

    (a) carry on a business under a name or other description which contains the words "European patent attorneys" or "European patent agents", or

    (b) otherwise describe itself, or permit itself to be described, as a firm which carries on the business of a "European patent attorney" or "European patent agent".

(4) A body corporate of which not less than the prescribed number or proportion of directors is on the European list may—

    (a) carry on a business under a name or other description which contains the words "European patent attorney" or "European patent agent", or

    (b) otherwise describe itself, or permit itself to be described as, a company which carries on the business of a "European patent attorney" or "European patent agent".

(5) Where the term "European patent attorney" or "European patent agent" may, in accordance

with this section, be used in reference to an individual, partnership or body corporate, it is equally permissible to use other expressions in reference to that person, or to his business or place of business, which are likely to be understood as indicating that he is entitled to be described as a "European patent attorney" or "European patent agent."

278 Use of the term "patent attorney": supplementary provisions.

(1) The term "patent attorney" may be used in reference to a solicitor, and a firm of solicitors may be described as a firm of "patent attorneys", without any contravention of section 276.
(2) No offence is committed under the enactments restricting the use of certain expressions in reference to persons not qualified to act as solicitors—
  (a) by the use of the term "patent attorney" in reference to a registered patent agent, or
  (b) by the use of the term "European patent attorney" in reference to a person on the European list.
(3) The enactments referred to in subsection (2) are section 21 of the M1. Solicitors Act 1974, section 31 of the M2. Solicitors (Scotland) Act 1980 and Article 22 of the M3. Solicitors (Northern Ireland) Order 1976.
Modifications etc. (not altering text)
C3. S. 278. (1) applied (with modifications) (23.12.2011) by The Legal Services Act 2007 (Designation as a Licensing Authority) (No. 2) Order 2011 (S.I. 2011/2866), arts. 1. (2), 8. (2)(3), Sch. 3
Marginal Citations
M11974 c. 37.
M21980 c. 46.
M3. S.I. 1976/582 (N.I.12).

279 Power to prescribe conditions, &c. for mixed partnerships and bodies corporate.

F9. . . . .
Amendments (Textual)
F9. S. 279 omitted (1.1.2010) and repealed (1.10.2011) by virtue of Legal Services Act 2007 (c. 29), ss. 185. (5), 210, 211, Sch. 23 (with ss. 29, 192, 193); S.I. 2009/3250, art. 2. (f)(i); S.I. 2011/2196, art. 2. (1)(h)(iii)

280 Privilege for communications with patent agents.

(1) This section applies to communications as to any matter relating to the protection of any invention, design, technical information, [F10or trade mark], or as to
  [F11. (a)] any matter involving passing off [F12, and
  (b) documents, material or information relating to any matter mentioned in paragraph (a).]
[F13. (2)Where a patent attorney acts for a client in relation to a matter mentioned in subsection (1), any communication, document, material or information to which this section applies is privileged from disclosure in like manner as if the patent attorney had at all material times been acting as the client's solicitor.]
(3) In subsection (2) "patent [F14attorney]" means—
  (a) a registered patent [F14attorney] or a person who is on the European list,
  (b) a partnership entitled to describe itself as a firm of patent [F15attorneys] or as a firm carrying on the business of a European patent attorney, F16. . .
  [F17. (ba)an unincorporated body (other than a partnership) entitled to describe itself as a patent attorney, or]

(c) a body corporate entitled to describe itself as a patent [F14attorney] or as a company carrying on the business of a European patent attorney.

(4) F18. . . . .

Amendments (Textual)

F10. Words in s. 280. (1) substituted (31.10.1994) by 1994 c. 26, s. 106. (1), Sch. 4 para. 8. (3); S.I. 1994/2550, art. 2

F11. Words in s. 280. (1) renumbered (1.1.2010) as s. 280. (1)(a) by virtue of Legal Services Act 2007 (c. 29), ss. 208. (1), 211, {Sch. 21 para. 77. (a)} (with ss. 29, 192, 193); S.I. 2009/3250, art. 2. (h) (with art. 9)

F12. S. 280. (1)(b) and preceding word inserted (1.1.2010) by Legal Services Act 2007 (c. 29), ss. 208. (1), 211, Sch. 21 para. 77. (b) (with ss. 29, 192, 193); S.I. 2009/3250, art. 2. (h) (with art. 9)

F13. S. 280. (2) substituted (1.1.2010) by Legal Services Act 2007 (c. 29), ss. 208. (1), 211, Sch. 21 para. 77. (c) (with ss. 29, 192, 193); S.I. 2009/3250, art. 2. (h) (with art. 9)

F14. Words in s. 280. (3) substituted (1.1.2010) by Legal Services Act 2007 (c. 29), ss. 280. (1), 211, Sch. 21 para. 77. (d)(i) (with ss. 29, 192, 193); S.I. 2009/3250, art. 2. (h) (with art. 9)

F15. Word in s. 280. (3) substituted (1.1.2010) by Legal Services Act 2007 (c. 29), ss. 208. (1), 211, Sch. 21 para. 77. (d)(ii) (with ss. 29, 192, 193); S.I. 2009/3250, art. 2. (h) (with art. 9)

F16. Word in s. 280. (3)(b) repealed (1.10.2011) by Legal Services Act 2007 (c. 29), ss. 210, 211, Sch. 23 (with ss. 29, 192, 193); S.I. 2011/2196, art. 2. (1)(h)(iii)

F17. S. 280. (3)(ba) inserted (1.1.2010) by Legal Services Act 2007 (c. 29), ss. 185. (6), 211 (with ss. 29, 192, 193); S.I. 2009/3250, art. 2. (f)(i) (with art. 9)

F18. S. 280. (4) omitted (1.1.2010) and repealed (1.10.2011) by virtue of Legal Services Act 2007 (c. 29), ss. 208. (1), 210, 211, Sch. 21 para 77. (e), Sch. 23 (with ss. 29, 192, 193); S.I. 2009/3250, art. 2. (h) (with art. 9); S.I. 2011/2196, art. 2. (1)(h)(iii)

281 Power of comptroller to refuse to deal with certain agents.

(1) This section applies to business under the M4. Patents Act 1949, the M5. Registered Designs Act 1949 or the M6. Patents Act 1977.

(2) The Secretary of State may make rules authorising the comptroller to refuse to recognise as agent in respect of any business to which this section applies—

(a) a person who has been convicted of an offence under section 88 of the Patents Act 1949, section 114 of the Patents Act 1977 or section 276 of this Act;

(b) [F19a person] whose name has been erased from and not restored to, or who is suspended from, the register of patent [F20attorneys] on the ground of misconduct;

(c) a person who is found by the Secretary of State to have been guilty of such conduct as would, in the case of [F21 a person] registered in the register of patent [F20attorneys], render [F22the person] liable to have [F23the person's] name erased from the register on the ground of misconduct;

(d) a partnership or body corporate of which one of the partners or directors is a person whom the comptroller could refuse to recognise under paragraph (a), (b) or (c) above.

(3) The rules may contain such incidental and supplementary provisions as appear to the Secretary of State to be appropriate and may, in particular, prescribe circumstances in which a person is or is not to be taken to have been guilty of misconduct.

(4) Rules made under this section shall be made by statutory instrument which shall be subject to annulment in pursuance of a resolution of either House of Parliament.

(5) The comptroller shall refuse to recognise as agent in respect of any business to which this section applies a person who neither resides nor has a place of business in the United Kingdom, the Isle of Man or another member State of the [F24. European Union].

Amendments (Textual)

F19. Words in s. 281. (2)(b) substituted (1.1.2010) by The Legal Services Act 2007 (Consequential Amendments) Order 2009 (S.I. 2009/3348), arts. 2. (1), 3. (2); S.I. 2009/3250, art.

2. (b)(i)

F20. Words in s. 281. (2) substituted (1.1.2010) by Legal Services Act 2007 (c. 29), ss. 208. (1), 211, Sch. 21 para. 78 (with ss. 29, 192, 193); S.I. 2009/3250, art. 2. (h) (with art. 9)

F21. Words in s. 281. (2)(c) substituted (1.1.2010) by The Legal Services Act 2007 (Consequential Amendments) Order 2009 (S.I. 2009/3348), arts. 2. (1), 3. (3)(a); S.I. 2009/3250, art. 2. (b)(i)

F22. Words in s. 281. (2)(c) substituted (1.1.2010) by The Legal Services Act 2007 (Consequential Amendments) Order 2009 (S.I. 2009/3348), arts. 2. (1), 3. (3)(b); S.I. 2009/3250, art. 2. (b)(i)

F23. Words in s. 281. (2)(c) substituted (1.1.2010) by The Legal Services Act 2007 (Consequential Amendments) Order 2009 (S.I. 2009/3348), arts. 2. (1), 3. (3)(c); S.I. 2009/3250, art. 2. (b)(i)

F24. Words substituted (22.4.2011) by The Treaty of Lisbon (Changes in Terminology) Order 2011 (S.I. 2011/1043), arts. 3, 4

Marginal Citations

M41949 c. 88.

M51949 c. 87.

M61977 c. 37.

Trade mark agents

F25282. . . . .

Amendments (Textual)

F25. S. 282 repealed (31.10.1994) by 1994 c. 26, s. 106. (2), Sch. 5; S.I. 1994/2550, art. 2

F26283. . . . .

Amendments (Textual)

F26. S. 283 repealed (31.10.1994) by 1994 c. 26, s. 106. (2), Sch. 5; S.I. 1994/2550, art. 2

F27284. . . . .

Amendments (Textual)

F27. S. 284 repealed (31.10.1994) by 1994 c. 26, s. 106. (2), Sch. 5; S.I. 1994/2550, art. 2

Supplementary

285 Offences committed by partnerships and bodies corporate.

(1) Proceedings for an offence under this Part alleged to have been committed by a partnership shall be brought in the name of the partnership and not in that of the partners; but without prejudice to any liability of theirs under subsection (4) below.

(2) The following provisions apply for the purposes of such proceedings as in relation to a body corporate—

(a) any rules of court relating to the service of documents;

(b) in England, Wales or Northern Ireland, Schedule 3 to the M7. Magistrates' Courts Act 1980 or Schedule 4 to the M8. Magistrates' Courts (Northern Ireland) Order 1981 (procedure on charge of offence).

(3) A fine imposed on a partnership on its conviction in such proceedings shall be paid out of the partnership assets.

(4) Where a partnership is guilty of an offence under this Part, every partner, other than a partner who is proved to have been ignorant of or to have attempted to prevent the commission of the offence, is also guilty of the offence and liable to be proceeded against and punished accordingly.

(5) Where an offence under this Part committed by a body corporate is proved to have been committed with the consent or connivance of a director, manager, secretary or other similar officer of the body, or a person purporting to act in any such capacity, he as well as the body corporate is guilty of the offence and liable to be proceeded against and punished accordingly.

Marginal Citations

M71980 c. 43.

M8. S.I. 1981/1675 (N.I. 26).

286 Interpretation.

In this Part—

"the comptroller" means the Comptroller-General of Patents, Designs and Trade Marks;

"director", in relation to a body corporate whose affairs are managed by its members, means any member of the body corporate;

"the European list" means the list of professional representatives maintained by the European Patent Office in pursuance of the European Patent Convention;

"registered patent [F28attorney"] has the meaning given by section 275 [F29. (2)];

F30. . . . .

Amendments (Textual)

F28. Words in s. 286 substituted (1.1.2010) by Legal Services Act 2007 (c. 29), ss. 208. (1), 211, Sch. 21 para. 79. (a) (with ss. 29, 192, 193); S.I. 2009/3250, art. 2. (h) (with art. 9)

F29. Word in s. 286 substituted (1.1.2010) by Legal Services Act 2007 (c. 29), ss. 208. (1), 211, Sch. 21 para. 79. (b) (with ss. 29, 192, 193); S.I. 2009/2350, art. 2. (h) (with art. 9)

F30. Definition in s. 286 repealed (31.10.1994) by 1994 c. 26, s. 106. (2), Sch. 5; S.I. 1994/2550, art. 2

Part VI Patents

Part VI Patents

F1287 Patents county courts: special jurisdiction.

. . . .

Amendments (Textual)

F1. Ss. 287-289 omitted (1.10.2013) by virtue of Crime and Courts Act 2013 (c. 22), s. 61. (3), Sch. 9 para. 30. (3); S.I. 2013/1725, art. 3. (c)

F1288 Financial limits in relation to proceedings within special jurisdiction of patents county court.

. . . .

Amendments (Textual)

F1. Ss. 287-289 omitted (1.10.2013) by virtue of Crime and Courts Act 2013 (c. 22), s. 61. (3), Sch. 9 para. 30. (3); S.I. 2013/1725, art. 3. (c)

F1289 Transfer of proceedings between High Court and patents county court.

. . . .

Amendments (Textual)
F1. Ss. 287-289 omitted (1.10.2013) by virtue of Crime and Courts Act 2013 (c. 22), s. 61. (3), Sch. 9 para. 30. (3); S.I. 2013/1725, art. 3. (c)

[F2290 Limitation of costs where pecuniary claim could have been brought in patents county court.

(1) Where an action is commenced in the High Court which could have been commenced in a patents county court and in which a claim for a pecuniary remedy is made, then, subject to the provisions of this section, if the plaintiff recovers less than the prescribed amount, he is not entitled to recover any more costs than those to which he would have been entitled if the action had been brought in the county court.
(2) For this purpose a plaintiff shall be treated as recovering the full amount recoverable in respect of his claim without regard to any deduction made in respect of matters not falling to be taken into account in determining whether the action could have been commenced in a patents county court.
(3) This section does not affect any question as to costs if it appears to the High Court that there was reasonable ground for supposing the amount recoverable in respect of the plaintiff's claim to be in excess of the prescribed amount.
(4) The High Court, if satisfied that there was sufficient reason for bringing the action in the High Court, may make an order allowing the costs or any part of the costs on the High Court scale or on such one of the county court scales as it may direct.
(5) This section does not apply to proceedings brought by the Crown.
(6) In this section "the prescribed amount" means such amount as may be prescribed by Her Majesty for the purposes of this section by Order in Council.
(7) No recommendation shall be made to Her Majesty to make an Order under this section unless a draft of the Order has been laid before and approved by a resolution of each House of Parliament.]
Amendments (Textual)
F2. S. 290 repealed (prosp.) by Courts and Legal Services Act 1990 (c. 41, SIF 37), ss. 124. (3), 125. (7), Sch. 20

F3291 Proceedings in patents county court.

. . . .

Amendments (Textual)
F3. S. 291 omitted (1.10.2013) by virtue of Crime and Courts Act 2013 (c. 22), s. 61. (3), Sch. 9 para. 30. (3); S.I. 2013/1725, art. 3. (c)

292 Rights and duties of registered patent agents in relation to proceedings in patents county court.

F4. . . . .
Amendments (Textual)
F4. S. 292 repealed (1.1.2010) by Legal Services Act 2007 (c. 29), ss. 208. (1), 210, 211, Sch. 21

Licences of right in respect of certain patents

293 Restriction of acts authorised by certain licences.

In paragraph 4. (2)(c) of Schedule 1 to the M1. Patents Act 1977 (licences to be available as of right where term of existing patent extended), at the end insert ", but subject to paragraph 4. A below", and after that paragraph insert—

"4. A(1)If the proprietor of a patent for an invention which is a product files a declaration with the Patent Office in accordance with this paragraph, the licences to which persons are entitled by virtue of paragraph 4. (2)(c) above shall not extend to a use of the product which is excepted by or under this paragraph.

(2) Pharmaceutical use is excepted, that is—

(a) use as a medicinal product within the meaning of the Medicines Act 1968, and

(b) the doing of any other act mentioned in section 60. (1)(a) above with a view to such use.

(3) The Secretary of State may by order except such other uses as he thinks fit; and an order may—

(a) specify as an excepted use any act mentioned in section 60. (1)(a) above, and

(b) make different provision with respect to acts done in different circumstances or for different purposes.

(4) For the purposes of this paragraph the question what uses are excepted, so far as that depends on—

(a) orders under section 130 of the Medicines Act 1968 (meaning of "medicinal product"), or

(b) orders under sub-paragraph (3) above,

shall be determined in relation to a patent at the beginning of the sixteenth year of the patent.

(5) A declaration under this paragraph shall be in the prescribed form and shall be filed in the prescribed manner and within the prescribed time limits.

(6) A declaration may not be filed—

(a) in respect of a patent which has at the commencement of section 293 of the Copyright, Designs and Patents Act 1988 passed the end of its fifteenth year; or

(b) if at the date of filing there is—

(i) an existing licence for any description of excepted use of the product, or

(ii) an outstanding application under section 46. (3)(a) or (b) above for the settlement by the comptroller of the terms of a licence for any description of excepted use of the product,

and, in either case, the licence took or is to take effect at or after the end of the sixteenth year of the patent.

(7) Where a declaration has been filed under this paragraph in respect of a patent—

(a) section 46. (3)(c) above (restriction of remedies for infringement where licences available as of right) does not apply to an infringement of the patent in so far as it consists of the excepted use of the product after the filing of the declaration; and

(b) section 46. (3)(d) above (abatement of renewal fee if licences available as of right) does not apply to the patent.".

Marginal Citations

M11977 c. 37.

294 When application may be made for settlement of terms of licence.

In Schedule 1 to the M2. Patents Act 1977, after the paragraph inserted by section 293 above, insert—

"4. B(1)An application under section 46. (3)(a) or (b) above for the settlement by the comptroller of the terms on which a person is entitled to a licence by virtue of paragraph 4. (2)(c) above is ineffective if made before the beginning of the sixteenth year of the patent.

(2) This paragraph applies to applications made after the commencement of section 294 of the Copyright, Designs and Patents Act 1988 and to any application made before the commencement of that section in respect of a patent which has not at the commencement of that section passed the end of its fifteenth year.".

Marginal Citations

M21977 c. 37.

Patents: miscellaneous amendments

295 Patents: miscellaneous amendments.

The M3. Patents Act 1949 and the M4. Patents Act 1977 are amended in accordance with Schedule 5.

Marginal Citations

M31949 c. 87.

M41977 c. 37.

Part VII Miscellaneous and General

Part VII Miscellaneous and General

Amendments (Textual)

F1. Ss. 296-296. ZF and cross-heading substituted (31.10.2003) for s. 296 and cross-heading by The Copyright and Related Rights Regulations 2003 (S.I. 2003/2498), reg. 24. (1) (with regs. 31-40)

[F2296 Devices designed to circumvent copy-protection.

(1) This section applies where—

  (a) a technical device has been applied to a computer program; and

  (b) a person (A) knowing or having reason to believe that it will be used to make infringing copies—

(i) manufactures for sale or hire, imports, distributes, sells or lets for hire, offers or exposes for sale or hire, advertises for sale or hire or has in his possession for commercial purposes any means the sole intended purpose of which is to facilitate the unauthorised removal or circumvention of the technical device; or

(ii) publishes information intended to enable or assist persons to remove or circumvent the technical device.

(2) The following persons have the same rights against A as a copyright owner has in respect of an infringement of copyright—

  (a) a person—

(i) issuing to the public copies of, or

(ii) communicating to the public,

the computer program to which the technical device has been applied;

(b) the copyright owner or his exclusive licensee, if he is not the person specified in paragraph (a);

(c) the owner or exclusive licensee of any intellectual property right in the technical device applied to the computer program.

(3) The rights conferred by subsection (2) are concurrent, and sections 101. (3) and 102. (1) to (4) apply, in proceedings under this section, in relation to persons with concurrent rights as they apply, in proceedings mentioned in those provisions, in relation to a copyright owner and exclusive licensee with concurrent rights.

(4) Further, the persons in subsection (2) have the same rights under section 99 or 100 (delivery up or seizure of certain articles) in relation to any such means as is referred to in subsection (1) which a person has in his possession, custody or control with the intention that it should be used to facilitate the unauthorised removal or circumvention of any technical device which has been applied to a computer program, as a copyright owner has in relation to an infringing copy.

(5) The rights conferred by subsection (4) are concurrent, and section 102. (5) shall apply, as respects anything done under section 99 or 100 by virtue of subsection (4), in relation to persons with concurrent rights as it applies, as respects anything done under section 99 or 100, in relation to a copyright owner and exclusive licensee with concurrent rights.

(6) In this section references to a technical device in relation to a computer program are to any device intended to prevent or restrict acts that are not authorised by the copyright owner of that computer program and are restricted by copyright.

(7) The following provisions apply in relation to proceedings under this section as in relation to proceedings under Part 1 (copyright)—

(a) sections 104 to 106 of this Act (presumptions as to certain matters relating to copyright); and

(b) section 72 of the [F3. Senior Courts Act 1981], section 15 of the Law Reform (Miscellaneous Provisions) (Scotland) Act 1985 and section 94. A of the Judicature (Northern Ireland) Act 1978 (withdrawal of privilege against self-incrimination in certain proceedings relating to intellectual property);

and section 114 of this Act applies, with the necessary modifications, in relation to the disposal of anything delivered up or seized by virtue of subsection (4).

(8) Expressions used in this section which are defined for the purposes of Part 1 of this Act (copyright) have the same meaning as in that Part.]

Amendments (Textual)

F2. Ss. 296-296. ZF and cross-heading substituted (31.10.2003) for s. 296 and cross-heading by The Copyright and Related Rights Regulations 2003 (S.I. 2003/2498), reg. 24. (1) (with regs. 31-40)

F3. S. 296. (7)(b): words wherever they occur in any enactment substituted (1.10.2009) by virtue of Constitutional Reform Act 2005 (c. 4), ss. 59, 148, Sch. 11 para. 1. (2); S.I. 2009/1604, art. 2

[F4296. ZACircumvention of technological measures

(1) This section applies where—

(a) effective technological measures have been applied to a copyright work other than a computer program; and

(b) a person (B) does anything which circumvents those measures knowing, or with reasonable grounds to know, that he is pursuing that objective.

(2) This section does not apply where a person, for the purposes of research into cryptography, does anything which circumvents effective technological measures unless in so doing, or in issuing information derived from that research, he affects prejudicially the rights of the copyright owner.

(3) The following persons have the same rights against B as a copyright owner has in respect of an infringement of copyright—

(a) a person—

(i) issuing to the public copies of, or

(ii) communicating to the public,

the work to which effective technological measures have been applied; and

(b) the copyright owner or his exclusive licensee, if he is not the person specified in paragraph (a).

(4) The rights conferred by subsection (3) are concurrent, and sections 101. (3) and 102. (1) to (4) apply, in proceedings under this section, in relation to persons with concurrent rights as they apply, in proceedings mentioned in those provisions, in relation to a copyright owner and exclusive licensee with concurrent rights.

(5) The following provisions apply in relation to proceedings under this section as in relation to proceedings under Part 1 (copyright)—

(a) sections 104 to 106 of this Act (presumptions as to certain matters relating to copyright); and

(b) section 72 of the [F5. Senior Courts Act 1981], section 15 of the Law Reform (Miscellaneous Provisions) (Scotland) Act 1985 and section 94. A of the Judicature (Northern Ireland) Act 1978 (withdrawal of privilege against self-incrimination in certain proceedings relating to intellectual property).

(6) Subsections (1) to (4) and (5)(b) and any other provision of this Act as it has effect for the purposes of those subsections apply, with any necessary adaptations, to rights in performances, publication right and database right.

(7) The provisions of regulation 22 (presumptions relevant to database right) of the Copyright and Rights in Databases Regulations 1997 (SI 1997/3032) apply in proceedings brought by virtue of this section in relation to database right.

Amendments (Textual)

F4. Ss. 296-296. ZF and cross-heading substituted (31.10.2003) for s. 296 and cross-heading by The Copyright and Related Rights Regulations 2003 (S.I. 2003/2498), reg. 24. (1) (with regs. 31-40)

F5. S. 296. ZA(5)(b): words wherever they occur in any enactment substituted (1.10.2009) by virtue of Constitutional Reform Act 2005 (c. 4), ss. 59, 148, Sch. 11 para. 1. (2); S.I. 2009/1604, art. 2

296. ZBDevices and services designed to circumvent technological measures

(1) A person commits an offence if he—

(a) manufactures for sale or hire, or

(b) imports otherwise than for his private and domestic use, or

(c) in the course of a business—

(i) sells or lets for hire, or

(ii) offers or exposes for sale or hire, or

(iii) advertises for sale or hire, or

(iv) possesses, or

(v) distributes, or

(d) distributes otherwise than in the course of a business to such an extent as to affect prejudicially the copyright owner,

any device, product or component which is primarily designed, produced, or adapted for the purpose of enabling or facilitating the circumvention of effective technological measures.

(2) A person commits an offence if he provides, promotes, advertises or markets—

(a) in the course of a business, or

(b) otherwise than in the course of a business to such an extent as to affect prejudicially the copyright owner,

a service the purpose of which is to enable or facilitate the circumvention of effective technological measures.

(3) Subsections (1) and (2) do not make unlawful anything done by, or on behalf of, law enforcement agencies or any of the intelligence services—

(a) in the interests of national security; or

(b) for the purpose of the prevention or detection of crime, the investigation of an offence, or the conduct of a prosecution,

and in this subsection " intelligence services " has the meaning given in section 81 of the Regulation of Investigatory Powers Act 2000.

(4) A person guilty of an offence under subsection (1) or (2) is liable—

(a) on summary conviction, to imprisonment for a term not exceeding three months, or to a fine not exceeding the statutory maximum, or both;

(b) on conviction on indictment to a fine or imprisonment for a term not exceeding two years, or both.

(5) It is a defence to any prosecution for an offence under this section for the defendant to prove that he did not know, and had no reasonable ground for believing, that—

(a) the device, product or component; or

(b) the service,

enabled or facilitated the circumvention of effective technological measures.

Amendments (Textual)

F4. Ss. 296-296. ZF and cross-heading substituted (31.10.2003) for s. 296 and cross-heading by The Copyright and Related Rights Regulations 2003 (S.I. 2003/2498), reg. 24. (1) (with regs. 31-40)

296. ZCDevices and services designed to circumvent technological measures: search warrants and forfeiture

(1) The provisions of sections 297. B (search warrants), 297. C (forfeiture of unauthorised decoders: England and Wales or Northern Ireland) and 297. D (forfeiture of unauthorised decoders: Scotland) apply to offences under section 296. ZB with the following modifications.

(2) In section 297. B the reference to an offence under section 297. A(1) shall be construed as a reference to an offence under section 296. ZB(1) or (2).

(3) In sections 297. C(2)(a) and 297. D(15) the references to an offence under section 297. A(1) shall be construed as a reference to an offence under section 296. ZB(1).

(4) In sections 297. C and 297. D references to unauthorised decoders shall be construed as references to devices, products or components for the purpose of circumventing effective technological measures.

Amendments (Textual)

F4. Ss. 296-296. ZF and cross-heading substituted (31.10.2003) for s. 296 and cross-heading by The Copyright and Related Rights Regulations 2003 (S.I. 2003/2498), reg. 24. (1) (with regs. 31-40)

296. ZDRights and remedies in respect of devices and services designed to circumvent technological measures

(1) This section applies where—

(a) effective technological measures have been applied to a copyright work other than a computer program; and

(b) a person (C) manufactures, imports, distributes, sells or lets for hire, offers or exposes for sale or hire, advertises for sale or hire, or has in his possession for commercial purposes any device, product or component, or provides services which—

(i) are promoted, advertised or marketed for the purpose of the circumvention of, or

(ii) have only a limited commercially significant purpose or use other than to circumvent, or

(iii) are primarily designed, produced, adapted or performed for the purpose of enabling or facilitating the circumvention of,
those measures.

(2) The following persons have the same rights against C as a copyright owner has in respect of an infringement of copyright—

(a) a person—

(i) issuing to the public copies of, or

(ii) communicating to the public,

the work to which effective technological measures have been applied;

(b) the copyright owner or his exclusive licensee, if he is not the person specified in paragraph (a); and

(c) the owner or exclusive licensee of any intellectual property right in the effective technological measures applied to the work.

(3) The rights conferred by subsection (2) are concurrent, and sections 101. (3) and 102. (1) to (4) apply, in proceedings under this section, in relation to persons with concurrent rights as they apply, in proceedings mentioned in those provisions, in relation to a copyright owner and exclusive licensee with concurrent rights.

(4) Further, the persons in subsection (2) have the same rights under section 99 or 100 (delivery up or seizure of certain articles) in relation to any such device, product or component which a person has in his possession, custody or control with the intention that it should be used to circumvent effective technological measures, as a copyright owner has in relation to any infringing copy.

(5) The rights conferred by subsection (4) are concurrent, and section 102. (5) shall apply, as respects anything done under section 99 or 100 by virtue of subsection (4), in relation to persons with concurrent rights as it applies, as respects anything done under section 99 or 100, in relation to a copyright owner and exclusive licensee with concurrent rights.

(6) The following provisions apply in relation to proceedings under this section as in relation to proceedings under Part 1 (copyright)—

(a) sections 104 to 106 of this Act (presumptions as to certain matters relating to copyright); and

(b) section 72 of the [F6. Senior Courts Act 1981], section 15 of the Law Reform (Miscellaneous Provisions) (Scotland) Act 1985 and section 94. A of the Judicature (Northern Ireland) Act 1978 (withdrawal of privilege against self-incrimination in certain proceedings relating to intellectual property);

and section 114 of this Act applies, with the necessary modifications, in relation to the disposal of anything delivered up or seized by virtue of subsection (4).

(7) In section 97. (1) (innocent infringement of copyright) as it applies to proceedings for infringement of the rights conferred by this section, the reference to the defendant not knowing or having reason to believe that copyright subsisted in the work shall be construed as a reference to his not knowing or having reason to believe that his acts enabled or facilitated an infringement of copyright.

(8) Subsections (1) to (5), (6)(b) and (7) and any other provision of this Act as it has effect for the purposes of those subsections apply, with any necessary adaptations, to rights in performances, publication right and database right.

(9) The provisions of regulation 22 (presumptions relevant to database right) of the Copyright and Rights in Databases Regulations 1997 (SI 1997/3032) apply in proceedings brought by virtue of this section in relation to database right.

Amendments (Textual)

F4. Ss. 296-296. ZF and cross-heading substituted (31.10.2003) for s. 296 and cross-heading by The Copyright and Related Rights Regulations 2003 (S.I. 2003/2498), reg. 24. (1) (with regs. 31-40)

F6. S. 296. ZD(6)(b): words wherever they occur in any enactment substituted (1.10.2009) by virtue of Constitutional Reform Act 2005 (c. 4), ss. 59, 148, Sch. 11 para. 1. (2); S.I. 2009/1604, art. 2

296. ZERemedy where effective technological measures prevent permitted acts

(1) In this section—

" permitted act " means an act which may be done in relation to copyright works, notwithstanding the subsistence of copyright, by virtue of a provision of this Act listed in Part 1 of Schedule 5. A;

" voluntary measure or agreement " means—

- any measure taken voluntarily by a copyright owner, his exclusive licensee or a person issuing copies of, or communicating to the public, a work other than a computer program, or

- any agreement between a copyright owner, his exclusive licensee or a person issuing copies of, or communicating to the public, a work other than a computer program and another party,

the effect of which is to enable a person to carry out a permitted act.

(2) Where the application of any effective technological measure to a copyright work other than a computer program prevents a person from carrying out a permitted act in relation to that work then that person or a person being a representative of a class of persons prevented from carrying out a permitted act may issue a notice of complaint to the Secretary of State.

(3) Following receipt of a notice of complaint, the Secretary of State may give to the owner of that copyright work or an exclusive licensee such directions as appear to the Secretary of State to be requisite or expedient for the purpose of—

(a) establishing whether any voluntary measure or agreement relevant to the copyright work the subject of the complaint subsists; or

(b) (where it is established there is no subsisting voluntary measure or agreement) ensuring that the owner or exclusive licensee of that copyright work makes available to the complainant the means of carrying out the permitted act the subject of the complaint to the extent necessary to so benefit from that permitted act.

(4) The Secretary of State may also give directions—

(a) as to the form and manner in which a notice of complaint in subsection (2) may be delivered to him;

(b) as to the form and manner in which evidence of any voluntary measure or agreement may be delivered to him; and

(c) generally as to the procedure to be followed in relation to a complaint made under this section;

and shall publish directions given under this subsection in such manner as in his opinion will secure adequate publicity for them.

(5) It shall be the duty of any person to whom a direction is given under subsection (3)(a) or (b) to give effect to that direction.

(6) The obligation to comply with a direction given under subsection (3)(b) is a duty owed to the complainant or, where the complaint is made by a representative of a class of persons, to that representative and to each person in the class represented; and a breach of the duty is actionable accordingly (subject to the defences and other incidents applying to actions for breach of statutory duty).

(7) Any direction under this section may be varied or revoked by a subsequent direction under this section.

(8) Any direction given under this section shall be in writing.

(9) This section does not apply to copyright works made available to the public on agreed contractual terms in such a way that members of the public may access them from a place and at a time individually chosen by them.

(10) This section applies only where a complainant has lawful access to the protected copyright work, or where the complainant is a representative of a class of persons, where the class of persons have lawful access to the work.

(11) Subsections (1) to (10) apply with any necessary adaptations to—

(a) rights in performances, and in this context the expression " permitted act " refers to an act that may be done by virtue of a provision of this Act listed in Part 2 of Schedule 5. A;

(b) database right, and in this context the expression " permitted act " refers to an act that may be done by virtue of a provision of this Act listed in Part 3 of Schedule 5. A; and

(c) publication right.

Amendments (Textual)

F4. Ss. 296-296. ZF and cross-heading substituted (31.10.2003) for s. 296 and cross-heading by The Copyright and Related Rights Regulations 2003 (S.I. 2003/2498), reg. 24. (1) (with regs. 31-40)

[F7296. ZEA.Remedy where restrictive measures prevent or restrict personal copying

(1) This section applies where an individual is prevented from making a personal copy of a copyright work, or is restricted in the number of personal copies of it which may be made, because of a restrictive measure applied by or on behalf of the copyright owner.

(2) That individual, or a person being a representative of a class of such individuals, may issue a notice of complaint to the Secretary of State.

(3) Following receipt of a notice of complaint, the Secretary of State may give to the owner of that copyright work or an exclusive licensee such directions as appear to the Secretary of State to be requisite or expedient for the purpose of—

(a) establishing whether any voluntary measure or agreement relevant to the copyright work subsists, or

(b) (where it is established there is no subsisting voluntary measure or agreement) ensuring that the owner or exclusive licensee of that copyright work makes available to the complainant or the class of individuals represented by the complainant the means of benefiting from section 28. B to the extent necessary to benefit from that section.

(4) In deciding whether to give such directions, the Secretary of State must consider whether the restrictive measure unreasonably prevents or restricts the making of personal copies, in particular having regard to—

(a) the right of the copyright owner to adopt adequate measures limiting the number of personal copies which may be made, and

(b) whether other copies of the work are commercially available on reasonable terms by or with the authority of the copyright owner in a form which does not prevent or unreasonably restrict the making of personal copies.

(5) The Secretary of State may also give directions—

(a) as to the form and manner in which a notice of complaint in subsection (2) may be delivered,

(b) as to the form and manner in which evidence of any voluntary measure or agreement may be delivered, and

(c) generally as to the procedure to be followed in relation to a complaint made under this section,

and shall publish directions given under this subsection in such manner as the Secretary of State thinks will secure adequate publicity for them.

(6) Subsections (5) to (8) of section 296. ZE—

(a) apply to directions under subsection (3)(a) or (b) as they apply to directions under section 296. ZE(3)(a) or (b), and

(b) apply to directions under subsection (5) as they apply to directions under section 296. ZE(4).

(7) This section does not apply to copyright works made available to the public on agreed contractual terms in such a way that members of the public may access them from a place and at a time individually chosen by them.

(8) In this section—

"restrictive measure" means any technology, device or component designed, in the normal course of its operation, to protect the rights of copyright owners, which has the effect of preventing a copyright work from being copied (in whole or in part) or restricting the number of copies which may be made;

"personal copy" means a copy of a copyright work which may be made under section 28. B;

"voluntary measure or agreement" has the same meaning as in section 296. ZE, except that the reference to carrying out a permitted act is to be read as a reference to making a personal copy.

(9) Subsections (1) to (8) apply with any necessary adaptations to—

(a) rights in performances, and in this context "personal copy" refers to a copy of a recording of a performance which may be made under paragraph 1. B of Schedule 2 without infringing the rights conferred by Chapter 2 of Part II (rights in performances), and

(b) publication right.]

Amendments (Textual)

F4. Ss. 296-296. ZF and cross-heading substituted (31.10.2003) for s. 296 and cross-heading by The Copyright and Related Rights Regulations 2003 (S.I. 2003/2498), reg. 24. (1) (with regs. 31-40)

F7. S. 296. ZEA inserted (1.10.2014) by The Copyright and Rights in Performances (Personal Copies for Private Use) Regulations 2014 (S.I. 2014/2361), regs. 1. (1), 3. (2) (with reg. 5) (but note that the amending S.I. was quashed with prospective effect by the High Court in the case of R (British Academy of Songwriters, Composers and Authors and others) v Secretary of State for Business, Innovation and Skills [2015] EWHC 2041 (Admin), 17 July 2015)

296. ZFInterpretation of sections 296. ZA to [F8296. ZEA]

(1) In sections 296. ZA to 296. ZE, "technological measures" are any technology, device or component which is designed, in the normal course of its operation, to protect a copyright work other than a computer program.

(2) Such measures are "effective" if the use of the work is controlled by the copyright owner through—

(a) an access control or protection process such as encryption, scrambling or other transformation of the work, or

(b) a copy control mechanism,

which achieves the intended protection.

(3) In this section, the reference to—

(a) protection of a work is to the prevention or restriction of acts that are not authorised by the copyright owner of that work and are restricted by copyright; and

(b) use of a work does not extend to any use of the work that is outside the scope of the acts restricted by copyright.

(4) Expressions used in sections 296. ZA to [F9296. ZEA] which are defined for the purposes of Part 1 of this Act (copyright) have the same meaning as in that Part.]

Amendments (Textual)

F4. Ss. 296-296. ZF and cross-heading substituted (31.10.2003) for s. 296 and cross-heading by The Copyright and Related Rights Regulations 2003 (S.I. 2003/2498), reg. 24. (1) (with regs. 31-40)

F8. Word in s. 296. ZF heading substituted (1.10.2014) by The Copyright and Rights in Performances (Personal Copies for Private Use) Regulations 2014 (S.I. 2014/2361), regs. 1. (1), 4. (3) (with reg. 5) (but note that the amending S.I. was quashed with prospective effect by the High Court in the case of R (British Academy of Songwriters, Composers and Authors and others) v Secretary of State for Business, Innovation and Skills [2015] EWHC 2041 (Admin), 17 July 2015)

F9. Word in s. 296. ZF(4) substituted (1.10.2014) by The Copyright and Rights in Performances (Personal Copies for Private Use) Regulations 2014 (S.I. 2014/2361), regs. 1. (1), 4. (3) (with reg. 5) (but note that the amending S.I. was quashed with prospective effect by the High Court in the case of R (British Academy of Songwriters, Composers and Authors and others) v Secretary of State for Business, Innovation and Skills [2015] EWHC 2041 (Admin), 17 July 2015)

[F10. Rights management information

Amendments (Textual)
F10. S. 296. ZG and cross-heading inserted (31.10.2003) by The Copyright and Related Rights
Regulations 2003 (S.I. 2003/2498), reg. 25 (with regs. 31-40)

296. ZGElectronic rights management information

(1) This section applies where a person (D), knowingly and without authority, removes or alters electronic rights management information which—

    (a) is associated with a copy of a copyright work, or

    (b) appears in connection with the communication to the public of a copyright work, and where D knows, or has reason to believe, that by so doing he is inducing, enabling, facilitating or concealing an infringement of copyright.

(2) This section also applies where a person (E), knowingly and without authority, distributes, imports for distribution or communicates to the public copies of a copyright work from which electronic rights management information—

    (a) associated with the copies, or

    (b) appearing in connection with the communication to the public of the work,

has been removed or altered without authority and where E knows, or has reason to believe, that by so doing he is inducing, enabling, facilitating or concealing an infringement of copyright.

(3) A person issuing to the public copies of, or communicating, the work to the public, has the same rights against D and E as a copyright owner has in respect of an infringement of copyright.

(4) The copyright owner or his exclusive licensee, if he is not the person issuing to the public copies of, or communicating, the work to the public, also has the same rights against D and E as he has in respect of an infringement of copyright.

(5) The rights conferred by subsections (3) and (4) are concurrent, and sections 101. (3) and 102. (1) to (4) apply, in proceedings under this section, in relation to persons with concurrent rights as they apply, in proceedings mentioned in those provisions, in relation to a copyright owner and exclusive licensee with concurrent rights.

(6) The following provisions apply in relation to proceedings under this section as in relation to proceedings under Part 1 (copyright)—

    (a) sections 104 to 106 of this Act (presumptions as to certain matters relating to copyright); and

    (b) section 72 of the [F11. Senior Courts Act 1981], section 15 of the Law Reform (Miscellaneous Provisions) (Scotland) Act 1985 and section 94. A of the Judicature (Northern Ireland) Act 1978 (withdrawal of privilege against self-incrimination in certain proceedings relating to intellectual property).

(7) In this section—

    (a) expressions which are defined for the purposes of Part 1 of this Act (copyright) have the same meaning as in that Part; and

    (b) " rights management information " means any information provided by the copyright owner or the holder of any right under copyright which identifies the work, the author, the copyright owner or the holder of any intellectual property rights, or information about the terms and conditions of use of the work, and any numbers or codes that represent such information.

(8) Subsections (1) to (5) and (6)(b), and any other provision of this Act as it has effect for the purposes of those subsections, apply, with any necessary adaptations, to rights in performances, publication right and database right.

(9) The provisions of regulation 22 (presumptions relevant to database right) of the Copyright and Rights in Databases Regulations 1997 (SI 1997/3032) apply in proceedings brought by virtue of this section in relation to database right.]

Amendments (Textual)

F11. S. 296. ZG(6)(b): words wherever they occur in any enactment substituted (1.10.2009) by virtue of Constitutional Reform Act 2005 (c. 4), ss. 59, 148, Sch. 11 para. 1. (2); S.I. 2009/1604, art. 2

[F12. Computer programs

Amendments (Textual)
F12. Cross heading and s. 296. A inserted (1.1.1993) by S.I. 1992/3233, reg.11

F13296. A Avoidance of certain terms.

(1) Where a person has the use of a computer program under an agreement, any term or condition in the agreement shall be void in so far as it purports to prohibit or restrict—
   (a) the making of any back up copy of the program which it is necessary for him to have for the purposes of the agreed use;
   (b) where the conditions in section 50. B(2) are met, the decompiling of the program; or
   [F14. (c)the observing, studying or testing of the functioning of the program in accordance with section 50. BA.]
(2) In this section, decompile, in relation to a computer program, has the same meaning as in section 50. B]
Amendments (Textual)
F13. S. 296. A inserted (1.1.1993) by S.I. 1992/3233, reg.11.
F14. S. 296. A(1)(c) substituted (31.10.2003) by The Copyright and Related Rights Regulations 2003 (S.I. 2003/2498), reg. 15. (4) (with regs. 31-40)

F15[Databases]

Amendments (Textual)
F15. S. 296. B and crossheading inserted (1.1.1998) by S.I. 1997/3032, reg. 10 (with Pt. IV)

296. B[F16 Avoidance of certain terms relating to databases]

Where under an agreement a person has a right to use a database or part of a database, any term or condition in the agreement shall be void in so far as it purports to prohibit or restrict the performance of any act which would but for section 50. D infringe the copyright in the database.
Amendments (Textual)
F16. S. 296. B inserted (1.1.1998) by S.I. 1997/3032, reg. 10 (with Pt. IV)

Fraudulent reception of transmissions

297 Offence of fraudulently receiving programmes.

(1) A person who dishonestly receives a programme included in a broadcasting F17. . . service provided from a place in the United Kingdom with intent to avoid payment of any charge applicable to the reception of the programme commits an offence and is liable on summary conviction to a fine not exceeding level 5 on the standard scale.
(2) Where an offence under this section committed by a body corporate is proved to have been committed with the consent or connivance of a director, manager, secretary or other similar officer of the body, or a person purporting to act in any such capacity, he as well as the body corporate is

guilty of the offence and liable to be proceeded against and punished accordingly.

In relation to a body corporate whose affairs are managed by its members "director" means a member of the body corporate.

Amendments (Textual)

F17. Words in s. 297. (1) repealed (31.10.2003) by The Copyright and Related Rights Regulations 2003 (S.I. 2003/2498), reg. 2. (2), Sch. 2 (with regs. 31-40)

[F18297. A Unauthorised decoders.

(1) A person commits an offence if he—

(a) makes, imports, distributes, sells or lets for hire or offers or exposes for sale or hire any unauthorised decoder;

(b) has in his possession for commercial purposes any unauthorised decoder;

(c) instals, maintains or replaces for commercial purposes any unauthorised decoder; or

(d) advertises any unauthorised decoder for sale or hire or otherwise promotes any unauthorised decoder by means of commercial communications.

(2) A person guilty of an offence under subsection (1) is liable—

[F19. (a)on summary conviction, to imprisonment for a term not exceeding six months, or to a fine not exceeding the statutory maximum, or to both;]]

(b) on conviction on indictment, to imprisonment for a term not exceeding [F20ten] years, or to a fine, or to both.

(3) It is a defence to any prosecution for an offence under this section for the defendant to prove that he did not know, and had no reasonable ground for believing, that the decoder was an unauthorised decoder.

(4) In this section—

"apparatus" includes any device, component or electronic data (including software);

"conditional access technology" means any technical measure or arrangement whereby access to encrypted transmissions in an intelligbile form is made conditional on prior individual authorisation;

"decoder" means any apparatus which is designed or adapted to enable (whether on its own or with any other apparatus) an encrypted transmission to be decoded;

"encrypted" includes subjected to scrambling or the operation of cryptographic envelopes, electronic locks, passwords or any other analogous application;

"transmission" means—

- any programme included in a broadcasting F21. . . service which is provided from a place in the United Kingdom or any other member State; or

- an information society service (within the meaning of Directive 98/34/EC of the European Parliament and of the Council of 22nd June 1998 F22, as amended by Directive 98/48/EC of the European Parliament and of the Council of 20th July 1998 F23) which is provided from a place in the United Kingdom or any other member State; and

"unauthorised", in relation to a decoder, means that the decoder is designed or adapted to enable an encrypted transmission, or any service of which it forms part, to be accessed in an intelligible form without payment of the fee (however imposed) which the person making the transmission, or on whose behalf it is made, charges for accessing the transmission or service (whether by the circumvention of any conditional access technology related to the transmission or service or by any other means).

Amendments (Textual)

F18. S. 297. A substituted (28.5.2000) by S.I. 2000/1175, art. 2. (2)

F19. S. 297. A(2)(a) substituted (20.11.2002) by 2002 c. 25, s. 1. (4)(a)(5); S.I. 2002/2749, art. 2

F20. Word in s. 297. A(2)(b) substituted (20.11.2002) by 2002 c. 25, s. 1. (4)(b)(5); S.I. 2002/2749, art. 2

F21. Words in s. 297. A(4) repealed (31.10.2003) by The Copyright and Related Rights

Regulations 2003 (S.I. 2003/2498), reg. 2. (2), Sch. 2 (with regs. 31-40)

F22. O.J. L204, 21.7.98, p.37

F23. O.J. L217, 5.8.98, p.18

[F24297. B Search warrants

(1) Where a justice of the peace (in Scotland, a sheriff or justice of the peace) is satisfied by information on oath given by a constable (in Scotland, by evidence on oath) that there are reasonable grounds for believing—

(a) that an offence under section 297. A(1) has been or is about to be committed in any premises, and

(b) that evidence that such an offence has been or is about to be committed is in those premises, he may issue a warrant authorising a constable to enter and search the premises, using such reasonable force as is necessary.

(2) The power conferred by subsection (1) does not, in England and Wales, extend to authorising a search for material of the kinds mentioned in section 9. (2) of the Police and Criminal Evidence Act 1984 (c. 60) (certain classes of personal or confidential material).

(3) A warrant under subsection (1)—

(a) may authorise persons to accompany any constable executing the warrant, and

(b) remains in force for [F25three months] from the date of its issue.

(4) In executing a warrant issued under subsection (1) a constable may seize an article if he reasonably believes that it is evidence that any offence under section 297. A(1) has been or is about to be committed.

(5) In this section " premises " includes land, buildings, fixed or moveable structures, vehicles, vessels, aircraft and hovercraft.]

Amendments (Textual)

F24. S. 297. B inserted (20.11.2002) by 2002 c. 25, s. 2. (4); S.I. 2002/2749, art. 2

F25. Words in s. 297. B(3)(b) substituted (1.1.2006) by Serious Organised Crime and Police Act 2005 (c. 15), ss. 174. (1), 178, Sch. 16 para. 6. (4); S.I. 2004/3495, art. 2. (1)(s) (subject to art. 2. (2))

[F26297. C Forfeiture of unauthorised decoders: England and Wales or Northern Ireland

(1) In England and Wales or Northern Ireland where unauthorised decoders have come into the possession of any person in connection with the investigation or prosecution of a relevant offence, that person may apply under this section for an order for the forfeiture of the unauthorised decoders.

(2) For the purposes of this section "relevant offence" means—

(a) an offence under section 297. A(1) (criminal liability for making, importing, etc. unauthorised decoders),

(b) an offence under the Trade Descriptions Act 1968,

[F27. (ba)an offence under the Business Protection from Misleading Marketing Regulations 2008,

(bb) an offence under the Consumer Protection from Unfair Trading Regulations 2008, or]

(c) an offence involving dishonesty or deception.

(3) An application under this section may be made—

(a) where proceedings have been brought in any court for a relevant offence relating to some or all of the unauthorised decoders, to that court, or

(b) where no application for the forfeiture of the unauthorised decoders has been made under paragraph (a), by way of complaint to a magistrates' court.

(4) On an application under this section, the court shall make an order for the forfeiture of any unauthorised decoders only if it is satisfied that a relevant offence has been committed in relation to the unauthorised decoders.

(5) A court may infer for the purposes of this section that such an offence has been committed in relation to any unauthorised decoders if it is satisfied that such an offence has been committed in relation to unauthorised decoders which are representative of the unauthorised decoders in question (whether by reason of being of the same design or part of the same consignment or batch or otherwise).

(6) Any person aggrieved by an order made under this section by a magistrates' court, or by a decision of such a court not to make such an order, may appeal against that order or decision—

(a) in England and Wales, to the Crown Court, or

(b) in Northern Ireland, to the county court.

(7) An order under this section may contain such provision as appears to the court to be appropriate for delaying the coming into force of the order pending the making and determination of any appeal (including any application under section 111 of the Magistrates' Courts Act 1980 (c. 43) or Article 146 of the Magistrates' Courts (Northern Ireland) Order 1981 (S.I. 1981/1675 (N.I. 26)) (statement of case)).

(8) Subject to subsection (9), where any unauthorised decoders are forfeited under this section they shall be destroyed in accordance with such directions as the court may give.

(9) On making an order under this section the court may direct that the unauthorised decoders to which the order relates shall (instead of being destroyed) be forfeited to a person who has rights or remedies under section 298 in relation to the unauthorised decoders in question, or dealt with in such other way as the court considers appropriate.]

Amendments (Textual)

F26. Ss. 297. C, 297. D inserted (20.11.2002) by 2002 c. 25, s. 5; S.I. 2002/2749, art. 2

F27. S. 297. C(2)(ba)(bb) and word substituted (26.5.2008) for word by The Consumer Protection from Unfair Trading Regulations 2008 (S.I. 2008/1277), reg. 1, Sch. 2 para. 44 (with reg. 28. (2)(3))

F28297. D Forfeiture of unauthorised decoders: Scotland

(1) In Scotland the court may make an order under this section for the forfeiture of unauthorised decoders.

(2) An order under this section may be made—

(a) on an application by the procurator-fiscal made in the manner specified in section 134 of the Criminal Procedure (Scotland) Act 1995 (c. 46), or

(b) where a person is convicted of a relevant offence, in addition to any other penalty which the court may impose.

(3) On an application under subsection (2)(a), the court shall make an order for the forfeiture of any unauthorised decoders only if it is satisfied that a relevant offence has been committed in relation to the unauthorised decoders.

(4) The court may infer for the purposes of this section that such an offence has been committed in relation to any unauthorised decoders if it is satisfied that such an offence has been committed in relation to unauthorised decoders which are representative of the unauthorised decoders in question (whether by reason of being of the same design or part of the same consignment or batch or otherwise).

(5) The procurator-fiscal making the application under subsection (2)(a) shall serve on any person appearing to him to be the owner of, or otherwise to have an interest in, the unauthorised decoders to which the application relates a copy of the application, together with a notice giving him the opportunity to appear at the hearing of the application to show cause why the unauthorised decoders should not be forfeited.

(6) Service under subsection (5) shall be carried out, and such service may be proved, in the

manner specified for citation of an accused in summary proceedings under the Criminal Procedure (Scotland) Act 1995 (c. 46).

(7) Any person upon whom notice is served under subsection (5) and any other person claiming to be the owner of, or otherwise to have an interest in, unauthorised decoders to which an application under this section relates shall be entitled to appear at the hearing of the application to show cause why the unauthorised decoders should not be forfeited.

(8) The court shall not make an order following an application under subsection (2)(a)—

(a) if any person on whom notice is served under subsection (5) does not appear, unless service of the notice on that person is proved, or

(b) if no notice under subsection (5) has been served, unless the court is satisfied that in the circumstances it was reasonable not to serve such notice.

(9) Where an order for the forfeiture of any unauthorised decoders is made following an application under subsection (2)(a), any person who appeared, or was entitled to appear, to show cause why the unauthorised decoders should not be forfeited may, within 21 days of the making of the order, appeal to the High Court by Bill of Suspension.

(10) Section 182. (5)(a) to (e) of the Criminal Procedure (Scotland) Act 1995 shall apply to an appeal under subsection (9) as it applies to a stated case under Part 2 of that Act.

(11) An order following an application under subsection (2)(a) shall not take effect—

(a) until the end of the period of 21 days beginning with the day after the day on which the order is made, or

(b) if an appeal is made under subsection (9) above within that period, until the appeal is determined or abandoned.

(12) An order under subsection (2)(b) shall not take effect—

(a) until the end of the period within which an appeal against the order could be brought under the Criminal Procedure (Scotland) Act 1995 (c. 46), or

(b) if an appeal is made within that period, until the appeal is determined or abandoned.

(13) Subject to subsection (14), where any unauthorised decoders are forfeited under this section they shall be destroyed in accordance with such directions as the court may give.

(14) On making an order under this section the court may direct that the unauthorised decoders to which the order relates shall (instead of being destroyed) be forfeited to a person who has rights or remedies under section 298 in relation to the unauthorised decoders in question, or dealt with in such other way as the court considers appropriate.

(15) For the purposes of this section—

[F29"relevant offence" means—

- an offence under section 297. A(1) (criminal liability for making, importing, etc unauthorised decoders),

- an offence under the Trade Descriptions Act 1968,

- an offence under the Business Protection from Misleading Marketing Regulations 2008,

- an offence under the Consumer Protection from Unfair Trading Regulations 2008, or

- any offence involving dishonesty or deception;]

"the court" means—

- in relation to an order made on an application under subsection (2)(a), the sheriff, and

- in relation to an order made under subsection (2)(b), the court which imposed the penalty.

Amendments (Textual)

F28. Ss. 297. C, 297. D inserted (20.11.2002) by 2002 c. 25, s. 5; S.I. 2002/2749, art. 2

F29. Words in s. 297. D(15) substituted (26.5.2008) by The Consumer Protection from Unfair Trading Regulations 2008 (S.I. 2008/1277), reg. 1, Sch. 2 para. 45 (with reg. 28. (2)(3))

[F30298 Rights and remedies in respect of apparatus, &c. for unauthorised reception of transmissions.

(1) A person who—

(a) makes charges for the reception of programmes included in a broadcasting F31. . . service provided from a place in the United Kingdom or any other member State,

(b) sends encrypted tranmissions of any other description from a place in the United Kingdom or any other member State, or

(c) provides conditional access services from a place in the United Kingdom or any other member State,

is entitled to the following rights and remedies.

(2) He has the same rights and remedies against a person—

(a) who—

(i) makes, imports, distributes, sells or lets for hire, offers or exposes for sale or hire, or advertises for sale or hire,

(ii) has in his possession for commercial purposes, or

(iii) instals, maintains or replaces for commercial purposes,

any apparatus designed or adapted to enable or assist persons to access the programmes or other transmissions or circumvent conditional access technology related to the programmes or other transmissions when they are not entitled to do so, or

(b) who publishes or otherwise promotes by means of commercial communications any information which is calculated to enable or assist persons to access the programmes or other transmissions or circumvent conditional access technology related to the programmes or other transmissions when they are not entitled to do so,

as a copyright owner has in respect of an infringement of copyright.

(3) Further, he has the same rights under section 99 or 100 (delivery up or seizure of certain articles) in relation to any such apparatus as a copyright owner has in relation to an infringing copy.

(4) Section 72 of the M1[F32. Senior Courts Act 1981], section 15 of the M2. Law Reform (Miscellaneous Provisions) (Scotland) Act 1985 and section 94. A of the M3. Judicature (Northern Ireland) Act 1978 (withdrawal of privilege against self-incrimination in certain proceedings relating to intellectual property) apply to proceedings under this section as to proceedings under Part I of this Act (copyright).

(5) In section 97. (1) (innocent infringement of copyright) as it applies to proceedings for infringement of the rights conferred by this section, the reference to the defendant not knowing or having reason to believe that copyright subsisted in the work shall be construed as a reference to his not knowing or having reason to believe that his acts infringed the rights conferred by this section.

(6) Section 114 applies, with the necessary modifications, in relation to the disposal of anything delivered up or seized by virtue of subsection (3) above.

(7) In this section "apparatus", "conditional access technology" and "encrypted" have the same meanings as in section 297. A, "transmission" includes transmissions as defined in that section and "conditional access services" means services comprising the provision of conditional access technology.]

Amendments (Textual)

F30. S. 298 substituted (25.5.2000) by S.I. 2000/1175, art. 2. (3)

F31. Words in s. 298. (1)(a) repealed (31.10.2003) by The Copyright and Related Rights Regulations 2003 (S.I. 2003/2498), reg. 2. (2), Sch. 2 (with regs. 31-40)

F32. S. 298. (4): words wherever they occur in any enactment substituted (1.10.2009) by virtue of Constitutional Reform Act 2005 (c. 4), ss. 59, 148, Sch. 11 para. 1. (2); S.I. 2009/1604, art. 2

Marginal Citations

M11981 c. 54.

M21985 c. 37.

M31978 c. 23.

299 Supplementary provisions as to fraudulent reception.

(1) Her Majesty may by Order in Council—

(a) provide that section 297 applies in relation to programmes included in services provided from a country or territory outside the United Kingdom, and

(b) provide that section 298 applies in relation to such programmes and to encrypted transmissions sent from such a country or territory.

F33. (2). . . . .

(3) A statutory instrument containing an Order in Council under subsection (1) shall be subject to annulment in pursuance of a resolution of either House of Parliament.

(4) Where sections 297 and 298 apply in relation to a broadcasting service F34. . . , they also apply to any service run for the person providing that service, or a person providing programmes for that service, which consists wholly or mainly in the sending by means of a telecommunications system of sounds or visual images, or both.

(5) In sections 297 [F35, 297. A] and 298, and this section, "programme"[F36and "broadcasting"], and related expressions, have the same meaning as in Part I (copyright).

Amendments (Textual)

F33. S. 299. (2) repealed by Broadcasting Act 1990 (c. 42, SIF 96), ss. 179. (2)(a), 203. (3), Sch. 21

F34. Words in s. 299. (4) repealed (31.10.2003) by The Copyright and Related Rights Regulations 2003 (S.I. 2003/2498), reg. 2. (2), Sch. 2 (with regs. 31-40)

F35. S. 299. (5): ", 297. A" inserted by Broadcasting Act 1990 (c. 42, SIF 96), s. 179. (2)(b)

F36. Words in s. 299. (5) substituted (31.10.2003) by The Copyright and Related Rights Regulations 2003 (S.I. 2003/2498), reg. 2. (1), Sch. 1 para. 3. (3) (with regs. 31-40)

Fraudulent application or use of trade mark

F37300. . . . .

Amendments (Textual)

F37. S. 300 repealed (31.10.1994) by 1994 c. 26, s. 106. (2), Sch. 5; S.I. 1994/2550, art. 2

Provisions for the benefit of [F38. Great Ormond Street Hospital for Children]

Amendments (Textual)

F38. Words in s. 301 cross-heading substituted (23.5.2016) by NHS (Charitable Trusts Etc) Act 2016 (c. 10), ss. 3. (2)(b), 5. (3)

301 Provisions for the benefit of [F39. Great Ormond Street Hospital for Children].

The provisions of Schedule 6 have effect for conferring on [F40. GOSH Children's Charity for the benefit of Great Ormond Street Hospital for Children] a right to a royalty in respect of the public performance, commercial publication [F41or communication to the public] of the play "Peter Pan" by Sir James Matthew Barrie, or of any adaptation of that work, notwithstanding that copyright in the work expired on 31st December 1987.

Amendments (Textual)

F39. Words in s. 301 heading substituted (23.5.2016) by NHS (Charitable Trusts Etc) Act 2016 (c. 10), ss. 3. (2)(a), 5. (3)

F40. Words in s. 301 substituted (23.5.2016) by NHS (Charitable Trusts Etc) Act 2016 (c. 10), ss. 3. (3), 5. (3)

F41. Words in s. 301 substituted (31.10.2003) by The Copyright and Related Rights Regulations 2003 (S.I. 2003/2498), reg. 2. (1), Sch. 1 para. 6. (2)(d) (with regs. 31-40)

Financial assistance for certain international bodies

302 Financial assistance for certain international bodies.

(1) The Secretary of State may give financial assistance, in the form of grants, loans or guarantees to—

(a) any international organisation having functions relating to trade marks or other intellectual property, or

(b) any [F42. EU] institution or other body established under any of the [F42. EU] Treaties having any such functions,

with a view to the establishment or maintenance by that organisation, institution or body of premises in the United Kingdom.

(2) Any expenditure of the Secretary of State under this section shall be defrayed out of money provided by Parliament; and any sums received by the Secretary of State in consequence of this section shall be paid into the Consolidated Fund.

Amendments (Textual)

F42. Words substituted (22.4.2011) by The Treaty of Lisbon (Changes in Terminology) Order 2011 (S.I. 2011/1043), arts. 3, 6

General

303 Consequential amendments and repeals.

(1) The enactments specified in Schedule 7 are amended in accordance with that Schedule, the amendments being consequential on the provisions of this Act.

(2) The enactments specified in Schedule 8 are repealed to the extent specified.

304 Extent.

(1) Provision as to the extent of Part I (copyright), Part II (rights in performances) and Part III (design right) is to be found in sections 157, 207 and 255 respectively; the extent of the other provisions of this Act is as follows.

(2) Parts IV to VII extend to England and Wales, Scotland and Northern Ireland, except that—

(a) sections 287 to 292 (patents county courts) extend to England and Wales only,

F43. (b). . . . .

(c) the amendments and repeals in Schedules 7 and 8 have the same extent as the enactments amended or repealed.

(3) The following provisions extend to the Isle of Man subject to any modifications contained in an Order made by Her Majesty in Council—

(a) sections 293 and 294 (patents: licences of right), and

(b) paragraphs 24 and 29 of Schedule 5 (patents: effect of filing international application for patent and power to extend time limits).

(4) Her Majesty may by Order in Council direct that the following provisions extend to the Isle of Man, with such exceptions and modifications as may be specified in the Order—

(a) Part IV (registered designs),

(b) Part V (patent agents),

(c) the provisions of Schedule 5 (patents: miscellaneous amendments) not mentioned in subsection (3) above,

(d) sections 297 to 299 (fraudulent reception of transmissions), and

(e) section 300 (fraudulent application or use of trade mark).

(5) Her Majesty may by Order in Council direct that sections 297 to 299 (fraudulent reception of transmissions) extend to any of the Channel Islands, with such exceptions and modifications as may be specified in the Order.

(6) Any power conferred by this Act to make provision by Order in Council for or in connection with the extent of provisions of this Act to a country outside the United Kingdom includes power to extend to that country, subject to any modifications specified in the Order, any provision of this Act which amends or repeals an enactment extending to that country.

Amendments (Textual)

F43. S. 304. (2)(b) omitted (23.5.2016) by virtue of NHS (Charitable Trusts Etc) Act 2016 (c. 10), ss. 3. (4), 5. (3)

305 Commencement.

(1) The following provisions of this Act come into force on Royal Assent—

paragraphs 24 and 29 of Schedule 5 (patents: effect of filing international application for patent and power to extend time limits);

section 301 and Schedule 6 (provisions for the benefit of the Hospital for Sick Children).

(2) Sections 293 and 294 (licences of right) come into force at the end of the period of two months beginning with the passing of this Act.

(3) The other provisions of this Act come into force on such day as the Secretary of State may appoint by order made by statutory instrument, and different days may be appointed for different provisions and different purposes.

Modifications etc. (not altering text)

C1. Power of appointment conferred by s. 305. (3) partly exercised: S.I. 1989/816, 955, 1032, 1303, 1990/1400, 2168

306 Short title.

This Act may be cited as the Copyright, Designs and Patents Act 1988.

Schedules

Schedule 1. CERTAIN PERMITTED USES OF ORPHAN WORKS

Section 76. A

Amendments (Textual)

F1. Sch. ZA1 inserted (29.10.2014) by The Copyright and Rights in Performances (Certain Permitted Uses of Orphan Works) Regulations 2014 (S.I. 2014/2861), reg. 3. (5), Sch. para. 1

PART 1 GENERAL PROVISIONS

Certain permitted uses of orphan works by relevant bodies

1.(1)A relevant body does not infringe the copyright in a relevant work in its collection which is an orphan work by—
(a) making the orphan work available to the public; or
(b) reproducing the orphan work for the purposes of digitisation, making available, indexing, cataloguing, preservation or restoration.
(2) A relevant body does not infringe the rights conferred by Chapter 2 of Part 2 by doing either of the following in relation to a relevant work in its collection which is an orphan work—
(a) making the orphan work available to the public; or
(b) reproducing the orphan work for the purposes of digitisation, making available, indexing, cataloguing, preservation or restoration.
(3) A relevant body does not commit an offence under section 107 or 198 by using an orphan work in a way which, by virtue of this Schedule, does not infringe copyright or the rights conferred by Chapter 2 of Part 2.
(4) This paragraph is subject to paragraph 6 (further requirements for use of orphan works).

Meaning of "relevant body", "relevant work" and "rightholder"

2.(1)In this Schedule "relevant body" means—
(a) a publicly accessible library, educational establishment or museum,
(b) an archive,
(c) a film or audio heritage institution, or
(d) a public service broadcasting organisation.
(2) Subject to sub-paragraph (4), in this Schedule "relevant work" means a work to which sub-paragraph (3) applies which is—
(a) a work in the form of a book, journal, newspaper, magazine or other writing which is contained in the collection of a publicly accessible library, educational establishment or museum, an archive or a film or audio heritage institution;
(b) a cinematographic or audiovisual work or a sound recording which is contained in the collection of a publicly accessible library, educational establishment or museum, an archive or a film or audio heritage institution; or
(c) a cinematographic or audiovisual work or a sound recording which was commissioned for exclusive exploitation by, or produced by, one or more public service broadcasting organisations on or before 31 December 2002 and is contained in the archives of that organisation or one or more of those organisations.
(3) This sub-paragraph applies to a work if—
(a) it is protected by copyright or rights conferred by Chapter 2 of Part 2, and
(b) the first publication or first broadcast of the work was in a member State.
(4) In this Schedule "relevant work" also includes a work listed in any of paragraphs (a) to (c) of sub-paragraph (2) which—
(a) is protected by copyright or rights conferred by Chapter 2 of Part 2, and
(b) has never been published or broadcast, but
(c) has been made publicly accessible by a relevant body with the consent of the rightholders,
as long as it is reasonable to assume that the rightholders would not oppose the use of the work as mentioned in paragraph 1. (1) or (2).
(5) References in this Schedule to a relevant work include—
(a) a work that is embedded or incorporated in, or constitutes an integral part of, a relevant work, and
(b) a performance in relation to which rights are conferred by Chapter 2 of Part 2 and which is

embedded or incorporated in, or constitutes an integral part of, a relevant work.

(6) In this Schedule "rightholder" in relation to a relevant work means—

(a) an owner of the copyright in the work,

(b) a licensee under an exclusive licence in relation to the work,

(c) a person with rights under Chapter 2 of Part 2 in relation to a performance recorded by the work, or

(d) a licensee under an exclusive licence in relation to those rights.

(7) In the application of sub-paragraph (6) to a performance by virtue of sub-paragraph (5), the reference in sub-paragraph (6)(c) to a performance recorded by the work is to be read as a reference to the performance.

(8) In this paragraph "public service broadcasting organisation" includes a public service broadcaster within the meaning of section 264 of the Communications Act 2003.

Meaning of "orphan work"

3.(1)For the purposes of this Schedule a relevant work is an orphan work if—

(a) there is a single rightholder in the work and the rightholder has not been identified or located, or

(b) there is more than one rightholder in the work and none of the rightholders has been identified or located,

despite a diligent search for the rightholder or rightholders having been carried out and recorded in accordance with paragraph 5.

(2) Subject as follows, a relevant work with more than one rightholder is also an orphan work for the purposes of this Schedule if—

(a) one or more of the rightholders has been identified or located, and

(b) one or more of the rightholders has not been identified or located despite a diligent search for the rightholder or rightholders having been carried out and recorded in accordance with paragraph 5.

Mutual recognition of orphan work status

4. A relevant work which is designated as an orphan work in another member   State is an orphan work for the purposes of this Schedule.

Diligent searches

5.(1)For the purposes of establishing whether a relevant work is an orphan work, a relevant body must ensure that a diligent search is carried out in good faith in respect of the work by consulting the appropriate sources for the category of work in question.

(2) The relevant body must carry out the diligent search prior to the use of the relevant work.

(3) The sources that are appropriate for each category of relevant work must as a minimum include—

(a) the relevant databases maintained by the Office for Harmonization in the Internal Market; and

(b) where there is no record that the relevant work is an orphan work in the databases referred to in paragraph (a), the relevant sources listed in Part 2 of this Schedule for that category.

(4) The Comptroller-General of Patents, Designs and Trade Marks may issue guidance on the appropriate sources to be consulted under this paragraph for any particular category of work.

(5) Subject to sub-paragraphs (6) to (8), a search of the sources mentioned in sub-paragraph (3)(b) must be carried out in the member State in which the relevant work was first published or broadcast.

(6) If the relevant work is a cinematographic or audiovisual work and the producer of the work has

his or her headquarters or habitual residence in a member State, the search must be carried out in the member State of the headquarters or habitual residence.

(7) If the relevant work falls within paragraph 2. (4), the search must be carried out in the member State where the organisation that made the work publicly accessible with the consent of the rightholders is established.

(8) If there is evidence to suggest that relevant information on rightholders is to be found in other countries, a relevant body carrying out a search in accordance with sub-paragraph (3)(b) must also consult the sources of information available in those other countries.

(9) A relevant body that makes use of orphan works in accordance with this Schedule must maintain records of its diligent searches and must provide the following information to the Office for Harmonization in the Internal Market—

(a) the results of the diligent searches which the relevant body has carried out and which first established that a work is an orphan work;

(b) the use that the relevant body makes of the orphan works;

(c) any change, pursuant to paragraph 7, of the orphan work status of a relevant work that the relevant body has used and in respect of which the relevant body has been supplied with evidence by a rightholder in accordance with paragraph 7. (2); and

(d) the contact information for the relevant body.

Further requirements for use of orphan works

6. This Schedule does not prevent the use by a relevant body of an orphan work as mentioned in paragraph 1 from infringing copyright or the rights conferred by Chapter 2 of Part 2 if—

(a) the revenues generated in the course of the use of the orphan work are used otherwise than for the exclusive purpose of covering the costs of the relevant body in digitising orphan works and making them available to the public;

(b) the relevant body uses the orphan work in order to achieve aims which are not related to its public-interest mission (and the aims which are to be treated as related to its public interest mission include, in particular, the preservation of, the restoration of, and the provision of cultural and educational access to, works contained in its collection);

(c) any rightholder who has been identified or located has, in relation to the rightholder's rights, not authorised the relevant body's use of the orphan work as mentioned in paragraph 1; or

(d) the relevant body fails, in the course of the permitted use of the orphan work, to acknowledge the name of any author of or other rightholder in the work who has been identified.

End of orphan work status

7.(1) This paragraph applies to a rightholder who has not been identified or located in relation to a relevant work.

(2) A rightholder may put an end to the orphan work status of a relevant work by providing evidence of his or her ownership of the rights to the Office for Harmonization in the Internal Market or to the relevant body which carried out the diligent search which first established that the relevant work is an orphan work.

(3) A relevant body that is using or has used the orphan work must within a reasonable period provide the rightholder with fair compensation for that body's use of the relevant work together with information on how the fair compensation has been calculated.

(4) If a relevant body and the rightholder cannot agree on the amount of compensation payable, either of them may apply to the Copyright Tribunal to determine the amount.

PART 2 SOURCES TO BE SEARCHED DURING DILIGENT SEARCH

Category of relevant work | Sources to be searched |
legal deposit, library catalogues and authority files maintained by libraries and other institutions;
the publishers' and authors' associations in the country in question;
 existing databases and registries, WATCH (Writers, Artists and their Copyright Holders), the ISBN (International Standard Book Number) and databases listing books in print;
the databases of the relevant collecting societies, including reproduction rights organisations;
sources that integrate multiple databases and registries, including VIAF (Virtual International Authority Files) and ARROW (Accessible Registries of Rights Information and Orphan Works).
2. Newspapers, magazines, journals and periodicals
 the ISSN (International Standard Serial Number) for periodical publications;
indexes and catalogues from library holdings and collections;
legal deposit;
the publishers' associations and the authors' and journalists' associations in the country in question;
the databases of relevant collecting societies including reproduction rights organisations.
the sources referred to in paragraphs 1 and 2;
the databases of the relevant collecting societies, in particular for visual arts, and including reproduction rights organisations;
the databases of picture agencies, where applicable.
legal deposit;
the producers' associations in the country in question;
databases of film or audio heritage institutions and national libraries;
databases with relevant standards and identifiers such as ISAN (International Standard Audiovisual Number) for audiovisual material, ISWC (International Standard Music Work Code) for musical works and ISRC (International Standard Recording Code) for sound recordings;
the databases of the relevant collecting societies, in particular for authors, performers, sound recording producers and audiovisual producers;
credits and other information appearing on the work's packaging;
databases of other relevant associations representing a specific category of rightholders.
5. Relevant works which have not been published or broadcast | Those sources that are listed in paragraphs 1 to 4 above which are appropriate to a relevant work which is unpublished.] |

Schedule 2. Regulation of licensing bodies

Amendments (Textual)
F1. Sch. A1 inserted (25.4.2013) by Enterprise and Regulatory Reform Act 2013 (c. 24), s. 103. (1), Sch. 22 para. 1

Codes of practice

1. (1)The Secretary of State may by regulations make provision for a licensing body to be required to adopt a code of practice that complies with criteria specified in the regulations.
(2) The regulations may provide that, if a licensing body fails to adopt such a code of practice, any code of practice that is approved for the purposes of that licensing body by the Secretary of State, or by a person designated by the Secretary of State under the regulations, has effect as a code of practice adopted by the body.
(3) The regulations must provide that a code is not to be approved for the purposes of provision under sub-paragraph (2) unless it complies with criteria specified in the regulations.
2. Regulations under paragraph 1 may make provision as to conditions that are to be satisfied, and

procedures that are to be followed—
(a) before a licensing body is required to adopt a code of practice as described in paragraph 1. (1);
(b) before a code of practice has effect as one adopted by a licensing body as described in paragraph 1. (2).

Licensing code ombudsman

3. (1)The Secretary of State may by regulations make provision—
(a) for the appointment of a person (the "licensing code ombudsman") to investigate and determine disputes about a licensing body's compliance with its code of practice;
(b) for the reference of disputes to the licensing code ombudsman;
(c) for the investigation and determination of a dispute so referred.
(2) Provision made under this paragraph may in particular include provision—
(a) about eligibility for appointment as the licensing code ombudsman;
(b) about the disputes to be referred to the licensing code ombudsman;
(c) requiring any person to provide information, documents or assistance to the licensing code ombudsman for the purposes of an investigation or determination;
(d) requiring a licensing body to comply with a determination of the licensing code ombudsman;
(e) about the payment of expenses and allowances to the licensing code ombudsman.

Code reviewer

4. (1)The Secretary of State may by regulations make provision—
(a) for the appointment by the Secretary of State of a person (the "code reviewer") to review and report to the Secretary of State on—
(i) the codes of practice adopted by licensing bodies, and
(ii) compliance with the codes of practice;
(b) for the carrying out of a review and the making of a report by that person.
(2) The regulations must provide for the Secretary of State, before appointing a person as the code reviewer, to consult persons whom the Secretary of State considers represent the interests of licensing bodies, licensees, members of licensing bodies, and the Intellectual Property Office.
(3) The regulations may, in particular, make provision—
(a) requiring any person to provide information, documents or assistance to the code reviewer for the purposes of a review or report;
(b) about the payment of expenses and allowances to the code reviewer.
(4) In this paragraph " member ", in relation to a licensing body, means a person on whose behalf the body is authorised to negotiate or grant licences.

Sanctions

5. (1)The Secretary of State may by regulations provide for the consequences of a failure by a licensing body to comply with—
(a) a requirement to adopt a code of practice under provision within paragraph 1. (1);
(b) a code of practice that has been adopted by the body in accordance with a requirement under provision within paragraph 1. (1), or that has effect as one adopted by the body under provision within paragraph 1. (2);
(c) a requirement imposed on the body under any other provision made under this Schedule;
(d) an authorisation under regulations under section 116. A or 116. B;
(e) a requirement imposed by regulations under section 116. A or 116. B;
(f) an authorisation under regulations under paragraph 1. A or 1. B of Schedule 2. A;
(g) a requirement imposed by regulations under paragraph 1. A or 1. B of that Schedule.

(2) The regulations may in particular provide for—

(a) the imposition of financial penalties or other sanctions;

(b) the imposition of sanctions on a director, manager or similar officer of a licensing body or, where the body's affairs are managed by its members, on a member.

(3) The regulations must include provision—

(a) for determining whether there has been a failure to comply with a requirement or code of practice for the purposes of any provision made under sub-paragraph (1);

(b) for determining any sanction that may be imposed in respect of the failure to comply;

(c) for an appeal against a determination within paragraph (a) or (b).

(4) A financial penalty imposed under sub-paragraph (2) must not be greater than £50,000.

(5) The regulations may provide for a determination within sub-paragraph (3)(a) or (3)(b) to be made by the Secretary of State or by a person designated by the Secretary of State under the regulations.

(6) The regulations may make provision for requiring a person to give the person by whom a determination within sub-paragraph (3)(a) falls to be made (the "adjudicator") any information that the adjudicator reasonably requires for the purpose of making that determination.

Fees

6. (1)The Secretary of State may by regulations require a licensing body to which regulations under any other paragraph of this Schedule apply to pay fees to the Secretary of State.

(2) The aggregate amount of fees payable under the regulations must not be more than the cost to the Secretary of State of administering the operation of regulations under this Schedule.

General

7. (1)The power to make regulations under this Schedule includes in particular power—

(a) to make incidental, supplementary or consequential provision, including provision extending or restricting the jurisdiction of the Copyright Tribunal or conferring powers on it;

(b) to make provision for bodies of a particular description, or carrying out activities of a particular description, not to be treated as licensing bodies for the purposes of requirements imposed under regulations under this Schedule;

(c) to make provision that applies only in respect of licensing bodies of a particular description, or only in respect of activities of a particular description;

(d) otherwise to make different provision for different purposes.

(2) Regulations under a paragraph of this Schedule may amend Part 1 or Part 2, or any other enactment or subordinate legislation passed or made before the paragraph in question comes into force, for the purpose of making consequential provision or extending or restricting the jurisdiction of the Copyright Tribunal or conferring powers on it.

(3) The power to make regulations is exercisable by statutory instrument.

(4) A statutory instrument containing regulations may not be made unless a draft of the instrument has been laid before and approved by a resolution of each House of Parliament.

8. References in this Schedule to a licensing body are to a body that is a licensing body for the purposes of Chapter 7 of Part 1 or Chapter 2 of Part 2, and references to licensees are to be construed accordingly.]

Schedule 3. Copyright: transitional provisions and savings

Section 170.

Modifications etc. (not altering text)

C1. Sch. 1 applied (with modifications) by S.I. 1989/1293, art. 4. (4)(5)(6)

C2. Sch. 1 applied (with modifications)(4.5.1993) by S.I. 1993/942, arts. 2. (3), 5, Sch. 4 (with art. 6)

C3. Sch. 1 applied (4.5.1993) by S.I. 1993/942, arts.4, 5, Sch. 4 (with art. 6)

C4. Sch. 1 applied (with modifications) (22.7.1999) by S.I. 1999/1751, arts. 2. (3), 3, 4. (3)-(5), 6, Sch. 5 (subject to arts. 5, 7) (as amended (22.4.2003) by S.I. 2003/774, arts. 2-5)

C5. Sch. 1 extended in part (with modifications) by The Copyright (Bermuda) Order 2003 (S.I. 2003/1517), art. 2, Sch. (the amendment coming into force in accordance with art. 1 of the amending S.I.)

C6. Sch. 1 extended in part (with modifications) by The Copyright (Gibraltar) Order 2005 (S.I. 2005/853), art. 2, Sch. (the amendment coming into force in accordance with art. 1 of the amending S.I.)

Introductory

1. (1)In this Schedule—

"the 1911 Act" means the M1. Copyright Act 1911,

"the 1956 Act" means the M2. Copyright Act 1956, and

"the new copyright provisions" means the provisions of this Act relating to copyright, that is, Part I (including this Schedule) and Schedules 3, 7 and 8 so far as they make amendments or repeals consequential on the provisions of Part I.

(2) References in this Schedule to "commencement", without more, are to the date on which the new copyright provisions come into force.

(3) References in this Schedule to "existing works" are to works made before commencement; and for this purpose a work of which the making extended over a period shall be taken to have been made when its making was completed.

Marginal Citations

M11911 c. 46.

M21956 c. 74.

2. (1)In relation to the 1956 Act, references in this Schedule to a work include any work or other subject-matter within the meaning of that Act.

(2) In relation to the 1911 Act—

(a) references in this Schedule to copyright include the right conferred by section 24 of that Act in substitution for a right subsisting immediately before the commencement of that Act;

(b) references in this Schedule to copyright in a sound recording are to the copyright under that Act in records embodying the recording; and

(c) references in this Schedule to copyright in a film are to any copyright under that Act in the film (so far as it constituted a dramatic work for the purposes of that Act) or in photographs forming part of the film.

General principles: continuity of the law

3. The new copyright provisions apply in relation to things existing at commencement as they apply in relation to things coming into existence after commencement, subject to any express provision to the contrary.

4. (1)The provisions of this paragraph have effect for securing the continuity of the law so far as the new copyright provisions re-enact (with or without modification) earlier provisions.

(2) A reference in an enactment, instrument or other document to copyright, or to a work or other subject-matter in which copyright subsists, which apart from this Act would be construed as referring to copyright under the 1956 Act shall be construed, so far as may be required for

continuing its effect, as being, or as the case may require, including, a reference to copyright under this Act or to works in which copyright subsists under this Act.

(3) Anything done (including subordinate legislation made), or having effect as done, under or for the purposes of a provision repealed by this Act has effect as if done under or for the purposes of the corresponding provision of the new copyright provisions.

(4) References (expressed or implied) in this Act or any other enactment, instrument or document to any of the new copyright provisions shall, so far as the context permits, be construed as including, in relation to times, circumstances and purposes before commencement, a reference to corresponding earlier provisions.

(5) A reference (express or implied) in an enactment, instrument or other document to a provision repealed by this Act shall be construed, so far as may be required for continuing its effect, as a reference to the corresponding provision of this Act.

(6) The provisions of this paragraph have effect subject to any specific transitional provision or saving and to any express amendment made by this Act.

Subsistence of copyright

5. (1)Copyright subsists in an existing work after commencement only if copyright subsisted in it immediately before commencement.

(2) Sub-paragraph (1) does not prevent an existing work qualifying for copyright protection after commencement—

(a) under section 155 (qualification by virtue of first publication), F1...

(b) by virtue of an Order under section 159 (application of Part I to countries to which it does not extend) [F2, or]

[F3. (c)where the work is an artistic work in which copyright subsists as a result of the disapplication of paragraph 6. (1) by paragraph 6. (1. A)]

Amendments (Textual)

F1. Word in Sch. 1 para. 5. (2)(a) omitted (6.4.2017) by virtue of The Copyright (Amendment) Regulations 2016 (S.I. 2016/1210), regs. 1, 2. (2)(a)

F2. Word in Sch. 1 para. 5. (2)(b) substituted (6.4.2017) by The Copyright (Amendment) Regulations 2016 (S.I. 2016/1210), regs. 1, 2. (2)(b)

F3. Sch. 1 para. 5. (2)(c) inserted (6.4.2017) by The Copyright (Amendment) Regulations 2016 (S.I. 2016/1210), regs. 1, 2. (2)(c)

6. (1)Copyright shall not subsist by virtue of this Act in an artistic work made before 1st June 1957 which at the time when the work was made constituted a design capable of registration under the M3. Registered Designs Act 1949 or under the enactments repealed by that Act, and was used, or intended to be used, as a model or pattern to be multiplied by an industrial process.

[F4. (1. A)Sub-paragraph (1) does not apply to an artistic work which was on 1st July 1995 protected under the law of another EEA state relating to copyright or related rights.]

(2) For this purpose a design shall be deemed to be used as a model or pattern to be multiplied by any industrial process—

(a) when the design is reproduced or is intended to be reproduced on more than 50 single articles, unless all the articles in which the design is reproduced or is intended to be reproduced together form only a single set of articles as defined in section 44. (1) of the Registered Designs Act 1949, or

(b) when the design is to be applied to—

(i) printed paper hangings,

(ii) carpets, floor cloths or oil cloths, manufactured or sold in lengths or pieces,

(iii) textile piece goods, or textile goods manufactured or sold in lengths or pieces, or

(iv) lace, not made by hand.

Amendments (Textual)

F4. Sch. 1 para. 6. (1. A) inserted (6.4.2017) by The Copyright (Amendment) Regulations 2016

(S.I. 2016/1210), regs. 1, 2. (3)
Marginal Citations
M31949 c. 88.
7. (1)No copyright subsists in a film, as such, made before 1st June 1957.

(2) Where a film made before that date was an original dramatic work within the meaning of the 1911 Act, the new copyright provisions have effect in relation to the film as if it was an original dramatic work within the meaning of Part I.

(3) The new copyright provisions have effect in relation to photographs forming part of a film made before 1st June 1957 as they have effect in relation to photographs not forming part of a film.

8. (1)A film sound-track to which section 13. (9) of the 1956 Act applied before commencement (film to be taken to include sounds in associated sound-track) shall be treated for the purposes of the new copyright provisions not as part of the film, but as a sound recording.

(2) However—

(a) copyright subsists in the sound recording only if copyright subsisted in the film immediately before commencement, and it continues to subsist until copyright in the film expires;

(b) the author and first owner of copyright in the film shall be treated as having been author and first owner of the copyright in the sound recording; and

(c) anything done before commencement under or in relation to the copyright in the film continues to have effect in relation to the sound recording as in relation to the film.

[F59. No copyright subsists in—

(a) a wireless broadcast made before 1st June 1957, or

(b) a broadcast by cable made before 1st January 1985;

and any such broadcast shall be disregarded for the purposes of section 14. (5) (duration of copyright in repeats).]

Amendments (Textual)
F5. Sch. 1 para. 9 substituted (31.10.2003) by The Copyright and Related Rights Regulations 2003 (S.I. 2003/2498), reg, 2. (1), {Sch. 1 para. 16. (a)} (with regs. 31-40)

Authorship of work

10. The question who was the author of an existing work shall be determined in accordance with the new copyright provisions for the purposes of the rights conferred by Chapter IV of Part I (moral rights), and for all other purposes shall be determined in accordance with the law in force at the time the work was made.

First ownership of copyright

11. (1)The question who was first owner of copyright in an existing work shall be determined in accordance with the law in force at the time the work was made.

(2) Where before commencement a person commissioned the making of a work in circumstances falling within—

(a) section 4. (3) of the 1956 Act or paragraph (a) of the proviso to section 5. (1) of the 1911 Act (photographs, portraits and engravings), or

(b) the proviso to section 12. (4) of the 1956 Act (sound recordings),

those provisions apply to determine first ownership of copyright in any work made in pursuance of the commission after commencement.

Duration of copyright in existing works

12. (1)The following provisions have effect with respect to the duration of copyright in existing

works.

The question which provision applies to a work shall be determined by reference to the facts immediately before commencement; and expressions used in this paragraph which were defined for the purposes of the 1956 Act have the same meaning as in that Act.

(2) Copyright in the following descriptions of work continues to subsist until the date on which it would have expired under the 1956 Act—

(a) literary, dramatic or musical works in relation to which the period of 50 years mentioned in the proviso to section 2. (3) of the 1956 Act (duration of copyright in works made available to the public after the death of the author) has begun to run;

(b) engravings in relation to which the period of 50 years mentioned in the proviso to section 3. (4) of the 1956 Act (duration of copyright in works published after the death of the author) has begun to run;

(c) published photographs and photographs taken before 1st June 1957;

(d) published sound recordings and sound recordings made before 1st June 1957;

(e) published films and films falling within section 13. (3)(a) of the 1956 Act (films registered under former enactments relating to registration of films).

(3) Copyright in anonymous or pseudonymous literary, dramatic, musical or artistic works (other than photographs) continues to subsist—

(a) if the work is published, until the date on which it would have expired in accordance with the 1956 Act, and

(b) if the work is unpublished, until the end of the period of 50 years from the end of the calendar year in which the new copyright provisions come into force or, if during that period the work is first made available to the public within the meaning of [F6section 12. (3)] (duration of copyright in works of unknown authorship), the date on which copyright expires in accordance with that provision;

unless, in any case, the identity of the author becomes known before that date, in which case [F7section 12. (2)] applies (general rule: life of the author [F8plus 70]).

(4) Copyright in the following descriptions of work continues to subsist until the end of the period of 50 years from the end of the calendar year in which the new copyright provisions come into force—

(a) literary, dramatic and musical works of which the author has died and in relation to which none of the acts mentioned in paragraphs (a) to (e) of the proviso to section 2. (3) of the 1956 Act has been done;

(b) unpublished engravings of which the author has died;

(c) unpublished photographs taken on or after 1st June 1957.

(5) Copyright in the following descriptions of work continues to subsist until the end of the period of 50 years from the end of the calendar year in which the new copyright provisions come into force—

(a) unpublished sound recordings made on or after 1st June 1957;

(b) films not falling within sub-paragraph (2)(e) above,

unless the recording or film is published before the end of that period in which case copyright in it shall continue until the end of the period of 50 years from the end of the calendar year in which the recording or film is published.

(6) Copyright in any other description of existing work continues to subsist until the date on which copyright in that description of work expires in accordance with sections 12 to 15 of this Act.

(7) The above provisions do not apply to works subject to Crown or Parliamentary copyright (see paragraphs 41 to 43 below).

Amendments (Textual)

F6. Words in Sch. 1 para. 12. (3)(b) substituted (31.10.2003) by The Copyright and Related Rights Regulations 2003 (S.I. 2003/2498), reg. 2. (1), Sch. 1 para. 18. (3)(a) (with regs. 31-40)

F7. Words in Sch. 1para. 12. (3) substituted (31.10.2003) by The Copyright and Related Rights Regulations 2003 (S.I.2003/2498), reg. 2. (1), Sch. 1 para. 18. (3)(b) (with regs. 31-40)

F8. Words in Sch. 1 para. 12. (3) substituted (31.10.2003) by The Copyright and Related Rights

Regulations 2003 (S.I. 2003/2498), reg. 2. (1), Sch. 1 para. 18. (3)(c) (with regs. 31-40)

Perpetual copyright under the Copyright Act 1775.

13. (1)The rights conferred on universities and colleges by the M4. Copyright Act 1775 shall continue to subsist until the end of the period of 50 years from the end of the calendar year in which the new copyright provisions come into force and shall then expire.

(2) The provisions of the following Chapters of Part I—

Chapter III (acts permitted in relation to copyright works),

Chapter VI (remedies for infringement),

Chapter VII (provisions with respect to copyright licensing), and

Chapter VIII (the Copyright Tribunal),

apply in relation to those rights as they apply in relation to copyright under this Act.

Marginal Citations

M41775 c. 53.

Acts infringing copyright

14. (1)The provisions of Chapters II and III of Part I as to the acts constituting an infringement of copyright apply only in relation to acts done after commencement; the provisions of the 1956 Act continue to apply in relation to acts done before commencement.

(2) So much of section 18. (2) as extends the restricted act of issuing copies to the public to include the rental to the public of copies of sound recordings, films or computer programs does not apply in relation to a copy of a sound recording, film or computer program acquired by any person before commencement for the purpose of renting it to the public.

(3) For the purposes of section 27 (meaning of "infringing copy") the question whether the making of an article constituted an infringement of copyright, or would have done if the article had been made in the United Kingdom, shall be determined—

(a) in relation to an article made on or after 1st June 1957 and before commencement, by reference to the 1956 Act, and

(b) in relation to an article made before 1st June 1957, by reference to the 1911 Act.

(4) For the purposes of the application of sections 31. (2), 51. (2) and 62. (3) (subsequent exploitation of things whose making was, by virtue of an earlier provision of the section, not an infringement of copyright) to things made before commencement, it shall be assumed that the new copyright provisions were in force at all material times.

(5) Section 55 (articles for producing material in a particular typeface) applies where articles have been marketed as mentioned in subsection (1) before commencement with the substitution for the period mentioned in subsection (3) of the period of 25 years from the end of the calendar year in which the new copyright provisions come into force.

(6) Section 56 (transfer of copies, adaptations, &c. of work in electronic form) does not apply in relation to a copy purchased before commencement.

(7) In section 65 (reconstruction of buildings) the reference to the owner of the copyright in the drawings or plans is, in relation to buildings constructed before commencement, to the person who at the time of the construction was the owner of the copyright in the drawings or plans under the 1956 Act, the 1911 Act or any enactment repealed by the 1911 Act.

15. (1)Section 57 (anonymous or pseudonymous works: acts permitted on assumptions as to expiry of copyright or death of author) has effect in relation to existing works subject to the following provisions.

(2) Subsection (1)(b)(i) (assumption as to expiry of copyright) does not apply in relation to—

(a) photographs, or

(b) the rights mentioned in paragraph 13 above (rights conferred by the M5. Copyright Act 1775).

(3) F9. . . . .

Amendments (Textual)
F9. Sch. 1 para. 15. (3) repealed (31.10.2003) by The Copyright and Related Rights Regulations 2003 (S.I. 2003/2498), reg. 2, Sch. 1 para. 16. (b), Sch. 2 (with regs. 31-40)
Marginal Citations
M51775 c. 53.

16. The following provisions of section 7 of the 1956 Act continue to apply in relation to existing works—

(a) subsection (6) (copying of unpublished works from manuscript or copy in library, museum or other institution);

(b) subsection (7) (publication of work containing material to which subsection (6) applies), except paragraph (a) (duty to give notice of intended publication);

(c) subsection (8) (subsequent broadcasting, performance, &c. of material published in accordance with subsection (7));

and subsection (9)(d) (illustrations) continues to apply for the purposes of those provisions.

17. Where in the case of a dramatic or musical work made before 1st July 1912, the right conferred by the 1911 Act did not include the sole right to perform the work in public, the acts restricted by the copyright shall be treated as not including—

(a) performing the work in public,

[F10. (b)communicating the work to the public, or]

(c) doing any of the above in relation to an adaptation of the work;

and where the right conferred by the 1911 Act consisted only of the sole right to perform the work in public, the acts restricted by the copyright shall be treated as consisting only of those acts.

Amendments (Textual)
F10. Sch. 1 para. 17. (b) substituted (31.10.2003) by The Copyright and Related Rights Regulations 2003 (S.I. 2003/2498), reg. 2. (1), Sch. 1 para. 4. (6) (with regs. 31-40)

18. Where a work made before 1st July 1912 consists of an essay, article or portion forming part of and first published in a review, magazine or other periodical or work of a like nature, the copyright is subject to any right of publishing the essay, article, or portion in a separate form to which the author was entitled at the commencement of the 1911 Act, or would if that Act had not been passed, have become entitled under section 18 of the M6. Copyright Act 1842.

Marginal Citations
M61842 c. 45.

Designs

19. (1)Section 51 (exclusion of copyright protection in relation to works recorded or embodied in design document or models) does not apply for ten years after commencement in relation to a design recorded or embodied in a design document or model before commencement.

(2) During those ten years the following provisions of Part III (design right) apply to any relevant copyright as in relation to design right—

(a) sections 237 to 239 (availability of licences of right), and

(b) sections 247 and 248 (application to comptroller to settle terms of licence of right).

(3) In section 237 as it applies by virtue of this paragraph, for the reference in subsection (1) to the last five years of the design right term there shall be substituted a reference to the last five years of the period of ten years referred to in sub-paragraph (1) above, or to so much of those last five years during which copyright subsists.

(4) In section 239 as it applies by virtue of this paragraph, for the reference in subsection (1)(b) to section 230 there shall be substituted a reference to section 99.

(5) Where a licence of right is available by virtue of this paragraph, a person to whom a licence was granted before commencement may apply to the comptroller for an order adjusting the terms of that licence.

(6) The provisions of sections 249 and 250 (appeals and rules) apply in relation to proceedings

brought under or by virtue of this paragraph as to proceedings under Part III.

(7) A licence granted by virtue of this paragraph shall relate only to acts which would be permitted by section 51 if the design document or model had been made after commencement.

(8) Section 100 (right to seize infringing copies, &c.) does not apply during the period of ten years referred to in sub-paragraph (1) in relation to anything to which it would not apply if the design in question had been first recorded or embodied in a design document or model after commencement.

(9) Nothing in this paragraph affects the operation of any rule of law preventing or restricting the enforcement of copyright in relation to a design.

Modifications etc. (not altering text)

C7. Sch. 1 para. 19. (1) excluded by S.I. 1989/1100, art. 10. (2)

C8. Sch. 1 para. 19. (2) modified by S.I. 1989/1100, art. 10. (3)

C9. Sch. 1 para. 19. (3) excluded by S.I. 1989/1100, art. 10. (3)

F1120. . . . .

Amendments (Textual)

F11. Sch. 1 para. 20 omitted (28.7.2016) by virtue of Enterprise and Regulatory Reform Act 2013 (c. 24), ss. 74. (3)(b), 103. (3); S.I. 2016/593, arts. 2. (1), 3 (with arts. 4, 5)

Abolition of statutory recording licence

21. Section 8 of the 1956 Act (statutory licence to copy records sold by retail) continues to apply where notice under subsection (1)(b) of that section was given before the repeal of that section by this Act, but only in respect of the making of records—

(a) within one year of the repeal coming into force, and

(b) up to the number stated in the notice as intended to be sold.

Moral rights

22. (1)No act done before commencement is actionable by virtue of any provision of Chapter IV of Part I (moral rights).

(2) Section 43 of the 1956 Act (false attribution of authorship) continues to apply in relation to acts done before commencement.

23. (1)The following provisions have effect with respect to the rights conferred by—

(a) section 77 (right to be identified as author or director), and

(b) section 80 (right to object to derogatory treatment of work).

(2) The rights do not apply—

(a) in relation to a literary, dramatic, musical and artistic work of which the author died before commencement; or

(b) in relation to a film made before commencement.

(3) The rights in relation to an existing literary, dramatic, musical or artistic work do not apply—

(a) where copyright first vested in the author, to anything which by virtue of an assignment of copyright made or licence granted before commencement may be done without infringing copyright;

(b) where copyright first vested in a person other than the author, to anything done by or with the licence of the copyright owner.

(4) The rights do not apply to anything done in relation to a record made in pursuance of section 8 of the 1956 Act (statutory recording licence).

24. The right conferred by section 85 (right to privacy of certain photographs and films) does not apply to photographs taken or films made before commencement.

Assignments and licences

25. (1)Any document made or event occurring before commencement which had any operation—
(a) affecting the ownership of the copyright in an existing work, or
(b) creating, transferring or terminating an interest, right or licence in respect of the copyright in an existing work,
has the corresponding operation in relation to copyright in the work under this Act.
(2) Expressions used in such a document shall be construed in accordance with their effect immediately before commencement.
26. (1)Section 91. (1) of this Act (assignment of future copyright: statutory vesting of legal interest on copyright coming into existence) does not apply in relation to an agreement made before 1st June 1957.
(2) The repeal by this Act of section 37. (2) of the 1956 Act (assignment of future copyright: devolution of right where assignee dies before copyright comes into existence) does not affect the operation of that provision in relation to an agreement made before commencement.
27. (1)Where the author of a literary, dramatic, musical or artistic work was the first owner of the copyright in it, no assignment of the copyright and no grant of any interest in it, made by him (otherwise than by will) after the passing of the 1911 Act and before 1st June 1957, shall be operative to vest in the assignee or grantee any rights with respect to the copyright in the work beyond the expiration of 25 years from the death of the author.
(2) The reversionary interest in the copyright expectant on the termination of that period may after commencement be assigned by the author during his life but in the absence of any assignment shall, on his death, devolve on his legal personal representatives as part of his estate.
(3) Nothing in this paragraph affects—
(a) an assignment of the reversionary interest by a person to whom it has been assigned,
(b) an assignment of the reversionary interest after the death of the author by his personal representatives or any person becoming entitled to it, or
(c) any assignment of the copyright after the reversionary interest has fallen in.
(4) Nothing in this paragraph applies to the assignment of the copyright in a collective work or a licence to publish a work or part of a work as part of a collective work.
(5) In sub-paragraph (4) "collective work" means—
(a) any encyclopaedia, dictionary, yearbook, or similar work;
(b) a newspaper, review, magazine, or similar periodical; and
(c) any work written in distinct parts by different authors, or in which works or parts of works of different authors are incorporated.
28. (1)This paragraph applies where copyright subsists in a literary, dramatic, musical or artistic work made before 1st July 1912 in relation to which the author, before the commencement of the 1911 Act, made such an assignment or grant as was mentioned in paragraph (a) of the proviso to section 24. (1) of that Act (assignment or grant of copyright or performing right for full term of the right under the previous law).
(2) If before commencement any event has occurred or notice has been given which by virtue of paragraph 38 of Schedule 7 to the 1956 Act had any operation in relation to copyright in the work under that Act, the event or notice has the corresponding operation in relation to copyright under this Act.
(3) Any right which immediately before commencement would by virtue of paragraph 38. (3) of that Schedule have been exercisable in relation to the work, or copyright in it, is exercisable in relation to the work or copyright in it under this Act.
(4) If in accordance with paragraph 38. (4) of that Schedule copyright would, on a date after the commencement of the 1956 Act, have reverted to the author or his personal representatives and that date falls after the commencement of the new copyright provisions—
(a) the copyright in the work shall revert to the author or his personal representatives, as the case may be, and
(b) any interest of any other person in the copyright which subsists on that date by virtue of any document made before the commencement of the 1911 Act shall thereupon determine.

29. Section 92. (2) of this Act (rights of exclusive licensee against successors in title of person granting licence) does not apply in relation to an exclusive licence granted before commencement.

Bequests

30. (1)Section 93 of this Act (copyright to pass under will with original document or other material thing embodying unpublished work)—
(a) does not apply where the testator died before 1st June 1957, and
(b) where the testator died on or after that date and before commencement, applies only in relation to an original document embodying a work.
(2) In the case of an author who died before 1st June 1957, the ownership after his death of a manuscript of his, where such ownership has been acquired under a testamentary disposition made by him and the manuscript is of a work which has not been published or performed in public, is prima facie proof of the copyright being with the owner of the manuscript.

Remedies for infringement

31. (1)Sections 96 and 97 of this Act (remedies for infringement) apply only in relation to an infringement of copyright committed after commencement; section 17 of the 1956 Act continues to apply in relation to infringements committed before commencement.
(2) Sections 99 and 100 of this Act (delivery up or seizure of infringing copies, &c.) apply to infringing copies and other articles made before or after commencement; section 18 of the 1956 Act, and section 7 of the 1911 Act, (conversion damages, &c.), do not apply after commencement except for the purposes of proceedings begun before commencement.
(3) Sections 101 to 102 of this Act (rights and remedies of exclusive licensee) apply where sections 96 to 100 of this Act apply; section 19 of the 1956 Act continues to apply where section 17 or 18 of that Act applies.
(4) Sections 104 to 106 of this Act (presumptions) apply only in proceedings brought by virtue of this Act; section 20 of the 1956 Act continues to apply in proceedings brought by virtue of that Act.
32. Sections 101 and 102 of this Act (rights and remedies of exclusive licensee) do not apply to a licence granted before 1st June 1957.
33. (1)The provisions of section 107 of this Act (criminal liability for making or dealing with infringing articles, &c.) apply only in relation to acts done after commencement; section 21 of the 1956 Act (penalties and summary proceedings in respect of dealings which infringe copyright) continues to apply in relation to acts done before commencement.
(2) Section 109 of this Act (search warrants) applies in relation to offences committed before commencement in relation to which section 21. A or 21. B of the 1956 Act applied; sections 21. A and 21. B continue to apply in relation to warrants issued before commencement.

Copyright Tribunal: proceedings pending on commencement

34. (1)The Lord Chancellor may, after consultation with the Lord Advocate, by rules make such provision as he considers necessary or expedient with respect to proceedings pending under Part IV of the 1956 Act immediately before commencement.
(2) Rules under this paragraph shall be made by statutory instrument which shall be subject to annulment in pursuance of a resolution of either House of Parliament.

Qualification for copyright protection

35. Every work in which copyright subsisted under the 1956 Act immediately before

commencement shall be deemed to satisfy the requirements of Part I of this Act as to qualification for copyright protection.

Dependent territories

36. (1)The 1911 Act shall remain in force as part of the law of any dependent territory in which it was in force immediately before commencement until—

(a) the new copyright provisions come into force in that territory by virtue of an Order under section 157 of this Act (power to extend new copyright provisions), or

(b) in the case of any of the Channel Islands, the Act is repealed by Order under sub-paragraph (3) below.

(2) An Order in Council in force immediately before commencement which extends to any dependent territory any provisions of the 1956 Act shall remain in force as part of the law of that territory until—

(a) the new copyright provisions come into force in that territory by virtue of an Order under section 157 of this Act (power to extend new copyright provisions), or

(b) in the case of the Isle of Man, the Order is revoked by Order under sub-paragraph (3) below;

and while it remains in force such an Order may be varied under the provisions of the 1956 Act under which it was made.

(3) If it appears to Her Majesty that provision with respect to copyright has been made in the law of any of the Channel Islands or the Isle of Man otherwise than by extending the provisions of Part I of this Act, Her Majesty may by Order in Council repeal the 1911 Act as it has effect as part of the law of that territory or, as the case may be, revoke the Order extending the 1956 Act there.

(4) A dependent territory in which the 1911 or 1956 Act remains in force shall be treated, in the law of the countries to which Part I extends, as a country to which that Part extends; and those countries shall be treated in the law of such a territory as countries to which the 1911 Act or, as the case may be, the 1956 Act extends.

(5) If a country in which the 1911 or 1956 Act is in force ceases to be a colony of the United Kingdom, section 158 of this Act (consequences of country ceasing to be colony) applies with the substitution for the reference in subsection (3)(b) to the provisions of Part I of this Act of a reference to the provisions of the 1911 or 1956 Act, as the case may be.

(6) In this paragraph "dependent territory" means any of the Channel Islands, the Isle of Man or any colony.

37. (1)This paragraph applies to a country which immediately before commencement was not a dependent territory within the meaning of paragraph 36 above but—

(a) was a country to which the 1956 Act extended, or

(b) was treated as such a country by virtue of paragraph 39. (2) of Schedule 7 to that Act (countries to which the 1911 Act extended or was treated as extending);

and Her Majesty may by Order in Council conclusively declare for the purposes of this paragraph whether a country was such a country or was so treated.

(2) A country to which this paragraph applies shall be treated as a country to which Part I extends for the purposes of sections 154 to 156 (qualification for copyright protection) until—

(a) an Order in Council is made in respect of that country under section 159 (application of Part I to countries to which it does not extend), or

(b) an Order in Council is made declaring that it shall cease to be so treated by reason of the fact that the provisions of the 1956 Act or, as the case may be, the 1911 Act, which extended there as part of the law of that country have been repealed or amended.

(3) A statutory instrument containing an Order in Council under this paragraph shall be subject to annulment in pursuance of a resolution of either House of Parliament.

Territorial waters and the continental shelf

38. Section 161 of this Act (application of Part I to things done in territorial waters or the United Kingdom sector of the continental shelf) does not apply in relation to anything done before commencement.

British ships, aircraft and hovercraft

39. Section 162 (British ships, aircraft and hovercraft) does not apply in relation to anything done before commencement.

Crown copyright

40. (1)Section 163 of this Act (general provisions as to Crown copyright) applies to an existing work if—
(a) section 39 of the 1956 Act applied to the work immediately before commencement, and
(b) the work is not one to which section 164, 165 or 166 applies (copyright in Acts, Measures and Bills and Parliamentary copyright: see paragraphs 42 and 43 below).
(2) Section 163 (1)(b) (first ownership of copyright) has effect subject to any agreement entered into before commencement under section 39. (6) of the 1956 Act.
41. (1)The following provisions have effect with respect to the duration of copyright in existing works to which section 163 (Crown copyright) applies.
The question which provision applies to a work shall be determined by reference to the facts immediately before commencement; and expressions used in this paragraph which were defined for the purposes of the 1956 Act have the same meaning as in that Act.
(2) Copyright in the following descriptions of work continues to subsist until the date on which it would have expired in accordance with the 1956 Act—
(a) published literary, dramatic or musical works;
(b) artistic works other than engravings or photographs;
(c) published engravings;
(d) published photographs and photographs taken before 1st June 1957;
(e) published sound recordings and sound recordings made before 1st June 1957;
(f) published films and films falling within section 13. (3)(a) of the 1956 Act (films registered under former enactments relating to registration of films).
(3) Copyright in unpublished literary, dramatic or musical works continues to subsist until—
(a) the date on which copyright expires in accordance with section 163. (3), or
(b) the end of the period of 50 years from the end of the calendar year in which the new copyright provisions come into force,
whichever is the later.
(4) Copyright in the following descriptions of work continues to subsist until the end of the period of 50 years from the end of the calendar year in which the new copyright provisions come into force—
(a) unpublished engravings;
(b) unpublished photographs taken on or after 1st June 1957.
(5) Copyright in a film or sound recording not falling within sub-paragraph (2) above continues to subsist until the end of the period of 50 years from the end of the calendar year in which the new copyright provisions come into force, unless the film or recording is published before the end of that period, in which case copyright expires 50 years from the end of the calendar year in which it is published.
42. (1)Section 164 (copyright in Acts and Measures) applies to existing Acts of Parliament and Measures of the General Synod of the Church of England.
(2) References in that section to Measures of the General Synod of the Church of England include Church Assembly Measures.

Parliamentary copyright

43. (1)Section 165 of this Act (general provisions as to Parliamentary copyright) applies to existing unpublished literary, dramatic, musical or artistic works, but does not otherwise apply to existing works.

(2) Section 166 (copyright in Parliamentary Bills) does not apply—

(a) to a public Bill which was introduced into Parliament and published before commencement,

(b) to a private Bill of which a copy was deposited in either House before commencement, or

(c) to a personal Bill which was given a First Reading in the House of Lords before commencement.

Copyright vesting in certain international organisations

44. (1)Any work in which immediately before commencement copyright subsisted by virtue of section 33 of the 1956 Act shall be deemed to satisfy the requirements of section 168. (1); but otherwise section 168 does not apply to works made or, as the case may be, published before commencement.

(2) Copyright in any such work which is unpublished continues to subsist until the date on which it would have expired in accordance with the 1956 Act, or the end of the period of 50 years from the end of the calendar year in which the new copyright provisions come into force, whichever is the earlier.

Meaning of "publication"

45. Section 175. (3) (construction of building treated as equivalent to publication) applies only where the construction of the building began after commencement.

Meaning of "unauthorised"

46. For the purposes of the application of the definition in section 178 (minor definitions) of the expression "unauthorised" in relation to things done before commencement—

(a) paragraph (a) applies in relation to things done before 1st June 1957 as if the reference to the licence of the copyright owner were a reference to his consent or acquiescence;

(b) paragraph (b) applies with the substitution for the words from "or, in a case" to the end of the words "or any person lawfully claiming under him"; and

(c) paragraph (c) shall be disregarded.

Schedule 4. Rights in performances: permitted acts

Section 189.
Modifications etc. (not altering text)
C1 Sch. 2 continued (31.10.2003) by virtue of The Copyright and Related Rights Regulations 2003 (S.I. 2003/2498) , reg. 33 (with regs. 31-40)

Introductory

1. (1)The provisions of this Schedule specify acts which may be done in relation to a performance

or recording notwithstanding the rights conferred by [F1this Chapter]; they relate only to the question of infringement of those rights and do not affect any other right or obligation restricting the doing of any of the specified acts.

(2) No inference shall be drawn from the description of any act which may by virtue of this Schedule be done without infringing the rights conferred by [F1this Chapter] as to the scope of those rights.

(3) The provisions of this Schedule are to be construed independently of each other, so that the fact that an act does not fall within one provision does not mean that it is not covered by another provision.

Amendments (Textual)

F1. Words in Sch. 2 para. 1. (1)(2) substituted (1.2.2006) by The Performances (Moral Rights, etc.) Regulations 2006 (S.I. 2006/18), reg. 2, Sch. para. 9 (with reg. 8)

[F2. Making of temporary copies

Amendments (Textual)

F2 Sch. 2 para. 1. A and cross-heading inserted (31.10.2003) by The Copyright and Related Rights Regulations 2003 (S.I. 2003/2498) , reg. 8. (2) (with regs. 31-40)

1. AThe rights conferred by [F3this Chapter] are not infringed by the making of a temporary copy of a recording of a performance which is transient or incidental, which is an integral and essential part of a technological process and the sole purpose of which is to enable—

(a) a transmission of the recording in a network between third parties by an intermediary; or

(b) a lawful use of the recording;

and which has no independent economic significance.]

Amendments (Textual)

F3 Words in Sch. 2 para. 1. A substituted (1.2.2006) by The Performances (Moral Rights, etc.) Regulations 2006 (S.I. 2006/18) , reg. 2 , Sch. para. 9 (with reg. 8)

[F4. Personal copies of recordings for private use

Amendments (Textual)

F4. Sch. 2 para. 1. B and cross-heading inserted (1.10.2014) by The Copyright and Rights in Performances (Personal Copies for Private Use) Regulations 2014 (S.I. 2014/2361), regs. 1. (1), 3. (3) (with reg. 5) (but note that the amending S.I. was quashed with prospective effect by the High Court in the case of R (British Academy of Songwriters, Composers and Authors and others) v Secretary of State for Business, Innovation and Skills [2015] EWHC 2041 (Admin), 17 July 2015)

1. B.(1)The making of a copy of a recording of a performance by an individual does not infringe the rights conferred by this Chapter provided that the copy—

(a) is a copy of—

(i) the individual's own copy of the recording, or

(ii) a personal copy of the recording made by the individual,

(b) is made for the individual's private use, and

(c) is made for ends which are neither directly nor indirectly commercial.

(2) In this paragraph "the individual's own copy" is a copy of a recording which—

(a) has been lawfully acquired by the individual on a permanent basis,

(b) is not an illicit recording, and

(c) has not been made under any provision of this Schedule which permits the making of a copy without infringing the rights conferred by this Chapter.

(3) In this paragraph a "personal copy" means a copy made under this paragraph.

(4) The rights conferred by this Chapter in a recording are infringed if an individual transfers a personal copy of the recording to another person (otherwise than on a private and temporary basis), except where the transfer is authorised by the rights owner.

(5) If the rights conferred by this Chapter are infringed as set out in sub-paragraph (4), a personal copy which has been transferred is for all purposes subsequently treated as an illicit recording.

(6) The rights conferred by this Chapter in a recording are also infringed if an individual, having made a personal copy of the recording, transfers the individual's own copy of the recording to another person (otherwise than on a private and temporary basis) and, after that transfer and without the consent of the rights owner, retains any personal copy.

(7) If the rights conferred by this Chapter are infringed as set out in sub-paragraph (6), any retained personal copy is for all purposes subsequently treated as an illicit recording.

(8) To the extent that a term of a contract purports to prevent or restrict the making of a copy which, by virtue of this paragraph, would not infringe any right conferred by this Chapter, that term is unenforceable.

(9) Expressions used but not defined in this paragraph have the same meaning as in section 28. B.]

[F5. Research and private study

Amendments (Textual)
F5. Sch. 2 paras. 1. C, 1. D and cross-headings inserted (1.6.2014) by The Copyright and Rights in Performances (Research, Education, Libraries and Archives) Regulations 2014 (S.I. 2014/1372), regs. 1, 3. (3)

1. C.(1)Fair dealing with a performance or a recording of a performance for the purposes of research for a non-commercial purpose does not infringe the rights conferred by this Chapter.

(2) Fair dealing with a performance or recording of a performance for the purposes of private study does not infringe the rights conferred by this Chapter.

(3) Copying of a recording by a person other than the researcher or student is not fair dealing if—

(a) in the case of a librarian, or a person acting on behalf of a librarian, that person does anything which is not permitted under paragraph 6. F (copying by librarians: single copies of published recordings), or

(b) in any other case, the person doing the copying knows or has reason to believe that it will result in copies of substantially the same material being provided to more than one person at substantially the same time and for substantially the same purpose.

(4) To the extent that a term of a contract purports to prevent or restrict the doing of any act which, by virtue of this paragraph, would not infringe any right conferred by this Chapter, that term is unenforceable.

(5) Expressions used in this paragraph have the same meaning as in section 29.

Copies for text and data analysis for non-commercial research

1. D.(1)The making of a copy of a recording of a performance by a person who has lawful access to the recording does not infringe any rights conferred by this Chapter provided that the copy is made in order that a person who has lawful access to the recording may carry out a computational analysis of anything recorded in the recording for the sole purpose of research for a non-commercial purpose.

(2) Where a copy of a recording has been made under this paragraph, the rights conferred by this Chapter are infringed if—

(a) the copy is transferred to any other person, except where the transfer is authorised by the rights owner, or

(b) the copy is used for any purpose other than that mentioned in sub-paragraph (1), except where the use is authorised by the rights owner.

(3) If a copy of a recording made under this paragraph is subsequently dealt with—

(a) it is to be treated as an illicit recording for the purposes of that dealing, and

(b) if that dealing infringes any right conferred by this Chapter, it is to be treated as an illicit recording for all subsequent purposes.

(4) To the extent that a term of a contract purports to prevent or restrict the making of a copy which, by virtue of this paragraph, would not infringe any right conferred by this Chapter, that term is unenforceable.

(5) Expressions used in this paragraph have the same meaning as in section 29. A.]

Criticism, reviews[F6, quotation] and news reporting

Amendments (Textual)

F6. Word in Sch. 2 para. 2 heading inserted (1.10.2014) by S.I. 2014/2356 reg. 4. (2)

2[F7. (1)Fair dealing with a performance or recording for the purpose of criticism or review, of that or another performance or recording, or of a work, does not infringe any of the rights conferred by [F8this Chapter] provided that the performance or recording has been made available to the public.

[F9. (1. ZA)The rights conferred by this Chapter in a performance or a recording of a performance are not infringed by the use of a quotation from the performance or recording (whether for criticism or review or otherwise) provided that—

(a) the performance or recording has been made available to the public,

(b) the use of the quotation is fair dealing with the performance or recording, and

(c) the extent of the quotation is no more than is required by the specific purpose for which it is used.]

(1. A)Fair dealing with a performance or recording for the purpose of reporting current events does not infringe any of the rights conferred by [F8this Chapter].]

[F10. (1. B)To the extent that a term of a contract purports to prevent or restrict the doing of any act which, by virtue of sub-paragraph (1. ZA), would not infringe any right conferred by this Chapter, that term is unenforceable.]

(2) Expressions used in this paragraph have the same meaning as in section 30.

Amendments (Textual)

F7 Sch. 2 para. 2. (1)(1. A) substituted (31.10.2003) for Sch. 2 para. 2. (1) by The Copyright and Related Rights Regulations 2003 (S.I. 2003/2498) , reg. 10. (2) (with regs. 31-40)

F8 Words in Sch. 2 para. 2. (1)(1. A) substituted (1.2.2006) by The Performances (Moral Rights, etc.) Regulations 2006 (S.I. 2006/18) , reg. 2 , Sch. para. 9 (with reg. 8)

F9. Sch. 2 para. 2. (1. ZA) inserted (1.10.2014) by The Copyright and Rights in Performances (Quotation and Parody) Regulations 2014 (S.I. 2014/2356), regs. 1, 4. (3)

F10. Sch. 2 para. 2. (1. B) inserted (1.10.2014) by The Copyright and Rights in Performances (Quotation and Parody) Regulations 2014 (S.I. 2014/2356), regs. 1, 4. (4)

[F11. Caricature, parody or pastiche

Amendments (Textual)

F11. Sch. 2 para. 2. A and cross-heading inserted (1.10.2014) by The Copyright and Rights in Performances (Quotation and Parody) Regulations 2014 (S.I. 2014/2356), regs. 1, 5. (2)

2. A.(1)Fair dealing with a performance or a recording of a performance for the purposes of caricature, parody or pastiche does not infringe the rights conferred by this Chapter in the performance or recording.

(2) To the extent that a term of a contract purports to prevent or restrict the doing of any act which, by virtue of this paragraph, would not infringe any right conferred by this Chapter, that term is unenforceable.

(3) Expressions used in this paragraph have the same meaning as in section 30. A.]

Incidental inclusion of performance or recording

3. (1)The rights conferred by [F12this Chapter] are not infringed by the incidental inclusion of a performance or recording in a sound recording, film [F13or broadcast].

(2) Nor are those rights infringed by anything done in relation to copies of, or the playing, showing [F14or communication to the public] of, anything whose making was, by virtue of sub-paragraph (1), not an infringement of those rights.

(3) A performance or recording so far as it consists of music, or words spoken or sung with music, shall not be regarded as incidentally included in a sound recording [F13or broadcast] if it is deliberately included.

(4) Expressions used in this paragraph have the same meaning as in section 31.

Amendments (Textual)

F12 Words in Sch. 2 para. 3. (1) substituted (1.2.2006) by The Performances (Moral Rights, etc.) Regulations 2006 (S.I. 2006/18) , reg. 2 , Sch. para. 9 (with reg. 8)

F13 Words in Sch. 2 para. 3. (1)(3) substituted (31.10.2003) by The Copyright and Related Rights Regulations 2003 (S.I. 2003/2498) , reg. 2. (1) , Sch. 1 para. 3. (1)(l)(m) (with regs. 31-40)

F14 Words in Sch. 2 para. 3. (2) substituted (31.10.2003) by The Copyright and Related Rights Regulations 2003 (S.I. 2003/2498) , reg. 2. (1) , Sch. 1 para. 6. (2)(e) (with regs. 31-40)

[F15. Disabled persons: copies of recordings for personal use

Amendments (Textual)

F15. Sch. 2 paras. 3. A-3. E and cross-headings inserted (1.6.2014) by The Copyright and Rights in Performances (Disability) Regulations 2014 (S.I. 2014/1384), regs. 1. (1), 3

3. A.(1)This paragraph applies if—

(a) a disabled person has lawful possession or lawful use of a copy of the whole or part of a recording of a performance, and

(b) the person's disability prevents the person from enjoying the recording to the same degree as a person who does not have that disability.

(2) The making of an accessible copy of the copy of the recording referred to in sub-paragraph (1)(a) does not infringe the rights conferred by this Chapter if—

(a) the copy is made by the disabled person or by a person acting on behalf of the disabled person,

(b) the copy is made for the disabled person's personal use, and

(c) the same kind of accessible copies of the recording are not commercially available on reasonable terms by or with the authority of the rights owner.

(3) If a person makes an accessible copy under this paragraph on behalf of a disabled person and charges the disabled person for it, the sum charged must not exceed the cost of making and supplying the copy.

(4) The rights conferred by this Chapter are infringed by the transfer of an accessible copy of a recording made under this paragraph to any person other than—

(a) a person by or for whom an accessible copy of the recording may be made under this paragraph, or

(b) a person who intends to transfer the copy to a person falling within paragraph (a), except where the transfer is authorised by the rights owner.

(5) An accessible copy of a recording made under this paragraph is to be treated for all purposes as an illicit recording if it is held by a person at a time when the person does not fall within sub-paragraph (4)(a) or (b).

(6) If an accessible copy of a recording made under this paragraph is subsequently dealt with—

(a) it is to be treated as an illicit recording for the purposes of that dealing, and

(b) if that dealing infringes any right conferred by this Chapter, it is to be treated as an illicit recording for all subsequent purposes.

Making and supply of accessible copies by authorised bodies

3. B.(1)If an authorised body has lawful possession of or lawful access to a copy of the whole or part of a recording of a performance (including a recording of a performance included in a broadcast), the body may, without infringing the rights conferred by this Chapter, make and supply accessible copies of the recording for the personal use of disabled persons.

(2) If an authorised body has lawful access to the whole or part of a broadcast, the body may, without infringing the rights conferred by this Chapter, make a recording of the broadcast, and make and supply accessible copies of the recording, for the personal use of disabled persons.

(3) But sub-paragraphs (1) and (2) do not apply if the same kind of accessible copies of the recording, or of the broadcast, are commercially available on reasonable terms by or with the consent of the rights owner.

(4) For the purposes of sub-paragraphs (1) and (2), supply "for the personal use of disabled persons" includes supply to a person acting on behalf of a disabled person.

(5) An authorised body which is an educational establishment conducted for profit must ensure that any accessible copies which it makes under this paragraph are used only for its educational purposes.

(6) An accessible copy made under this paragraph must be accompanied by a statement that it is made under this paragraph, unless it is accompanied by an equivalent statement in accordance with section 31. B(7).

(7) If an accessible copy is made under this paragraph of a recording which is in copy-protected electronic form, the accessible copy must, so far as is reasonably practicable, incorporate the same or equally effective copy protection (unless the rights owner agrees otherwise).

(8) An authorised body which has made an accessible copy of a recording under this paragraph may supply it to another authorised body which is entitled to make accessible copies of the recording under this paragraph for the purposes of enabling that other body to make accessible copies of the recording.

(9) If an authorised body supplies an accessible copy it has made under this paragraph to a person or authorised body as permitted by this paragraph and charges the person or body for it, the sum charged must not exceed the cost of making and supplying the copy.

(10) If an accessible copy of a recording made under this paragraph is subsequently dealt with—

(a) it is to be treated as an illicit recording for the purposes of that dealing, and

(b) if that dealing infringes any right conferred by this Chapter, it is to be treated as an illicit recording for all subsequent purposes.

Making and supply of intermediate copies by authorised bodies

3. C.(1)An authorised body which is entitled to make an accessible copy of a recording of a performance under paragraph 3. B may, without infringing the rights conferred by this Chapter, make a copy of the recording ("an intermediate copy") if this is necessary in order to make the accessible copy.

(2) An authorised body which has made an intermediate copy of a recording under this paragraph may supply it to another authorised body which is entitled to make accessible copies of the recording under paragraph 3. B for the purposes of enabling that other body to make accessible copies of the recording.

(3) The rights conferred by this Chapter are infringed by the transfer of an intermediate copy made under this paragraph to a person other than another authorised body as permitted by sub-paragraph (2), except where the transfer is authorised by the rights owner.

(4) If an authorised body supplies an intermediate copy to an authorised body under sub-paragraph (2) and charges the body for it, the sum charged must not exceed the cost of making and supplying the copy.

Accessible and intermediate copies: records

3. D.(1)An authorised body must keep a record of—

(a) accessible copies it makes under paragraph 3. B,

(b) intermediate copies it makes under paragraph 3. C, and

(c) the persons to whom such copies are supplied.

(2) An authorised body must allow the rights owner or a person acting for the rights owner, on giving reasonable notice, to inspect the records at any reasonable time.

Paragraphs 3. A to 3. D: interpretation and general

3. E.(1)This paragraph supplements paragraphs 3. A to 3. D and includes definitions.

(2) "Disabled person" means a person who has a physical or mental impairment which prevents the person from enjoying a recording of a performance to the same degree as a person who does not have that impairment, and "disability" is to be construed accordingly.

(3) But a person is not to be regarded as disabled by reason only of an impairment of visual function which can be improved, by the use of corrective lenses, to a level that is normally acceptable for reading without a special level or kind of light.

(4) An "accessible copy" of a recording of a performance means a version of the recording which enables the fuller enjoyment of the recording by disabled persons.

(5) An accessible copy—

(a) may include facilities for navigating around the version of the recording, but

(b) must not include any changes to the recording which are not necessary to overcome the problems suffered by the disabled persons for whom the accessible copy is intended.

(6) To the extent that a term of a contract purports to prevent or restrict the doing of any act which, by virtue of paragraph 3. A, 3. B or 3. C, would not infringe any right conferred by this Chapter, that term is unenforceable.

(7) "Authorised body" and "supply" have the meaning given in section 31. F, and other expressions used in paragraphs 3. A to 3. D but not defined in this paragraph have the same meaning as in sections 31. A to 31. BB.]

[F16. Illustration for instruction

Amendments (Textual)

F16. Sch. 2 para. 4 substituted (1.6.2014) by The Copyright and Rights in Performances (Research, Education, Libraries and Archives) Regulations 2014 (S.I. 2014/1372), regs. 1, 4. (4)

4.(1)Fair dealing with a performance or a recording of a performance for the sole purpose of illustration for instruction does not infringe the rights conferred by this Chapter provided that the dealing is—

(a) for a non-commercial purpose, and

(b) by a person giving or receiving instruction (or preparing for giving or receiving instruction).

(2) To the extent that a term of a contract purports to prevent or restrict the doing of any act which, by virtue of this paragraph, would not infringe any right conferred by this Chapter, that term is unenforceable.

(3) Expressions used in this paragraph have the same meaning as in section 32.]

Playing or showing sound recording, film, [F17or broadcast]at educational establishment

Amendments (Textual)

F17 Words in heading preceding Sch. 2 para. 5 substituted (31.10.2003) by The Copyright and Related Rights Regulations 2003 (S.I. 2003/2498) , reg. 2. (1) , Sch. 1 para. 2. (2) (with regs. 31-40)

5. (1)The playing or showing of a sound recording, film [F18or broadcast] at an educational establishment for the purposes of instruction before an audience consisting of teachers and pupils at the establishment and other persons directly connected with the activities of the establishment is not a playing or showing of a performance in public for the purposes of infringement of the rights conferred by [F19this Chapter] .

(2) A person is not for this purpose directly connected with the activities of the educational establishment simply because he is the parent of a pupil at the establishment.

(3) Expressions used in this paragraph have the same meaning as in section 34 and any provision made under section 174. (2) with respect to the application of that section also applies for the purposes of this paragraph.

Amendments (Textual)

F18 Words in Sch. 2 para. 5. (1) substituted (31.10.2003) by The Copyright and Related Rights Regulations 2003 (S.I. 2003/2498) , reg. 2. (1) , Sch. 1 para. 3. (1)(n) (with regs. 31-40)

F19 Words in Sch. 2 para. 5. (1) substituted (1.2.2006) by The Performances (Moral Rights, etc.) Regulations 2006 (S.I. 2006/18) , reg. 2 , Sch. para. 9 (with reg. 8)

[F20. Recording by educational establishments of broadcasts

Amendments (Textual)

F20. Sch. 2 paras. 6, 6. ZA and cross-headings substituted (1.6.2014) for Sch. 2 para. 6 and cross-heading by The Copyright and Rights in Performances (Research, Education, Libraries and Archives) Regulations 2014 (S.I. 2014/1372), regs. 1, 4. (5)

6.(1)A recording of a broadcast, or a copy of such a recording, may be made by or on behalf of an educational establishment for the educational purposes of that establishment without infringing any of the rights conferred by this Chapter in relation to any performance or recording included in it, provided that the educational purposes are non-commercial.

(2) The rights conferred by this Chapter are not infringed where a recording of a broadcast or a copy of such a recording, made under sub-paragraph (1), is communicated by or on behalf of the educational establishment to its pupils or staff for the non-commercial educational purposes of that establishment.

(3) Sub-paragraph (2) only applies to a communication received outside the premises of the establishment if that communication is made by means of a secure electronic network accessible only by the establishment's pupils and staff.

(4) Acts which would otherwise be permitted by this paragraph are not permitted if, or to the extent that, licences are available authorising the acts in question and the educational establishment responsible for those acts knew or ought to have been aware of that fact.

(5) If a recording made under this paragraph is subsequently dealt with—

(a) it is to be treated as an illicit recording for the purposes of that dealing, and

(b) if that dealing infringes any right conferred by this Chapter, it is to be treated as an illicit recording for all subsequent purposes.

(6) In this paragraph "dealt with" means—

(a) sold or let for hire,

(b) offered or exposed for sale or hire, or

(c) communicated otherwise than as permitted by sub-paragraph (2).

(7) Expressions used in this paragraph (other than "dealt with") have the same meaning as in section 35 and any provision made under section 174. (2) with respect to the application of that section also applies for the purposes of this paragraph.

Copying and use of extracts of recordings by educational establishments

6. ZA.(1)The copying of extracts of a recording of a performance by or on behalf of an educational establishment does not infringe any of the rights conferred by this Chapter in the recording provided that the copy is made for the purposes of instruction for a non-commercial purpose.

(2) The rights conferred by this Chapter are not infringed where an extract of a recording of a performance, made under sub-paragraph (1), is communicated by or on behalf of the educational establishment to its pupils or staff for the purposes of instruction for a non-commercial purpose.

(3) Sub-paragraph (2) only applies to a communication received outside the premises of the establishment if that communication is made by means of a secure electronic network accessible only by the establishment's pupils and staff.

(4) Not more than 5% of a recording may be copied under this paragraph by or on behalf of an educational establishment in any period of 12 months.

(5) Acts which would otherwise be permitted by this paragraph are not permitted if, or to the extent that, licences are available authorising the acts in question and the educational establishment responsible for those acts knew or ought to have been aware of that fact.

(6) The terms of a licence granted to an educational establishment authorising acts permitted by this paragraph are of no effect so far as they purport to restrict the proportion of a recording which may be copied (whether on payment or free of charge) to less than that which would be permitted by this paragraph.

(7) If a recording made under this paragraph is subsequently dealt with—

(a) it is to be treated as an illicit recording for the purposes of that dealing, and

(b) if that dealing infringes any right conferred by this Chapter, it is to be treated as an illicit recording for all subsequent purposes.

(8) In this paragraph "dealt with" means—

(a) sold or let for hire,

(b) offered or exposed for sale or hire, or

(c) communicated otherwise than as permitted by sub-paragraph (2).

(9) Expressions used in this paragraph (other than "dealt with") have the same meaning as in section 36 and any provision made under section 174. (2) with respect to the application of that section also applies for the purposes of this paragraph.]

F21 [Lending of copies by educational establishments]

Amendments (Textual)

F21 Sch. 2 para. 6. A and crossheading inserted (1.12.1996) by S.I. 1996/2967 , reg. 20. (3) (with Pt. III)

[F226. A(1)The rights conferred by [F23this Chapter] are not infringed by the lending of copies of a recording of a performance by an educational establishment.

(2) Expressions used in this paragraph have the same meaning as in section 36. A; and any provision with respect to the application of that section made under section 174. (2) (instruction given elsewhere than an educational establishment) applies also for the purposes of this paragraph.]

Amendments (Textual)

F22 Sch. 2 para. 6. A inserted (1.12.1996) by S.I. 1996/2967 , reg. 20. (3) (with Pt. III)

F23 Words in Sch. 2 para. 6. A(1) substituted (1.2.2006) by The Performances (Moral Rights, etc.) Regulations 2006 (S.I. 2006/18) , reg. 2 , Sch. para. 9 (with reg. 8)

F24 [Lending of copies by libraries or archives]

Amendments (Textual)

F24 Sch. 2 para. 6. B and crossheading inserted (1.12.1996) by S.I. 1996/2967 , reg. 20. (3) (with Pt. III)

[F25 6. B (1) The rights conferred by [F26 this Chapter] are not infringed by the lending of copies of a recording of a performance by a F27 ... library or archive (other than a public library) which is not conducted for profit.

[F28. (A1)The rights conferred by this Chapter are not infringed by the following acts by a public library in relation to a book within the public lending right scheme—

(a) lending the book;

(b) in relation to an audio-book or e-book, copying or issuing a copy of the book as an act incidental to lending it.

(A2) Expressions used in sub-paragraph (A1) have the same meaning as in section 40. A(1).]

F29. (2)...............................].

Amendments (Textual)

F25. Sch. 2 para. 6. B inserted (1.12.1996) by S.I. 1996/2967, reg. 20. (3) (with Pt. III)

F26. Words in Sch. 2 para. 6. B(1) substituted (1.2.2006) by The Performances (Moral Rights, etc.) Regulations 2006 (S.I. 2006/18), reg. 2, Sch. para. 9 (with reg. 8)

F27. Word in Sch. 2 para. 6. B(1) omitted (1.6.2014) by virtue of The Copyright and Rights in Performances (Research, Education, Libraries and Archives) Regulations 2014 (S.I. 2014/1372), reg. 1, Sch. para. 8. (a)

F28. Sch. 2 para. 6. B(A1)(A2) inserted (30.6.2014) by Digital Economy Act 2010 (c. 24), ss. 43. (8)(a), 47. (3)(d); S.I. 2014/1659, art. 2

F29. Sch. 2 para. 6. B(2) omitted (1.6.2014) by virtue of The Copyright and Rights in Performances (Research, Education, Libraries and Archives) Regulations 2014 (S.I. 2014/1372), reg. 1, Sch. para. 8. (b)

Modifications etc. (not altering text)

C2. Sch. 2 para. 6. B modified (1.12.1996) by S.I. 1996/2967, reg. 35 (with Pt. III)

[F30 Libraries and educational establishments etc : making recordings of performances available through dedicated terminals

Amendments (Textual)

F30. Sch. 2 paras. 6. C-6. H and cross-headings inserted (1.6.2014) by The Copyright and Rights in Performances (Research, Education, Libraries and Archives) Regulations 2014 (S.I. 2014/1372), regs. 1, 6

6. C.(1)The rights conferred by this Chapter in a recording of a performance are not infringed by an institution specified in sub-paragraph (2) communicating the recording to the public or making it available to the public by means of a dedicated terminal on its premises, if the conditions in sub-paragraph (3) are met.

(2) The institutions are—

(a) a library,

(b) an archive,

(c) a museum, and

(d) an educational establishment.

(3) The conditions are that the recording or a copy of the recording—

(a) has been lawfully acquired by the institution,

(b) is communicated or made available to individual members of the public for the purposes of research or private study, and

(c) is communicated or made available in compliance with any purchase or licensing terms to which the recording is subject.

Copying by librarians: supply of single copies to other libraries

6. D.(1)A librarian may, if the conditions in sub-paragraph (2) are met, make a single copy of the

whole or part of a published recording of a performance and supply it to another library, without infringing any rights conferred by this Chapter in the recording.

(2) The conditions are—

(a) the copy is supplied in response to a request from a library which is not conducted for profit, and

(b) at the time of making the copy the librarian does not know, or could not reasonably find out, the name and address of a person entitled to authorise the making of a copy of the recording.

(3) Where a library makes a charge for supplying a copy under this paragraph, the sum charged must be calculated by reference to the costs attributable to the production of the copy.

(4) To the extent that a term of a contract purports to prevent or restrict the doing of any act which, by virtue of this paragraph, would not infringe any right conferred by this Chapter, that term is unenforceable.

Copying by librarians etc : replacement copies of recordings

6. E.(1)A librarian, archivist or curator of a library, archive or museum may, without infringing any rights conferred by this Chapter, make a copy of a recording of a performance in that institution's permanent collection—

(a) in order to preserve or replace that recording in that collection, or

(b) where a recording in the permanent collection of another library, archive or museum has been lost, destroyed or damaged, in order to replace the recording in the collection of that other library, archive or museum,

provided that the conditions in sub-paragraphs (2) and (3) are met.

(2) The first condition is that the recording is—

(a) included in the part of the collection kept wholly or mainly for the purposes of reference on the institution's premises,

(b) included in a part of the collection not accessible to the public, or

(c) available on loan only to other libraries, archives or museums.

(3) The second condition is that it is not reasonably practicable to purchase a copy of the recording to achieve either of the purposes mentioned in sub-paragraph (1).

(4) The reference in sub-paragraph (1)(b) to a library, archive or museum is to a library, archive or museum which is not conducted for profit.

(5) Where an institution makes a charge for supplying a copy to another library, archive or museum under sub-paragraph (1)(b), the sum charged must be calculated by reference to the costs attributable to the production of the copy.

(6) To the extent that a term of a contract purports to prevent or restrict the doing of any act which, by virtue of this paragraph, would not infringe any right conferred by this Chapter, that term is unenforceable.

Copying by librarians: single copies of published recordings

6. F.(1)A librarian of a library which is not conducted for profit may, if the conditions in sub-paragraph (2) are met, make and supply a single copy of a reasonable proportion of a published recording without infringing any of the rights in the recording conferred by this Chapter.

(2) The conditions are—

(a) the copy is supplied in response to a request from a person who has provided the librarian with a declaration in writing which includes the information set out in sub-paragraph (3), and

(b) the librarian is not aware that the declaration is false in a material particular.

(3) The information which must be included in the declaration is—

(a) the name of the person who requires the copy and the material which that person requires,

(b) a statement that the person has not previously been supplied with a copy of that material by any library,

(c) a statement that the person requires the copy for the purposes of research for a non-commercial purpose or private study, will use it only for those purposes and will not supply the copy to any other person, and

(d) a statement that to the best of the person's knowledge, no other person with whom the person works or studies has made, or intends to make, at or about the same time as the person's request, a request for substantially the same material for substantially the same purpose.

(4) Where a library makes a charge for supplying a copy under this paragraph, the sum charged must be calculated by reference to the costs attributable to the production of the copy.

(5) Where a person ("P") makes a declaration under this paragraph that is false in a material particular and is supplied with a copy of a recording which would have been an illicit recording if made by P—

(a) P is liable for infringement of the rights conferred by this Chapter as if P had made the copy, and

(b) the copy supplied to P is to be treated as an illicit recording for all purposes.

(6) To the extent that a term of a contract purports to prevent or restrict the doing of any act which, by virtue of this paragraph, would not infringe any right conferred by this Chapter, that term is unenforceable.

Copying by librarians or archivists: single copies of unpublished recordings

6. G.(1)A librarian or archivist may make and supply a single copy of the whole or part of a recording without infringing any of the rights conferred by this Chapter in the recording, provided that—

(a) the copy is supplied in response to a request from a person who has provided the librarian or archivist with a declaration in writing which includes the information set out in sub-paragraph (2), and

(b) the librarian or archivist is not aware that the declaration is false in a material particular.

(2) The information which must be included in the declaration is—

(a) the name of the person who requires the copy and the material which that person requires,

(b) a statement that the person has not previously been supplied with a copy of that material by any library or archive, and

(c) a statement that the person requires the copy for the purposes of research for a non-commercial purpose or private study, will use it only for those purposes and will not supply the copy to any other person.

(3) But the rights conferred by this Chapter are infringed if—

(a) the recording had been published or communicated to the public before the date it was deposited in the library or archive, or

(b) the rights owner has prohibited the copying of the recording,

and at the time of making the copy the librarian or archivist is, or ought to be, aware of that fact.

(4) Where a library or archive makes a charge for supplying a copy under this paragraph, the sum charged must be calculated by reference to the costs attributable to the production of the copy.

(5) Where a person ("P") makes a declaration under this paragraph that is false in a material particular and is supplied with a copy of a recording which would have been an illicit recording if made by P—

(a) P is liable for infringement of the rights conferred by this Chapter as if P had made the copy, and

(b) the copy supplied to P is to be treated as an illicit recording for all purposes.

Paragraphs 6. B to 6. G: interpretation

6. H.Expressions used in paragraphs 6. B to 6. G have the same meaning as in sections 40. A to 43.]

[F31. Certain permitted uses of orphan works

Amendments (Textual)
F31. Sch. 2 para. 6. I and cross-heading inserted (29.10.2014) by The Copyright and Rights in Performances (Certain Permitted Uses of Orphan Works) Regulations 2014 (S.I. 2014/2861), regs. 1, 3. (4)
6. I.(1)The rights conferred by this Chapter are not infringed by a relevant body in the circumstances set out in paragraph 1. (2) of Schedule ZA1 (subject to paragraph 6 of that Schedule).
(2) "Relevant body" has the meaning given by that Schedule.]

Copy of work required to be made as condition of export

7. (1)If an article of cultural or historical importance or interest cannot lawfully be exported from the United Kingdom unless a copy of it is made and deposited in an appropriate library or archive, it is not an infringement of any right conferred by [F32this Chapter] to make that copy.
(2) Expressions used in this paragraph have the same meaning as in section 44.
Amendments (Textual)
F32 Words in Sch. 2 para. 7. (1) substituted (1.2.2006) by The Performances (Moral Rights, etc.) Regulations 2006 (S.I. 2006/18) , reg. 2 , Sch. para. 9 (with reg. 8)

Parliamentary and judicial proceedings

8. (1)The rights conferred by [F33this Chapter] are not infringed by anything done for the purposes of parliamentary or judicial proceedings or for the purpose of reporting such proceedings.
(2) Expressions used in this paragraph have the same meaning as in section 45.
Amendments (Textual)
F33 Words in Sch. 2 para. 8. (1) substituted (1.2.2006) by The Performances (Moral Rights, etc.) Regulations 2006 (S.I. 2006/18) , reg. 2 , Sch. para. 9 (with reg. 8)

Royal Commissions and statutory inquiries

9. (1)The rights conferred by [F34this Chapter] are not infringed by anything done for the purposes of the proceedings of a Royal Commission or statutory inquiry or for the purpose of reporting any such proceedings held in public.
(2) Expressions used in this paragraph have the same meaning as in section 46.
Amendments (Textual)
F34 Words in Sch. 2 para. 9. (1) substituted (1.2.2006) by The Performances (Moral Rights, etc.) Regulations 2006 (S.I. 2006/18) , reg. 2 , Sch. para. 9 (with reg. 8)

Public records

10. (1)Material which is comprised in public records within the meaning of the M1. Public Records Act 1958, the M2. Public Records (Scotland) Act 1937 or the M3. Public Records Act (Northern Ireland) 1923 [F35, or in Welsh public records (as defined in [F36the Government of Wales Act 2006]),] which are open to public inspection in pursuance of that Act, may be copied, and a copy may be supplied to any person, by or with the authority of any officer appointed under

that Act, without infringing any right conferred by [F37this Chapter].

(2) Expressions used in this paragraph have the same meaning as in section 49.

Amendments (Textual)

F35 Words in Sch. 2 para. 10. (1) inserted (1.4.1999) by 1998 c. 38 , s. 125 , Sch. 12 para. 29 (with ss. 139. (2) , 143. (2)); S.I. 1999/782 , art. 2

F36 Words in Sch. 2 para. 10. (1) substituted by Government of Wales Act 2006 (c. 32) , s. 160. (1) , Sch. 10 para. 32 (with Sch. 11 para. 22), the amending provision coming into force immediately after "the 2007 election" (held on 3.5.2007) subject to s. 161. (4)(5) of the amending Act, which provides for certain provisions to come into force for specified purposes immediately after the end of "the initial period" (which ended with the day of the first appointment of a First Minister on 25.5.2007) - see ss. 46, 161. (1)(4)(5) of the amending Act.

F37 Words in Sch. 2 para. 10. (1) substituted (1.2.2006) by The Performances (Moral Rights, etc.) Regulations 2006 (S.I. 2006/18) , reg. 2 , Sch. para. 9 (with reg. 8)

Marginal Citations

M1 1958 c. 51 .

M2 1937 c. 43 .

M3 1923 c. 20 (N.I.) .

Acts done under statutory authority

11. (1)Where the doing of a particular act is specifically authorised by an Act of Parliament, whenever passed, then, unless the Act provides otherwise, the doing of that act does not infringe the rights conferred by [F38this Chapter] .

(2) Sub-paragraph (1) applies in relation to an enactment contained in Northern Ireland legislation as it applies to an Act of Parliament.

(3) Nothing in this paragraph shall be construed as excluding any defence of statutory authority otherwise available under or by virtue of any enactment.

(4) Expressions used in this paragraph have the same meaning as in section 50.

Amendments (Textual)

F38 Words in Sch. 2 para. 11. (1) substituted (1.2.2006) by The Performances (Moral Rights, etc.) Regulations 2006 (S.I. 2006/18) , reg. 2 , Sch. para. 9 (with reg. 8)

Transfer of copies of works in electronic form

12. (1)This paragraph applies where a recording of a performance in electronic form has been purchased on terms which, expressly or impliedly or by virtue of any rule of law, allow the purchaser to make further recordings in connection with his use of the recording.

(2) If there are no express terms—

(a) prohibiting the transfer of the recording by the purchaser, imposing obligations which continue after a transfer, prohibiting the assignment of any consent or terminating any consent on a transfer, or

(b) providing for the terms on which a transferee may do the things which the purchaser was permitted to do,

anything which the purchaser was allowed to do may also be done by a transferee without infringement of the rights conferred by [F39this Chapter], but any recording made by the purchaser which is not also transferred shall be treated as an illicit recording for all purposes after the transfer.

(3) The same applies where the original purchased recording is no longer usable and what is transferred is a further copy used in its place.

(4) The above provisions also apply on a subsequent transfer, with the substitution for references in sub-paragraph (2) to the purchaser of references to the subsequent transferor.

(5) This paragraph does not apply in relation to a recording purchased before the commencement

of [F40this Chapter].

(6) Expressions used in this paragraph have the same meaning as in section 56.

Amendments (Textual)

F39 Words in Sch. 2 para. 12. (2) substituted (1.2.2006) by The Performances (Moral Rights, etc.) Regulations 2006 (S.I. 2006/18) , reg. 2 , Sch. para. 8 (with reg. 8)

F40 Words in Sch. 2 para. 12. (5) substituted (1.2.2006) by The Performances (Moral Rights, etc.) Regulations 2006 (S.I. 2006/18) , reg. 2 , Sch. para. 9 (with reg. 8)

Use of recordings of spoken works in certain cases

13. (1)Where a recording of the reading or recitation of a literary work is made for the purpose—

(a) of reporting current events, or

(b) of [F41communicating to the public] the whole or part of the reading or recitation,

it is not an infringement of the rights conferred by [F42this Chapter] to use the recording (or to copy the recording and use the copy) for that purpose, provided the following conditions are met.

(2) The conditions are that—

(a) the recording is a direct recording of the reading or recitation and is not taken from a previous recording or from a broadcast F43. . . ;

(b) the making of the recording was not prohibited by or on behalf of the person giving the reading or recitation;

(c) the use made of the recording is not of a kind prohibited by or on behalf of that person before the recording was made; and

(d) the use is by or with the authority of a person who is lawfully in possession of the recording.

(3) Expressions used in this paragraph have the same meaning as in section 58.

Amendments (Textual)

F41 Words in Sch. 2 para. 12 substituted (31.10.2003) by The Copyright and Related Rights Regulations 2003 (S.I. 2003/2498) , reg. 2. (1) , Sch. 1 para. 12. (b) (with regs. 31-40)

F42 Words in Sch. 2 para. 13. (1) substituted (1.2.2006) by The Performances (Moral Rights, etc.) Regulations 2006 (S.I. 2006/18) , reg. 2 , Sch. para. 9 (with reg. 8)

F43 Words in Sch. 2 para. 13. (2)(a) repealed (31.10.2003) by The Copyright and Related Rights Regulations 2003 (S.I. 2003/2498) , reg. 2. (2) , Sch. 2 (with regs. 31-40)

Recordings of folksongs

14. (1)A recording of a performance of a song may be made for the purpose of including it in an archive maintained by a [F44body not established or conducted for profit] without infringing any of the rights conferred by [F45this Chapter] , provided the conditions in sub-paragraph (2) below are met.

(2) The conditions are that—

(a) the words are unpublished and of unknown authorship at the time the recording is made,

(b) the making of the recording does not infringe any copyright, and

(c) its making is not prohibited by any performer.

[F46. (3)A single copy of a recording made in reliance on sub-paragraph (1) and included in an archive referred to in that sub-paragraph may be made and supplied by the archivist without infringing any right conferred by this Chapter, provided that—

(a) the copy is supplied in response to a request from a person who has provided the archivist with a declaration in writing which includes the information set out in sub-paragraph (4), and

(b) the archivist is not aware that the declaration is false in a material particular.

(4) The information which must be included in the declaration is—

(a) the name of the person who requires the copy and the recording which is the subject of the request,

(b) a statement that the person has not previously been supplied with a copy of that recording by any archivist, and

(c) a statement that the person requires the copy for the purposes of research for a non-commercial purpose or private study, will use it only for those purposes and will not supply the copy to any other person.

(5) Where an archive makes a charge for supplying a copy under this paragraph, the sum charged must be calculated by reference to the costs attributable to the production of the copy.

(6) Where a person ("P") makes a declaration under this paragraph that is false in a material particular and is supplied with a copy of a recording which would have been an illicit recording if made by P—

(a) P is liable for infringement of the rights conferred by this Chapter as if P had made the copy, and

(b) the copy supplied to P is to be treated as an illicit recording for all purposes.

(7) In this paragraph references to an archivist include a person acting on behalf of an archivist.

(8) Expressions used in this paragraph have the same meaning as in section 61.]

Amendments (Textual)

F44. Words in Sch. 2 para. 14. (1) substituted (1.6.2014) by The Copyright and Rights in Performances (Research, Education, Libraries and Archives) Regulations 2014 (S.I. 2014/1372), regs. 1, 7. (3)

F45 Words in Sch. 2 para. 14. (1)(3) substituted (1.2.2006) by The Performances (Moral Rights, etc.) Regulations 2006 (S.I. 2006/18) , reg. 2 , Sch. para. 9 (with reg. 8)

F46. Sch. 2 para. 14. (3)-(8) substituted (1.6.2014) for Sch. 2 para. 14. (3)(4) by The Copyright and Rights in Performances (Research, Education, Libraries and Archives) Regulations 2014 (S.I. 2014/1372), regs. 1, 7. (4)

F47 [Lending of certain recordings]

Amendments (Textual)

F47 Sch. 2 para. 14. A and crossheading inserted (1.12.1996) by S.I. 1996/2967 , reg. 20. (3) (with Pt. III)

F4814. A(1)The Secretary of State may by order provide that in such cases as may be specified in the order the lending to the public of copies of films or sound recordings shall be treated as licensed by the performer subject only to the payment of such reasonable royalty or other payment as may be agreed or determined in default of agreement by the Copyright Tribunal.

(2) No such order shall apply if, or to the extent that, there is a licensing scheme certified for the purposes of this paragraph under paragraph 16 of Schedule 2. A providing for the grant of licences.

(3) An order may make different provision for different cases and may specify cases by reference to any factor relating to the work, the copies lent, the lender or the circumstances of the lending.

(4) An order shall be made by statutory instrument; and no order shall be made unless a draft of it has been laid before and approved by a resolution of each House of Parliament.

(5) Nothing in this section affects any liability under section 184. (1)(b) (secondary infringement: possessing or dealing with illicit recording) in respect of the lending of illicit recordings.

(6) Expressions used in this paragraph have the same meaning as in section 66.

Amendments (Textual)

F48 Sch. 2 para. 14. A inserted (1.12.1996) by S.I. 1996/2967 , reg. 20. (3) (with Pt. III)

Playing of sound recordings for purposes of club, society, &c

15. F49. . . . .

Amendments (Textual)

F49 Sch. 2 para. 15 omitted (1.1.2011) by virtue of The Copyright, Designs and Patents Act 1988 (Amendment) Regulations 2010 (S.I. 2010/2694) , art. 3. (2)

Incidental recording for purposes of broadcast F50. . .

Amendments (Textual)
F50 Words in heading preceding Sch. 2 para. 16 repealed (31.10.2003) by The Copyright and Related Rights Regulations 2003 (S.I. 2003/2498) , reg. 2. (2) , Sch. 2 (with regs. 31-40)
16. (1)A person who proposes to broadcast a recording of a performance F51. . . in circumstances not infringing the rights conferred by [F52this Chapter] shall be treated as having consent for the purposes of [F53this Chapter] for the making of a further recording for the purposes of the broadcast F51. . . .

(2) That consent is subject to the condition that the further recording—

(a) shall not be used for any other purpose, and

(b) shall be destroyed within 28 days of being first used for broadcasting the performance F51. . . .

(3) A recording made in accordance with this paragraph shall be treated as an illicit recording—

(a) for the purposes of any use in breach of the condition mentioned in sub-paragraph (2)(a), and

(b) for all purposes after that condition or the condition mentioned in sub-paragraph (2)(b) is broken.

(4) Expressions used in this paragraph have the same meaning as in section 68.

Amendments (Textual)
F51 Words in Sch. 2 para. 16. (1)(2)(b) repealed (31.10.2003) by The Copyright and Related Rights Regulations 2003 (S.I. 2003/2498) , reg. 2. (2) , Sch. 2 (with regs. 31-40)
F52 Words in Sch. 2 para. 16. (1) substituted (1.2.2006) by The Performances (Moral Rights, etc.) Regulations 2006 (S.I. 2006/18) , reg. 2 , Sch. para. 9 (with reg. 8)
F53 Words in Sch. 2 para. 16. (1) substituted (1.2.2006) by The Performances (Moral Rights, etc.) Regulations 2006 (S.I. 2006/18) , reg. 2 , Sch. para. 10 (with reg. 8)

Recordings for purposes of supervision and control of broadcasts and [F54other services]

Amendments (Textual)
F54 Words in heading preceding Sch. 2 para. 17 substituted (31.10.2003) by The Copyright and Related Rights Regulations 2003 (S.I. 2003/2498) , reg. 2. (1) , Sch. 1 para. 2. (1) (with regs. 31-40)
17. (1)The rights conferred by [F55this Chapter] are not infringed by the making or use by the British Broadcasting Corporation, for the purpose of maintaining supervision and control over programmes broadcast by them [F56or included in any on-demand programme service provided by them], of recordings of those programmes.

[F57. (2)The rights conferred by [F55this Chapter] are not infringed by anything done in pursuance of—

[F58. (a)section 167. (1) of the Broadcasting Act 1990, section 115. (4) or (6) or 117 of the Broadcasting Act 1996 or paragraph 20 of Schedule 12 to the Communications Act 2003;]

(b) a condition which, [F59 by virtue of section 334. (1) of the Communications Act 2003] , is included in a licence granted under Part I or III of that Act or Part I or II of the Broadcasting Act 1996; F60 . . .

(c) a direction given under section 109. (2) of the Broadcasting Act 1990 (power of [F61. OFCOM] to require production of recordings etc).

[F62. (d)section 334. (3) [F63, 368. O(1) or (3)] of the Communications Act 2003.]

[F64. (3) The rights conferred by [F55 this Chapter] are not infringed by the use by OFCOM in connection with the performance of any of their functions under the Broadcasting Act 1990, the Broadcasting Act 1996 or the Communications Act 2003 of—

(a) any recording, script or transcript which is provided to them under or by virtue of any provision of those Acts; or

(b) any existing material which is transferred to them by a scheme made under section 30 of the Communications Act 2003.]]

(4) In subsection (3), "existing material" means—

(a) any recording, script or transcript which was provided to the Independent Television Commission or the Radio Authority under or by virtue of any provision of the Broadcasting Act 1990 or the Broadcasting Act 1996; and

(b) any recording or transcript which was provided to the Broadcasting Standards Commission under section 115. (4) or (6) or 116. (5) of the Broadcasting Act 1996.

[F65. (5)Copyright is not infringed by the use by an appropriate regulatory authority designated under section 368. B of the Communications Act 2003, in connection with the performance of any of their functions under that Act, of any recording, script or transcript which is provided to them under or by virtue of any provision of that Act.

(6) In this section " on-demand programme service " has the same meaning as in the Communications Act 2003 (see section 368. A of that Act).]

Amendments (Textual)

F55 Words in Sch. 2 para. 17. (1)(2)(3) substituted (1.2.2006) by The Performances (Moral Rights, etc.) Regulations 2006 (S.I. 2006/18) , reg. 2 , Sch. para. 9 (with reg. 8)

F56 Words in Sch. 2 para. 17. (1) inserted (19.12.2009) by The Audiovisual Media Services Regulations 2009 (S.I. 2009/2979) , reg. 12. (3)(a)

F57 Sch. 2 para. 17. (2)(3) substituted (1.10.1996 for certain purposes and 1.4.1997 otherwise) by 1996 c. 55 , s. 148. (1) , Sch. 10 Pt. III para. 32 (with s. 43. (6)); S.I. 1996/2120 , art. 4. (1) , Sch. 1 ; S.I. 1997/1005 , art. 4

F58 Sch. 2 para. 17. (2)(a) substituted (29.12.2003) by Communications Act 2003 (c. 21) , ss. 406 , 411 , Sch. 17 para. 93. (2)(a) (with Sch. 18); S.I. 2003/3142 , art. 3 , Sch. 1 (with art. 11)

F59 Words in Sch. 2 para. 17. (2)(b) substituted (29.12.2003) by Communications Act 2003 (c. 21) , ss. 406 , 411 , Sch. 17 para. 93. (2)(b) (with Sch. 18); S.I. 2003/3142 , art. 3 , Sch. 1 (with art. 11)

F60 Word in Sch. 2 para. 17. (2)(b) repealed (29.12.2003) by Communications Act 2003 (c. 21) , ss. 406 , 411 , Sch. 19. (1) (with Sch. 18 , Sch. 19. (1) Note 1); S.I. 2003/3142 , art. 3 , Sch. 1 (with art. 11)

F61 Word in Sch. 2 para. 17. (2)(c) substituted (29.12.2003) by Communications Act 2003 (c. 21) , ss. 406 , 411 , Sch. 17 para. 93. (2)(c) (with Sch. 18); S.I. 2003/3142 , art. 3 , Sch. 1 (with art. 11)

F62 Sch. 2 para. 17. (2)(d) inserted (29.12.2003) by Communications Act 2003 (c. 21) , ss. 406 , 411 , Sch. 17 para. 93. (2)(d) (with Sch. 18); S.I. 2003/3142 , art. 3 , Sch. 1 (with art. 11)

F63 Words in Sch. 2 para. 17. (2)(d) inserted (19.12.2009) by The Audiovisual Media Services Regulations 2009 (S.I. 2009/2979) , reg. 12. (3)(b)

F64 Sch. 2 para. 17. (3)(4) substituted (29.12.2003) for Sch. 2 para. 17. (3) by Communications Act 2003 (c. 21) , ss. 406 , 411 , Sch. 17 para. 93. (3) (with Sch. 18); S.I. 2003/3142 , art. 3 , Sch. 1 (with art. 11)

F65 Sch. 2 para. 17. (5)(6) inserted (19.12.2009) by The Audiovisual Media Services Regulations 2009 (S.I. 2009/2979) , reg. 121. (3)(c)

Modifications etc. (not altering text)

C3 Sch. 2 para. 17 modified (20.7.2004) The Contracting Out (Functions relating to Broadcast Advertising) and Specification of Relevant Functions Order 2004 (S.I. 2004/1975) , art. 9. (1)(3) (with reg. 5)

[F66. Recording for the purposes of time-shifting

Amendments (Textual)

F66. Sch. 2 para. 17. A and preceding heading inserted (31.10.2003) by The Copyright and

Related Rights Regulations 2003 (S.I. 2003/2498), reg. 19. (3) (with regs. 31-40)

17. A(1)The making in domestic premises for private and domestic use of a recording of a broadcast solely for the purpose of enabling it to be viewed or listened to at a more convenient time does not infringe any right conferred by [F67this Chapter] in relation to a performance or recording included in the broadcast.

(2) Where a recording which would otherwise be an illicit recording is made in accordance with this paragraph but is subsequently dealt with—

(a) it shall be treated as an illicit recording for the purposes of that dealing; and

(b) if that dealing infringes any right conferred by [F67this Chapter] , it shall be treated as an illicit recording for all subsequent purposes.

(3) In sub-paragraph (2), " dealt with " means sold or let for hire, offered or exposed for sale or hire or communicated to the public.

(4) Expressions used in this paragraph have the same meaning as in section 70.]

Amendments (Textual)

F67 Words in Sch. 2 para. 17. A(1)(2)(b) substituted (1.2.2006) by The Performances (Moral Rights, etc.) Regulations 2006 (S.I. 2006/18) , reg. 2 , Sch. para. 9 (with reg. 8)

[F68. Photographs of broadcasts

Amendments (Textual)

F68. Sch. 2 para. 17. B and preceding heading inserted (31.10.2003) by The Copyright and Related Rights Regulations 2003 (S.I. 2003/2498), reg. 20. (2) (with regs. 31-40)

17. B(1)The making in domestic premises for private and domestic use of a photograph of the whole or any part of an image forming part of a broadcast, or a copy of such a photograph, does not infringe any right conferred by [F69this Chapter] in relation to a performance or recording included in the broadcast.

(2) Where a recording which would otherwise be an illicit recording is made in accordance with this paragraph but is subsequently dealt with—

(a) it shall be treated as an illicit recording for the purposes of that dealing; and

(b) if that dealing infringes any right conferred by [F69this Chapter] , it shall be treated as an illicit recording for all subsequent purposes.

(3) In sub-paragraph (2), " dealt with " means sold or let for hire, offered or exposed for sale or hire or communicated to the public.

(4) Expressions used in this paragraph have the same meaning as in section 71.]

Amendments (Textual)

F69 Words in Sch. 2 para. 17. B(1)(2)(b) substituted (1.2.2006) by The Performances (Moral Rights, etc.) Regulations 2006 (S.I. 2006/18) , reg. 2 , Sch. para. 9 (with reg. 8)

Free public showing or playing of broadcast F70. . .

Amendments (Textual)

F70 Words in heading preceding Sch.2 para. 18 repealed (31.10.2003) by The Copyright and Related Rights Regulations 2003 (S.I. 2003/2498) , reg. 2. (2) , Sch. 2 (with regs. 31-40)

18. (1)The showing or playing in public of a broadcast F71. . . to an audience who have not paid for admission to the place where the broadcast F71. . . is to be seen or heard does not infringe any right conferred by [F72this Chapter] in relation to a performance or recording included in—

(a) the broadcast F71. . ., or

(b) any sound recording [F73. (except so far as it is an excepted sound recording)] or film which is played or shown in public by reception of the broadcast F71. . . .

[F74. (1. A)The showing or playing in public of a broadcast to an audience who have not paid for admission to the place where the broadcast is to be seen or heard does not infringe any right conferred by [F72this Chapter] in relation to a performance or recording included in any excepted sound recording which is played in public by reception of the broadcast, if the playing or showing of that broadcast in public—

(a) F75 . . . .

(b) is necessary for the purposes of—

(i) repairing equipment for the reception of broadcasts;

(ii) demonstrating that a repair to such equipment has been carried out; or

(iii) demonstrating such equipment which is being sold or let for hire or offered or exposed for sale or hire.]

(2) The audience shall be treated as having paid for admission to a place—

(a) if they have paid for admission to a place of which that place forms part; or

(b) if goods or services are supplied at that place (or a place of which it forms part)—

(i) at prices which are substantially attributable to the facilities afforded for seeing or hearing the broadcast F76. . . , or

(ii) at prices exceeding those usually charged there and which are partly attributable to those facilities.

(3) The following shall not be regarded as having paid for admission to a place—

(a) persons admitted as residents or inmates of the place;

(b) persons admitted as members of a club or society where the payment is only for membership of the club or society and the provision of facilities for seeing or hearing broadcasts F76. . . is only incidental to the main purposes of the club or society.

(4) Where the making of the broadcast F76. . . was an infringement of the rights conferred by [F72this Chapter] in relation to a performance or recording, the fact that it was heard or seen in public by the reception of the broadcast F76. . . shall be taken into account in assessing the damages for that infringement.

(5) Expressions used in this paragraph have the same meaning as in section 72.

Amendments (Textual)

F71 Words in Sch. 2 para. 18. (1) repealed (31.10.2003) by The Copyright and Related Rights Regulations 2003 (S.I. 2003/2498) , reg. 2. (2) , Sch. 2 (with regs. 31-40)

F72 Words in Sch. 2 para. 18. (1)(1. A)(4) substituted (1.2.2006) by The Performances (Moral Rights, etc.) Regulations 2006 (S.I. 2006/18) , reg. 2 , Sch. para. 9 (with reg. 8)

F73 Words in Sch. 2 para. 18. (1)(b) inserted (31.10.2003) by The Copyright and Related Rights Regulations 2003 (S.I. 2003/2498) , reg. 21. (2)(a) (with regs. 31-40)

F74 Sch. 2 para. 18. (1. A) inserted (31.10.2003) by The Copyright and Related Rights Regulations 2003 (S.I. 2003/2498) , reg. 21. (2)(b) (with regs. 31-40)

F75 Sch. 2 para. 18. (1. A)(a) omitted (1.1.2011) by virtue of The Copyright, Designs and Patents Act 1988 (Amendment) Regulations 2010 (S.I. 2010/2694) , art. 4. (2)

F76 Words in Sch. 2 para. 18. (2)(b)(i)(3)(4) repealed (31.10.2003) by The Copyright and Related Rights Regulations 2003 (S.I. 2003/2498) , reg. 2. (2) , Sch. 2 (with regs. 31-40)

[F77. Reception and re-transmission of [F78wireless broadcast by cable]]

Amendments (Textual)

F77 Crossheading substituted (1.10.1996) by 1996 c. 55 , s. 138 , Sch. 9 para. 5 (with s. 43. (6)); S.I. 1996/2120 , art. 4. (1) , Sch. 1

F78 Words in heading preceding Sch. 2 para. 19 substituted (31.10.2003) by The Copyright and Related Rights Regulations 2003 (S.I.2003/2498) , reg. 22. (3)(a) (with regs. 31-40)

F7919. . . . .

Amendments (Textual)

F79. Sch. 2 para. 19 repealed (31.7.2017) by Digital Economy Act 2017 (c. 30), ss. 34. (1)(b), 118. (6); S.I. 2017/765, reg. 2. (n)

F8019. A. . . . .

Provision of sub-titled copies of broadcast F81. . .

[F83. Recording of broadcast for archival purposes

21.(1)A recording of a broadcast or a copy of such a recording may be made for the purpose of being placed in an archive maintained by a body which is not established or conducted for profit without infringing any right conferred by this Chapter in relation to a performance or recording included in the broadcast.

(2) To the extent that a term of a contract purports to prevent or restrict the doing of any act which, by virtue of this paragraph, would not infringe any right conferred by this Chapter, that term is unenforceable.

(3) Expressions used in this paragraph have the same meaning as in section 75.]

Schedule 5. LICENSING OF PERFORMERS' ... RIGHTS

Licensing schemes and licensing bodies

1. (1)In [F3this Chapter] a "licensing scheme" means a scheme setting out—
(a) the classes of case in which the operator of the scheme, or the person on whose behalf he acts, is willing to grant performers' property right licences, and
(b) the terms on which licences would be granted in those classes of case;
and for this purpose a "scheme" includes anything in the nature of a scheme, whether described as a scheme or as a tariff or by any other name.
(2) In [F3this Chapter] a "licensing body" means a society or other organisation which has as its main object, or one of its main objects, the negotiating or granting, whether as owner or prospective owner of a performer's property rights or as agent for him, of performers' property right licences, and whose objects include the granting of licences covering the performances of more than one performer.

(3) In this paragraph "performers' property right licences" means licences to do, or authorise the doing of, any of the things for which consent is required under section 182. A, [F4182. B, 182. C or 182. CA] .

(4) References in [F5this Chapter] to licences or licensing schemes covering the performances of more than one performer do not include licences or schemes covering only—

(a) performances recorded in a single recording,

(b) performances recorded in more than one recording where—

(i) the performers giving the performances are the same, or

(ii) the recordings are made by, or by employees of or commissioned by, a single individual, firm, company or group of companies. For purpose a group of companies means a holding company and its subsidiaries within the meaning of [F6section 1159 of the Companies Act 2006].

[F7. (5)Schedule A1 confers powers to provide for the regulation of licensing bodies.]

Amendments (Textual)

F3. Words in Sch. 2. A para. 1. (1)(2) substituted (1.2.2006) by The Performances (Moral Rights, etc.) Regulations 2006 (S.I. 2006/18), reg. 2, Sch. para. 9 (with reg. 8)

F4. Words in Sch. 2. A para. 1. (3) substituted (31.10.2003) by The Copyright and Related Rights Regulations 2003 (S.I. 2003/2498), reg. 7. (4)(a) (with reg. 31-40)

F5. Words in Sch. 2. A para. 1. (4) substituted (1.2.2006) by The Performances (Moral Rights, etc.) Regulations 2006 (S.I. 2006/18), reg. 2, Sch. para. 8 (with reg. 8)

F6. Words in Sch. 2. A para. 1. (4) substituted (1.10.2009) by The Companies Act 2006 (Consequential Amendments, Transitional Provisions and Savings) Order 2009 (S.I. 2009/1941), art. 2. (1), Sch. 1 para. 98. (b) (with art. 10)

F7. Sch. 2. A para. 1. (5) inserted (25.4.2013) by Enterprise and Regulatory Reform Act 2013 (c. 24), s. 103. (1), Sch. 22 para. 4

[F8. Power to provide for licensing of orphan rights

Amendments (Textual)

F8. Sch. 2. A paras. 1. A-1. D and cross-heading inserted (25.4.2013) by Enterprise and Regulatory Reform Act 2013 (c. 24), s. 103. (1), Sch. 22 para. 5

1. A(1)The Secretary of State may by regulations provide for the grant of licences to do, or authorise the doing of, acts to which section 182, 182. A, 182. B, 182. C, 182. CA, 183 or 184 applies in respect of a performance, where—

(a) the performer's consent would otherwise be required under that section, but

(b) the right to authorise or prohibit the act qualifies as an orphan right under the regulations.

(2) The regulations may—

(a) specify a person or a description of persons authorised to grant licences, or

(b) provide for a person designated in the regulations to specify a person or a description of persons authorised to grant licences.

(3) The regulations must provide that, for a right to qualify as an orphan right, it is a requirement that the owner of the right has not been found after a diligent search made in accordance with the regulations.

(4) The regulations must provide for any licence—

(a) to have effect as if granted by the missing owner;

(b) not to give exclusive rights;

(c) not to be granted to a person authorised to grant licences.

(5) The regulations may apply in a case where it is not known whether a performer's right subsists, and references to a right, to a missing owner and to an interest of a missing owner are to be read as including references to a supposed right, owner or interest.

Extended collective licensing

1. B(1)The Secretary of State may by regulations provide for a licensing body that applies to the Secretary of State under the regulations to be authorised to grant licences to do, or authorise the doing of, acts to which section 182, 182. A, 182. B, 182. C, 182. CA, 183 or 184 applies in respect of a performance, where the right to authorise or prohibit the act is not owned by the body or a person on whose behalf the body acts.

(2) An authorisation must specify the acts to which any of those sections applies that the licensing body is authorised to license.

(3) The regulations must provide for the rights owner to have a right to limit or exclude the grant of licences by virtue of the regulations.

(4) The regulations must provide for any licence not to give exclusive rights.

General provision about licensing

1. C(1)This paragraph and paragraph 1. D apply to regulations under paragraphs 1. A and 1. B.

(2) The regulations may provide for a body to be or remain authorised to grant licences only if specified requirements are met, and for a question whether they are met to be determined by a person, and in a manner, specified in the regulations.

(3) The regulations may specify other matters to be taken into account in any decision to be made under the regulations as to whether to authorise a person to grant licences.

(4) The regulations must provide for the treatment of any royalties or other sums paid in respect of a licence, including—

(a) the deduction of administrative costs;

(b) the period for which sums must be held;

(c) the treatment of sums after that period (as bona vacantia or otherwise).

(5) The regulations must provide for circumstances in which an authorisation to grant licences may be withdrawn, and for determining the rights and obligations of any person if an authorisation is withdrawn.

(6) The regulations may include other provision for the purposes of authorisation and licensing, including in particular provision—

(a) for determining the rights and obligations of any person if a right ceases to qualify as an orphan right (or ceases to qualify by reference to any rights owner), or if a rights owner exercises the right referred to in paragraph 1. B(3), while a licence is in force;

(b) about maintenance of registers and access to them;

(c) permitting the use of a work for incidental purposes including an application or search;

(d) for a right conferred by section 205. C to be treated as having been asserted under section 205. D;

(e) for the payment of fees to cover administrative expenses.

1. D(1)The power to make regulations includes power—

(a) to make incidental, supplementary or consequential provision, including provision extending or restricting the jurisdiction of the Copyright Tribunal or conferring powers on it;

(b) to make transitional, transitory or saving provision;

(c) to make different provision for different purposes.

(2) Regulations under any provision may amend this Part, or any other enactment or subordinate legislation passed or made before that provision comes into force, for the purpose of making consequential provision or extending or restricting the jurisdiction of the Copyright Tribunal or conferring powers on it.

(3) Regulations may make provision by reference to guidance issued from time to time by any person.

(4) The power to make regulations is exercisable by statutory instrument.

(5) A statutory instrument containing regulations may not be made unless a draft of the instrument has been laid before and approved by a resolution of each House of Parliament.]

References and applications with respect to licensing schemes

2. Paragraphs 3 to 8 (references and applications with respect to licensing schemes) apply to licensing schemes operated by licensing bodies in relation to a performer's property rights which cover the performances of more than one performer, so far as they relate to licences for—
(a) copying a recording of the whole or any substantial part of a qualifying performance, F9 . . .
[F10. (aa)making such a recording available to the public in the way mentioned in section 182. CA(1), or.]
(b) renting or lending copies of a recording to the public;
and in those paragraphs "licensing scheme" means a licensing scheme of any of those descriptions.
Amendments (Textual)
F9. Sch. 2. A para. 2: word "or" appearing at the end of sub-para. (a) repealed (31.10.2003) by virtue of The Copyright and Related Rights Regulations 2003 (S.I. 2003/2498), reg. 2. (2), Sch. 2 (with regs. 31-40)
F10. Sch. 2. A para. 2. (aa) substituted (31.10.2003) for word "or" appearing at the end of sub-para. (a) by virtue of The Copyright and Related Rights Regulations 2003 (S.I. 2003/2498), reg. 7. (4)(b) (with regs. 31-40)

Reference of proposed licensing scheme to tribunal

3. (1)The terms of a licensing scheme proposed to be operated by a licensing body may be referred to the Copyright Tribunal by an organisation claiming to be representative of persons claiming that they require licences in cases of a description to which the scheme would apply, either generally or in relation to any description of case.
(2) The Tribunal shall first decide whether to entertain the reference, and may decline to do so on the ground that the reference is premature.
(3) If the Tribunal decides to entertain the reference it shall consider the matter referred and make such order, either confirming or varying the proposed scheme, either generally or so far as it relates to cases of the description to which the reference relates, as the Tribunal may determine to be reasonable in the circumstances.
(4) The order may be made so as to be in force indefinitely or for such period as the Tribunal may determine.

Reference of licensing scheme to tribunal

4. (1)If while a licensing scheme is in operation a dispute arises between the operator of the scheme and—
(a) a person claiming that he requires a licence in a case of a description to which the scheme applies, or
(b) an organisation claiming to be representative of such persons,
that person or organisation may refer the scheme to the Copyright Tribunal in so far as it relates to cases of that description.
(2) A scheme which has been referred to the Tribunal under this paragraph shall remain in operation until proceedings on the reference are concluded.
(3) The Tribunal shall consider the matter in dispute and make such order, either confirming or varying the scheme so far as it relates to cases of the description to which the reference relates, as the Tribunal may determine to be reasonable in the circumstances.
(4) The order may be made so as to be in force indefinitely or for such period as the Tribunal may determine.

Further reference of scheme to tribunal

5. (1)Where the Copyright Tribunal has on a previous reference of a licensing scheme under paragraph 3 or 4, or under this paragraph, made an order with respect to the scheme, then, while the order remains in force—
(a) the operator of the scheme,
(b) a person claiming that he requires a licence in a case of the description to which the order applies, or
(c) an organisation claiming to be representative of such persons,
may refer the scheme again to the Tribunal so far as it relates to cases of that description.
(2) A licensing scheme shall not, except with the special leave of the Tribunal, be referred again to the Tribunal in respect of the same description of cases—
(a) within twelve months from the date of the order on the previous reference, or
(b) if the order was made so as to be in force for 15 months or less, until the last three months before the expiry of the order.
(3) A scheme which has been referred to the Tribunal under this paragraph shall remain in operation until proceedings on the reference are concluded.
(4) The Tribunal shall consider the matter in dispute and make such order, either confirming, varying or further varying the scheme so far as it relates to cases of the description to which the reference relates, as the Tribunal may determine to be reasonable in the circumstances.
(5) The order may be made so as to be in force indefinitely or for such period as the Tribunal may determine.

Application for grant of licence in connection with licensing scheme

6. (1)A person who claims, in a case covered by a licensing scheme, that the operator of the scheme has refused to grant him or procure the grant to him of a licence in accordance with the scheme, or has failed to do so within a reasonable time after being asked, may apply to the Copyright Tribunal.
(2) A person who claims, in a case excluded from a licensing scheme, that the operator of the scheme either—
(a) has refused to grant him a licence or procure the grant to him of a licence, or has failed to do so within a reasonable time of being asked, and that in the circumstances it is unreasonable that a licence should not be granted, or
(b) proposes terms for a licence which are unreasonable,
may apply to the Copyright Tribunal.
(3) A case shall be regarded as excluded from a licensing scheme for the purposes of sub-paragraph (2) if—
(a) the scheme provides for the grant of licences subject to terms excepting matters from the licence and the case falls within such an exception, or
(b) the case is so similar to those in which licences are granted under the scheme that it is unreasonable that it should not be dealt with in the same way.
(4) If the Tribunal is satisfied that the claim is well-founded, it shall make an order declaring that, in respect of the matters specified in the order, the applicant is entitled to a licence on such terms as the Tribunal may determine to be applicable in accordance with the scheme or, as the case may be, to be reasonable in the circumstances.
(5) The order may be made so as to be in force indefinitely or for such period as the Tribunal may determine.

Application for review of order as to entitlement to licence

7. (1)Where the Copyright Tribunal has made an order under paragraph 6 that a person is entitled to a licence under a licensing scheme, the operator of the scheme or the original applicant may apply to the Tribunal to review its order.

(2) An application shall not be made, except with the special leave of the Tribunal—

(a) within twelve months from the date of the order, or of the decision on a previous application under this paragraph, or

(b) if the order was made so as to be in force for 15 months or less, or as a result of the decision on a previous application under this paragraph is due to expire within 15 months of that decision, until the last three months before the expiry date.

(3) The Tribunal shall on an application for review confirm or vary its order as the Tribunal may determine to be reasonable having regard to the terms applicable in accordance with the licensing scheme or, as the case may be, the circumstances of the case.

Effect of order of tribunal as to licensing scheme

8. (1)A licensing scheme which has been confirmed or varied by the Copyright Tribunal—

(a) under paragraph 3 (reference of terms of proposed scheme), or

(b) under paragraph 4 or 5 (reference of existing scheme to Tribunal),

shall be in force or, as the case may be, remain in operation, so far as it relates to the description of case in respect of which the order was made, so long as the order remains in force.

(2) While the order is in force a person who in a case of a class to which the order applies—

(a) pays to the operator of the scheme any charges payable under the scheme in respect of a licence covering the case in question or, if the amount cannot be ascertained, gives an undertaking to the operator to pay them when ascertained, and

(b) complies with the other terms applicable to such a licence under the scheme,

shall be in the same position as regards infringement of performers' property rights as if he had at all material times been the holder of a licence granted by the rights owner in question in accordance with the scheme.

(3) The Tribunal may direct that the order, so far as it varies the amount of charges payable, has effect from a date before that on which it is made, but not earlier than the date on which the reference was made or, if later, on which the scheme came into operation.

If such a direction is made—

(a) any necessary repayments, or further payments, shall be made in respect of charges already paid, and

(b) the reference in sub-paragraph (2)(a) to the charges payable under the scheme shall be construed as a reference to the charges so payable by virtue of the order. No such direction may be made where sub-paragraph (4) below applies.

(4) An order of the Tribunal under paragraph 4 or 5 made with respect to a scheme which is certified for any purpose under paragraph 16 has effect, so far as it varies the scheme by reducing the charges payable for licences, from the date on which the reference was made to the Tribunal.

(5) Where the Tribunal has made an order under paragraph 6 (order as to entitlement to licence under licensing scheme) and the order remains in force, the person in whose favour the order is made shall if he—

(a) pays to the operator of the scheme any charges payable in accordance with the order or, if the amount cannot be ascertained, gives an undertaking to pay the charges when ascertained, and

(b) complies with the other terms specified in the order,

be in the same position as regards infringement of performers' property rights as if he had at all material times been the holder of a licence granted by the rights owner in question on the terms specified in the order.

References and applications with respect to licensing by licensing

bodies

9. Paragraphs 10 to 13 (references and applications with respect to licensing by licensing bodies) apply to licences relating to a performer's property rights which cover the performance of more than one performer granted by a licensing body otherwise than in pursuance of a licensing scheme, so far as the licences authorise—

(a) copying a recording of the whole or any substantial part of a qualifying performance, F11 . . .

[F12. (aa)making such a recording available to the public in the way mentioned in section 182. CA(1), or.]

(b) renting or lending copies of a recording to the public;

and references in those paragraphs to a licence shall be construed accordingly.

Amendments (Textual)

F11. Sch. 2. A para. 9: word "or" appearing at the end of sub-para. (a) repealed (31.10.2003) by virtue of The Copyright and Related Rights Regulations 2003 (S.I. 2003/2498), reg. 2. (2), Sch. 2 (with regs. 31-40)

F12. Sch. 2. A para. 9. (aa) substituted (31.10.2003) for word "or" appearing at the end of sub-para. (a) by virtue of The Copyright and Related Rights Regulations 2003 (S.I. 2003/2498), reg. 7. (4)(b) (with regs. 31-40)

Reference to tribunal of proposed licence

10. (1)The terms on which a licensing body proposes to grant a licence may be referred to the Copyright Tribunal by the prospective licensee.

(2) The Tribunal shall first decide whether to entertain the reference, and may decline to do so on the ground that the reference is premature.

(3) If the Tribunal decides to entertain the reference it shall consider the terms of the proposed licence and make such order, either confirming or varying the terms as it may determine to be reasonable in the circumstances.

(4) The order may be made so as to be in force indefinitely or for such period as the Tribunal may determine.

Reference to tribunal of expiring licence

11. (1)A licensee under a licence which is due to expire, by effluxion of time or as a result of notice given by the licensing body, may apply to the Copyright Tribunal on the ground that it is unreasonable in the circumstances that the licence should cease to be in force.

(2) Such an application may not be made until the last three months before the licence is due to expire.

(3) A licence in respect of which a reference has been made to the Tribunal shall remain in operation until proceedings on the reference are concluded.

(4) If the Tribunal finds the application well-founded, it shall make an order declaring that the licensee shall continue to be entitled to the benefit of the licence on such terms as the Tribunal may determine to be reasonable in the circumstances.

(5) An order of the Tribunal under this paragraph may be made so as to be in force indefinitely or for such period as the Tribunal may determine.

Application for review of order as to licence

12. (1)Where the Copyright Tribunal has made an order under paragraph 10 or 11, the licensing body or the person entitled to the benefit of the order may apply to the Tribunal to review its order.

(2) An application shall not be made, except with the special leave of the Tribunal—

(a) within twelve months from the date of the order or of the decision on a previous application under this paragraph, or

(b) if the order was made so as to be in force for 15 months or less, or as a result of the decision on a previous application under this paragraph is due to expire within 15 months of that decision, until the last three months before the expiry date.

(3) The Tribunal shall on an application for review confirm or vary its order as the Tribunal may determine to be reasonable in the circumstances.

Effect of order of tribunal as to licence

13. (1)Where the Copyright Tribunal has made an order under paragraph 10 or 11 and the order remains in force, the person entitled to the benefit of the order shall if he—

(a) pays to the licensing body any charges payable in accordance with the order or, if the amount cannot be ascertained, gives an undertaking to pay the charges when ascertained, and

(b) complies with the other terms specified in the order,

be in the same position as regards infringement of performers' property rights as if he had at all material times been the holder of a licence granted by the rights owner in question on the terms specified in the order.

(2) The benefit of the order may be assigned—

(a) in the case of an order under paragraph 10, if assignment is not prohibited under the terms of the Tribunal's order; and

(b) in the case of an order under paragraph 11, if assignment was not prohibited under the terms of the original licence.

(3) The Tribunal may direct that an order under paragraph 10 or 11, or an order under paragraph 12 varying such an order, so far as it varies the amount of charges payable, has effect from a date before that on which it is made, but not earlier than the date on which the reference or application was made or, if later, on which the licence was granted or, as the case may be, was due to expire. If such a direction is made—

(a) any necessary repayments, or further payments, shall be made in respect of charges already paid, and

(b) the reference in sub-paragraph (1)(a) to the charges payable in accordance with the order shall be construed, where the order is varied by a later order, as a reference to the charges so payable by virtue of the later order.

General considerations: unreasonable discrimination

14. (1)In determining what is reasonable on a reference or application under this Schedule relating to a licensing scheme or licence, the Copyright Tribunal shall have regard to—

(a) the availability of other schemes, or the granting of other licences, to other persons in similar circumstances, and

(b) the terms of those schemes or licences,

and shall exercise its powers so as to secure that there is no unreasonable discrimination between licensees, or prospective licensees, under the scheme or licence to which the reference or application relates and licensees under other schemes operated by, or other licences granted by, the same person.

(2) This does not affect the Tribunal's general obligation in any case to have regard to all relevant circumstances.

Application to settle royalty or other sum payable for lending

15. (1)An application to settle the royalty or other sum payable in pursuance of paragraph 14. A of

Schedule 2 (lending of certain recordings) may be made to the Copyright Tribunal by the owner of a performer's property rights or the person claiming to be treated as licensed by him.

(2) The Tribunal shall consider the matter and make such order as it may determine to be reasonable in the circumstances.

(3) Either party may subsequently apply to the Tribunal to vary the order, and the Tribunal shall consider the matter and make such order confirming or varying the original order as it may determine to be reasonable in the circumstances.

(4) An application under sub-paragraph (3) shall not, except with the special leave of the Tribunal, be made within twelve months from the date of the original order or of the order on a previous application under that sub-paragraph.

(5) An order under sub-paragraph (3) has effect from the date on which it is made or such later date as may be specified by the Tribunal.

Certification of licensing schemes

16. (1) A person operating or proposing to operate a licensing scheme may apply to the Secretary of State to certify the scheme for the purposes of [F13 paragraph F14 ... 14. A F15 ... of Schedule 2 (F14 ... lending of certain recordings F15 ...)] .

(2) The Secretary of State shall by order made by statutory instrument certify the scheme if he is satisfied that it—

(a) enables the works to which it relates to be identified with sufficient certainty by persons likely to require licences, and

(b) sets out clearly the charges (if any) payable and the other terms on which licences will be granted.

(3) The scheme shall be scheduled to the order and the certification shall come into operation for the purposes of [F16the relevant paragraph] of Schedule 2—

(a) on such date, not less than eight weeks after the order is made, as may be specified in the order, or

(b) if the scheme is the subject of a reference under paragraph 3 (reference of proposed scheme), any later date on which the order of the Copyright Tribunal under that paragraph comes into force or the reference is withdrawn.

(4) A variation of the scheme is not effective unless a corresponding amendment of the order is made; and the Secretary of State shall make such an amendment in the case of a variation ordered by the Copyright Tribunal on a reference under paragraph 3, 4 or 5, and may do so in any other case if he thinks fit.

(5) The order shall be revoked if the scheme ceases to be operated and may be revoked if it appears to the Secretary of State that it is no longer being operated according to its terms.

Amendments (Textual)

F13. Words in Sch. 2. A para. 16. (1) substituted (31.10.2003) by The Copyright and Related Rights Regulations 2003 (S.I. 2003/2498), reg. 2. (1), Sch. 1 para. 17. (a) (with regs. 31-40)

F14. Words in Sch. 2. A para. 16. (1) omitted (1.6.2014) by virtue of The Copyright and Rights in Performances (Research, Education, Libraries and Archives) Regulations 2014 (S.I. 2014/1372), reg. 1, Sch. para. 9

F15. Words in Sch. 2. A para. 16. (1) omitted (1.6.2014) by virtue of The Copyright and Rights in Performances (Disability) Regulations 2014 (S.I. 2014/1384), reg. 1. (1), Sch. para. 6

F16. Words in Sch. 2. A para. 16. (3) substituted (31.10.2003) by The Copyright and Related Rights Regulations 2003 (S.I. 2003/2498), reg. 2. (1), Sch. 1 para. 17. (b) (with regs. 31-40)

Powers exercisable in consequence of competition report

17 [F17. (1) Sub-paragraph (1. A) applies where whatever needs to be remedied, mitigated or prevented by the Secretary of State, [F18 or (as the case may be) the Competition and Markets

Authority] under section 12. (5) of the Competition Act 1980 or section 41. (2), 55. (2), 66. (6), 75. (2), 83. (2), 138. (2), 147. (2) [F19 , 147. A(2)] or 160. (2) of, or paragraph 5. (2) or 10. (2) of Schedule 7 to, the Enterprise Act 2002 (powers to take remedial action following references to the [F20 Competition and Markets Authority] in connection with public bodies and certain other persons, mergers or market investigations etc.) consists of or includes—

(a) conditions in licences granted by the owner of a performer's property rights restricting the use to which a recording may be put by the licensee or the right of the owner to grant other licenses, or

(b) a refusal of an owner of a performer's property rights to grant licences on reasonable terms.

(1. A)The powers conferred by Schedule 8 to the Enterprise Act 2002 include power to cancel or modify those conditions and, instead or in addition, to provide that licences in respect of the performer's property rights shall be available as of right.

(2)The references to anything permitted by Schedule 8 to the Enterprise Act 2002 in section 12. (5. A) of the Competition Act 1980 and in sections 75. (4)(a), 83. (4)(a), 84. (2)(a), 89. (1), 160. (4)(a), 161. (3)(a) and 164. (1) of, and paragraphs 5, 10 and 11 of Schedule 7 to, the Act of 2002 shall be construed accordingly.]]

(3) [F21. The Secretary of State[F22or (as the case may be) the Competition and Markets Authority.]] shall only exercise the powers available by virtue of this paragraph if he [F23or it] is satisfied that to do so does not contravene any Convention relating to performers' rights to which the United Kingdom is a party.

(4) The terms of a licence available by virtue of this paragraph shall, in default of agreement, be settled by the Copyright Tribunal on an application by the person requiring the licence; and terms so settled shall authorise the licensee to do everything in respect of which a licence is so available.

(5) Where the terms of a licence are settled by the Tribunal, the licence has effect from the date on which the application to the Tribunal was made.

Amendments (Textual)

F17. Sch. 2. A para. 17. (1)(1. A)(2) substituted (20.6.2003 for certain purposes and 29.12.2004 otherwise) for Sch. 2. A para. 17. (1)(2) by 2002 c. 40, ss. 278. (1), 279, Sch. 25 para. 18. (5)(a); S.I. 2003/1397, arts. 2, 3. (1), Sch. (with arts. 4-12); S.I. 2004/3233, art. 2, Sch. (with arts. 3-5)

F18. Words in Sch. 2. A para. 17. (1) substituted (1.4.2014) by The Enterprise and Regulatory Reform Act 2013 (Competition) (Consequential, Transitional and Saving Provisions) Order 2014 (S.I. 2014/892), art. 1. (1), Sch. 1 para. 59. (a)(i) (with art. 3)

F19. Word in Sch. 2. A para. 17. (1) inserted (1.4.2014) by The Enterprise and Regulatory Reform Act 2013 (Competition) (Consequential, Transitional and Saving Provisions) Order 2014 (S.I. 2014/892), art. 1. (1), Sch. 1 para. 59. (a)(ii) (with art. 3)

F20. Words in Sch. 2. A para. 17. (1) substituted (1.4.2014) by The Enterprise and Regulatory Reform Act 2013 (Competition) (Consequential, Transitional and Saving Provisions) Order 2014 (S.I. 2014/892), art. 1. (1), Sch. 1 para. 59. (a)(iii) (with art. 3)

F21. Words in Sch. 2. A para. 17. (3) substituted (20.6.2003 for certain purposes and 29.12.2004 otherwise) by 2002 c. 40, ss. 278. (1), 279, Sch. 25 para. 18. (5)(b)(i); S.I. 2003/1397, arts. 2, 3. (1), Sch. (with arts. 4-12); S.I. 2004/3233, art. 2, Sch. (with arts. 3-5)

F22. Words in Sch. 2. A para. 17. (3) substituted (1.4.2014) by The Enterprise and Regulatory Reform Act 2013 (Competition) (Consequential, Transitional and Saving Provisions) Order 2014 (S.I. 2014/892), art. 1. (1), Sch. 1 para. 59. (b) (with art. 3)

F23. Words in Sch. 2. A para. 17. (3) inserted (20.6.2003 for certain purposes and 29.12.2004 otherwise) by 2002 c. 40, ss. 278. (1), 279, Sch. 25 para. 18. (5)(b)(ii); S.I. 2003/1397, arts. 2, 3. (1), Sch. (with arts. 4-12); S.I. 2004/3233, art. 2, Sch. (with arts. 3-5)

Modifications etc. (not altering text)

C1. Sch. 2. A para. 17. (1) amended (20.6.2003) by The Enterprise Act 2002 (Protection of Legitimate Interests) Order 2003 (S.I. 2003/1592), Sch. 4 para. 7. (3)(a)

C2. Sch. 2. A para. 17. (2) amended (20.6.2003) by The Enterprise Act 2002 (Protection of Legitimate Interests) Order 2003 (S.I. 2003/1592), Sch. 4 para. 7. (3)(b)

Schedule 6. Registered designs: minor and consequential amendments of 1949 Act

Section 272.

Modifications etc. (not altering text)

C1. Sch. 3 extended (with modifications) (Isle of Man) (9.12.2001) by S.I. 2001/3678, art. 3, Sch. 3

C2. Sch. 3 extended (Isle of Man) (with modifications) (11.11.2013) by The Registered Designs (Isle of Man) Order 2013 (S.I. 2013/2533), arts. 1, 3. (2), Sch. 2

Section 3: proceedings for registration

F11. . . . .

Amendments (Textual)

F1. Sch. 3 para. 1 repealed (9.12.2001) by S.I. 2001/3949, reg. 9. (2), Sch. 2 (with transitional provisions in regs. 10-14)

Section 4: registration of same design in respect of other articles, etc.

F22. . . . .

Amendments (Textual)

F2. Sch. 3 para. 2 repealed (9.12.2001) by S.I. 2001/3949, reg. 9. (2), Sch. 2 (with transitional provisions in regs. 10-14)

Section 5: provisions for secrecy of certain designs

3. (1)Section 5 of the Registered Designs Act 1949 is amended as follows.

(2) For "a competent authority" or "the competent authority", wherever occurring, substitute " the Secretary of State "; and in subsection (3)(c) for "that authority" substitute " he ".

(3) For subsection (2) substitute—

"(2)The Secretary of State shall by rules make provision for securing that where such directions are given—

(a) the representation or specimen of the design, and

(b) any evidence filed in support of the applicant's contention that the appearance of an article is material (for the purposes of section 1. (3) of this Act),

shall not be open to public inspection at the Patent Office during the continuance in force of the directions."

F3. (4). . . . .

(5) Omit subsection (5).

Amendments (Textual)

F3. Sch. 3 para. 3. (4) repealed (9.12.2001) by S.I. 2001/3949, reg. 9. (2), Sch. 2 (with transitional provisions in regs. 10-14)

Section 6: provisions as to confidential disclosure, etc.

F44. . . . .

Amendments (Textual)

F4. Sch. 3 para. 4 repealed (9.12.2001) by S.I. 2001/3949, reg. 9. (2), Sch. 2 (with transitional provisions in regs. 10-14)

Section 9: exemption of innocent infringer from liability for damages

5. In section 9 of the M1. Registered Designs Act 1949 (exemption of innocent infringer from liability for damages), in subsections (1) and (2) for "copyright in a registered design" substitute " the right in a registered design ".
Marginal Citations
M11949 c. 88.

Section 11: cancellation of registration

F56. . . . .
Amendments (Textual)
F5. Sch. 3 para. 6 repealed (9.12.2001) by S.I. 2001/3949, reg. 9. (2), Sch. 2 (with transitional provisions in regs. 10-14)

Section 14: registration where application has been made in convention country

7. In section 14 of the Registered Designs Act 1949 (registration where application has been made in convention country), for subsections (2) and (3) substitute—
"(2)Where an application for registration of a design is made by virtue of this section, the application shall be treated, for the purpose of determining whether that or any other design is new, as made on the date of the application for protection in the convention country or, if more than one such application was made, on the date of the first such application.
(3) Subsection (2) shall not be construed as excluding the power to give directions under section 3.
(4) of this Act in relation to an application made by virtue of this section.".

Section 15: extension of time for application under s.14 in certain cases

8. In section 15. (1) of the M2. Registered Designs Act 1949 (power to make rules empowering registrar to extend time for applications under s.14) for "the Board of Trade are satisfied" substitute " the Secretary of State is satisfied " and for "they" substitute " he ".
Marginal Citations
M21949 c. 88.

Section 16: protection of designs communicated under international agreements

F69. . . . .
Amendments (Textual)
F6. Sch. 3 para. 9 repealed (9.12.2001) by S.I. 2001/3949, reg. 9. (2), Sch. 2 (with transitional provisions in regs. 10-14)

Section 19: registration of assignments, &c.

10. In section 19 of the Registered Designs Act 1949 (registration of assignments, &c.), after subsection (3) insert—
"(3. A)Where design right subsists in a registered design, the registrar shall not register an interest under subsection (3) unless he is satisfied that the person entitled to that interest is also entitled to a corresponding interest in the design right.
(3. B)Where design right subsists in a registered design and the proprietor of the registered design is also the design right owner, an assignment of the design right shall be taken to be also an assignment of the right in the registered design, unless a contrary intention appears.".

Section 20: rectification of the register

11. In section 20 of the Registered Designs Act 1949 (rectification of the register), after subsection (4) add—
"(5)A rectification of the register under this section has effect as follows—
    (a) an entry made has effect from the date on which it should have been made,
    (b) an entry varied has effect as if it had originally been made in its varied form, and
    (c) an entry deleted shall be deemed never to have had effect,
nless, in any case, the court directs otherwise.".

Section 22: inspection of registered designs

12. (1)Section 22 of the Registered Designs Act 1949 (inspection of registered designs) is amended as follows.
(2) For subsection (1) substitute—
"(1)Where a design has been registered under this Act, there shall be open to inspection at the Patent Office on and after the day on which the certificate of registration is issued—
    (a) the representation or specimen of the design, and
    (b) any evidence filed in support of the applicant's contention that the appearance of an article is material (for the purposes of section 1. (3) of this Act).
This subsection has effect subject to the following provisions of this section and to any rules made under section 5. (2) of this Act.".
(3) In subsection (2), subsection (3) (twice) and subsection (4) for "representation or specimen of the design" substitute " representation, specimen or evidence ".

Section 23: information as to existence of right in registered design

13. For section 23 of the M3. Registered Designs Act 1949 (information as to existence of right in registered design) substitute—

"23 Information as to existence of right in registered design.

On the request of a person furnishing such information as may enable the registrar to identify the design, and on payment of the prescribed fee, the registrar shall inform him—
    (a) whether the design is registered and, if so, in respect of what articles, and
    (b) whether any extension of the period of the right in the registered design has been granted,
and shall state the date of registration and the name and address of the registered proprietor.".
Marginal Citations
M31949 c. 88.

Section 25: certificate of contested validity of registration

14. In section 25 of the Registered Designs Act 1949 (certificate of contested validity of registration), in subsection (2) for "the copyright in the registered design"substitute " the right in the registered design ".

Section 26: remedy for groundless threats of infringement proceedings

15. (1)Section 26 of the Registered Designs Act 1949 (remedy for groundless threats of infringement proceedings) is amended as follows.
(2) In subsections (1) and (2) for "the copyright in a registered design" substitute " the right in a registered design ".
(3) After subsection (2) insert—
"(2. A)Proceedings may not be brought under this section in respect of a threat to bring proceedings for an infringement alleged to consist of the making or importing of anything.".

Section 27: the court

16. For section 27 of the Registered Designs Act 1949 (the court) substitute—

"27 The court.

(1) In this Act "the court" means—
    (a) in England and Wales the High Court or any patents county court having jurisdiction by virtue of an order under section 287 of the Copyright, Designs and Patents Act 1988,
    (b) in Scotland, the Court of Session, and
    (c) in Northern Ireland, the High Court.
(2) Provision may be made by rules of court with respect to proceedings in the High Court in England and Wales for references and applications under this Act to be dealt with by such judge of that court as the Lord Chancellor may select for the purpose.".

Section 28: the Appeal Tribunal

17. (1)Section 28 of the Registered Designs Act 1949 (the Appeal Tribunal) is amended as follows.
(2) For subsection (2) (members of Tribunal) substitute—
"(2)The Appeal Tribunal shall consist of—
    (a) one or more judges of the High Court nominated by the Lord Chancellor, and
    (b) one judge of the Court of Session nominated by the Lord President of that Court.".
(3) In subsection (5) (costs), after "costs" (twice) insert " or expenses ", and for the words from "and any such order" to the end substitute—
"and any such order may be enforced—
    (a) in England and Wales or Northern Ireland, in the same way as an order of the High Court;
    (b) in Scotland, in the same way as a decree for expenses granted by the Court of Session.".
(4) For subsection (10) (seniority of judges) substitute—
"(10)In this section "the High Court" means the High Court in England and Wales; and for the purposes of this section the seniority of judges shall be reckoned by reference to the dates on which they were appointed judges of that court or the Court of Session.".
(5) The amendments to section 28 made by section 10. (5) of the M4. Administration of Justice

Act 1970 (power to make rules as to right of audience) shall be deemed always to have extended to Northern Ireland.
Marginal Citations
M41970 c. 31.

Section 29: exercise of discretionary powers of registrar

18. In section 29 of the M5. Registered Designs Act 1949 (exercise of discretionary powers of registrar) for "the registrar shall give" substitute " rules made by the Secretary of State under this Act shall require the registrar to give ".
Marginal Citations
M51949 c. 88.

Section 30: costs and security for costs

19. For section 30 of the Registered Designs Act 1949 (costs and security for costs) substitute—

"30 Costs and security for costs.

(1) Rules made by the Secretary of State under this Act may make provision empowering the registrar, in any proceedings before him under this Act—
    (a) to award any party such costs as he may consider reasonable, and
    (b) to direct how and by what parties they are to be paid.
(2) Any such order of the registrar may be enforced—
    (a) in England and Wales or Northern Ireland, in the same way as an order of the High Court;
    (b) in Scotland, in the same way as a decree for expenses granted by the Court of Session.
(3) Rules made by the Secretary of State under this Act may make provision empowering the registrar to require a person, in such cases as may be prescribed, to give security for the costs of—
    (a) an application for cancellation of the registration of a design,
    (b) an application for the grant of a licence in respect of a registered design, or
    (c) an appeal from any decision of the registrar under this Act,
and enabling the application or appeal to be treated as abandoned in default of such security being given.".

Section 31: evidence before registrar

20. For section 31 of the M6. Registered Designs Act 1949 (evidence before registrar) substitute—

"31 Evidence before registrar.

Rules made by the Secretary of State under this Act may make provision—
    (a) as to the giving of evidence in proceedings before the registrar under this Act by affidavit or statutory declaration;
    (b) conferring on the registrar the powers of an official referee of the Supreme Court as regards the examination of witnesses on oath and the discovery and production of documents; and
    (c) applying in relation to the attendance of witnesses in proceedings before the registrar the rules applicable to the attendance of witnesses in proceedings before such a referee.".
Marginal Citations
M61949 c. 88.

Section 32: power of registrar to refuse to deal with certain agents

21. Section 32 of the Registered Designs Act 1949 (power of registrar to refuse to deal with certain agents) is repealed.

Section 33: offences under s.5 (secrecy of certain designs)

22. (1)Section 33 of the Registered Designs Act 1949 (offences under s.5 (secrecy of certain designs)) is amended as follows.
(2) In subsection (1), for paragraphs (a) and (b) substitute—
"(a)on conviction on indictment to imprisonment for a term not exceeding two years or a fine, or both;
(b) on summary conviction to imprisonment for a term not exceeding six months or a fine not exceeding the statutory maximum, or both.".
(3) Omit subsection (2).
(4) The above amendments do not apply in relation to offences committed before the commencement of Part IV.

Section 34: falsification of register, &c.

23. (1)In section 34 of the Registered Designs Act 1949 (falsification of register, &c.) for "shall be guilty of a misdemeanour" substitute—
"shall be guilty of an offence and liable—
(a) on conviction on indictment to imprisonment for a term not exceeding two years or a fine, or both;
(b) on summary conviction to imprisonment for a term not exceeding six months or a fine not exceeding the statutory maximum, or both.".
(2) The above amendment does not apply in relation to offences committed before the commencement of Part IV.

Section 35: fine for falsely representing a design as registered

24. (1)Section 35 of the M7. Registered Designs Act 1949 (fine for falsely representing a design as registered) is amended as follows.
(2) In subsection (1) for the words from "a fine not exceeding £50" substitute " a fine not exceeding level 3 on the standard scale ".
(3) In subsection (2)—
(a) for "the copyright in a registered design" substitute " the right in a registered design ";
(b) for "subsisting copyright in the design" substitute " subsisting right in the design under this Act "; and
(c) for the words from "a fine" to the end substitute " a fine not exceeding level 1 on the standard scale ".
(4) The amendment in sub-paragraph (2) does not apply in relation to offences committed before the commencement of Part IV.
Marginal Citations
M71949 c. 88.

Section 35. A: offence by body corporate - liability of officers

25. (1)In the Registered Designs Act 1949 after section 35 insert—

"35. A Offence by body corporate: liability of officers.

(1) Where an offence under this Act committed by a body corporate is proved to have been committed with the consent or connivance of a director, manager, secretary or other similar officer of the body, or a person purporting to act in any such capacity, he as well as the body corporate is guilty of the offence and liable to be proceeded against and punished accordingly.

(2) In relation to a body corporate whose affairs are managed by its members "director" means a member of the body corporate.".

(2) The above amendment does not apply in relation to offences committed before the commencement of Part IV.

Section 36: general power to make rules, &c.

26. (1)Section 36 of the Registered Designs Act 1949 (general power to make rules, &c.) is amended as follows.

(2) In subsection (1) for "the Board of Trade" and "the Board" substitute " the Secretary of State ", and for "as they think expedient" substitute " as he thinks expedient ".

(3) For the words in subsection (1) from "and in particular" to the end substitute the following subsections—

"(1. A)Rules may, in particular, make provision—

   (a) prescribing the form of applications for registration of designs and of any representations or specimens of designs or other documents which may be filed at the Patent Office, and requiring copies to be furnished of any such representations, specimens or documents;

   (b) regulating the procedure to be followed in connection with any application or request to the registrar or in connection with any proceeding before him, and authorising the rectification of irregularities of procedure;

   (c) providing for the appointment of advisers to assist the registrar in proceedings before him;

   (d) regulating the keeping of the register of designs;

   (e) authorising the publication and sale of copies of representations of designs and other documents in the Patent Office;

   (f) prescribing anything authorised or required by this Act to be prescribed by rules.

(1. B)The remuneration of an adviser appointed to assist the registrar shall be determined by the Secretary of State with the consent of the Treasury and shall be defrayed out of money provided by Parliament.".

Section 37: provisions as to rules and Orders

27. (1)Section 37 of the M8. Registered Designs Act 1949 (provisions as to rules and orders) is amended as follows.

(2) Omit subsection (1) (duty to advertise making of rules).

(3) In subsections (2), (3) and (4) for "the Board of Trade" substitute " the Secretary of State ".
Marginal Citations
M81949 c. 88.

Section 38: proceedings of the Board of Trade

28. Section 38 of the Registered Designs Act 1949 (proceedings of the Board of Trade) is repealed.

Section 39: hours of business and excluded days

29. In section 39 of the Registered Designs Act 1949 (hours of business and excluded days), in subsection (1) for "the Board of Trade" substitute " the Secretary of State ".

Section 40: fees

30. In section 40 of the Registered Designs Act 1949 (fees) for "the Board of Trade" substitute " the Secretary of State ".

Section 44: interpretation

31. (1)In section 44 of the Registered Designs Act 1949 (interpretation), subsection (1) is amended as follows.

F7. (2). . . . .

(3) At the appropriate place insert—

""author" in relation to a design, has the meaning given by section 2. (3) and (4);".

(4) Omit the definition of "copyright".

F7. (5). . . . .

(6) For the definition of "court" substitute—

""the court" shall be construed in accordance with section 27 of this Act;".

(7) In the definition of "design" for "subsection (3) of section one of this Act" substitute " section 1. (1) of this Act ".

(8) At the appropriate place insert—

""employee", "employment" and "employer" refer to employment under a contract of service or of apprenticeship,".

(9) Omit the definition of "Journal".

(10) In the definition of "prescribed" for "the Board of Trade" substitute " the Secretary of State ".

Amendments (Textual)

F7. Sch. 3 para. 31. (2)(5) repealed (9.12.2001) by S.I. 2001/3949, reg. 9. (2), Sch. 2 (with transitional provisions in regs. 10-14)

Section 45: application to Scotland

32. In section 45 of the M9. Registered Designs Act 1949 (application to Scotland), omit paragraphs (1) and (2).

Marginal Citations

M91949 c. 88.

Section 46: application to Northern Ireland

33. (1)Section 46 of the Registered Designs Act 1949 (application to Northern Ireland) is amended as follows.

(2) Omit paragraphs (1) and (2).

(3) For paragraph (3) substitute—

"(3)References to enactments include enactments comprised in Northern Ireland legislation:".

(4) After paragraph (3) insert—

"(3. A)References to the Crown include the Crown in right of Her Majesty's Government in Northern Ireland:".

(5) In paragraph (4) for "a department of the Government of Northern Ireland" substitute " a Northern Ireland department ", and at the end add " and in relation to a Northern Ireland

department references to the Treasury shall be construed as references to the Department of Finance and Personnel ".

Section 47: application to Isle of Man

34. For section 47 of the Registered Designs Act 1949 (application to Isle of Man) substitute—

"47 Application to Isle of Man.

This Act extends to the Isle of Man, subject to any modifications contained in an Order made by Her Majesty in Council, and accordingly, subject to any such Order, references in this Act to the United Kingdom shall be construed as including the Isle of Man.".

Section 47. A: territorial waters and the continental shelf

35. In the Registered Designs Act 1949, after section 47 insert—

"47. A Territorial waters and the continental shelf.

(1) For the purposes of this Act the territorial waters of the United Kingdom shall be treated as part of the United Kingdom.
(2) This Act applies to things done in the United Kingdom sector of the continental shelf on a structure or vessel which is present there for purposes directly connected with the exploration of the sea bed or subsoil or the exploitation of their natural resources as it applies to things done in the United Kingdom.
(3) The United Kingdom sector of the continental shelf means the areas designated by order under section 1. (7) of the Continental Shelf Act 1964.".

Section 48: repeals, savings and transitional provisions

36. In section 48 of the Registered Designs Act 1949 (repeals, savings and transitional provisions), omit subsection (1) (repeals).

Schedule 1: provisions as to Crown use of registered designs

37. (1)The First Schedule to the M10. Registered Designs Act 1949 (provisions as to Crown use of registered designs) is amended as follows.
(2) In paragraph 2. (1) after "copyright" insert " or design right ".
(3) In paragraph 3. (1) omit "in such manner as may be prescribed by rules of court".
(4) In paragraph 4. (2) (definition of "period of emergency") for the words from "the period ending" to "any other period" substitute " a period ".
(5) For paragraph 4. (3) substitute—
"(3)No Order in Council under this paragraph shall be submitted to Her Majesty unless a draft of it has been laid before and approved by a resolution of each House of Parliament.".
Marginal Citations
M101949 c. 88.

Schedule 2: enactments repealed

38. Schedule 2 to the Registered Designs Act 1949 (enactments repealed) is repealed.

Schedule 7. The Registered Designs Act 1949 as amended Arrangement of Sections

Section 273.

Modifications etc. (not altering text)

C1. Sch. 4 extended (with modifications) (Isle of Man) (9.12.2001) by S.I. 2001/3678, art. 3, Sch. 3

C2. Sch. 4 extended (Isle of Man) (with modifications) (11.11.2013) by The Registered Designs (Isle of Man) Order 2013 (S.I. 2013/2533), arts. 1, 3. (2), Sch. 2

Registrable designs and proceedings for registration

1. Designs registrable under Act.
2. Proprietorship of designs.
3. Proceedings for registration.
4. Registration of same design in respect of other articles.
5. Provision for secrecy of certain designs.
6. Provisions as to confidential disclosure, &c.

Effect of registration, &c.

7. Right given by registration.
8. Duration of right in registered design.
8. ARestoration of lapsed right in design.
8. BEffect of order for restoration of right.
9. Exemption of innocent infringer from liability for damages.
10. Compulsory licence in respect of registered design.
11. Cancellation of registration.
11. APowers exercisable for protection of the public interest.
11. BUndertaking to take licence of right in infringement proceedings.
12. Use for services of the Crown.

International arrangements

13. Orders in Council as to convention countries.
14. Registration of design where application for protection in convention country has been made.
15. Extension of time for applications under s.14 in certain cases.
16. Protection of designs communicated under international agreements.

Register of designs, &c.

17. Register of designs.
18. Certificate of registration.
19. Registration of assignments, &c.
20. Rectification of register.
21. Power to correct clerical errors.
22. Inspection of registered designs.

23. Information as to existence of right in registered design.

24... ... ...

Legal proceedings and appeals

25. Certificate of contested validity of registration.
26. Remedy for groundless threats of infringement proceedings.
27. The court.
28. The Appeal Tribunal.

Powers and duties of registrar

29. Exercise of discretionary powers of registrar.
30. Costs and security for costs.
31. Evidence before registrar.
32... ... ...
33. Offences under s.5.
34. Falsification of register, &c.
35. Fine for falsely representing a design as registered.
35. AOffence by body corporate: liability of officers.

Rules, &c.

36. General power of Secretary of State to make rules, &c.
37. Provisions as to rules and Orders.
38... ... ...

Supplemental

39. Hours of business and excluded days.
40. Fees.
41. Service of notices, &c., by post.
42. Annual report of registrar.
43. Savings.
44. Interpretation.
45. Application to Scotland.
46. Application to Northern Ireland.
47. Application to Isle of Man.
47. ATerritorial waters and the continental shelf.
48. Repeals, savings and transitional provisions.
49. Short title and commencement.
Schedules:
Schedule 1—Provisions as to the use of registered designs for the services of the Crown and as to rights of third parties in respect of such use.
Schedule 2—... ... ...
An Act to consolidate certain enactments relating to registered designs.
[16th December 1949]

Registrable designs and proceedings for registration

Designs registrable under Act.

1. (1)In this Act "design" means features of shape, configuration, pattern or ornament applied to an article by any industrial process, being features which in the finished article appeal to and are judged by the eye, but does not include—
(a) a method or principle of construction, or
(b) features of shape or configuration of an article which—
(i) are dictated solely by the function which the article has to perform, or
(ii) are dependent upon the appearance of another article of which the article is intended by the author of the design to form an integral part.
(2) A design which is new may, upon application by the person claiming to be the proprietor, be registered under this Act in respect of any article, or set of articles, specified in the application.
(3) A design shall not be registered in respect of an article if the appearance of the article is not material, that is, if aesthetic considerations are not normally taken into account to a material extent by persons acquiring or using articles of that description, and would not be so taken into account if the design were to be applied to the article.
(4) A design shall not be regarded as new for the purposes of this Act if it is the same as a design—
(a) registered in respect of the same or any other article in pursuance of a prior application, or
(b) published in the United Kingdom in respect of the same or any other article before the date of the application,
or if it differs from such a design only in immaterial details or in features which are variants commonly used in the trade.
This subsection has effect subject to the provisions of sections 4, 6 and 16 of this Act.
(5) The Secretary of State may by rules provide for excluding from registration under this Act designs for such articles of a primarily literary or artistic character as the Secretary of State thinks fit.

Proprietorship of designs.

2. (1)The author of a design shall be treated for the purposes of this Act as the original proprietor of the design, subject to the following provisions.
(1. A)Where a design is created in pursuance of a commission for money or money's worth, the person commissioning the design shall be treated as the original proprietor of the design.
(1. B)Where, in a case not falling within subsection (1. A), a design is created by an employee in the course of his employment, his employer shall be treated as the original proprietor of the design.
(2) Where a design, or the right to apply a design to any article, becomes vested, whether by assignment, transmission or operation of law, in any person other than the original proprietor, either alone or jointly with the original proprietor, that other person, or as the case may be the original proprietor and that other person, shall be treated for the purposes of this Act as the proprietor of the design or as the proprietor of the design in relation to that article.
(3) In this Act the "author" of a design means the person who creates it.
(4) In the case of a design generated by computer in circumstances such that there is no human author, the person by whom the arrangements necessary for the creation of the design are made shall be taken to be the author.

Proceedings for registration.

3. (1)An application for the registration of a design shall be made in the prescribed form and shall be filed at the Patent Office in the prescribed manner.

(2) An application for the registration of a design in which design right subsists shall not be entertained unless made by the person claiming to be the design right owner.

(3) For the purpose of deciding whether a design is new, the registrar may make such searches, if any, as he thinks fit.

(4) The registrar may, in such cases as may be prescribed, direct that for the purpose of deciding whether a design is new an application shall be treated as made on a date earlier or later than that on which it was in fact made.

(5) The registrar may refuse an application for the registration of a design or may register the design in pursuance of the application subject to such modifications, if any, as he thinks fit; and a design when registered shall be registered as of the date on which the application was made or is treated as having been made.

(6) An application which, owing to any default or neglect on the part of the applicant, has not been completed so as to enable registration to be effected within such time as may be prescribed shall be deemed to be abandoned.

(7) An appeal lies from any decision of the registrar under this section.

Registration of same design in respect of other articles, etc.

4. (1)Where the registered proprietor of a design registered in respect of any article makes an application—

(a) for registration in respect of one or more other articles, of the registered design, or

(b) for registration in respect of the same or one or more other articles, of a design consisting of the registered design with modifications or variations not sufficient to alter the character or substantially to affect the identity thereof,

the application shall not be refused and the registration made on that application shall not be invalidated by reason only of the previous registration or publication of the registered design: Provided that the right in a design registered by virtue of this section shall not extend beyond the end of the period, and any extended period, for which the right subsists in the original registered design.

(2) Where any person makes an application for the registration of a design in respect of any article and either—

(a) that design has been previously registered by another person in respect of some other article; or

(b) the design to which the application relates consists of a design previously registered by another person in respect of the same or some other article with modifications or variations not sufficient to alter the character or substantially to affect the identity thereof,

then, if at any time while the application is pending the applicant becomes the registered proprietor of the design previously registered, the foregoing provisions of this section shall apply as if at the time of making the application the applicant had been the registered proprietor of that design.

Provisions for secrecy of certain designs.

5. (1)Where, either before or after the commencement of this Act, an application for the registration of a design has been made, and it appears to the registrar that the design is one of a class notified to him by the Secretary of State as relevant for defence purposes, he may give directions for prohibiting or restricting the publication of information with respect to the design, or the communication of such information to any person or class of persons specified in the directions.

(2) The Secretary of State shall by rules make provision for securing that where such directions are given—

(a) the representation or specimen of the design, and

(b) any evidence filed in support of the applicant's contention that the appearance of an article is material (for the purposes of section 1. (3) of this Act), shall not be open to public inspection at the Patent Office during the continuance in force of the directions.

(3) Where the registrar gives any such directions as aforesaid, he shall give notice of the application and of the directions to the Secretary of State, and thereupon the following provisions shall have effect, that is to say:—

(a) the Secretary of State shall, upon receipt of such notice, consider whether the publication of the design would be prejudicial to the defence of the realm and unless a notice under paragraph (c) of this subsection has previously been given by that authority to the registrar, shall reconsider that question before the expiration of nine months from the date of filing of the application for registration of the design and at least once in every subsequent year;

(b) for the purpose aforesaid, the Secretary of State may, at any time after the design has been registered or, with the consent of the applicant, at any time before the design has been registered, inspect the representation or specimen of the design, or any such evidence as is mentioned in subsection (2)(b) above, filed in pursuance of the application;

(c) if upon consideration of the design at any time it appears to the Secretary of State that the publication of the design would not, or would no longer, be prejudicial to the defence of the realm, he shall give notice to the registrar to that effect;

(d) on the receipt of any such notice the registrar shall revoke the directions and may, subject to such conditions, if any, as he thinks fit, extend the time for doing anything required or authorised to be done by or under this Act in connection with the application or registration, whether or not that time has previously expired.

(4) No person resident in the United Kingdom shall, except under the authority of a written permit granted by or on behalf of the registrar, make or cause to be made any application outside the United Kingdom for the registration of a design of any class prescribed for the purposes of this subsection unless—

(a) an application for registration of the same design has been made in the United Kingdom not less than six weeks before the application outside the United Kingdom; and

(b) either no directions have been given under subsection (1) of this section in relation to the application in the United Kingdom or all such directions have been revoked:

Provided that this subsection shall not apply in relation to a design for which an application for protection has first been filed in a country outside the United Kingdom by a person resident outside the United Kingdom.

... ...

Provisions as to confidential disclosure, etc.

6. (1)An application for the registration of a design shall not be refused, and the registration of a design shall not be invalidated, by reason only of—

(a) the disclosure of the design by the proprietor to any other person in such circumstances as would make it contrary to good faith for that other person to use or publish the design;

(b) the disclosure of the design in breach of good faith by any person other than the proprietor of the design; or

(c) in the case of a new or original textile design intended for registration, the acceptance of a first and confidential order for goods bearing the design.

(2) An application for the registration of a design shall not be refused and the registration of a design shall not be invalidated by reason only—

(a) that a representation of the design, or any article to which the design has been applied, has been displayed, with the consent of the proprietor of the design, at an exhibition certified by the Secretary of State for the purposes of this subsection;

(b) that after any such display as aforesaid, and during the period of the exhibition, a representation of the design or any such article as aforesaid has been displayed by any person without the consent of the proprietor; or

(c) that a representation of the design has been published in consequence of any such display as is mentioned in paragraph (a) of this subsection,
if the application for registration of the design is made not later than six months after the opening of the exhibition.

(3) An application for the registration of a design shall not be refused, and the registration of a design shall not be invalidated, by reason only of the communication of the design by the proprietor thereof to a government department or to any person authorised by a government department to consider the merits of the design, or of anything done in consequence of such a communication.

(4) Where an application is made by or with the consent of the owner of copyright in an artistic work for the registration of a corresponding design, the design shall not be treated for the purposes of this Act as being other than new by reason only of any use previously made of the artistic work, subject to subsection (5).

(5) Subsection (4) does not apply if the previous use consisted of or included the sale, letting for hire or offer or exposure for sale or hire of articles to which had been applied industrially—
(a) the design in question, or
(b) a design differing from it only in immaterial details or in features which are variants commonly used in the trade,
and that previous use was made by or with the consent of the copyright owner.

(6) The Secretary of State may make provision by rules as to the circumstances in which a design is to be regarded for the purposes of this section as "applied industrially" to articles, or any description of articles.

Effect of registration, &c.

Right given by registration.

7. (1) The registration of a design under this Act gives the registered proprietor the exclusive right—
(a) to make or import—
(i) for sale or hire, or
(ii) for use for the purposes of a trade or business, or
(b) to sell, hire or offer or expose for sale or hire,
an article in respect of which the design is registered and to which that design or a design not substantially different from it has been applied.

(2) The right in the registered design is infringed by a person who without the licence of the registered proprietor does anything which by virtue of subsection (1) is the exclusive right of the proprietor.

(3) The right in the registered design is also infringed by a person who, without the licence of the registered proprietor makes anything for enabling any such article to be made, in the United Kingdom or elsewhere, as mentioned in subsection (1).

(4) The right in the registered design is also infringed by a person who without the licence of the registered proprietor—
(a) does anything in relation to a kit that would be an infringement if done in relation to the assembled article (see subsection (1)), or
(b) makes anything for enabling a kit to be made or assembled, in the United Kingdom or elsewhere, if the assembled article would be such an article as is mentioned in subsection (1);
and for this purpose a "kit" means a complete or substantially complete set of components intended to be assembled into an article.

(5) No proceedings shall be taken in respect of an infringement committed before the date on which the certificate of registration of the design under this Act is granted.

(6) The right in a registered design is not infringed by the reproduction of a feature of the design which, by virtue of section 1. (1)(b), is left out of account in determining whether the design is registrable.

Duration of right in registered design.

8. (1)The right in a registered design subsists in the first instance for a period of five years from the date of the registration of the design.

(2) The period for which the right subsists may be extended for a second, third, fourth and fifth period of five years, by applying to the registrar for an extension and paying the prescribed renewal fee.

(3) If the first, second, third or fourth period expires without such application and payment being made, the right shall cease to have effect; and the registrar shall, in accordance with rules made by the Secretary of State, notify the proprietor of that fact.

(4) If during the period of six months immediately following the end of that period an application for extension is made and the prescribed renewal fee and any prescribed additional fee is paid, the right shall be treated as if it had never expired, with the result that—

(a) anything done under or in relation to the right during that further period shall be treated as valid,

(b) an act which would have constituted an infringement of the right if it had not expired shall be treated as an infringement, and

(c) an act which would have constituted use of the design for the services of the Crown if the right had not expired shall be treated as such use.

(5) Where it is shown that a registered design—

(a) was at the time it was registered a corresponding design in relation to an artistic work in which copyright subsists, and

(b) by reason of a previous use of that work would not have been registrable but for section 6. (4) of this Act (registration despite certain prior applications of design),

the right in the registered design expires when the copyright in that work expires, if that is earlier than the time at which it would otherwise expire, and it may not thereafter be renewed.

(6) The above provisions have effect subject to the proviso to section 4. (1) (registration of same design in respect of other articles, &c.).

Restoration of lapsed right in design.

8. A(1)Where the right in a registered design has expired by reason of a failure to extend, in accordance with section 8. (2) or (4), the period for which the right subsists, an application for the restoration of the right in the design may be made to the registrar within the prescribed period.

(2) The application may be made by the person who was the registered proprietor of the design or by any other person who would have been entitled to the right in the design if it had not expired; and where the design was held by two or more persons jointly, the application may, with the leave of the registrar, be made by one or more of them without joining the others.

(3) Notice of the application shall be published by the registrar in the prescribed manner.

(4) If the registrar is satisfied that the proprietor took reasonable care to see that the period for which the right subsisted was extended in accordance with section 8. (2) or (4), he shall, on payment of any unpaid renewal fee and any prescribed additional fee, order the restoration of the right in the design.

(5) The order may be made subject to such conditions as the registrar thinks fit, and if the proprietor of the design does not comply with any condition the registrar may revoke the order and give such consequential directions as he thinks fit.

(6) Rules altering the period prescribed for the purposes of subsection (1) may contain such transitional provisions and savings as appear to the Secretary of State to be necessary or expedient.

Effect of order for restoration of right.

8. B(1)The effect of an order under section 8. A for the restoration of the right in a registered design is as follows.

(2) Anything done under or in relation to the right during the period between expiry and restoration shall be treated as valid.

(3) Anything done during that period which would have constituted an infringement if the right had not expired shall be treated as an infringement—

(a) if done at a time when it was possible for an application for extension to be made under section 8. (4); or

(b) if it was a continuation or repetition of an earlier infringing act.

(4) If after it was no longer possible for such an application for extension to be made, and before publication of notice of the application for restoration, a person—

(a) began in good faith to do an act which would have constituted an infringement of the right in the design if it had not expired, or

(b) made in good faith effective and serious preparations to do such an act,

he has the right to continue to do the act or, as the case may be, to do the act, notwithstanding the restoration of the right in the design; but this does not extend to granting a licence to another person to do the act.

(5) If the act was done, or the preparations were made, in the course of a business, the person entitled to the right conferred by subsection (4) may—

(a) authorise the doing of that act by any partners of his for the time being in that business, and

(b) assign that right, or transmit it on death (or in the case of a body corporate on its dissolution), to any person who acquires that part of the business in the course of which the act was done or the preparations were made.

(6) Where an article is disposed of to another in exercise of the rights conferred by subsection (4) or subsection (5), that other and any person claiming through him may deal with the article in the same way as if it had been disposed of by the registered proprietor of the design.

(7) The above provisions apply in relation to the use of a registered design for the services of the Crown as they apply in relation to infringement of the right in the design.

Exemption of innocent infringer from liability for damages.

9. (1)In proceedings for the infringement of the right in a registered design damages shall not be awarded against a defendant who proves that at the date of the infringement he was not aware, and had no reasonable ground for supposing, that the design was registered; and a person shall not be deemed to have been aware or to have had reasonable grounds for supposing as aforesaid by reason only of the marking of an article with the word "registered" or any abbreviation thereof, or any word or words expressing or implying that the design applied to the article has been registered, unless the number of the design accompanied the word or words or the abbreviation in question.

(2) Nothing in this section shall affect the power of the court to grant an injunction in any proceedings for infringement of the right in a registered design.

Compulsory licence in respect of registered design.

10. (1)At any time after a design has been registered any person interested may apply to the registrar for the grant of a compulsory licence in respect of the design on the ground that the design is not applied in the United Kingdom by any industrial process or means to the article in respect of which it is registered to such an extent as is reasonable in the circumstances of the case;

and the registrar may make such order on the application as he thinks fit.

(2) An order for the grant of a licence shall, without prejudice to any other method of enforcement, have effect as if it were a deed executed by the registered proprietor and all other necessary parties, granting a licence in accordance with the order.

(3) No order shall be made under this section which would be at variance with any treaty, convention, arrangement or engagement applying to the United Kingdom and any convention country.

(4) An appeal shall lie from any order of the registrar under this section.

Cancellation of registration.

11. (1)The registrar may, upon a request made in the prescribed manner by the registered proprietor, cancel the registration of a design.

(2) At any time after a design has been registered any person interested may apply to the registrar for the cancellation of the registration of the design on the ground that the design was not, at the date of the registration thereof, new..., or on any other ground on which the registrar could have refused to register the design; and the registrar may make such order on the application as he thinks fit.

(3) At any time after a design has been registered, any person interested may apply to the registrar for the cancellation of the registration on the ground that—

(a) the design was at the time it was registered a corresponding design in relation to an artistic work in which copyright subsisted, and

(b) the right in the registered design has expired in accordance with section 8. (4) of this Act (expiry of right in registered design on expiry of copyright in artistic work);

and the registrar may make such order on the application as he thinks fit.

(4) A cancellation under this section takes effect—

(a) in the case of cancellation under subsection (1), from the date of the registrar's decision,

(b) in the case of cancellation under subsection (2), from the date of registration,

(c) in the case of cancellation under subsection (3), from the date on which the right in the registered design expired,

or, in any case, from such other date as the registrar may direct.

(5) An appeal lies from any order of the registrar under this section.

Powers exercisable for protection of the public interest.

11. A(1)Where a report of the Monopolies and Mergers Commission has been laid before Parliament containing conclusions to the effect—

(a) on a monopoly reference, that a monopoly situation exists and facts found by the Commission operate or may be expected to operate against the public interest,

(b) on a merger reference, that a merger situation qualifying for investigation has been created and the creation of the situation, or particular elements in or consequences of it specified in the report, operate or may be expected to operate against the public interest,

(c) on a competition reference, that a person was engaged in an anti-competitive practice which operated or may be expected to operate against the public interest, or

(d) on a reference under section 11 of the Competition Act 1980 (reference of public bodies and certain other persons), that a person is pursuing a course of conduct which operates against the public interest,

the appropriate Minister or Ministers may apply to the registrar to take action under this section.

(2) Before making an application the appropriate Minister or Ministers shall publish, in such manner as he or they think appropriate, a notice describing the nature of the proposed application and shall consider any representations which may be made within 30 days of such publication by persons whose interests appear to him or them to be affected.

(3) If on an application under this section it appears to the registrar that the matters specified in the Commission's report as being those which in the Commission's opinion operate, or operated or may be expected to operate, against the public interest include—

(a) conditions in licences granted in respect of a registered design by its proprietor restricting the use of the design by the licensee or the right of the proprietor to grant other licences, or

(b) a refusal by the proprietor of a registered design to grant licences on reasonable terms,

he may by order cancel or modify any such condition or may, instead or in addition, make an entry in the register to the effect that licences in respect of the design are to be available as of right.

(4) The terms of a licence available by virtue of this section shall, in default of agreement, be settled by the registrar on an application by the person requiring the licence; and terms so settled shall authorise the licensee to do everything which would be an infringement of the right in the registered design in the absence of a licence.

(5) Where the terms of a licence are settled by the registrar, the licence has effect from the date on which the application to him was made.

(6) An appeal lies from any order of the registrar under this section.

(7) In this section "the appropriate Minister or Ministers" means the Minister or Ministers to whom the report of the Monopolies and Mergers Commission was made.

Undertaking to take licence of right in infringement proceedings.

11. B(1)If in proceedings for infringement of the right in a registered design in respect of which a licence is available as of right under section 11. A of this Act the defendant undertakes to take a licence on such terms as may be agreed or, in default of agreement, settled by the registrar under that section—

(a) no injunction shall be granted against him, and

(b) the amount recoverable against him by way of damages or on an account of profits shall not exceed double the amount which would have been payable by him as licensee if such a licence on those terms had been granted before the earliest infringement.

(2) An undertaking may be given at any time before final order in the proceedings, without any admission of liability.

(3) Nothing in this section affects the remedies available in respect of an infringement committed before licences of right were available.

Use for services of the Crown.

12. The provisions of the First Schedule to this Act shall have effect with respect to the use of registered designs for the services of the Crown and the rights of third parties in respect of such use.

International Arrangements

Orders in Council as to convention countries.

13. (1)His Majesty may, with a view to the fulfilment of a treaty, convention, arrangement or engagement, by Order in Council declare that any country specified in the Order is a convention country for the purposes of this Act:

Provided that a declaration may be made as aforesaid for the purposes either of all or of some only of the provisions of this Act, and a country in the case of which a declaration made for the purposes of some only of the provisions of this Act is in force shall be deemed to be a convention country for the purposes of those provisions only.

(2) His Majesty may by Order in Council direct that any of the Channel Islands, any colony,... shall be deemed to be a convention country for the purposes of all or any of the provisions of this Act; and an Order made under this subsection may direct that any such provisions shall have effect, in relation to the territory in question, subject to such conditions or limitations, if any, as may be specified in the Order.

(3) For the purposes of subsection (1) of this section, every colony, protectorate, territory subject to the authority or under the suzerainty of another country, and territory administered by another country... under the trusteeship system of the United Nations, shall be deemed to be a country in the case of which a declaration may be made under that subsection.

Registration of design where application for protection in convention country has been made.

14. (1)An application for registration of a design in respect of which protection has been applied for in a convention country may be made in accordance with the provisions of this Act by the person by whom the application for protection was made or his personal representative or assignee:

Provided that no application shall be made by virtue of this section after the expiration of six months from the date of the application for protection in a convention country or, where more than one such application for protection has been made, from the date of the first application.

(2) Where an application for registration of a design is made by virtue of this section, the application shall be treated, for the purpose of determining whether that or any other design is new, as made on the date of the application for protection in the convention country or, if more than one such application was made, on the date of the first such application.

(3) Subsection (2) shall not be construed as excluding the power to give directions under section 3.

(4) of this Act in relation to an application made by virtue of this section.

(4) Where a person has applied for protection for a design by an application which—

(a) in accordance with the terms of a treaty subsisting between two or more convention countries, is equivalent to an application duly made in any one of those convention countries; or

(b) in accordance with the law of any convention country, is equivalent to an application duly made in that convention country,

he shall be deemed for the purposes of this section to have applied in that convention country.

Extension of time for applications under s.14 in certain cases.

15. (1)If the Secretary of State is satisfied that provision substantially equivalent to the provision to be made by or under this section has been or will be made under the law of any convention country, he may make rules empowering the registrar to extend the time for making application under subsection (1) of section 14 of this Act for registration of a design in respect of which protection has been applied for in that country in any case where the period specified in the proviso to that subsection expires during a period prescribed by the rules.

(2) Rules made under this section—

(a) may, where any agreement or arrangement has been made between His Majesty's Government in the United Kingdom and the government of the convention country for the supply or mutual exchange of information or articles, provide, either generally or in any class of case specified in the rules, that an extension of time shall not be granted under this section unless the design has been communicated in accordance with the agreement or arrangement;

(b) may, either generally or in any class of case specified in the rules, fix the maximum extension which may be granted under this section;

(c) may prescribe or allow any special procedure in connection with applications made by virtue of this section;

(d) may empower the registrar to extend, in relation to an application made by virtue of this section, the time limited by or under the foregoing provisions of this Act for doing any act, subject to such conditions, if any, as may be imposed by or under the rules;

(e) may provide for securing that the rights conferred by registration on an application made by virtue of this section shall be subject to such restrictions or conditions as may be specified by or under the rules and in particular to restrictions and conditions for the protection of persons (including persons acting on behalf of His Majesty) who, otherwise than as the result of a communication made in accordance with such an agreement or arrangement as is mentioned in paragraph (a) of this subsection, and before the date of the application in question or such later date as may be allowed by the rules, may have imported or made articles to which the design is applied or may have made any application for registration of the design.

Protection of designs communicated under international agreements.

16. (1)Subject to the provisions of this section, the Secretary of State may make rules for securing that, where a design has been communicated in accordance with an agreement or arrangement made between His Majesty's Government in the United Kingdom and the government of any other country for the supply or mutual exchange of information or articles,—

(a) an application for the registration of the design made by the person from whom the design was communicated or his personal representative or assignee shall not be prejudiced, and the registration of the design in pursuance of such an application shall not be invalidated, by reason only that the design has been communicated as aforesaid or that in consequence thereof—

(i) the design has been published or applied, or

(ii) an application for registration of the design has been made by any other person, or the design has been registered on such an application;

(b) any application for the registration of a design made in consequence of such a communication as aforesaid may be refused and any registration of a design made on such an application may be cancelled.

(2) Rules made under subsection (1) of this section may provide that the publication or application of a design, or the making of any application for registration thereof shall, in such circumstances and subject to such conditions or exceptions as may be prescribed by the rules, be presumed to have been in consequence of such a communication as is mentioned in that subsection.

(3) The powers of the Secretary of State under this section, so far as they are exercisable for the benefit of persons from whom designs have been communicated to His Majesty's Government in the United Kingdom by the government of any other country, shall only be exercised if and to the extent that the Secretary of State is satisfied that substantially equivalent provision has been or will be made under the law of that country for the benefit of persons from whom designs have been communicated by His Majesty's Government in the United Kingdom to the government of that country.

(4) References in the last foregoing subsection to the communication of a design to or by His Majesty's Government or the government of any other country shall be construed as including references to the communication of the design by or to any person authorised in that behalf by the government in question.

Register of designs, etc.

Register of designs.

17. (1)The registrar shall maintain the register of designs, in which shall be entered—

(a) the names and addresses of proprietors of registered designs;

(b) notices of assignments and of transmissions of registered designs; and

(c) such other matters as may be prescribed or as the registrar may think fit.

(2) No notice of any trust, whether express, implied or constructive, shall be entered in the register of designs, and the registrar shall not be affected by any such notice.

(3) The register need not be kept in documentary form.

(4) Subject to the provisions of this Act and to rules made by the Secretary of State under it, the public shall have a right to inspect the register at the Patent Office at all convenient times.

(5) Any person who applies for a certified copy of an entry in the register or a certified extract from the register shall be entitled to obtain such a copy or extract on payment of a fee prescribed in relation to certified copies and extracts; and rules made by the Secretary of State under this Act may provide that any person who applies for an uncertified copy or extract shall be entitled to such a copy or extract on payment of a fee prescribed in relation to uncertified copies and extracts.

(6) Applications under subsection (5) above or rules made by virtue of that subsection shall be made in such manner as may be prescribed.

(7) In relation to any portion of the register kept otherwise than in documentary form—

(a) the right of inspection conferred by subsection (4) above is a right to inspect the material on the register; and

(b) the right to a copy or extract conferred by subsection (5) above or rules is a right to a copy or extract in a form in which it can be taken away and in which it is visible and legible.

(8) Subject to subsection (11) below, the register shall be prima facie evidence of anything required or authorised to be entered in it and in Scotland shall be sufficient evidence of any such thing.

(9) A certificate purporting to be signed by the registrar and certifying that any entry which he is authorised by or under this Act to make has or has not been made, or that any other thing which he is so authorised to do has or has not been done, shall be prima facie evidence, and in Scotland shall be sufficient evidence, of the matters so certified.

(10) Each of the following—

(a) a copy of an entry in the register or an extract from the register which is supplied under subsection (5) above;

(b) a copy or any representation, specimen or document kept in the Patent Office or an extract from any such document,

which purports to be a certified copy or certified extract shall, subject to subsection (11) below, be admitted in evidence without further proof and without production of any original; and in Scotland such evidence shall be sufficient evidence.

(11) In the application of this section to England and Wales nothing in it shall be taken as detracting from section 69 or 70 of the Police and Criminal Evidence Act 1984 or any provision made by virtue of either of them.

(12) In this section "certified copy" and "certified extract" means a copy and extract certified by the registrar and sealed with the seal of the Patent Office.

Certificate of registration.

18. (1)The registrar shall grant a certificate of registration in the prescribed form to the registered proprietor of a design when the design is registered.

(2) The registrar may, in a case where he is satisfied that the certificate of registration has been lost or destroyed, or in any other case in which he thinks it expedient, furnish one or more copies of the certificate.

Registration of assignments, etc.

19. (1)Where any person becomes entitled by assignment, transmission or operation of law to a

registered design or to a share in a registered design, or becomes entitled as mortgagee, licensee or otherwise to any other interest in a registered design, he shall apply to the registrar in the prescribed manner for the registration of his title as proprietor or co-proprietor or, as the case may be, of notice of his interest, in the register of designs.

(2) Without prejudice to the provisions of the foregoing subsection, an application for the registration of the title of any person becoming entitled by assignment to a registered design or a share in a registered design, or becoming entitled by virtue of a mortgage, licence or other instrument to any other interest in a registered design, may be made in the prescribed manner by the assignor, mortgagor, licensor or other party to that instrument, as the case may be.

(3) Where application is made under this section for the registration of the title of any person, the registrar shall, upon proof of title to his satisfaction—

(a) where that person is entitled to a registered design or a share in a registered design, register him in the register of designs as proprietor or co-proprietor of the design, and enter in that register particulars of the instrument or event by which he derives title; or

(b) where that person is entitled to any other interest in the registered design, enter in that register notice of his interest, with particulars of the instrument (if any) creating it.

(3. A)Where design right subsists in a registered design, the registrar shall not register an interest under subsection (3) unless he is satisfied that the person entitled to that interest is also entitled to a corresponding interest in the design right.

(3. B)Where design right subsists in a registered design and the proprietor of the registered design is also the design right owner, an assignment of the design right shall be taken to be also an assignment of the right in the registered design, unless a contrary intention appears.

(4) Subject to any rights vested in any other person of which notice is entered in the register of designs, the person or persons registered as proprietor of a registered design shall have power to assign, grant licences under, or otherwise deal with the design, and to give effectual receipts for any consideration for any such assignment, licence or dealing.

Provided that any equities in respect of the design may be enforced in like manner as in respect of any other personal property.

(5) Except for the purposes of an application to rectify the register under the following provisions of this Act, a document in respect of which no entry has been made in the register of designs under subsection (3) of this section shall not be admitted in any court as evidence of the title of any person to a registered design or share of or interest in a registered design unless the court otherwise directs.

Rectification of register.

20. (1)The court may, on the application of any person aggrieved, order the register of designs to be rectified by the making of any entry therein or the variation or deletion of any entry therein.

(2) In proceedings under this section the court may determine any question which it may be necessary or expedient to decide in connection with the rectification of the register.

(3) Notice of any application to the court under this section shall be given in the prescribed manner to the registrar, who shall be entitled to appear and be heard on the application, and shall appear if so directed by the court.

(4) Any order made by the court under this section shall direct that notice of the order shall be served on the registrar in the prescribed manner; and the registrar shall, on receipt of the notice, rectify the register accordingly.

(5) A rectification of the register under this section has effect as follows—

(a) an entry made has effect from the date on which it should have been made,

(b) an entry varied has effect as if it had originally been made in its varied form, and

(c) an entry deleted shall be deemed never to have had effect,

unless, in any case, the court directs otherwise.

Power to correct clerical errors.

21. (1)The registrar may, in accordance with the provisions of this section, correct any error in an application for the registration or in the representation of a design, or any error in the register of designs.

(2) A correction may be made in pursuance of this section either upon a request in writing made by any person interested and accompanied by the prescribed fee, or without such a request.

(3) Where the registrar proposes to make any such correction as aforesaid otherwise than in pursuance of a request made under this section, he shall give notice of the proposal to the registered proprietor or the applicant for registration of the design, as the case may be, and to any other person who appears to him to be concerned, and shall give them an opportunity to be heard before making the correction.

Inspection of registered designs.

22. (1)Where a design has been registered under this Act, there shall be open to inspection at the Patent Office on and after the day on which the certificate of registration is issued—

(a) the representation or specimen of the design, and

(b) any evidence filed in support of the applicant's contention that the appearance of an article is material (for the purposes of section 1. (3) of this Act).

This subsection has effect subject to the following provisions of this section and to any rules made under section 5. (2) of this Act.

(2) In the case of a design registered in respect of an article of any class prescribed for the purposes of this subsection, no representation, specimen or evidence filed in pursuance of the application shall, until the expiration of such period after the day on which the certificate of registration is issued as may be prescribed in relation to articles of that class, be open to inspection at the Patent Office except by the registered proprietor, a person authorised in writing by the registered proprietor, or a person authorised by the registrar or by the court:

Provided that where the registrar proposes to refuse an application for the registration of any other design on the ground that it is the same as the first-mentioned design or differs from that design only in immaterial details or in features which are variants commonly used in the trade, the applicant shall be entitled to inspect the representation or specimen of the first-mentioned design filed in pursuance of the application for registration of that design.

(3) In the case of a design registered in respect of an article of any class prescribed for the purposes of the last foregoing subsection, the representation, specimen or evidence shall not, during the period prescribed as aforesaid, be inspected by any person by virtue of this section except in the presence of the registrar or of an officer acting under him; and except in the case of an inspection authorised by the proviso to that subsection, the person making the inspection shall not be entitled to take a copy of the representation, specimen or evidence or any part thereof.

(4) Where an application for the registration of a design has been abandoned or refused, neither the application for registration nor any representation, specimen or evidence filed in pursuance thereof shall at any time be open to inspection at the Patent Office or be published by the registrar.

Information as to existence of right in registered design.

23. On the request of a person furnishing such information as may enable the registrar to identify the design, and on payment of the prescribed fee, the registrar shall inform him—

(a) whether the design is registered and, if so, in respect of what articles, and

(b) whether any extension of the period of the right in the registered design has been granted, and shall state the date of registration and the name and address of the registered proprietor.

... ...

Legal proceedings and appeals

Certificate of contested validity of registration.

25. (1)If in any proceedings before the court the validity of the registration of a design is contested, and it is found by the court that the design is validly registered, the court may certify that the validity of the registration of the design was contested in those proceedings.
(2) Where any such certificate has been granted, then if in any subsequent proceedings before the court for infringement of the right in the registered design or for cancellation of the registration of the design, a final order or judgment is made or given in favour of the registered proprietor, he shall, unless the court otherwise directs, be entitled to his costs as between solicitor and client: Provided that this subsection shall not apply to the costs of any appeal in any such proceedings as aforesaid.

Remedy for groundless threats of infringement proceedings.

26. (1)Where any person (whether entitled to or interested in a registered design or an application for registration of a design or not) by circulars, advertisements or otherwise threatens any other person with proceedings for infringement of the right in a registered design, any person aggrieved thereby may bring an action against him for any such relief as is mentioned in the next following subsection.
(2) Unless in any action brought by virtue of this section the defendant proves that the acts in respect of which proceedings were threatened constitute or, if done, would constitute, an infringement of the right in a registered design the registration of which is not shown by the plaintiff to be invalid, the plaintiff shall be entitled to the following relief, that is to say:—
(a) a declaration to the effect that the threats are unjustifiable;
(b) an injunction against the continuance of the threats; and
(c) such damages, if any, as he has sustained thereby.
(2. A)Proceedings may not be brought under this section in respect of a threat to bring proceedings for an infringement alleged to consist of the making or importing of anything.
(3) For the avoidance of doubt it is hereby declared that a mere notification that a design is registered does not constitute a threat of proceedings within the meaning of this section.

The court.

27. (1)In this Act "the court" means—
(a) in England and Wales, the High Court or any patents county court having jurisdiction by virtue of an order under section 287 of the Copyright, Designs and Patents Act 1988,
(b) in Scotland, the Court of Session, and
(c) in Northern Ireland, the High Court.
(2) Provision may be made by rules of court with respect to proceedings in the High Court in England and Wales for references and applications under this Act to be dealt with by such judge of that court as the Lord Chancellor may select for the purpose.

The Appeal Tribunal.

28. (1)Any appeal from the registrar under this Act shall lie to the Appeal Tribunal.
(2) The Appeal Tribunal shall consist of—
(a) one or more judges of the High Court nominated by the Lord Chancellor, and

(b) one judge of the Court of Session nominated by the Lord President of that Court.

(2. A)At any time when it consists of two or more judges, the jurisdiction of the Appeal Tribunal—

(a) where in the case of any particular appeal the senior of those judges so directs, shall be exercised in relation to that appeal by both of the judges, or (if there are more than two) by two of them, sitting together, and

(b) in relation to any appeal in respect of which no such direction is given, may be exercised by any one of the judges;

and, in the exercise of that jurisdiction, different appeals may be heard at the same time by different judges.

(3) The expenses of the Appeal Tribunal shall be defrayed and the fees to be taken therein may be fixed as if the Tribunal were a court of the High Court.

(4) The Appeal Tribunal may examine witnesses on oath and administer oaths for that purpose.

(5) Upon any appeal under this Act the Appeal Tribunal may by order award to any party such costs or expenses as the Tribunal may consider reasonable and direct how and by what parties the costs or expenses are to be paid; and any such order may be enforced—

(a) in England and Wales or Northern Ireland, in the same way as an order of the High Court;

(b) in Scotland, in the same way as a decree for expenses granted by the Court of Session.

... ...

(7) Upon any appeal under this Act the Appeal Tribunal may exercise any power which could have been exercised by the registrar in the proceeding from which the appeal is brought.

(8) Subject to the foregoing provisions of this section the Appeal Tribunal may make rules for regulating all matters relating to proceedings before it under this Act, including right of audience.

(8. A)At any time when the Appeal Tribunal consists of two or more judges, the power to make rules under subsection (8) of this section shall be exercisable by the senior of those judges: Provided that another of those judges may exercise that power if it appears to him that it is necessary for rules to be made and that the judge (or, if more than one, each of the judges) senior to him is for the time being prevented by illness, absence or otherwise from making them.

(9) An appeal to the Appeal Tribunal under this Act shall not be deemed to be a proceeding in the High Court.

(10) In this section "the High Court" means the High Court in England and Wales; and for the purposes of this section the seniority of judges shall be reckoned by reference to the dates on which they were appointed judges of that court or the Court of Session.

Powers and duties of Registrar

Exercise of discretionary powers of registrar.

29. Without prejudice to any provisions of this Act requiring the registrar to hear any party to proceedings thereunder, or to give to any such party an opportunity to be heard, rules made by the Secretary of State under this Act shall require the registrar to give to any applicant for registration of a design an opportunity to be heard before exercising adversely to the applicant any discretion vested in the registrar by or under this Act.

Costs and security for costs.

30. (1)Rules made by the Secretary of State under this Act may make provision empowering the registrar, in anyproceedings before him under this Act—

(a) to award any party such costs as he may consider reasonable, and

(b) to direct how and by what parties they are to be paid.

(2) Any such order of the registrar may be enforced—

(a) in England and Wales or Northern Ireland, in the same way as an order of the High Court;

(b) in Scotland, in the same way as a decree for expenses granted by the Court of Session.

(3) Rules made by the Secretary of State under this Act may make provision empowering the registrar to require a person, in such cases as may be prescribed, to give security for the costs of—

(a) an application for cancellation of the registration of a design,

(b) an application for the grant of a licence in respect of a registered design, or

(c) an appeal from any decision of the registrar under this Act,

and enabling the application or appeal to be treated as abandoned in default of such security being given.

Evidence before registrar.

31. Rules made by the Secretary of State under this Act may make provision—

(a) as to the giving of evidence in proceedings before the registrar under this Act by affidavit or statutory declaration;

(b) conferring on the registrar the powers of an official referee of the [F1 Senior Courts] as regards the examination of witnesses on oath and the discovery and production of documents; and

(c) applying in relation to the attendance of witnesses in proceedings before the registrar the rules applicable to the attendance of witnesses in proceedings before such a referee.

... ...

Amendments (Textual)

F1. Sch. 4 para. 31. (b): words substituted (1.10.2009) by Constitutional Reform Act 2005 (c. 4), ss. 59, 148, Sch. 11 para. 4; S.I. 2009/1604, art. 2

Offences

Offences under s.5.

33. (1)If any person fails to comply with any direction given under section five of this Act or makes or causes to be made an application for the registration of a design in contravention of that section, he shall be guilty of an offence and liable—

(a) on conviction on indictment to imprisonment for a term not exceeding two years or a fine, or both;

(b) on summary conviction to imprisonment for a term not exceeding six months or a fine not exceeding the statutory maximum, or both.

... ...

Falsification of register, etc.

34. If any person makes or causes to be made a false entry in the register of designs, or a writing falsely purporting to be a copy of an entry in that register, or produces or tenders or causes to be produced or tendered in evidence any such writing, knowing the entry or writing to be false, he shall be guilty of an offence and liable—

(a) on conviction on indictment to imprisonment for a term not exceeding two years or a fine, or both;

(b) on summary conviction to imprisonment for a term not exceeding six months or a fine not exceeding the statutory maximum, or both.

Fine for falsely representing a design as registered.

35. (1)If any person falsely represents that a design applied to any article sold by him is registered in respect of that article, he shall be liable on summary conviction to a fine not exceeding level 3 on the standard scale; and for the purposes of this provision a person who sells an article having stamped, engraved or impressed thereon or otherwise applied thereto the word "registered", or any other word expressing or implying that the design applied to the article is registered, shall be deemed to represent that the design applied to the article is registered in respect of that article.

(2) If any person, after the right in a registered design has expired, marks any article to which the design has been applied with the word "registered", or any word or words implying that there is a subsisting right in the design under this Act, or causes any such article to be so marked, he shall be liable on summary conviction to a fine not exceeding level 1 on the standard scale.

Offence by body corporate: liability of officers.

35. A(1)Where an offence under this Act committed by a body corporate is proved to have been committed with the consent or connivance of a director, manager, secretary or other similar officer of the body, or a person purporting to act in any such capacity, he as well as the body corporate is guilty of the offence and liable to be proceeded against and punished accordingly.

(2) In relation to a body corporate whose affairs are managed by its members "director" means a member of the body corporate.

Rules, etc.

General power of Secretary of State to make rules, etc.

36. (1)Subject to the provisions of this Act, the Secretary of State may make such rules as he thinks expedient for regulating the business of the Patent Office in relation to designs and for regulating all matters by this Act placed under the direction or control of the registrar or the Secretary of State.

(1. A)Rules may, in particular, make provision—

(a) prescribing the form of applications for registration of designs and of any representations or specimens of designs or other documents which may be filed at the Patent Office, and requiring copies to be furnished of any such representations, specimens or documents;

(b) regulating the procedure to be followed in connection with any application or request to the registrar or in connection with any proceeding before him, and authorising the rectification of irregularities of procedure;

(c) providing for the appointment of advisers to assist the registrar in proceedings before him;

(d) regulating the keeping of the register of designs;

(e) authorising the publication and sale of copies of representations of designs and other documents in the Patent Office;

(f) prescribing anything authorised or required by this Act to be prescribed by rules.

(1. B)The remuneration of an adviser appointed to assist the registrar shall be determined by the Secretary of State with the consent of the Treasury and shall be defrayed out of money provided by Parliament.

(2) Rules made under this section may provide for the establishment of branch offices for designs and may authorise any document or thing required by or under this Act to be filed or done at the Patent Office to be filed or done at the branch office at Manchester or any other branch office established in pursuance of the rules.

Provisions as to rules and Orders.

37. (1)... ... ...

(2) Any rules made by the Secretary of State in pursuance of section 15 or section 16 of this Act, and any order made, direction given, or other action taken under the rules by the registrar, may be made, given or taken so as to have effect as respects things done or omitted to be done on or after such date, whether before or after the coming into operation of the rules or of this Act, as may be specified in the rules.

(3) Any power to make rules conferred by this Act on the Secretary of State or on the Appeal Tribunal shall be exercisable by statutory instrument; and the Statutory Instruments Act 1946 shall apply to a statutory instrument containing rules made by the Appeal Tribunal in like manner as if the rules had been made by a Minister of the Crown.

(4) Any statutory instrument containing rules made by the Secretary of State under this Act shall be subject to annulment in pursuance of a resolution of either House of Parliament.

(5) Any Order in Council made under this Act may be revoked or varied by a subsequent Order in Council.

... ...

Supplemental

Hours of business and excluded days.

39. (1)Rules made by the Secretary of State under this Act may specify the hour at which the Patent Office shall be deemed to be closed on any day for purposes of the transaction by the public of business under this Act or of any class of such business, and may specify days as excluded days for any such purposes.

(2) Any business done under this Act on any day after the hour specified as aforesaid in relation to business of that class, or on a day which is an excluded day in relation to business of that class, shall be deemed to have been done on the next following day not being an excluded day; and where the time for doing anything under this Act expires on an excluded day, that time shall be extended to the next following day not being an excluded day.

Fees.

40. There shall be paid in respect of the registration of designs and applications therefor, and in respect of other matters relating to designs arising under this Act, such fees as may be prescribed by rules made by the Secretary of State with the consent of the Treasury.

Service of notices, &c., by post.

41. Any notice required or authorised to be given by or under this Act, and any application or other document so authorised or required to be made or filed, may be given, made or filed by post.

Annual report of registrar.

42. The Comptroller-General of Patents, Designs and Trade Marks shall, in his annual report with respect to the execution of the Patents Act 1977, include a report with respect to the execution of this Act as if it formed a part of or was included in that Act.

Savings.

43. (1)Nothing in this Act shall be construed as authorising or requiring the registrar to register a design the use of which would, in his opinion, be contrary to law or morality.

(2) Nothing in this Act shall affect the right of the Crown or of any person deriving title directly or indirectly from the Crown to sell or use articles forfeited under the laws relating to customs or excise.

Interpretation.

44. (1)In this Act, except where the context otherwise requires, the following expressions have the meanings hereby respectively assigned by them, that is to say—

"Appeal Tribunal" means the Appeal Tribunal constituted and acting in accordance with section 28 of this Act as amended by the Administration of Justice Act 1969;

"article" means any article of manufacture and includes any part of an article if that part is made and sold separately;

"artistic work" has the same meaning as in Part I of the Copyright, Designs and Patents Act 1988;

"assignee" includes the personal representative of a deceased assignee, and references to the assignee of any person include references to the assignee of the personal representative or assignee of that person;

"author", in relation to a design, has the meaning given by section 2. (3) and (4);

... ...

"corresponding design", in relation to an artistic work, means a design which if applied to an article would produce something which would be treated for the purposes of Part I of the Copyright, Designs and Patents Act 1988 as a copy of that work;

"the court" shall be construed in accordance with section 27 of this Act;

"design" has the meaning assigned to it by section 1. (1) of this Act;

"employee", "employment" and "employer" refer to employment under a contract of service or of apprenticeship;

... ...

"prescribed" means prescribed by rules made by the Secretary of State under this Act;

"proprietor" has the meaning assigned to it by section two of this Act;

"registered proprietor" means the person or persons for the time being entered in the register of designs as proprietor of the design;

"registrar" means the Comptroller-General of Patents Designs and Trade Marks;

"set of articles" means a number of articles of the same general character ordinarily on sale or intended to be used together, to each of which the same design, or the same design with modifications or variations not sufficient to alter the character or substantially to affect the identity thereof, is applied.

(2) Any reference in this Act to an article in respect of which a design is registered shall, in the case of a design registered in respect of a set of articles, be construed as a reference to any article of that set.

(3) Any question arising under this Act whether a number of articles constitute a set of articles shall be determined by the registrar; and notwithstanding anything in this Act any determination of the registrar under this subsection shall be final.

(4) For the purposes of subsection (1) of section 14 and of section 16 of this Act, the expression "personal representative", in relation to a deceased person, includes the legal representative of the deceased appointed in any country outside the United Kingdom.

Application to Scotland.

45. In the application of this Act to Scotland—

... ...

- The expression "injunction" means "interdict"; the expression "arbitrator"means "arbiter";
- the expression "plaintiff" means "pursuer"; the expression "defendant" means "defender".

Application to Northern Ireland.

46. In the application of this Act to Northern Ireland—

... ...

(3) References to enactments include enactments comprised in Northern Ireland legislation:

(3. A)References to the Crown include the Crown in right of Her Majesty's Government in Northern Ireland:

(4) References to a government department shall be construed as including references to a Northern Ireland department, and in relation to a Northern Ireland department references to the Treasury shall be construed as references to the Department of Finance and Personnel.

... ...

Application to Isle of Man.

47. This Act extends to the Isle of Man, subject to any modifications contained in an Order made by Her Majesty in Council, and accordingly, subject to any such Order, references in this Act to the United Kingdom shall be construed as including the Isle of Man.

Territorial waters and the continental shelf.

47. A(1)For the purposes of this Act the territorial waters of the United Kingdom shall be treated as part of the United Kingdom.

(2) This Act applies to things done in the United Kingdom sector of the continental shelf on a structure or vessel which is present there for purposes directly connected with theexploration of the sea bed or subsoil or the exploitation of their natural resources as it applies to things done in the United Kingdom.

(3) The United Kingdom sector of the continental shelf means the areas designated by order under section 1. (7) of the Continental Shelf Act 1964.

Repeals, savings, and transitional provisions.

48. (1)... ... ...

(2) Subject to the provisions of this section, any Order in Council, rule, order, requirement, certificate, notice, decision, direction, authorisation, consent, application, request or thing made, issued, given or done under any enactment repealed by this Act shall, if in force at the commencement of this Act, and so far as it could have been made, issued, given or done under this Act, continue in force and have effect as if made, issued, given or done under the corresponding enactment of this Act.

(3) Any register kept under the Patents and Designs Act 1907 shall be deemed to form part of the corresponding register under this Act.

(4) Any design registered before the commencement of this Act shall be deemed to be registered under this Act in respect of articles of the class in which it is registered.

(5) Where, in relation to any design, the time for giving notice to the registrar under section 59 of the Patents and Designs Act 1907 expired before the commencement of this Act and the notice was not given, subsection (2) of section 6 of this Act shall not apply in relation to that design or any registration of that design.

(6) Any document referring to any enactment repealed by this Act shall be construed as referring to the corresponding enactment of this Act.

(7) Nothing in the foregoing provisions of this section shall be taken as prejudicing the operation of section 38 of the Interpretation Act 1889 (which relates to the effect of repeals).

Short title and commencement.

49. (1)This Act may be cited as the Registered Designs Act 1949.
(2) This Act shall come into operation on the first day of January, nineteen hundred and fifty, immediately after the coming into operation of the Patents and Designs Act 1949.

FIRST SCHEDULE

Provisions as to the Use of Registered Designs for the Services of the Crown and as to the Rights of Third Parties in Respect of such Use

Use of registered designs for services of the Crown

1. (1)Notwithstanding anything in this Act, any Government department, and any person authorised in writing by a Government department, may use any registered design for the services of the Crown in accordance with the following provisions of this paragraph.
(2) If and so far as the design has before the date of registration thereof been duly recorded by or applied by or on behalf of a Government department otherwise than in consequence of the communication of the design directly or indirectly by the registered proprietor or any person from whom he derives title, any use of the design by virtue of this paragraph may be made free of any royalty or other payment to the registered proprietor.
(3) If and so far as the design has not been so recorded or applied as aforesaid, any use of the design made by virtue of this paragraph at any time after the date of registration thereof, or in consequence of any such communication as aforesaid, shall be made upon such terms as may be agreed upon, either before or after the use, between the Government department and the registered proprietor with the approval of the Treasury, or as may in default of agreement be determined by the court on a reference under paragraph 3 of this Schedule.
(4) The authority of a Government department in respect of a design may be given under this paragraph either before or after the design is registered and either before or after the acts in respect of which the authority is given are done, and may be given to any person whether or not he is authorised directly or indirectly by the registered proprietor to use the design.
(5) Where any use of a design is made by or with the authority of a Government department under this paragraph, then, unless it appears to the department that it would be contrary to the public interest so to do, the department shall notify the registered proprietor as soon as practicable after the use is begun, and furnish him with such information as to the extent of the use as he may from time to time require.
(6) For the purposes of this and the next following paragraph "the services of the Crown" shall be deemed to include—
(a) the supply to the government of any country outside the United Kingdom, in pursuance of an agreement or arrangement between Her Majesty's Government in the United Kingdom and the government of that country, of articles required—
(i) for the defence of that country; or
(ii) for the defence of any other country whose government is party to any agreement or arrangement with Her Majesty's said Government in respect of defence matters;
(b) the supply to the United Nations, or the government of any country belonging to that organisation, in pursuance of an agreement or arrangement between Her Majesty's Government and that organisation or government, of articles required for any armed forces operating in pursuance of a resolution of that organisation or any organ of that organisation;

and the power of a Government department or a person authorised by a Government department under this paragraph to use a design shall include power to sell to any such government or to the said organisation any articles the supply of which is authorised by this sub-paragraph, and to sell to any person any articles made in the exercise of the powers conferred by this paragraph which are no longer required for the purpose for which they were made.

(7) The purchaser of any articles sold in the exercise of powers conferred by this paragraph, and any person claiming through him, shall have power to deal with them in the same manner as if the rights in the registered design were held on behalf of His Majesty.

Rights of third parties in respect of Crown use

2. (1)In relation to any use of a registered design, or a design in respect of which an application for registration is pending, made for the services of the Crown—

(a) by a Government department or a person authorised by a Government department under the last foregoing paragraph; or

(b) by the registered proprietor or applicant for registration to the order of a Government department,

the provisions of any licence, assignment or agreement made, whether before or after the commencement of this Act, between the registered proprietor or applicant for registration or any person who derives title from him or from whom he derives title and any person other than a Government department shall be of no effect so far as those provisions restrict or regulate the use of the design, or any model, document or information relating thereto, or provide for the making of payments in respect of any such use, or calculated by reference thereto; and the reproduction or publication of any model or document in connection with the said use shall not be deemed to be an infringement of any copyright or design right subsisting in the model or document.

(2) Where an exclusive licence granted otherwise than for royalties or other benefits determined by reference to the use of the design is in force under the registered design then—

(a) in relation to any use of the design which, but for the provisions of this and the last foregoing paragraph, would constitute an infringement of the rights of the licensee, sub-paragraph (3) of the last foregoing paragraph shall have effect as if for the reference to the registered proprietor there were substituted a reference to the licensee; and

(b) in relation to any use of the design by the licensee by virtue of an authority given under the last foregoing paragraph, that paragraph shall have effect as if the said sub-paragraph (3) were omitted.

(3) Subject to the provisions of the last foregoing sub-paragraph, where the registered design or the right to apply for or obtain registration of the design has been assigned to the registered proprietor in consideration of royalties or other benefits determined by reference to the use of the design, then—

(a) in relation to any use of the design by virtue of paragraph 1 of this Schedule, sub-paragraph (3) of that paragraph shall have effect as if the reference to the registered proprietor included a reference to the assignor, and any sum payable by virtue of that sub-paragraph shall be divided between the registered proprietor and the assignor in such proportion as may be agreed upon between them or as may in default of agreement be determined by the court on a reference under the next following paragraph; and

(b) in relation to any use of the design made for the services of the Crown by the registered proprietor to the order of a Government department, sub-paragraph (3) of paragraph 1 of this Schedule shall have effect as if that use were made by virtue of an authority given under that paragraph.

(4) Where, under sub-paragraph (3) of paragraph 1 of this Schedule, payments are required to be made by a Government department to a registered proprietor in respect of any use of a design, any person being the holder of an exclusive licence under the registered design (not being such a licence as is mentioned in sub-paragraph (2) of this paragraph) authorising him to make that use of the design shall be entitled to recover from the registered proprietor such part (if any) of those

payments as may be agreed upon between that person and the registered proprietor, or as may in default of agreement be determined by the court under the next following paragraph to be just having regard to any expenditure incurred by that person—

(a) in developing the said design; or

(b) in making payments to the registered proprietor, other than royalties or other payments determined by reference to the use of the design, in consideration of the licence;

and if, at any time before the amount of any such payment has been agreed upon between the Government department and the registered proprietor, that person gives notice in writing of his interest to the department, any agreement as to the amount of that payment shall be of no effect unless it is made with his consent.

(5) In this paragraph "exclusive licence" means a licence from a registered proprietor which confers on the licensee, or on the licensee and persons authorised by him, to the exclusion of all other persons (including the registered proprietor), any right in respect of the registered design.

Compensation for loss of profit

2. A(1)Where Crown use is made of a registered design, the government department concerned shall pay—

(a) to the registered proprietor, or

(b) if there is an exclusive licence in force in respect of the design, to the exclusive licensee,

compensation for any loss resulting from his not being awarded a contract to supply the articles to which the design is applied.

(2) Compensation is payable only to the extent that such a contract could have been fulfilled from his existing manufacturing capacity; but is payable notwithstanding the existence of circumstances rendering him ineligible for the award of such a contract.

(3) In determining the loss, regard shall be had to the profit which would have been made on such a contract and to the extent to which any manufacturing capacity was under-used.

(4) No compensation is payable in respect of any failure to secure contracts for the supply of articles to which the design is applied otherwise than for the services of the Crown.

(5) The amount payable under this paragraph shall, if not agreed between the registered proprietor or licensee and the government department concerned with the approval of the Treasury, be determined by the court on a reference under paragraph 3; and it is in addition to any amount payable under paragraph 1 or 2 of this schedule.

(6) In this paragraph—

"Crown use", in relation to a design, means the doing of anything by virtue of paragraph 1 which would otherwise be an infringement of the right in the design; and

"the government department concerned", in relation to such use, means the government department by whom or on whose authority the act was done.

Reference of disputes as to Crown use

3. (1)Any dispute as to—

(a) the exercise by a Government department, or a person authorised by a Government department, of the powers conferred by paragraph 1 of this Schedule,

(b) terms for the use of a design for the services of the Crown under that paragraph,

(c) the right of any person to receive any part of a payment made under paragraph 1. (3), or

(d) the right of any person to receive a payment under paragraph 2. A,

may be referred to the court by either party to the dispute.

(2) In any proceedings under this paragraph to which a Government department are a party, the department may—

(a) if the registered proprietor is a party to the proceedings, apply for cancellation of the registration of the design upon any ground upon which the registration of a design may be cancelled on an application to the court under section twenty of this Act;

(b) in any case, put in issue the validity of the registration of the design without applying for its cancellation.

(3) If in such proceedings as aforesaid any question arises whether a design has been recorded or applied as mentioned in paragraph 1 of this Schedule, and the disclosure of any document recording the design, or of any evidence of the application thereof, would in the opinion of the department be prejudicial to the public interest, the disclosure may be made confidentially to counsel for the other party or to an independent expert mutually agreed upon.

(4) In determining under this paragraph any dispute between a Government department and any person as to terms for the use of a design for the services of the Crown, the court shall have regard to any benefit or compensation which that person or any person from whom he derives title may have received, or may be entitled to receive, directly or indirectly from any Government department in respect of the design in question.

(5) In any proceedings under this paragraph the court may at any time order the whole proceedings or any question or issue of fact arising therein to be referred to a special or official referee or an arbitrator on such terms as the court may direct; and references to the court in the foregoing provisions of this paragraph shall be construed accordingly.

Special provisions as to Crown use during emergency

4. (1)During any period of emergency within the meaning of this paragraph, the powers exercisable in relation to a design by a Government department, or a person authorised by a Government department under paragraph 1 of this Schedule shall include power to use the design for any purpose which appears to the department necessary or expedient—

(a) for the efficient prosecution of any war in which His Majesty may be engaged;

(b) for the maintenance of supplies and services essential to the life of the community;

(c) for securing a sufficiency of supplies and services essential to the well-being of the community;

(d) for promoting the productivity of industry, commerce and agriculture;

(e) for fostering and directing exports and reducing imports, or imports of any classes, from all or any countries and for redressing the balance of trade;

(f) generally for ensuring that the whole resources of the community are available for use, and are used, in a manner best calculated to serve the interests of the community; or

(g) for assisting the relief of suffering and the restoration and distribution of essential supplies and services in any part of His Majesty's dominions or any foreign countries that are in grave distress as the result of war;

and any reference in this Schedule to the services of the Crown shall be construed as including a reference to the purposes aforesaid.

(2) In this paragraph the expression "period of emergency" means a period beginning on such date as may be declared by Order in Council to be the commencement, and ending on such date as may be so declared to be the termination, of a period of emergency for the purposes of this paragraph.

(3) No Order in Council under this paragraph shall be submitted to Her Majesty unless a draft of it has been laid before and approved by a resolution of each House of Parliament.

... ...

Schedule 8. Patents: miscellaneous amendments

Section 295.

Withdrawal of application before publication of specification

1. In section 13. (2) of the M1. Patents Act 1949 (duty of comptroller to advertise acceptance of and publish complete specification) after the word "and", in the first place where it occurs, insert ", unless the application is withdrawn,".

Marginal Citations
M1 1949 c. 87.

Correction of clerical errors

2. (1)In section 15 of the M2. Patents Act 1977 (filing of application), after subsection (3) insert—
"(3. A)Nothing in subsection (2) or (3) above shall be construed as affecting the power of the comptroller under section 117. (1) below to correct errors or mistakes with respect to the filing of drawings.".

(2) The above amendment applies only in relation to applications filed after the commencement of this paragraph.

Marginal Citations
M2 1977 c. 37.

Supplementary searches

3. (1)Section 17 of the Patents Act 1977 (preliminary examination and search) is amended as follows.

(2) In subsection (7) (supplementary searches) for "subsection (4) above" substitute "subsections (4) and (5) above" and for "it applies" substitute "they apply".

(3) After that subsection add—
"(8)A reference for a supplementary search in consequence of—

  (a) an amendment of the application made by the applicant under section 18. (3) or 19. (1) below, or

  (b) a correction of the application, or of a document filed in connection with the application, under section 117 below,

shall be made only on payment of the prescribed fee, unless the comptroller directs otherwise.".

4. In section 18 of the Patents Act 1977 (substantive examination and grant or refusal of patent), after subsection (1) insert—
"(1. A)If the examiner forms the view that a supplementary search under section 17 above is required for which a fee is payable, he shall inform the comptroller, who may decide that the substantive examination should not proceed until the fee is paid; and if he so decides, then unless within such period as he may allow—

  (a) the fee is paid, or

  (b) the application is amended so as to render the supplementary search unnecessary,

he may refuse the application.".

5. In section 130. (1) of the Patents Act 1977 (interpretation), in the definition of "search fee", for "section 17 above" substitute "section 17. (1) above".

Application for restoration of lapsed patent

6. (1)Section 28 of the Patents Act 1977 (restoration of lapsed patents) is amended as follows.

(2) For subsection (1) (application for restoration within period of one year) substitute—
"(1)Where a patent has ceased to have effect by reason of a failure to pay any renewal fee, an application for the restoration of the patent may be made to the comptroller within the prescribed period.

(1. A)Rules prescribing that period may contain such transitional provisions and savings as appear

to the Secretary of State to be necessary or expedient.".

(3) After subsection (2) insert—

"(2. A)Notice of the application shall be published by the comptroller in the prescribed manner.".

(4) In subsection (3), omit paragraph (b) (requirement that failure to renew is due to circumstances beyond proprietor's control) and the word "and" preceding it.

This amendment does not apply to a patent which has ceased to have effect in accordance with section 25. (3) of the M3. Patents Act 1977 (failure to renew within prescribed period) and in respect of which the period referred to in subsection (4) of that section (six months' period of grace for renewal) has expired before commencement.

(5) Omit subsections (5) to (9) (effect of order for restoration).

Marginal Citations

M31977 c. 37.

7. After that section insert—

"28. A Effect of order for restoration of patent.

(1) The effect of an order for the restoration of a patent is as follows.

(2) Anything done under or in relation to the patent during the period between expiry and restoration shall be treated as valid.

(3) Anything done during that period which would have constituted an infringement if the patent had not expired shall be treated as an infringement—

(a) if done at a time when it was possible for the patent to be renewed under section 25. (4), or

(b) if it was a continuation or repetition of an earlier infringing act.

(4) If after it was no longer possible for the patent to be so renewed, and before publication of notice of the application for restoration, a person—

(a) began in good faith to do an act which would have constituted an infringement of the patent if it had not expired, or

(b) made in good faith effective and serious preparations to do such an act,

he has the right to continue to do the act or, as the case may be, to do the act, notwithstanding the restoration of the patent; but this right does not extend to granting a licence to another person to do the act.

(5) If the act was done, or the preparations were made, in the course of a business, the person entitled to the right conferred by subsection (4) may—

(a) authorise the doing of that act by any partners of his for the time being in that business, and

(b) assign that right, or transmit it on death (or in the case of a body corporate on its dissolution), to any person who acquires that part of the business in the course of which the act was done or the preparations were made.

(6) Where a product is disposed of to another in exercise of the rights conferred by subsection (4) or (5), that other and any person claiming through him may deal with the product in the same way as if it had been disposed of by the registered proprietor of the patent.

(7) The above provisions apply in relation to the use of a patent for the services of the Crown as they apply in relation to infringement of the patent.".

8. In consequence of the above amendments—

(a) in section 60. (6)(b) of the M4. Patents Act 1977, for "section 28. (6)" substitute "section 28. A(4) or (5)"; and

(b) in sections 77. (5), 78. (6) and 80. (4) of that Act, for the words from "section 28. (6)" to the end substitute "section 28. A(4) and (5) above, and subsections (6) and (7) of that section shall apply accordingly.".

Marginal Citations

M41977 c. 37.

Determination of right to patent after grant

9. (1)Section 37 of the Patents Act 1977 (determination of right to patent after grant) is amended as follows.

(2) For subsection (1) substitute—

"(1)After a patent has been granted for an invention any person having or claiming a proprietary interest in or under the patent may refer to the comptroller the question—

(a) who is or are the true proprietor or proprietors of the patent,

(b) whether the patent should have been granted to the person or persons to whom it was granted, or

(c) whether any right in or under the patent should be transferred or granted to any other person or persons;

and the comptroller shall determine the question and make such order as he thinks fit to give effect to the determination.".

(3) Substitute "this section"—

(a) in subsections (4) and (7) for "subsection (1)(a) above", and

(b) in subsection (8) for "subsection (1) above".

10. In section 74. (6) (meaning of "entitlement proceedings"), for "section 37. (1)(a) above" substitute "section 37. (1) above".

Employees' inventions

11. (1)In section 39 of the Patents Act 1977 (right to employees' inventions), after subsection (2) add—

"(3)Where by virtue of this section an invention belongs, as between him and his employer, to an employee, nothing done—

(a) by or on behalf of the employee or any person claiming under him for the purposes of pursuing an application for a patent, or

(b) by any person for the purpose of performing or working the invention,

shall be taken to infringe any copyright or design right to which, as between him and his employer, his employer is entitled in any model or document relating to the invention.".

(2) In section 43 of the M5. Patents Act 1977 (supplementary provisions with respect to employees' inventions), in subsection (4) (references to patents to include other forms of protection, whether in UK or elsewhere) for "in sections 40 to 42" substitute "in sections 39 to 42.".

Marginal Citations

M51977 c. 37.

Undertaking to take licence in infringement proceedings

12. (1)Section 46 of the Patents Act 1977 (licences of right) is amended as follows.

(2) In subsection (3)(c) (undertaking to take licence in infringement proceedings) after the words "(otherwise than by the importation of any article" insert "from a country which is not a member State of the European Economic Community".

(3) After subsection (3) insert—

"(3. A)An undertaking under subsection (3)(c) above may be given at any time before final order in the proceedings, without any admission of liability.".

Power of comptroller on grant of compulsory licence

13. In section 49 of the Patents Act 1977 (supplementary provisions with respect to compulsory licences), omit subsection (3) (power to order that licence has effect to revoke existing licences

and deprive proprietor of power to work invention or grant licences).

Powers exercisable in consequence of report of Monopolies and Mergers Commission

14. For section 51 of the Patents Act 1977 (licences of right: application by Crown in consequence of report of Monopolies and Mergers Commission) substitute—

"51 Powers exercisable in consequence of report of Monopolies and Mergers Commission.

(1) Where a report of the Monopolies and Mergers Commission has been laid before Parliament containing conclusions to the effect—
(a) on a monopoly reference, that a monopoly situation exists and facts found by the Commission operate or may be expected to operate against the public interest,
(b) on a merger reference, that a merger situation qualifying for investigation has been created and the creation of the situation, or particular elements in or consequences of it specified in the report, operate or may be expected to operate against the public interest,
(c) on a competition reference, that a person was engaged in an anti-competitive practice which operated or may be expected to operate against the public interest, or
(d) on a reference under section 11 of the Competition Act 1980 (reference of public bodies and certain other persons), that a person is pursuing a course of conduct which operates against the public interest,
the appropriate Minister or Ministers may apply to the comptroller to take action under this section.
(2) Before making an application the appropriate Minister or Ministers shall publish, in such manner as he or they think appropriate, a notice describing the nature of the proposed application and shall consider any representations which may be made within 30 days of such publication by persons whose interests appear to him or them to be affected.
(3) If on an application under this section it appears to the comptroller that the matters specified in the Commission's report as being those which in the Commission's opinion operate, or operated or may be expected to operate, against the public interest include—
(a) conditions in licences granted under a patent by its proprietor restricting the use of the invention by the licensee or the right of the proprietor to grant other licences, or
(b) a refusal by the proprietor of a patent to grant licences on reasonable terms
he may by order cancel or modify any such condition or may, instead or in addition, make an entry in the register to the effect that licences under the patent are to be available as of right.
(4) In this section "the appropriate Minister or Ministers" means the Minister or Ministers to whom the report of the Commission was made.".

Compulsory licensing: reliance on statements in competition report

15. In section 53. (2) of the M6. Patents Act 1977 (compulsory licensing: reliance on statements in reports of Monopolies and Mergers Commission)—
(a) for "application made in relation to a patent under sections 48 to 51 above" substitute "application made under section 48 above in respect of a patent"; and
(b) after "Part VIII of the Fair Trading Act 1973" insert "or section 17 of the Competition Act 1980".
Marginal Citations

Crown use: compensation for loss of profit

16. (1)In the Patents Act 1977, after section 57 insert—

"57. A Compensation for loss of profit.

(1) Where use is made of an invention for the services of the Crown, the government department concerned shall pay—

(a) to the proprietor of the patent, or

(b) if there is an exclusive licence in force in respect of the patent, to the exclusive licensee,

compensation for any loss resulting from his not being awarded a contract to supply the patented product or, as the case may be, to perform the patented process or supply a thing made by means of the patented process.

(2) Compensation is payable only to the extent that such a contract could have been fulfilled from his existing manufacturing or other capacity; but is payable notwithstanding the existence of circumstances rendering him ineligible for the award of such a contract.

(3) In determining the loss, regard shall be had to the profit which would have been made on such a contract and to the extent to which any manufacturing or other capacity was under-used.

(4) No compensation is payable in respect of any failure to secure contracts to supply the patented product or, as the case may be, to perform the patented process or supply a thing made by means of the patented process, otherwise than for the services of the Crown.

(5) The amount payable shall, if not agreed between the proprietor or licensee and the government department concerned with the approval of the Treasury, be determined by the court on a reference under section 58, and is in addition to any amount payable under section 55 or 57.

(6) In this section "the government department concerned", in relation to any use of an invention for the services of the Crown, means the government department by whom or on whose authority the use was made.

(7) In the application of this section to Northern Ireland, the reference in subsection (5) above to the Treasury shall, where the government department concerned is a department of the Government of Northern Ireland, be construed as a reference to the Department of Finance and Personnel.".

(2) In section 58 of the M7. Patents Act 1977 (reference of disputes as to Crown use), for subsection (1) substitute—

"(1)Any dispute as to—

(a) the exercise by a government department, or a person authorised by a government department, of the powers conferred by section 55 above,

(b) terms for the use of an invention for the services of the Crown under that section,

(c) the right of any person to receive any part of a payment made in pursuance of subsection (4) of that section, or

(d) the right of any person to receive a payment under section 57. A,

may be referred to the court by either party to the dispute after a patent has been granted for the invention.";

and in subsection (4) for "under this section" substitute "under subsection (1)(a), (b) or (c) above".

(3) In section 58. (11) of the Patents Act 1977 (exclusion of right to compensation for Crown use if relevant transaction, instrument or event not registered), after "section 57. (3) above)" insert ", or to any compensation under section 57. A above,".

(4) The above amendments apply in relation to any use of an invention for the services of the Crown after the commencement of this section, even if the terms for such use were settled before commencement.

Marginal Citations

Right to continue use begun before priority date

17. For section 64 of the Patents Act 1977 (right to continue use begun before priority date) substitute—

"64 Right to continue use begun before priority date.

(1) Where a patent is granted for an invention, a person who in the United Kingdom before the priority date of the invention—

(a) does in good faith an act which would constitute an infringement of the patent if it were in force, or

(b) makes in good faith effective and serious preparations to do such an act,

has the right to continue to do the act or, as the case may be, to do the act, notwithstanding the grant of the patent; but this right does not extend to granting a licence to another person to do the act.

(2) If the act was done, or the preparations were made, in the course of a business, the person entitled to the right conferred by subsection (1) may—

(a) authorise the doing of that act by any partners of his for the time being in that business, and

(b) assign that right, or transmit it on death (or in the case of a body corporate on its dissolution), to any person who acquires that part of the business in the course of which the act was done or the preparations were made.

(3) Where a product is disposed of to another in exercise of the rights conferred by subsection (1) or (2), that other and any person claiming through him may deal with the product in the same way as if it had been disposed of by the registered proprietor of the patent.".

Revocation on grounds of grant to wrong person

18. In section 72. (1) of the M8. Patents Act 1977 (grounds for revocation of patent), for paragraph (b) substitute—

"(b)that the patent was granted to a person who was not entitled to be granted that patent;".

Marginal Citations
M81977 c. 37.

Revocation where two patents granted for same invention

19. In section 73 of the Patents Act 1977 (revocation on initiative of comptroller), for subsections (2) and (3) (revocation of patent where European patent (UK) granted in respect of same invention) substitute—

"(2)If it appears to the comptroller that a patent under this Act and a European patent (UK) have been granted for the same invention having the same priority date, and that the applications for the patents were filed by the same applicant or his successor in title, he shall give the proprietor of the patent under this Act an opportunity of making observations and of amending the specification of the patent, and if the proprietor fails to satisfy the comptroller that there are not two patents in respect of the same invention, or to amend the specification so as to prevent there being two patents in respect of the same invention, the comptroller shall revoke the patent.

(3) The comptroller shall not take action under subsection (2) above before—

(a) the end of the period for filing an opposition to the European patent (UK) under the European Patent Convention, or

(b) if later, the date on which opposition proceedings are finally disposed of;

and he shall not then take any action if the decision is not to maintain the European patent or if it is amended so that there are not two patents in respect of the same invention.

(4) The comptroller shall not take action under subsection (2) above if the European patent (UK) has been surrendered under section 29. (1) above before the date on which by virtue of section 25. (1) above the patent under this Act is to be treated as having been granted or, if proceedings for the surrender of the European patent (UK) have been begun before that date, until those proceedings are finally disposed of; and he shall not then take any action if the decision is to accept the surrender of the European patent.".

Applications and amendments not to include additional matter

20. For section 76 of the M9. Patents Act 1977 (amendments of applications and patents not to include added matter) substitute—

"76 Amendments of applications and patents not to include added matter.

(1) An application for a patent which—

(a) is made in respect of matter disclosed in an earlier application, or in the specification of a patent which has been granted, and

(b) discloses additional matter, that is, matter extending beyond that disclosed in the earlier application, as filed, or the application for the patent, as filed,

may be filed under section 8. (3), 12 or 37. (4) above, or as mentioned in section 15. (4) above, but shall not be allowed to proceed unless it is amended so as to exclude the additional matter.

(2) No amendment of an application for a patent shall be allowed under section 17. (3), 18. (3) or 19. (1) if it results in the application disclosing matter extending beyond that disclosed in the application as filed.

(3) No amendment of the specification of a patent shall be allowed under section 27. (1), 73 or 75 if it—

(a) results in the specification disclosing additional matter, or

(b) extends the protection conferred by the patent.".

Marginal Citations
M91977 c. 37.

Effect of European patent (UK)

21. (1)Section 77 of the Patents Act 1977 (effect of European patent (UK)) is amended as follows.

(2) For subsection (3) (effect of finding of partial validity on pending proceedings) substitute—

"(3)Where in the case of a European patent (UK)—

(a) proceedings for infringement, or proceedings under section 58 above, have been commenced before the court or the comptroller and have not been finally disposed of, and

(b) it is established in proceedings before the European Patent Office that the patent is only partially valid,

the provisions of section 63 or, as the case may be, of subsections (7) to (9) of section 58 apply as they apply to proceedings in which the validity of a patent is put in issue and in which it is found that the patent is only partially valid.".

(3) For subsection (4) (effect of amendment or revocation under European Patent Convention) substitute—

"(4)Where a European patent (UK) is amended in accordance with the European Patent Convention, the amendment shall have effect for the purposes of Parts I and III of this Act as if the specification of the patent had been amended under this Act; but subject to subsection (6)(b) below.

(4. A)Where a European patent (UK) is revoked in accordance with the European Patent Convention, the patent shall be treated for the purposes of Parts I and III of this Act as having been revoked under this Act.".

(4) In subsection (6) (filing of English translation), in paragraph (b) (amendments) for "a translation of the amendment into English" substitute "a translation into English of the specification as amended".

(5) In subsection (7) (effect of failure to file translation) for the words from "a translation" to "above" substitute "such a translation is not filed".

The state of the art: material contained in patent applications

22. In section 78 of the M10. Patents Act 1977 (effect of filing an application for a European patent (UK)), for subsection (5) (effect of withdrawal of application, &c.) substitute—

"(5)Subsections (1) to (3) above shall cease to apply to an application for a European patent (UK), except as mentioned in subsection (5. A) below, if—

(a) the application is refused or withdrawn or deemed to be withdrawn, or

(b) the designation of the United Kingdom in the application is withdrawn or deemed to be withdrawn,

but shall apply again if the rights of the applicant are re-established under the European Patent Convention, as from their re-establishment.

(5. A)The occurrence of any of the events mentioned in subsection (5)(a) or (b) shall not affect the continued operation of section 2. (3) above in relation to matter contained in an application for a European patent (UK) which by virtue of that provision has become part of the state of the art as regards other inventions.".

Marginal Citations
M101977 c. 37.

Jurisdiction in certain proceedings

23. Section 88 of the Patents Act 1977 (jurisdiction in legal proceedings in connection with Community Patent Convention) is repealed.

Effect of filing international application for patent

24. (1)Section 89 of the Patents Act 1977 (effect of filing international application for patent) is amended as follows.

(2) After subsection (3) insert—

"(3. A)If the relevant conditions are satisfied with respect to an application which is amended in accordance with the Treaty and the relevant conditions are not satisfied with respect to any amendment, that amendment shall be disregarded.".

(3) After subsection (4) insert—

"(4. A)In subsection (4)(a) "a copy of the application" includes a copy of the application published in accordance with the Treaty in a language other than that in which it was filed.".

(4) For subsection (10) (exclusion of certain applications subject to European Patent Convention) substitute—

"(10)The foregoing provisions of this section do not apply to an application which falls to be treated as an international application for a patent (UK) by reason only of its containing an indication that the applicant wishes to obtain a European patent (UK); but without prejudice to the application of those provisions to an application which also separately designates the United Kingdom.".

(5) The amendments in this paragraph shall be deemed always to have had effect.

(6) This paragraph shall be repealed by the order bringing the following paragraph into force.

25. For section 89 of the M11. Patents Act 1977 (effect of filing international application for patent) substitute—

"89 Effect of international application for patent.

(1) An international application for a patent (UK) for which a date of filing has been accorded under the Patent Co-operation Treaty shall, subject to—

section 89. A (international and national phases of application), and

section 89. B (adaptation of provisions in relation to international application),

be treated for the purposes of Parts I and III of this Act as an application for a patent under this Act.

(2) If the application, or the designation of the United Kingdom in it, is withdrawn or (except as mentioned in subsection (3)) deemed to be withdrawn under the Treaty, it shall be treated as withdrawn under this Act.

(3) An application shall not be treated as withdrawn under this Act if it, or the designation of the United Kingdom in it, is deemed to be withdrawn under the Treaty—

   (a) because of an error or omission in an institution having functions under the Treaty, or

   (b) because, owing to circumstances outside the applicant's control, a copy of the application was not received by the International Bureau before the end of the time limited for that purpose under the Treaty,

or in such other circumstances as may be prescribed.

(4) For the purposes of the above provisions an application shall not be treated as an international application for a patent (UK) by reason only of its containing an indication that the applicant wishes to obtain a European patent (UK), but an application shall be so treated if it also separately designates the United Kingdom.

(5) If an international application for a patent which designates the United Kingdom is refused a filing date under the Treaty and the comptroller determines that the refusal was caused by an error or omission in an institution having functions under the Treaty, he may direct that the application shall be treated as an application under this Act, having such date of filing as he may direct.

89. A International and national phases of application.

(1) The provisions of the Patent Co-operation Treaty relating to publication, search, examination and amendment, and not those of this Act, apply to an international application for a patent (UK) during the international phase of the application.

(2) The international phase of the application means the period from the filing of the application in accordance with the Treaty until the national phase of the application begins.

(3) The national phase of the application begins—

   (a) when the prescribed period expires, provided any necessary translation of the application into English has been filed at the Patent Office and the prescribed fee has been paid by the applicant; or

   (b) on the applicant expressly requesting the comptroller to proceed earlier with the national phase of the application, filing at the Patent Office—

(i) a copy of the application, if none has yet been sent to the Patent Office in accordance with the Treaty, and

(ii) any necessary translation of the application into English,

and paying the prescribed fee.

For this purpose a "copy of the application" includes a copy published in accordance with the Treaty in a language other than that in which it was originally filed.

(4) If the prescribed period expires without the conditions mentioned in subsection (3)(a) being

satisfied, the application shall be taken to be withdrawn.

(5) Where during the international phase the application is amended in accordance with the Treaty, the amendment shall be treated as made under this Act if—

(a) when the prescribed period expires, any necessary translation of the amendment into English has been filed at the Patent Office, or

(b) where the applicant expressly requests the comptroller to proceed earlier with the national phase of the application, there is then filed at the Patent Office—

(i) a copy of the amendment, if none has yet been sent to the Patent Office in accordance with the Treaty, and

(ii) any necessary translation of the amendment into English;

otherwise the amendment shall be disregarded.

(6) The comptroller shall on payment of the prescribed fee publish any translation filed at the Patent Office under subsection (3) or (5) above.

89. B Adaptation of provisions in relation to international application.

(1) Where an international application for a patent (UK) is accorded a filing date under the Patent Co-operation Treaty—

(a) that date, or if the application is re-dated under the Treaty to a later date that later date, shall be treated as the date of filing the application under this Act,

(b) any declaration of priority made under the Treaty shall be treated as made under section 5. (2) above, and where in accordance with the Treaty any extra days are allowed, the period of 12 months specified in section 5. (2) shall be treated as altered accordingly, and

(c) any statement of the name of the inventor under the Treaty shall be treated as a statement filed under section 13. (2) above.

(2) If the application, not having been published under this Act, is published in accordance with the Treaty it shall be treated, for purposes other than those mentioned in subsection (3), as published under section 16 above when the conditions mentioned in section 89. A(3)(a) are complied with.

(3) For the purposes of section 55 (use of invention for service of the Crown) and section 69 (infringement of rights conferred by publication) the application, not having been published under this Act, shall be treated as published under section 16 above—

(a) if it is published in accordance with the Treaty in English, on its being so published; and

(b) if it is so published in a language other than English—

(i) on the publication of a translation of the application in accordance with section 89. A(6) above, or

(ii) on the service by the applicant of a translation into English of the specification of the application on the government department concerned or, as the case may be, on the person committing the infringing act.

The reference in paragraph (b)(ii) to the service of a translation on a government department or other person is to its being sent by post or delivered to that department or person.

(4) During the international phase of the application, section 8 above does not apply (determination of questions of entitlement in relation to application under this Act) and section 12 above (determination of entitlement in relation to foreign and convention patents) applies notwithstanding the application; but after the end of the international phase, section 8 applies and section 12 does not.

(5) When the national phase begins the comptroller shall refer the application for so much of the examination and search under section 17 and 18 above as he considers appropriate in view of any examination or search carried out under the Treaty.".

Marginal Citations

M111977 c. 37.

Proceedings before the court or the comptroller

26. In the M12. Patents Act 1977, after section 99 (general powers of the court) insert—

"99. A Power of Patents Court to order report.

(1) Rules of court shall make provision empowering the Patents Court in any proceedings before it under this Act, on or without the application of any party, to order the Patent Office to inquire into and report on any question of fact or opinion.
(2) Where the court makes such an order on the application of a party, the fee payable to the Patent Office shall be at such rate as may be determined in accordance with rules of court and shall be costs of the proceedings unless otherwise ordered by the court.
(3) Where the court makes such an order of its own motion, the fee payable to the Patent Office shall be at such rate as may be determined by the Lord Chancellor with the approval of the Treasury and shall be paid out of money provided by Parliament.

99. B Power of Court of Session to order report.

(1) In any proceedings before the Court of Session under this Act the court may, either of its own volition or on the application of any party, order the Patent Office to inquire into and report on any question of fact or opinion.
(2) Where the court makes an order under subsection (1) above of its own volition the fee payable to the Patent Office shall be at such rate as may be determined by the Lord President of the Court of Session with the consent of the Treasury and shall be defrayed out of moneys provided by Parliament.
(3) Where the court makes an order under subsection (1) above on the application of a party, the fee payable to the Patent Office shall be at such rate as may be provided for in rules of court and shall be treated as expenses in the cause.".
Marginal Citations
M121977 c. 37.
27. For section 102 of the M13. Patents Act 1977 (right of audience in patent proceedings) substitute—

"102 Right of audience, &c. in proceedings before comptroller.

(1) A party to proceedings before the comptroller under this Act, or under any treaty or international convention to which the United Kingdom is a party, may appear before the comptroller in person or be represented by any person whom he desires to represent him.
(2) No offence is committed under the enactments relating to the preparation of documents by persons not legally qualified by reason only of the preparation by any person of a document, other than a deed, for use in such proceedings.
(3) Subsection (1) has effect subject to rules made under section 281 of the Copyright, Designs and Patents Act 1988 (power of comptroller to refuse to recognise certain agents).
(4) In its application to proceedings in relation to applications for, or otherwise in connection with, European patents, this section has effect subject to any restrictions imposed by or under the European Patent Convention.

102. A Right of audience, &c. in proceedings on appeal from the comptroller.

(1) A solicitor of the Supreme Court may appear and be heard on behalf of any party to an appeal under this Act from the comptroller to the Patents Court.

(2) A registered patent agent or a member of the Bar not in actual practice may do, in or in connection with proceedings on an appeal under this Act from the comptroller to the Patents Court, anything which a solicitor of the Supreme Court might do, other than prepare a deed.

(3) The Lord Chancellor may by regulations—

(a) provide that the right conferred by subsection (2) shall be subject to such conditions and restrictions as appear to the Lord Chancellor to be necessary or expedient, and

(b) apply to persons exercising that right such statutory provisions, rules of court and other rules of law and practice applying to solicitors as may be specified in the regulations;

and different provision may be made for different descriptions of proceedings.

(4) Regulations under this section shall be made by statutory instrument which shall be subject to annulment in pursuance of a resolution of either House of Parliament.

(5) This section is without prejudice to the right of counsel to appear before the High Court.".

Marginal Citations

M131977 c. 37.

Provision of information

28. In section 118 of the M14. Patents Act 1977 (information about patent applications, &c.), in subsection (3) (restriction on disclosure before publication of application: exceptions) for "section 22. (6)(a) above" substitute "section 22. (6) above".

Marginal Citations

M141977 c. 37.

Power to extend time limits

29. In section 123 of the Patents Act 1977 (rules), after subsection (3) insert—

"(3. A)It is hereby declared that rules—

(a) authorising the rectification of irregularities of procedure, or

(b) providing for the alteration of any period of time,

may authorise the comptroller to extend or further extend any period notwithstanding that the period has already expired.".

Availability of samples of micro-organisms

30. In the Patents Act 1977 after section 125 insert—

"125. A Disclosure of invention by specification: availability of samples of micro-organisms.

(1) Provision may be made by rules prescribing the circumstances in which the specification of an application for a patent, or of a patent, for an invention which requires for its performance the use of a micro-organism is to be treated as disclosing the invention in a manner which is clear enough and complete enough for the invention to be performed by a person skilled in the art.

(2) The rules may in particular require the applicant or patentee—

(a) to take such steps as may be prescribed for the purposes of making available to the public samples of the micro-organism, and

(b) not to impose or maintain restrictions on the uses to which such samples may be put, except as may be prescribed.

(3) The rules may provide that, in such cases as may be prescribed, samples need only be made available to such persons or descriptions of persons as may be prescribed; and the rules may identify a description of persons by reference to whether the comptroller has given his certificate as to any matter.

(4) An application for revocation of the patent under section 72. (1)(c) above may be made if any of the requirements of the rules cease to be complied with.".

Schedule 9. PERMITTED ACTS TO WHICH SECTION 296ZE APPLIES

Section 296. ZE
Amendments (Textual)
F1 Sch. 5. A inserted (31.10.2003) by The Copyright and Related Rights Regulations 2003 (S.I. 2003/2498) , reg. 24. (2) , Sch. 3 (with regs. 31-40)

PART 1. Copyright exceptions

section 29 (research and private study)

[F2section 29. A (copies for text and data analysis for non-commercial research)]
Amendments (Textual)
F2 Words in Sch. 5. A Pt. 1 inserted (1.6.2014) by The Copyright and Rights in Performances (Research, Education, Libraries and Archives) Regulations 2014 (S.I. 2014/1372) , reg. 1 , Sch. para. 10. (2)(d)

section 31. A [F3. (disabled persons: copies of works for personal use)"]
Amendments (Textual)
F3. Words in Sch. 5. A Pt. 1 substituted (1.6.2014) by The Copyright and Rights in Performances (Disability) Regulations 2014 (S.I. 2014/1384), reg. 1. (1), Sch. para. 7. (2)(a)

section 31. B [F4. (making and supply of accessible copies by authorised bodies)]
Amendments (Textual)
F4. Words in Sch. 5. A Pt. 1 substituted (1.6.2014) by The Copyright and Rights in Performances (Disability) Regulations 2014 (S.I. 2014/1384), reg. 1. (1), Sch. para. 7. (2)(b)

[F5section 31. BA (making and supply of intermediate copies by authorised bodies)]
Amendments (Textual)
F5. Words in Sch. 5. A Pt. 1 substituted (1.6.2014) by The Copyright and Rights in Performances (Disability) Regulations 2014 (S.I. 2014/1384), reg. 1. (1), Sch. para. 7. (2)(c)

[F6section 32 (illustration for instruction)]
Amendments (Textual)
F6 Words in Sch. 5. A Pt. 1 substituted (1.6.2014) by The Copyright and Rights in Performances (Research, Education, Libraries and Archives) Regulations 2014 (S.I. 2014/1372) , reg. 1 , Sch. para. 10. (2)(a)

section 35 (recording by educational establishments of broadcasts)

[F7section 36 (copying and use of extracts of works by educational establishments)]
Amendments (Textual)
F7 Words in Sch. 5. A Pt. 1 substituted (1.6.2014) by The Copyright and Rights in Performances (Research, Education, Libraries and Archives) Regulations 2014 (S.I. 2014/1372) , reg. 1 , Sch. para. 10. (2)(b)

F8 ...
Amendments (Textual)
F8 Words in Sch. 5. A Pt. 1 omitted (1.6.2014) by virtue of The Copyright and Rights in Performances (Research, Education, Libraries and Archives) Regulations 2014 (S.I. 2014/1372) , reg. 1 , Sch. para. 10. (2)(c)

F8 ...

F8 ...

[F2section 41 (copying by librarians: supply of single copies to other libraries)]

F8 ...

[F2 section 42 (copying by librarians etc : replacement copies of works)]

[F2section 42. A (copying by librarians: single copies of published works)]

F8 ...

[F2section 43 (copying by librarians or archivists: single copies of unpublished works)]

section 44 (copy of work required to be made as condition of export)

section 45 (Parliamentary and judicial proceedings)

section 46 (Royal Commissions and statutory inquiries)

section 47 (material open to public inspection or on official register)

section 48 (material communicated to the Crown in the course of public business)

section 49 (public records)

section 50 (acts done under statutory authority)

section 61 (recordings of folksongs)

section 68 (incidental recording for purposes of broadcast)

section 69 (recording for purposes of supervision and control of broadcasts)

section 70 (recording for purposes o
f time-shifting)

section 71 (photographs of broadcasts)

F9 ...

Amendments (Textual)

F9. Sch. 5. A Pt. 1 entry omitted (1.6.2014) by virtue of The Copyright and Rights in Performances (Disability) Regulations 2014 (S.I. 2014/1384), reg. 1. (1), Sch. para. 7. (2)(d)

[F10section 75 (recording of broadcast for archival purposes)]

Amendments (Textual)

F10 Words in Sch. 5. A Pt. 1 substituted (1.6.2014) by The Copyright and Rights in Performances (Research, Education, Libraries and Archives) Regulations 2014 (S.I. 2014/1372) , reg. 1 , Sch. para. 10. (2)(e)

PART 2. Rights in performances exceptions

[F11paragraph 1. C of Schedule 2 (research and private study)][F11paragraph 1. D of Schedule 2 (copies for text and data analysis for non-commercial research)][F12[F13paragraph 3. A of Schedule 2 (disabled persons: copies of recordings for personal use)][F13paragraph 3. B of Schedule 2 (making and supply of accessible copies by authorised bodies)] [F13paragraph 3. C of Schedule 2 (making and supply of intermediate copies by authorised bodies)]paragraph 4 of Schedule 2 (illustration for instruction)] [F14paragraph 6 of Schedule 2 (recording by educational establishments of broadcasts)] [F11paragraph 6. ZA of Schedule 2 (copying and use of extracts of recordings by educational establishments)][F11paragraph 6. D of Schedule 2 (copying by librarians: supply of single copies to other libraries)][F11paragraph 6. E of Schedule 2 (copying by librarians etc: replacement copies of recordings)][F11paragraph 6. F of Schedule 2 (copying by librarians: single copies of published   recordings)][F11paragraph 6. G of Schedule 2 (copying by librarians or archivists: single copies of unpublished recordings)]paragraph 7 of Schedule 2 (copy of work required to be made as condition of export)paragraph 8 of Schedule 2 (Parliamentary and judicial proceedings) paragraph 9 of Schedule 2 (Royal Commissions and statutory inquiries) paragraph 10 of Schedule 2 (public records) paragraph 11 of Schedule 2 (acts done under statutory authority) paragraph 14 of Schedule 2 (recordings of folksongs) paragraph 16 of Schedule 2 (incidental recording for purposes of broadcast) paragraph 17 of Schedule 2 (recordings for purposes of supervision and control of broadcasts)paragraph 17. A of Schedule 2 (recording for the purposes of time-shifting) paragraph 17. B of Schedule 2 (photographs of broadcasts) F15... paragraph 21 of Schedule 2 (recording of broadcast for archival purposes)]

Amendments (Textual)

F11. Words in Sch. 5. A Pt. 2 inserted (1.6.2014) by The Copyright and Rights in Performances (Research, Education, Libraries and Archives) Regulations 2014 (S.I. 2014/1372), reg. 1, Sch. para. 10. (3)(c)

F12 Words in Sch. 5. A Pt. 2 substituted (1.6.2014) by The Copyright and Rights in Performances (Research, Education, Libraries and Archives) Regulations 2014 (S.I. 2014/1372) , reg. 1 , Sch. para. 10. (3)(a)

F13. Words in Sch. 5. A Pt. 2 inserted (1.6.2014) by The Copyright and Rights in Performances

PART 3. Database right exceptions

regulation 20 of and Schedule 1 to the Copyright and Rights in Databases Regulations 1997 (S.I. 1997/3032)]

Schedule 10. Provisions for the Benefit of Great Ormond Street Hospital for Children

Section 301.
Amendments (Textual)
F1. Words in Sch. 6 heading substituted (23.5.2016) by NHS (Charitable Trusts Etc) Act 2016 (c. 10), ss. 3. (5), 5. (3)

Interpretation

1. (1)In this Schedule—
[F2 "GOSH Children's Charity" means Great Ormond Street Hospital Children's Charity (company registration number 9338724);]
 "the Hospital" means [F3. Great Ormond Street Hospital for Children],
F4...
 "the work" means the play "Peter Pan" by Sir James Matthew Barrie.
(2) Expressions used in this Schedule which are defined for the purposes of Part I of this Act (copyright) have the same meaning as in that Part.
Amendments (Textual)
F2. Definition in Sch. 6 para. 1. (1) inserted (23.5.2016) by NHS (Charitable Trusts Etc) Act 2016 (c. 10), ss. 3. (7)(a), 5. (3)
F3. Words in Sch. 6 para. 1. (1) substituted (23.5.2016) by NHS (Charitable Trusts Etc) Act 2016 (c. 10), ss. 3. (7)(b), 5. (3)
F4. Definition in Sch. 6 para. 1. (1) omitted (23.5.2016) by virtue of NHS (Charitable Trusts Etc) Act 2016 (c. 10), ss. 3. (7)(c), 5. (3)

Entitlement to royalty

2. (1)[F5. GOSH Children's Charity is] entitled, subject to the following provisions of this Schedule, to a royalty in respect of any public performance, commercial publication [F6or communication to the public] of the whole or any substantial part of the work or an adaptation of it.
(2) Where [F7. GOSH Children's Charity is] or would be entitled to a royalty, another form of remuneration may be agreed.

Amendments (Textual)
F5. Words in Sch. 6 para. 2. (1) substituted (23.5.2016) by NHS (Charitable Trusts Etc) Act 2016 (c. 10), ss. 3. (8)(a), 5. (3)
F6. Words in Sch. 6 para. 2. (1) substituted (31.10.2003) by The Copyright and Related Rights Regulations 2003 (S.I. 2003/2498), reg. 2. (1), Sch. 1 para. 6. (2)(f) (with regs. 31-40)
F7. Words in Sch. 6 para. 2. (2) substituted (23.5.2016) by NHS (Charitable Trusts Etc) Act 2016 (c. 10), ss. 3. (8)(b), 5. (3)
Modifications etc. (not altering text)
C1. Sch. 6 para. 2: power to amend conferred (23.5.2016) by NHS (Charitable Trusts Etc) Act 2016 (c. 10), s. 5. (3), Sch. 2 para. 5. (2)(a)

Exceptions

3. No royalty is payable in respect of—
(a) anything which immediately before copyright in the work expired on 31st December 1987 could lawfully have been done without the licence, or further licence, of the [F8copyright owner at that time]; or
(b) anything which if copyright still subsisted in the work could, by virtue of any provision of Chapter III of Part I of this Act (acts permitted notwithstanding copyright), be done without infringing copyright.

Amendments (Textual)
F8. Words in Sch. 6 para. 3. (a) substituted (23.5.2016) by NHS (Charitable Trusts Etc) Act 2016 (c. 10), ss. 3. (9), 5. (3)

Saving

4. No royalty is payable in respect of anything done in pursuance of arrangements made before the passing of this Act.

Procedure for determining amount payable

5. (1)In default of agreement application may be made to the Copyright Tribunal which shall consider the matter and make such order regarding the royalty or other remuneration to be paid as it may determine to be reasonable in the circumstances.
(2) Application may subsequently be made to the Tribunal to vary its order, and the Tribunal shall consider the matter and make such order confirming or varying the original order as it may determine to be reasonable in the circumstances.
(3) An application for variation shall not, except with the special leave of the Tribunal, be made within twelve months from the date of the original order or of the order on a previous application for variation.
(4) A variation order has effect from the date on which it is made or such later date as may be specified by the Tribunal.
F9[(5) The provisions of Chapter VIII of Part I (general provisions relating to the Copyright Tribunal) apply in relation to the Tribunal when exercising any jurisdiction under this paragraph.]

Amendments (Textual)
F9. Sch. 6 para. 5. (5) added (1.12.1996) by S.I. 1996/2967, reg. 24. (3) (with Pt. III)

[F10 Sums received to be held for the benefit of the Hospital

Amendments (Textual)
F10. Sch. 6 para. 6 and crossheading substituted (23.5.2016) by NHS (Charitable Trusts Etc) Act

2016 (c. 10), ss. 3. (10), 5. (3)

6. The sums received by GOSH Children's Charity by virtue of this Schedule, after deduction of any relevant expenses, are to be held by it for the purposes of the Hospital.]

Right only for the benefit of the Hospital

7. (1)The right of [F11. GOSH Children's Charity] under this Schedule may not be assigned and shall cease if [F12. GOSH Children's Charity purports] to assign or charge it.

(2) The right F13... shall cease if the Hospital ceases to have a separate identity or ceases to have purposes which include the care of sick children.

F14. (3).............................

Amendments (Textual)

F11. Words in Sch. 6 para. 7. (1) substituted (23.5.2016) by NHS (Charitable Trusts Etc) Act 2016 (c. 10), ss. 3. (11)(a)(i), 5. (3)

F12. Words in Sch. 6 para. 7. (1) substituted (23.5.2016) by NHS (Charitable Trusts Etc) Act 2016 (c. 10), ss. 3. (11)(a)(ii), 5. (3)

F13. Words in Sch. 6 para. 7. (2) omitted (23.5.2016) by virtue of NHS (Charitable Trusts Etc) Act 2016 (c. 10), ss. 3. (11)(b), 5. (3)

F14. Sch. 6 para. 7. (3) omitted (23.5.2016) by virtue of NHS (Charitable Trusts Etc) Act 2016 (c. 10), ss. 3. (11)(c), 5. (3)

Schedule 11. Consequential amendments: general

Section 303. (1).

Amendments (Textual)

F1 Sch. 5. A inserted (31.10.2003) by The Copyright and Related Rights Regulations 2003 (S.I. 2003/2498) , reg. 24. (2) , Sch. 3 (with regs. 31-40)

British Mercantile Marine Uniform Act 1919 (c.62)

1. For section 2 of the British Mercantile Marine Uniform Act 1919 (copyright in distinctive marks of uniform) substitute—

2" Right in registered design of distinctive marks of uniform.

The right of the Secretary of State in any design forming part of the British mercantile marine uniform which is registered under the Registered Designs Act 1949 is not limited to the period prescribed by section 8 of that Act but shall continue to subsist so long as the design remains on the register.".

Chartered Associations (Protection of Names and Uniforms) Act 1926 (c.26)

2 In section 1. (5) of the Chartered Associations (Protection of Names and Uniforms) Act 1926 for "the copyright in respect thereof" substitute " the right in the registered design " .

Patents, Designs, Copyright and Trade Marks (Emergency) Act 1939 (c.107)

3. (1)The Patents, Designs, Copyright and Trade Marks (Emergency) Act 1939 is amended as follows.

(2) In section 1 (effect of licence where owner is enemy or enemy subject)—

(a) in subsection (1) after "a copyright" and "the copyright" insert " or design right " ;

(b) in subsection (2) after "the copyright" insert " or design right " and for "or copyright" substitute " , copyright or design right " .

(3) In section 2 (power of comptroller to grant licences)—

(a) in subsection (1) after "a copyright", "the copyright" (twice) and "the said copyright" insert " or design right " and for "or copyright" (twice) substitute " , copyright or design right " ;

(b) in subsections (2) and (3) for ", or copyright" substitute " , copyright or design right " ;

(c) in subsection (4) and in subsection (5) (twice), after "the copyright" insert " or design right " ;

(d) in subsection (8)(c) for "or work in which copyright subsists" substitute " work in which copyright subsists or design in which design right subsists " .

(4) In section 5 (effect of war on international arrangements)—

(a) in subsection (1) for "section twenty-nine of the Copyright Act 1911" substitute " section 159 or 256 of the Copyright, Designs and Patents Act 1988 (countries enjoying reciprocal copyright or design right protection) " ;

(b) in subsection (2) after "copyright" (four times) insert " or design right " and for "the Copyright Act 1911" (twice) substitute " Part I or III of the Copyright, Designs and Patents Act 1988 " .

(5) In section 10. (1) (interpretation) omit the definition of "copyright", and for the definitions of "design", "invention", "patent" and "patentee" substitute—

" " design " has in reference to a registered design the same meaning as in the Registered Designs Act 1949, and in reference to design right the same meaning as in Part III of the Copyright, Designs and Patents Act 1988;

" invention " and " patent " have the same meaning as in the Patents Act 1977. ".

Crown Proceedings Act 1947 (c.44)

4. (1)In the Crown Proceedings Act 1947 for section 3 (provisions as to industrial property) substitute—

3" Infringement of intellectual property rights.

(1) Civil proceedings lie against the Crown for an infringement committed by a servant or agent of the Crown, with the authority of the Crown, of—

   (a) a patent,

   (b) a registered trade mark or registered service mark,

   (c) the right in a registered design,

   (d) design right, or

   (e) copyright;

but save as provided by this subsection no proceedings lie against the Crown by virtue of this Act in respect of an infringement of any of those rights.

(2) Nothing in this section, or any other provision of this Act, shall be construed as affecting—

   (a) the rights of a government department under section 55 of the Patents Act 1977, Schedule 1 to the Registered Designs Act 1949 or section 240 of the Copyright, Designs and Patents Act 1988 (Crown use of patents and designs), or

   (b) the rights of the Secretary of State under section 22 of the Patents Act 1977 or section 5 of the Registered Designs Act 1949 (security of information prejudicial to defence or public safety).".

(2) In the application of sub-paragraph (1) to Northern Ireland—

(a) the reference to the Crown Proceedings Act 1947 is to that Act as it applies to the Crown in right of Her Majesty's Government in Northern Ireland, as well as to the Crown in right of Her Majesty's Government in the United Kingdom, and

(b) in the substituted section 3 as it applies in relation to the Crown in right of Her Majesty's Government in Northern Ireland, subsection (2)(b) shall be omitted.

Patents Act 1949 (c.87)

5 In section 47 of the Patents Act 1949 (rights of third parties in respect of Crown use of patent), in the closing words of subsection (1) (which relate to the use of models or documents), after "copyright" insert " or design right " .

Public Libraries (Scotland) Act 1955 (c.27)

F2 6 . . . .

Amendments (Textual)

F2. Sch. 7 para. 6 repealed (1.12.1996) by S.I. 1996/2967, reg. 11. (7) (with Pt. III)

London County Council (General Powers) Act 1958 (c.xxi)

7. In section 36 of the London County Council (General Powers) Act 1958 (power as to libraries: provision and repair of things other than books) for subsection (5) substitute—

"(5)Nothing in this section shall be construed as authorising an infringement of copyright.".

Public Libraries and Museums Act 1964 (c.75)

F3 8 . . . .

Amendments (Textual)

F3. Sch. 7 para. 8 repealed (1.12.1996) by S.I. 1996/2967, reg. 11. (7) (with Pt. III)

Marine, &c., Broadcasting (Offences) Act 1967 (c.41)

9. F4 . . . .

Amendments (Textual)

F4. Sch. 7 para. 9 repealed (8.2.2007) by Wireless Telegraphy Act 2006 (c. 36), ss. 124, 125. (1), 126. (2), Sch. 9 Pt. 1 (with Sch. 8 Pt. 1)

Medicines Act 1968 (c.67)

10. (1)Section 92 of the Medicines Act 1968 (scope of provisions restricting promotion of sales of medicinal products) is amended as follows.

(2) In subsection (1) (meaning of "advertisement") for the words from "or by the exhibition" to "service" substitute " or by means of a photograph, film, sound recording, broadcast or cable programme, " .

(3) F5 . . . .

(4) For subsection (6) substitute—

"(6)In this section "film", "sound recording", "broadcast", "cable programme", "cable programme service", and related expressions, have the same meaning as in Part I of the Copyright, Designs and Patents Act 1988 (copyright).".

Amendments (Textual)

Post Office Act 1969 (c.48)

11 In Schedule 10 to the Post Office Act 1969 (special transitional provisions relating to use of patents and registered designs), in the closing words of paragraphs 8. (1) and 18. (1) (which relate to the use of models and documents), after "copyright" insert " or design right " .

Merchant Shipping Act 1970 (c.36)

12. In section 87 of the Merchant Shipping Act 1970 (merchant navy uniform), for subsection (4) substitute—
"(4)Where any design forming part of the merchant navy uniform has been registered under the Registered Designs Act 1949 and the Secretary of State is the proprietor of the design, his right in the design is not limited to the period prescribed by section 8 of that Act but shall continue to subsist so long as the design remains registered.".

Taxes Management Act 1970 (c.9)

13. In section 16 of the Taxes Management Act 1970 (returns to be made in respect of certain payments)—
(a) in subsection (1)(c), and
(b) in subsection (2)(b),
 for "or public lending right" substitute " , public lending right, right in a registered design or design right " .

Tribunals and Inquiries Act 1971 (c.62)

F6 14 . . . .
Amendments (Textual)
F6. Sch. 7 para. 14 repealed (1.10.1992) by Tribunals and Inquiries Act 1992 (c. 53), ss. 18. (2), 19. (2), Sch. 4 Pt.I

Fair Trading Act 1973 (c.41)

15. F7 . . . .
Amendments (Textual)
F7. Sch. 7 para. 15 repealed (20.6.2003) by 2002 c. 40, ss. 278. (2), 279, Sch. 26; S.I. 2003/1397, art. 2. (1), Sch.

House of Commons Disqualification Act 1975 (c.24)

16 In Part II of Schedule 1 to the House of Commons Disqualification Act 1975 (bodies of which all members are disqualified), at the appropriate place insert " The Copyright Tribunal " .

Northern Ireland Assembly Disqualification Act 1975 (c.25)

17 In Part II of Schedule 1 to the Northern Ireland Assembly Disqualification Act 1975 (bodies of which all members are disqualified), at the appropriate place insert " The Copyright Tribunal " .

Restrictive Trade Practices Act 1976 (c.34)

18. (1)The Restrictive Trade Practices Act 1976 is amended as follows.

(2) In Schedule 1 (excluded services) for paragraph 10 (services of patent agents) substitute—

"10. The services of registered patent agents (within the meaning of Part V of the Copyright, Designs and Patents Act 1988) in their capacity as such.";

 and in paragraph 10. A (services of European patent attorneys) for "section 84. (7) of the Patents Act 1977" substitute " Part V of the Copyright, Designs and Patents Act 1988 " .

(3) In Schedule 3 (excepted agreements), after paragraph 5. A insert—

" Design right

5. B(1)This Act does not apply to—

(a) a licence granted by the owner or a licensee of any design right,

(b) an assignment of design right, or

(c) an agreement for such a licence or assignment,

if the licence, assignment or agreement is one under which no such restrictions as are described in section 6. (1) above are accepted, or no such information provisions as are described in section 7. (1) above are made, except in respect of articles made to the design; but subject to the following provisions.

(2) Sub-paragraph (1) does not exclude a licence, assignment or agreement which is a design pooling agreement or is granted or made (directly or indirectly) in pursuance of a design pooling agreement.

(3) In this paragraph a " design pooling agreement " means an agreement—

(a) to which the parties are or include at least three persons(the "principal parties") each of whom has an interest in one or more design rights, and

(b) by which each principal party agrees, in respect of design right in which he has, or may during the currency of the agreement acquire, an interest to grant an interest (directly or indirectly) to one or more of the other principal parties, or to one or more of those parties and to other persons.

(4) In this paragraph—

" assignment ", in Scotland, means assignation; and

" interest " means an interest as owner or licensee of design right.

(5) This paragraph applies to an interest held by or granted to more than one person jointly as if they were one person.

(6) References in this paragraph to the granting of an interest to a person indirectly are to its being granted to a third person for the purpose of enabling him to make a grant to the person in question.".

Resale Prices Act 1976 (c. 53)

19 In section 10. (4) of the Resale Prices Act 1976 (patented articles: articles to be treated in same way), in paragraph (a) after "protected" insert " by design right or " .

Patents Act 1977 (c. 37)

20 In section 57 of the Patents Act 1977 (rights of third parties in respect of Crown use of patent), in the closing words of subsection (1) (which relate to the use of models or documents), after "copyright" insert " or design right " .

21. In section 105 of the Patents Act 1977 (privilege in Scotland for communications relating to patent proceedings), omit "within the meaning of section 104 above", make the existing text

subsection (1) and after it insert—

"(2)In this section—

" patent proceedings " means proceedings under this Act or any of the relevant conventions, before the court, the comptroller or the relevant convention court, whether contested or uncontested and including an application for a patent; and

" the relevant conventions " means the European Patent Convention, the Community Patent Convention and the Patent Co-operation Treaty. ".

22. In section 123. (7) of the Patents Act 1977 (publication of case reports by the comptroller)—

(a) for "and registered designs" substitute " registered designs or design right " ,

(b) for "and copyright" substitute " , copyright and design right " .

23. In section 130. (1) of the Patents Act 1977 (interpretation), in the definition of "court", for paragraph (a) substitute—

"(a)as respects England and Wales, the High Court or any patents county court having jurisdiction by virtue of an order under section 287 of the Copyright, Designs and Patents Act 1988;".

Unfair Contract Terms Act 1977 (c. 50)

24 In paragraph 1 of Schedule 1 to the Unfair Contract Terms Act 1977 (scope of main provisions: excluded contracts), in paragraph (c) (contracts relating to grant or transfer of interest in intellectual property) after "copyright" insert " or design right " .

Judicature (Northern Ireland) Act 1978 (c. 23)

25 In section 94. A of the Judicature (Northern Ireland) Act 1978 (withdrawal of privilege against self-incrimination in certain proceedings relating to intellectual property), in subsection (5) (meaning of "intellectual property") after "copyright" insert " or design right " .

Capital Gains Tax Act 1979 (c. 14)

F8 26 . . . .

Amendments (Textual)

F8. Sch. 7 para. 26 repealed (6.3.1992 with effect as mentioned in s. 289. (1)(2) of the repealing Act) by Taxation of Chargeable Gains Act 1992 (c. 12), ss. 289, 290, Sch.12 (with s. 201. (3), Sch. 11 paras. 22, 26. (2), 27)

British Telecommunications Act 1981 (c. 38)

27. F9 . . . .

Amendments (Textual)

F9. Sch. 7 para. 27 repealed (25.7.2003 for specified purposes and 29.12.2003 otherwise) by Communications Act 2003 (c. 21), ss. 406, 408, 411, Sch. 19. (1) (with Sch. 18, Sch. 19. (1) Note 1); S.I. 2003/1900, arts. 1. (2), 2. (1), 3. (1), Sch. 1 (with art. 3. (2) (as amended (8.12.2003) by S.I. 2003/3142, art. 1. (3))); S.I. 2003/3142, art. 3, Sch. 1 (with art. 11)

[F10. Senior Courts Act 1981] (c. 54)

Amendments (Textual)

F10. Sch. 7 para. 28 cross-heading: words wherever they occur in any enactment substituted (1.10.2009) by virtue of Constitutional Reform Act 2005 (c. 4), ss. 59, 148, Sch. 11 para. 1. (2); S.I. 2009/1604, art. 2

28. (1)The [F11. Senior Courts Act 1981] is amended as follows.

(2) In section 72 (withdrawal of privilege against self-incrimination in certain proceedings relating to intellectual property), in subsection (5) (meaning of "intellectual property") after "copyright" insert " , design right " .

(3) In Schedule 1 (distribution of business in the High Court), in paragraph 1. (i) (business assigned to the Chancery Division: causes and matters relating to certain intellectual property) for "or copyright" substitute " , copyright or design right " .

Amendments (Textual)

F11. Sch. 7 para. 28: words wherever they occur in any enactment substituted (1.10.2009) by virtue of Constitutional Reform Act 2005 (c. 4), ss. 59, 148, Sch. 11 para. 1. (2); S.I. 2009/1604, art. 2

F12 29 , 30.. . . . .

Amendments (Textual)

F12. Sch. 7 paras. 29, 30 repealed by Broadcasting Act 1990 (c. 42, SIF 96), s. 203. (3), Sch. 21 (the repeal being in force subject, as to para. 29, as mentioned in S.I. 1990/2347 art. 3. (3))

Companies Act 1985 (c. 6)

[F1331. (1)Part XII of the Companies Act 1985 (registration of charges) is amended as follows.

(2) In section 396 (registration of charges in England and Wales: charges which must be registered), in subsection (1)(j) for the words from "on a patent" to the end substitute " or on any intellectual property " , and after subsection (3) insert—

"(3. A) The following are " intellectual property " for the purposes of this section—

  (a) any patent, trade mark, service mark, registered design, copyright or design right;

  (b) any licence under or in respect of any such right.".

(3) In section 410 (registration of charges in Scotland: charges which must be registered), in subsection (4)(c) (incorporeal moveable property) after subparagraph (vi) insert—

"(vii)a registered design or a licence in respect of such a design,

(viii)a design right or a licence under a design right,".]

Amendments (Textual)

F13. Sch. 7 para. 31 repealed (prosp.) by Companies Act 1989 (c. 40, SIF 27), ss. 212, 215. (2), Sch. 24

Law Reform (Miscellaneous Provisions) (Scotland) Act 1985 (c. 73)

32 In section 15 of the Law Reform (Miscellaneous Provisions) (Scotland) Act 1985 (withdrawal of privilege against self-incrimination in certain proceedings relating to intellectual property), in subsection (5) (meaning of "intellectual property") after "copyright" insert " or design right " .

Atomic Energy Authority Act 1986 (c. 3)

33 In section 8. (2) of the Atomic Energy Authority Act 1986 (powers of Authority as to exploitation of research: meaning of "intellectual property"), after "copyrights" insert " , design rights " .

Education and Libraries (Northern Ireland) Order 1986 (S.I. 1986/594 (N.I.3))

F14 34 . . . .

Amendments (Textual)

F14. Sch. 7 para. 34 repealed (16.1.1994) by S.I. 1993/2810 (N.I. 12), arts. 1. (2), 50. (2), Sch.5 and expressed to be repealed (1.12.1996) by S.I. 1996/2967, reg. 11. (7) (with Pt. III)

Companies (Northern Ireland) Order 1986 (S.I. 1986/1032 (N.I.6))

35. F15 . . . .

Amendments (Textual)

F15. Sch. 7 para. 35 repealed (1.10.2009) by The Companies Act 2006 (Consequential Amendments, Transitional Provisions and Savings) Order 2009 (S.I. 2009/1941), art. 2. (2), Sch. 2 (with art. 10)

Income and Corporation Taxes Act 1988 (c. 1)

36. (1)The Income and Corporation Taxes Act 1988 is amended as follows.

(2) In section 83 (fees and expenses deductible in computing profits and gains of trade) for "the extension of the period of copyright in a design" substitute " an extension of the period for which the right in a registered design subsists " .

(3) F16 . . . .

(4) F17 . . . .

(5) F17 . . . .

(6) F17 . . . .

(7) In section 821 (payments made under deduction of tax before passing of Act imposing income tax for that year), in subsection (3) (payments subject to adjustment) after paragraph (a) insert—

   "(aa)any payment for or in respect of a right in a design to which section 537. B applies; and".

(8) In Schedule 19 (apportionment of income of close companies), in paragraph 10. (4) (cessation or liquidation: debts taken into account although creditor is participator or associate), in paragraph (c) (payments for use of certain property) for the words from "tangible property" to "extend)" substitute—

"(i)tangible property,

(ii) copyright in a literary, dramatic, musical or artistic work within the meaning of Part I of the Copyright, Designs and Patents Act 1988 (or any similar right under the law of a country to which that Part does not extend), or

(iii) design right,".

(9) In Schedule 25 (taxation of UK-controlled foreign companies: exempt activities), in paragraph 9. (1)(a) (investment business: holding of property) for "patents or copyrights" substitute " or intellectual property " and after that subparagraph insert—

"(1. A) In sub-paragraph (1)(a) above " intellectual property " means patents, registered designs, copyright and design right (or any similar rights under the law of a country outside the United Kingdom). ".]

Amendments (Textual)

F16. Sch. 7 para. 36. (3) repealed (6.4.2005 with effect as mentioned in s. 883 of the repealing Act) by Income Tax (Trading and Other Income) Act 2005 (c. 5), ss. 883, 884, Sch. 3 (with savings and transitional provisions in Sch. 2)

F17. Sch. 7 para. 36. (4)(5)(6) repealed (6.4.2007 with effect as mentioned in s. 1034 of the repealing Act) by Income Tax Act 2007 (c. 3), ss. 1031, 1034, Sch. 3 Pt. 1 (with savings and transitional provisions in Sch. 2)

Schedule 12. Repeals

Section 303. (2).

Amendments (Textual)

F1 Sch. 5. A inserted (31.10.2003) by The Copyright and Related Rights Regulations 2003 (S.I. 2003/2498) , reg. 24. (2) , Sch. 3 (with regs. 31-40)

1939 c. 107. | Patents, Designs, Copyright and Trade Marks (Emergency) Act 1939. | In section 10(1), the definition of "copyright". |

1945 c. 16. | Limitation (Enemies and War Prisoners) Act 1945. | In sections 2(1) and 4(a), the reference to section 10 of the Copyright Act 1911. |

1949 c. 88. | Registered Designs Act 1949. | In section 3(2), the words "or original". |

| | Section 5(5). |

| | In section 11(2), the words "or original". |

| | In section 14(3), the words "or the Isle of Man". |

| | Section 32. |

| | Section 33(2). |

| | Section 37(1). |

| | Section 38. |

| | In section 44(1), the definitions of "copyright" and "Journal". |

| | In section 45, paragraphs (1) and (2). |

| | In section 46, paragraphs (1) and (2). |

1949 c. 88.—cont. | Registered Designs Act 1949.—cont. | Section 48(1). |

| | In Schedule 1, in paragraph 3(1), the words "in such manner as may be prescribed by rules of court". |

| | Schedule 2. |

1956 c. 74. | Copyright Act 1956. | The whole Act. |

1957 c. 6. | Ghana Independence Act 1957. | In Schedule 2, paragraph 12. |

1957 c. 60. | Federation of Malaya Independence Act 1957. | In Schedule 1, paragraphs 14 and 15. |

1958 c. 44. | Dramatic and Musical Performers' Protection Act 1958. | The whole Act. |

1958 c. 51. | Public Records Act 1958. | Section 11. |

| | Schedule 3. |

1960 c. 52. | Cyprus Independence Act 1960. | In the Schedule, paragraph 13. |

1960 c. 55. | Nigeria Independence Act 1960. | In Schedule 2, paragraphs 12 and 13. |

1961 c. 1. | Tanganyika Independence Act 1961. | In Schedule 2, paragraphs 13 and 14. |

1961 c. 16. | Sierra Leone Independence Act 1961. | In Schedule 3, paragraphs 13 and 14. |

1961 c. 25. | Patents and Designs (Renewals, Extensions and Fees) Act 1961. | The whole Act. |

1962 c. 40. | Jamaica Independence Act 1962. | In Schedule 2, paragraph 13. |

1962 c. 54. | Trinidad and Tobago Independence Act 1962. | In Schedule 2, paragraph 13. |

1963 c. 53. | Performers' Protection Act 1963. | The whole Act. |

1964 c. 46. | Malawi Independence Act 1964. | In Schedule 2, paragraph 13. |

1964 c. 65. | Zambia Independence Act 1964. | In Schedule 1, paragraph 9. |

. . . F2. | | |

1964 c. 93. | Gambia Independence Act 1964. | In Schedule 2, paragraph 12. |

1966 c. 24. | Lesotho Independence Act 1966. | In the Schedule, paragraph 9. |

1966 c. 37. | Barbados Independence Act 1966. | In Schedule 2, paragraph 12. |

1967 c. 80. | Criminal Justice Act 1967. | In Parts I and IV of Schedule 3, the entries relating to the Registered Designs Act 1949. |

1968 c. 56. | Swaziland Independence Act 1968. | In the Schedule, paragraph 9. |

1968 c. 67. | Medicines Act 1968. | In section 92(2)(a), the words from "or embodied" to "film". |

| | Section 98. |

1968 c. 68. | Design Copyright Act 1968. | The whole Act. |

1971 c. 4. | Copyright (Amendment) Act 1971. | The whole Act. |
1971 c. 23. | Courts Act 1971. | In Schedule 9, the entry relating to the Copyright Act 1956. |
1971 c. 62. | Tribunals and Inquiries Act 1971. | In Schedule 1, paragraph 24. |
1972 c. 32. | Performers' Protection Act 1972. | The whole Act. |
1975 c. 24. | House of Commons Disqualification Act 1975. | In Part II of Schedule 1, the entry relating to the Performing Right Tribunal. |
1975 c. 25. | Northern Ireland Assembly Disqualification Act 1975. | In Part II of Schedule 1, the entry relating to the Performing Right Tribunal. |
1977 c. 37. | Patents Act 1977. | Section 14(4) and (8). |
	In section 28(3), paragraph (b) and the word "and" preceding it.
	Section 28(5) to (9).
	Section 49(3).
	Sections 72(3).
	Sections 84 and 85.
	Section 88.
	Section 104.
	In section 105, the words "within the meaning of section 104 above".
	Sections 114 and 115.
	Section 123(2)(k).
	In section 130(1), the definition of "patent agent".
	In section 130(7), the words "88(6) and (7),".
	In Schedule 5, paragraphs 1 and 2, in paragraph 3 the words "and 44(1)" and "in each case", and paragraphs 7 and 8.
1979 c. 2.	Customs and Excise Management Act 1979.	In Schedule 4, the entry relating to the Copyright Act 1956.
1980 c. 21.	Competition Act 1980.	Section 14.
1981 c. 68.	Broadcasting Act 1981.	Section 20(9)(a).
1982 c. 35.	Copyright Act 1956 (Amendment) Act 1982.	The whole Act.
1983 c. 42.	Copyright (Amendment) Act 1983.	The whole Act.
1984 c. 46.	Cable and Broadcasting Act 1984.	Section 8(8).
	Section 16(4) and (5).
	Sections 22 to 24.
	Section 35(2) and (3).
	Sections 53 and 54.
	In section 56(2), the definition of "the 1956 Act".
	In Schedule 5, paragraphs 6, 7, 13 and 23.
1985 c. 21. | Films Act 1985. | Section 7(2). |
1985 c. 41. | Copyright (Computer Software) Amendment Act 1985. | The whole Act. |
1985 c. 61. | Administration of Justice Act 1985. | Section 60. |
1986 c. 39. | Patents, Designs and Marks Act 1986. | In Schedule 2, paragraph 1(2)(a), in paragraph 1(2)(k) the words "subsection (1)(j) of section 396 and" and in paragraph 1(2)(1) the words "subsection (2)(i) of section 93". |
1988 c. 1. | Income and Corporation Taxes Act 1988. | In Schedule 29, paragraph 5.] |
Amendments (Textual)
F2. In Sch. 8 entry relating to the Malta Independence Act 1964 repealed (5.11.1993) by 1993 c. 50 s. 1. (1), Sch. 1 Pt.XVI

Open Government Licence v3.0

The full licence if available at the following address:
http://www.nationalarchives.gov.uk/doc/open-government-licence/version/3/

Printed in Great Britain
by Amazon